The Mormon Vanguard Brigade of 1847

Norton Jacob's Record

Photograph of a charcoal portrait of Norton Jacob. Artist, photographer, and date are unknown. Courtesy of the LDS Church Archives.

The Mormon Vanguard Brigade of 1847

Norton Jacob's Record

~

Edited by

Ronald O. Barney

~

Utah State University Press
Logan, Utah

Utah State University Press
Logan, Utah 84322-7800
www.usu.edu/usupress

Manufactured in the United States of America
Printed on acid-free paper

Cover illustrations courtesy of the LDS Church Archives, except for back cover image of Great Salt Lake, which is from Frederick Piercy, *Route from Liverpool to Great Salt Lake Valley* (1855).

Library of Congress Cataloging-in-Publication Data

Jacob, Norton, 1804-1879.
The Mormon vanguard brigade of 1847 : Norton Jacob's record / edited by Ronald O. Barney.
p. cm.
Includes bibliographical references and index.
ISBN 0-87421-609-5 (hardcover : alk. paper) — ISBN 0-87421-610-9 (pbk. : alk. paper)
1. Jacob, Norton, 1804-1879—Diaries. 2. Mormon pioneers—Diaries. I. Barney, Ronald O., 1949- II. Jacob, Norton, 1804-1879. Record of Norton Jacob. III. Title.
BX8695.J33A3 2005
289.3'092--dc22

2005006156

To Marilyn,

who for me has been my constant companion,

my support and pleasure

Contents

Illustrations

Acknowledgments

I APPRECIATE THE ASSISTANCE OF SEVERAL MEMBERS of the Norton Jacob family in the preparation of this work. Steven Gunn Jacob, a great-great-grandson of Norton, has encouraged the project for years and, by way of his family organization, has underwritten the production of maps augmenting this volume. I am especially grateful for the encouragement of another Jacob descendant, a great-grandson, Lloyd M. Gerber. Indeed, it was Lloyd Gerber who actuated this project into something more than talk. With Preston Gerber, a great-great-great-grandson of Norton, Lloyd financed preliminary work on Norton Jacob's life. Lloyd's persistence to insure the work's completion has done just that. Other Jacob family members have also made helpful contributions in the production of this work. R. Douglas Jacob, another great-great-grandson of Jacob, has also encouraged the project and helped in the preparation of the transcription of Norton Jacob's diary appearing in this book. Rachael Gerber, a great-great-great-granddaughter of Jacob, also assisted in the preparation of the Jacob diary transcription.

I am grateful for the encouragement of friends and colleagues whose expertise and careful scholarship on Mormonism and the Saints' western journey I have called upon to strengthen my work. W. Randall Dixon of the LDS Church Archives, the foremost scholar of early Salt Lake City, has critiqued several chapters of the manuscript and made a number of helpful suggestions, including the identification of the location of Jacob's residences in Salt Lake City. Michael N. Landon, also a colleague at the LDS Church Archives and an expert of western trails and travel, has read the entire manuscript and made numerous corrections and recommendations preventing me from including mistakes I otherwise would have made. His encouragement has been especially helpful to me. William G. Hartley, whose expertise on Mormon emigration and the post-Nauvoo sojourn of the Saints is unparalleled, has also read the manuscript and made numerous corrections and recommendations steering me from mistakes and otherwise providing helpful insight into the period. I am also grateful for the contributions to this project from colleagues William W. Slaughter who has helped with the illustrations and otherwise has benefitted my work. April Williamson has been especially helpful in preparation of the illustrations in the book. My colleagues Ronald G. Watt and Melvin L. Bashore have provided source material and guidance on the project. M. Guy Bishop did preliminary work on the Jacob family and helped prepare the transcription of Jacob's diary for editing and annotation. I also thank Ronald W. Walker, David Packard, and John W. Welch for information they provided to me, amplifying this story. I am also very grateful to Marlene Kettley, an expert on Mormonism in Illinois during the period of the Saints' 1840s tenure there, who has been very helpful to me in providing information about Mormons and geographical sites in Illinois, especially for particulars of Norton Jacob's missionary journey to Indiana and Michigan in 1844. I thank Robert Calhoon for information he provided about his ancestor, Aaron Smith, and Lydia and Don Westover who provided information about Howard Egan.

I also thank the staff, my colleagues, at the LDS Church Archives and the LDS Church History Library in Salt Lake City, Utah. They have been unfailingly competent and professional. The staff and Church Service Missionaries of the Family History Library, in Salt Lake City, Utah, have been helpful in every way when called upon for information. I am also grateful to the staff of the Illinois State Historical Library in Springfield, Illinois, and to the Special Collections staff at the University of Utah's Marriott Library in Salt Lake City for their assistance.

I am especially appreciative for the support of my family while producing this work. My wife, Marilyn Stafford, has been patient and very supportive. My children, Joshua and his wife Colette, my daughter Alison and her husband Sean, and my son Christian have all encouraged the project. Without their support, I simply would never have completed the work.

John R. Alley and his colleagues at Utah State University Press have been very helpful in bringing this work to fruition. Tom Child prepared the maps for the book. After all the assistance I have received, the interpretation of Norton Jacob's diary and his life, as represented in this volume, is my own, for which I accept responsibility.

Introduction

THERE IS, FOR MODERN OBSERVERS, NOTHING quite like the eyewitness account of a significant historic event. And a first-hand view of a protracted epic is, being so rare, almost more than one can hope for.[1] Norton Jacob, a Massachusetts son born just two centuries ago, penned, over a period of nine years beginning in 1844, one of the finer and more illuminating first-person accounts of the removal of the Church of Jesus Christ of Latter-day Saints from the Mississippi River Valley to their new homeland in the West's Great Basin. From the confusion following their prophet's martyrdom in June 1844, to the Saints' 1846 expulsion from Illinois and initial drive across Iowa's miry winter bog, to temporary quarters at wilderness's edge on the Missouri River, and finally to their Great Basin refuge, Jacob's record explicates a time of singular significance in Mormon history. The chronicle's highpoint is his daily report of the 1847 vanguard expedition to the West. It is one of a handful of the most descriptive contemporary records illustrating the beginnings of the westward hegira of Mormonism.[2] And though it is, as the noted overland trail historian and bibliographer Merrill Mattes has written, "less publicized than [William] Clayton's and [Howard] Egan's [accounts]," Jacob's diary of the formidable venture "is exceptional in the keenness of observations and richness of detail."[3] Also found in the account is Jacob's record of his family's

1. In the particular genre of westward travel narratives, in contrast to most important historical events or settings, the adventure proved so compelling that "the participants wrote about it like no other period in history, except perhaps the Civil War years." Still, in the whole of westward emigration, only "one in every two hundred fifty emigrants jotted down the details of his or her journey—either in a diary, in letters, or as reminiscences." Walker, "'Written Under Very Adverse Circumstances'," 4.
2. The 1847 vanguard journey of the Latter-day Saints to the Great Basin was of great importance to Norton Jacob. It is the crux of his story. Of the 124 pages composing Norton Jacob's record from 1844 to 1852, the six months describing the trek to the Salt Lake Valley and the return to Winter Quarters comprise 44 percent of the extant account. (Another sixteen leaves at the end of the record, apparently containing text, were later cut from the bound volume.)
3. Mattes, *Platte River Road Narratives*, 101.

subsequent transit to the Great Basin in 1848 and their settlement in the Salt Lake Valley. Norton Jacob's personal chronicle of the familiar story reveals anew to the modern reader particulars of a time when Mormonism acquired a new and enduring identity.

That identity has been furbished by icons constructed to insure the feat is never forgotten, at least by the Saints. Not only has the pioneer vanguard been honored yearly in late July throughout Utah's communities since the mid-nineteenth century, the cultural symbols traditionally used to etch memories into a people's consciousness would please even the Hebrew prophets.[4] Monuments (one of them the largest in Utah), parades (one of them among the largest in the United States), pageants, plays, musicals, books, hymns, songs, poems, and art, as well as other venerations, attest to the importance of the trek to those who have inherited the legacy. Celebrations of some enormity every fifty years after the arrival of the Mormon pilgrims in 1847, most recently the sesquicentennial in 1997, have proven historically to be among Utah's most heralded commemorations.[5] The pioneer vanguard of 1847 is of consequence to both Mormons and Americans who recognize the importance of the West's settlement. Jacob's chronicle is, to those who are generations removed, one of the most revealing illuminators of that journey.

The cross-country expedition was an arduous one. The difficulties of overland travel in antebellum America, however, failed to discourage the hardy, desperate, and adventurous whose minds mused about the wonderland of the American West for themselves and for their families. As the young country's western borders incrementally moved westward, word of trans-Mississippi charms circulated through eastern cities and hamlets. Fur traders, government explorers, and missionaries, besides burnishing the Pacific slope's luster, further swelled America's appetite for expansion. Already decades in the making by the time the Mormons joined the westward cavalcade, movement to the western country by several thousand Americans had followed trails-turned-highways hugging numerous rivers like the Platte, Sweetwater, Snake, Columbia, Humboldt, and Truckee. These waterways, mostly unnavigable, proved the life-blood of western travel as they coursed through the grasslands, prairies, plains, high plateaus, mountain passes and valleys supplying, besides water to the emigrants, provender for the overlanders' animals. What massages our chimerical imaginations today, romanticizing the wonders of America-in-

4. Deuteronomy 6, in particular verse 12, "beware lest thou forget."
5. The requirements for re-enacting the 1847 trek fifty years later in 1897 would have been too close to the hardships of the actual journey to quicken the imaginations of those honoring the 1847 pioneers to carry out such a feat. Advances in technology buffered the difficulties for those who commemorated the event in the twentieth century. For a description of the centennial re-enactment in 1947 see Cannon, *Centennial Caravan*, and for the 1997 sesquicentennial re-enactment see Newbold, *In Our Fathers' Footsteps*, and Lloyd, "Pioneer Trek 1997."

the-rough, proved to be something less than idyllic to those who gambled their futures upon Eden's promise.[6]

Modern readers have difficulty comprehending the formidable difficulty of the journey for mid-nineteenth-century sojourners bound for the West. What took the 1847 Mormon vanguard one hundred eleven days to traverse[7]—just over a thousand miles—the handcart Saints, a decade later, accomplished in sixty to eighty days. The Pony Express and stage coaches in the early 1860s compressed the length of travel to a week or two. Still later, the journey by rail car took but two days. Today one can drive it in less than twenty-four hours or fly over it in two.[8] The distorted perspectives from extended time and technological convenience makes an account like Jacob's all the more important to moderns attempting to harness time while venturing to understand the past.

Jacob's account is also important when considered in light of his subordinate social status within Mormonism. "Once, historians looked only at society's upper crust," according to historian Howard Zinn. It was only "the leaders and others," Zinn continues, "who made the headlines and whose words and deeds survived as historical truth. In our lifetimes, [however,] this has begun to change. Shifting history's lens from the upper rungs to the lower, we are learning more than ever about the masses of people who did the work that made society tick."[9] Jacob and his kind were those who objectified the visions conjured by their leaders, the followers who provided the grist for their leaders' greatness. And while the traditionally lesser-regarded voices will never supercede in relative importance history's most visible and arguably more influential characters, there can be no claim for thorough, contextual, or comprehensive history without representation from the second, third, and fourth tiers of society, no matter the time or event considered.

Jacob represents that visibly under-represented class of Saints whose calloused hands, sun-burned necks, modest expectations, and quiet voices are too frequently obscured and who have been, for the most part, relegated to a lack of importance inordinately disproportional to their significance to

---

6. The literature regarding America's obsession with and movement to the West is vast and, therefore, unwieldy. The finest analysis and summary of nineteenth-century westward travel is John Unruh's *The Plains Across*. Merrill Mattes's *The Great Platte River Road*, though limited to describing travel from eastern Nebraska to eastern Wyoming, provides an excellent overview of the wide scope of the overland experience.
7. A useful exercise to better understand the geographical scope of the venture to the Great Basin is a review of William Clayton's *Latter-day Saints' Emigrants' Guide*, published the year after the vanguard's trek. Clayton, using the figures he gleaned during the 1847 journey from the use of his innovative "roadometer," breaks the entire expedition into brief segments, increments as short as a mile and a half, describing the physical characteristics and notable sites of the journey. See Stanley Kimball's edited version of Clayton's *Guide*.
8. Buckley, "Crossing the Great Plains," 8.
9. Zinn, preface to Raphael, *A People's History of the American Revolution*.

societal progress and cultural stability. Were it not for the seemingly small but steady incremental advances made by Mormonism's common folks—the followers—the religion would have stalled and collapsed into something far less than its current consequential status. In the spirit of satisfying the interest in understanding a fuller, more accurate, and complete record of the Mormon character, one that pries into the shaded corners of the past, Jacob's record stands as a declaration for authentic history.

Jacob's observations of Mormonism's recovery from shrinking confidence in the wake of Nauvoo's debacle to its independent swagger in the Great Basin can detour the reader's attention from the diarist's personal drama during the period. We know from Jacob and elsewhere little about his early life. But whoever he was, like so many of his contemporaries, the religion of the Latter-day Saints transformed Jacob's world. From relocating his residence to straining family relationships, the new faith altered his connections to several of a person's most important concerns. The effect was, at the outset, unsettling, to say the least. In affiliating, at the age of thirty-six, with Joseph Smith's religion, in spite of initial opposition from his entire family and at a time when the religion's almost universally unsavory reputation tainted anyone who bore its stigma, Jacob demonstrated an independence and self-assurance that speaks volumes about his personal world view and self-identity. The gauntlet of public disdain moved him not an inch from his self-determined course. This characteristic of resolution, of course, likely had other manifestations in Jacob's personality not featured in this protracted episode of his life.

Regrettably, the Jacob diary does not prove psychoanalytically revealing of particulars of his personal traits and idiosyncracies. It lacks introspection. Nor does it reveal the man's hearth-side behavior and thought. The nine years covered by Jacob's record, for the most part, describe a tumultuous time of tenuous and volatile circumstances. The contemporary contextual evidence still extant also provides little assistance to the modern reader in making known Jacob's persona, except for several stereotypical attributes we associate with the frontier: pioneer toughness, resilience to adversity, and unyielding determinism. Still, there is a character revealed through the significant event the diary illuminates that helps us to understand the motives, objectives, and achievement of adherents of nineteenth-century Mormonism.

Mormonism

The Church of Jesus Christ of Latter-day Saints, born in New York and raised through a rough childhood on America's antebellum hinterland, struggled into its adolescent identity as it fled its inhospitable motherland in 1846–1847. Severing its parental tether to step into the age of majority, Mormonism in its eighteenth year, journeyed into the western wilderness and forever after solidified its religious personality and stiffened its people's backbones to sustain a growing and more complex corpus. The Mormons' migration to the West proved to be the threshold over which the Latter-day Saints emerged into maturity. Brigham Young reminded his followers on 25 October 1846, of "the nature of our journey & suffering" to date. But "in ten years," he said, "it would be one of the most interesting histories in the world."[10] So it was, at least to the Saints. One of Mormonism's most important nineteenth-century figures, a vanguard brigade participant himself, Wilford Woodruff, defined in 1859 the singular importance of the Nauvoo to Salt Lake Valley journey. To Thomas L. Kane, Mormonism's unlikely nineteenth-century advocate, Woodruff wrote that the trek was "one of the most stirring and prominent events in the dealings of God with this people in their rise and progress."[11]

The Latter-day Saint exodus from the Mississippi and Missouri river valleys to the Great Basin of the American West is a rival for the most important event, though protracted, that ever occurred within Mormonism. Certainly the seminal foundational events empowering Joseph Smith to establish the Church of Jesus Christ of Latter-day Saints are, to Mormons, supreme in influence and effect upon what Mormonism became. But the 1846–1847 western trek initiated an episodic period that engendered the momentum to mold the dissimilar portions of the religion into an enduring, vivified organism. The initial pilgrimage, combined with the emigrant companies that immediately followed, "served as the foundation to all that came after."[12] For a generation, year after year, companies of trail-worn Mormons descended from the Wasatch's canyons having endured a unique transformational religious sacrament that shaped their spiritual and cultural identity. Americans and Europeans, who populated Mormonism in its first two generations, acquired similar characteristics.

Preponderantly poor, a certain equanimity emerged among the Mormon sojourners during the overland journey. By wooden wagon drawn by oxen, horses, or mules, on foot or horseback, pushing and pulling carts, tens of thousands trudged for months at a time across the North American landscape. A homogeneity of participation, by the very nature of what they believed and what they had done, marked their experience. Upon their arrival, by families or as individuals, the pilgrims procured that indelible identity as being one among those who had gathered to Zion. It was not something that singled one out among his or her contemporaries, for each and all were among the gathered. Nevertheless, for the first generation the recognition that one

---

10. Stout, *On the Mormon Frontier*, 1:206.
11. Wilford Woodruff to Thomas L. Kane, 8 March 1859, Historian's Office, Letterpress Copybooks, v. 1, p. 727–730. Richard Bennett recently echoed Woodruff's view, stating: "the coming of Brigham Young and his band of faithful followers was a defining moment in the history of Mormonism, of the state of Utah, and of America." Bennett, *We'll Find the Place*, xiii.
12. Bennett, *We'll Find the Place*, xiv.

had made the journey qualified them for something beyond their baptismal membership in the LDS Church. They now had stories to tell: not someone else's story, their own. The crucible of crossing the plains proved to be the catalyst that transformed the Latter-day Saints from disparate groups and individuals into something they previously were not.

This change of status, while mostly immeasurable, nevertheless actuated, in significant ways, the sojourners. The stories coalesced and bound together the pioneers and their posterity. There was a biogenetic strain, of sorts, to the inheritance. To the pioneers, and their descendants alike, attachment to the exodus to Zion meant more than participation in a heroic event. "Although [Mormonism is] called 'The Church of Jesus Christ of Latter-day Saints' and may very well be in theological definition a church," declares noted religious historian Martin Marty, "I perceive it more as a people." Marty speaks of the societal qualities that weave frayed and tangential strands into a garment. "What's interesting about the Mormons," he explains, "is that they are from a mixed ethnic stock not much different from the rest of the majority and yet they are a distinct people." It is a "story," he says, a common story, that "makes a people."[13] The primary event vivifying this metamorphosis from disparate fragments into a mutual entity included months of incessant walking, ubiquitous clouds of dust, chronic fatigue, sleep under the stars, and bouts of gastrointestinal distress. The shared experience, harrowing to some, adventure for others, but, for most, just the most arduous endeavor of their lives, is underestimated by those who misunderstand Mormonism's substantial success. For while the trek is now generations removed from reality, its effect still melds the Latter-day Saints.

As important as this story may be to not only the settlement of the West but to the nation's growth in the nineteenth century, its significance has been relegated to something less than consequential by many modern observers. One explanation for this apparent neglect is measured by the accountant's game; what do the numbers reveal? On a ledger book, how does the Mormon vanguard, or, for that matter, the entire Mormon migration, fit within the chronicle of American history? How significant were 148 Mormon pilgrims trudging their way westward across the continent? "Between 1840 and 1860," according to historian Richard White, "approximately 300,000 people traveled to the Far West on the overland trails. Of them, 53,000 went to Oregon, 200,000 to California (120,000 during the Gold Rush years), and 43,000 went to Utah."[14]

13. Marty, "It Finally All Depends on God," 46. This generalization, of course, refers to the entirety of the Mormon exodus to Utah. Frankly, the vanguard's venture was not the story of a people, but the story of the male half of the people. The story of a people, by definition, is a narrative where at least half the tale describes females. The neglect of women in this account comes of an information hole, not an ignorance of their importance to the story of Mormonism.

14. White, *It's Your Misfortune*, 189.

Less than 50,000 Mormons compared to over a quarter million of their countrymen in a score of years. The contrast of the 148 who composed the 1847 Mormon vanguard to the 4,500 who coursed the Oregon Trail for the west coast that year is even more stark.[15] In the light of this comparison, compared to contemporary American sojourners, the simple power of numbers places the Mormon venture short of the extraordinary place it holds in the Mormon panorama. But misjudging, by the numbers, the relative importance of this story and its expanded implications regarding the history of the West distorts for the modern observer the significant contribution to American history made by these zealous characters.

Besides the sometimes misleading exercise of appraising relevance by comparing numbers, the Mormon trek's importance is also lessened by what Jan Shipps, the long-tenured Mormon observer, has argued is the "shallow coverage" given the Mormon story by historians of the West who consign the Mormon epic to "the western history ghetto." "[T]he Mormon story," she claims, "must somehow seem un-Western to many who study, theorize, and write about the history of the American West," concluding that "many, if not most, historians of the West shape the western story like a doughnut, circling all around the Great Basin, taking into account and telling nearly every western story except the Mormon one."[16] Noted historian Patricia Limerick endorses Shipps's recognition of the disparity. "Mormon history," Limerick notes, "is one of the most compelling, distinctive, and instructive components of [western] regional history; yet under the terms of the old, frontier school of Western American history," Mormon history finds itself "dismissed and marginalized."[17]

A Much Chronicled Journey

Despite national and regional neglect, the Mormon exodus remains an oft-told story within Mormonism. Indeed, Walter Nugent has stated recently: "Much has been written about the 1847 trek of several hundred Latter-day Saints under Brigham Young from Council Bluffs, Iowa, along the north bank of the Platte River through the South pass to the shore of the Great Salt Lake."[18] So what is the justification for yet another volume added to the Mormon story?

---

15. Unruh, *Plains Across*, 119.
16. Shipps, *Sojourner in the Promised Land*, 21. Kenneth Owens also draws attention to this neglect in *Gold Rush Saints*, 27–28, 360–370.
17. Limerick, "Peace Initiative," 6. Stewart Udall recently criticized some interpreters of western development who have "warped" our understanding of the settlement of the West by "diminish[ing] the importance of the community-building work of settlers who came to stay." This group included, according to Stewart, Protestant and Catholic missionaries, immigrant farmers, and Mormons. Udall, *Forgotten Founders*, 6. See also Ferenc Morton Szasz, "How Religion Created an Infrastructure for the Mountain West" in Shipps and Silk, *Religion and Public Life*, 49–68.
18. Nugent, *Into the West*, 80. Nugent's generalization is correct, though the place of origin for the 1847 trek was Winter Quarters, in Nebraska, rather than Council Bluffs, Iowa.

Richard Bennett's authoritative volume on the Mormon vanguard's trek west, *We'll Find the Place*, published for the event's sesquicentennial celebration in 1997, was justified, in part, because, as he said, "While so much has been written, the surprise is that so much of the story has never been told."[19] Despite Bennett's commendable overview of the Mormon exodus into the West, much of the story *still* remains to be told. Bennett's treatment of the exodus provides the surrounding context for the Mormon vanguard's creation and execution. He explains, as well, by way of fresh and insightful interpretation, the vanguard's leader's motivations, ordeal, and accomplishment during the spring and summer of 1847. Missing from Bennett's portrayal, however, except for brief excerpts, are the actual voices of the journey, the contemporary records of its participants. These voices of the trail illuminate the story in authentic ways impossible for any modern narrative or analysis to convey.

Several dozen who were numbered among the 1847 Mormon pioneer vanguard created personal accounts of the endeavor.[20] Many are contemporary records, a handful or so of which are first-rate portrayals of the journey. (A few participants wrote reminiscent documents.) Just two years after Brigham Young's brigade entered the Salt Lake Valley, Orson Pratt serially published his diary of the trek in the *Latter-day Saints' Millennial Star* (in England) as "Interesting Items Concerning the Journeying of the Latter-day Saints from the City of Nauvoo, Until Their Location in the Valley of the Great Salt Lake." While Pratt's fine report was thus first published somewhat contemporarily (and later republished in 1924–1926 and 1975), the other personal accounts of the journey did not become publicly available until decades after the event and only after the deaths of their creators. In 1886, seven years after William Clayton's demise, his diary for April-July 1847 was excerpted in the LDS Church's *Juvenile Instructor*. Clayton's diary has proven to be the most comprehensive and informative contemporary narrative of the 1847 trek. Its later publication in 1921 as *William Clayton's Journal: A Daily Record of the Journey of the Original Company of "Mormon" Pioneers from Nauvoo, Illinois, to the Valley of the Great Salt Lake*, remains the most important of 1847 accounts.[21] In 1911–1912 Erastus Snow's diary of the period was printed

19. Bennett, *We'll Find the Place*, xiii.
20. Most of these accounts were acquired and are now preserved by the LDS Church Archives, originally known as the Historian's Office. See Melvin Bashore's and Linda Haslam's *Mormon Pioneer Companies Crossing the Plains (1847–1868) Narratives* for the extant accounts of the trek's participants, contemporary and retrospective, and their present whereabouts in Utah. (Some 1847 accounts may be found outside Utah, such as Howard Egan's original diary which can be found at Yale University's Beinecke Library.) Bashore's and Haslam's important compilation also identifies the surviving accounts found in Utah repositories or libraries of every known company of LDS emigrants to Utah prior to 1869.
21. A more recent publication of William Clayton's journal *An Intimate Chronicle: The Journals of William Clayton* (1995), edited by George D. Smith, contains an abbreviated, and therefore incomplete, form of Clayton's 1847 diary.

serially in the LDS Church's *Improvement Era* as "From Nauvoo to Salt Lake in the Van of the Pioneers" (and later, in 1948, as "Journey to Zion" in the *Utah Humanities Review*). Snow's account was followed in 1917 by Howard Egan's account of the trek, *Pioneering the West, 1846 to 1878: Major Howard Egan's Diary*. Following these significant publications, the diaries of Heber C. Kimball (kept by Clayton and published in 1939–1940), John Brown (1941), Appleton Milo Harmon (1946), Lorenzo Dow Young (1946), Horace K. Whitney (1947, excerpts), William A. Empey (1949), Albert Perry Rockwood (1968), Brigham Young (1971, compiled by clerks), Charles Alfred Harper (ca. 1971), Wilford Woodruff (1983), Levi Jackman (1986), and, mostly recently, Thomas Bullock (1997), were printed.[22] With the exception of Bullock's diary, and an incomplete version of Clayton's, all previous accounts are now out-of-print.[23]

Not only are most of the previously published records of the pioneer diarists generally unavailable except through libraries, several of the most important of the primary records remain unpublished. These include the journals of George A. Smith and Amasa M. Lyman, (both kept by Albert Carrington). Both are significant and merit publication. Many of the other accounts from those composing the pioneer vanguard were brief recollections or records,

---

22. See this volume's bibliography for full citations of these publications.
23. Several compilations provide important overviews of the 1847 trek and the Mormon Trail. A number contain excerpts of diary entries of the vanguard company to illustrate the venture's scope. The unpublished ones include two prepared by the LDS Church Historian's Office: Church Emigration, 1831–1869, and Journal History of the Church, which both recount the 1847 journey. The published ones include two by Andrew Jenson, "The Pioneers of 1847" (1890) and *Day by Day with the Utah Pioneers* (1897, 1934, and various republications), Preston Nibley's *Exodus to Greatness* (1947), Hal Knight's and Stanley Kimball's *111 Days to Zion* (1978), and Carol Madsen's *Journey to Zion* (1997).

    Other compilations contain biographical sketches and appraisals of those constituting the vanguard company. The published chronicles are Andrew Jenson's *Day by Day* (1897, 1934), Kate Carter's "They Came in '47" (1947), Kate Carter's "The First Company to Enter Salt Lake Valley" (1959), Susan Black's "Impact of the Original Pioneer Company" (1984), and the "1847 Pioneers," *Deseret News, 1997–98 Church Almanac* (1996), the latter and Carter's containing the most complete biographical sketches of the Mormon vanguard. For information about the women and children who accompanied the vanguard, see Adams, "She's Going."

    The important narratives portraying the Mormon pioneer story of 1846–1847 include Wallace Stegner's *The Gathering of Zion* (1964), Joseph Brown's *The Mormon Trek West* (1980), Richard Holzapfel's *Their Faces toward Zion* (1996), William Slaughter's and Michael Landon's *Trail of Hope* (1997), Susan Black's and William Hartley's *The Iowa Mormon Trail* (1997), and Richard Bennett's *We'll Find the Place* (1997). Stanley Kimball's *Historic Sites and Markers along the Mormon and Other Great Western Trails* (1988), characterizes the Mormon Trail and the modern monuments commemorating important sites along the trail.

    A Public Broadcasting System documentary directed by Lee Groberg and written by Heidi Swinton, *Trail of Hope: The Story of the Mormon Trail* (1997), adds a significant multi-media dimension to the topic.

some of which have been published, while others remain unpublished and obscure.

Place of Norton Jacob's Account

While William Clayton's and Thomas Bullock's accounts may be the most universally instructive portrayals of the 1847 journey, Norton Jacob's record of the trek begs the attention of all students of the Mormon exodus to Utah, if not a significant place in the historic chronicles of the entire overland venture. First printed as a typescript in 1949 (reprinted in 1953) by family members, that limited edition of "The Record of Norton Jacob" lacked the interpretive annotation required to properly place the journey in context and to illustrate its importance in Mormon literature as personal narrative.[24] Jacob's straightforward, legible, and well-written chronicle makes accessible the view of one of the expedition's rank-and-file, in contrast to the more visible records written by and for the company's leaders (Clayton and Bullock). Jacob and most of his less visible Mormon contemporaries, lack, in today's cultural market, an acknowledgment that it was people laboring at his level who actually bore the weight of the Mormon kingdom. Responding affirmatively to their leaders' direction, Jacob's sort ultimately determined whether initiatives, projects, or programs were successfully completed or derailed by indifference or malcontent.

Several levels of leadership in 1847 managed the company of 148 persons, including fourteen "captains of ten." Norton Jacob was appointed captain of the twelfth ten. Though lacking the authority of one of the expedition's visible leaders, Jacob's account represents a blue-collar point of view necessary to understand the full scope of the Mormon vanguard. His record can be likened to Solomon Carvalho's portrayal of John C. Fremont's 1853 expedition to the West,[25] or Frederick Dellenbaugh's portrait of John Wesley Powell's exploration of the Colorado River in 1871–1872,[26] accompanying accounts of significant epics which provide a broadened perspective on the historic ventures. Jacob documents particulars of not only the vanguard's journey to the West but also their return to Winter Quarters later in the year, an arguably more interesting segment of the venture that is barely known.[27] His earlier personal observations of the unsettling aftermath of the assassinations

24. Jacob and Jacob, *Record of Norton Jacob*. The LDS Church Historian's Office used Jacob's diary in the compilation of a unpublished day-by-day account of the pioneer venture produced between 1923 and 1926. Historian's Office, Pioneers of 1847, Church Emigration, 1831–1869.
25. Carvalho, *Incidents of Travel*.
26. Dellenbaugh, *A Canyon Voyage*.
27. Wallace Stegner's *The Gathering of Zion*, pages 173–196, and this editor's biography of Lewis Barney, one of Jacob's ten, give some dimension to the return of the vanguard with some Mormon Battalion veterans to Winter Quarters. *One Side by Himself*, 106–116.

of Joseph and Hyrum Smith, the final efforts to finish Nauvoo's temple, the Saints' removal from Nauvoo to what became the Mormon settlements on the Missouri River, and preparations there for the 1847 hegira to Utah provide a splendid context preparatory to the vanguard's trek. Another dimension that augments this first-person witness just described is Jacob's chronicle of 1848, when he removed his wife and children from western Iowa and returned to the Salt Lake Valley, to settle his family. Jacob's perspective of the complicated segments of the Mormons' removal from the Midwest to the Great Basin adds significantly to the literature describing the initial Anglo settlement of Utah, and illuminating Mormon purposes and strategies for survival in their escape to the western wilderness.[28]

"The Record of Norton Jacob"

The original manuscript of the document edited here was donated by Jacob family members in 1949 to the LDS Church Historian's Office (now the Church Archives, Family and Church History Department, The Church of Jesus Christ of Latter-day Saints, Salt Lake City, Utah), where it is available to researchers. (The title of the record, as catalogued in the LDS Church Archives, is Norton Jacob (1804–1879), Reminiscence and Journal, 1844 May–1852 January.) The record, self-titled by Jacob as "The Record of Norton Jacob," compared to documents of a similar genre, is unusual in size. The volume is rectangular in shape, 16.5 inches (42 cm.) in height, and 6.5 inches (16.5 cm.) in width. The bound volume originally had 156 pages (78 leaves). However, the final 32 pages (16 leaves), or 20 percent of the account, were trimmed from the book. It is assumed that the extricated pages contained text. It is not known how many years into Norton Jacob's life beyond 1852 the missing pages represented. It is also not known by whom or why the action of removing the pages, which undoubtedly injures Jacob's life record, was perpetrated. (The typescript of Jacob's record, prepared in 1949, contains all of the journal that is extant, except for the final few lines of the account, where Jacob begins telling of disharmony between himself and his second wife.)

Source references to some materials in annotations herein are cited as the published or typescript versions of the texts, which tend to be more accessible to the reader than original documents. A compilation of biographical notes, identifying those mentioned by Jacob in his account, has been appended to the journal. Where information could not be found regarding a very few named by Jacob, their sketch does not appear in the footnotes or biographical notes. A short form of citation of sources used in annotating the volume is used throughout the book. Full bibliographic citations can be found in the bibliography.

---

28. Narrative overviews of the Mormon venture during this period are found in Leonard, *Nauvoo*, 418–619; Bennett, *Mormons at the Missouri*; and Bennett, *We'll Find the Place*.

The Jacob diary, documents, and photographs annotate and illustrate the text are used courtesy of the Church Archives, The Church of Jesus Christ of Latter-day Saints. While I am an employee of the LDS Church Archives, this work is not sponsored by nor approved by the Church of Jesus Christ of Latter-day Saints. Nor has the final product received the church's endorsement.

EDITORIAL PROCEDURES

Several different styles for transcribing historical documents from holograph to typescript exist that are accepted by the community of documentary and scholarly editors in representing modern productions of texts. The document's characteristics often dictate the style in which the item will be rendered. The method of transcription employed in this project, because Jacob wrote with relative clarity, without many incidental corrections, uses components of more than one style, which is allowable if used consistently throughout the text. The Jacob record is, in my judgment, best represented to the modern reader by a combination of the methods of "diplomatic" and "expanded" transcription as described by Michael Stevens and Steven Burg. The characteristics of these forms include "transfer[ing] the text of a document into modern type [by using] symbols such as arrows, carets, and brackets to indicate the document's stylistic details and appearance," and "standardizing accidentals, datelines, and signatures" as well as "mark[ing] paragraphs with indentations" absent the "attempt to reproduce the excessive spacing and physical layout of the text of documents."[29] This transcription of Norton Jacob's original diary represents my ambition to make Jacob's work accessible to the modern reader while attempting to reproduce the manuscript as closley as possible.

Spelling and capitalization are rendered as written by Jacob. Silent punctuation has been added to both Jacob's account and to some of his contemporaries' accounts used in the footnotes, primarily by way of periods or commas, to render the text more understandable to the reader. Some of Jacob's punctuation not conforming to modern usage has been altered, such as periods or commas silently replacing em dashes where appropriate. Also, equal signs in the original text, as in "Sweet=water," have been modernized to hyphens, rendering "Sweet-water."

[Brackets] indicate the editor's alteration of or addition to the text. Insertions into the text by Jacob are shown by <angle brackets>. Hyphens in hyphenated words in the original text are eliminated. Ordinal superscripts, such as 12th, are lowered to the line, i.e., 12th. Numbers with fractions are represented as a whole number with a space before the fraction. Strikeouts and erasures are shown as ~~strikeouts~~. Write-overs are shown as <angle brackets> with the corrected word or words shown as a ~~strikeout~~. The abbreviation,

29. Stevens and Burg, *Editing Historical Documents*, 76.

"&c," used by Jacob represents etcetera. Underlining is represented by *italics*. Ampersands (&), signifying the word *and*, have been retained in the text. Jacob's use, still fairly common in the nineteenth century, of the antiquated *long s*, particularly to precede a standard *s* when rendering a double *s*, as in *paſs* for *pass*, has been modernized to a standard *ss*. Abbreviations for ante meridiem and post meridiem, A.M. and P.M., often written as large capitals by Jacob, are standardized in small capitals.

Editorial marks on the pages, presumably supplied by the editors of the 1949/1953 transcription of the Jacob diary, obscure the original text in numerous instances. While most of Jacob's original writing is discernible, there are, in cases of capitalization primarily, occasions where conjecture is represented in my rendition of Jacob's text.

Mileage figures, either totals from Winter Quarters or daily figures, are sometimes insertions made by Jacob above the line or entered at the bottom of a page. When insertions of mileage appear mid-sentence, interrupt the narrative, or are written at the page's bottom, they are included at sentence's end or at the end of the day's entry, common to many of Jacob's other mileage entries.

Jacob's inclusion of latitude, i.e., Lat 49° 28' 28", supplied by Orson Pratt, were usually inserted above the line in the Jacob diary as insertions, though occasionally they were included as part of the text. For the sake of uniformity, the measurements are placed at the end of the day's entry in which the figure appear.

~

His Life

~

SHEFFIELD, MASSACHUSETTS'S VILLAGE CEMETERY, Bow Wow by name, became the final resting place for several generations of Norton Jacob's family, whose antecedents arrived in Britain's American colonies in the first quarter of the seventeenth century. Native American claims and rights in southwestern Massachusetts, where Sheffield sat, had been extinguished by a growing Anglo presence and colonial government in 1724. Within a generation, the Jacob and Kellogg families, Norton's ancestors, called the frontier village home. By the time Norton's grandfather Richard Jacob, Jr., was born there in 1760, during the French and Indian War, Sheffield was the most populous settlement in Berkshire County.[1] A dozen years later, however, the county's residents were reticent to completely endorse the anti-British sentiment espoused by their Boston brothers. But the revolutionary spirit soon stirred the region, and Sheffield's citizens joined the patriotic breach against their motherland. Richard's son Udney Hay, named after the Revolutionary War figure, was born in Sheffield in 1781.[2]

The dominant influence in Sheffield for generations was Congregationalism, whose "prescribed orthodoxy meant Calvinism." Norton Jacob, born there 11 August 1804 to Udney Hay and Elizabeth Hubbard Jacob, grew up in a religious climate where church and state melded to shape the character of the community, which grew to 2,500 residents by 1820.[3] When Norton was about eight years of age, Udney broke his family's patrilocal tradition in Sheffield and relocated over one hundred miles westward to the Finger Lakes region of New York, temporarily residing at Scipio in Cayuga County. This was followed by a brief stay two counties to the east in Chenango County, New York. By 1822 Udney moved his family westward again, this time much

---

1. Both Norton Jacob's paternal great-grandfather and grandfather settled in Sheffield before the birth of Norton's father.
2. Hoogs, *Sheffield, Massachusetts*, 18; Preiss, *Sheffield*, 36–38, 42, 73. Udney Hay was a colonial colonel in the Revolutionary War and a deputy quartermaster general, who organized a black military unit of 125 men, thirty being free blacks, called the First Rhode Island Regiment. He later became involved in Vermont politics. Lopriano, "Pompey Lamb Revisited."
3. Preiss, *Sheffield*, 19, 21, 51.

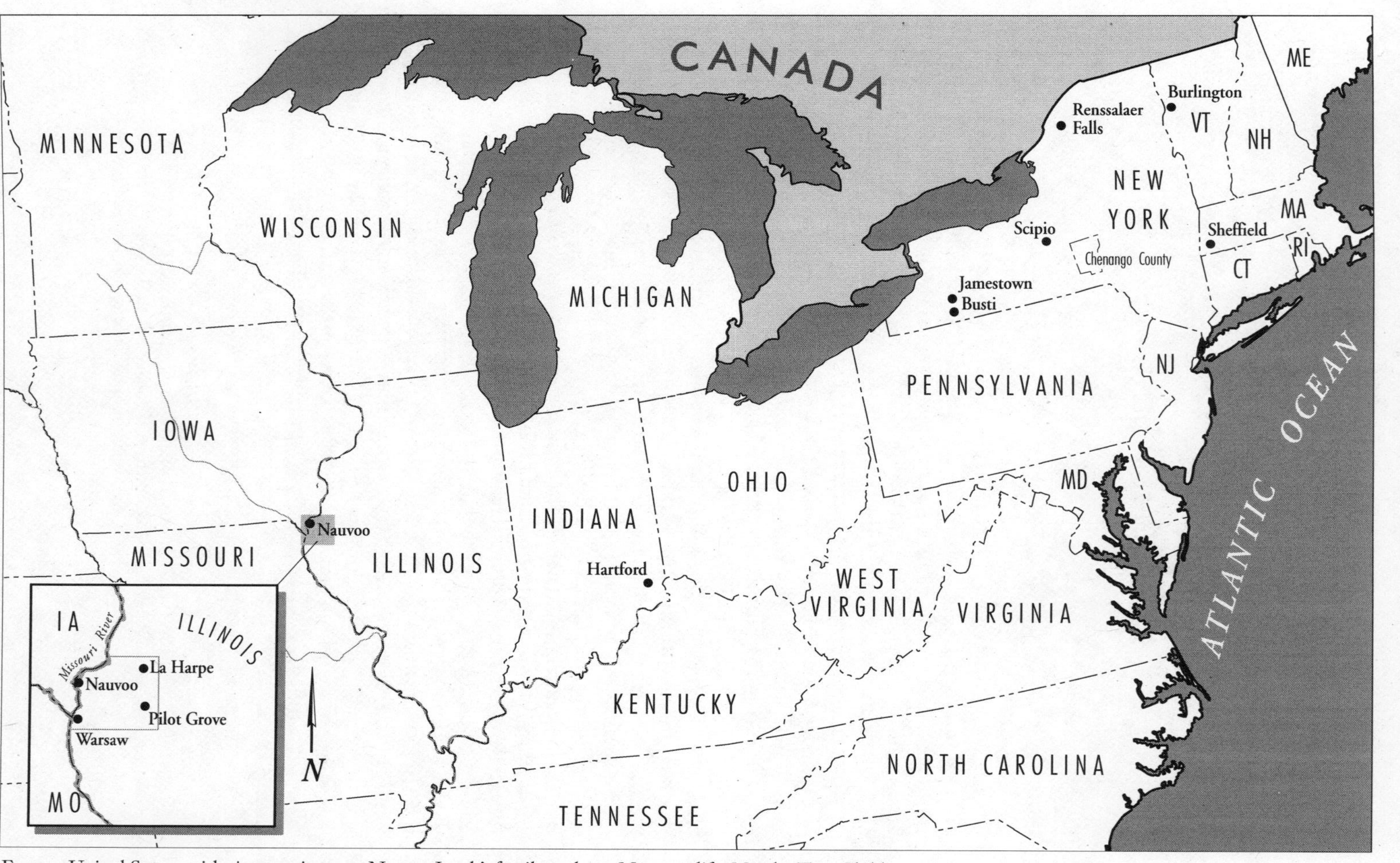

Eastern United States, with sites pertinent to Norton Jacob's family and pre-Mormon life. Map by Tom Child.

deeper into the interior, to Hartford in southeastern Indiana. But a handful of years later, one of his seven children, Jason, recalled, his father returned for a time to New York.[4]

As Norton Jacob's father jockeyed for a suitable location to permanently establish himself, the son came of age. Having relocated himself to western New York at Busti in Chautauqua County, twenty-six-year-old Norton married Emily Heaton, a nineteen-year-old woman from Burlington, Vermont, on 20 November 1830. The following May a female child arrived in their household. Elsie Pamelia would be the first of eleven children born to the couple. Three years later, after apparently moving a short distance to Jamestown in the same county, Oliver Barr Jacob, the Jacobs' first surviving son, joined the family. (The year previous, little Benjamin had died shortly after birth.) Later in the year, after Oliver's birth in January 1834, Norton and Emily packed their young family together and moved a third of a continent westward to the edge of civilization, on the east bank of the Mississippi River.

Illinois, a state since 1818 and the object of one of the most effective real estate promotions in American history in the 1820s and 1830s, drew hopefuls from every sector of eastern America. Norton Jacob grasped the promising opportunity and settled at Warsaw, in Hancock County, Illinois, whose western boundary was the great Father of Waters. Citizens of the several river towns upstream from St. Louis, Missouri, calculated strategies to tap the increasing river traffic for commercial increase. Jacob joined the contest and in 1834 built Hancock County's first mill "run by Wilcox & Co., at Warsaw."[5] There his family continued to grow with the birth of Lucian in 1836. The following year Norton's younger brother Stephen moved to Pilot Grove, just twenty miles northeast of Warsaw on the Illinois prairie.[6] It is not known if Norton preceded his brother or if the younger Jacob's move lured his older brother to the county's eastern sector, but by 1838 Norton had relocated his family to Pilot Grove. Settled but a few years earlier by folks from Virginia, Ohio, Kentucky, and New York, the township's mix of northerners and southerners seemed to work. Boasting "a wide expanse of prairie, covered with ducks and deer and waving grass and wild flowers,"[7] the township's landscape was much different than the eastern woodlands that served the Jacobs for generations.

The Jacob brothers' success on Illinois's rich prairie proved compelling to the rest of the family as well. In 1838 Norton's father Udney moved his family to Hancock County and settled a few miles north of his children in the county's northeastern sector, in Durham Township not far from the only settlement

4. Gregg, *History of Hancock County, Illinois*, 921–922.
5. Gregg, *History of Hancock County, Illinois*, 849–850.
6. Stephen Jacob's property is shown in Pilot Grove Township, Hancock County, Illinois, in an 1859 plat map of the county. *Map of Hancock County, Illinois*.
7. Gregg, *History of Hancock County, Illinois*, 841.

in the area, La Harpe.[8] The village of La Harpe, named for an early French explorer in the area, emerged in the early 1830s. Coupled with "as excellent a body of prairie as can be found in the county," the region was also "well timbered, skirting two branches of Crooked Creek."[9] Another of Norton's brothers, Jason, two years his junior, also established himself in the county, marrying there in 1839.[10] Hancock County, with its attendant allurements for settlement and frontier progress and prosperity, worked satisfactorily for a couple of Norton's siblings for decades. But while Norton's father and siblings forged their familial and economic futures, his own radically transformed.

Somewhat coincidental to the Jacob family establishing themselves in Illinois, the luckless followers of Joseph Smith, known as Mormons, found themselves finally expelled from the state of Missouri, where they had lobbied, in several locations since 1831, for acceptance against some pretty cold shoulders. Their collectiveness, as well as their religious heterodoxy, did not play well anywhere in republican Christian America. Refugees to western Illinois in 1839, the Mormons' plight in Missouri had become known throughout the region. Illinoisans initially showed them much sympathy. But as the Saints increasingly occupied the western peninsula of Hancock County and beyond, their presence became more than a curiosity to the county's earlier residents. With Mormon numbers and influence increasing, a proportional amount of antipathy mounted towards them. For a minority of locals, though, the religion's unusualness provoked interest. One of the latter was curious Norton Jacob.

Jacob later noted that during 1840's summer season he read a booklet written in reply to one of the anti-Mormon works of the time. The Mormon author of the volume, Parley Pratt, one of Mormonism's most important literary constructionists, set him to thinking. Pratt had declared, according to Jacob, "some important Prophesies which appeared to me to be related to those found in the Bible, which led me into a new field of inquiry; for I fuly believed the Prophets, & that whatever the Lord had spoken by them would . . . be fulfiled in his own due time."[11] Over the ensuing fall and winter Jacob continued his investigation of the provocative religion, listening to "some of the Elders preach," and reading "with much interest" Pratt's *Voice of Warning* (1837). As the climax to Jacob's study, Zenos Gurley, a Mormon elder from

8. Udney H. Jacob, is identified in Hancock County land records for 1842 as having purchased 120 acres (80 and 40 acres, worth $400 and $120, respectively) in Township 7, Range 6. Hancock (Ill.: County) Assessor's Office, Books of Assessment, 1840, 1842, and 1850, p. 51.
9. Gregg, *History of Hancock County, Illinois*, 892.
10. Jason Kellogg Jacob's property in 1859 is shown in a plat map of Durham Township, Hancock County, Illinois. *Map of Hancock County, Illinois*; Gregg, *History of Hancock County, Illinois*, 921–922.
11. Norton Jacob's statements found in this biographical sketch come from the beginning of chapter 1 of this volume.

Nauvoo, the center of the Mormon gathering in Hancock County, shook the recently established moorings in the county's northeastern sector by baptizing fifty-two people, "the first class of society," in six days. Jacob was one of them; on 15 March 1841, at age thirty-six, he crossed the Mormon threshold.

Immediately, Gurley's new convert felt a wall of familial resistance. Besides his wife and her father, who were skeptics, Norton wrote, "My Father, Mother, Brothers, & Sisters opposed me violently. my Fat[h]er said he had rather heard I was dead than that I was a Mormon." Sixty-year-old Udney Hay Jacob's own exegesis of biblical religion, ancient and modern, ran counter to Joseph Smith's reconfiguration of Jesus's religion away from that of the rest of American Christianity. He undoubtedly could tell that Mormonism's dye had washed deeply his son's thinking, and he was concerned about the eternal salvation of Norton's soul. At this stage, Udney was anything but passive about the new religion. While Norton's life after encountering the Latter-day Saints is straightforward and understandable, his father's track in and around Mormonism deviated enigmatically and unpredictably until the last years of the elder Jacob's life. The Jacob patriarch's connection to Mormonism remains today controversial, if amusing, considering the antipodal beliefs he periodically held. It is even likely the case that Udney's inordinate interest in Christianity raised Norton's consciousness about the religious world he encountered in Hancock County, directly resulting in Norton's curiosity about Mormonism. But Udney was not just interested in religion, he philosophically roamed the political arena as well.

Letters Udney Jacob wrote in March 1840 indicate he had produced a manuscript concerning religion, demonstrating, for the time, some sophistication of thought. A 3 March 1840 letter to a Mormon acquaintance, prior to Udney's son's interest in the Latter-day Saints, illustrates his deduction, by dissecting New Testament texts, that baptism for the remission of sins, for example, was not necessary. Jesus, he reasoned, had redeemed a repentant world of their sins, and as his disciples were among the repentant, those, including the Mormons, who required baptism for the remission of sins of believers made "an idol of their own works, as much as if they had made a graven image and worshipped it." Indeed, he continued, those "who teach that we must be baptized in order to receive the Holy Spirit, might as well teach that we must first love God in order to make him love us. It is precisely the same idea in a different form." He pledged to his Mormon friends that his purpose in arousing their attention to their error was "that you might be saved from the bitterness and false wrath erected in you by sorcery."[12]

But Udney was not content to sway only the Hancock County locals regarding his religious thinking. Later that month, the elder Jacob, claiming to be "a watchman upon the wals of Zion and seeing the sword approaching," wrote to Martin Van Buren, the United States president, then in the middle

12. Jacob to Granger, 3 March 1840.

of the 1840 campaign for reelection, to inform the president that "I hold in my hands a manuscript, which if it was published seasonably, and sufficiently circulated, would . . . be the certain means of insureing your Election." Without giving detail in his letter about his political strategies, he also issued a warning about the Latter-day Saints: "I know them to be deluded and [a] dangerous set of fanatics," and "I am informed [that Joseph Smith] is determined to throw his weight with all his deluded followers into the scale against you."[13] This would not be the last time Udney's religious and biblical views stirred the climate of Hancock County.

After witnessing his family's resistance to his Mormon affiliation, Norton Jacob determined that living amidst his kin "was no place for me." His half interest in eighty acres at Pilot Grove, which he jointly purchased in October 1840 with his brother Stephen, he liquidated in full to his brother, and in the fall of 1841 he built a temporary home closer to Nauvoo. He relocated his family to the Mormon capital the following year, in November 1842. By this time he had been ordained to the lay priesthood, to the office of elder, and had refashioned his temporal and spiritual infrastructure to absorb all that was Mormon. In Nauvoo his children—Elsie, Oliver, and Lucian—were schooled and Norton became trustee of one of the numerous schools conducted in the city.[14] He also joined the city's military unit, the Nauvoo Legion.[15] Norton had cast his lot with the Saints.[16] It was an ultimate gesture from which he would never retreat.

While Norton was preparing his home and his young family for habitation in Nauvoo, his father Udney stirred Mormonism itself, though a full understanding of his impact at the time and later remains speculative. The controversy surrounding Udney Hay Jacob's thirty-seven-page booklet published in 1842, commonly called *The Peacemaker*, was the means by which the elder Jacob reached wider public awareness.[17] Using biblical

---

13. Jacob to Van Buren, 19 March 1840. There is no evidence from Van Buren's extant papers that he actually received the letter or, if he did, replied to it. It is clear from the letter's content that Jacob was soliciting financial assistance to have his manuscript published.
14. The report for Lavina Whipple's school, of which Norton Jacob was a trustee in late 1843 and early 1844, show his children's regular attendance during January and February 1844. Other school records showing his children's participation, if any, are not extant. Hancock (Ill. : County) School Commissioner, Nauvoo School Schedules, 1842–1845.
15. Nauvoo Legion, Files 1841–1845.
16. This apparent adherence to everything Mormon included voting patterns. For example, in the Hancock County, Illinois, election of 1 August 1842, for which the voting record survives for Nauvoo residents, Jacob is shown as having voted for the candidates supported by the rest of the Saints. Thomas Ford, then in Mormon favor, received 454 votes in Nauvoo to that of his opponent who had 5. Other candidates for the offices of Lieutenant Governor, Senate and House Representatives, Sheriff, and Coroner, received similar results based upon Mormon endorsement or not. This block voting contributed to the irreparable fracture between the Saints and the county's residents. Illinois. Hancock County. Nauvoo Precinct, Election Returns, 1842 Aug. 1.
17. It is apparent that the text of *The Peacemaker* represents portions of the manuscript on religion created by Udney Jacob referred to earlier.

precedent, the treatise addresses gender relations and, in particular, marital behavior according to God's intention for the human family. Explicating diverse matters such as fornication, adultery, divorce, and barrenness, while lamenting the contemporary situation of familial matters in the country, Udney Jacob brashly argued, in conclusion, for the reinstitution of Old Testament polygamy. While Norton's father was still not a Mormon (he later would be) and apparently lacked funds to self-publish, the job was printed in Nauvoo, Illinois, with Joseph Smith listed as publisher: this at a time when plural marriage among the Saints was very limited in practice and still secret. Adding to the intrigue, Joseph Smith, through Nauvoo's church organ, the *Times and Seasons*, promptly condemned the piece.[18] While there was some impact from the pamphlet's publication at the time, the little work eventually reached outside its initial limited influence.[19]

Norton Jacob's tenure in Nauvoo, practicing Mormonism, reinforced his commitment to his religion. Besides his wife finally embracing the faith in July 1843, he wrote that he "had closely observed the course & proceedings

18. Joseph Smith denounced the piece as "an unmeaning rigmarole of nonsence [*sic*], folly, and trash." *Times and Seasons* 4, no. 2 (1 December 1842): 32.

For preliminary investigations into the pamphlet and its author, see Godfrey, "A New Look at the Alleged Little Known Discourse," 49–53; Foster, "A Little Known Defense of Polygamy from the Mormon Press in 1842," 21–34, and Foster, *Religion and Sexuality*, 174–177. Lawrence Foster's conclusion that Jacob and Joseph Smith were collaborative in the production of the pamphlet is unlikely. In Udney's 6 January 1844 letter to Joseph Smith, whom Jacob states that he had never met, Jacob, while announcing that he had been by this time baptized a Mormon, quizzed Smith about several theological particulars without once mentioning his pamphlet, its implications, or any prior association. As Peter Crawley has recently explained, John Taylor on 17 August 1845, while rebutting William Smith's negative contentions about the Twelve Apostles of the same date, also denounced claims of Joseph Smiths's collaboration in Jacob's pamphlet, which he called a "corrupt book." Also, Udney Jacob's March 1851 letter to Brigham Young contains language clearly indicating that his production of *The Peacemaker* was not with church approval, much less collaboration. Udney Jacob's work was demonstrably his own. Udney Jacob to Joseph Smith, 6 January 1844; Crawley, *A Descriptive Bibliography of the Mormon Church*, 211–212, 412–413.

19. The pamphlet had a life that continued to affect Mormonism after publication, despite institutional condemnation. The visit of John Scott, one of Norton Jacob's close associates, to Burlington, Iowa, in 1848 illustrates, in part, the work's impact. He wrote that upon visiting the settlement containing about fifteen LDS families, he encountered "some wild ideas" held by the Mormon locals. Specifically, he said, Udney Jacob's "small work," *The Peacemaker*, is "held more sacred than the Roman prayer book by the Catholic[s]." After some effort, he persuaded those in the small congregation who had the pamphlet to surrender the publication to him, after which he "made a burnt of[fe]ring of them," eventually restoring "tranquility" to the branch. Scott, Journals, March 1848.

Its unintended reach, with grizzly and horrific results, extended into the twentieth century. Brothers Dan and Ron Lafferty, who murdered their sister-in-law and her infant daughter in Utah County, Utah, in 1984, built their radical and extreme religious views in part from reading Udney Jacob's 1842 pamphlet justifying polygamy as God's law. Krakauer, *Under the Banner of Heaven*, 88–90, 115–116.

of the principal men but especialy the Phrophet Joseph [Smith], & all tended to strengthen my faith." Jacob's metamorphism into Mormonism equipped him with a motivation to foster the religion beyond his dooryard. Early in 1844, Joseph Smith inaugurated a move to place the Saints' Missouri plight, coupled with an increasing perception of hostility from Illinois authorities, before the American public. In that election year, Smith determined to campaign for the United States presidency. The means to popularize the Mormon leaders' candidacy, along with declarations of Mormon religious legitimacy, was a missionary force turned electioneers. Norton Jacob was one of the many called upon to undertake the quixotic task. At the April 1844 church conference, the strategy "to set forth [Smith's] Claims to the People" was established. Jacob's assignment was Michigan. Wearing the ministerial cloak for the first time cheered him.

The course of Norton Jacob's life over the following eight years is the burden of the rest of this volume and will not be considered here beyond brief overview. Jacob's missionary endeavor to Michigan was interrupted by the assassination of Joseph and Hyrum Smith in June 1944. Returning to the Mormon seat at Nauvoo, he witnessed the religion's internal struggle to regroup and coalesce. Jacob seems to have readily accepted Brigham Young and the Twelve Apostles as heirs of Smith's mantle. Thereafter in late 1845 and early 1846, Jacob played an important role in finishing the Nauvoo Temple, in construction since 1841, and there, with his wife, received their much anticipated religious endowments. Aligning with Young and the Twelve meant exile. Early 1846 found Jacob involved in making family and community preparations for their literal errand into the American wilderness. The Jacobs, as an extended family, crossed the Mississippi River in late spring in the second wave of Mormon emigres bound at the time for the Missouri River. There, on the Nebraska side, near modern Omaha, they relocated, like the rest of the Saints, to several temporary settlements until they fixed upon the site of Winter Quarters, now headquarters of the refugee church.[20]

Mormonism's geographical destiny was not on America's prairie or plain. It was in her mountains. The following spring, thirty-seven-year-old Jacob elected, upon invitation, to join the pioneer vanguard, whose objective it was to identify the Great Basin site where the Saints would reestablish themselves and a new era of Mormonism. Jacob's significant chronicle of the 1847 endeavor includes accounts of both the trek to the Great Basin and the return to Winter Quarters, where he reunited with his family, who had moved to western Iowa's Pottawattamie County. He repeated in 1848, this time with his family, his journey of 1847. This overland venture came with a heavy price; his oldest son Oliver, ill from the journey's start, died at Independence Rock, mostly enervating his family.

---

20. Jacob and his family lived in the northwestern-most sector of Winter Quarters.

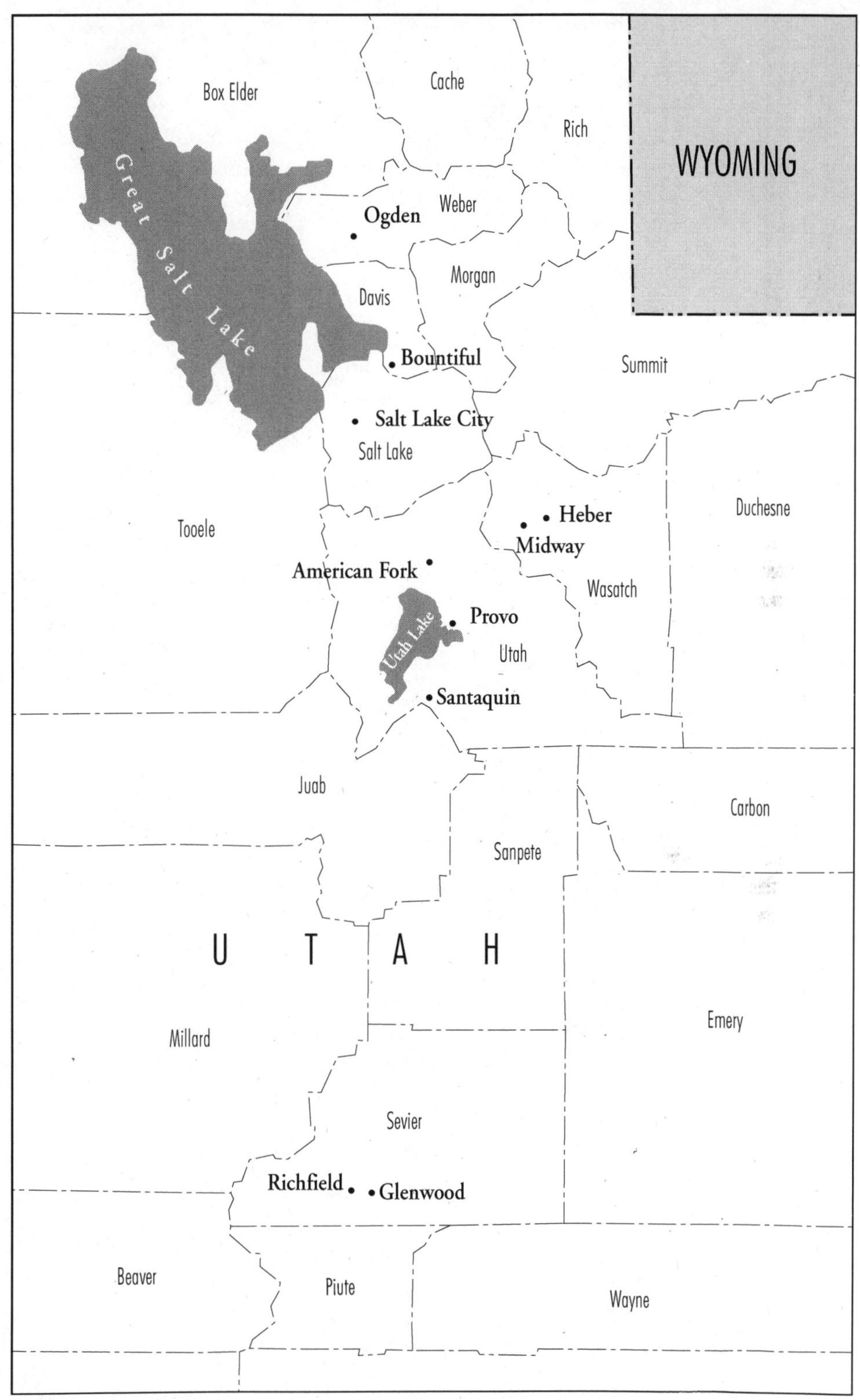

Utah locations where Norton Jacob resided. Map by Tom Child.

Once in Utah, Jacob, known as a carpenter, millwright, and mechanic, immediately found employment constructing a mill in Bountiful, Utah, with skills he had gained from mill building in Warsaw, Illinois, and on Turkey Creek at Winter Quarters, Nebraska. Other similar construction projects followed. Besides working at mill sites in Utah County[21] and the Salt Lake Valley, he was in January 1850 appointed foreman of the joiners and carpenters in the LDS Church's remarkably effective public works program in Great Salt Lake City.[22] In 1855 he moved his family north to Weber County, where he superintended construction of a sixty-six foot bridge spanning the Weber River at its canyon's mouth.[23] Jacob's substantial skill, in short supply in Mormonism's agrarian culture, earned him a considerable reputation among his fellow Saints.

For a time, it appeared that Jacob would become a Mormon urbanite centered in Great Salt Lake City. Before his temporary move to Weber County to build the bridge, he lived in the Salt Lake 17th Ward near the temple site and in the 16th Ward, where he was appointed one of the presidents of the LDS Church's 14th Quorum of Seventy.[24] Upon returning to Salt Lake City after his venture on the Weber, he lived on North Temple Street in the 16th Ward, a few blocks west of where he had previously lived.[25] His family gathered around him. Udney Jacob, after his September 1849 arrival in Utah, moved near Norton in Salt Lake City,[26] also living in the 16th Ward. Apparently Udney remained

---

21. At Jacob Houtz's mill site in Springville, Utah, Jacob was hired "to make and install the machinery, which consisted of a millwheel, the wheel pit, two sets of burrs and screens to separate the flour from the bran. The burrs were made from quartsite [*sic*] blasted from the mountain near Garfield Beach, and the gypsum used to cement the burrs was obtained from the mouth of Hobble Creek Canyon." Carter, "Pioneer Mills and Milling," 3:28–29; Roberts, "Pioneer Mills and Milling," 7:96.
22. At a meeting of church officials on 26 January 1850, Truman O. Angell was appointed architect of church projects with Jacob foreman of the same. Journal History, 26 January 1850; Young, *Manuscript History, 1847–1850*, 275; Jenson, *Latter-day Saint Biographical Encyclopedia*, 4:708.
23. Jacob penned a letter to the editor of the *Deseret News* on 9 May 1855 stating that his crew had just completed a "strong and durable structure, spanning, with an arch of 66 feet, the turbulent and angry flood poured out of Weber Kanyon." Giving details of the formidable feat he claimed the bridge would endure "as long as the mountain pine, of which it is made, will last." Journal History, 9 May 1855; *Our Pioneer Heritage*, 2:609. (Jacob's family is shown to be living in Weber County in 1856 when the territorial census was taken.)
24. Journal History, 25 May 1854.
25. Norton Jacob lived on the southeast corner of Block 104, on Lot 1, which is just northwest of and caddy-corner to today's LDS Conference Center in Salt Lake City, Utah. Norton sold this property to Orson Hyde in November 1852 and purchased, the previous month, Lot 3 on Block 98, presently located on the north side of North Temple Street between 400 and 500 West in the city. This latter lot he sold in November 1854 to Almon W. Babbitt. My thanks to W. Randall Dixon of the LDS Church Archives for identifying these properties in extant Salt Lake City records, which also included Udney Hay Jacob's residence, mentioned below.
26. Udney Jacob's residence in Salt Lake City, Utah, was just west of his son, the present location of which is on the northwest corner of North Temple Street and 600 West. See

at this Salt Lake City residence until his passing in April 1860.[27] Coincident to Udney's passing, something, for which no explanation survives, moved Norton to relocate. After a decade near Mormonism's expanding center, Norton, now the family patriarch, recast his lot for Utah's rural regions.

A dozen years after settling in Utah, Norton Jacob moved his family to a high mountain valley forty-five miles east of Salt Lake City, first called Timpanogos Valley, then Provo River Valley, and later Heber Valley. The vale, over a mile high, fifteen miles long, and ten wide, became the principal settlement of Utah's Wasatch County. By the summer of 1860, Jacob had located his family in the east side of Heber's fort, named after Mormon leader Heber Kimball, just prior to the place being designated a ward.[28] There he was soon invited to give a principal speech at the 24th of July celebration about his experience with the vanguard in 1847.[29] In 1862 he relocated his family to the nearby fledgling fort of what became Midway, later dubbed "Little Switzerland" because of its alpine character, where he housed his family in a cabin on the fort's north wall.[30] While in Midway he was appointed and later elected Wasatch County justice of the peace in 1862 for one of two precincts.[31] Religiously, he served in 1863–1864 as the presiding church elder in the small settlement on the west side of Heber Valley at Snake Creek, which was later incorporated into Midway.[32] Norton's children with Emily, though she died

---

Udney Hay Jacob's land transaction with Samuel Langfield (Lot 2 of Block 61 in Plat C) in Salt Lake City on 17 November 1857. John Pack Papers.

27. *Deseret News*, 16 May 1860. Udney married again when he took another wife, Phylotte Greene Pack, a widow, not long after his arrival in Utah. In 1852 Phylotte, then seventy-six years old, wrote to Brigham Young requesting to be sealed to Udney whom she described as "a good man, a kind husband, and . . . anxious to do all he can to advance the Kingdom of our God, and to be obedient in all things." One inexplicable feature of this communication is her claim that "Altho I am now near 77 years old, I am far advanced in a State of Pregnancy." Pregnancy? Her plea was that her marital sealing to Udney could take place before her "confinement." Phylotte Jacob to Brigham Young, 2 March 1852.

    Family records indicate there was another marriage of Udney to Elizabeth Piggett (born in Ireland in 1783), though nothing more could be found by the editor about the union.

28. A traveler to "the valley of the Timpanogos" in October 1860 reported that he found "fifty families" already settled there, having "inclosed two thousand acres of farm and meadow land" with another "five hundred acres . . . under cultivation." Journal History, 28 October 1860; Mortimer, *How Beautiful upon the Mountains*, 15.

29. Journal History, 24 July 1860.

30. *Under Wasatch Skies*, 21.

31. Journal History, 22 March 1862, 4 August 1862; Mortimer, *How Beautiful upon the Mountains*, 17, 663; Jenson, *Latter-day Saints Biographical Encyclopedia*, 4:708.

32. Snake Creek, first settled in 1859 and aptly named for the remarkable number of rattlesnakes on the creek, was eventually combined in 1866 with another small settlement, Mound City, to form Midway, Utah. About the time that Jacob moved his family to the valley, about a dozen families lived at Snake Creek. Esshom, *Pioneers and Prominent Men of Utah*, 956; Journal History, 28 October 1860; Jenson, *Encyclopedic History of the Church*, 500–501.

coincident to his move to Heber Valley, matured there, where they lived for a generation.[33] But with his children coming of age and starting their own families, Norton was not content to remain there.

Jacob's circumstances were driven, in part, from his marital arrangements. With Emily Heaton Jacob, whom he had married in 1830, he had eleven children, six of whom reached the age of majority. Subscribing to Mormonism completely, Jacob after his removal to Utah became a polygamist. He married his first plural wife, Maria Van Valkenburg (born in 1835 in New York), in 1851. Their union had difficulties, which he described (though part of his report was later torn from his diary), and they apparently had no children. He also married as a plural wife Eliza Elizabeth Graham (born in New York in 1828) in 1859, six months before his first wife died. Four children were born to this union. His final marriage, according to available records, was to Sarah Wood Clark (born in Ohio in 1818, who had become a Mormon in 1850). They also had no children, but it was Sarah with whom Norton spent the last years of his life.

Leaving his maturing family in Heber Valley, Norton relocated to the Wasatch Front in Utah Valley where he lived for a time at Santaquin and at American Fork,[34] though he maintained close ties to Heber City and Midway. His tenure in Utah Valley was brief. In 1873, again with unknown motives, he removed, with his wife Sarah, south to Glenwood, Utah, in south-central Utah's Sevier River Valley. First settled in the 1860s, Sevier Valley was emptied of white settlers for nearly five years during the Black Hawk War in the 1860s and early 1870s. Glenwood was, in 1873, just reestablishing itself. The mile-high village, located seven miles east of Richfield, the valley's most populous community, was composed of almost 500 settlers in 1874, and was one of the Sevier Valley's more substantial settlements.[35] From the time of his arrival he served as clerk of the local Mormon ward, recording the minutes of meetings with his steady hand,[36] and he was known as the community's first historian.[37] The settlement's primary activity during Jacob's tenure there was the United Order, a cooperative economic enterprise universal throughout Mormon Utah at the time. Jacob subscribed, which included the symbol of his commitment to the significant endeavor: rebaptism in 1875.[38] It was in Glenwood that Norton Jacob lived the remainder of his life. Other than a county tax assessment for 1877 which showed him with assets totaling only $250 ($200 in land, a $10 horse, and other taxable property of $40), which was not far from average in the poverty-stricken Sevier settlements, the nature

33. Mortimer, *How Beautiful upon the Mountains*, 225–226, 228, 397, 661–663, 747–748.
34. 1870 Census; *Our Pioneer Heritage*, 2:610.
35. Glenwood Ward, Record of Members.
36. Jacob's minute-taking lasted from 1 October 1873 to 9 September 1877. Glenwood Ward, Record of Members.
37. Glenwood Ward, Record of Members; Warnock and Warnock, *Our Own Sevier*, 229.
38. Glenwood Ward, Record of Members.

and quality of his life are not known due to the absence of records.[39] He died there thirty days after the new year in 1879.[40]

Norton Jacob's place in the Mormon galaxy is important because he felt constrained to document a significant period in his life. And while records regarding several hundred of Jacob's contemporaries survive, hundreds, even thousands, more of his contemporaries who lived no less interesting, complicated, and contributive lives, remain virtually unknown. Modern writers' and readers' preoccupations with elites and celebrity further veil Mormonism's majority in its early decades. Jacob's record provides access to the mainstream world of Mormonism, a blue-collar view, in its transitory years after Joseph Smith's martyrdom when the Saints reinvented themselves.

39. Sevier County, Utah, Tax Assessment and Military Enlistment Records, 1873–1918.
40. Glenwood Ward, Record of Members; Jenson, *Latter-day Saints Biographical Encyclopedia*, 4:708.

Reminiscence and 1844

NORTON JACOB, FORTY YEARS OLD IN 1844, begins his record with a memoir of his investigation of and entry into The Church of Jesus Christ of Latter-day Saints in 1840–1841. Jacob's embrace of a religion held in derision by its neighbors wherever its membership located, besides a suspicious media, was met by his family similarly. Having emigrated to Hancock County, the western-most county in Illinois, in the mid-1830s, the Jacobs witnessed the Mormon arrival in Nauvoo, Illinois, and their expansion into the county. The tension likely escalated when Norton physically separated from his parents and siblings and moved to Nauvoo–—the Mormon center—–in 1842. His wife Emily, whom he described as being skeptical of his affiliation with Joseph Smith's church, and his children remained aloof from Norton's faith until 1843.

It was in mid-1844 that Norton Jacob, clearly captivated by his newfound faith, entered the Mormon missionary corp preaching the Mormon gospel and Joseph Smith's candidacy for the United States presidency. Crossing northern Illinois and Indiana, he finally entered his field of labor in southern Michigan. It was there that he heard of the murders of Joseph and Hyrum Smith in Carthage, Illinois. There in Michigan, also, James Jesse Strang made his initial bid to succeed Joseph Smith. Jacob, with Strang's brother-in-law Moses Smith, reported Strang's challenge to Nauvoo, notifying the Mormon Twelve Apostles that there was a rival to their leadership of the devastated church. Jacob and the rest of the Mormons in Hancock County, for the remainder of 1844, preserved body and soul in an atmosphere of uncertainty.

I was first led to investigate the principles & doctrines of the Church of Jesus Christ of Latter day Saintss in the summer of 1840 by reading a little pamphlet which I think was entitled "A Review of Leroy Sunderland's Review of Mormonism Unveiled" by Parley P. Pratt.[1] In this work there [were] some

1. The forty-seven page response in 1838 of Parley P. Pratt—*Mormonism Unveiled: Zion's Watchman Unmasked and Its Editor, Mr. L. R. Sunderland, Exposed*—countered the Rev. LaRoy Sunderland's fifty-four page critique of Mormonism titled *Mormonism Exposed and*

important Prophesies which appeared to me to be related to those found in the Bible, which led me into a new field of inquiry; for I fuly believed the Prophets, & that whatever the Lord had spoken by them would would be fulfiled in his own due time. During the fall & winter folowing I heard some of the Elders preach, obtain<ed> the "Voice of Warning by P. P. Pratt which I read with much interest[2] & on the 15th of March 1841, I was baptis[ed] by Elder Zenos Gurly at Laharp.[Hancock County, Illinois].[3]

My Father, Mother, Brothers, & Sisters opposed me violently. my Fat[h]er said he had rather heard I was dead than that I was a Mormon.[4] I found it was no place for me where I then lived which was at Pilot Grove, Hancock Co., Ill.[5] I had heard much of the sufferings and persecutions of the Saints in Mo., and a Kindred Spirit with theirs soon led me to gather up with them

---

Refuted. First appearing earlier in the year serially in a Methodist publication, Sunderland's polemic used E.D. Howe's *Mormonism Unveiled* (1834) for grist, and Pratt's earlier work, *Voice of Warning* (1837) as a foil. Pratt's response to Sunderland is the earliest extant printed Mormon reply to an anti-Mormon work. Crawley, *Descriptive Bibliography of the Mormon Church*, 15, 76–79.

2. Parley P. Pratt's *A Voice of Warning*, published in 1837 and over 220 pages in length, was not only one of the earliest explanations of Mormonism, it was also one of the most significant doctrinal and theological works about the faith produced in the nineteenth century. Pratt's style and arguments served as a model for many of the apologetic pamphlets produced after its publication. Crawley, *Descriptive Bibliography of the Mormon Church*, 69–71.

3. Zenos Hovey Gurley, in March 1841, reported to the editors of Nauvoo's *Times and Seasons* that he had recently, in six days, baptized fifty-two people in the La Harpe, Illinois, area. Norton Jacob may have been numbered among this substantial missionary harvest. *Times and Seasons* 2, no. 10 (15 March 1841): 350.

   La Harpe, a well-timbered sector of land in the northeastern corner of Hancock County, Illinois, about twenty-two miles east and north of Nauvoo, was the only village in La Harpe Township. The village's first settler in 1831, helped lay out the site in 1836. A Mormon congregation grew in the village, undoubtedly initiated through the work of Zenos Gurley. Gregg, *History of Hancock County*, 892.

4. Udney Hay Jacob, Norton's father, was initially so opposed to Mormonism that he wrote a letter on 19 March 1840 to U.S. President Martin Van Buren where he denounced Mormons as a "deluded and dangerous set of fanatics." Two of Norton's brothers, Stephen and Jason, unlike their father who later reconsidered and became a Mormon, remained aloof from their kin's religious inclinations. Udney H. Jacob to Martin Van Buren, 19 March 1840.

5. Pilot Grove, Hancock County, Illinois, established in 1830, was also known, due to Jacob family residence there, as Jacob Corner. The township was named for a stand of timber which stood alone on the Illinois prairie. Located in Section 4 of the township, the village was located about two and one half miles northeast of Burnside, Illinois. A cemetery is the only reminder of the village of between thirty and forty people. Some of Pilot Grove's earliest settlers became Mormons, and an LDS branch was located there during the 1840s. Anti-Mormon sentiment rose so high there in the mid-1840s that Mormon opponents prided themselves as "Brick Batters," determined to clear the area of Latter-day Saints. Gregg, *History of Hancock County, Illinois*, 841.

to Nauvoo, their new city, the founding of which I had watched with much interest.[6] ow[n]ing a small farm with my brother Stephen [Jacob], I sold out my half to him for $250, to be paid in five equal anual instalments in produce delivered in the city of Nauvoo.[7] I now prepared to move my family there. I built m[e] a house on the Prarie 7 miles from the city & moved into it in the fal of '41.[8] I here gatherd together materiels to build in the city & the first of Nov. 1842 I removed my family to the City of the Saints.[9]

I have said that I had watched it from its foundation. by this <I> mean that I had closely observed the course & proceedings of the principal men but especialy the Phrophet Joseph [Smith] & all tended to strengthen my faith. I <was> present at the laying of the corner stone of the Temple, a most beautiful day it was, the 6th day of April 1841.[10] There was a Splndid military parade & review of the Nauvoo Legion under the command of the Lieutenant General Joseph Smith.[11] there was also present in command

---

6. The establishment of Nauvoo, Illinois, as headquarters of the LDS Church in the 1840s is explained in Flanders, *Nauvoo*, 23–56; Miller and Miller, *Nauvoo*, 18–40; and Leonard, *Nauvoo*, 41–61.
7. Udney H. Jacob and his sons Stephen and Jason K. are shown in the 1842 tax assessment for Hancock County, Illinois, as living near each other in Range 6N 6W in Hancock County, Illinois. Stephen, 39 in the census of 1850, with his wife and seven children, and Jason K., 43 in 1850, with his wife and five children, are also shown still living there. Jason K. served as Durham Township supervisor and auditor in the mid-1860s. Hancock (Ill. : County) Assessor's Office, Books of Assessment, 1840, 1842, and 1850, p. 183; Ballowe, Jewell, and Lundgren, *1850 Census of Illinois, Hancock County*, 107, 194; Blender, *This Township Called Durham*, 693.
8. The precise location of this home is not known.
9. Hancock County land records for Nauvoo, do not show a property purchase by Jacob at this time, suggesting that initially he did not secure title to his property. However, two transactions in his wife Emily's name, one in May 1844 for $50 on Cutler Street a mile or so east and north of the Nauvoo Temple, and the other in May 1845 for $100 a couple of miles east and south of the temple, show purchases by the Jacobs' of Nauvoo property. Nauvoo (Ill.) Registry of Deeds, 1843–1846, Book B, 316–317.

   By the end of 1842 when Jacob moved to Nauvoo, the city had flowered into a city of about 4000, one of the largest communities in Illinois. The Illinois capital of Springfield was of comparable size, though Chicago outdistanced both cities in population at this time. Black, "How Large was the Population of Nauvoo?" 91–94; Leonard, *Nauvoo*, 179.
10. Laying the Nauvoo Temple's cornerstones was a significant event in Mormon history. In the aftermath of the expulsion of the Mormons from Missouri, a significant structure like the temple, symbolizing permanence and strength, was of great consequence to the Latter-day Saints. Held on the eleventh anniversary of the church's organization, the events of the day, were conducted in two segments. The first was a military parade featuring the Nauvoo Legion and its officers, followed by the cornerstone ceremony conducted with precise decorum and order. A overview of the day is recounted in Smith, *History of the Church*, 4:326–331; and Leonard, *Nauvoo*, 233–234.
11. The military role was just one change of garb for Joseph Smith, whose multi-dimensional role in Mormonism, from the political to the religious arena, warmed him to his followers. Conversely, Smith's ubiquitous presence and authority in Mormon life alienated him from outsiders who feared him to be a demagogue.

Brigadier Don Carlos Smith, a noble looking young man who not long after fell <a> prey to the power of the destroyer. J[ohn]. C. Bennet held command as Major General on that day, and after he had formed the troops in treble lines around the consecrated spot, all the General and field officers gathered in within the place [m]arked out for the walls. not much had [b]een excavated then except about the corners where trenches had been sunk to the depth of the intended basement and filed with rough walls so as to receive the corner stones which were cut and hewn. 'twas now about midday. a countless multitude thronged around the Marsheled lines filed with much wonder & curiosity to Know what all this would amount to. manny strange murmurs ran through <the> waveing throng to see the Prophet, the master spirit of the Glitering scene, mount a scaffold at the South East corner in full Military Costume acompanied by many of his fellow officers & friends! aye, and some pretended friends too. T[homas] C Sharp was there. manny were detailed from the ranks to hold within <the> walls the loosed horses & among the rest I ~~the~~ held that of T. C. Sharp while he with other visitors took his seat beside the Prophet, a mean hypocritical knave. I believe he here imbibed that Spirit of rancor which since <has> been so freely manifested against the Saints for he envied that magesty & magnanimity ~~to~~ which he had not the honesty and courage to emulate.[12] After a Lecture delivered by Sydney Rigdon,[13] the South East Corner Stone was laid by Joseph as first President of the Church. The multitude now dispersed & Joseph & his fellow officers & friends retired for refreshments. In the afternoon the other ~~four~~ three c[o]rners were laid in due form, the South West by the "Twelve," as traveling high Council abroad, the North West by the Bishop [Vinson] Knight, as President of the Lesser Priesthood,[14] and I believe the North <E> by the Building Commitee.[15]

The pomp associated with the Nauvoo Legion at this event was the military organization's first major display before Nauvoo's citizens. The presentation was hardly paralleled thereafter. As will be seen, the Legion became an important entity in Jacob's life, particularly during the time after the expulsion of the Mormons from Illinois. Miller and Miller, *Nauvoo*, 98; Leonard, *Nauvoo*, 118.

12. Thomas Sharp, a young newspaperman from Warsaw, Illinois, with a wary neighborly curiosity in April 1841, would, the following month, draw a broad line between the Saints and other county residents, due, primarily, to the increasing numbers of Mormons and their interests in determining politic influence in the county. Thereafter, Sharp became one of the most influential opponents of Mormonism in Illinois. Many Mormons later considered him directly responsible for the murders of Joseph and Hyrum Smith. Leonard, *Nauvoo*, 83, 679n61–62.
13. Sidney Rigdon's speech for 6 April 1841 is recounted in Smith, *History of the Church*, 4:327–329.
14. Information about the role of the Lesser or Aaronic Priesthood in the LDS Church is found in Hartley, "From Men to Boys," 80–136. See the overview of the church's priesthood role in the note below.
15. The day's events are described in Smith, *History of the Church*, 4:326–331; Swinton, *Sacred Stone*, 45–46; and Leonard, *Nauvoo*, 233–235.

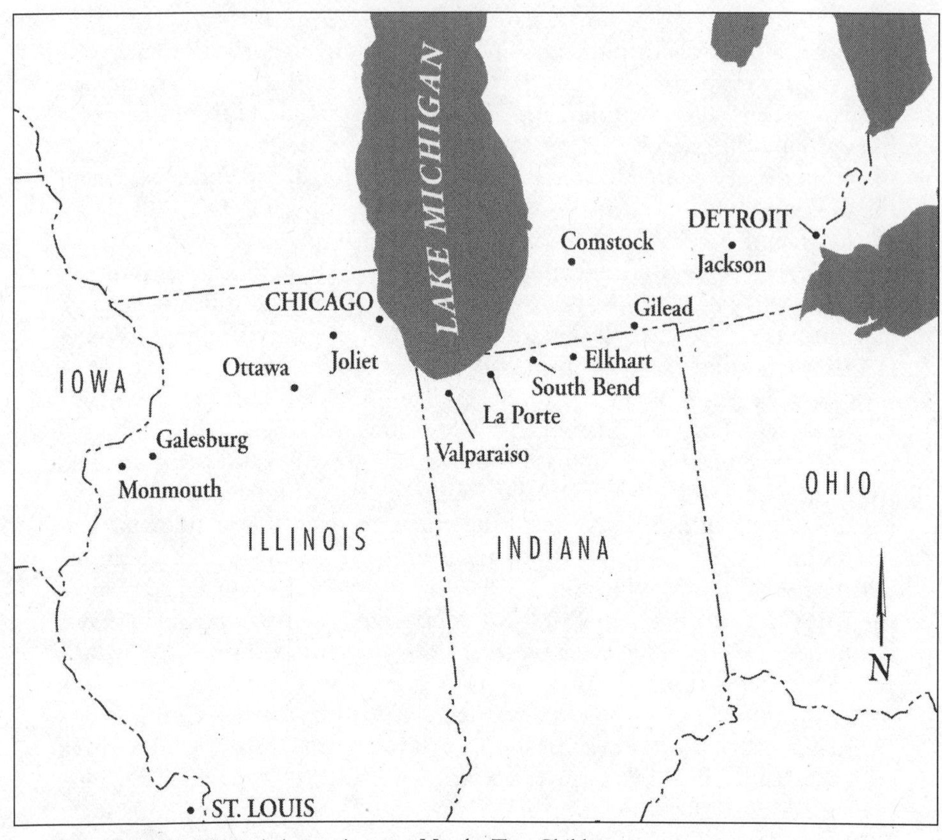

Norton Jacob's 1844 missionary journey. Map by Tom Child.

At this conference I was ordained into the Elders Quorum.[16] My wife's Father Elias Heaton, who had lived in my family for several years, died at my house the 10th day of Sept. 1842. he was a verry friendly well meaning man but rather Sceptical. being destitue of faith, he could not be a Mormon. Wee buried him

16. During the Saints' tenure in Kirtland, Ohio, from 1831–1838, a lay priesthood, with two divisions, was established buttressing the church's hierarchical structure. Its purpose was the distribution of authority and responsibility, investing a feature of ownership in the minds of the recipients. The duty of the lesser priesthood, known as the Aaronic Priesthood, was the outward practice, or liturgy, of Mormon worship. The higher, or Melchizedek, priesthood was administrative in function and responsibility. As the organization expanded and matured in Nauvoo, the every-man-his-own-priest structure had a complicated success that explains, in part, the Saints' progress in making Mormonism such an integral role in its adherents' lives. A portrayal of the expression of this unique lay priesthood at this time is found in Hartley, "Nauvoo Stake, Priesthood Quorums, and the Church's First Wards," 57–80.

The elders, part of the greater or higher priesthood, had administrative and missionary responsibility. See Dorius, "Elder," 326–327; and Hartley, "Nauvoo Stake, Priesthood Quorums, and the Church's First Wards," 67–69.

in the City of the Saints, where we hope through our assistance he will come forth in the resurection.[17] My wife [Emily Heaton Jacob], like her Father, was naturaly Sceptical, but by means of the instructi[on] she received, by living with the Saints & hearing the Prophet [Joseph Smith] preach, she was induced to be baptised in July 1843 in the city of Nauvoo & about the same time our Daughter Elsie [Pamelia Jacob] & oldest <son> Oliver [Barr Jacob] were baptised.[18]

At the Spring conference 1844, Bro Joseph [Smith] directed that all the Elders of Israel should go into the vineyard. he had previously been nominated for President of the United States & part of the business of the Elders would be to set forth his Claims to the People.[19] I took a mission to the State <of> Michigan

---

17. Elias Heaton, sixty-three, died from typhus fever in Nauvoo, Illinois. Cook, *Nauvoo Deaths and Marriages*, 35.

    A later insertion into Jacob's record by his son Ira N. Jacob reads: "I was baptized for him [Heaton] in the Salt Lake Temple." This action refers to the Mormon practice of baptism for the dead, vicariously gathering the dead into the Mormon Kingdom. The rite is based on the New Testament text in I Cor. 15:29, the theology of which Joseph Smith initiated in the LDS Church in Nauvoo in August 1840.

18. The LDS Church has a well-deserved reputation for its record-keeping legacy. However, for the early decades of the church's history, the absence of early membership records is common. While some information is not extant, in most cases, this type of record apparently was not created at the time. As far as can be determined, most early membership information about the Jacob family does not exist. For information about early record keeping among the Mormons, see Jessee, "Joseph Smith and the Beginning of Mormon Record Keeping."

19. Joseph Smith's entrance into the nation's political arena was a significant step for him personally and for the Latter-day Saints as a people. In the aftermath of the Saints' debacle in Missouri, followed by several years of disappointment in federal and state governments in obtaining redress for their losses there, Smith on 8 February 1844 announced his candidacy for the United States presidency. At the 8 February meeting, Smith explained:

    > I would not have suffered my name to have been used by my friends on any wise as president of the united States or candidate for that office If I & my friends Could have had the privilege of enjoying our religious & civel rights as American Citizen[s] even those rights which the Constitution guarantee unto all her Citizens alike. But this we as a people have been denied from the beginning. Woodruff, *Journal*, 2:349.

    His premature death in June 1844 prevented the full expression of his run for the American presidency.

    Over three hundred church missionaries, including the Twelve Apostles, fanned out eastward from Nauvoo in the spring of 1844 to popularize their prophet's political hopes. Willard Richards explained the intent was for church elders to "go forth by hundreds or thousands and search the land, preaching religion and politics." Willard Richards to James Arlington Bennett, 4 March 1844, *History of the Church*, 6:232. For descriptions of Smith's political objectives at this time, see Poll, "Joseph Smith and the Presidency, 1844," 17–21; Hickman, "Political Legacy of Joseph Smith," 22–27; Allen, "Was Joseph Smith a Serious Candidate," 21–22; Garr, "Joseph Smith: Candidate," 151–168; Van Orden, "William W. Phelps," 88–90; and Leonard, *Nauvoo*, 327–340. The inauguration of Smith's presidential campaign, particularly for the end of January, February, and the first of March 1844 is found in *History of the Church*, 6:187–233.

& on the 14th day of May [1844] I started in company with Elders Charles Rich, David Ful[l]mer & Moses Smith, in a two horse carriage. ~~wich~~[20]

<~~Tues~~ Tuesday> May 14 [1844] Traveled 45 m[iles]. Stopd at Center Grove [Warren County, Illinois] with Mr [Elijah] Hannah.[21]

15th [May 1844] to Monmouth [Warren County, Illinois], 8 m[iles]. a little beyond was caut in a rain Storm. having got severely drenched, wee went but 4 m[iles] farther and stopped with brother [Justus] Ames [Eames].[22]

16th [May 1844] rained till nearly noon when wee passed on through Galesburg [Knox County, Illinois] to Walnut Creek [now Altoona, Knox County, Illinois][23] 28 m[iles]. stopd with Mr. Leef.[24]

17th [May 1844] passed through Providence [Bureau County, Illinois], 27 miles, Indian Town[ship] & 3 m[iles] beyond stoped with an Abolitionist.

18th [May 1844] passed through Princeton [Bureau County, Illinois] 3 m[iles] & over 7 m[iles] to J[esse]. Weeksom's [Wixom's], Troy Grove [Township, LaSalle County, Illinois] 18 m[iles]. Mrs [Artimesia] Weeksom is Sister of Br [Charles] Rich & belongs to the Church. ~~19th.~~ in the evening Bro [David] Fulmer Lectured on Politics & I preceded him by reading Joseph [Smith]'s "Views" & making some remarks.[25] the people appeared well satisfed.

---

20. There was precedent for this unusual missionary initiative. The previous year in June 1843, Joseph Smith was arrested upon questionable terms by Missouri and Illinois lawmen who intercepted him while he visited family in Dixon, Illinois. After his release he called eighty-two missionaries to spread throughout Illinois to "preach the gospel and disabuse the public mind with regard to [his] arrest or capture." Smith, *An American Prophet's Record*, 393; *Times and Seasons* 4, no. 15 (15 June 1843): 240.
21. An Elijah Hannah is identified in Section 17 of Warren County, Illinois, in the 1840 federal census.
22. Justus Eames and his wife Betsey were baptized in September 1837 by Wilford Woodruff on the Fox Islands in Maine. They were, according to Woodruff, "the first baptized upon the Islands of the sea . . . in these last days by an Elder of Israel." Woodruff, *Journal*, 1:174. Their Illinois home served as a resting stop for many Saints en route to and from Nauvoo. They lived at the time on Cedar Creek (not the one in Warren County), three miles from Galesburg, Illinois. While visiting the Eames' on 11 May 1845, Woodruff noted that they had a "pleasant place of 100 acres, 40 in corn." Woodruff, *Journal*, 2:394, 396.
23. Moses Smith previously moved to Walnut Creek in 1840, about sixty miles northeast of Nauvoo. Smith helped organize a branch of the LDS Church there that soon numbered over 100 adherents. Smith's life is recounted in Clark, "Moses Smith."
24. Charles C. Rich identified the man's surname as Leek. The 1840 federal census identifies two men named Leak, Conrad and Wesner, who lived in Knox County, Illinois.
25. The "Views" Jacob mentions was the textual platform for Joseph Smith's candidacy for the U.S. presidency: *General [Joseph] Smith's Views of the Powers and Policy of the*

19th Sunday [May 1844] passed on to Ottawa [La Salle County, Illinois],[26] where wee expected to find the brethren assembled in conference but whe[n] <wee> got to old Father [David] Sanger wee found that he thought mormonism so unpopular, although a Saint, that he had sent the conference away up to Newark [Kendall County, Illinois] 20 m[iles], <on> Fox River, away.[27] wee posted in the rain, after taking some refreshment & arrived Just as conference was breaking up.[28] here were two of the "Twelve," Wilford Woodruff & George A. Smith. wee Stopd at Br [Asa] Manchester's withe them.

20th [May 1844] remained here. there was a hevy frost this morning. in evening wee had a Pollitical Lecture. I first read the "Views," when Brethren [David] Fulmer & G[eorge]. A. Smith folowed. Br Smith made some ironical remarks on the Goverment which gave offense to a Doct [Griffin] Smith[29] wh[o] raised quite a row, but by the power of God it was soon quieted.

21st [May 1844] travled to Juliet [Joliet, Will County, Illinois], 30 m[iles]. Staid at Sister [Martha] Denison's.[30] in the evening Brethren [Wilford] Woodruff & [David] Fulmer ~~&~~ Lectured on Politics.

22 [May 1844] here wee parted with ~~the~~ Brethren [George] Smith & [Wilford] Woodruff & went to a Mr Hew's, 13 m[iles].

23d [May 1844] passed through Lockport [Will County, Illinois] to Thorn Grove [Cook County, Illinois], 30 m[iles]. Staid with Br [Osmyn] D[e]uel.

Government of the United States. First published as a twelve-page pamphlet in Nauvoo in February 1844, it was reprinted several more times in several different cities later in the spring. While Joseph Smith established the general principles of the text, William W. Phelps authored *Views*. Crawley, *Descriptive Bibliography of the Mormon Church*, 244–247; Woodruff, *Journal*, 2:349. For an overview of the creation of the pamphlet and of its meaning, see Crawley, *Descriptive Bibliography of the Mormon Church*, 244–247; and Hickman, "Political Legacy of Joseph Smith," 22–27, followed by a facsimile of the pamphlet.

26. An active branch of the LDS Church functioned in Ottawa, Illinois.
27. An LDS Church branch had been established in Newark, Illinois, by William O. Clark on 1 March 1844.
28. Branches represented at the Newark conference on 18–19 May 1844 were Newark, La Salle, Ottawa, Bureau, Pleasant Grove, Indian Creek, Big Vermillion, and French Creek, with church members at the conference totaling 133 members, 10 elders, and 1 teacher. George Smith noted Norton Jacob's arrival in Newark at the end of the conference. *Times and Seasons* 5, no. 11 (1 June 1844): 557–558 (reprinted in *History of the Church*, 6:399–401); Smith, "My Journal," (June 1948): 279–280.
29. This may be Griffin Smith (ca. 30), a physician from Canada living in Big Grove Township, Kendall County, Illinois, according to the 1850 census.
30. This may be Martha Denny who lived east of Joliet, Illinois. She was a widow when Lysander Denny married her in Nauvoo. George Smith said the group "put up with Sister Dana." Smith, "My Journal," (June 1948): 280.

24 [May 1844] to Indiana Branch,[31] 33 m[iles]. Stoped with Sister Dewy, a widow.[32]

25 [May 1844] passed throug Valparaiso [Porter County, Indiana] & Laport [La Porte County, Indiana] 22 [miles?] to J Cunningham's 8 m[iles] on Rolling Prarie. he is a Brother of Lester Dewy. remained here over Sunday.

26th [May 1844] Elders [David] Fulmer & [Charles] Rich[33] preached at old Mr Caswell's, a Universalist.

27 [May 1844] passed through South Bend [St. Joseph County, Indiana], 23 m[iles]. Mish[a]waka, [St. Joseph County, Indiana]. 4 m[iles]. Elkhart [Elkhart County, Indiana], 12 m[iles] to Tibbit's Tavern, 2 m[iles]. Sign "Live & let Live," a good hearted sort of man.[34] Passed on to Comstock, Kalamazoo Co., Mich[igan].[35]

on the first of June [1844][36] attended a conference at Br Ezekiel Lee's.[37] By this conference Moses Smith & myself were sent to Branch Co.

---

31. An LDS Church branch existed in Indiana, Lake County, Illinois.
32. Charles Rich's entry for the day is similar to Jacob's, but continues the statement about "Sister Dewey" with "[and visited] Br Kinsey one miles from Valperazo." Rich, Diary, 24 May 1844.
33. Charles Rich's experience during this period is described in Arrington, *Charles C. Rich*, 79–81.
34. Charles Rich suggested that it was a "Br Tibets" who was proprietor of the "Live and let live Tavern." Rich, Diary, 13 July 1844.
35. Comstock is located just east of the regional center of Kalamazoo in Kalamazoo County, Michigan. An LDS Church branch was located there at the time.
36. Charles Rich's diary accounts for the last four days of May, 1844, which may have involved Jacob. Rich traveled in St. Joseph County and Branch County, Michigan. Wilford Woodruff noted in his diary that Norton Jacob and Moses Smith arrived at Lee's place for the conference on 30 May 1844, "which with us all together made a large company." Woodruff, *Journal*, 2:403.
37. The Comstock, Michigan, conference (also called the Kalamazoo Conference) held 31 May–1 June 1844, was attended by "125 members, [and] 35 elders," representing eight branches and "scattered" Saints. (Branches represented were Kalamazoo, Grand Prairie, Atsego, Pawpaw, Albion, Calhoun, Florence, St. Joseph, Mottville, St. Joseph, and Barry.) The meetings, presided over by Wilford Woodruff and George Smith, were held in Ezekiel Lee's "barn," though it was also referred to it as his "school house." Minutes of the conference were published in the *Times and Seasons* and are found in Woodruff's journal for 1–2 June 1844, which included representation of Joseph Smith's presidential candidacy, the intent of which was "to unite the nation," and also contained discussion "of our persecution, loss of our rights appeal to Mo & the nation being rejected, the danger the goverment was in &c." When the conference concluded, a "warmth of friendship & <feeling of> kindness . . . that marks the noble & generous soul was manifest by many of the assembly." Dunn, Journals, 5 September 1843, 31 May–1 June 1844; "Kalamazoo conference," *Times and Seasons*, (15 July 1844): 579–580; Woodruff, *Journal*, 2:403–406; Smith, "My Journal," (July 1948): 322.

[Michigan][38] to Preach & Lecture in favor of Gen. Joseph Smith for President of the United States. Here I commenced my first Preaching of the Gospel of the new & everlasting covenant.[39]

wee continued to labor here [Branch County, Michigan] until the first of July [1844] when wee attended a State convention at Jackson [Jackson County, Michigan] for the purpose of nominating Presidential Electors. wee met many of the Brethren from different parts of the State. Br Chalrles C. Rich Presided.[40]

wee met on the 5th [July 1844] in the court House but a few of the Citizens attended. a report had Just reached us that our Beloved Prophet Joseph & Patriarch Hiram Smith were Murdered in Carthge Jail.[41] But wee did not believe the Story and proceeded to nominate our Electors.[42] When Moses Smith returned to Branch Co. [Michigan] & I up to Oakland Co. [Michigan] to exchange our heavy two Horse [carriage] for a one Horse Buggy. I returned through Jackson [Michigan] to [blank] where I met with Br Zebedee Coultrin [Coltrin] at house of Brother [blank] where I tarried several days.

on the 15th [July 1844] wee held a conference here[43] when wee receive[d] a letter from Br Charles C Rich in Indiana on his way hom to Nauvoo

---

38. Branch County is located in south central Michigan on the border with Indiana. A list of men appointed to missions in Michigan and Indiana, found in Charles Rich's 1844 diary, indicates that "M. Smith" was assigned to Hillsdale County, Michigan, just east of Branch County, and "N. Jacob" was appointed to Branch County, Michigan.
39. Electioneering for Joseph Smith for the U.S. presidency was just an added dimension to the proselytizing efforts of the LDS missionaries, who continued to preach the Mormon "Gospel of the new & everlasting covenant."
40. At the Comstock (Kalamazoo) Conference meeting of 1 June 1844 "It was moved and Carried that we sustain Elders Charles C. Rich & Harry [Harvey] Green, in their appointment to preside over the State of Michigan assigned them by the quorum of the Twelve." Woodruff, *Journal*, 2:405. The political campaign and establishment of church branches in Michigan by Jacob and his associates, including Rich, is described in Arrington, *Charles C. Rich*, 79–81.
41. The Smith brothers were killed by Hancock County, Illinois, mobocrats from several county sectors on 27 June 1844 in the county jail where they were held on charges of inciting riot and treason stemming from the destruction of the *Nauvoo Expositor's* on 10 June 1844. Jacob learned the rumor was true ten days later on 15 July 1844.
42. The political convention held in Jackson, Michigan, on 5–6 July 1844 was called to appoint "presidential Electors for the State of Michigan" in the upcoming election. The Mormon elders represented "the friends of Jeffersonian Democracy." At the meeting on 6 July Charles Rich spoke first, followed by Norton Jacob, clerk of the convention in whose hand the minutes were kept, who set "forth in the first place the duties of the President." After identifying constitutional provisions for the executive branch's duties, Jacob complained about the president's neglect in responding to the Saints' plight, coupled with other government ineptitude. Jackson, Michigan, Convention Minutes; Arrington, *Charles C. Rich*, 81.
43. This conference at Jackson, Michigan, was not one of the scheduled apostolic conferences such as the one held on 1 June 1844 in Comstock, Michigan.

[Illinois], which fully confirmed the report of the death of the Prophets [Joseph and Hyrum Smith].[44] Br Harvey Green presided at this conference. I now returned to branch Co. [Michigan] where my wife's Mother [Mary Heaton] lived,[45] also her sister Lucretia ~~married~~ wife of Ebenezer Mudge. the old Lady listened with considerable interest while the others tu[r]ned a deaf ear to the Gospel. I found Moses [Smith] completely discomfitted by <the> news <of> the Prophet's death[46] & he could preach verry little afterwards 'till another catastrope hapened him, which <I will> relate in due time, while I felt to proclaim with loud voic to Priest & People that the blood of the Prophets they had Slain should most assuredly be visited upon

44. Jacob's terse acknowledgment of Joseph and Hyrum Smith's death belies the effect their demise had on LDS Church members. Having heard rumors of the killings previously and obtaining confirming information of the stinging reality, undoubtedly blunted Jacob's emotions. A fellow missionary in Maryland at the time, Jacob Hamblin, recorded what probably gets closer to the feeling felt by Jacob and his sort upon hearing the awful news.

    we was often presented with the public papers with diferant accounts of the deth of the Prophet. we did not consid<e>r our Selvs ~~any obligations~~ to believe them. I know I fel<t> very meloncoly and my Sperit<s> deprest. ~~Augus<t>~~ July <14> I asertaind from a privet letter the truth that the Prophet and ~~Pa~~ Patriarch ware Marterd. my feelings I will not attempt to ~~dis~~ describe. for a moment all was lost. I was on my way to Cragors town to fill ~~an a~~ an apointment. ~~I~~ I thought I could not Preach and that I was under no obligation to in as mutch as they had kiled the man that God had Sent to restore all things. I could not refrain from weeping. I turned aside to giv vent to my feelings as I was a bout to leeve the Road. ~~I~~ I met two or three purs<on>. one of them observd I wonder what will become of Elder Hamblins Morman President. I could hardly restrain myself. I felt as ~~if I coul~~ if I could be ani~~lated th~~ an<n>ilated it would be ~~of~~ a gre<a>t ble<s>ing to me. I stopt ~~my~~ under a tree. the thoughts that the Prophet was dead was more than I could well endure. thare apeard to be the wate of a Mountain on me. I thought it would crush me to deth. at length believing it must be the power of the Devel an knowing that thare was Some thing rong, I Preyd to my Hevnly father for his Holy Spirit. after a little all was wright. Hamblin, Journal, 24–27.

45. It appears that after the death of her husband, Elias, in 1842, Mary Heaton moved to Michigan to live with her sister Lucretia Mudge.
46. The death of Joseph Smith completely enervated the Latter-day Saints for a time. Having led the church for fourteen years, and there being no established procedure for succession, Smith's demise created an atmosphere forcing the Mormons to choose from several alternatives for their religious future, including the possibility in some minds of Mormonism's dissolution. Of this crisis, George Q. Cannon later remembered, "how men's minds were indulged in; the guesses, the anticipations, some thinking one man would be chosen, and others that some one else would be. Many of the people were at an entire loss to know who would take charge of the church affairs." Cannon, 8 October 1877, *Journal of Discourses*, 19:231.

    Brigham Young and the Twelve Apostles proved, for the majority, the most formidable option, although James Jesse Strang, Sidney Rigdon, Alpheus Cutler, Lyman Wight, the Smith family, and others each attracted a number of church members. Several years were required for clear delineations to emerge defining the various fragments of the church. An overview of the alternatives for Mormon leadership after Joseph Smith's death and the process leading to Brigham Young's succession of the LDS Church presidency is found in Leonard, *Nauvoo*, 418–459.

this Generation.[47]

Wee continued laboring 'till about the first of August [1844] when wee met with Br[ethre]n H[arvey] Green,[48] Crandal Dun[n], and some eight or ten other Elders and held a conference in Florence, St Joseph Co. [Michigan].[49] While here the famous James J. Strang & Aaron Smith, Brother to Moses [Smith], came along with their revelation to gather the Saints & build up Voree in Wisconsin.[50] It being a letter purporting to < be> written by Br Joseph Smith & mailed in Nauvoo Just before his death. The letter carried upon its <face> the marks of a base forgery being written throughout in Printed characters. the Post mark was Black whil that issued from the office was uniformly red.[51] But above all, <the> contents of the thing was altgether

47. Wilford Woodruff's language at the time describing his anger at the Smiths' deaths was similar to Jacob's: "They were murdered to appeas the wrath of a gentile mob as Christ was by a Jewish mob. Peace be to thy ashes, the most glorious resurrection to thy bodies and the American gentile nation answer for thy blood before the bar of God." Woodruff, *Journal*, 2:413.
48. Harvey Green, one of those in charge of LDS Church activity in Michigan, was voted by the assembly to preside at this conference. This was the common protocol for appointing the presiding officer of a church conference at this time, though the person elected to preside may not have been the one holding the highest ecclesiastical office in attendance at the conference.
49. The conference was held "at the Rice schoolhouse" in Florence, a township in St. Joseph County, located in southwestern Michigan, sharing a border with Indiana. On 3 August, Jacob preached to conference attendees "on the gathering of saints and building of Zion." Dunn, Journal, 3 August 1844.
50. On 5 August, James Strang, according to Crandell Dunn, "Presented a revelation witch he said was ritten by bro Jos<e>ph Smith to him setting forth his claims to be the Prophet and seer of the church, and that he should plant a stake of the church [in] Westconcin [Wisconsin] teritory and that Aaron Smith should be his councellors." After listening to Strang's claims, Dunn said, "I Pronounced it a fals one and counceld him to return home to Nauvoo. he said he would. I told him to say nothing about the geathering at vorea [Voree, Wisconsin]. he said he would not say any thing about the geathering to vorea, till it was sanctioned by the twelve." Dunn, Journal, 5 August 1844.

    The "special conference," composed of twelve priesthood holders, according to minutes of the meeting, chose as their business "a certain letter from Joseph Smith to James J. Strang, a copy of which is hereunto annexed." Norton Jacob and Moses Smith were "constituted a committee to carry said letter to the authorities of the church at Nauvoo." (The letter allegedly from Joseph Smith to Strang was copied with the conference minutes which are found in the Joseph Smith Collection, Supplement, in the LDS Church Archives.)
51. Crandell Dunn confronted James Strang himself on 5 August 1844 in Florence Township, Michigan, regarding the questionable postmark. Examining Strang's alleged revelation, he said to Strang "that they had two letter stamps at the post-office in Nauvoo, or else his was a forged one, as I had three letters from the office about the same time his was mailed, which gave me a few chances to test his. His was stamped with black ink, and the letters (or type) were one size larger than the three which I had, and they were stamped with red ink." Countered with the contrary evidence, Strang, according to Dunn, dropped his head "as if he had been knocked down." Dunn to Appleby, 4 August 1846, *Millennial Star*, 93.

bombastic unlike the work of God & dishonorable to <the> name of Joseph Smith, whose signature it bore in <a> hand he never wrote, But named Moses & Aaron as coleagues with Strang which completely unshiped Moses & <he> was never good for anny thing afterwards.[52] The thing no doubt was framed by Aaron Smith & James J. Strang.[53]

The conference directed them to go immediately to Nauvoo, where was the proper authority to decide upon their pretentions, but Aaron absolutely refused,[54] & so they passed on East seeking Proselites.[55]

The 12th of this month [August 1844], wee met again in conference in Gilead, Branch Co. [Michigan][56] where I Baptised Pamela [Freeman], the Wife of Esq. Freeman.[57] this was the first person that I had ever baptised. Shortly after this there were some 7 or 8 added to the Church in this place. I now started in company <with> Moses Smith for Nauvoo [Illinois] bearing a copy of Strang's revelation. I arrived at home the 24 day of August [1844] & found my family well except ~~Elizabeth~~ Emma, the youngest.

August 24 [1844]. I arrived at Home in company with Moses Smith. the next day met in council with the "Twelve"[58] when the folly of the Strang Revelation was fully made manifest & Moses warned to follow <the> counsil ~~or he~~ <of the Twel[v]e> or he would be sure to fall, which has since been verified, for he went off into the woods with Emit [James Emmett][59] & his property & family

52. This appears to be the "catastrophe" affecting Moses Smith that Jacob referred to at the 15 July 1844 conference described earlier.
53. The course of James Strang's life and his challenge to Mormonism is recounted in Quaife, *Kingdom of Saint James*; Fitzpatrick, *King Strang Story*; and Noord, *King of Beaver Island*.
54. At the afternoon session of the conference on 5 August, Jacob preached to the assembly, "after[which] J Strang & Aaron smith manifested a bad spirit." Crandell Dunn then confronted Strang about the forged revelation he purported to have received from Joseph Smith. Dunn, Journal, 5 August 1844.
55. Coincident to the events involving Jacob in Michigan, a conference was held in Nauvoo on 8 August 1844 where the present and future leadership of Mormonism was discussed in light of Joseph Smith's murder. It was at an afternoon meeting on that date where scores later claimed to witness what has been called by Mormons a "transfiguration" of Brigham Young into the persona of Joseph Smith. From this event, most Latter-day Saints lined up behind Young and the Twelve Apostles as Smith's successors. For a discussion of the 8 August 1844 event, see Jorgensen, "The Mantle of the Prophet Joseph," and Mouritsen, *Mantle*.
56. Crandell Dunn, on 10 August, reported that the two-day conference in Gilead, Michigan, was held "at Mr freemans Barn," where Moses Smith preached and was followed by "El[der] Norton Jacob." Dunn, Journal, 10 August 1844.
57. Crandell Dunn wrote that the baptism of Pamela Freeman took place on 11 August 1844.
58. The minutes of the Florence Township, Michigan, conference, along with a copy of the letter dated 18 June 1844, allegedly written by Joseph Smith to James J. Strang just prior to Smith's death, were presented to the council by Norton Jacob and Moses Smith.
59. James Emmett took a collection of Latter-day Saints across Iowa in 1844–1846, eventually landing at Camp Vermillion, near present-day Burbank, South Dakota, on the Missouri River. Emmett's venture, ostensibly to complement the Saints' plan to evacuate Nauvoo,

are all scattered from him.[60]

Oct. 6 [1844] Conference assembled in the grove East of Temple when Br Brigham Young was fully established by a unanimous vote of the whole congregation as President of the whole Church.[61] At this conference I was ordained into the tenth Quorum of Sevnty.[62]

on the 27th of Oct [1844] my youngest <Daughter Emma> ~~my~~ died of Black canker.[63]

Illinois, in their move westward, provoked the censure of LDS Church leaders. Moses Smith aligned with Emmett for only a brief period. Emmett's westward venture and eventual fracture with Mormonism is found in Hartley, *My Best for the Kingdom*, 137–177, 187–237.

60. The effect of Jacob's report to Nauvoo authorities the last week of August 1844 was an item addressed "TO THE SAINTS," published in the city's *Times and Seasons*. James Strang and Aaron Smith, it stated, had been "circulating" a false revelation, recruiting Saints to settle in Wisconsin, and were "thereby leading the saints astray." As of 26 August 1844, Strang and Smith, it continued, were "cut off from the church . . . By order of the Council of the Twelve [Apostles]." *Times and Seasons* 5, no. 16 (2 September 1844): 631.

    Moses Smith's life after his disengagement with the LDS Church is reported in Clark, "Moses Smith," 155–170.

61. The LDS Church's fall conference was the first held since Joseph Smith's death. Brigham Young, in the aftermath of Sidney Rigdon's claim to lead the church, sermonized at the conference on the legitimacy of the Twelve Apostles to lead the church. Minutes for the morning meeting on Monday, 7 October, read, in part,: "Elder W. W. Phelps moved that we uphold Brigham Young the president of the quorum of the Twelve, as one of the Twelve and first presidency of the church. The motion was duly seconded, and put to the church by Elder John Smith and carried unanimously." The Twelve Apostles, with Brigham Young at the lead, would function as the church's First Presidency. However, it was not until December 1847, at Orson Hyde's home, southeast of Kanesville, Iowa, after Young's return to the Missouri River settlements from the Salt Lake Valley, that he and two counselors, Heber Kimball and Willard Richards, were formalized as the church's new First Presidency succeeding Smith and his counselors. *Times and Seasons* 5, no. 20 (1 November 1844): 692; Bennett, *Mormons at the Missouri*, 199–212.

62. One of the orders of the conference was that "The presidents of seventies will organize all the seventies . . . . We want them organized and begin to fill up the second quorum and then the third and the fourth to the tenth." By the end of the year, sixteen seventy's quorums had been organized. Thirty-five quorums were organized before the Mormons were driven from Nauvoo. The office of seventy, another tier in the Mormon priesthood, ostensibly had the duty of the church's missionary work. *Times and Seasons* 5, no. 20 (1 November 1844): 695. Jacob was later assigned to the 14th Quorum of Seventy.

63. Emma Jacob's death of "Black Canker," probably diphtheria, was a month shy of her second birthday.

1845

A CONSTRAINED UNEASINESS SETTLED OVER HANCOCK COUNTY, Illinois, for most of a year in the aftermath of the Smith brothers' assassinations. As fall dawned in 1845, bad decisions, misunderstanding, and polemical politics led to hot words and then exasperated aggression on Hancock County's prairie, kindling a full breach with bullets flying and fires burning. Before winter, Brigham Young, now the primary leader of the Latter-day Saints, recognized the inevitable. His people's destiny was removal from Illinois to some distant site or sites, out of reach of their countrymen. Amidst this precarious setting, the Nauvoo Temple's completion for the purpose of hosting the Mormons' most sacred, empowering ordinances became paramount. Norton Jacob's carpentry skills played an important role for the project. By the end of the year, the entire Mormon enterprise focused on preparing for exodus.

~~

Towards the close of Jan. 1845 I commenced work on the Temple as a Steady hand. during the Spring & Summer I w[r]ought constantly, being Foreman of all the framing of the Roof & Tower.[1]

---

1. Jacob's role in the LDS Church's effort to finish the Nauvoo Temple, in construction since 1841, was consequential. As the limestone walls of the structure rose on the bluff overlooking the Mississippi River to the west, carpenters, fifteen in number since the previous December, had been preparing timbers to furbish the structure's interior. Jacob and the other carpenters teamed with hundreds of others to bring the project to fruition. A description of the roof's construction is found in Colvin, *Nauvoo Temple*, 150–152.

   In light of Joseph Smith's death and the increasingly obvious conclusion that the Mormons would have to abandon Nauvoo, the momentum to finish the Nauvoo Temple is significant in understanding Mormon thinking and theology. Marshaling the resources of Nauvoo's skilled and unskilled workmen, church leaders determined the edifice would be completed, no matter the apparent folly in finishing a building they would not utilize. Events transpiring in the temple during the winter of 1845–1846, which the workers could only imagine at this time, proved the endeavor's worth for the Saints.

   Overviews of the sequence and highpoints of the temple's construction can be found in Miller and Miller, *Nauvoo*, 107–117; Colvin, *Nauvoo Temple*, 15–37; and Leonard, *Nauvoo*, 242–255.

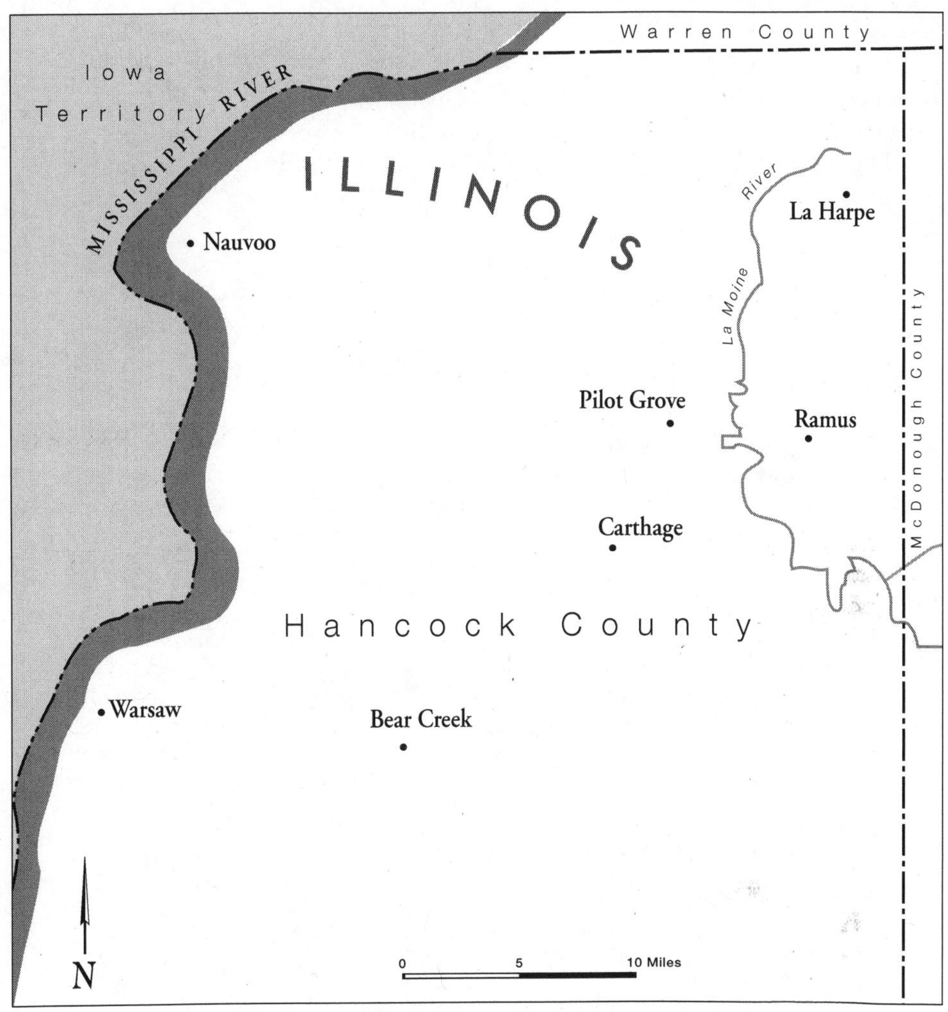

Hancock County, Illinois. Map by Tom Child.

on the 24th of May [1845], about 6 o clock A.M., the Cap Stone was Laid on the S East corner.[2]

on the 16th of August [1845] I finished framing the Tower and on the 18 [August 1845] commenced the Nauvoo House.[3]

2. Explaining the necessity of the temple-building endeavor, even in unfavorable circumstances, Brigham Young stated at the ceremony: "The last stone is now laid upon the Temple and I pray the Almighty in the name of Jesus to defend us in this place and sustain us until the Temple is finished and we have all got our endowments." Smith, *History of the Church*, 7:417–418.
3. The Nauvoo House, whose construction at the south end of Nauvoo's Main Street

on the 23d [August 1845] they finished raising the Dome of the Tower & all hands partook of a feast of Melons in the Attick Story.[4]

The first of Sept. [1845] there began to be rumors of the Mob meeting in several parts of the County of Hancok[5] & on the 10th day of Sept. [1845]

---

adjacent to Joseph Smith's home, was contemplated by Smith at the same time he received a revelation to erect the Nauvoo Temple. (Doctrine and Covenants 124: 22–24, 56–82, 111–122.) The former structure was to be a hotel to accommodate visitors to the Saints' city. The building's cornerstone was set on 2 October 1841, and by 18 August 1845 "the basement walls had been raised to the square, ready for brickwork to begin." Unlike the temple, the construction of which became the Saints' focus, this structure was never completed, though a reconfigured remnant of it, owned by the Community of Christ, today stands adjacent to Smith's Homestead and Mansion House on the Mississippi River's bank. Miller and Miller, *Nauvoo*, 124–126.

4. The description of the dome and tower of the temple (including a photograph of the same), as well as a description of the temple's attic, is found in Colvin, *Nauvoo Temple*, 143–145, 210–218.

5. Following the assassinations of Joseph and Hyrum Smith on 27 June 1844, the non-Mormon population of Hancock County, Illinois, expected the Saints to fragment and Nauvoo to shrivel. A year-long peace, of sorts, prevailed in the county, anticipating the Saints' removal. In May 1845 the trial for those accused of the Smiths' murders commenced, ending in acquittal of those charged. In the August 1845 county elections, candidates supported by the Saints carried several county offices. County residents chafed under the continuing political domination of the Mormons, an issue that only added to the friction between the two groups. The Mormons, despite their plans to remove, appeared, to their neighbors, intent on staying. There could be no peaceful resolution to the dilemma. The acquittal of those accused of engineering the Smiths' murders is discussed in Oaks and Hill, *Carthage Conspiracy*. For a general overview of the two-year Hancock County conflict see Hamilton, "From Assassination to Expulsion," 214–230; and Leonard, *Nauvoo*, 463–550.

Latter-day Saints, believing it was their doctrine and theology that aroused their neighbors to hatred, failed to recognize that wherever they dominated a region they brought out the worst in their neighbors, who, without proximity to the Mormons, were as benign as any other local population in the United States. When confronted by a growing concentration of Mormons, the non-Mormons, according to Robert Flanders,

> were eventually excited to uneasiness, then to hostility toward the sect. To be sure, the Mormon religion was unorthodox, but the nation knew and tolerated many unorthodox sects. Contemporary observers did not regard individual Mormons as fanatics or find them, as individuals, very different from thousands of others of Yankee descent who spread across the upper Midwest during the first half of the nineteenth century. But Mormonism, the gentiles [non-Mormons] observed, was more than the unorthodox doctrine of ardent believers. It was a burgeoning, centralized, corporate sect committed to action upon its beliefs—and those beliefs entailed the reordering of society and the conversion of the world. It was the Mormon Church in action that aroused its neighbors. Flanders, *Nauvoo*, 3.

The complicated climate fostering the explosion of vigilante violence employed in September 1845 by the *old settlers* against Mormons living in the outlying farms of Hancock County, where not only homesteads were destroyed but men were murdered, is difficult to comprehend. By September 1845, the region's most vindictive opponents of Smith's religion exacted a hatred against their fellow Americans paralleling that executed

they commnced burning house & grain in the ~~So~~ Morl[e]y Settlement in the South part of the County.[6] they continued their devastations through the week[7] & on Tuesday the 16th [September 1845] <the> Military were caled together.[8] As I had Command of the 5th com[pany] of Artille[r]y, I met with

---

by Missouri's residents against the Saints in the previous decade. A year later, a military assault upon Nauvoo to completely rout the Saints from the county capped the non-Mormons' determination to rid themselves of Latter-day Saints. For the *old settlers'* views of the Mormon intrusion into Hancock County, see Hallwas, "Mormon Nauvoo from a Non-Mormon Perspective," 160–180; and Hallwas and Launius, *Cultures in Conflict*. The Latter-day Saint view is represented by Leonard, *Nauvoo*, 463–550.

6. Solomon Hancock, a resident of Yelrome, Morley's settlement, wrote on 13 September 1845 to Nauvoo church leaders of the trauma inflicted on Saints in and around his settlement, requesting counsel:

> On Wednesday the 10th [September] all of a sudden, the mob rushed upon Edmund Durfee and destroyed some property, and set fire to both of his buildings, they then dispersed; Bro. Durfee with his family then put the fire out. The same day in the evening they shot at our guard and missed them, the mob then fled a small distance and soon set fire to the house of John Edmondson, and in a few minutes the house was in flames. On the morning of the 11th they again set fire to the buildings of Edmund Durfee, and fired upon some of his children without hitting them; they then proceeded to the old shop of Father [Isaac] Morley's and set fire to both his shops, firing at the same time upon J[ames] C. Snow, as they supposed, and thought they had killed him, it proved however to be Clark Hallett who escaped unhurt; they then set fire to J. C. Snow's house, and fled hom to Lima. In the afternoon the mob came on again and set fire to Father Whiting's chair shop, Walter Cow, Cheney Whiting and Azariah Tuttle's houses, at evening they retreated back again. On the morning of the 12th we held a council and selected two men to go and make proposals to sell, but got no particular answer. Last evening they set on fire three buildings, near Esq. Walker's; and this morning we expect them to renew their work of destruction. Williams and Roosevelt were in Lima yesterday. The mob is determined to destroy us; . . . Do for us, what you think us best; we will do as you tell us. Jessee, "John Taylor Nauvoo Journal," 89–90.

Morley's settlement, (also then known as Yelrome–Isaac Morley's surname spelled backwards–and now known as Tioga) is located in the southwestern sector of Hancock County, Illinois. For a discussion of the torching of Morley's Settlement, see Hartley, *The Burning of Morley's Settlement*.

7. A spokesman for the local settlers described the vigilante tactics of those intent on driving the Mormons from Hancock County:

> The houses burnt were mostly log cabins of not much value, though some pretty good dwellings were included. The manner was to go to the house and warn the inmates out—that they were going to burn it. Usually there would be no show of resistance; but all hands, burners and all, would proceed to take out the goods and place them out of danger. When the goods were all securely removed, the torch would be applied, and the house consumed. Then on to another. We are not aware that a correct count was ever made of the number they burned; but our informant states that there were probably 70 or 80. Some accounts have placed it as high as 125. Gregg, *History of Hancock County*, 374.

8. With the Mormons of Hancock County under siege, Mormons and their sympathizers became both defensive and offensive in action. On 13 September 1845, Hancock County sheriff Jacob Backenstos called for the county's law-abiding citizens to volunteer for a posse he was raising to quell the vigilante assaults in the county. Two days later, Brigham

<the> [first] Regmt [Regiment] in the Masonic Hall when it was reorganized,[9] & after ward I reorganized my com[pany] having Georg P. Stiles, first Liut., M[ephibosheth]. Serrine [Sirrine], 2d, W[illia]m Burton, 3d, & Charles Dalton, Ensign. On this day wee received inteligence of the death of one notorious Mobber by the hands of ~~the~~ one of the Sherrifs Posse. the name of the one Killed was Franklin B. [A.] Worrel[l].[10]

on the 17th [September 1845] the Legion was called out when attended at the head of my company.[11]

Young reactivated a division–the second cohort of the first regiment–of the nearly dormant Nauvoo Legion to ready themselves for county duty if called upon. Leonard, *Nauvoo*, 528.

An overview of the inception, organization, and implementation of the Nauvoo Legion, provided for in Nauvoo's city charter, is found in Gardner, "The Nauvoo Legion," 181–197; and Leonard, *Nauvoo*, 112–118.

9. The Nauvoo Legion had been disbanded by the Illinois legislature earlier in 1845. Faced with the reality of the need for self-protection because of the surge of Hancock County violence, the Legion unofficially reorganized. "The first regiment, second cohort . . . met and organized, choosing the old officers, to place themselves in readiness to act at the sheriff's call." Jacob's attachment to the artillery division was part of this reorganization. Brigham Young to Samuel Brannan, 15 September 1845, Smith, *History of the Church*, 7:445.

10. Franklin Worrell, on 16 September 1845, was killed by Orrin Porter Rockwell, in defense of county sheriff Jacob Backenstos. Mormons stated at the time that Rockwell had interrupted Worrell who, with several others, were after Backenstos to do him harm. Worrell's supporters claim he was merely "passing on the road from Carthage to Warsaw [Illinois], with the view of ascertaining the facts as to disturbances" in other parts of the county. Worrell's death, because he was viewed as a patriot by county residents intent on eliminating the Mormon presence in their county, only exacerbated the mounting hostility toward the Saints. Two days after his death, the *Warsaw Signal's* editor, Thomas Sharp, editorialized: "Poor Frank, he was one of the noblest spirits in our county, and his death has kindled and will kindle a flame that can never be quenched until every Mormon has left the vicinity." Such threats, not unlike those proposed earlier in Missouri, found the ears of Mormon leaders. Inflamed passions in Hancock County were sufficiently high, that the day after Worrell's death, Brigham Young announced to vigilante leaders that if the Mormons were left alone they would leave the county the following spring. *Warsaw Signal*, 17 September 1845; Leonard, *Nauvoo*, 529–531; Schindler, *Orrin Porter Rockwell*, 144–146; Gregg, *History of Hancock County, Illinois*, 340; and Hallwas and Launius, *Cultures in Conflict*, 275–278.

11. The Nauvoo Legion, the city's militia founded upon provisions stipulated in the city's charter, was first activated in February 1841. Although the organization is widely referenced, "little has been published on the Legion and its function in Nauvoo beyond well-known accounts of particular actions." By 1844 the Legion "seems to have been organized but not fully mobilized." The Legion, once a function of the Illinois militia, was later jettisoned as a state entity. Saunders, "Officers and Arms," 140, 145. A comprehensive history of the Nauvoo Legion in Illinois is being prepared at present by Richard Bennett, Susan Black, and Donald Cannon.

The Legion was divided into two brigade-size organizations called cohorts, the second one, of which Jacob was a part, was the "foot troops" or infantry. This cohort was

1845 13

On this day wee received intelligence
of the death of one notorious Mobber
by the hands of one of the Sheriffs
Posse. the name of the one killed was
Franklin A. Worrel. On the 17th the
Legion was called out. when attended at the
head of my Company. On the 18th I was called by Br
Brigham to work on the Temple & left my
Company in command of S. P. Hiles first Lieu
A Detachment of Cavelry was sent out on the
Evening of the 16th & on the 17th about 2 ocl P.M
fell in with some of the house burners on
Bear Creek when they immediately fled
& being pursued by our men two of
them mob were shot dead & one
wounded. Our men were acting as a
Posse comitatus under immediate
command of the Sherrif. On the
same day annother detachment was
sent out under Col Markham the next
day another strong detachment went
under the Sherrif & Gen. Miller
they having come in the night before
and On Saturday the 20 all the Mobbers
having all fled across the Missisippi,
our troops entered Warsaw in
triumph. Sunday Br Brigham
preached verry encouraging to
the Saints. A Signal staff being
erected on top of the Tower, it was
arranged that a white flag should
be a signal for assembling the
troops. This evening the signal was
hoisted about sunset. When wee
were collected it was found to be a false
alarm. A horseman having com
in from Carthage stating that a
mob was in sight which
proved to be a deligation sent
from McDonah & Schuyler Co to
enquire into our difficulties. 50
horseman however, went to Carth
-age under Col Markham. On the 22
a detachment was sent to Ramus
& another to Laharp to prevent any
outbreaks in the East part of the
Co & on Wednesday the 24th 40
horsemen were sent for to Laharp
go to Laharp the Mob still gath
ering in the adjoining Cos.

Handwriting of Norton Jacob. Courtesy of the LDS Church Archives.

on the 18th [September 1845] I <was> called by Br Brigham to work on the Temple & left my com[pany]. in command of G. P. Stiles, first Liut. [A] Dtachment of Cavelry [was] sent out on the Evening of the 16th [September 1845]. on the 17th [September 1845] about 2 ocl P.M. fell in with some of the house burners on Bear Creek [Hancock County, Illinois][12] when they immediately fled & being pursued by our men two of ~~them~~ mob were ~~s~~shot dead & one wounded.[13] our men were acting as a Posse comitatus under immediate command of the Sherrif [Jacob Backenstos]. on the [obscure word crossed out] same day annother detachment was sent out under Col [Stephen] Markum [Markham]. the next day another Strong detachment went under the Sherrif & Gen [George] Miller, they having come in the night before and on Saturday the ~~19~~ 20th [September 1845] the mobbers having all fled across the Missisippi, our troops entered Warsaw in triumph.[14]

Sunday [21 September 1845] Br Brigham [Young] preached verry encouraging to the Saints. a Signal staff being erected on top of the Tower, it was arranged

---

composed of "five regimental staffs and as many as sixteen companies." (The Artillery unit, to which Jacob was attached, was one of the regiments.) The hierarchy of command included, in descending order, a colonel, lieutenant colonel, major, quartermaster sergeant, and sergeant major. The Nauvoo Legion's Second Cohort "totaled 1,751 men." Saunders, "Officers and Arms," 140–141.

12. Bear Creek, twenty-eight miles south of Nauvoo in Hancock County, received its name "from a crooked and ugly stream which meanders through it." The area was half prairie and half timber. First settled in about 1835, it was the location of a small congregation of Latter-day Saints. Gregg, *History of Hancock County, Illinois*, 608.

13. Another participant reported the killing and wounding of three men. Leonard, *Nauvoo*, 531–532.

14. One of the posse's participants, William Burton, wrote, "this body of men were generally Saints. I also volunteered to go, and I rode for near two weeks in various parts of the County, some of the time night & day. we camped near the Mobocratic head Quarters. they fearing an attack from us fled & crossed the Mississippi into Missouri. However previous to this some of them we caught in the act of burning, who ran as soon as they saw us. we persued them & some were shot. we finally suceeded in suppressing them <&> stoped their career for a while." Burton, Diaries, v. 9.

    Another volunteer, George Laub, wrote, "This posey [posse] consisted of Saints, for our Enemy was also his [Jacob Backenstos] Enemy. I was called on & went fourth as one of the possey accompanyed by about Two hundred in one Company. We traveld at the rate of Twelve Miles, nearly all night, till we got to the place of randesvoos where we was welcomed by Brother Markems. Stephen Markems [Markham] as colonel of a ridgment [regiment] of brethren who had gone before we did. We marched nearly to the Enemy camp. There was Some five or Six hundred of the Eenemy. There was five or Six houses on fire when Some of our brethren was Scouting, and the Lord Speeded the animels of the brethren so that the house burners could not get out of the [way] & Severl was shot dead. This frightened the residew So they Seased their burning for a Short time." England, "George Laub," 163.

    There was a sense of relief in Nauvoo when reports of these events reached the resident's ears leading them to believe that thereafter the "Mob promis[ed] not to molest us." Knight, "Journal of Thomas Bullock," [20 September 1845], 20. The week's explosive action is recounted in Leonard, *Nauvoo*, 528–533.

that a white flagg should be a signal for assembling the troops. this evening the Signal was hoisted about sunset.[15] when wee were colected it was found to be a false alarm, a horseman having com in from Carthage [Hancock County, Illinois][16] stating that a mob had hove in sight, which proved to be a deligation sent from MaDonah [McDonough] & Shyler [Schuyler] Co[unties]. [Illinois] to enquire into our difficulties.[17] 50 horseman, however, went to Carthage under Col [Stephen] Markum.

on the 22d [September 1845] a ditachment was sent to Ramus [Hancock County, Illinois][18] & another to Laharp to prevent any outbreak in the East part of the Co[unty].,[19] & on Wednesday the 24th [September 1844] 40 ~~more~~ horsemen were sent for to ~~Laharp~~ go to Laharp, the Mob still gathering in the adjoining Co.

Wednesday Sept 24 [1845] A delegation arrived from Quincy [Adams County, Illinois] stating that the People were much incensed against us since those men were killed.[20] The Devil appears to be much enraged at the Saints, a pretty good Sign that [we] are doing the will of God. I remember Br Josep Smith said some two years ago the about the time the Temple was

15. The method of signaling the Saints to rally was employed the previous day as well, as Zina Diantha Huntington Jacobs stated: "The first thing I saw as I looked toward the Temple just as the sun was risen, a white flag, a signature to gather. A company is called for to assist a company that is out to execute the Laws of the Land to put down the mob." Beecher, "All Things Move in Order in the City," [20 September 1845] 320.
16. Carthage, county seat of Hancock County, Illinois, and located about fifteen miles southeast of Nauvoo, was first settled in 1831. "[B]eing in the midst of an extensive prairie, [Carthage] was not settled as early as the western and eastern portions of the county." The community was designated as county seat in 1833. Gregg, *History of Hancock County, Illinois*, 687.
17. McDonough and Schuyler counties are the adjoining counties to the east of Hancock County, Illinois.
18. Ramus, Illinois, located about twenty miles east of Nauvoo, became one of the more populated Mormon centers in Hancock County. Perhaps 400 to 500 people once populated the community. Later called Macedonia (today Webster), the village was first laid out in 1840. An overview of the community during this difficult period is found in Rugh, "Those Who Labor in the Earth," 92–155; Gregg, *History of Hancock County, Illinois*, 475.
19. For another view of the property destruction and threats made by some Hancock County citizens against Mormons near Carthage, the center of the county, see Barney, *One Side by Himself*, 76–81.
20. The men killed, of course, were those who fell under the retaliation of the posse noted above. The "Quincy Committee" from Adams County soon assumed an ameliorating force between the Mormons and their hostile neighbors. A decision from the "Committee," which met on 22 September 1845, called for Brigham Young and the Saints to declare their intentions for the future. This, of course, elicited from the Saints the promise to leave the following year. Hamilton, "From Assassination to Expulsion," 223. A brief overview of the committee's involvement regarding the Mormons is found in Leonard, *Nauvoo*, 534–536.

finished all Hell would be raised. This day the "Twelve" & some others went to Carthage to demand their trial on a charge of High Treason & were all acquited.[21]

25th [September 1845] a delegation having arrived from Quincy yesterday had an interview with the "Twelve" today. they ~~b~~ brought a copy of resolutions passed by a large meeting of the citizens of Quincy requesting the Saints to leav the State in Six months & a written answer to be returned by the Twelve stating in explicit terms what they would do in the premises.[22] Accordingly they returned an answer setting forth the facts concerning our grievances,[23] that wee had suffered the Mob to burn some 50 houses & much grain, turning sick women & children out in the hot Sun by day & the damp dewe of Night without offering anny resistance until called upon by the legal authorities of the County to viz: the Sherrif [Jacob Backenstos], who was not a member of our community, yet because he came upon them while in the act of burning a house & as they fled & would not be arrested two of them were shot. the republecan Spirit of the people was raised to boiling heat. God deliver me from such a goverment!! and may Ep[h]raim spedily reclaim his inheritance & the cursed Gentiles swept from the Land according to the promise of the Lord![24] The Twelve pro<po>sed in their answer to leave next season provided wee could be secured in the enjoyment of peace until then & be paid for our property. wee [will] then remove to a place so remote that there would be no danger of anny more collision.[25]

---

21. The group, which included "the Twelve & a number of other Gentlemen," upon their arrival visited the Carthage jail where fifteen months before Joseph and Hyrum Smith were shot. After arousing "feelings of horror" caused by seeing the "marks w[h]ere the balls penetrated" the walls of the jail and witnessing "the blood on the floor," they were notified they were wanted for trial. Particulars of the proceedings are found in Stout, *On the Mormon Frontier*, 1:72–73.
22. The Quincy, Illinois, delegation, after meeting with Mormon leaders, sent letters the first week of October 1845 to them outlining stipulations for the Saints to evacuate Hancock County the next spring. The letters of 1–2 October and the "Resolutions by the citizens of Quincy" of 3 October, as printed in the *Quincy Whig*, are printed in Smith, *History of the Church*, 7:449–453.
23. LDS Church leaders replied to the delegation on 1 October 1845. Besides articulating their grievances regarding lawless retribution heaped upon them, church leaders acknowledged that they would leave Illinois the following spring "when grass grows and water runs." Hamilton, "From Assassination to Expulsion," 223.
24. Ephraim's inheritance anticipates the restoration of God's promises to ancient Israel, according to Mormons. Because of Ephraim's rebellion centuries ago, they were scattered among the non-believing nations. Ephraim, in Genesis 48:13–20, received the covenant of God's special occupation with them as his chosen people, to be fulfilled in the last days. See "Ephraim," *Encyclopedia of Mormonism*, 1:461–462.
25. Other first-hand accounts of the incendiary events leading to the Mormon compromise wherein they promised to evacuate the Nauvoo peninsula are detailed in Stout, *On the Mormon Frontier*, 1:62–73; and Barney, *Anson Call*, 134–137.

Father Alp[h]eus Cutler proposed to me this day to go with him with my family on an expedition next Spring. I agreed to go. he is to take a hundred families, as also Reynol[d]s Cahoon. Father [Isaac] Morley & [Samuel] Bent ~~t~~ are to take a hundred families each.[26] Upon counciling withe my Brethren I found it was best not to go with Father Cutler.[27]

27th [September 1845] at 4 oclock the Artillery was called together when Col. [John] Scott proceeded to lay before us the order of arrangement for the future with regard to our opperations. having acertained the amount of our arms, Teams, horses &c., informed us that from this time forth all wee had would be under the drection of our proper officrs, the orders coming from the Head dow[n] to the comman[d]ants of companies who would be held responsable for all their Teams, &c. wee were commanded to secrete our cannon,[28] ~~this~~ as the <Governer> [Thomas Ford] was expected to pay us a visit, & from past example of his taking away our arms, wee were aprehensive that he <might> want to borrow them. the smallest gun was assigned to my Com[pany].[29]

28th [September 1845] News arrived that the Governor had sent on troops to assist in administering the Law in Hancock Co., Gen. J[ohn]. J. Hardin commanding.[30] he immediately dismissed all the Sherrif's Posse that were on

26. As early as 28 August 1845, plans were hatched for 3,000 able-bodied male Mormons to travel to Alta California preparatory to the whole of Mormondom joining them. On 9 September 1845, LDS Church leaders had halved the number, determining "that a company of 1500 men be selected to go to Great Salt Lake valley." By 11 October 1845 the plan had been adjusted to include a full complement of twenty-five companies of 100 emigrants each to emigrate westward in 1846. This plan failed to materialize. Bennett, *Mormons at the Missouri*, 14; Smith, *History of the Church*, 7:439, 442, 481–482; Leonard, *Nauvoo*, 557.
27. Jacob does not explain the reason he neglected to join Alpheus Cutler's group, which, at this time, was an important component of the design to move the LDS Church westward. Later, however, Jacob's family lived near the west branch of the Nishnabotna River, in proximity to Cutler and those he led on Silver Creek, in Pottawattamie County, Iowa, which will be described later.
28. Wandle Mace, whose duty it was to prepare the cannon for duty, wrote: "Some old cannon had been brought to Nauvoo from New Orleans, which had lain in the salt water until they had become very rusty . . . . [Brigham Young] told me to take them into the basement of the Temple and rebore them and get them ready for action. I accordingly called upon two or three of the brethren to help me, and we took them by night into the basement, white washed the windows to prevent observation, and went to work." Mace, Autobiography, 103.
29. The Nauvoo Legion's Second Cohort was equipped with three cannons, along with 220 small arms. One of the cannons was the "Old Sow," the carronade which accompanied the vanguard to Utah in 1847. Saunders, "Officers and Arms," 144–145.
30. John Hardin was the brigadier general (later the major general) of the Illinois state militia at this time. See John Hardin's public correspondence concerning the Mormons, 1–10

duty to return home & issued orders that not more than four persons armed should assemble together in the county except his troops.[31]

Oct 5 1845. It being the Sabbath, meeting was held in the Temple, it being now all enclosed.[32] the meeting was opend by prayr by President Brigham Young. when after he & some others had made a few remarks Elder [John] Taylor spoke at considerable length on the prospects before us, that Peace being now restored wee had nothing to do but finish & dedicate the Temple & prepare to remove in a body next Spring, stating that he should feel to rejoice when he had got beyond the bounds of the Christians for he wo[u]ld not then have to carry his Six Shooter in his pocket ~~then~~ all the time as he had since the ~~B~~ Bloodsuckers ~~under~~ tried to suck his blood in Carthage Jail. In the afternoon 4 companies were drawn out begining with No 1 under the Twelve, No 2 under Capt. [Samuel] Bent, No 3 under Capt. [Alpheus] Cutler, & No 4 under Capt. [Isaac] Morley. they received some generel instruction from Br Brigham & then 5 Teams were drawn out of each com[pany]. to work on the Temple & for the Church.

6th [October 1845] ~~Co~~ A General Conference of the Church met in the Temple, opend by Prayer by Br Parley P Pratt. after a beautiful Hymn sung by the Choir, the President then stated that the first business would be to present the Authorities of the Church for consideration & approval, when Br Brigham Young was unanimously sustained as President of the Church & the [president] of the Twelve, & the members of that Quorum were sustained except W[illia]m Smith, o[b]jection being made by P. P. Pratt, when by a unanimous vote he was rejected.[33] objection was made by Br Almon Babbitt to Br Lyman Wight on account of his separating & not being with the Twelve.

October 1845, in Johannsen, *Letters of Stephen A. Douglas*, 120–27, 137. An overview of Hardin's actions during this period is found in Leonard, *Nauvoo*, 533–539.

31. "It took until Sunday, September 28, nine days after Carthage was commandeered by Backenstos's posse, for Governor Ford's army under General Hardin to reach Carthage and dismiss the occupying posse." Hamilton, "From Assassination to Expulsion," 223.

    Jacob failed to note the "convention" held in Carthage, Illinois, days later on 1–2 October 1845 when the county's anti-Mormons resolved their determination to expel the Saints from their region. See the proceedings in Hallwas and Launius, *Cultures in Conflict*, 304–309.

32. The inauguration of meetings in the temple was considered of great significance to the Mormons. "Through the indefatigable exertions, unceasing industry, and heaven-blessed labors, in the midst of trials, tribulations, poverty, and worldly obstacles, solemnized in some instances, by death, about five thousand saints had inexpressible joy and great satisfaction to meet for the first time in the House of the Lord in the City of Joseph." Smith, *History of the Church*, 7:456.

33. A report of the meeting found in Smith, *History of the Church*, 7:458–459, states that it was Orson, rather than Parley Pratt who objected to William Smith's place with the Twelve Apostles. The course of William Smith's life after the death of his brothers until his excommunication is described in Edwards, "William B. Smith," 142–46.

Br H[eber]. C. Kimbal [stated] that Br Wight was with a small com[pany] & no one here was able to tell whether he was doing well or ill so he proposed that his case be laid over which was agreed to.[34] In the afternoon wee received a rich treat from P. P. Pratt on the first principle ~~of God~~ contained in the command to multiply & replenish the Earth, showing that principle was turned aside by the foolish & wicked Laws of the Gentiles preventing man from enjoying his inheritance according to the law of God.

7th [October 1845] Preaching by Br Amasa Lyman showing the reason why God had dealt with his People in the way he had for the last 15 years in [order] to prepare them & bring about his purposes.[35] In the afternoon the congregation was sudenly dismissed by Father John Smith before it was fully convened, teling them [to] go immediately home & prepare for the worst. all this alarm was occasioned by some of Gen. [John] Hardin's troops coming in to search for theives & stolen property & they found some property which was claimed by Mr Crawford, who was said to be one of the house burners. they also took one man by the name of Gardner & one by the name of Smith.

8th [October 1845] Br Brigham [Young] commenced in the morning by denouncing such characters in the most severe terms & took measures to [have] them all cut off from the Church.[36] after he got through Mother [Lucy Mack] Smith, Joseph [Smith]'s Mother, addressed the congregation abou<t> an hour concerning the history of herself & family in bringing forth the Book of Mormmon. she said it was eighteen years ago last monday since she commenced preaching the gospel, being caled upon by Joseph to go & tell Martin Harris & family that he [Joseph Smith] had got the Plates & he wanted him to take an a[l]phabet of the characters & carry them to the learned men to decypher ~~them~~.[37] in the afternoon, passed a resolution that the Twelve & all others should immediately settle with the Truties [Trustees] in trust[38] when after appointing comittees to sell property preparatory to mooving &

34. The presentation, acceptance, and in one case the rejection of William Smith, of church authorities at this conference is noted in Smith, *History of the Church*, 7:458–460. Lyman Wight's life after Joseph Smith's death and his dissonance with Brigham Young and his erstwhile apostolic quorum are addressed in Wight, *Wild Ram of the Mountain*, 227–311.
35. A report of Amasa Lyman's sermon is found in Smith, *History of the Church*, 7:468–469.
36. Thomas Bullock, one of Brigham Young's clerks, reported that Young "spoke on the subject of thieves and warned the brethren not to receive any stolen goods into their house." Knight "Journal of Thomas Bullock" [8 October 1845], 24–25.
37. The minutes of Lucy Smith's words preserved by the LDS Church are printed in Walker, "Lucy Mack Smith Speaks to the Nauvoo Saints," 278–284. A contemporary summary of Lucy Smith's words can be found in *Times and Seasons* 6, no. 16 (1 November 1845): 1013–1014. See also Smith, *History of the Church*, 7:470–473.
38. Joseph Smith became Trustee-in-Trust for the church in 1841 and on 9 August 1844, two months after his death, Bishops Newel Whitney and George Miller succeeded him as jointly appointed Trustees-in-Trust for the LDS Church. Arrington, *Brigham Young*, 118; Smith, *History of the Church*, 7:247.

appointing W[illia]m W Phelps to write <6> School Books for the instruction of Children.[39] the co[n]ference adjournd 'till the 6th day of next April. this night I was directed by Col. [John] Scott to bring my cannon to the North side of the Temple wich I did accompanied by Lieut [William] Burton & one of our men.

9th [October 1845] The Sevnties held a general conference this morning in <the> Temple, & there was also a council by the first Presidency for sending persons abroad to settle up business preparatory to removing in the Spring.[40] this night at 12 oclock I was called ~~by Adgt. Repshur~~ to come immediately to the Temple. Col [John] Scott & 12 or 15 others were there. wee went to work & prepared a place behind some large piles of Lumber & stowed away our four pieces of Artillery[41] having heard that Gen. [John] Hardin's Posse were coming in from Carthage to demand all the persons that were in command of the Shiriff's Posse in the late disturbances. if they were not given up they would immediately make war upon the City.

10th [October 1845] I worked upon <the> Ars[e]nal.[42] in <the> afternoon commenced Bishop [Newel] Whitney's Barn. at 10 oclock at night I <was> called by Agt [Adjutant Daniel] Repshur to go & notify my com[pany] to meet at the Temple at 3 oclck in the morning, when wee met there & having deposited our arms went home for Breakfast. Several Regiments were gatherd in different parts of the city & remained on the watch during the day from the Tower of <the> Temple. ~~of~~ with good glasses wee were enabled to overlook the Praries for 15 or 20 mils, & not having seen anny movment of men during the day, at 10 oclk at night o<u>r Regmt was discharged, it being a false alarm.

17th [October 1845] Finished the Bishop's [Newel Whitney] Barn & raised it.

18th [October 1845] Returned to work at the Temple replacing the lower Girders, they having lain 4 years in the weather exposed were so decayed as not to be safe.

---

39. The intent of this action was to institute a Mormon-controlled educational program, free of non-LDS influence, including textbooks. Incidents causing a hastened departure of the Saints from Nauvoo preempted preparation of the school books for the Mormon children. Smith, *History of the Church*, 7:474–475; Miller and Miller, *Nauvoo*, 91–92.
40. A brief note summarizing Joseph Young's message, as senior president of the Seventies, is found in Smith, *History of the Church*, 7:481.
41. See footnote 28 in this chapter.
42. Nauvoo's arsenal or armory was planned in September 1844 and built just west of the temple. Because Illinois governor Thomas Ford ordered the Nauvoo Legion to disarm, thereby eliminating the need for a munitions depot, the arsenal was finished as a school. Leonard, *Nauvoo*, 478.

Sunday 19th [October 1845] I attended a general coference of the Sevnties in the Temple when I was called to act as one of the sevn Presidents of the 14th Quorum, to suply the vacancy caused by the Death of Br Jonathan Dunham.[43] I was ordained under the hands of Presd Joseph Young & Arza Adams. after the business was done the congregation of the Saints assembled and was addresd by Br Orson Hide [Hyde], frst giving an account of his success in procureing canvass for the Tabernacle. he had got it not by loans from the rich who held on to their money, but by begging & some voluntary donations he had in his mission of some three months to the East obtained $1800 dolars, $600 more than was necessary to purchace the canvass.[44] He then gave us a verry spirited dicourse on the "children of Jerusalem refusing to [be] gathered together by Jesus"[45] & applyed the subject to the present scituation of the Saints in being driven out from among the Gentiles, after which Elder [John] Taylor read to the congregation two letters written by W[illia]m Smith (he havig gone to Galena [Jo Daviess County, Illinois]) in which he Speaks evil of the Saints at Nauvoo & threatens B[righam]. Young. after the reading Br Brigham made some remarks showing the folly of his course, yea the wickedness of his conduct in trying to injure his friends. 'twas then unanimously resolved that W[illia]m Smith be cut off from the church & given into the hands of the Lord.[46]

20th [October 1845] This morning I put my name in Br M[ephibosheth]. Serrine's company to go West. he was Just starting for Michigan to gather up the Brethren & appointed me one of a committee of three to attend to the business of the com[pany] in his absence. in the evening I met with the com[pany].[47] when it was agreed that I should go the next day in search of timber for waggons.

---

43. Jonathan Dunham died on 28 July 1845 while on a short exploring expedition searching for a route to the West. Leonard, *Nauvoo*, 514.
44. The 4000 yards of canvas, shipped for Nauvoo on 17 September 1845 and costing $1,050, was intended for a portable tabernacle, elliptical in shape, to be located near the front of the temple which faced west. With intentions to hold 10,000 persons, the structure was to be 250 x 125 feet. Watson, "The Nauvoo Tabernacle," 416–421; Leonard, *Nauvoo*, 479–480.
45. Orson Hyde's perspective on this was born of personal experience in Europe and Palestine in 1839–1841. Hyde, *Orson Hyde*, 111–150.
46. William Smith, already a church apostle since 1835, had been church patriarch since 24 May 1845. In August 1845 Brigham Young managed to offend Smith by limiting the scope of his authority due to Smith's recalcitrance. From Smith's public dissonance, LDS Church leaders rejected him as church patriarch and as an apostle on 6 October 1845. He was unchurched two weeks later on 19 October. Bates and Smith, *Lost Legacy*, 93–94. Smith's career is described in Edwards, "William B. Smith," 140–157; Smith, *History of the Church*, 7:483.
47. Mephibosheth Sirrine was appointed captain of the 23rd of the 25 companies of 100 Mormon emigrants who were to prepare for a spring 1846 departure for the West. Smith, *History of the Church*, 7:482.

21st [October 1845] Went in com[pany]. with Br Wandel [Wandle] Mace up the river Bluffs in search of timber. found some on Br [Adolphus] Babcock's land <5 miles> and engaged it for the com[pany]. he thought he would come in withe us.

October 1845 22d I Went with 4 men & two teams to get the timber. Br [Adolphus] Babcock now wished me to put down his name in our company which was No 23.[48]

23d [October 1845] Continued geting timber. this night I was caled by Adgt [Daniel] Repshur between 11 & 12 oclock to warn out all <of> my company to meet at the Temple at 7 oclock next morning. when ~~most~~ assembled there was but few of my men required and those mounted. the rest were dismissed. I continued geting timber till Friday the 31st [October 1845] when I returned to work at the Temple.

Saturday [1 November 1845] my father Udney H. Jacob came to my house from Pilot Grove & in the evening he said he now fuly believed this work (Mormonism) to be true. indeed he now k[n]ew it to <be> the work of God foretold by the Prophets. but when he was baptised two Years ago he did *not kn*ow it to be true. I was much rejoced to hear this & it was soon arranged that he should be <re>baptised on the morrow.[49] there had been some difficulty in the Branch in Pilot Grove which had caused him to request his name to be taken from the record. but all was now right. I had frequently told my wife that he wo[u]ld come back into the Church for I had ~~had~~ a dream to that effect. The rest of my Kindred are as hard as the nether mill Stone.[50]

Sunday 2d of Nov. [1845] wee went to meeting at the Temple. Br Orsen Hide preached & he gave transgrisors a warning not to go with us to the West in the Spring as the Law of God would be put in force against all thieves & disorderly persons. he gave them cl[e]arly to understand that they would be droped out by the way.[51] he was folowed by Br H[eber] Kimble stiring the People up to finish the Temple. he said he had rather go into the Wilderness with a pack on his back & his wife with a bundle of clothes under her arm & have the Temple finished than to go with his waggon loaded down with gold!!

48. This is Mephibosheth Sirrine's company, the 23rd of 25, referred to in the footnote for 20 October 1845.
49. See Quinn, "Practice of Rebaptism at Nauvoo."
50. Despite Norton's statement about his kin's coldness toward Mormonism, his brother Stephen, still living in Hancock County in 1880, was noted as having taken "no part in the Mormon war" of 1845–1846. Gregg, *History of Hancock County, Illinois*, 849–850, 921–922.
51. For a discussion of the Saints' concept of the imputation of the Law of God for violations of the civic and moral code, see the following chapter containing the report and notes about Brigham Young's sermon of 13 September 1846.

William Weeks's architectural plan for the Nauvoo Temple. Courtesy of the LDS Church Archives.

& the Temple not finished! I went withe Bro Zenos Gurly in the afternoon ~~& my Father~~ to the river where I baptized <my Father> & Br Gurly assisted to confirm him a member in the Church of Jesus Christ of latterday Saints.

Monday Nov 3 1845 Br W[illia]m Weeks, the architect of the Temple, requested me this morning to go ahead & put in the Truss timbers for the lower floor of the Temple. continued to work at the Temple through the week.

Satturday evening [8 November 1845] had a meeting of our com[pany]. No 23, for the West. the brethren were verry anxious that I should go to work in the Shop <& assist in> making waggons for the expedition.

Sunday [9 November 1845] I applyed to Br [William] Weeks informing him of their request but he would not consent that I should go. there was a meeting in upper part of the Temple as the lower floor was taken up when Br Brigham [Young] recom<en>ded that the several companys should make out a bill of Iron requisite for waggons[52] & send with what money they could raise by Br [Joseph] Haywood [Heywood][53] to Quincy next tuesday. consequently there was a special meeting of our com[pany]. calld this evening when wee borrowed $50 of a Sister Green whose husband had returned to Michigan to sell his property. Br Rogers took the money to carry to Br Haywood.

Monday 10th [November 1845] upon aplication of Br Wandel Mace, Br [William] <Weeks> concluded to let me go to work at waggons.[54] Br Moses Deming furnished me with $30 to purchase Pine Lumber out of a raft just arrivd for waggon boxes,[55] one dollar of which was mysteriously lost in counting.

---

52. The endeavor to build wagons for emigration was so extensive that "Teams are sent to all parts of the county to purchase iron," resulting in "blacksmiths [being] at work night and day." Smith, *History of the Church*, 7:536.
53. This is probably Joseph Leland Heywood.
54. By the end of November 1845 wagon-making had become Nauvoo's primary industry; "wheelwrights, carpenters and cabinetmakers are nearly all foremen wagon makers, and many [who are] not mechanics are at work in every part of the town preparing timber for making wagons." Before long, wagon-making shops were "established at the Nauvoo House, Masonic Hall, and Arsenal" with "nearly every shop in town" being "employed in making wagons." The result at this time was just over 1,500 ready for use, with another 1,900 under construction. Regrettably, in the press to prepare the vehicles for departure, it was determined, once the first emigrants reached Winter Quarters, that only 1,000 of the wagons built were fit for travel to the Missouri River. The thousand good ones were then used to shuttle the refugees across Iowa. Smith, *History of the Church*, 7:535–536; Leonard, *Nauvoo*, 558.
55. A late November report stated that timber for wagon-making "is cut and brought into the city green; hub, spoke, and felloe timber boiled in salt and water, and other parts

11th [November 1845] commenced in conexion with Br [Wandle] Mace & others to prepare a shop for work.[56]

15th [November 1845] This evening our Com[pany]. No 23 met at O[ren] Jeffords house when the co[mpany]. was organized by elcting Moses Deming, ~~PC~~ Chairman of the co[mpany]. Wandel Mace, Boss of the Waggon Shop, & myself Trea[s]urer of the co[mpany]. afterwards Moses Deming was elcted Capt. of all the Teams & W[illia]m Burton, Commissary of the company.[57]

17th [November 1845] This day Bro <W[illia]m> Weeks the Achitect of the Temple came to the Shop & said that I must return to take charge of the framing at the Temple. I replyed that I left there by his permission & do as he said, & on Tuesday, the 18th of Nov. [1845], again commenced work there. about this time there was a Br [Edmund] Durphy [Durfee][58] shot by the mob at Lima [Adams County, Illinois]. The Brethren rapidly pushing forward the finishing of the rooms in the Attick Story preparatory to the Endowment.[59]

26 [November 1845] This evening at a meeting of our co[mpany]. at the Shop, Moses Deming requested the Brethren to excuse him from acting longer as chairman on account of his deafness, as he coul[d] <not> readily hear the remarks of persons speaking. his request was complyed withe when

---

kiln dried." All resources were considered in the haste to construct the vehicles for an imminent departure. "All the fences for miles around were searched for oak rails that would do to work into wagon timber," one of the locals reported. With iron being scarce, "many wagons were made with wooden tires." Smith, *History of the Church*, 7:535–536; Leonard, *Nauvoo*, 558.

56. Of Wandle Mace's wagon-making activity, he wrote: the "Wagon Companies were organized to make wagons for the journey to the Rocky Mountains. There was quite a number of such companies, in fact the whole people was interested in some one of them. I was called upon to superintend the one called the Michigan Wagon Com[p]any's shop. I made a Boring and Mortising machine to facilitate the work, there was much to do and little time to do it." Mace, Autobiography, 109.
57. In Mephibosheth Sirrine's absence, sent to Michigan on church assignment, Moses Deming was voted to replace Sirrine as the head of the 23rd company. After Sirrine's return to the body of the Saints in February 1846, he resumed his leadership of the 23rd emigrating company. See Jacob's entry for 14 February 1846 in the next chapter.
58. Edmund (also spelled Edmond) Durfee, after relocating to Missouri and then to Hancock County, Illinois, near Morley's settlement, saw his home burned in September by an anti-Mormon mob. He fled to Nauvoo but returned to his farm in mid-November to harvest his crop. While dousing a haystack fired by the mob, vigilantes-in-wait shot and killed him on 15 November 1845. The alleged perpetrators were apprehended, but later released. See Durfee's troubles in footnote 6 in this chapter and the overview of the circumstances of his death in Hartley, *The 1845 Burning of Morley's Settlement and Murder of Edmund Durfee*. See also Smith, *History of the Church*, 7:523–531.
59. Anticipating the reception of spiritual endowments from God, believed by Mormons to equip them with extraordinary Godly knowledge and power, characterized Mormon expectations from their earliest existence. Prince, *Power from on High*, 16–21, 115–148.

they proceeded [to] elect me <to act> as the chairman. I was still employed in puting in the lower flooring timbers of the Temple, & the upper rooms being finished & completely furnished., was dedicated[60] & on ~~the~~ Wednesday, the 10th day of Dec. 1845, the Twelve commenced the washing & anointing in the Temple of the Lord!![61]

On Friday the 12th [December 1845] Br W[illia]m Weeks came to me & said he wanted me to go ~~ho~~ home & prepare myself & Wife & come to the Temple at ~~noon~~ 12 oclock A.M. ready to receive our endowments.[62] Wee most joyfuly complyed with the request & at about 5 oclock P.M. Wee were washed & anointed in the House of the Lord. it was the most interesting Scene of all my life & one that afforded the most Peace & Joy that wee had ever experienced since wee were Married, which has been over 15 years. ~~Brs Weeks was~~ Brethren W[illia]m Weeks, Truman 0. Angel[l], Charles C. Rich, George W. Harris, James A[l]lred, & W[illia]m Felshaw were the first that received their endowments in this House of the Lord ~~this time~~ which took place on this day, the time before having been occupied in the washing & anointing those that had before received their endowments under the hands of Joseph ~~the~~ Smithe the Prophet, which he confered upon them one year ago last winter. After those six went in with their wives, Amos Fielding, Noah Packerd [Packard], Samuel Rolf[e], A[a]ron Johnson, W[illia]m Snow, Wil[l]ard Snow, Erastus Snow, [William] Player & myself with our wives were called in & all passed through the endowment ~~together~~ at the same time.[63]

---

60. The temple's attic was dedicated for ceremonial purposes on 30 November 1845. Particulars of the meeting are found in Smith, *History of the Church*, 7:534–535; Clayton, *An Intimate Chronicle*, 192–193.

61. Religious rituals practiced by Latter-day Saints are of two forms, both considered sacred by church members. The first type are public ordinances, such as baptism and communion, which were introduced in Mormonism at its outset. The second type, non-public and associated with Mormon temples, were implemented incrementally as Mormons built their sacred structures in Kirtland and Nauvoo. The washings and anointings, ordinances associated with Mormon temples, are initiatory to the Mormon endowment and sealing.

    The main room of the attic story of the temple, where the ordinances were conducted, was "eighty-eight feet two inches long and twenty-eight feet eight inches wide. It is arched over, and the arch is divided into six spaces by cross beams to support the roof. There are six small rooms on each side about fourteen feet square." Smith, *History of the Church*, 7:542. Once the temple's attic was completed, temple ordinances were offered to the church's rank and file in rooms set aside for the rituals. The temple's ordinances and their chronological context are described in Brown, "Temple Ordinances," 5–21; Leonard, *Nauvoo*, 255–265.

62. Those, including carpenters, who had labored on the temple, according to previous instructions by Joseph Smith, were among the first to receive temple ordinances. Leonard, *Nauvoo*, 261.

63. "[T]he First Presidency of the Seventy and their wives and others numbering in all twenty-eight males and twenty-seven females received the ordinances of endowment" on

on Sunday the 14 [December 1845] attended a General conference of the Sevnties in the concert Hall[64] when B A[lbert]. P[erry]. Rockwood Presided & there was about $30 raised to purchase clothing for the purpose of carrying the Sevnties throug the Endowments.[65] I still continued to work at the Temple rejoiceing in being countd worthy to [be] associated with the Lord's Holy anointed ones. this week my Father visited me after being absent from the city some time. he appeared to be much perplexed about his business and seemed inclined to tarry at his home at Pilot Grove through the winter but I perswaded him to come & live with my family and endeavor to obtain a K[n]owledge of the things pertaining to the fullness of the Priesthood & Kingdom of God in the Last days. he tarried till Sunday the 21st [December 1845] when upon my recomdation he was ordained into the Elders Quorum. about the middle of this week the weather set in verry cold. I foun[d] Widow Stoel & family were suffering intensely living in a cold open house with out firewood. I called upon her as I went to my work in the morning and told her to take her children and go to my house. afterwards with the assistance of Father I removed her beds etc <&> she tarried with us. on Tuesday 23 [December 1845] my Father removed his clothing &c and took up his abode with us. we all lived together now verry hapily ~~on~~ enjoying the comfort of the holy Gost. on the 21st [December 1845] I with my wife first had the exqusit pleasure of meeting with <the> holy order of the Lord's anointed in his holy house whose Motto is "Holiness to the Lord."

The enimies of the Lord this week got out warrants for the aprehension of the Twelve and the deputy Marshall of this District came here with some dozen Soldier and aprehended a man by the name of W[illia]m Miller supposing him to be Br Brigham Young, took him out to Carthage where they found out their mistake and were chagriened to think they had missed <their> aim.[66] may God grant <that> they may always be foiled in <their> attempts and fall into their own pit which they <have> prepared for the Saints.

---

12 December 1845, requiring Brigham Young and others to officiate in the Temple until midnight. Smith, *History of the Church*, 7:544.

64. Sometimes also called the Music Hall, the Concert Hall was located a block north of the Nauvoo Temple. Miller and Miller, *Nauvoo*, 128.

65. The Mormon endowment ritual requires white ceremonial clothing.

66. Of the 23 December 1845 incident, Brigham Young stated: "William Miller put on my cap and Brother [Heber] Kimball's cloak and went downstairs meeting the marshal and his assistants at the door [of the temple]." Action against Young "on a writ from the United States court, charg[ed] him with counterfeiting the coin of the United States." The identity deception lasted until the Young/Miller ruse was discovered at a Carthage, Illinois, tavern. The event has become famous in Mormon circles as an illustration of the ineptness of Illinois authorities. Smith, *History of the Church*, 7:549–551.

The pursuit of Young and other church leaders at this time by officials bent on saddling church leaders with alleged violations of the law proved to be the catalyst provoking the Saints to accelerate their departure from Nauvoo, resulting in the winter withdrawal of the first wave of Saints the following February.

On Monday the 28th [December 1845] Br Noah Rogers arrived direct from the Sandwich Islands and was joyfuly received by his friends and brethren.[67] The Marshall returned and searched the Temple for the Twelve but when he came where they was they want there and he went away as cheap as he came.

67. Noah Rogers, Addison Pratt, Benjamin Grouard, and Knowlton Hanks left Nauvoo, Illinois, on 1 June 1843 for a mission to the Pacific Islands, the first foreign language mission in Mormon history. After departing New Bedford, Massachusetts, the first three named landed on Tubuai in April 1844, Hanks having died en route. Rogers returned to the United States while Pratt and Grouard continued their missions for several more years. The story of this mission is told in Ellsworth and Perrin, *Seasons of Faith and Courage*.

1846

PREPARATIONS TO ABANDON THE MORMON CAPITAL of Nauvoo escalated through the winter. The sacred ordinances of the temple, still under construction, were made available to all who desired and qualified for the blessing. The last day of religious temple activity in the first week of February was almost coincident to the first exile crossing the Mississippi River. Over the next eight months, thousands of Saints traversed the Iowa landscape en route to temporary respite at the Missouri River. Jacob and his family crossed the Mississippi mid-June in concert with the bulk of the Mormon refugees that year. First at Cold Spring, then Cutler's Park, before the founding of Winter Quarters, Jacob held his family together in the refugee camps. There he also formed part of the newly re-energized Nauvoo Legion, raised to prevent encroachment by enemies yet again. His considerable construction skills, once applied to Nauvoo's temple, were later plied upon Brigham Young's Turkey Creek mill in Winter Quarters' north sector. There he planned for his family's journey into the wilderness.

~~

Sunday January 11th 1846. I met with the congregaton of the Lord on the second floor of the Temple. Brethren [Benjamin] Clap[p], John Young & Father [Freeman] Nickerson[1] Spoke to the people, and wee had a good meeting. It is a time of trouble ~~the~~ and the Twelve ~~were~~ are prepareing to leave a country where they are hunted like wild beasts by a black hearted set of Mobbers. this evening a nu[m]ber of such scoundrels under the character of Goverment Troops went to the house of Br Andrew Colton in the midest of the night and took him out of his bed under a charge of horse Stealing. they went also to Br [James] Ea[s]tmans[2] Stable and broke it open looking for the stolen horse but found him not. But they took their prisoner off to Carthage. Tthe Police were in <soon> pursuit, and some of the rascals whoo staid till morning were driven off by our Police and were told by Capt. [Hosea] Stout[3]

1. This is probably Freeman Nickerson.
2. This may be James Eastman.
3. This is probably Hosea Stout.

that if they came back and were found runing through the streets at Night he would kill them, and left the city in great rage.

Tuesday the 13th [January 1846] having been permited to leave the work at the Temple, <I> commenced again at our waggon Shop, and I went over the river after timber. This evening at 6 oclock I attended prayers among the anointed ones in the Temple.[4]

continued work ~~here~~ for the shop through the week.

Sunday [18 January 1846] attended meeting in the second Story of the Temple. Br [Benjamin] C<l>app preached & Br John Young Spoke. Prophesied the all the Saints that would obey the commandments of God he [God] would bring them out from among this Nation with a high hand & an outstreced arm.[5]

Monday the 19th [January 1846] went with my wife to the Temple in the morning to attend to our Sealing but there was a council to be held which put other business. I went into that council to represent M[ephisbosheth]. Serrine's co[mpany].[6] the business of the council was to acertain how many were ready to start for the West. not being in possesion of all the facts, the President Br Brigham Young appointed next Sunday at two oclock to make report of all men & Teams that could be ready to depart on short notice.

In the evening I went into the holy of holies[7] with Emily my wife where by Pres. Brigham Young we were according to the holy order of the Priesthood Sealed together for time and all eternity and Sealed up unto eternal life and against all sin except the sin against the Holy G[h]ost.[8] may God keep us faithful in his ordinences amen!

---

4. The "anointed ones," in this instance, were those who had been endowed in the Nauvoo Temple.
5. John Young's language reported by Jacob is common to one of Joseph Smith's revelations received in Kirtland, Ohio, in 1834, which reads, in part: "For ye are the children of Israel, and of the seed of Abraham, and ye must needs be led out of bondage by power, and with an stretched-out arm. And as your fathers were led at the first, even so shall the redemption of Zion be." Doctrine and Covenants 103:17–18. (See also Doctrine and Covenants 136:22.) The optimistic bravado of the Latter-day Saints contributed to their success in exiting Illinois.
6. This concerns Mephibosheth Sirrine's 23rd of 25 companies of 100 emigrants of which Jacob became a part in October 1845.
7. The Holy of Holies is a compartment within the Nauvoo Temple, based on a similarly named part of ancient Israel's tabernacle in the wilderness described in Exodus 25.
8. The Mormon sealing ceremony, conducted by the authority of church leaders, and different from the bestowal of the endowment which was also being conducted simultaneously in the temple, joins a man and woman to an eternal marital relationship in contrast to a mortal marital connection ending at the death of either spouse. The theology and authority for the ordinance stems from the New Testament statement in Matthew 16:19 where Jesus gave the apostle Peter authority to "bind on earth" and "in heaven." The ritual was implemented first on 7 January 1846 when four couples were united at an altar constructed in the temple's attic. See Brown, "Temple Ordinances," 16–18; and

Satterday 24 [January 1846] a meeting of the People was caled in the house of the Lord to elct ~~additional~~ three Trustees to assist the Trustees in Trust, N[ewel]. K. Whitney & George Miller.[9] when they shall leave here that the business may be done in their absence. Brethren Almon W. Babbitt, John Fulmer, & ~~Doct. Bernhisal were chosen~~ Br [Joseph] Haywood were chosen, & Henry Miller & Doct. [John] Bernhisel were nominated to assist the Nauvoo house committee, it being the <intention> to proceed with that work & the Temple the ensuing season so as to employ the Brethren until they can sell their property & prepare to move.[10] query, will the mob let them?

on Sunday 25th [January 1846] I remained at home in the forenoon & employed myself in writing the Genealegy of our family as I received from my Father [Udney Jacob].[11] in the afternoon I went & delivered my report at the meeting of the Captains of hundreds.

Monday 26th [January 1846] in the afternoon I went with Father [Udney Jacob], my wife Emily [Heaton Jacob] & Sister [Philanda] Loveredg[12] & her

---

Colvin, *Nauvoo Temple*, 93–96. Another component of the temple sealing ordinance for Latter-day Saints, includes the provision for joint eternal salvation for the husband and wife through compliance to God's commands. The concept is explained in Doctrine and Covenants 132:19. The Jacobs' ordinance was recorded in the *Nauvoo Temple Endowment Register*, 6–7.

9. Newel Whitney and George Miller, both Mormon bishops, were appointed on 9 August 1844 as trustees-in-trust "to settle the affairs of the late Trustee-in-Trust, Joseph Smith." Whitney and Miller struggled interpersonally, evidenced by William Clayton's observation two months earlier when he described them as being "at antipodes with each other in nearly all their operations." Smith, *History of the Church*, 7:247; Clayton, *An Intimate Chronicle*, 191 [17 November 1845]. At the same time administrative meetings were held in the temple, ordinances sacred to Mormons also continued to be performed. For this date, "One hundred and fifty-one persons received ordinances in the Temple." Smith, *History of the Church*, 7:573.

10. Among the responsibilities initially given to the five trustees, besides serving as a "committee to dispose of [church] property and effects and aid in emigrating," as well as liquidating church debts, was to supervise "enclos[ing] the Nauvoo House and complet[ing] the first story of the Temple." Later Almon Babbitt, Joseph Heywood, and John Fullmer were designated as "trustees for the building of the Temple," (Brigham Young's design for the three included Babbitt's role as "lawyer," Fullmer's as "bulldog and growl," and Heywood "to settle debts"). Henry Miller and John Bernhisel were appointed as "trustees or committee for the building of the Nauvoo House." Smith, *History of the Church*, 7:569, 576; Bennett, *We'll Find the Place*, 317. The careers of these men as church trustees is considered in Bennett, *We'll Find the Place*, 317–323.

11. Genealogical connections are important to Mormons and have from this early day been a major feature of Latter-day Saints theology. See Allen, Embry, and Mehr, *Hearts Turned to the Fathers*, 11–31, for an overview of the theological concept and implementation of the belief into Mormonism. See Appendix 1 for Jacob's list of family connections which prefaces his diary.

12. This refers to Philanda Marsh Loveridge (1792–), from Massachusetts, and her son Alexander H. Loveridge (1828–1905), born in New York.

Son [Alexander] to Father John Smith's, the Patriarch,[13] to get our Patriarchal Blessings.[14] Father was well pleased with his Blessing. he said, "Bro Smith, I Know you are a true prophet for you have told me the truth." Emily too was much strengthened in her faith.

Tuesday [27 January 1846] in afternoon & evening My [Seventies] Quorum met at the old Printing office & had a feast. our Wives, Daughter[s] & mothers partook with us in the festivity. we had <a> time of great rejoiceing t[o]gether and yet mingled with a sober feeling.

"City of Joseph, Jan 26, 1846

A Blessing by John Smith Patriach upon the head of Norton Jacob, Son of Udney & Elizabeth, born 11th August 1804, Berkshire Co., Mass. Brother Norton, Beloved of the Lord, I lay my hands on thy head by the authority given <me> of Jesus of Nazereth, place upon thee all <the> blessings of Abraham, Isaac and Jacob, the Priesthood and power which was given to the house of Israel, which shall be sealed upon thy head in fulness in due time. no power <on> earth shall be able to destroy thy faith because thy heart is honest. notwithstanding, 'tis thy duty to watch & pray lest ye enter into temptation because of the weakness of the flesh. the Lord delighteth in thee, & hath given his Angels charge to watch over thee continualy. it is left to thy choice in what part of the Vinyeard thou wilt labor. the whispering of the Spirit is, thy greatest labor is among the Lamanites.[15] thou shalt have prosperity at

---

13. The office of church patriarch was lineal within the Smith family at the time. John Smith, Joseph Smith Jr.'s uncle, became church patriarch following the deaths of John's brother, Joseph Smith Sr., and Hyrum Smith, Joseph Sr.'s son, and the excommunication of another of Joseph Sr.'s sons, William. John Smith's tenure as church patriarch is described in Bates and Smith, *Lost Legacy*, 104–122.
14. Patriarchal blessings are prophetic pronouncements given to individual members by ordained patriarchs within Mormonism. The blessings may include language of hope and encouragement, along with promises of particular blessings in mortality, as well as connecting the recipient to a heritage within ancient Israel. It is a practice that continues within the faith. Mormon patriarchal blessings are explained in Bates and Smith, *Lost Legacy*, 8; Mortimer, "Patriarchal Blessings," 3:1066–1067. Norton Jacob received two other patriarchal blessings late in life, one in 1876 and then in 1878, the year before he died.
15. A racial/ethnic designation found in the Book of Mormon, the "Lamanites" in Mormon jargon, are Native Americans, who, the Saints declare, are descendants of the Book of Mormon peoples who came to the western hemisphere about 600 B.C.E. For the background and role of the Book of Mormon to Latter-day Saints see Givens, *By the Hand of Mormon*. Jacob's attention having been drawn to an awareness of Lamanites may help explain his initial interest later in the year in Alpheus Cutler, who had designs on preaching Mormonism to the Native Americans when called to do so by Joseph Smith. At the same time that Cutler calculated to carry a mission to the Indians, he strained his relations with LDS Church leaders who withdrew their support of his ambitions. Jorgensen, "The Old Fox," 154, 161, 164, 169.

all times & in all places. wherever thy lot is cast, thou shalt have exceeding <faith> to work miracles in the eyes of the People. Thousands shall believe thy testimony. obey the Gospel. thou shalt lead them to Zion[16] & no power shall stay thine hand. thou shalt be able to control the elements by the power of the Prieshood vested in thee. no miracle shall be too hard for thee to perform when it shall be for the Salvation of men. Thou shalt have an inheritance in the Land of Joseph[17] with thy Brethren. raise up a numerous posterity to keep thy name in remembrance & the name of thy Fathers to all generations. Be diligent Brother, to follow the council of those who are ~~set~~ appointed to lead the Church, & thou shalt inherit every blessing which your heart desires even eternal life. I seal this blessing upon thee, & thy posterity in common with thy companion, Amen!" (a true copy)

"City of Joseph, Jany 26th 1846

A Blessing by John Smith Patriarch upon the head of Emily Jacob, Daughter of Elias & Mary Heaton, Born Nov 28th, 1810, Chittenden Co., Vermont. Sister Emily, By the authority vested in me to bless the fatherless, I place my my hands upon thy head in the name of Jesus of Nazareth [and] Seal upon thee the Priesthood with all the blessings of the new and everlasting covenant which was Sealed upon the Children of Joseph,[18] for this [is] thy lineage, the same as thy companion. thou hast a right to all the blessings which is sealed upon his head, for a woman can have but little power in the Priesthood without a man. thou shalt be blest in thy Basket & in thy Store, and in all things that you put your hand to do. thy family shall be blest with health, peace and plnty. there shall be no lack in thine house. the destroyer shall not disturb thy peace. thou shalt be blest with health and Strength beyond all <thy> fears, even like the Daughters of Israel when they were in bondage in Egypt. ~~Comfort thy heart 'tis privilege to have faith to converse is Th~~

thou shalt have <the> ministering of Angels to comfort thy heart. tis thy privilege to have faith to converse with them as with thy friends. thy children shall increase about thee and become verry numerous like Jacob and be honorable in the house of Israel. none shall excell them. thy days and years shall be multiplied upon thy head according to thy desire of thine heart. thou shalt partake of all the Blessings of the Redeemers Kingdon, worlds without end. inasmuch as thou art faithful, these words shall not fail. amen" (a true copy.)

---

16. The concept of Zion held several meanings for the Latter-day Saints, including a specific place with an apocalyptic destiny, the site of Independence, Missouri, and any place where the "pure in heart" gathered. For an overview of the Mormon view of Zion, see Sorensen, "Zion," 4:1624–1626.
17. This is a reference to the geography where Joseph Smith had promised a divine inheritance to his followers.
18. This refers to Joseph, the biblical figure who descended from Abraham, Isaac, and Jacob.

Sunday 1st Feb. [1846] there was meeting in the Temple. Br Orson Pratt spoke to <the> People, when Br Brigham Young said that Moses Smith wanted to set forth the doctrines & claims of James J Strang. Moses then arose & read some of Strang's productions & made some comments & warned the People to flee to Voree, Strang's new city in Wisconsin, where he promised them Peace & safety. he however recognized the authority of the Twelve. after he had done, Br Brigham said he would make no comment but Simply ask the People if they had heard the voice of the Good Shepherd in what had been advanced, when No!! resounded all over the house. taws [twas] proposed that Moses Smith be cut off from the Church, wich was carried unanimously. Strang & Aaron Smith was also cut off.[19] many have been deluded by Strangism & ~~some~~ <one> of them, <a> President of Sevnties.[20] this evening met with my [Seventies] Qu<o>rum (14th) ~~&~~ when they were notified [to] be at the Templ wednesday morning at 7 oclk to receive their endowments.

At 5 oclock Wednesday, 4th [February 1846][21] I repaired to the Templ where I found the Brethren & Sisters recreating themselves with music & dancing after their Labors as the Endowments were adjourned for two days.[22]

Friday [6 February 1846] the Endowments were continud.[23] in the evening I again repaired to the House of the Lord with my Father Udney [Jacob], my Wife Emily [Jacob], my Daughter Elsie P. [Jacob], & Miss Matilda Stoel [Stowell]. in the cours of the night my Father, Daughter, & Miss Matilda all received their washing & anointing, & about 11 oclock I, with my Wife

19. Church leaders had published notice in the *Times and Seasons* of their having, on 26 August 1844, "cut off from the church of Jesus Christ of Latter-day Saints" James Strang and Aaron Smith. This action before a church body ratified their previous decision. *Times and Seasons* 5, no. 16, (2 September 1844): 631.
20. For James Strang's effect on Brigham Young's and the Twelve Apostle's leadership at this time, see Bennett, *We'll Find the Place*, 12–18. The Seventies president referred to here may have reference to Josiah Butterfield (1795–1871) who was excommunicated in October 1844.
21. A wintery 4 February 1846 was the day the Mormon exile from Nauvoo was initiated, with emigrant wagons first crossing the Mississippi River to Iowa.
22. It appears that dancing within the Nauvoo Temple began on 30 December 1845 as a spontaneous impulse "to have a little season of recreation" after the labors of the day involving the administration of temple ordinances to the Saints. For a time Brigham Young endorsed the religious aspect of dancing stating that as the "temple was a Holy place, . . . when we danced, we danced unto the Lord, and that no person would be allowed to come on to this floor, and afterwards mingle with the wicked." The wicked, he said, "had no right to dance," as "dancing and music belonged to the Saints." On 9 February 1846, however, Young discontinued the activity contending "that all dancing and merriment should cease, lest the brethren and sisters be carried away by vanity." Smith, *History of the Church*, 7:557, 566; Clayton, *Intimate Chronicle*, 247.
23. "Five hundred and twelve persons received the first ordinances of endowment in the Temple" on 6 February 1846. Smith, *History of the Church*, 7:580.

Emily, received ~~second~~ my Secnd anointing [and] was ordaind a King & Priest unto God in room No. 4.[24]

Sunday Feb. 8th 1846 at 9 Oclock A.M. the Endowments were Stoped in the House of the Lord & the vails were taken down. the People were then called out into the grove West of <the> Temple where wee were addressed by Prisednt Joseph Young, who is President of all the Sevnties, there being 32 Quorums. Br Jedediah Grant & Benj. Clapp also of the first Council of the Sevnties spoke to the People. when Brethren [Orson] Hide, [John] Taylor, P[arley]. P Pratt & Brigham Young gave vent to their feelings by addressing the People for the last time in Nauvoo. Br Brigham warned them that grieveious wolves would come in among the Sheep when they were gone, not sparing the flock, that from among themselves men would spring up speaking perverse thing to turn men away from the truth. he said they would start tomorrow.[25] Some of the Brethren have crossed over three or four days ago, and they are crossing all the time.[26]

Monday [9 February 1846] about 4 4 oclock P.M. a fire broke out in the Temple by a Stove pipe in the main deck roof. for some time it lookd rather fearful, but by cuting up ~~the~~ a portion of the Deck & roof of it was subdued after doing about $100 damage.[27]

Friday Feb. 13th [1846] Br M[ephibosheth]. Serrine arrived from Michigan having had good success in his mission. about sevnty families are on their way to this place fully fitted & prepared to go on West as soon as they arrive.

Satturday morning [14 February 1846] I went with Br [Mephibosheth] Serrine to visit Br Brigham young & get council from him concerning our future

24. This temple ordinance is described in Leonard, *Nauvoo*, 260–261; and Brown, "Temple Ordinances," 18–19.
25. In a meeting of the Twelve Apostles that day, Brigham Young related that they prayed to God that he would bless "our intended move to the west," and petitioned that he would "enable us some day to finish the Temple, and dedicate it to him, and we would leave it is in his hands to do as he pleased; and to preserve the building as a monument to Joseph Smith." Smith, *History of the Church*, 7:580. William Huntington's observations for the day stated that it was "a *solemn time* . . . ever to be remembered. Many were backing out, leaving the Church and following a false prophet by the name of *Strang*." Huntington quoted in Bennett, *Mormons at the Missouri*, 20.
26. Before the winter month of February was over, probably more than 2,000 had crossed the Mississippi and settled six miles westward on Sugar Creek, in Iowa Territory.
27. Thomas Bullock described the cause of the fire to be a stove in the building over-heating while the "clothing in the Temple was being washed and dried in the upper room." He continued that the "wood work caught fire and burned from the railing to the ridge about 16 feet North and South and about 10 feet East and West." Also, the "shingles on the north side were broken through in many places." Knight, "Journal of Thomas Bullock," 49.

opperations.[28] he was stopping at his Brother Joseph Young's, having sent his baggage waggons across the river the night before. he appeared to <be> in good Spirits & was well pleased with what Br Serrine done & told him <to> organize his co[mpany]. & Keep them together & start as soon as possible across the country to Council Bluffs on the Massourie river with their teams, while a Steam Boat should be chartered to carry the Mill irons, Goods & heavy Baggage around by water to the same place.[29]

Sunday 15th [February 1846] Br Brigham Young with his family crossed the river & went out to Sugar Creek where the Brethren who are going West in this first company have formed a camp.[30] this day I visited at Br C[harles]. W. Wandel[l]'s & had a verry agreeable pleasant time.

on Wednesday the 11th [February 1846] my Father [Udney Jacob] was ordained a High Priest.[31]

Sunday 22d [February 1846] a meeting was convened in the Temple on the first floor. ~~it was a~~ the room was yet unfinishd. Br Benjamin Clapp began the meeting by prayer. he had proceeded some little time when a slight cra<c>k was heard in the floor and being laid on truss girders they settled a little, when suddenly the People began to scream vehemently, as though they expected [the] house to fall on them, [and] instantly rushed in every direction & some began to break the sash & glass. several windows were thus broken & men plunged out like mad cats upon the frozen ground & stones below.[32] twas in vain to attempt to restore order & President [Brigham] Young directed

28. Mephibosheth Sirrine's meeting with Brigham Young, concerned, of course, the status of the 23rd company of emigrants in their preparation for removal to the West.
29. Fluctuating plans had been developing for months about the timing and method of evacuating Nauvoo. For example, on 18 January, Brigham Young's history includes this insight into preparations: "A meeting of the captains of Emigrant Companies was held in the attic story of the Temple, to ascertain the number ready and willing to start should necessity compel our instant removal." The plan Jacob noted here had been established for some time. Smith, *History of the Church*, 7:569.
30. The Sugar Creek camp, six miles west of Montrose, Iowa, was the staging ground for the push across Iowa, which began on 1 March 1846. The camp may have lined the creek for a mile. Kimball, *Historic Sites and Markers*, 24.
31. The LDS office of high priest forms a stratum of the Melchizedek, or higher, priesthood in church administration. Its place as the upper tier of the higher priesthood had not yet developed, as the office of seventy was then elevated over that of the high priest. Hartley, "Nauvoo Stake, Priesthood Quorums, and the Church's First Wards," 70; Clayton, *Intimate Chronicle*, 195, 213 [14 December 1845].
32. Brigham Young, having temporarily returned to Nauvoo from Sugar Creek, stated the furor over the "new truss floor" settling was caused by the cracking of "an inch-board or some light timber underneath [the floor]." It was reported that "some jumped out of the windows smashing the glass and all before them." One man jumping out the window "broke his arm and smashed his face, another broke his leg," and, Young added, "both were apostates." Many of the rest "jumped up and down with all their might crying Oh!

32 especialy concerning the followers of James J Strang - Br Brigham spoke also & said he was surprised that People did not know any better than to get frightned because the floor of the Temple setled a little & forbid appointing any more meetings there without an order from the Twelve he said he was not at troubled about Strangism any who wished to follow Strang he wanted them to go by all means the Lord did not want any who were desirous of following the Devil—

At three oclock the Seventies held a general conference at the Concert Hall where wee were addresed by our President Joseph Young & Orson Hide there was much of the Good Spirit manifest - in the evening I attended a meeting of my Quorum when Chaney Gaylord was Cut of from the Church of Jesus Christ of Latterday Saints for apostacy [illegible] Joining the Strangites—

Sunday 1st of March I went in company with Brethren Lerrine, O Terry, Jackson Bagly & Frost over to the Camp the winter having been Cold had frozen the river over the Second time this winter, wee crossed on the ice & went out six miles to the Camp wee found the Camp of Israel in motion striking their tents to move on a Sabbath days Journey father, wee found them in good spirits having President Brigham Young & the Twelve in their midst - when wee returned home wee found John E. Page one of the Twelve had been declareing himself opposed to the course of his Brethren - Br Hide replyed to him in such a way as to show that Page had been remiss in his duty ever

Handwriting of Norton Jacob. Courtesy of the LDS Church Archives.

the People to go out into the Grove although it was cold.[33] Br O[son] Hide addressed them some time on the subject of Apostasy, more especialy concerning the followers of James J Strang.[34] Br Brigham spoke also & said he was surprised that people did not Know any better than to get frightned because the floor of the Temple settled a little & forbid appointing any more meetings there without an order from the Twelve. he said he was not at [all] troubled about Strangism. any who wished to follow Strang, he wanted them to go. by all means the Lord did not want any who were desirous of following the Devil.

at three oclock the Sevnties held a general conference at the Concert Hall where wee were addresed by our President, Joseph Young, & Orson Hide. there was much of the Good Spirit ma[n]ifest. in the evening I attended a meeting of my Quorum when Cha[u]nc[e]y Gaylord[35] was cut of[f] from the Church of Jesus Christ of Latterday Saints for apostacy for Joing the Strangites.

Sunday ~~28th~~ <1st of March [1846]> I went in company with Brethren [Mephisbosheth] Serrine, O[tis] Terry, Jackson,[36] [Eli] Bagley[37] & [Burr] Frost[38] over tto the camp [Sugar Creek]. the <weather> having been cold had frozen the river over the Second time this winter.[39] wee crossed on the ice & went out six miles to the camp. wee found the Camp of Israel in motion,

---

Oh!! Oh!!! as though they could not settle the floor fast enough." Smith, *History of the Church*, 7:594.

33. After adjourning to the adjacent grove, where the "snow was about a foot deep," Brigham Young said he told the people they could now "jump up and down as much as they pleased." Smith, *History of the Church*, 7:594.
34. James Strang initially wielded significant momentum in drawing many fragments of Mormonism toward his leadership. "Several outstanding leaders and personalities were going with Strang, including William Marks, former president of the Nauvoo Stake, John E. Page, an apostle until his excommunication in February 1846, William Smith, Joseph Smith's younger brother and former member of the Quorum of the Twelve, Lucy Mack Smith, Joseph's aging mother, Judge George H. Adams, and William McLellen [*sic*]." Bennett, *Mormons at the Missouri*, 18–19.
35. Mormon priesthood quorums in the nineteenth century had authority to discipline their members, including the extreme action of excommunication.
36. The identity of this Jackson is not known. Six male Jackson's were heads of household in the 1850 census in Pottawattamie County, Iowa, where many Saints were gathered.
37. This may be Eli Bagley.
38. This is probably Burr Frost.
39. The area's temperature varied between 12° below zero to 20° above zero Fahrenheit for most of the last week of February 1846.
40. Before the advance teams' departure on 1 March 1846, the inhumanely cold, final week of February 1846 was a flurry of activity plotting the next westward advance of the Saints, which included Bishop George Miller's small group going a few days in advance of the advance teams. Stephen Markham, who on 23 February was instructed to send a company to another campground between Sugar Creek and Bonaparte Mills, was just one of several who were assigned duty to find one or more routes in which the Saints could cross Iowa. Smith, *History of the Church*, 595.

striking their tents to move on a sabbath days Journey farther.[40] wee found them in good S<p>irits having President Brigham Young & the Twelve in their midst. when wee returned home wee found John E. Page, one of the Twelve, had been declareing himself opposed to the course of his Brethren. Br [Orson] Hide replyd to him in such a way as to show that he <(Page)> had been remiss in his duty ever since he undertook to go with Elder Hide to Jerusalem. Then Elder Hide read a ~~let~~ communication from the Council dated Feb ninth in which they withdrew the hand of fellowship from Br John E. Page. the congregation sanctioned <the> act, by which he was severed from the Church,[41] only a few Strangites voting in his favor.[42]

~~June~~ I continued work at the waggon Shop until about the first of May [1846] when I got a waggon for my winter's work.[43] Father [Udney Jacob] bought him one and proceeded to fit them up for the Journey west. he married the Widow [Lovisa Comstock] Snyder & on the 17th of May [1846] at 9 oclok P.M. I Married Jesse Snyder (younget Son of the Widow) to my Daughter Elsie Pamel[i]a [Jacob].[44] Father, Jesse & myself went up into McDonah [McDonough] co. [Illinois][45] & bought 14 Steers & 2 hefers of John Huston[46] at $20 apiece, an exorbitant price. wee immediately took them across the river to Br George Snyder's camp & left Oliver [Jacob] to take care of them.

---

41. John Page was formally excommunicated from the LDS Church on 27 June 1846.
42. Jacob's reference to James Strang's followers in the midst of church meetings, where business was conducted and decisions were made, indicates the lines between the various factions within Mormonism were still somewhat blurred.
43. Mormon emigrant wagons, states Richard Bennett, were patterned after the Murphy wagon, a high-plains freight wagon which was an alternative to the Conestoga wagon. The Mormon wagon beds were nine to ten feet long, four feet wide, with sides being two feet high. Caulking sealed the bed for river crossings. A waterproof canvas held by five or six hickory bows covered the rectangular box. Large wooden wheels with iron tires, the front ones smaller than the hind wheels for maneuverability, moved the wagon and its contents across the terrain. Bennett, *We'll Find the Place*, 64n56. See also Davis, "Where have All the Wagons Gone," 16–39, which describes a variety of wagons used for overland travel, including the Murphy wagon.

    On 30 April the finally-completed Nauvoo Temple, which had occupied so much of Jacob's energy and resources, was privately dedicated, followed by a public ceremony on 1 May 1846.
44. Udney Jacob's first wife, Norton's mother, Elizabeth Hubbard, was still living at this time. She apparently did not embrace Mormonism, perhaps leading to estrangement or divorce before Udney joined with the Saints. Family records indicate Elizabeth Hubbard Jacob died about 1871.

    Elsie Pamelia Jacob turned fifteen years old just four days previous to her marriage. Norton Jacob, having Mormon priesthood authority, had performed at least two other marriages, the latter ones being performed in Nauvoo in 1843. Cook, *Nauvoo Deaths and Marriages*, 107, 109.
45. McDonough County, Illinois, borders Hancock County to the east.
46. Though Jacob complained about the price of the stock bought from John Huston, it appears from a letter that Jacob wrote in 1848 that he held the man in high regard.

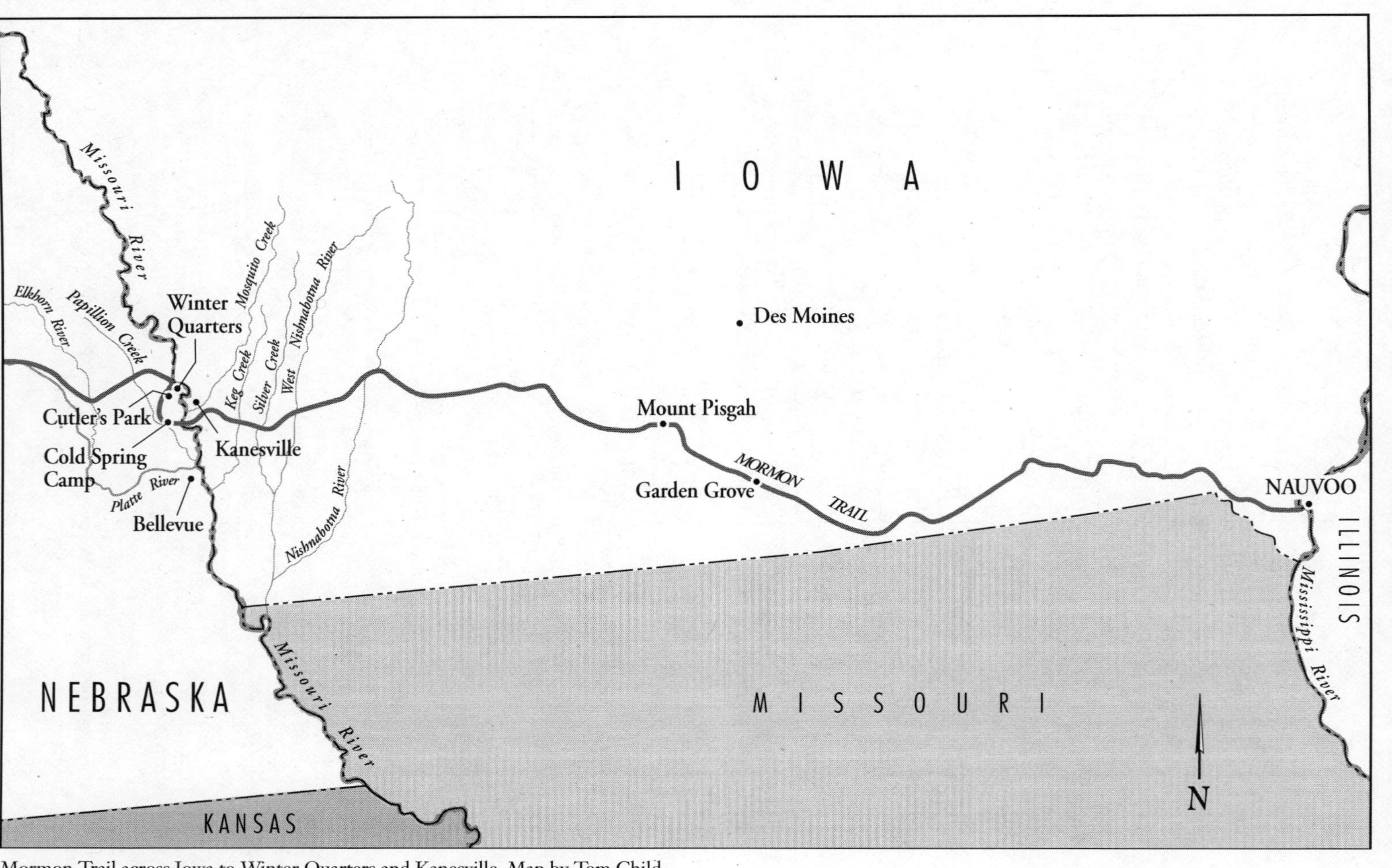

Mormon Trail across Iowa to Winter Quarters and Kanesville. Map by Tom Child.

on the 28th of May [1846] wee cross over with our two Waggons and families & then commenced breaking our Steers.[47]

June 17th [1846] left the bank of the Misssisippi for the camp of Israel to the West with my family composed as follows, Myself,[48] my Wife Emily, Daughter Elsie P. [Snyder] & her Hu<s>band Jesse Snyder, my Sons Oliver B. [Jacob], Lucian L. [Jacob], Ira N. [Jacob], & Joseph Jacob, together with my Father Udney [Jacob][49] & his Wife [Lovisa Jacob] and Sister [Ann] Boice [Boyce][50] & her Son W[illia]m [Boyce].[51] the first night Father's horse strayed off which hindered us several days. at length he was found & wee proceded on our Journey with variou[s] success.[52] passed a large Settlement of the Brethren called Mt Pisgah on Grand river.[53]

on Tuesday the 21st of July [1846] wee had good weather the whole rout[54] & arrived at Council Bluff[55] near the mouth of the Great Platte [River] on the Missourie [River] the <24th> ~~last~~ day of July [1846].[56] Here I met with Br

47. The Jacob family departed Nauvoo in the second wave of Mormon exiles. The first group were the two to three thousand that left in February–March 1846. The second session, though protracted, constituted nearly ten thousand people, and was by far the largest emigration from Nauvoo. The third and last group to leave Nauvoo were the so-called poor Saints, who hung on until the assault by Mormon enemies finally drove them across the Mississippi River in September 1846. See Hartley, "The Pioneer Trek," 32–34.
48. Norton Jacob was forty-one years of age when he left Nauvoo.
49. Udney Hay Jacob was sixty five at the time of this venture.
50. This may be Ann Geldard Boyce (1798–1846), who was born in England.
51. This may be William Boyce.
52. The multi-faceted routes and means for the crossing of Iowa by the Saints in 1846 are described in Kimball, "The Iowa Trek of 1846," 36–45; and Kimball, "The Mormon Trail Network in Iowa, 1838–1863," 321–336.
53. Mt. Pisgah, Union County, Iowa, located 172 miles from Nauvoo, was, like Garden Grove, another temporary Mormon settlement to assist the Saints crossing Iowa. The settlement was initiated on 11 May 1846. Brigham Young, after arriving at the Missouri River, returned to Mt. Pisgah from 6–9 July to recruit able-bodied men for the Mormon Battalion. Sixty-six men volunteered. The way-stations of Garden Grove and Mt. Pisgah are described in Gentry, "The Mormon Way Stations," 27–48.
54. The Mormon refugees who left Nauvoo in February and March of the year suffered excruciating hardships due to the inclement weather and horrific traveling conditions. The second wave of emigrants, of which the Jacobs were a part, had a much easier transit of Iowa departing in the late spring.
55. Council Bluffs refers to the area now known by that name in Pottawattamie County, Iowa, (first called by the Mormons Miller's Hollow, after Henry Miller, and still later, until 1853, Kanesville, after Thomas Kane), though the designation of Council Bluffs earlier referred to other sites in the region, including what became Bellevue, Nebraska.
56. By this time, the Brigham Young-led Mormons, who had arrived at the Missouri River on 14 June 1846, had carved out camps on both the Nebraska and Iowa sides of the Missouri. Just three days earlier the Mormon Battalion, having been recruited over the previous month, and finally mustered on 16 July, departed camp for their journey to the American Southwest to serve the United States in its war with Mexico. The Mormon crossing of Iowa in 1846, including the recruitment of the Mormon Battalion, is described in Bennett, *Mormons at the Missouri*, 13–67.

Heber C Kimbal who counciled me to cross the Missourie & join his family in the Camp of Israel. accordingly wee crossed over on the 30th [July 1846],[57] ~~where we~~ except Sister [Ann] Boice & Son, who taried with Br George Snyder. 4 miles from the river wee Joined the Camp of Israll with President Brigham Young at its head, accompanyed by sveral of his Brethren of the Twelve.[58] wee camped with Br Heber [Kimball]'s company.

Satterday the first of August [1846] he [Heber Kimball] came & introduced to me Sister Flora Clarinda Gleason[59] who had come with Bro [Reynolds] Cahoon & wished a place to reside. I was well pleased to receive her into my family.

Monday evening [3 August 1846] our whole camp was called to Br Heber [Kimball]'s Tent when after some remarks by him a vote was taken (there being about 70 present) to proceed up the [Missouri] river in search of a place for winter quarters.[60]

Tuesday [4 August 1846] proceeded six or eight miles.

Wednesday [5 August 1846] went about as far & camped near the largest body of Timber wee had seen.[61]

Thursday [6 August 1846] Br Brigham [Young]'s camp came up & after a day or two spent in examining the surrounding country a council was held <at> Br Heber [Kimball]'s encampment when a vote was taken to remain here during the winter.[62] we are twenty <miles> from the Otto [Oto] vilage[63] near the

57. On another front of the Saints' emigration, the previous day more than 200 Mormons led by Samuel Brannan aboard the ship *Brooklyn* docked in what was later called San Francisco, California. Coincident to the day of departure of the first refugees from Nauvoo, 4 February 1846, Brannan and his group sailed from New York City for a voyage around Cape Horn in South America to California. Brannan, traveling eastward from California, intersected the vanguard one year later on the high plains of Wyoming. Bagley, *Scoundrel's Tale*, 131–168, 203–226.
58. The first camp headquarters for the Saints on the Missouri River's west side was Cold Spring, about fifteen miles north of the post at Bellevue, Nebraska. It was from Cold Spring, now a part of Omaha, Nebraska, that the Saints gathered during the heat of July 1846. After their temporary stay there, they continued northward looking for "winter quarters." Bennett, *Mormons at the Missouri*, 68.
59. Flora Clarinda Gleason (1819–1900), was unmarried at the time.
60. Concerning the size of the Mormon camp, two days previously it was reported that the "council of the Twelve with about three hundred wagons are now encamped about four miles west of the Missouri river, and scores of wagons still crossing." Young, *Manuscript History, 1846–1847*, 290.
61. Brigham Young accompanied the group on this day. Young, *Manuscript History, 1846–1847*, 296.
62. This was the location for the second camp headquarters (after Cold Spring), a place that came to be called Cutler's Park. Named after Alpheus Cutler who discovered the location

ferry, about 3 miles from from the Missourie river.

Col Joh[n] Scot of <the> Artillery requested me to come and take my place in the Artillery.[64] Br Heber <c.> Kimbal being my Spiritual Father in the Church,[65] I asked his council upon the Subject & <he> told me to go with Br Scot if <I> wished to. accordngly on Thursday the 13th of August [1846] I moved my waggon a short distance & camped with the Artllery compny leaving Father Udney [Jacob] & his wife [Lovisa] <&> my Daughter [Elsie Snyder] & her Husband [Jesse Snyder] in Father Heber's Encampment.[66]

---

along the "divide" between the Missouri and Elkhorn rivers, the Nebraska site of Cutler's Park lay about fourteen miles north of Cold Spring and three miles west of the Missouri River. Hosea Stout described the main camp as being "situated on the prairie in two divisions and located on two ridges forming a beautiful sight." Brigham Young and Heber Kimball each led one of the two divisions of refugees. Of course, Cutler's Park, despite its initial approval as the site for the Mormons to winter, was soon replaced by what came to be known as Winter Quarters, nearer the Missouri River. Bennett, *Mormons at the Missouri*, 68; Stout, *On the Mormon Frontier*, 1:184.

63. The Oto Indians, located in proximity to the confluence of the Platte and Missouri rivers since the late eighteenth century where they settled after a historic presence in Wisconsin, had encountered Anglos previously when Marquette and Joliet and Lewis and Clark visited them during their continental explorations. Their language was a derivation of Siouan and they are closely related to the Iowa and Missouri tribes, all once Winnebagos. Their several villages were composed of oven-shaped earth houses, though they used teepees on hunting expeditions. By the time of the Mormon presence they numbered about 1,000. Waldman, *Encyclopedia of Native American Tribes*, 172.

64. Soon after the Saints gathered to the Missouri River, Brigham Young exhibited an anxiousness about revitalizing the Nauvoo Legion. With the Mormon Battalion depleting crucial manpower from the Mormon center, the defensive role of a reinvigorated Nauvoo Legion became increasingly important. On 27 July 1846 Hosea Stout, after being instructed by Young, wrote: "I now began to see what his designs were in relation to the military for he still intended to recognize the organization of the Nauvoo Legion." On 8 August 1846, Stout reported Young "to be very anxious to have the military put in opperation and have the officers of the Legion to take their places." Young's concern translated into "332 privates and 70 commissioned & non-commissioned officers in the two Divisions of the camp" by the 28th of the same month, as reported by Stout. Despite the small numbers at this time and lack of formality, the military character of the camp preparatory to the westward journey influenced much that transpired, with the military and civic functions of the exiles melded for organization and security. Stout, *On the Mormon Frontier*, 1:181,184,188.

65. This references a familial practice among Mormons at the time wherein non-blood-related persons and their families were connected through "adoption" to larger family organizations generally headed by a church authority. At this time the importance of such familial structure was great. The importance of the "Law of Adoption" to leading church families in the relocation of the Saints to the West ebbed within a year or so. The practice during this time is described in Stout, *On the Mormon Frontier*, 1:178, 178n50, 290n59. See also Irving, "The Law of Adoption."

66. The entire "Camp of Israel" at this time was "Divided into two grand divisions," one headed by Brigham Young and the other by Heber Kimball. Young's camp, led by Albert Rockwood, totaled "324 men and boys over ten years, 359 wagons, 146 horses, 1264 oxen, 49 mules, 828 cows and 416 sheep." Heber Kimball's division "showed a total of 228 men,

Sunday 16th [August 1846] Capt John Farnum [Farnham] died in our camp. I made his coffin out of rough boards & <wee> buried him near an Indian mound. went to work, all hands, this week fencing our Encampment. Some four or five of our men were sick together [with] the Col. [John Scott], leaving but 9 or 10 fit for duty.

Satter 22d [August 1846] received a notice from the Col. [John Scott] to <meet> at his Quarters at 6 oclock P.M. in <a> council of officers of the Artillry Regmt as an order had been issued by <Gen.> Brigham Young to fill up four companies. none but Capt. [John] Little [Lytle][67] & myself attended. the case of Major John Pack came up who abandoned the Regmt and declined Serveing at a perilous time in Nauvoo when, accordng to our records, the Sherrif of Hancock co. called us out as a Posse to Suppress the mob. the vacancy was filled at that time by electing Capt Stephen H God[d]ard to serve in his place. now Major Pack comes up & claims his place in the Regmt. Council decided that he could not legaly do so inasmuch as several officers had been promoted to fill vacancies occasioned by his neglect of duty & it would be wrong now to take away their rights.

Monday 24 [August 1846] Edward M. Green came into our co[mpany]. & wee commenced cutting our hay.[68] continued at our hay through the week.

Satterday 29 [August 1846] Some of the Omahaw Indians,[69] by request of President [Brigham] Young & council, came & camped here when a council was held with them in which they agreed that wee might winter on their Lands, but they chose that wee should Build & make the most of our improvements some 15 miles above here, near the Garrison,[70] as they intend <to> locate &

---

230 wagons, 83 horses, 741 oxen, 105 young cattle, 340 cows and 244 sheep." Stout, *On the Mormon Frontier*, 1:186; 311.

67. This is probably John Lytle.
68. The importance of harvesting hay/grass for the emigrants' animals was of great significance. Brigham Young ordered on 7 August, while selecting a settlement site, to ignore obtaining timber for building homes "till hay is gathered." Young, *Manuscript History, 1846–1847*, 298.
69. The Omaha Indians once lived in the Ohio River valley before relocating westward. The Kaw, Osage, Ponca, and Quapaws also derived from the same Ohio River peoples. After separating from the Ponca, the Omaha moved to their Missouri River locale in eastern Nebraska between the Platte and Niobrara rivers early in the nineteenth century. Their language was Siouan. Described as Plains Indians, they used earth lodges in winter and mobile teepees in the summer. They were historic opponents of the Sioux. Waldman, *Encyclopedia of Native American Tribes*, 167–168.
70. The Garrison likely refers to abandoned Fort Atkinson, named after Colonel Henry Atkinson and first established in 1819 (though it was originally called Camp Missouri). With most of travel to the West in the 1820s going more southerly via Santa Fe, the army determined in 1827 to decommission the post. Frazer, *Forts of the West*, 84–85.
71. The town would become Winter Quarters.
72. The Cutler Park council took place on 28 August 1846. The Omaha and Oto nations'

make a Town there.[71] they would permit us to rema<in> one or two years.[72]

Saturday Sept 5th [1846] continued to work at the hay through the past week. this day two young lads by the names of [Daniel] Barnum & [Pelatiah] Brown[73] were severely whiped by the Marshal [Horace Eldredge] of Cutler's Park (which is the name given to this place) for the crime of seduction.[74]

Friday 11th [September 1846][75] I received the following notice from Col. [John] Scott

---

delegation was led by chief Big Elk, "a man sixty two years of age," and his son Standing Elk, "a man about 32 years of age," with their entourage, including Logan Fontenelle, their interpreter who was "a half breed, a young man of a very penetrating look, and something of a schollar. . . . aged about 24 years," and seventy other chiefs and braves. The Saints were represented by the Twelve Apostles and the local High Council. They all crowded into a large double tent in the Saints' makeshift settlement. The treat proved beneficial for both sides. The Omahas negotiated promises from the Mormons to be sparing in their use of local resources, while at the same time eliciting a promise of assistance from the exiles in agricultural production and other things. The Native Americans recommended the Saints move still farther north to undisputed Omaha lands where the latter's presence would serve as a buffer between the Omaha and their enemies, the Sioux. Of course, the Omahas' generosity provided a two-year cushion allowing the destitute Saints two years to recover their stance, giving them flexibility to adjust their plans to transport their people to the West. The Omaha chiefs signed on 31 August 1846 an agreement endorsing this negotiation. Stout, *On the Mormon Frontier*, 188; Bennett, *Mormons at the Missouri*, 70–73. For an overview of Mormon relations with Native Americans in what is now Iowa and Nebraska see Coates, "Refugees, Friends, and Foes," 65–90.

73. Daniel Branum and Pelatiah Brown were the sons, respectively, of Job V. Branum and, probably, Pelatiah Brown, Sr.
74. The Daniel Barnum/Pelatiah Brown affair was a significant event as it, according to Hosea Stout, inaugurated the imputation of the biblical "Law of God" for infractions of the moral and civil code. While biblical law called for the most extreme penalty for violation of God's commands, the thunder of proscriptive rhetoric rather than the implementation of corporal or capital punishment was most often meted by the Mormons to transgressors. See the discussion of the Saints' concept of activating the Law of God for violations of the civic and moral code associated with the report and notes about Brigham Young's sermon of 13 September 1846 found in this chapter. According to Brigham Young's record, besides Barnum and Brown, Jackson Clothier was also involved in "illicit intercourse with females." The young men in question, with the young women, "had been out for fifteen nights in succession untill after two o'clock" and, according to the charge made against them, the boys had had "carnal communication with the girls," though the males denied the charge. The biblical penalty for the acts was death, which Daniel Barnum initially thought might be his fate. However, Barnum, Brown, and Clothier were whipped with "18 hard lashes" as penalty for their misdeed. Stout, *On the Mormon Frontier*, 1:190–192; Young, *Manuscript History, 1846–1847*, 369. (For comparison, sixteen months later a man among the Saints received "39 lash[es] on his bare back" for stealing a horse. Journal History, 17 January 1848.)
75. This is the date, 11 September 1846, that Brigham Young and the Twelve Apostles selected the site of what became Winter Quarters, Nebraska. Home sites were identified beginning 23 September 1846. Bennett, *Mormons at the Missouri*, 73. A description of the rudimentary nature of the homes built in Winter Quarters to temporarily house the exiled

Head Quarters, Artillery Regmt, Cutler's Park, Sept 11th 1846
Capt. Norton Jacob

Sir, you are hereby notified to enquire after the commissioned and noncommissioned officers of your company and notify them to [a]ppear with yourself in person at my Quarters on Sunday Evening at six oclock Sept 13th herein. fail not for wee must meet in council to transact some Important business. you will please give ~~to~~ attention to order and fail not.[76]

John Scott, Col.[77]

Sunday 13th [September 1846] Attended meeting at the Stand.[78] Br Orson Pratt Spoke on the necesity of obtaining K[n]owledge, that the Elders frequenty, for the want thereof, made Statements that were incorrect or failed ~~failed~~ to prove correct posis<t>ions not Knowing how to apply Evidence. for instance, many would say that the five Senses were the only inlets of Human Kowledg, wereas much of our <Knowledge> is received by mental perception, reasoning and reflection. again the Sectarian world say that about six thousand years ago God made all things out of not[h]ing, when it can be demonstrated <that> light is thirty thousand years in coming from the fixed Stars to the Earth. consquently that light was in existance at least 24 thousand years before this Earth.[79] Br Heber [Kimball] Spoke upon the fuss made by some persons about those boys being whiped.[80] some went and hid themselves saying they would Shoot anny boddy who should undertake to whip them, which he regarded as a pretty sure sign of their guilt. the whping had been done by order of the council and he would support his brethren in the course they had taken.[81]

Saints is found in a report written by Church Historian Willard Richards, reproduced in Young, *Manuscript History, 1846–1847*, 486–488.

76. This military document and the description by Jacob of events that soon followed are evidence that the exodus was conducted under a cloud of fear and anxiety felt by the Saints concerning what they might encounter. Jacob's inclusion in his diary account of this order and the military activity that follows illustrates his own consciousness about the gravity of the precarious situation in which the Mormons found themselves.
77. A letter sent by John Scott to church leaders was received the following day, 12 September, wherein Scott asked permission to locate at a particular spot for the winter. Brigham Young said it was "Voted that he [Scott] has the privilege of locating where he has selected . . . and that some of the cannon be prepared for immediate use so that they may be directed to any point where they may be needed." Young, *Manuscript History, 1846–1847*, 381.
78. The Stand was undoubtedly like the one adjacent to the temple in Nauvoo, a wooden structure which elevated the speaker to be seen and heard by the congregation.
79. Hosea Stout noted that Orson Pratt, whose theme was "the organization of worlds & the planetary system," also "said that we could distinctly see with a common spy glass in the constellation of Orion (in the Sword of Orion) unorganized matter enough to make many millions of worlds as large as the sun." Stout, *On the Mormon Frontier*, 1:193.
80. This refers to Daniel Branum, Pelatiah Brown, and Jackson Clothier.
81. Illustrating the division the corporal punishment of the young men caused within the

President Young spoke verry severely upon the course taken by some in undertakeing to Stir up strife in the camp because some boys had been whipped, they having been neglected by their own Fathers. he thought the Marshal had not whipped them severe enough or <they> would hold their toungs. besides, some middl aged men were engaged in encourageing them in their course, a thing they ought to be ashamed of. if they wished thus to corrupt themselves, he wanted them to leave the Camp of Israel and go away among the Gentiles. But if they remained here they must observe order & decorum. and he Swore twice in the name of Israel's God that such vile conduct should [not] be allowed in this Camp, for <if> they could not [be] governed without, the Law of God should be executed & that would make short work.[82]

In the Evening met the council at Col. [John] Scott's Quarters. present Col. John Scott, Capt. John Litle, Capt Harrison Burgess & myself. Ordered that four companies of at Least 20 men each raised within the week & that report be made here next Sunday Evening at 6 oclock.[83]

Monday 14th [September 1846] I went out as usual with the Brethren to work at the hay when after wee got into the meadow, in geting off the waggon, one of the oxen Kicked me severely on the left side which so disabled me that I was

---

Mormon camp, some believing the whipping to be cruel and barbaric, Heber Kimball told Hosea Stout after the meeting that "one Brother refused to give him [Kimball] his hand because he supposed he [Kimball] was one who gave council to have the boys whipped." After Kimball explained to the man that the decision was a collective one, made by the "High Council," the objector was satisfied, according to Kimball, that Kimball "had nothing to do with it." Stout, *On the Mormon Frontier*, 1:192.

82. The reference by church leaders to the "Law of God," mentioned several times by Jacob in his record, referred to biblical law where matters such as murder, adultery, bestiality, blasphemy, and stealing (thievery) were capital offenses punishable by death. See, e.g., Exodus 22:19; Leviticus 20:10; 24:16–17. Brigham Young and church leaders were interested in equipping their people with righteousness for the Second Advent of Jesus, which many Saints believed would occur within their time. Strict adherence to the commandments of God, as described in the Bible and Book of Mormon, therefore, was the objective for the Saints collectively and individually. This concept of behavioral expectation and the ostensible penalty for violating God's commands is crucial in understanding the Latter-day Saints' view of themselves as modern Israel and the manner in which church members were governed. The ominous rhetoric threatening the activation of the Law of God characterized Mormon preachments for more than a decade. The day before this public meeting on 13 September, Brigham Young met with the Twelve Apostles and the High Council and commenting on this matter said, "Some boys have been whipped in camp, and it is right." Then generalizing about iniquity in the camp Young said, "If we allow men to come here and set up their own plans, three years will not roll around before we will have cutting of throats here." Young, *Manuscript History, 1846–1847*, 380–381. Other accounts of Young's words on 13 September 1846 are also found in Ibid., 383–384, and Stout, *On the Mormon Frontier*, 1:193.
83. These figures, after all that had been said about the westward journey, illustrate the difficulty of implementing the Saints' plan to organize and transport the exiles.

obliged to quit work. remained till monday following unable to work.

~~Mo~~monday 21st [September 1846] ground sythes. at night about 9 oclock an alrm was made and wee were directed to get the two six-pounders out and prepare for action.[84] Capts [John] Litle and [Harrison] Burgess mustered about [blank] additional men & wee were on duty 'till about 3 oclock A.M. when all turned in but the gaards. in the morning by the direction [of] Col. [John] Scot, I drilled some of the men at the manual of the piece. about ten oclock all the camp of Israel was called together under arms when it was organized by President [Brigham] Young and the Council <into> one Regmt. of four battalians consisting of four companies each of 25 men rank and file. Stephen Markum was elected col., Hosea Stout Lieut., col. John Scot first major, Henry Heriman second Major, and John Gleason third Major.[85] Gene[r]al B[righam] Young made a speach to the Brethre in which <he> claimed the right of being commander in Chief of all the forces of the Saints, which was accorded by a unanimous <vote> of all present.[86] wee were then dismissed & returned to our camp, viz the Artillery Battalion composed of Capt. [John] Litle's co[mpany]., Capt [James] Flack's, Capt Burgesse's & my own. after wee arrived <at> our

---

84. The alarm was prompted by a report Brigham Young received from Peter Sarpy, who operated the trading post south of Winter Quarters, "that two gentlemen (confidentially) from Missouri had informed him that the Missourians were collecting with the Sheriff of Missouri at their head designing to come up and attack the saints, that they had writs for the Twelve and others." So much fear shrouded the Mormon camp that "Some were ready to go into fits almost." Taking the rumor seriously, though it proved to be just a rumor, Brigham Young "sent two spies northward and two southward" to ascertain the potential threat of another round of government intervention in their affairs. Anxiety from this event actuated Young's weeks-long desire to revitalize the Saints' military structure, then somewhat loosely organized, into a formalized defensive mechanism. Clayton, *An Intimate Chronicle*, 289; Stout, *On the Mormon Frontier*, 1:195; Young, *Manuscript History, 1846–1847*, 392.
85. The organizational particulars Jacob describes vary with more official information about the meeting. The variance may be explained by a lack of information being distributed to all in attendance during Brigham Young's establishment of the military structure of the camp of Israel. Young called the meeting for the purpose "to organize and take care of ourselves in this savage country and prepare for going over the mountains." Young also asked those assembled "if they would take the officers in the Nauvoo Legion or choose new ones." A unanimous vote confirmed the existing organization. While efforts to organize militarily earlier, as Jacob's record of 13 September describes, were somewhat haphazard, the alarm provoked something definite. Eleven men were assigned as captains to "form companies of twenty-five each" under the direction of Stephen Markham, as Colonel, and Hosea Stout, as Lieut. Colonel, of the 1st Battalion of Infantry. The artillery unit to which Jacob was assigned, under John Scott's leadership, was composed of sixty-three men. Young, *Manuscript History, 1846–1847*, 392.
86. The military atmosphere of the camp, already pervading the westward migration of the Saints, was now officially organized, and in light of the perceived threat of government intervention was clearly a defensive measure to protect the Saints in their extremely vulnerable situation. See Jacob's note below where he continues on the events of the day after the entry for 25 September 1846.

camp wee were dismissed till 5 oclock P.M. when three companies, Flack's, Burgess' & my own, met & elected one Lieut. & two Seargeant's each, when wee were dismissed by Major John Scot.

Thursday 24th [September 1846] This morning a verry <si[n]gular> incident occured in our camp. Before the organization above related, Col. [John] Scot had received an order from Gen. B[righam] Young to send one of the four pieces of Ordinance in his possession to Bishop [George] Miller's camp, two hundred miles abov here at the mouth of the Punkaw [Ponca] river.[87] In compliance with that order wee had prepared the four-pounder, & drew up written instructions for the manual of the piece.[88] this morning the Bishop's ~~<agent> came to receive the gun. Just as he was hiching on his team, Col. Stephen Markum came up, his Adjutent~~ Agent Jacob Houtz[89] came to receive the gun. Just as he was hitching on his team Col Stephen Markum came up. His Adjutant, Major [John] Bills, was also present. The team being hitched on the gun-carriage, Says Br Scot, "who is to rec[e]ipt for this gun?" Col. Markum replyed, "Brigham has ordered me to take charge of the guns and have them put in order." Says Br Scot, "This property has long since been put in my possesion with orders from Br Brigham not to let anny of it go <without> orders from him, & taking a receipt. moreover, I have Just receipted for these oxen and no man shall take them away without <giveing> a receipt." Says Markum, "how did *you* come to recipt for them?" as though he had been doing that which he should not have done. Scot replyed, "Gen. Young to<l>d me to do so. accordingly I have given one like this, Received of Zerah Pulsapher [Zera Pulsipher] one yoke of oxen to be used in hauling a cannon up to Bishop Miller's camp." Says Markum, "who's here to take them?" (The oxen) some

---

87. The request for a cannon, with "two coil of large rope," had been delivered to Brigham Young on 4 August by two of Bishop George Miller's camp. The very capable bishop had been assigned in June 1846 by Young to lead an advance company of Mormons as far as Fort Laramie to prepare for the Saints' anticipated move west. After initial plans were modified, Miller's company, melded with another company of Saints led by James Emmett, were invited by a Ponca Indian chief to winter near a Ponca village in northeastern Nebraska. Church leaders apparently approved the proposal. A caravan numbering between 160 and 175 wagons coursed northward across Nebraska in August 1846 and finally settled near the confluence of the Niobrara and Missouri rivers, about 150 miles northwest of Winter Quarters. Internal conflict and disease afflicted the company. Eventually Miller rejected LDS Church leaders' proposals for moving the Saints westward, as well as what he perceived to be their usurpation of authority. Miller eventually broke from the church. Young, *Manuscript History, 1846–1847*, 294, 427, 456; Hartley, *My Best for the Kingdom*, 209–229, which also provides an overview of the ventures involving Miller and Emmett in 1846–1847.

88. Four yoke of oxen were committed to haul the cannon to Miller's camp at Ponca. Young, *Manuscript History, 1846–1847*, 393.

89. Jacob Houtz was assisted by Vincent Shurtleff from the Ponca settlement. It had taken them nine days to reach Winter Quarters. Young, *Manuscript History, 1846–1847*, 387–388.

one replyed, "Br Houtz here is Millers Agent. Says ~~Markum "Then let him receipt for them." They all then started towards Br Scot's Tent, Br Houtz remarking to his Teamster, "you may turn the team around, I suppose. Col. Scot will <not> let it go out of the yard 'till the gun is recipted for." Says Markum, "Yes, drive it out of~~ Houtz, "I will receipt for them. none but a damd fool would object to what Col. Scot requires." Says Col. Markum, "Lets go and fix it" and they all started towards Col. Scot's Tent, Br Houts remarking to his Teamster, "You may turn the team around. I suppose Col. Scot will not let the gun go out of the yard until it is receipted for." "Yes," Says Markum, "Drive it out of the yard. I'le bear you out in it." Br Scot turned round, Saying, "Col. Markum, that gun shall not go out of this yard 'till I have a receipt for it." Says Markum, "I swear it Shall," & immediaetly caught the whip out of the driver's hand, exclaiming, "John Scot, I'le straighten you." Scot unhooked the lead cattle's chain, when Markum collared him. Scot also seized him and held him off at arms end, Saying Sternly, "Markum, you Shall not come into this yard & interfere with my business." Markum calld out to his Adjutant Bills, "Go and bring a Force to take away this gun. Bring a force, I say. I command you to bring a force!" And away scampered Agt Bills, telling every man he met to gather up forthwith to the Publick Square armed and equipt, for terible things were expected! Some said afterwards they did not Know where the Public square was. But some ten or dozen particular friends happened to think that the little triangular spot occupied by the Atillry must be the Public square![90] so on they came with rifle and musket, Sword & Spear, and passed round outside of the yard where they formed a line with their backs towards the mouths of those terrible guns! that the Agt. sending by one of the Gene[r]al's Aides the night after the alarm, Commanded Col. Scot to have the priming drawn out of, lest it get wet, when there had been neither shot nor priming in them for the last six months at least. It reminds one of Don Quixots attack upon the windmill,[91] for if those great guns had ~~have~~ bellowed there would have been a deal of wind! But to return to the parties at the gun, They soon both relinquished their hold, Br Scot rema[r]king calmly, "Markum, the thing I requre of you is reasonabl. Br Young has given me charge of this property. I dont care a dam for Joseph Young, & nobody else. I'le have a Force here to take it." Says Markum, "I can raise a Force too." Says Scot, "But look here, Col. Markum. you show no authority from Gen. Young for the course you are pursuing." [obscure word struck out] Here Markum hesitated à little, & Br Houtz again offered to <do as> ~~thing~~ he had done before, when all three proceeded drectly to the Tent,

---

90. This will not be Jacob's last illustration of human folly in the Mormons' extreme circumstances during the exodus and settlement in the West. Jacob's humorous characterization of the incident gives insight into his personality.

91. This, of course, references Miguel de Cervantes's seventeenth-century novel *Don Quixote*, where the protagonist imagines doing great things in unreal settings, specifically Don Quixote tilting against windmills.

and a receipt for the gun & oxen was made out and signed by Br Jacob Houtz some time before the redoubtable Force under command of Capt. Charles Bird arrived, Who came without anny orders from his superior officer, Major John Gleason. co<n>s<e>quently, like fools, they came as a Mob! and Col. Markum suffered them to stay as long as they pleased, without disperseing or dismising them 'till they went away as they came, like fools with their fingers in their mouths. While Br Jacob Houtz hitched on to his cannon again & drove off in triumph. All this happened about ten oclock A.M. Some time in the afternoon Col. Markum came into the yard enquiring for "Br Scot." he soon found him, when Lo and behold!! he wanted to see if the receipt taken by Br Scot held Br Houtz responsable for the delivery of that cannon to Bishop Miller, for if it did not, he would send on a man to take poss[ess]ion of it & see that it was so deliverd. Query, would he not have had another fight for it?

Friday 25 [September 1846] This morning wee received inteligence of a hard fought battle at Nauvoo a week ago last Satturday[92] in which Br W[illia]m Anderson, his son [Augustus] & another man [David Norris] <were killed>[93]

Note: At <the> time of the organization on the 22d [September 1846] Gen [Brigham] Young Said the camp was about <to> remove down to the river for Winter Quarters and that he wanted a company of 25 men under the command of some suitabl person to reconaiter [reconnoiter] the country to the South, to search for crossing places on the Elk-horn, Platte river, & other streams and also to seek for good places to winter stock so that wee might travel in the winter or next spring, for companies would have to be selected to hunt & search out countries & places which wee had never thought of. He also said that he had appointed Col. A[lbert]. P. Rockwood to be his aiddacamp to carry messages and do business for [obscure character crossed out] his name, to be his mouthpiece, for when sent to do anny thing, he Knew enough to stop when he had done it and <not> proceed to do his own errant in addition and but feew men Knew enough for that. Therefore he wanted all the people

92. Daniel Wells and William Cutler were the visitors from Nauvoo, delivering mail and supplying information about the situation in Nauvoo. Young, *Manuscript History, 1846–1847*, 395.

93. William Anderson, his son Augustus, and David Norris were killed on Saturday, 12 September during the anti-Mormon military assault on Nauvoo that eventually drove the remaining Saints from the city. The elder Anderson "was shot in the breast by a musket ball. He lived fifteen minutes." The younger Anderson and Norris were killed by cannon balls. William Clayton, on 25 September 1846 in the Mormon camp, heard that the "mob fired 62 shots with the cannon and 10 rounds with the muskets making 12,000 musket balls only killing 3 and wounding 3." Littlefield, *The Martyrs*, 105; Clayton, *An Intimate Chronicle*, 291. The circumstances of the "Battle of Nauvoo" are detailed in Leonard, *Nauvoo*, 599–616. The expulsion in September 1846 of the last remnant of Mormons to go west from Nauvoo and their September-November 1846 journey from the Mississippi to Missouri River is personally chronicled in Bullock, *Camp of the Saints*, 66–99.

to receive Br Rockwood as his Mouth Piece, Just as though <the> commands sent by him & the words spoken were spoken & commanded by himself. Br Brigham then called upon the people to sanction it by their votes, which they did.[94] From this and other things that have transpired, I have come to the conclusion that it is the policy and intention to put down every Spirit in the Camp of Israel that would seek to establish a selvish independance, & that Br Rockwood is to be made an instrument ~~to~~ to accomplish that thing, as he is Br Brighams eldest son by adoption.[95] Well, I say Amen, for there must be less of that Spirit before a proper union can prevail among the saints.

While Col. [Stephen] Markum's Force were formed in the manner before mentioned in this record, Br H[eber]. C. Kimbal came up & Spoke against such a proceeding, saying that the Brethren should not let their passions govern them, But act with calmness and moderation. How, said he, could the Twelve ever get along with their business if they were to take fire at every obstacle that was thrown in their way.

In presence of Br Kimbal & some others who had also come to see what was going on, a short explanation took place between Markum & [John] Scot, when they mutually agreed that what had passed should not interupt or break their friendship and they gave each other the hand of fellowship. But it <made> quite a stir in the Camp of Israel, as officious persons can yet be found among the Saints who seek to promote discord and stir up Strife. well may the Lord reward them for the iniquitous practices, and hasten the time when righteousness & the Law of God shall prevail, & tyrrany and oppression be purged out from among the People of the Lord, yea, & <be> driven from the face of the Earth.[96]

Thursday, Friday, & Satturday [24, 25, 26 September 1846] the whole Camp of Israel were in motion, moving down to their winter Quarters on the river at the mouth of Turkey Creek where they have laid out a city on a beautiful cite on a high second Bottom where they intend to build a water mill on Turkey Creek.[97]

---

94. Brigham Young's designation of himself as the military commander and Albert Rockwood as his second reminds the reader of the martial influence of the Mormon transit to the West, which melded rather harmoniously with Young's and the Twelve Apostle's ecclesiastical roles of leadership of the Latter-day Saints.

95. The "law of adoption," referenced earlier, which characterized the Brigham Young-Albert Perry Rockwood relationship is explained in Irving, "The Law of Adoption."

96. The differences between Stephen Markham and John Scott were eventually considered by the Winter Quarters High Council on 26 November 1846 where it was "decided [there was] no cause of action." Young, *Manuscript History, 1846–1847*, 465.

97. In searching for a suitable place to build a temporary headquarters for the church, it was determined that Turkey Creek, with a "twenty or twenty five feet fall sufficient for two runs of four feet stones," would be an excellent site on which to build a mill. Brigham Young examined the mill site on 28 September, though the general area had been selected for settlement on 11 September 1846. Turkey Creek ran in the northern sector of what

Satturday [26 September 1846] Br [John] Scott went down to see Brigham [Young] & Heber [Kimball] to as<c>ertain where they intended to have the Artillery Camp for the winter. he met with rather a cool reception from Brigham, as those officious persons above alluded to had filled his ears with various false statements concerning the affair between Scot & [Stephen] Markum. But after listening to Br Scot's defence of his conduct, he appeared better pleased with the course he had taken in that matter, when the conversation was turned by Br Brigham upon the subject of the post which he wished Major Scott to occupy with his Artellery, immediately North of the City on the opposite side of Turkey Creek.

Sunday [27 September 1846] Some five or six of our company, together with Major [John] Scot & myself, took a two Horse waggon and went down to search out the spot for our encampment. About 80 rods North of the head of Main Street in small valley, well shelterd from the winds of winter by the surrounding hills, wee found one of the best Springs of living water that has been found in this part of the Country, <&> here wee determined to fix our Camp.

Monday 28th [September 1846] Commenced moving our camp & continued engaged at it for 3 or 4 days. Our camp was now composed of the following named persons: Major John Scot & family, Capt. Norton Jacob & family, Capt. James M. Flack, Lieut. Thomas King and family, John Robbinson[98] & family, Caleb Baldwin & family, W[illia]m. Robison & family, Timothy King & family, James McGaw in charge of Br [Lucius] Scovil's family (who has gone on a mission to England),[99] James Baldwin, James Keeler, Edward Pugh, Moses Vince, John Grosebeck [Groesbeck] & family. Br Scot had, some time ago, taken a Job of work of Presbyterian Missionary down at the Oto vilage which is called Belview [Bellevue, Nebraska].[100]

---

became Winter Quarters. Journal History, 20 September 1846; Young, *Manuscript History,1846–1847*, 377, 395. See Richard Bennett's discussion of the mill in *Mormons at the Missouri*, 114–115. Winter Quarters was located just fifteen miles north of Bellevue, located near the mouth of the Platte River. The Saints' two-year sojourn at Winter Quarters is described in Bennett, *Mormons at the Missouri*, 73–147.

98. It is not certain which of the four John Robinsons in the LDS Church at this time this references.

99. Lucius Scovil returned to Winter Quarters from his mission to England on 3 October 1847.

100. In 1846 the Presbyterian Board of Missions in New York City, sent the Rev. Edward McKinney and his wife to establish a mission to the Omaha and Oto Indians at Bellevue, Nebraska, Nebraska's first settlement presently located just south of Omaha. The mission, which the Mormons apparently helped construct, consisted of a two-story cottonwood log building, thirty-six by eighty feet. It "contained six rooms, in addition to four rooms in each of the two L's" in which the building was shaped. The "building was designed to accommodate the mission family, the assistants, and forty Indian pupils." The building was not completed until 1848. Goss, *Bellevue*, 4–5; *Old Bellevue*, 20.

Monday [29 September 1846] John Groesbeck & family went down to commence said Job of work.

Teusday [30 September 1846] Thomas R. King & family & James Baldwin went down also, Timothy King went also on Monday.

Sunday Oct 4th [1846] I went to meeting over in the city or Big Camp [Winter Quarters]. Br Orson Pratt Preached a good Gospel Sermon.[101] In the afternoon there was a business meeting.[102] Br [Asahel] Lathrop & [John] Hill[103] had Just arrived from up the river. They had l[e]ft their families together with some 8 or ten others about 70 miles above this place, having broken off from Bishop [George] Miller's camp because of <the> oppression ~~that~~ and disorder that prevails there.[104] they had found extensive Rush Bottoms where they had stoped, and President [Brigham] Young said it was his intention to send his cattle up there to winter them & thought it advisable for some families to go up there, that those that wished might prepare to winter their stock on the Rushes.

Monday 5th [October 1846] Our moving being accomplishd, Brethren [John] Scott, [James] Flack, [James] Keeler, & [James] McGaw went down to assist about the Job.[105] Befor leaving, Major Scott placed me in charge of the camp under the following order:

> Artillery Camp Oc. 5th 1846
> Capt. N. Jacob
> Sir: you are hereby authorised and Commanded To take charge of the Artillery Camp In my absence and also of the Battalion if necesity require it. John Scott, Major.

---

101. Hosea Stout reported that Orson Pratt's sermon for 4 October concerned "the first principles of the Gospel, as there were some present who did not belong to the Church." Stout, *On the Mormon Frontier*, 1:203.
102. At this meeting Orson Pratt, Amasa Lyman, and Wilford Woodruff "divided the city [Winter Quarters] into thirteen wards and appointed a bishop over each." Young, *Manuscript History, 1846–1847*, 404, 425.
103. Though there were as many as a half dozen John Hills in the LDS Church at this time, the Hill this references is probably John Hill (1814–1863).
104. Asahel Lathrop, one of the Miller/Emmett company, apparently had a falling out the previous month with company leaders and, with "a cluster of discontented people, . . . moved farther down the Missouri [from the Ponca camp where George Miller located] to their own site." Miller's arbitrary rule managed to offend others, such as when he cancelled church meetings after 30 November 1846. His lieutenants held meetings anyway. Hartley, *My Best for the Kingdom*, 217, 223.
105. The "Job" refers to constructing the Presbyterian Mission at Bellevue, Nebraska, described above.

I was not able to work much this week by reason of a large swelling under my left arm.

Sunday 11th Oct [1846] I lanced it [the swelling under his arm], when discharged verry freely & I was soon able to work again. This <day> all hands were out in the rain selecting our cattle out of the big Herd which had Just been brot down from up the river about six miles.[106]

Sunday 18th [October 1846] I went down to work on the missionary Job and worked one week, when through the mean, undermining conduct of [James] McGaw, Thomas King & [John] Groesbeck, Br [John] Scott & the remander of our co[mpany] were discharged from the work by our missionary employer, [Edward] McKiney[107] & King. Groesbeck & J[ames]. Baldwin were employed by him to ~~to~~ finish the Job!

These men were influenced in this by a Spirit of covetousness & insubordination which more fully manifested itself after they returned to camp by their drawing off & making a division in the co[mpany]. McGaw, John Robinson, Tho. King, Tim. King & Groesbeck drew off, by which our working co[mpany] was so reduced that we foun[d] ourselves under the necesity of seperating our business & work <each> by himself. During my absence below, Father returned from the botoms above here where he had went to winter & came into the Artellery camp.

I comenced building my house about the first of Nov. [1846] in which I was employed about 3 weeks,[108] when I went to work on President [Brigham] Young's Grist mill.[109] I worked 7 days when I was prevented doing anny thing by <a> swelling on my hand for about 3 weeks. about this time Pres'd Young called the People together at the Stand on the council Lot and gave them a severe Chastisement for their sins and transgressions of the Law of God, telling them that they must repent immediately & bring forth works

106. Brigham Young's account reported the fury of the three-hour rain where the "cattle were so uneasy they could not be kept on the prairie." Upon retrieving the cattle, according to Hosea Stout, "The herd allmost filled the Town." Young, *Manuscript History, 1846–1847*, 411; Stout, *On the Mormon Frontier*, 1:204.

107. This, of course, is a reference to the Presbyterian mission to the Omahas, established at Bellevue, Nebraska, by Edward McKinney in 1846.

108. Jacob and his family numbering six, along with his father Udney and his wife, found themselves living in the Winter Quarters 21st Ward located in the northwestern-most sector of Winter Quarters on the north side of Turkey Creek. Bishop's List of Widows, Women whose Husbands are in the Army and others.

109. On 19 December 1846, Brigham Young reported that the lower story of the flouring mill on Turkey Creek was completed. Historian's Office, Manuscript History, Winter Quarters, 19 December 1846. Jacob's work on Young's mill on Turkey Creek, in the north sector of Winter Quarters, anticipated his work on constructing several mills in Utah.

of righteousness or they would be all swept from the face of the Earth, that the Thieves need not undertake [to] go with the Saints from this Camp for when wee should leave here for the West, the Law of God in every particular wo<u>ld take full effect & that woud cut the matter short, even as short as the man who went to cut [obscure character struck out] a dog's tail off and by <mistake> he cut it close behind his ears! He did not want to go anny further into the wilderness without an entire & thoroug reformation, for wee should all be destroyed by the Lamanites as were the Neph<i>tes of old, and finaly concluded by saying that notwithstanding what he had said, he still Knew this to be the best people there was on the Earth.[110] I should conclude from all this that the inhabitants of the Earth are nigh unto that period of destruction Spoken of by Israel's Prophets.

25th of Nov. [1846] the whole Camp of Winter Quarters was divided into [obscure character struck out] Bishopricks[111] under the direction of the High Council for the purpose of taking care of the Poor which included the wives of those men who volunteered & went into the army last July, about 500 men. This [the recruitment of the Mormon Battalion] was a measure that seemed to be necssary in order to turn away the Jealousy of the General Government and secure its protection in some <degree> to the Saints.

---

110. The substance of this sermon as reported by Jacob, is very much like sermons delivered by Brigham Young on 15 and 20 December 1846. On 20 December, after identifying the peoples' transgressions, he warned that he "would prefer traveling over the mountains with the Twelve only than to be accompanied with the wicked and those who continued to commit iniquity; and warned those who lied and stole and followed Israel, that they would have their heads cut off, for that was the law of God and it would be executed." Stout, *On the Mormon Frontier*, 1:218; Young, *Manuscript History, 1846–1847*, 479–480.

111. On 25 November the High Council of Winter Quarters determined to expand the city's thirteen wards (congregations), each led by a bishop, into twenty-two "smaller wards." Jacob with his family, as noted earlier, lived in the 21st Ward on the north side of Turkey Creek. Jacob's role in the ward was to serve as clerk. Young, *Manuscript History, 1846–1847*, 464; Bishop's List of Widows, Women whose Husbands are in the Army and others.

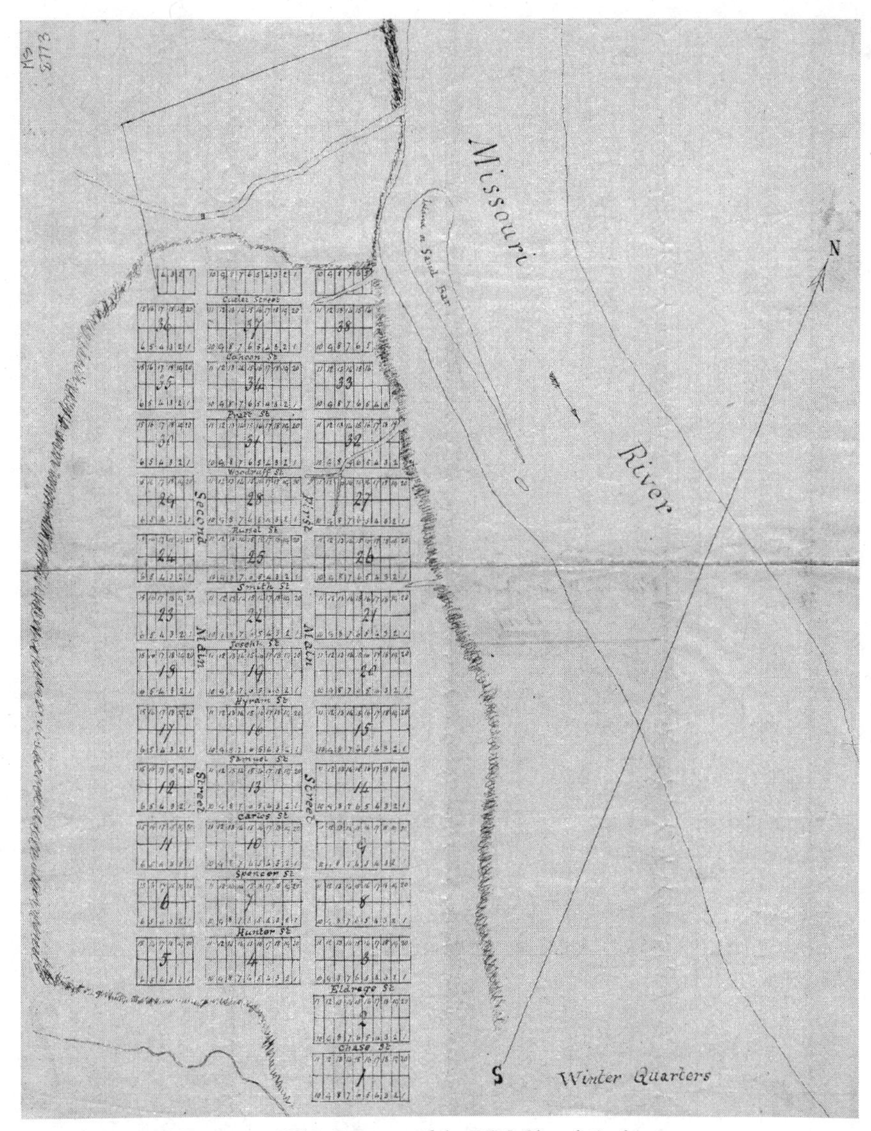

Plan of Winter Quarters, ca. 1846. Courtesy of the LDS Church Archives.

January–April 1847

WHILE MANY UNKNOWNS, NOT THE LEAST of which was their ultimate geographical objective, hovered over the Saints after a winter on the Missouri River, Norton Jacob was recruited to join the vanguard of Mormon emigration to the West. He settled his family on the Iowa side of the Missouri in Pottawattamie County while he ventured with his comrades. He was appointed one of fourteen captains of ten as the twelve dozen who composed the company organized in mid-April in eastern Nebraska. By the end of the month the pilgrims had traced the north bank of the Loup Fork River before crossing it and breaking south to join the Platte River, the great highway to the West.

14th January 1847 The Lord gave a revelation to the Church through the "Twelve" entitled "Tth[e] word and will of the Lord concerning the Saints in their Journeyings to the West."[1] Let all the camp of Israel be organised into companies of Hundreds, fifties & tens, with a President and two councilers to each company &c. Under this revelation the Camp was organised & about the first of Feb. [1847] I was appointed a capt of the eighth ten in the third hundred 2d grand division under H[eber]. C. Kimbal.[2]

1. Jacob's reflective entry regarding the "Word and Will of the Lord," a 14 January 1847 revelation from Jesus to Brigham Young, defined not only the organizational structure for the western journey, it also denoted the Saints as modern Israel; "I am the Lord your God, even the God of your fathers, the God of Abraham and of Isaac and Jacob. I am he who led the children of Israel out of the land of Egypt; and my arm is stretched out in the last days, to save my people Israel." (Doctrine and Covenants 136:21–22.) The structure, akin to their travel across Iowa, called for "captains of hundreds, captains of fifties, and captains of tens, with a president and his two counselors at their head, under the direction of the Twelve Apostles." (Doctrine and Covenants 136:3) The declaration (revelation) was apparently first presented to the Saints for confirmation on Sunday, 7 February 1847. The text of the revelation was added to the Mormon canon—the Doctrine and Covenants—in 1876. Young, *Manuscript History, 1846–1847*, 522.
2. "The Captains of Hundred met in the Council House and appointed their captains of tens; who in turn chose their ten men," according to Brigham Young, who also stated that he "approved the form drawn up by Thos. Bullock for organizing the companies." Young,

About the first of March I [was] selected for one of the Pioneers to go and seek out the place where the Lord promised in the revelation refered to above to establish a Steak [stake] of Zion.[3]

15th [March 1847] In complyance with Br Heber [Kimball]'s council I went down to where Br Joel Ricks is settled on West Branch of the Nishnebotana [River][4] to see if I could get any assistance to help me to go with the Pioneers. Br Ricks & family appeared glad to see me and treated me very kindly. Br Ricks verry readily agreed to send a two Horse team with me and take care of my family while I should go along with the Twelve as a Pioneer.

Friday March 26th [1847] at 10 oclock the People were called together by the ringing of the old Temple bell when a Special conferance was held preparatory to the departure of the Pioneers.[5] Br Brigham [Young] chastened the People severely for being so covetous and withholding their means in fitting out the Pioneers and proposed that the Pioneers keep the word of Wisdom.[6]

Manuscript History, 1846–1847, 519. The structure Jacob described changed by the time of the pioneer vanguard's departure in April 1847.

3. A "stake of Zion" was a center of gathering for the Mormon faithful, such as those at Kirtland, Nauvoo, and Winter Quarters, where the full scope of Mormon belief and practice was enacted. In this instance, the particular "stake of Zion" referred to was, of course, the one to be established in what would become Salt Lake City, Utah.

   The designation "Pioneers" held meaning for the Saints beyond the dictionary definition. The "Pioneers" was the official title placed upon those who would forge a path for those who would follow them to the Rocky Mountains.

   In plans disseminated in November 1846, church leaders explained that their original intent was to depart Winter Quarters in early March 1847 in order to arrive in the Great Basin by 1 June. Bennett, "Finalizing Plans for the Trek West," 102. Beating the non-Mormon emigration to the trail (to better access animal feed and diminish potential conflict), initiating a settlement for those who followed, and planting a crop for fall harvest (wherever they landed) held the highest priority in the church leaders' plan. However, a multiplicity of complications modified Young's early plans.

4. Apparently the camp where Joel Ricks temporarily settled was one of several Mormon enclaves located near the Nishnabotna branches, a number of which have been forgotten to history. The West Branch of the Nishnabotna River, flowing in a southwesterly direction, drained the central part of what would become Pottawattamie and later Mills County, Iowa, in the southwestern sector of the state. Keg Creek served as the drainage for the west portion of the county, while the East Branch of the Nishnabotna drained the east. Other, smaller, streams in western Iowa emptied into the Nishnabotna branches which, in turn, poured into the Missouri River near the border of Iowa and Missouri. *History of Mills County, Iowa*, 324.

5. See Watt, "A Tale of Two Bells," for a discussion of the fate of the Nauvoo Temple's bell.

6. Brigham Young's lifetime views, practice, and expectations for the Saints regarding the Saints' health code, the Word of Wisdom, is discussed in Peterson and Walker, "Brigham Young's Word of Wisdom Legacy." The code includes advocation of the use of grains, vegetables, fruits, with meat to be used sparingly. It also included a proscription against the use of coffee, tea, alcohol, and tobacco.

The following is a return of the eigthth Ten N. Jacob Capt in Capt Roundy's Company being the 3d Company in the 2d Grand division under H. C. Kimbal

45

Names	Age	Teamsters	Waggons	Horses	Mules	Yoke of oxen	Cows	Sheep	Provisions: Flour	Meal	Wheat	Corn	Meat	Groceries	Remarks: Tools, Seeds, Cash
Norton Jacob No 1	32	1	1	-	-	1	1	-	150	50	-	-	50		1 chest of Joiner Tools, one 2 year old Heifer
Emily Jacob	36	Carryed with the Pioneers one peck White Beans & some Tools													
Oliver B. Jacob	13	1													
Lucian H Jacob	11	1													
Ira N. Jacob	6														
Joseph Jacob	2														
Udney H. Jacob No 2	66	1	1	1	-	1½	3	-	40	40	-	-	-		1 yearling Colt one 2 year old Heifer Stray ½ bu Beans Cash $10.00
Louisa S Jacob	57														
James Goff No 3	38	1	1	-	-	1	1								
Mary Goff	35														
Sarah Jane Goff	15														
Elisha Goff	10														
Aaron J Goff	6														
James Goff Jun	1														
Catherine An Van Vilzer	9														
German Elsworth No 4	31	1	1	-	-	1	4	4	70	-	-	9			1 Plough 3 bu Wheat
Spedy Elsworth	26														
Elizabeth Elsworth	7														
Epraim Elsworth	5														
Evaline Elsworth	4														
Esther Elsworth	2														
Minerva Elsworth	1														
David Elsworth No 5	42	1	1	-	-	1	2	-	-	-	4	1			1½ Bu Buck Wheat 1 Plough Shire axe ho[e]
Catherine Elsworth	41	Sent with the Pioneers ½ Bu Buck Wheat													
James Elsworth	12														
Lucinda Elsworth	10														
Epraim Elsworth	5														
Anna Elsworth	3														

This page and facing page: proposed roster of Norton Jacob's Eighth Ten, early 1847. Courtesy of the LDS Church Archives.

Anna Ellsworth 3

Joel Ricks No. 6 41 1 6 7 – 14 15 12 | 3 Ploughshares
Eleanor Ricks 39 | Sent with the Pioneers | Axes &c one X cut Saw Cash $15.00
Thomas E. Ricks 18 | one Two Horse Team
Lewis Ricks 16 | Waggon & harness
Sally Ann Ricks 14 | two Bu corn one Do meal
Claranda Ricks 12 | one Sett Plough Irons one
Temperance Ricks 10
Wm Ricks 8 | hoe $1.00 cash. 6 yds Shiring 12 75
Jonathan Ricks 6 | 14 lbs Pork 4 56
Mary E. Ricks 4
Josiah Ricks 2

Benjmin Cross No 7 57 1 1 – – 1 3 Sent with Pioneers | ½ bu corn 1 Peck Potatoes
½ bu corn 1 Peck Potatoes
Roxana Cross 54 Beans Pumpkin Squash & onion Seeds

Wm Steel No 8 41 1 1 – – ½ 3 9 | 2 Bu Buck Wheat
Margaret Steel 37
James Steel 15 1
Loisa Steel 8
Amanda Steel 3
Leonne Steel 10 months

Thomas Whittle No 9 34 1 2 – – 3 3 5 150 | 1 Plough 2 Bu Wheat one 2 year old Heifer
Mary Whittle 29
Olive Whittle 13 | Sent with Pioneers
John C Whittle 11 | one Bu Corn 3 Do meal
Mary E. Whittle 9
George Whittle 6
Zerah Whittle 4
Emiline Whittle 2

Cary Burdick No. 10 51 1 1 – – 1 1 – 1 50 – 30 | 1 Plough
Polly Burdick 40 | Sent with Pioneers | 1 Sett Harrow teeth augers Chisels &c
Jackson Burdick 20 1 | 2 quts Beans & Corn 1 onion Seed
AnnJenett Burdick 16 | 1 pr Jacks 37 ½ thread | 1 X cut Saw
Jess Burdick 11 1 | mend Boots ,50 | 1½ Bu Buck Wheat
Norton Jacob

Charles Harper my companion in the Pioneers furnished 4 Bu. corn 1 Plough bolt, 31¼ also 108 lbs of Crackers 50 lbs Flour 1½ Bu meal 25 lbs meat

Monday 29th March [1847] all the <Pioneers> met at the council House when they were assigned to the Several Waggons & directed to hold themselves ready to move when called for.[7] Charles Harper was my companion. wee immediately proceeded to make some necessary preperations. In the mean time I received the following orders:

> Winter Quarters March 30<th> 1847
> Capt. Norton Jacob
> Sir, I hereby leave the cannon[8] that is fitted for the Pioneers in your care, and under your command, until otherwise disposed of by Gen. B[righam]. Young.
> Signed John Scott, Col.

After I returned from Br [Joel] Ricks, Br Heber [Kimball] counciled me to send my family down to where Br Ricks lives to tarry through the summer or to go on West with him. accordingly I sent <a> letter to Br Ricks to that effect, as I had sold my house [in Winter Quarters] to Br [Addison] Everet[t] for cloth & Powder to help fit me out.

April 5th [1847][9] I receieved directions from General B[righam]. Young [to]

Among other things he said that day, Young also spoke to those who were going to stay at Winter Quarters by counseling "those living in dug outs to get houses on the top of the ground to live during the summer, or they would be sick." He warned about hostility towards the region's Native Americans explaining that domesticated animals, fruits, and vegetables were thought by the Indians to be "their mode of living to kill and eat." To the Saints who would steal, his threat was severe stating they should "be dealt with according to law," understood to include the potential of capital punishment. In the afternoon Young spoke again: "I preached to the saints in the afternoon, and told them that it would be necessary for those who followed the Pioneers to take eighteen months provisions. A committee would be appointed and each wagon examined. The Pioneers would probably stay on the other side of the Mountains until the snow began to fill up the gaps in the mountains. If mob violence should render it necessary for all to remove, take your cows, put your loads on their backs and fasten your children on the top. Where the saints do all they can the Lord will do the rest." Young, *Manuscript History, 1846–1847*, 530, 541.

7. At this 29 March meeting Young explained that "Twenty-five Pioneers reported themselves ready to start on their western journey" and that "thirty-two more reported themselves ready to start within two days." He "notified those who desired to start on the Pioneer journey to do so in the morning." Young, *Manuscript History, 1846–1847*, 543.

8. This cannon has reference to the "old sow," the only piece of artillery carried by the vanguard. Nicknamed after a sow who unearthed the weapon from its hiding place, the gun was not a "true cannon (which is longer and heavier)" but was a "short-barreled, low-muzzle-velocity carronade, built for shipboard use." Likely cast between 1790 and 1810, the bore carried "a 12-pound solid shot." Leonard, "Cannon was First 'Pulpit,'" 17 March 1990.

   Not for offensive purposes, but believing the "old sow" might be advantageous in passing through Indian country, which it was, the weapon served to "frighten the Indians and to let them know that we had big guns in camp." Barney, *One Side By Himself*, 99.

9. The inconvenience and sacrifice exhibited by some members of the vanguard to equip themselves and leave their families was significant and is difficult to comprehend today.

procure a team and feed for it from the several captains in the camp [and] to draw the Cannon. I found it difficult for them to raise it. only got three Horses & two sets of harness this day.

April 6th 1847 The ~~great~~ anniversary of the rise & organization of the Church.[10] a Special Conference was held in Winter Quarters,[11] Br John Smith Presiding. Br Brigham [Young] addresse[d] the congregation a short time. Said that on the morrow he intended to start on his Journey West, then pro[po]sed that conference proceed to do its Business.[12] Father John Smith arose & said that he was not in good health & should call upon Br W[illiam]. W. Phelps to bring forward the business of the conference when he arose & stated that the first Business woul[d] be to present the "Twelve" & try their standing in the church when they were sever[al]ly presented [and] unanimously sustained [in] their offices excep[t] Lyman Wight, the wild Ram of the Mountains.[13] Br Heber C. Kimbal said he had seen him some time ago in a Dream. run hymself up to his knees in the mud & they had to pull him out. So they finaly concluded to let him remain there at present. The High Council & Sevn first

---

On this day, 5 April 1847, George Smith buried his newborn son who died the previous day. Three days later he left his rudimentary dwelling for the West. With the Twelve Apostles, of which he was one, he returned to Winter Quarters on 12 April. Rejoining the emigrant company on April 14th, he again left his family, this time with "cornmeal enough to last . . . three days, but no other provisions." Three family members were left ill, including his youngest daughter who had "inflamation of the brain" and was not expected to live. Smith was informed on 19 April, by express, that his daughter had perished two days previously. Smith (Carrington), History, 5, 8, 19 April 1847.

10. The Saints celebrated the church's 6 April 1830 organization annually beginning in 1832.

11. Brigham Young, in August 1847, characterized the progress of Winter Quarters before the vanguard departed the site in April 1847: "We succeeded in building upwards of 700 houses, most of them more comfortable than are usually found on the borders of the western states, and many of them are very good, and most of this was accomplished in less than three months. We also built a first rate flouring mill, which cost several thousand dollars and is moved by water power." (Andrew Jenson estimated that as many as 1000 dugouts and homes were constructed in the settlement.) Historian's Office, Manuscript History, Winter Quarters, 7 August 1847.

12. Itching to get started, Erastus Snow called the business "unimportant" and was pleased that Brigham Young adjourned the meeting as "the Pioneer company were about ready and anxious to be on their journey westward." Snow, "Journey," (April 1948): 107.

13. The hierarchy of the church was officially reconstituted at this crucial time as a new phase of Mormonism was inaugurated. Besides endorsing the Twelve Apostles by those in attendance, despite their reticence in supporting Lyman Wight, Brigham Young noted that he "was sustained as President of the church and of the Twelve apostles." Those that would be later recognized as general authorities of the church, including the presidents "of all the Seventies," the "presiding Bishop," and the "Patriarch in the Church" were also sustained, as well as "members of the High Council." Young, *Manuscript History, 1846–1847*, 546–547.

Wight's designation as the "wild ram of the mountains," was a pseudonym coined by William W. Phelps, who characterized other members of the Twelve Apostles with designations suiting their particular personas. Leonard, *Nauvoo*, 444.

Presidents of the Seventies were then presented and unanimously sustained. The President of the High Priests Quorum, Georg Miller, they chose not to meddle with now. the fact is Br George has the Spirit of apostacy & will soon break off to the South and lead many uneasy Spirits with him.[14] hence the Brethren of the Twelve were willing to let the leaven of the Pharisees, which <is> hypocracy, work out the condemnation of all such as choose to cherish it. Br Heber now proposed to speak of <a> mystery which he wanted the People to pay attention to & moved that they forthwith help the Pioneers off by furnishing one Horse & some feed which was soon raised. this now completed my team &c for the cannon. I had procured the assistance <of> Col. Stephen Markum to drive the team.

Wednesday 7th April [1847] about noon I left my family and Started on the great expedition with the Pioneers to the West.[15] President B[righam]. Young & his Teams started at the same time.[16] wee also had <the> cannon along, a six Pounder. wee traveled about 10 miles on the Divide up the river & camped about Sun set near a small grove in a Hollow where we were somewhat shielded from the North wind which was very cold.[17]

---

14. Brigham Young's earlier entreaties to George Miller had born sour fruit. Increasingly Miller's differences with Young and the Twelve Apostles were manifest in estrangement. See Bennett, "A Samaritan had passed by."
15. For this day Charles A. Harper wrote: "left my home in Winter Quarters April 7, 1847 in a wagon with Norton Jacobs belonging to H.C. Kimball's Division and journey about 7 miles when we camped for the night." Harper, *Diary*, 15.

    Likely somewhat common to the separation of each of the vanguard from their families, Erastus Snow stated, "I called my family together and dedicated them unto the Lord, and commanded them to serve the Lord with all their hearts, and cultivate peace and love, and hearken to the whisperings of the Holy Spirit and pray much. . . . I then laid my hands upon my children and blessed them beginning with the youngest . . . blessing each according to the fulness of my heart in the power of the Holy Ghost. I then administered to my wife Artimesia blessing her and rebuking her weakness, and giving her a charge toward her family." Snow, "Journey," (April 1948): 107–108.
16. This inauspicious beginning initiated the creation of a cross-country emigrant road now recognized by the U. S. federal government as a national trail, The "Mormon Pioneer National Historic Trail," a portion of which is covered by Interstate 80 in Nebraska. Detailed maps of the "Mormon Pioneer Trail" illustrating the route and the trail's important points are found in three volumes by Stanley Kimball: *Discovering Mormon Trails* (1979), *Historic Sites and Markers* (1988), and *Historic Resource Study* (1991). Important maps of the Oregon and California trails, which merge with the Mormon Trail in Wyoming, are found in two volumes by Gregory Franzwa: *Maps of the Oregon Trail* (1982), and *Maps of the California Trail* (1999).

    Three excellent, up-to-date maps of the Oregon, California, and Mormon trails, published jointly by three agencies of U. S. federal government—the National Park Service, the Bureau of Land Management, and the Forest Service—are currently available from the agencies and at visitor's centers, government and private, associated with the trails.
17. As the various fragments of the pioneer camp had not yet coalesced, Thomas Bullock's first night on the trail was "on the prairie, without food or water." Bullock, *Camp of the Saints*, 117.

Thursday [8 April 1847] Tarried in camp. President [Brigham] Young went up to where some of the Brethren are prepareing to farm some 4 or 5 miles above here. Br [Albert] Rockwood <&> several others went back to Town to do some business. towards evening Br Brigham returned & news arrived that Parley P. Pratt had returned from England & John Taylor was hourly expected. in consequence of this the President returned home as they probably [will] hold a council before we leave.[18]

Friday 9th [April 1847] Still remained encamped having received some addition to our numbers, now over 30 waggons.[19] The weather is pleasant, white frost at night. the grass [is] Just beginning to start up. 1/2 past two oclock the "Twelve" all returned except Parley [Pratt and John Taylor] from Town & wee all moved on.[20] Heber [Kimball]s Division also came up and now <wee> numbered 64 waggons & carriages.[21] wee traveled about 8 miles & camped in the Prarie at a fine Spring of water.[22]

Satturday 10th [April 1847] Moved on about 7 oclck, a verry cold North wind blowing, but softened towards evening & became verry pleasant when we hove in sight of the Elk Horn river & the valley of the Great Platte ~~spread~~ affording a full view of the river stretched away for many miles to the west like a line of Silver glistening in the setting Sun through the scattered Timber upon its banks.[23] <Total 18 m[iles]> about half an hour before the Sun set four waggons dcended the Bluff & came onto the banks of the [Elk]Horn where

18. Learning of Parley Pratt's and John Taylor's return, Brigham Young with the Twelve returned to Winter Quarters. He stated that they "held a council, when Elder Pratt made a report of his mission." Young, *Manuscript History, 1846–1847*, 547.

    Young waited for the two Apostles' arrival for some time. Besides this disappointment, Young scolded his two associates for their determination to remain in Winter Quarters to take care of their families instead of joining the vanguard. Pratt and Taylor followed the vanguard two months later when the second contingent of Mormon emigrants departed for the Great Basin. Bennett, *We'll Find the Place*, 85–86.

19. While waiting for those who had returned to Winter Quarters, the "brethren danced one cotillion to wile away the time." Bullock, *Camp of the Saints*, 118.

20. The call to "hitch up & be ready" by Orson Pratt aroused "cheerfulness into every man." Bullock, *Camp of the Saints*, 118.

21. The size of the vanguard fluctuated until 18 April when Ellis Eames left the group. As of 11 April the company included seventy-two wagons and 135 men. Smith (Carrington), History, 11 April 1847.

22. Mundane tasks were required of everyone from the outset. At this camp, Brigham Young, Heber Kimball, and Willard Richards "went to cutting grass for their cattle with knives & afterwards inspected teams to see that all was right." Bullock, *Camp of the Saints*, 118.

23. Six months later in the first week of October, in proximity to the Elkhorn River, Hosea Stout, anticipating the arrival of the vanguard on their return to Winter Quarters, wrote that upon climbing "to the Bluffs" he "took a good view of the Horn & platte bottoms or plains all then in full bloom which lay before us in a beautifull leavel as far as we could see with good spy glasses. It was altogether the best and most splendid view I ever had of a praire country." Stout, *On the Mormon Frontier*, 1:278.

were some dozen other waggons. here wee camped. the rest of the <company> stoped back about 4 miles.[24] <20 miles travld.>

Sunday 11th [April 1847] after breakfast wee commenced crossing ove[r] on a raft made of dry cottonwood Loggs on <which> the Brethren had crossed 23 waggons. before this morning by 10 oclock wee had 16 over when the other part of the Camp came up. by 4 oclock P.M. wee had got them all over & formed our camp half a mile below on the Bank.[25] This Stream [the Elkhorn River] is about one hundred and fifty feet wide. Just one week ago the first Pioneers camped on the opposite bank, Stephen H. Goddard & Tarlton Lewis. The weather now has become warm. grass grows fast. our Horses are turned out to graze & are doing verry well. This camp is ascertained by Br Orson Pratt to be 2[0] miles South of West of Winter Quarters. our last days travel 20 miles.

Monday 12th [April 1847] The "Twelve" & some others return to Winter Quarters.[26] I went with them to bring up my cow & rifle Gun.[27] went across

---

24. Howard Egan said that the group with which he journeyed camped six miles from the Elkhorn River. Egan, *Pioneering*, 21.
25. Thomas Bullock stated for this day that "All the teams belonging to the company were crossed by 20 minutes to 10, on a Raft, when President B. Young, H. C. Kimball, and Bishop Whitney drove up, & immediately afterwards some of the Wagons of the second part of the Pioneer Camp came in sight, when they were continued to be crossed over, and at 20 minutes to 4 the 72nd Wagon was rafted over, thus making 69 Pioneer Wagons, 3 return Wagons (72), 3 return men, 136 Pioneers, 2 Women & 2 children." Bullock, *Camp of the Saints*, 119.
26. Brigham Young reported that upon yet another return to Winter Quarters, a council was held where Parley Pratt "reported that he had brought some means" from England, which Young received for the benefit of the Saints. At this council Young also appointed Thomas Bullock to be the official clerk of the camp, to "keep a journal of the Pioneer journey." (See Bullock, *Camp of the Saints*.) The following day on 13 April leaders met again where John Taylor reported his mission to England and the condition of the Saints there to the council. At this gathering Pratt also "exhibited two Sextants, two Barometers, two artificial horizons, one circle of reflection, several thermometers and a Telescope which he had brought from England." Pratt's brother Orson utilized some of this equipment to define their westward trek en route. Young returned with his comrades to the camp of the vanguard on 14 April. Young, *Manuscript History, 1846–1847*, 548.

    The return to Winter Quarters took a toll on church leaders. The evening of their return on 12 April, George Smith wrote: "I went to bed feeling much tired and bruised by riding horseback 35 miles on a rough going nag." Smith (Carrington), History, 12 April 1847.
27. Charles Harper, for 12 April, wrote: "Monday morning the 12th, the Twelve all left to go back in Winter Quarters. . . . N. Jacobs returned with the Twelve to Winter Quarters." Harper, *Diary*, 15. Concerning those who did not return to Winter Quarters, Howard Egan wrote that "the rest of us [went] on, by counsel, in order to cross an extensive bottom of twelve miles before the water should rise and the roads get muddy. Accordingly we went on and encamped on the banks of the Platte river. . . . Here we intend to remain until the Twelve Apostles return." Egan, *Pioneering*, 22.

in about 4 hours some thing like 18 miles. I found Br Joel Ricks had Started my family over the River but my goods and cow was this being hindered from crossing by the Wind.[28] so it all hapened right. I did not get a chance to see enny of my family but Lucian [Jacob] & Elsie [Jacob] Snyder.

Tuesday 13th [April 1847] got ready & started back with A[ppleton] Harmon in one of Heber's [Kimball] waggons. Campd 4 miles from Town [Winter Quarters]. Rowzel [Roswell] Stephens [Stevens] & A[ddition] Everett were <with us>.

Wednesday, 14th [April 1847][29] Early in the morning heard some Indians whooping & a gun fired. soon four of them came to us & were verry Saucy because wee would not give them our provisions.[30] one of them offered to shoot one of our cows [31] but they finaly went away by our giving them two ears of corn apiece.[32] Started on in the course of the day fell in company & camped with Bre[thren] Brigham [Young], [Ezra] Benson, & [Willard] Richards, & 7 or 8 others 5 miles from the ferry on the [Elk]Horn.

Thursday, 15th [April 1847] Moved down crossed the Horn & went up-to the camp 12 miles above on the bank of the Platte. arrived about the midle of the

---

28. It is likely that Joel Ricks planned to relocate Jacob's family in proximity to his on the Nishnabotna's west branch.

29. Several diarists stated that it rained during the morning as the camp prepared for their journey. Egan, *Pioneering*, 23; Bullock, *Camp of the Saints*, 120.

30. Fear of attack and depredation from Native Americans was among the vanguard's gravest concerns. Two months later on 19 June, soon after the second Mormon emigrating companies crossed the Elkhorn River, Jacob Weatherby, a teamster who had already embarked on the westward journey, was returning with one man and two women to Winter Quarters with mail when he was attacked by three Indians. He "was shot by one of the Indians, thro' the body, while endeavoring to prevent them robbing his wagon." He died the following day. Sessions, *Mormon Midwife*, 85; Snow, *Personal Writings*, 180; Historian's Office, Pioneers of 1847, Church Emigration, 1831–1849.

31. Addison Everett, with whom Jacob traveled, noted the incident though he dated it as 13 April. He wrote that "Early in the morning we ware visited by 4 Omah haw indians who demanded food. not receiving as much as they wished they drawed thare Bows charged with steel pointed arrows at Brother N Jacobs cow but being spoken to sharply they desisted[?]. we started on and traveled until 8 1/2 OC[lock] P.M." Everett, Diary, 13 April 1847.

32. Thomas Bullock wrote that "Four Omaha Indians came rushing down upon us, waiving their standards covered with Turkies Feathers, hallowing and yelling like Savages, which frightened my cattle [so much] that they broke away from the tongue & ran as if they were mad two or three miles in the direction the [*sic*] of Winter Quarters. . . . We had to allay their excitement by giving them our bread. They were not satisfied with that, but demanded more to take with them. After that was given them, one had the boldness to come to my Wagon & attempt to take the front of my Wagon Cover to make him a head dress, but I repelled him & he went away in anger. We then hitched up & started on our journey." Bullock, *Camp of the Saints*, 120–121.

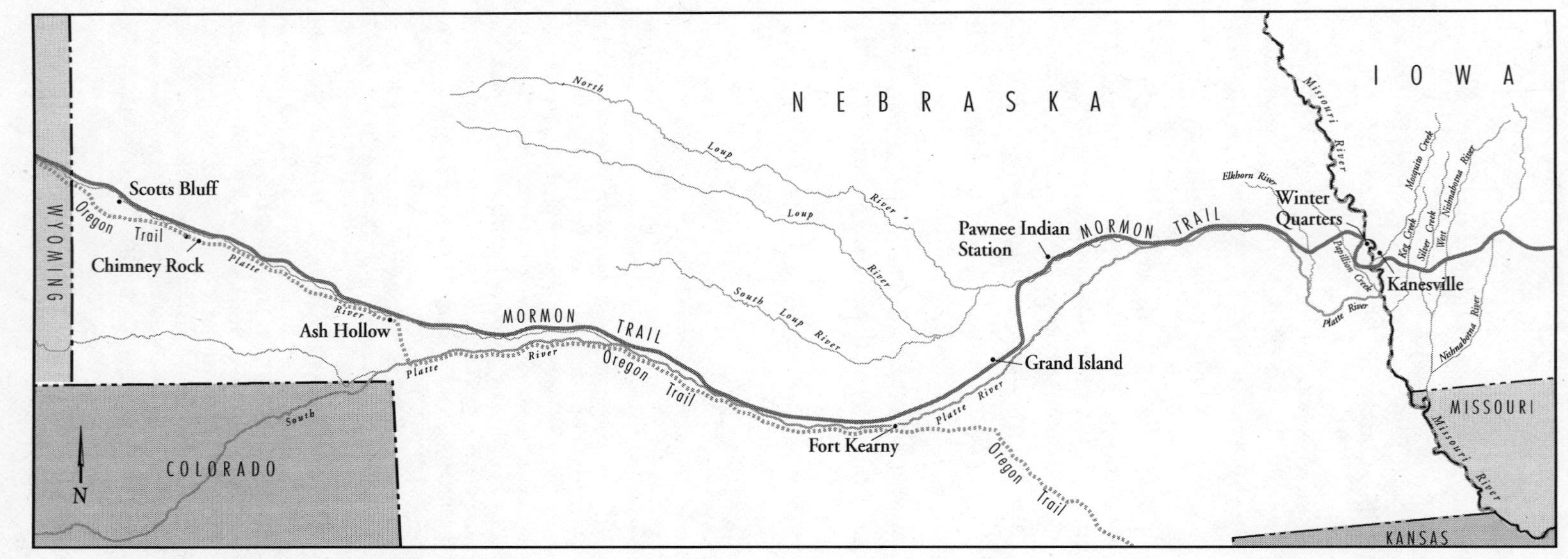

Mormon Trail across Nebraska. Map by Tom Child.

afternoon.[33] some of the Brethren were engaged setting their Waggon Tires. Total 50 m[iles].

In the evening we were called together by the sound of the Bugle when President [Brigham] Young delivered a short lecture upon the necesity of being vigalent holy & righteous before God, that <wee may> be successful in our present mission watching & Praying continualy.[34] he then appointed tomorrow morning at 8 oclock to meet & organze the camp for Journeying, stating that when organized the camp would <be> summoned to rise in the morning by the Sound of the Bugle, also to attend Prayers, & also for the camp to go ahead.[35]

---

33. William Clayton said, after arriving with the others, that "This camp is about twelve miles from the Elk Horn and about 47 from Winter Quarters." Clayton, *Journal*, 74.
34. The vanguard was Brigham Young's. If there had to be a singular character identified as imperative to the pioneer expedition, that character would have to be Young. That is how history has honored him. But just what was his role during the journey? Certainly, in preparation for the final lap to the West, he was the mastermind of the remarkable endeavor to escape Nauvoo, the enervating trudge across Iowa (the most difficult feature of the entire western journey for the Saints), and the city-builder who temporarily headquartered several thousand of the bedraggled Saints on the Missouri River. However, based upon the contemporary evidence—the diary accounts of the journey—he was not a micro-managing autocrat; he was not the lone decision maker for important matters; he was not the muscle which moved the expedition. His role, once the caravan embarked, proved, mostly, to be manager and facilitator. Young often found himself in the background, almost, depending on the vanguard's military organization to function. The substantial company nearly ran itself. He appeared, of course, when he was needed, as he was from time to time. But to characterize Brigham Young's influence upon the trek by what happened on 28–29 May 1847 when, at Scotts Bluff he excoriated the company for their idleness, card playing, and practical jokes, imposing his will upon the company which caused some to quake in his looming shadow, is to distort his impact upon the vanguard. When, for example, Young became ill for the last two weeks of the venture, there was hardly a pause in the voyage's momentum. The vanguard's other leaders and the pioneers themselves quickly formed the requisite adjustments to traveling arrangements, divided the company into two groups, and engineered the vanguard to its destination. When Young entered the Salt Lake Valley on 24 July 1847, two days after the advance groups did the same, streams had already been dammed, crops planted, and exploring parties were already traversing their new homeland.
35. Brigham Young's "short lecture" that evening laid out for the company's participants the nature of their westward journey, a highly disciplined venture cued by the bugle. The men were told that the expedition was to be organized and regulated. The bugle would "blow when he wanted them together . . . immediately." They were to "stop for nothing." At night, he said, the "bugle would blow when it was bed time [and] the bugle would blow <in the morning> when it was time to get up." Private and collective prayers to "heavenly Farther" were central to their plan and were to be a daily function of the camp. And, after guards were selected for the night, "the bugle blowed" and they "all went to bed except the guards." Because of the confrontation the previous day, Young said that he also "informed the brethren that I had intimations that the Pawnee Indians were advised to rob us." Atwood, Journal, 15 April 1847; Young, *Manuscript History, 1846–1847*, 548–549.

Friday 16th [April 1847] called together by the sound of the Bugle at 8 oclock when upon numbering there was found to be onehundred & forty three men 3 women & two children. wee have also 73 waggons.[36] Br George A Smith Spoke upon the necesity of strictness of Dicipline in order to [secure] our own preservation. He was followed by H[eber]. C. Kimbal who said he felt like saying a few words. he was going along & wanted if there was anny along <who> did not like to obey the necessary rules of the camp without murmuring to turn back now for he had been on a similar mission (though not for the purpose of seeking a Location) in company with Joseph Smith when some murmured against him, their leader & 18 of them died with the plague in two days.[37] After being numbered & formed in two lines in a circle around the waggon carrying the Leather Boat[38] all kneeled down when Br Brigham [Young] addressed the Lord by Prayer & dedicated the mission and all wee have to the Lord God of Israel.[39] then those Brethren Spoke I have mentioned

---

36. William Clayton's account names the participants, states the number of wagons at 72, and also enumerates their livestock: "93 horses, 52 mules, 66 oxen, 19 cows, and 17 dogs, and chickens." Clayton, *Journal*, 76.

    Howard Egan numbered only 89 horses, but also listed in his account their provisions, which are significant: "Flour 1228 lbs., meat 865 lbs., sea biscuit 125 lbs., beans 296 lbs., bacon 241 lbs., corn for teams 2869 lbs., buckwheat 300 lbs., dried beef 25 lbs., groceries 290 3/4 lbs., sole leather 15 lbs., oats 10 bus., rape [a thick oil extracted from the rapeweed used as a lubricant] 40 lbs., seeds 71 lbs., cross-cut saw 1, axes 6, scythe 1, hoes 3, logs chains 5, spade 1, crowbar 1, tent 1, keg of powder 25 lbs., lead 20 lbs., codfish 40 lbs., garden seeds 50 lbs., plows 2, bran 3 1/2 bus., 1 side of harness leather, whip saw 1, iron 16 lbs., nails 16 lbs., 1 sack of salt 200 lbs., saddles 2, tool chest worth $75, 6 pair of double harness worth about $200, total amount of breadstuff 2507 lbs. at $55.40." The total value of the materials was placed at $1592.87 1/2. Egan, *Pioneering*, 24.
37. This refers to the journey of Zion's Camp from Kirtland, Ohio, to Jackson County, Missouri, in May-June 1834. The ostensible purpose of the paramilitary march composed of 205 or so personnel in two divisions was the hope of recovering property taken by locals from the Saints the previous year in Missouri. Coincident to complaints by camp participants the group was afflicted with cholera. While chroniclers number those who died from the cholera at between thirteen and eighteen, historian of the venture, James L. Bradley, states that 30 percent of the camp had cholera with fourteen dying. Bradley, *Zion's Camp, 1834*, 207. A memorial marker to those who died in the Mound Grove Cemetery in Independence, Missouri, identifies fifteen who died, including two women.
38. The leather boat, known as the "revenue cutter," refers to the small craft that was used to ferry equipment across rivers, streams, and creeks along the way. Erastus Snow stated that Brigham Young "secured and brought with him Father Eldredge's leather skiff for the use of the fishermen. It was placed upon the running gears of a light wagon in the stead of a box and carried the fishing apparatus, and was drawn by two horses." Snow, "Journey," (April 1948): 110–111.
39. Brigham Young's providential view of the Saints' exile from Illinois, at a time when the universal feeling among Mormons that their rights had been violated in their expulsion from Illinois, was expressed when he stated in June 1846, according to Daniel Davis, "that he could see the Hand of the Lord in our Being Drove out of Nauvoo." Still, as noted by Addison Everett, Young's petition to God at this time was delivered in "the Most rational and fervent manner I ever heard." Davis, Diary, 21 June 1846; Everett, Diary, 16 April 1847.

when Bishop N[ewel] K. Whitney addressed us stating that he was going back to tarry awhile & would do all he could to help off the families of those who were going ahead in this expedition. his heart was full & he did [not] know how to express his feelings. felt like saying that wee should be prospered & he would bless us in the name of the Lord God of Israel—and Br Brigham said he felt like saying Amen. President Young now proceeded to organise the camp & caled upon the Brethren to nominate thei[r] officers. he move[d] that wee organize into companys for Journeying and Military defence of hundreds fifties & tens.[40] Stephen Markum was elected capt of hundred, also A[lbert] P. Rockwood is capts of fifty, Tarlton Lewis, Stephen H Godard, John Pack, & Howard Egan.[41] Stepen Markum was then elected capt of the Guard and directed to draw out fifty men for a standing guard which was divided into cos of ten and a capt to each ten. I was chosen ~~capt~~ one of the Guard and capt of the third ten.[42] wee moved on about three miles & camped for the night.[43] a tremendous cold North wind sprung up which caused it to freeze severely so that the ground was frozen next morning.[44]

Satturday 17th [April 1847] About 9 oclock wee moved on and Bishops [Newel] Whitney & [Joseph] Nobles[45] with some others returned to Winter Quarters. Porter Rockwell, Jack Redden, & Br [Jesse] Little Just from Philadelphia

---

40. The military connotation was not just analogy. The company being "organized in a military capacity" evoked the image of discipline, purpose, and order that Brigham Young intended for the vanguard's venture into the West. Young, *Manuscript History, 1846–1847*, 549.
41. The language of Jacob's account somewhat distorts the organization. Stephen Markham and Albert Rockwood were captains of hundreds, "Tarlton Lewis, James Case, Addison Everett, John Pack and Shadrach Roundy were elected Captains of Fifties." Young, *Manuscript History, 1846–1847*, 549. See completed structure on following page.
42. This designation of Jacob as captain of the third ten of the guard should not be confused with his appointment the following day as captain of the Mormon vanguard's twelfth ten, of a total of fourteen tens. (See Jacob's entry for 17 April 1847.) Previous to and outside this latter organization, "Colonel [Stephen] Markham was appointed captain of a standing guard and he picked out 48 men, 12 at a time, to stand one-half of the night." Smith (Carrington), History, 16 April 1847.
43. Thomas Bullock stated the camp traveled "about 4 *miles* and encamped again at 10 minutes to 4 near a Cotton Wood Grove where there was a pretty good sprinkling of green grass, which the cattle ate with avidity. Also some rushes that were in the timber, on the river bank & Island." Bullock, *Camp of the Saints*, 123.

    As the Mormon vanguard inaugurated the last leg of their exilic journey from Illinois, they joined with many of their adventurous countrymen with an eye on the western horizon. While roughly 2,200 Mormons crossed the plains in 1847, later in the year 4,000 American emigrants pushed westward to Oregon with another 450 en route to California. Unruh, *Plains Across*, 119.
44. Despite the cold weather, from which William Clayton "took a very bad cold," he described "The country in the neighborhood of the Elk Horn [as] one of the most beautiful I ever saw." Clayton, *Journal*, 78.
45. This is likely Joseph Noble.

returned to Winter Quarters yesterday to bring up some presents &c sent by col. [Thomas] Kane of Philadelphia to the Twelve. wee traveled about 7 miles and camped alongside a fine grove of cottonwood, wind still cold.[46] in the evening wee were called together by the sound of the Bugle when the President [Brigham Young] directed the capts to arrange their several company's.[47] when they were formed in a colum of tens en masse the President now proposed the question whether <the> camp in a military point of view should consist of one or two Regiments. It <was> decided that wee be one Regiment & Stephen Markum was elected coln. John Pack first Major & Shadrac Roundy second major.[48] wee have 14 Tens commanded by Wilford Woodruff captn of first ten, Ezra T. Benson 2d, Phineas H. Young 3d, Luke Johnson 4th, Stephen H. Godard 5th, James Case 6th, Seth Taft 7th, Charles Shumway 8th, Howard Egan 9th, Appleton Harmon 10th, John S. Higby 11th, Norton Jacob 12, John Brown 13th, and Joseph Matthews Capt. of the 14th Ten.[49] The following is a List of my Ten. Charles A. Harper, George Woodward, George Mills, Andrew S. Gibbons, Lewis Barney, Stephen Markum, John W. Norton, Joseph Hancock.

A List of the third Ten in the Guard: Norton Jacob Capt., Addison Everett, W[illia]m. Wadsworth [Wordsworth], John W. Norton, Francis M. Pomeroy, Lyman Curtis, Horace M. Frink, <Erastus Snow>, Levi N. Kendall, excused Hance [Hans] C. Hanson [Hansen], W[illia]m. O. A. Smoot.

Captains of Ten in the Guard Tarlton Lewis 1st, W[illia]m. Emp[e]y 2d, Norton Jacob 3rd, Barnaby [Barnabas] Adams 4th, Edson Whipple 5th

It was moved & carryed that B[righam]. Young be General & Commander in Chief of the expedition & A[lbert]. P. Rockwood and H[eber]. C. Kimbal be appointed his aides.

Sunday 18th [April 1847] wee tarryed in camp.[50] my Ten was on Guard from

46. The "morning was cold and the wind northwest," stated Howard Egan, the temperature standing at 26°at 8 A.M., according to George Smith (Carrington). Further, he said, "the wind [was] blowing very strong, which made it very disagreeable, as it was a sandy road." Egan, *Pioneering*, 25; Smith (Carrington), History, 17 April 1847.
47. Among other items of instruction, Brigham Young also counseled that "every man who walked to carry a loaded gun, and every teamster to have his where he could easily lay his hands on it." The following day he reiterated the command: "Every man who does not drive a team to walk by the side of his wagon with his gun loaded and and [caps] handy." Smith (Carrington), History, 17–18 April 1847.
48. "President Young," according to Howard Egan, "said it was necessary to have a military organization before we left this place." Besides Stephen Markham, John Pack, and Shadrach Roundy, Egan stated that "Thomas Tanner" was also "to take command of the camp [cannon]." Egan, *Pioneering*, 25.
49. The entire vanguard is listed by tens in Appendix 2 in this volume.
50. Of their Sabbath pause, Howard Egan stated, "Today, being the day set apart by the Almighty God for His people to rest, we do not intend to travel." He also complained that during the day the "wind continued to blow so hard, and it was so cold, it was thought wisdom not to call the brethren together to have meeting." Egan, *Pioneering*, 25–26.

12 till 5 oclock <a.m.> last night. a Trader's waggon laden with Furs & Peltry came down from the Pawnees and camped about 30 rods below us. they were two days from Pawnee.[51] today there was 7 Traders waggons arived from above & stoped 2 or 3 hours where the other camped.[52] This evening the Presidt [Brigham Young] called together the captains of the camp when it was agreed that wee rise by the sound of the Bugle and attend <Prayer> at 5 A. M.. and move forward at 7 a.m. the extra men march with guns in hand by the side of their waggons and the Teamsters with theirs where they can lay their hand upon it. also that the Camp all retire for Prayer & rest by the Sound of the Bugle at 1/2 past 8 p.m.[53] John [Thomas] Tanner was appointed by Gen ~~M~~ Young to select a squad and take command of the Cannon which of course relieved me. our course from the [Elk]Horn has been about N. West. afternoon became more warm. Total 60 m[iles].

Monday 19th [April 1847] Bugle sounded at 5 & at 7 a.m. when wee pursued our Journey having a very pleasant morning.[54] traveled 15 miles & halted to

---

51. A description of the Pawnee Indians, at this time, including their interaction with the Saints, is found in Hyde, *Pawnee Indians*, 224–230.
52. The merchandise, owned by Peter Sarpy who had a trading post just downriver from Winter Quarters on the Missouri River, was identified as "three wagons loaded with furs" accompanied by "four or five pack mules." Egan, *Pioneering*, 25; Snow, "Journey," (April 1948): 110.
53. Brigham Young's account for the day states, "Rules were drawn up for the government of the Camp." Howard Egan included the particulars of these "LAWS OR RULES" levied on the camp:

> 1.- After this date the horn or bugel shall be blown every morning at 5 a.m., when every man is expected to arise and pray: then attend to his team, get breakfast and have everything finished so that the camp may start by 7 o'clock.
> 2.- Each extra man is to travel on the off side of the team with his gun on his shoulder, loaded, and each driver have his gun so placed that he can lay hold of it at a moment's warning. Every man must have a piece of leather over the nipple of his gun, or if it is a flintlock, in the pan, having caps and powder-flask ready.
> 3.- The brethren will halt for an hour about noon, and they must have their dinner ready cooked so as not to detain the camp for cooking.
> 4.- When the camp halts for the night, wagons are to be drawn in a circle, and the horses to be all secured inside the circle when necessary.
> 5.- The horn will blow at 8:30 p.m., when every man must return to his wagon and pray, except the night guard, and be in bed by 9 o'clock, at which time all fires must be put out.
> 6.- The camp is to travel in close order, and no man to leave the camp twenty rods without orders, from the Captain.
> 7.- Every man is to put as much interest in taking care of his brother's cattle, in preserving them, as he would his own, and no man will be indulged in idleness.
> 8.- Every man is to have his gun and pistol in perfect order.
> 9.- Let all start and keep together, and let the cannon ["old sow"] bring up the rear, and the company guard to attend it, traveling along with the gun, and see that nothing is left behind at each stopping place." Young, *Manuscript History, 1846–1847*, 550; Egan, *Pioneering*, 23–24.

54. The camp's method of travel this day was "in double file." Clayton, *Journal*, 81.

feed on the bank of the River <Platte> at 1/2 past one oclock.[55] wee formed in a circle with the forward ends of our waggons outward.[56] here Porter Rockwell, [Jackson] Reding [Redden], [Jesse] Little & <(another young)> <Thomas Brown>[57] man overtook us having left Winter Quarters yesterday morning.[58] wee are now at the North bend of the Platte Latitude 41° 27' according <to> an observation made today at 12 oclock A.M. [noon] by Br Orson Pratt. The Latitude of Winter quarters is by his observation 41° 19'.[59] Our cours[e] today is West. from where wee halted wee traveled 8 miles & camped in <a> semicircle with each end resting upon the bank of the River in an open Praree. The bottoms are verry broad 10 or 12 miles, destitute of Timber. yesterday Br [Ellis] Eames went back sick.[60]

Tuesday 20th [April 1847] 7 Waggon went forward early with Capt [John] Higby to a Lake 15 miles to fish. The Camp moved on 10 miles and halted for dinner. here P[orter] Rockwell & T[homas] Brown had a fine chase after three deer but did not get them.[61] wee moved on to where the fishermen were who had caut above two hundred fine fish.[62] here wee camped in a semicircle

55. En route they passed several small lakes where several of the camp shot ducks. Clayton, *Journal*, 81.
56. The configuration of the wagons was "in order to have our horses and cattle in the center to secure them from the Indians, with the guard placed outside of the wagons." Egan, *Pioneering*, 26.
57. Thomas Brown's inclusion with the pioneer vanguard provokes questions that extant evidence does not answer. Just two months earlier Brigham Young received a report from Hosea Stout, a police official in Winter Quarters, that Brown had threatened members of the governing Twelve Apostles, not to mention that he was wanted for murder by an Iowa sheriff. Brown became particularly problematic to Jacob on his return to Winter Quarters later in the year.
58. Jesse Little, a brother-in-law of Brigham Young, had just returned from church work on the east coast and, hardly having time to light, joined the pioneers. The men from Winter Quarters brought mail which was distributed through the camp.
59. Once familiar with the scientific instruments provided by John Taylor and his brother Parley, the ever confident Orson Pratt, "was convinced that his own readings were more accurate than [John] Fremont's," [whose published report gave readings] although his (Pratt's) "own efforts at determining longitude" were "very rough." England, *Life and Thought of Orson Pratt*, 122.
60. Some, like Howard Egan, were uncharitable in Ellis Eames's departure: "Ellis Ames returned from this place in consequence of sickness, so he said, but I think he is weak in the faith." Egan, *Pioneering*, 25.
61. William Clayton said Porter Rockwell and Thomas Brown chased the deer "four or five miles, but did not succeed in taking any of them." Clayton, *Journal*, 84.
62. The "fishermen" found a small lake within a mile or two of the road and, with the "revenue cutter" and seine (net), had a lively day of fishing. William Clayton identified three of the several fishermen who provided a welcome feast of the 200 fish for the overlanders as John Higbee, Luke Johnson, and Stephen Markham. "The fish were distributed around the camp according to the number of persons in each wagon," Clayton explained, "generally two to a wagon, and the brethren enjoyed a good supper on fish." Clayton, *Journal*, 84–85.

the ends resting on a slough opposite a wooded Island.[63]

Wednesday 21st [April 1847] Started at the usual time. traveled 12 miles over the best tract of high bottom land that wee have seen with a pretty good <supply> of Cottonwood timber along the river.[64] wee halted on the bank of the Loup Fork of the Platte.[65] here is the main boddy of the Pawnee Indians.[66] large numbers of them flocked around us & stole a pair of bridles & <a> copper wash pan. The President gave their chief some tobacco & other small presents with which they were much dissatisfied[67] & we proceeded on 8 miles & camped on the bank of the Loup in a strong position & in consequence of <the> hostile feeling of the Indians the President called out a guard of fifty men.[68] I was out on the Picquet [picket] from 12 till 5 oclk A.M. and notwithstanding our fears the night passed off quietly.[69] this afternoon wee

---

63. The arrangement of the wagons was a defensive measure, which also included placing the "oxen and cattle inside of the circle." Egan, *Pioneering*, 27.

64. Cottonwood trees proved useful to emigrants and their animals. The previous day cottonwoods were "cut down for the horses to browse on, which they eat readily." Young, *Manuscript History, 1846–1847*, 550.

65. Rather than following the Platte as its course bent southwesterly near present-day Columbus, Nebraska, which would have required a river crossing at the Loup Fork River, the vanguard continued westward by following the Loup Fork on its north bank for approximately fifty miles before breaking due south for nearly twenty miles to reconnect with the Platte River.

66. The Mormons' initial encounter with the Pawnee, "who seemed very friendly," soon deteriorated. Smith (Carrington), History, 21 April 1847.

67. The Pawnee delegation, composed of "Two of the chiefs and a number of the Indians," with the chief riding "a mule [and] the rest . . . on foot," arrived in camp and, at the outset, "appeared very friendly" but "wanted presents." Among the Native Americans there was "a young Indian . . . that could talk some English." After providing the primary chief, whom Horace Whitney identified as "Sisketuk," with "powder and lead, tobacco and salt, flour and other trinkets," Brigham Young "proposed to shake hands and part in friendship," but the chief, with anger, refused. Through his interpreter the chief said the whites' offering was "heap . . . too little." He complained that the whites were not only "rich," but that they "would kill and drive away their buffalo," and that the whites "should go back," which was emphasized more than once. Egan, *Pioneering*, 27; Atwood, Journal, 21 April 1847; Whitney, Diary, 21 April 1847; Snow, "Journey," (April 1847): 111.

68. William Clayton also wrote that Brigham Young "called for volunteers to stand guard and about 100 volunteered amongst whom were all the twelve except Dr. [Willard] Richards. This guard was divided into two companies of fifty each, one company to stand the first half the night, and the remainder the last half." Clayton, *Journal*, 87.

69. "Out of the companies," William Clayton wrote, "a party were stationed as a picket guard some distance from the camp, the balance stood near the camp." To increase their ability to discern the subtle Indians, "Mules were stationed with the picket guard to help them notice the approach of Indians." Those so fortunate to sleep did so "with their clothes on" to respond immediately in case of attack. Clayton, *Journal*, 87–88; Young, *Manuscript History, 1846–1847*, 550; Smith (Carrington), History, 21 April 1847.

    Lewis Barney, one of Jacob's ten, wrote regarding the rest of the camp: "we lay by our wagons and teams all night with our guns in our arms Expecting an attack from the Indians." Barney, Autobiography and diary, 33.

had quite a refreshing shower of rain which caused the Buffalo grass to cover the Prarie with a smiling green.[70] The Squaws at the vilage wee passed were busily engaged in digging roots while their Lords were walking about like Kentucky Negro drivers perfectly listless and Idle.[71] wee camped at the mouth of Looking Glass Creek.[72]

Thursday 22 [April 1847] Moved on in a cool morning 2 miles. crossed the Looking Glass Creek, which showed plainly that wee had left the muddy Sloughs & creeks of Missourie for the bottom was hard white sand & the water clear as crystal.[73] halted after going 10 miles for dinner at the ford of Beaver Creek. This <is> an excelent country of rich Land and heavy groves of Timber on the River. Latitude of this crossing <of Beaver creek a good mill Stream> 41° 25' 13". Total 128 m[iles].

This is a most delightful country of undulating Prairie & Gentle slopes crowned with the richest kind of grass, that serves to feed those immense herds of Buffalo that graze oupon these western plains, though by the by wee have not seen anny yet. This country is so beautifuly addapted to cultivation that there is driven from the mind all idea of its being a wild waste in the wilderness![74] "The fields in the wood;" and one is continualy looking out for the Habitations of man. weel [well] towards evening wee sure<ly> found one, a deserted Missionary station that [was] established about eight years ago for the benefit of the Pawnee Indians[75] but the continued wars between that Tribe

70. "The buffalo grass," wrote Clayton, "is very short and curly like the hair on a buffalo robe." Clayton, *Journal*, 88.

71. While this passage could be read more than one way, it likely reflects general attitudes among the Mormons at the time toward African-Americans or their southern masters, which, of course, mirrored the views of other northern white Americans. Three black men were among the vanguard: Green Flake, Oscar Crosby, and Hark Lay. There is no evidence of complaint from extant diaries regarding their service or contribution to the journey. See Carter, "The Negro Pioneer," 8:500–504; "1847 Pioneers," *Deseret News, 1997–98 Church Almanac*, 129, 133–134, 141–142; Coleman, "Blacks in Utah History," 118.

72. "Father [Heber] Kimball said to call it Looking Glass creek, because it was very clear," wrote Howard Egan. Egan, *Pioneering*, 28.

73. "When the Mormons crossed it, the well-timbered Looking Glass Creek was sixteen feet wide and two feet deep." Bullock, *Camp of the Saints*, 127n49.

74. Howard Egan described the area as "the prettiest location that I have seen this side of the Mississippi river." Egan, *Pioneering*, 28.

75. With the financial backing of the American Board of Commissioners for Foreign Missions, a collaboration of the Presbyterian and Congregational churches, Samuel Parker, with John Dunbar and Samuel Allis, inaugurated the Christianizing of the Pawnee Indians in 1834. It was a significant endeavor by the devoted missionaries which expanded to include about thirty whites. Continuing hostilities between the Pawnee and their nemesis, the Lakota Sioux, postponed a permanent mission until 1841 when a small community was established on Plumb Creek, a small tributary of the Loup River. For the five years the mission operated, the Lakota's regular raids and dissension between the white missionaries regarding which methodology could be best employed to interest the

& the Sioux finaly caused the Missionaries to flee down to Belview [Bellevue, Nebraska] <on the Missouri> last Summer.[76] So wee quietly took possession of the farm yard and found abundance of good hay & corn fodder.[77] no wonder that Indians have contended for this Spot for it is one of surpassing beauty. They have had several battles in this neighbourhood when the Missionary women & children had to secrete themselves in their cellar.[78] From where we halted to this place is about 7 miles.

Pawnee in Christianity (not one of the Pawnee converted), eventually broke the spirits of the missionaries. After a raid by the Lakota's in mid-June 1846 where the Pawnee village and mission were raided, sacked, and burned, the missionaries abandoned the mission on 18 June 1846. Jensen, "The Pawnee Mission, 1834–1846," 301–310; Potter, "A Note on the Samuel Allis Family," 1–4; Hartley, *My Best for the Kingdom*, 210. See John Dunbar's 30 June 1846 letter describing the events that drove him and his family away from the mission. "Letters Concerning the Presbyterian Mission," 683–686. See also Samuel Allis's view of the endeavor in Allis, "Forty Years Among the Indians," 151–157.

Located about 134 miles from Winter Quarters in present-day Nance County, Nebraska, twenty miles west of Columbus, Nebraska, the missionary station, near the junction of the Cedar and Loup rivers, had been, according to William Clayton, "deserted last fall" and that what remained had apparently been "left to rot." Clayton, *Journal*, 90–91. A detailed description of the Indian farm as the Mormons found it is recorded in Clayton, *Journal*, 95–101.

76. See Jacob's entry and the footnote concerning the Rev. Edward McKinney's missionary station for the Omaha and Oto Indians in 1846 at Bellevue, Nebraska, for 28 September 1846 in the previous chapter.

77. The Mormons already knew about the Pawnee missionary station. The previous August fourteen families, formerly attached to Bishop George Miller's company, had moved to the unoccupied complex to weather the winter season under the leadership of Jacob Gates. They lasted only until October 1846 before returning to the Saints' settlements on the Missouri. Upon returning from their late summer hunt, the Pawnees visited the missionary station where the Mormons arranged with the Pawnee to utilize the station's resources. Young, *Manuscript History, 1846–1847*, 290, 374; Hartley, *My Best for the Kingdom*, 216. See Samuel Allis's complaint below regarding the Mormon's occupation of the station that winter.

The missionary station, noted as "quite a large farm fenced [with] some very good buildings on it," was configured as "buildings . . . on three sides of a hollow square, with the south side picketed" and the "blacksmith shop [being] about 200 yards lower down." Addison Everett, on entering the premises, wrote that they "found a large stack of hay a[nd] plenty of corn and some 20 or 22 Bushels of corn Belonging to Br [Andrew] Shumway he having camped here last fall." Egan, *Pioneering*, 28; Smith (Carrington), History, 23 April 1847; Everett, Diary, 22 April 1847.

Lewis Barney, one of Jacob's ten, described "the building and cellars built by the natives" as: "Several Large rooms supposed to be Council rooms built in a round or Circular form Sufficient to accomodate Several hundred persons and aranged with Seats all round the inside of the structur. There were also Several large Cellars dug in the ground seven or eight feet deep, Some of them measureing from 15 to 20 feet across the Center with a hole on the top large enough to admit a man. this was the only entrance to these sulteraneous apartments arranged for the purpose of storing provisions." Barney, Autobiography and diary, 33.

78. James Case, a member of the Mormon vanguard who had worked at the missionary station, explained that at the time of attack the "Pawnees were all away at the time, but

Friday 23d [and 24th April 1847] We tarryed while a party went to examine the Ford across the Loup fork. meanwhile Capt. John [Thomas] Tanner who has been appointed Capt. of the Gun is engaged drilling his men. about noon the President [Brigham Young] returned with his party who had been to e[x]plore the Ford of the Loup Fork and reported it to be verry bad. Col. [Albert] Rockwood at the same time proclaimed the General orders of the day, First that Bishop [Tarlton] Lewis select a party to go ahead & prepare for building a raft also that the Teamsters hitch on [and] move forward carrying 2 or 3 rails each to cover the raft. President Young had proclaimed the evening before that no one should <carry> anny property away from here that did not belong to him. the Wood, water, hay, and fodder, use what they wanted, but nothing more.[79] he now told the Brethren that if they wanted anny of the Ploughs or Iron to purchase [them] of Father James Case[80] who had formerly been in the employ of the Missionaries at this place & they were indebted to him.[81] he therefore would sell some of their property to obtain his debt, and write to the Missionarys giving them an account of what he had done.[82]

---

about 20 children, which the missionaries secreted and soon after left, for fear the Sioux would find them and burn them out." Smith (Carrington), History, 23 April 1847.

A few years previous to this on 27 June 1843, in a devastating raid by the Lakota, the Pawnees lost nearly all of their horses, having one-half of their lodges burned, and sixty-seven of the tribe killed, including the village chief. Two years later the Ponca Indians attacked the village, this time assaulting the white missionaries there. It is little wonder the Pawnee and their Christian benefactors were frightened by rival tribes. Jensen, "The Pawnee Mission, 1834–1846," 307–308.

79. William Clayton and Howard Egan also noted Brigham Young's instructions to Clayton stating that Brigham told the camp that they could "use the fodder and hay for their teams, but forbade any man carrying anything away, even to the value of one cent." Clayton, *Journal*, 91; Egan, *Pioneering*, 28.

80. James Case had worked as a government farmer at the missionary station for seven years and had become a Mormon while working there. The previous year in 1846, leaving the missionary station, Case arrived at the Mormon camp on the Missouri on 27 July 1846. With him he had "a wagon load of goods in company with six other wagons of [George] Miller's, with missionary and government property, which had been removed from Pawnee Village through fear of the [Sioux] Indians." The displaced Protestant missionaries had "arranged for Bishop Miller's company to go to the station, salvage possessions, and haul them back to Bellevue [Nebraska]." Young, *Manuscript History, 1846–1847*, 286; Hartley, *My Best for the Kingdom*, 210.

81. William Clayton wrote that "[James] Case lived as government farmer and received $300.00 a year for it, but when Major Harvey learned at the last payday, which was last November, that father Case had joined the 'Mormons' he very politely dismissed him from the government service." Clayton, *Journal*, 90.

82. One of the Presbyterian missionaries, Samuel Allis on 8 February 1847, reported the negative effect upon the mission of the fourteen Mormon families under Jacob Gates who occupied the abandoned station from August to October 1846: "The govt. buildings at Pawnee are all burned, and the Mormons have Injured the Mission houses considerable." It is not known if his general perception of Latter-day Saints may have influenced his appraisal of the Mormons at the mission: "Notwithstanding their high pretensions, I consider them a poor deluded theivish, immoral set of beings, who will cause sitizens of

Bill of Iron & Ploughs received of James Case by the 12th Ten to carry upon shares—Norton Jacob Capt.} 76 lbs of Iron; Stephen Markum 104 lbs of Iron, one Plough & one Shire, four Waggon Boxes; George Mills 2 Ploughs & 37 lbs of Iron; Joseph Hancock one Breaking Plough & 62 lbs of Iron.[83]

About 4 oclock P.M. wee arrived on the bank of the river at the Ford Just below the old Pawnee Town, 5 miles.[84] The Brethren were about discouraged with regard to the rafting business, & some partly unloaded their Waggons & commenced fording. Professor [Orson] Pratt went in with his carriage first, got his horses swamped in the Quicks Sand, had to take them of[f] his carriage & with the assistance of 5 or 6 men got them out.[85] Three other waggons got [over] by doubling teams with a good deal of difficulty. The conclusion now was to go up a little above & ferry over the goods in the Leather Boat & cross

---

the Und states trouble wherever they go." "Letter Concerning the Presbyterian Mission," 739–740; Hyde, *Pawnee Indians*, 226.

83. "There is a large quantity of good bar iron," William Clayton wrote, "and a number of plows, which the brethren put into their wagons on the terms proposed by father Case." George Smith (Carrington) numbered the materials as "seventeen good plough irons, some iron for ploughs, three wagon wheels, etc., etc." Clayton, *Journal*, 92; Smith (Carrington), History, 22 April 1847.

84. "[B]eautifully situated on the north bank of the Loup [Fork River]," the Pawnee town near the missionary station "was the noted village of First Grand Band of the Second Division of the Grand Pawnee Nation" which had been inhabited, according to James Case, by "about six thousand inhabitants." Described as "hav[ing] been and are yet a terror to all the western tribes," despite being victimized by the Sioux, the Pawnees had a substantial presence in the area. According to one Mormon account, the "range of the Pawnee town just above our camp occupies some ten acres of ground, and were partially fortified by an embankment of earth and sod nearly finished." The account continued that "there were upwards of two hundred lodges built in a circular form averaging from twenty to sixty feet in diameter inside, and from 15 to 30 feet in height, with a covered entrance of some 5 to 10 feet all covered with earth. Interspersed promiscuously were the stables for the horses made of poles fastened in the ground upright and close together, and bound at the height of one head by poles lashed ~~together~~ around horizontally. Their cache holes for securing their corn and [blank] also dug promiscuously, the opening being from 18 inches to 2 feet, and lined with grass, matting or puncheon [a heavy, broad piece of roughly dressed timber with one side hewed flat]." Smith (Carrington), History, 23 April 1847.

Case, apparently, explained to his companions that a "Pawnee can have as many wives as he can buy," but "after a girl was once sold and became a widow, or was deserted, she then married, if at all, without price." He further described the burial practice of the Pawnees which was evidenced by a nearby burial ground: "Upon the slope and elevation are the graves of their braves, and noted men, who are placed in their graves in a sitting posture. The whole [is] then covered with poles and matting and a circular mound of earth and sod raised over it to the height of from four to six feet." Smith (Carrington), History, 23 April 1847.

85. Regarding Orson Pratt's crossing, Lewis Barney wrote, "He got half way over When the horses mired down. 8 or 10 men geathered hold of them and Soon draged them to Shore. the Stream was full of men ready to drag the teams out when they got Stuck. By the time orson Pratt got Safe on the opposite Bank there was 6 or 8 teams Plunging along through the Sand. By the time they got over there was ten or 15 more in the river." Barney, Autobiography and diary, 37–38.

the waggons empty. <Total 140 [miles]> accordingly wee proceeded up about 3/4 of a mile & camped immediately below the ruins of the Pawnee vilage on a high Bluff bank in the usual semicircular form. My Ten was on guard from 7 P.A. [P.M.] till midnight. A council of officers was called in the evening to consult upon the best method to adopt for crossing the river. it [is] some four hundred yards wide, shallow, full of bars, and one entire bed of Quick Sand constantly changiing its position by the force of the current.[86] It [was] finaly concluded to build two rafts in the morning out of the dry poles at the vilage & at the same time commence crossing the goods in the Boat, & Col. direct the crossing of the Teams.[87] he proceeded the next morning to set stakes in different places across the Stream so as to follow one track and thereby pack the sand & make it more firm.[88] President Young commenced crossing his loading in the Boat.[89] Br Heber [Kimball] proposed to his boys to double teans and take our loads in our waggons as wee could not all go over in the Boat today. so at it wee went & put on three and four teams to a waggon and took over all our effects long before the first division got theirs over with the aid of the Boat. I crossed my Ten in about 3 hours. by the time wee had half of us got over the road had become tolerably firm. At 4 oclock the whole camp had passed over without anny accident for which wee felt truly thankful to our heavenly Father.[90] wee now moved up the river & camped 4 miles. <Lat 41.20.31">

Sunday 25th [April 1847] Remained encamped on the south bank of the Loup Fork. last night a horse belonging to B[righam]. Young choked to death by his <halter>. At 4 oclock P.M. the camp was called together for Pu[b]lick worship.[91] after singing Prayer by H[eber]. C. Kimbal when the President Said there was liberty for anny one to speak ~~who chose~~ when Br Erastus Snow remarked that

86. The quicksand proved so treacherous that one man who, after crossing the Loup Fork realized he had left his gun on the river's opposite side, "tryed to Cross the River afoot but was unable to do so as the quicksand would let him Sink down So he Could Scarcely get out of the water." After several unsuccessful attempts at crossing, he "was obliged to Come back to Camp with out his Riffle." Barney, Autobiography and diary, 34.

87. The rafts built were "about sixteen feet long each to carry over our goods on the morrow." Young, *Manuscript History, 1846–1847*, 551.

88. Lewis Barney wrote, "the bed got hard So the Wagons rattled over the sand like they were traveling over rocks and the Whole Camp Soon was Safe on the other Side." Barney, Autobiography and diary, 38.

89. Brigham Young's "carriage was drawn to the sand bar by men with a long rope." Clayton, *Journal*, 93.

90. The crossing of Loup Fork was such a formidable challenge to the neophyte venturers, Lewis Barney concluded that "The Crossing of this River was as plain a manifestation of the interposition of Divine Providence as any that is recorded in modern times." Barney, Autobiography and diary, 38.

91. William Clayton said the meeting was called "Soon after 5:00 P.M. . . . at the wagon of President Young." Clayton, *Journal*, 103. Jacob's account of the speeches given this day is the most extensive extant.

he felt deeply interested in our present mission, that he had never left home more freely or [with] so little regret, he had not had a feeling of turning back, but was never so happy in his life. Father James Case also expressed similar feelings, said it was a new business to him but he never felt so well in his life. he had traveled with the [Protestant] Missionarys when they came up into this country & <they> constantly <were> contending whereas in this camp all was peace & harmony. Br George A. Smith said he was with the camp [Zion's Camp] that came up to Mo. in 1834. that camp was not as orderly as this has been but there was a murmering which caused the Spirit of the Lord to rest upo[n] "Joseph" and he prophesied that they would [suffer] for it & he could not prevent it but counceled them to repent that peradventure the Lord would lighten the Scourge. they expected that some of them were to fall in battle as they were going to fight the Missouryans, but the word of the Lord came that they must turn back, no fighting but ~~soon~~ the Cholera broke out among them and 18 were soon laid under the sod & whoever attemted to rebuke the disease by [the] laying on of hands were sure to be taken immediately.[92] <Total 144 [miles]> he reccomended that the brethren be very careful not to destroy animal life unnecessaryly but use all they wanted & let the remainder live. at this moment a wolf was seen walking up towards the camp. sveral were for starting immediately to kill him, when President Young asked whether wee had better continue our meeting or go and Kill the wolf? When all unanimously agreed to continue our meeting and let the wolf live as wee had no sheep for him to kill & he could do us no harm.[93] The President now said he would make some remarks. he was well pleased with the proceeding of the camp thus far. he had no doubt the Lord had led us & would continue to lead if wee were faithful. all these matters were right but there was some items of business he would mention. It was necessary there should be a <daily> report from the several Tens that their men were all on hand that the roll should be caled twice a day to acertain if anny were missing. he would also speak of the guard. his Horse got killed through carelessness of the guard. they [were] so technical about countersigns [and] keeping the men on their post that they wold let a horse choak to death & not go and relieve him.[94] I then

92. See footnote about Zion's Camp for 16 April 1847.

93. Thomas Bullock reported that "while G. A. Smith was relating the Prophet Joseph's instructions not to kill any of the animals or birds, or any thing created by Almighty God that had life, for the sake of destroying it, a large Wolf came out of the Wood on our right hand & walked very leisurely within about 50 rods past our camp; as much as to say the Devil & I are determined to prove whether you will practice what is now taught." Bullock, *Camp of the Saints*, 132.

94. William Clayton, who mistakenly identified the horse as belonging to Brigham Young's brother Phinehas, described the horses death: "It appears he was tied to a stake with a chain near a steep hole in the ravine, and either stepped back or lay down and rolled over into the hole, and the chain being short he was choked to death, having no power to extricate himself. This is a grievous loss for there are no more teams in the camp than what are absolutely necessary, and in fact, there are hardly enough to get along very comfortably." Clayton, *Journal*, 94.

asked the privileg of making some remarks with reference to the conduct of the guard as I was the officer of the first watch & knew that the Horse was not killed during my watch & the men attended to their duty faithfuly. I then asked [whether] a man should be permited to leave his post during the time of his watch observing that one of my men did do it for a short time but soon returned. The President replyed [that] if a man saw anny difficulty among the horses or cattle in anny part of the camp it was his duty to go and relieve them even if he had to disobey his officer & then report himself and the officer. and with regard to a countersign, it was perfect nonsense in this camp, and he wanted all gentile technicalitys to be laid aside. Such regulations as were common in an army of such persons was not applicable to us, ~~wanted~~ and he wanted the Brethren to learn one principle now.[95] There was much said about oppression in this church. he would ask if the Twelve "oppressed anny body." The answer by the congregation was no. The earth, said he, is composed of small particles. so [is] the Knowledge of God [in] small degrees, making use of every little principle as it was manifested to the mind. The more a man had of the Spirit of God the more he was disposed to break off every yoke, while ~~most~~ <many> [of] the Elders that were in authority ~~in this~~ were disposed to tyrranize over those placed under them as had bee<n> manifested in the Army (refering to the Mormon Battalion).

In the evening a council of officers was called and some 25 hunters selected to hunt the Buffalo.[96] The Land on this side of [the] river [is] dry, sandy, and [has] a thin soil. The President also reccomended that the several Tens select two men each to cook and that they be exempt from all other dutys.

Monday 26th [April 1847] About 4 oclock A.M. two shots were fired by the Guard at 5 or 6 Indians who were creeping into the camp.[97] the Bugle was sounded & all hands called to arms. the gunners loaded ready for action but the Indians fled and nothing more was seen of them except their Mocasin

95. "Remarks were made by several," reported Howard Egan, "and instructions given by President Young, chiefly in reference to the folly of conforming to Gentile customs on an expedition of this nature." Egan, *Pioneering*, 29.

96. Knowing the camp approached buffalo country, the hunters were selected to put "an end to every man's running ahead with his gun to scare away the game." After the designation of the hunters, Young "stated that no man must leave the camp to hunt but those men." Both Clayton and Bullock identify eight horseback hunters and eleven who were to hunt on foot. The Twelve Apostles, however, were given "the privilege of hunting when they have a mind to." Snow, "Journey," (April 1948): 113; Atwood, Journal, 25 April 1847; Clayton, *Journal*, 103; Bullock, *Camp of the Saints*, 132.

The designation of hunter was highly desired by some in the camp who were not selected. One of Jacob's ten, Lewis Barney, was particularly chagrined to be overlooked in the selection of the hunters, only, several weeks later, to gain the privilege which served as the highlight of his journey with the vanguard. Barney, *One Side by Himself*, 98–101.

97. Several others, including William Clayton, said the alarm was raised at "about 3:30" when "The day was just breaking . . . [and] the moon had just gone down [with] The air being extremely cold and fires put out." Clayton, *Journal*, 104.

tracks affter day light in the sand. at an early hour wee were on our Journey & traveled about 8 miles over a dry, sandy prarie with little grass & halted for dinner opposite an old Indian vilage which is desertion.[98] ~~moved on~~ moved on and camped on ~~Small~~ <~~Sand~~> <Gravel> Creek [blank] 7 miles.[99] This morning wee organized My Ten (12th) for cooking, selected Charles A. Harper Chief cook & Andrew S. Gibbons assistant. yesterday President Young in speaking of his dead Horse said he had scolded some for which he would now ask pardon of Col. Wright for he was the only man that had a legal right to find fault & murmer. whoever therefore <whoever> had anny grumbling to do must call on Col. Wright for permission, & he was then formaly elected to the office of Grumbler.[100] This Col. Wright is no other than Henry G. Sherwood one of the High Council who ~~relieved~~ assumed the cognoman of Col. Wright last summer when returning from the camp of Israel to get his family for the purpose of traveling without being known by the Mob. Well, this arrangment of making him Chief grumbler for the camp had an ecelent [excellent] effect in puting a check upon some fractious persons especialy one by the name of [Solomon] Chamberlin who had all the time been quarreling with his Team or some body [or] another but after this he was tolerable decent. This evening Just after sunset two Horses were run off suppo<sed that the Indians got them>.[101] our course today about West. <Lat 41° 17' 2 1">

Tuesday 27 [April 1847] After 12 oclock A.M. I was on Guard with my Ten. during the watch two wolves were shot at by the Guard but no Indians made their appearance. Started this morning to go across to the Platte, a south course.[102] Porter Rockwell, Thomas Brown, Joseph Mathews & [Jesse] Little

---

98. Having crossed Loup Fork previously to return to the Platte, they found at this point, "There is no road here, consequently, President Young, Kimball and some others went ahead on horseback to hunt out the best track." Egan, *Pioneering*, 30; Clayton, *Journal*, 105. Thomas Bullock said they made "an entire new road, on the South side of the Loup Fork." En route to Grand Island they broke new road for several miles. Bullock, *Camp of the Saints*, 133, 135–136.

99. Thomas Bullock said at this point, Elk Sand Creek as identified by Will Bagley, "The face of the country is now beginning to change [having] had to cross many Sloughs & small ridges." He also said "The large trees disappear & instead thereof have small stunted scrubby trees & willows on the margin of the River." Though they had seen none, they found evidence of buffalo in this area. Bagley in Bullock, *Camp of the Saints*, 133. It was also on this day, Charles Harper wrote, "I saw for the first time 4 antelope on the other side of the Platt [though] some of the men saw them the morning before." Harper, *Diary*, 19.

100. This insight into Brigham Young's skill in leading the motley composition of the camp with humor, as well as removing from himself the onus of correction, illustrates a feature of his success in guiding the Camp of Israel.

101. About a dozen men, including Brigham Young, "went in pursuit" of the stolen horses, but "returned unsuccessful at 1/2 past 10." Bullock, *Camp of the Saints*, 134.

102. The Saints' encounter with the Platte, 1030 miles long, the great highway to the West, was of some significance. Their route was fixed by this broad stream bisecting the Great Plains before flowing into the Missouri River, stretching 800 miles before its proximity to the Sweetwater River in Wyoming. Meaning "shallow" in French, the Platte, in

went back in search of the Horses that were stolen last night. wee traveled about 11 miles and halted in a small vale where wee found pretty good grass but wee had <to> dig for water & could not obtain enough ~~to~~ so as to water Stock.[103] the Thermometer stood at 86° & the heat was verry oppressive to the ox teams.[104] they travel in the rear ~~something like~~ about twenty of them.[105] moved on to a beautiful little creek <caled Prarie creek> in the open Prarie 5 miles and camped. our Horses found plenty of grass. Just after wee left the place where wee halted some of our hunters killed an Antelope. Soon after wee stoped at our camping place the Boys came up who had been in pursuit of the Stolen Horses. they fell in with 15 naked Pawnees, some of the verry fellows that came around where wee halted down at the first Pawnee vilage. <Total 175 m[iles] > They tried to get hold of our men's Horses but <were> detered by their six Shooters.[106] they then made off when our Boys rod[e] back a short distance & the fellows fired several guns at them. our men Shouted when they put off as fast as they could run. there is no doubt they had the Horses hid in the brush. If they had been a little stronger ~~force~~ they m<ight have got them>. < Lat 41° 9' 26">

Wednesday 28th [April 1847] Tarryed ~~in cas~~ a little while this morning to let our Teams feed and recruit their energies after the fatieging march of yesterday without water. About 9 oclock wee got under way. The most distresing accident happened last evening that has occured since wee started. A Brother

---

contrast to the other great navigable American waterways familiar to the pioneer camp, was humorously characterized as being "a mile wide and an inch deep, too thin to plow, too thick to drink." Levi Jackman, although stating the water to be "healthey and good," later described the Platte as being "wide, shale watter, full of iselands" and that the "water is like the missieares [Missouri River], it has the appearance of dirty soap suds." www.octa-trails.org/JumpingOffToday/VirtualTour/PlatteNE.asp; Hartley, "Gathering the Dispersed Nauvoo Saints," 19; Jackman, Diary, 16 May 1847.

The most comprehensive description of *The Great Platte River Road* across Nebraska, variously called the Oregon, California, and Mormon trails, is Merrill Mattes important volume of the same name. Mattes's volume focuses on the road from Nebraska's Fort Kearny to Wyoming's Fort Laramie. "The Great Platte River Valley" is described, 238–263.

103. "The brethren set to work," wrote Thomas Bullock, "& dug three wells, getting to water which has a very copperas like taste." Bullock, *Camp of the Saints*, 134.

104. The heat was compounded by "a light shower with very heavy wind," accompanied by "thunder and lightening." Egan, *Pioneering*, 30.

105. The oppressive heat that day caused the ox teams, after traveling about two miles, to give out. They "had to stop and feed." Clayton, *Journal*, 108.

106. William Clayton elaborated that the Pawnee were "all naked except the breech cloth, and armed with rifles and bows and arrows. The Indians advanced toward [us] but the brethren motioned and told them to stop and held their rifles and pistols ready to meet them. When the Indians saw this they began to holler 'bacco! bacco!'" Told that the whites had no tobacco, the Indians looked for other "gifts." When one of them approached Joseph Mathews intent on relieving him of his horse's bridle, Thomas Brown "cocked his pistol and pointed at the Indian shouting if he did not leave he would kill him." As the Pawnee retreated, the Mormons turned back to their camp when "the Indians fired six shots at them with their rifles and the brethren immediately faced about at which the Indians fled towards the timber below." Clayton, *Journal*, 109–110.

by the name of [Mathew] Ivory had set down his gun by the side of Capt. John Brown's waggon. Just after wee stopped a gust of wind came up attended with some rain. some one picked up the gun & put it into the waggon. Capt. Brown went <to> pull out his Coat. it cau[gh]t on the cock of the gun when it went off sending the ball through some clothing bags, set it on fire, passed out at the hind end of the waggon close by 2 or 3 men, and ~~wen~~ broke the fore leg of Lewis Barney's Mare, a fine animal, as he was l<e>ading [her] past the waggon.[107] when wee left some one shot her to put her out of her misery.[108] Br [Rodney] Badger furnished his mare to help haul Br Barney's waggon. wee traveled 10 miles ~~to the ban~~ in a S Westerly direction and halted on the bank of the Platte opposite Grand Island. Continued our course S Westerly 6 miles and camped in a circle on the Bank of Wood Creek.[109] Total 16 m[iles].

Thursday 29 [April 1847][110] ~~travled~~ <Travled> about 3 miles ~~to~~ where wee

---

107. Lewis Barney's account of the accident reads, "one of the Bretheren [John Brown] had been out and Came in wet. he went to his wagon to get his Coat. at the same time I Started with my horses to take them out to feed. As I was leading them along by the hind end of his wagon he took hold of his Coat to pull it out of the wagon. it Caught the hammer of his Riffle and fired it off, the ball passing through a bundle of Cloths, out through the hind gate and Struck one of my Mares, braking her Shoulder bone to pieces." Barney also noted, "had the mare [not] Stoped the ball it would have Struck me." Barney, Autobiography and diary, 34. Charles Harper lamented, "we have lost 4 hourses within a few days by nothing by carelessness." Harper, *Diary* 19–20.

108. The day after the accident, Lewis Barney wrote, "Finding the Mare's Shoulder very much swelld and in great Misery, It was thought advisable to Shoot her and put her out of her misery. So I got Luk Johnson to kill her." Barney, Autobiography and diary, 34–35.

    The importance of domestic animals to nineteenth-century Americans on the move cannot be overstated. Godfrey, "No Small Miracle," 3–16. Notwithstanding the well organized and well equipped vanguard, the loss of Barney's horses negatively affected travel for Barney both to the Salt Lake Valley and his return to Winter Quarters. Barney, *One Side by Himself*, 98, 109–110.

109. At the end of this day, Erastus Snow exulted, "The country we have passed over today is the most beautiful I ever beheld—a continuous unbroken plain covered with green grass, from one to six inches high as far as the eye can see extending in all directions, without any timber or other objects to obstruct the vision except the timber on Grand Island." Snow, "Journey," (April 1948): 114.

110. William Clayton, on 29 April, left the first of many "guide boards" along the trail, every ten miles after their arrival at Fort Laramie, supplying information about the vanguard and about the route to those who would follow. On 5 July, the first company of the second wave of Mormon emigrants bound for the Great Basin that year found the first board. John Smith, Joseph Smith, Jr.'s uncle and part of the second emigrating company, wrote upon finding the board that they found "the First Trace of our Bretheren who have gone Before us & we were highly Pleased." Smith, Journal, 5 July 1847.

    While there were instances where the vanguard used buffalo skulls to communicate with those who followed—such as the instance where Jedediah Grant showed Eliza Snow on 14 July 1847 a buffalo skull which read: "All well—feed bad—we only 300 ms. from W."—the method was unusual. Before the expresses sent by messengers in August, communication from the vanguard to the following companies was usually by way of "guide boards" written by William Clayton. Snow, *Personal Writings*, 184.

<found> grass for <our> Teams & stoped & got Brea[k]fast.[111] one mile further [we] crossed wood River ~~creek~~, a good sized mill stream.[112] saw some Antelope,[113] passed on up the Platte about 6 miles & halted. here I found a white mineral Substance lying on the groun[d] in considerable quantities <not crystalized> supposed to be salts of Nitre.[114] I also found a deer's horn completely preserved by lying with the prongs down in the ground on ~~and~~ a spot where the salts <was> plenty while the other one lying with the prongs up were [obscure characters crossed out] roted of[f] to the beam. from here moved on 9 miles & camp[ed] on the bank of a slough of the river which is as muddy as the Missouri.[115] Total 19 mi[les]. I was on guard with my Ten till midnight. The Bottoms here are fertile.

Friday 30th [April 1847] Started at 8 oclock ~~and~~ traveled 10 miles and halted on a small creek where the grass was more abundant than anny place wee had seen.[116] A tremendous cold wind sprang up from the North this affternoon which rendered the weather verry uncomfortable.[117] after going 7 mils wee camped in open Prarie destitute of wood and water.[118]

111. William Clayton breakfasted that day "on goose and mouldy bread." Clayton, *Journal*, 112.
112. Using Augustus Mitchell's famous 1846 map of the trans-Mississippi West, they identified Wood River's designation. Noting the "large body of beautiful level land between th[e] creek and the Platte, with a quick soil and sufficient timber," George Smith (Carrington) suggested "if [the land] was used carefully," it could support "quite a large settlement." The river's crossing occurred "about five miles west of present Grand Island, Nebraska." Smith (Carrington), History, 29 April 1847; Bagley in Bullock, *Camp of the Saints*, 136n67.
113. William Clayton indicated they "Saw many antelope, and the brethren had a good chance to kill one, but they missed it, although three of them shot at it." Clayton, *Journal*, 113.
114. William Clayton stated the "white substance . . . seems to ooze out of the ground around here, and tastes like salt, but not so strong as common salt." Clayton, *Journal*, 113.
115. "[E]verything . . . is shrinking up," William Clayton complained, "for the wind is perfectly dry and parching; there is no moisture to it. Even my writing desk is splitting with the drought." Clayton, *Journal*, 112.
116. At this place William Clayton reported, "There are immense patches of blue grass which from appearances, the buffalo are fond of. There are also numerous patches of buffalo grass which is very short, thick on the ground, and curly like the hair on a buffalo's hide, and much resembling it, except in color." Oddly, Brigham Young's account for the day reads: "Very little grass for the animals." Clayton, *Journal*, 113; Young, *Manuscript History, 1846–1847*, 552.

    Concerning their route for the previous few days, Clayton wrote, "We have thus far followed the Indian trail, but it is now so grown over and so old it is scarce discernible." Clayton, *Journal*, 114.
117. At sundown the temperature stopped at 41°, prompting William Clayton's statement that it was so cold "that every man wants his overcoat on and a buffalo robe over it." Smith (Carrington), History, 30 April 1847; Clayton, *Journal*, 115.
118. Here Erastus Snow said, "for the first time we resorted to Buffalo manure for fuel and found it better than we had expected. We also sunk a well about six feet and found water." Thomas Bullock also described the use of a new cooking tool: "At Luke Johnson's fire I saw a Buffalo Skull made ~~for~~ a chimney—the smoke coming out at two holes between the horns, combined the useful & ludicrous." Snow, "Journey," (April 1948): 114; Bullock, *Camp of the Saints*, 136.

~

May 1847

~

Two weeks into their journey, the Mormon overlanders entered the legendary realm of the American bison in central Nebraska. Dazzled and astonished by the sheer number of the behemoths of the plains, the Saints killed the beasts for food and some for sport. The Oregon/California trail followed the Platte River's south bank while the Saints' route paralleled the Platte River's meanderings on the north side as they climbed to the high Wyoming plains. By the end of the month they passed the sites now part of western trail mystique including Ash Hollow, Chimney Rock, and Scotts Bluff. They were also in the country of the Sioux Indians, a number of "the noble looking fellows" whom they peacefully encountered. At month's end they were within a day's walk of Fort Laramie.

~~

Satturday May, 1<st>, 1847[1] A cold uncomfortable morning.[2] Started before Breakfast & traveled about 8 miles when ~~when~~ wee discovered a drove of Buffalo ~~wee~~ and halted while five or six hunters Started in pursuit. Shot one but did not get it.[3] Started on a few miles when a large Band of Buffalo was discovered grazeing quietly along the side of the Bluff about 3 miles from us.[4] wee pursued our Journey along in sight of them some distance when a

---

1. This was a significant day for the pioneers, "a romantic day," as Erastus Snow described it. Two weeks into their journey on 1 May, they finally encountered the American bison of which so much had been imagined. William Clayton wrote, "This being the first day buffalo has been seen on our journey and in fact the first ever seen by any except about five or six of the brethren, it excited considerable interest and pleasure in the breasts of the brethren, and as may be guessed, the teams moved slowly and frequently stopped to watch their movement." Snow, "Journey," (April 1948): 115; Clayton, *Journal*, 117–118. Clayton's detail of the day consumes eight pages in the published account, 116–124.
2. The "Thermometer at sunrise [was] 30°." Smith (Carrington), History, 1 May 1847.
3. Luke Johnson, Porter Rockwell, and Thomas Brown were the three who pursued the first of the buffalo sighted. Johnson shot one, "but it escaped into the herd; & owing to the rugged country they were unable to follow it." Bullock, *Camp of the Saints*, 142.
4. "Willard Richards counted 65 [buffalo], William Clayton counted 72, & Orson Pratt 74 by the assistance of their Telescopes." Bullock, *Camp of the Saints*, 142.

   Describing the legendary beasts, Clayton wrote, "the appearance of the wild buffalo at a distance is somewhat singular. The color of the back and about half way down

council of the Hunters was held and a plan adapted for the chase & some 8 or ten Horsemen started in pursuit, while the camp moved on. presently an Antelope started up.[5] Professor [Orson] Pratt shot at him & he led off towards the Herd of Buffalo with two dogs in pursuit. <Total 235 [miles]> they all ran right in among them when they began to huddle up together & roll off to the west along <the> verge of the Bluff, some time before the Hunters came up with them. but having taken a circuit around on the hills & the Herd halted ~~a~~ our Hunters [obscure word crossed out] after a little time came down upon them in gallant stile. A cloud of dust was soon raised which almost hid the dark rooling [rolling] herd below.[6] wee could scarsely hear their guns but with the help of our [spy] glasses wee could see them drop down a dark spot now [and] then upon <the> green Prarie. in a little more than an hour our Hunters came in having slaughtered one Bull, three cows, & 5 calves. While the pursuit was going on one of our men at the head of the advancing colum of waggons shot a calf lying where its Mother had left it. in fact the ground wee were now <on> looked like an old summer pasture, so completely was it fed off by the Buffalo & wild geese, but bad as it was wee were compeled to halt & camp so as to take care of our Meat. wee soon found a place on the bank of a small creek partly dry. wee called it Buffalo Creek. some light waggons were dispatched for the Meat & about dark it was all in.[7]

one Hunter Joseph Hancock who started on foot when the first party went out this morning, did not come in at night fall. in the morning a good deal of anxiety prevailed among us lest the Indians had found & robbed him, but a little after Sunris he came in bringing a piece of a Buffalo cow he had killed.[8] with three men he went back after his meat but the wolves had taken the greater part.[9] they However killed two Antelopes and brought in the meat.

---

the sides is a light brown, the rest is a very dark brown. The shoulder appears slightly rounding and humped. When running, the large shaggy head hangs low down, about half way in height between the ground and the top of the shoulder. They canter like any ox or cow, but appear far more cumbersome and heavy, especially about the fore parts, which look larger than they really are on account of the long, thick matty hair. They run tolerably fast, but a good horse will easily gain on them. They will run a long time without diminishing their speed." The chase was worth it. "Their meat is very sweet and tender as veal." Clayton, *Journal*, 124.

5. Antelope, "a medium between the deer and goat," with "hair like a deer and forked horns," were, like the bison, also unfamiliar to most members of the camp. Jackman, Journal, 3 May 1847.
6. William Clayton and Erastus Snow numbered the herd at nearly 200 buffalo. Clayton, *Journal*, 119; Snow, "Journey," (April 1948): 115.
7. "The game came into camp at dark and was equally divided among the several tens," wrote Erastus Snow, "Journey," (April 1948): 115.
8. Fearing for Joseph Hancock's safety, Erastus Snow stated, "guns were fired and Bugle sounded to let him know (if he were in hearing) our whereabouts." Snow, "Journey," (April 1948): 115.
9. After having killed a buffalo cow, Thomas Bullock related, Joseph Hancock protected his kill from wolves by shooting at the scavengers, having to fence in the cow "with stakes,"

I was <on> the first watch with my Ten. in the fore part of the night two Buffalo calves approached the guard when one of them fired & wounded one of the calves in the thigh. when they fled the men pursued & caut the wounded one which made in all 12 Buffalo wee got besides several that were mortaly wounded during the chase. another young Buffalo passed close by one <of> my men on Guard but he did not shoot at it. This Buffalo chase took place opposite the head of Grand Island.[10] Lat[itude] 40° 41'42".

Sunday 2d [May 1847][11] All hands were busy, some cooking, some drying meat, and some <making> Horse halters & Laryets [lariats] out of the Buffalo hides.[12] There were plenty of Buffalo in sight through the day but the Brethren were directed not to Kill them.[13] about noon President [Brigham] Young started with a party up the Platte to look out a better place for camping & returned about 3 A.M. [P.M.] reported good <feed> some 2 miles above.[14] the Bugle sounded for gathering up the Teams to move. when wee ~~found~~ proceeded up & camped on the bank of a nother creek. The distance from where wee halted Satterday to this place [is] 10 miles.

Monday 3d [May 1847] Orders came from President [Brigham] Young to tarry here today for the purpose of hunting Buffalo. twenty hunters were sent out, accompanyed by 3 waggons for a still hunt.[15] A party of 15 men

---

before "He lay down on the Prairie for the night." Bullock, *Camp of the Saints*, 143.

10. Having traveled eighteen miles on 1 May, the night's camp settled "a little above the head of Grand Island, Nebraska. (Travel for the day was impeded, in part, from "some ox teams [being] weak for want of food.") Grand Island, on the Platte River, was the site originally designated by church leaders as their objective to quarter for the winter of 1846–1847. What became Winter Quarters was determined to be a better location than Grand Island, in part, because of regional instability from the rivalry of the Sioux and Pawnee which prevailed in the area. Snow, "Journey," (April 1948): 115; Smith (Carrington), History, 1 May 1847; Bennett, *We'll Find the Place*, 44.
11. The morning was "cold but clear," with the "Thermometer at sunrise [being] 20°." Nearly an inch of ice had formed in camp buckets in the night. Egan, *Pioneering*, 32; Smith (Carrington), History, 2 May 1847.
12. "The meat was cut up in strips," Thomas Bullock wrote, "& part dried over the fire to preserve it for future use," while at the same time "The hides were cut up into ropes & thongs & stretched between Stakes." Egan wrote that "This morning we cut up a quarter of a buffalo cow and salted it down." Bullock, *Camp of the Saints*, 143; Egan, *Pioneering*, 32.
13. Besides being Sunday, with Brigham Young giving "orders not to shoot on the Sabbath day," the "five large [buffalo] and seven calves" killed on Saturday were sufficient to satisfy the camp for the moment. Bullock, *Camp of the Saints*, 144; Clayton, *Journal*, 125.
14. Landscape in the area was marked by "prairie dog holes, which cover one thousand acres of land, and by the buffalo licks, caused by the buffalo licking up the saltish white deposit (saline efforessence [efflorescence] of Fremont), which had covered the soil thickly for the last forty miles." Smith (Carrington), History, 2 May 1847.
15. Only two buffalo this day were brought into camp by the hunters. Smith (Carrington), History, 3 May 1847.

was also sent up the river to reconoiter the country as it was believed that Indians were near for the Prarie had been burning ahead for 3 days and last night came down within a mile of us.[16] <Total 245 [miles].> I was one of the reconoitering party. Br Seth [Ezra] Benson our captain, [and] 4 of us started on ahead. a mile from camp in some willows wee discovered a camp which had contained some 50 wickiups or Lodges. the camp fires were still burning. a large body of Indians had left them upon our approach into the neighborhood on Satrerday. Br [James] Case who has been with the Pawnee Missionarys for 8 years,[17] expressed it as his opinion that this party is the Grand Pawnees who live below on the other side of the Platte. their object is to destroy the grass by burning & drive off the Buffalo so that wee cannot subsist ourselves & teams.[18] wee proceeded about 10 miles & found the Prarie burnt & burning as far as wee could see.[19] some Antelope attracted our attention. Br [William] Empey, on a fleet animal, started to get round them & turn them toward us. he succeeded in getting beyond the main body & was proceeding round some straglers, when he sudenly came close upon a large body of Indians secreted with their Ponys in a low piece of ground near the bank of the river. they began to mount & start in the direction of our party when <he> returned to us at full speed and gave the alarm that a war party of Indians was coming down upon us.[20] Our captain direc<t>ed that wee retire immediately towards the camp. the Indians now showed themselves about a mile from us. wee retired at a pretty smart trot. The reason wee chose to avoid them is that they are the Band that robed the emigrants last spring, & not visiting our camp it is evident that their design is to watch until they can get the advantage of us, frighten our Horses & take a spoil, but wee are ready for them. wee have our cannon loaded with canister Shot.[21] on our return to camp President Young

16. With the need to replenish the food stock, to determine the course of travel, and to secure the company from Indian threats, Thomas Bullock described the duties for the day: "Orders were given for 20 men to go out on the hunt, & 15 to go & search out a road & another camping place, while some were appointed to watch the cattle; & all the rest were ordered to stay in camp." Bullock, *Camp of the Saints*, 144.
17. See Jacob's entry and editor's notes for 23–24 April 1847.
18. See Jacob's entry and editor's notes for 21 April 1847.
19. Another of the reconnoitering party, Erastus Snow, after ten miles of surveillance finding "only here and there a patch of grass not burned," wrote that the Pawnee's strategy to destroy the pioneers' prairie feed was nearly successful: the grass "had so far [been] destroyed . . . that our teams could not be sustained." Snow, "Journey," (April 1948): 116.
20. William Empey estimated the body of Indians to number nearly 300. Bullock, *Camp of the Saints*, 144; Clayton, *Journal*, 126.
21. "Till now the wheels bearing our cannon had been encumbered with a wagon bed and other loading," wrote Erastus Snow. "[T]hese were removed and it was ordered that henceforth the cannon be hauled in the rear of the company ready for immediate use." Snow, "Journey," (April 1948): 116.

    William Clayton stated that the "cannon was unlimbered [th]at night and prepared for action in case it should be needed." The "cannon was fired about 9 P.M. to let the Indians know we had one." The following morning the cannon thundered again at 4 A.M. Clayton, *Journal*, 127; Smith (Carrington), History, 3–4 May 1847.

directed 20 men to go after the Hunters. a part of them have Just returned & report but one Buffalo seen today.

They brought in two Antelopes. Col. [Stephen] Markum with the men that went after [the] hunters came in at ~~dark~~ nightfall bringing two Buffalo calves. they fell in with a small herd some four or five miles below the camp on the bottom & gave chace. Br [William] dykes dismounted from his Mule to shoot, a dangerous practice, for the Mule broke from him and ran directly after the herd who took to the Bluffs. one man pursued until he found his horse could not stand it. when Col. Markum came up, & being better mounted, after a chace of 2 or 3 miles caught the Mule. Horses frequently get lost in this way by throwing their riders in a chace, take off with the fleeing herd, and are never recovered.

Two of our Blacksmiths set up their Bellows and have been at work today repairing waggons.[22] ~~Here is thousan~~ There are thousands & thousands of acres of Land here covered with Prarie Dog Towns. they burrow in the ground like manny other small animals & are about the size of a large gray Squirrel.[23] Several ~~of~~ have been Killed by the Brethren & are esteemed good meat.

Tuesday 4th [May 1847] This is the third morning wee have had a white frost but the wind is South & [there is] prospect of warmer weather. About 8 oclock the camp was called together.[24] Coln [Stephen] Markum said he wanted the men all to start at the Sound of the Bugle to gather their cattle & Teams so that wee should not be hindred in [our] Journey by Some men laging behind. He then said he wanted another Ten form<d> in the guard. he wanted men to volunteer for that purpose, which was soon done. President [Brigham] Young then remarked that wee had proceeded thus far without much commanding or scolding & it would not be necessary, especialy the scolding, if all men were disposed to do right. but it was necessary that the rules & regulations of the camp be observed strictly from this time forth & they should be read to the camp every 2 or 3 days & especialy on Sunday. but this is not the <time for> preaching but for doing, & it [is] necessary for every man to be vigilant & seek his neigbors welfare as much as his own. it must be so in this camp; it must be so in the whole Church; and not a man would find admitance into the Kingdom of God who did not act upon this principle. it is necessary to carry <this principle> Just so far as not to indulge people in negligence & idleness. Some men, & there [are] those in this camp, who, if you take care of their

---

22. This was also a day for wagon and other repairs by the blacksmiths: "[Thomas] Tanner and [James] Davenport are fixing their forges to do some repairing, shoeing, etc.," including Hosea Cushing's wagon which "had some of the tires set." Clayton, *Journal*, 126; Egan, *Pioneering*, 33.

23. William Clayton wrote that prairie dogs looked "much like a squirrel, only the body is thicker and the tail short and no bush on it." Clayton, *Journal*, 125.

24. To remind the Indians of their power, at 4 A.M. the "cannon was fired . . . which awoke the entire camp." Others of the company reported the meeting commencing at 7:30 A.M. Bullock, *Camp of the Saints*, 144; Clayton, *Journal*, 127; Egan, *Pioneering*, 33.

cattle & Teams, ~~woul[d]~~ <will> sit down & do nothing. but the time has come that if men violate the rules & regulations of the camp they must be punished. the captains of Tens are required to organize thier companys & see that no man leaves his Ten at anny time unless he is directed to by their proper officers for if men will persist in stragling away from the camp without orders they will be rob[b]ed and abused by the Indians. he required that the captains keep with [their] companys & the men stay with their waggons or they would be chastised severely. he now asked if the camp would sanction this proposition when it <was> unanimously approved.[25] About 9 A.M. the camp got under way. after traveling 2 miles a Half-Breed Frenchman [Charles Beaumont], one of nine men in the employ of [Peter] Sarpey as Indian traders, came across the river to us having discovered our Waggons.[26] he forded the river on foot which is above a mile wide at this place.[27] They were direct from Fort Larimie in 16 days with ox Teams, 3 Waggons. By the request of President Young he tarryd until letters could be written to send to Winter Quarters. in about an hour wee dispatched three men across the river with him to carry the package of <52> letters[28] & deliver them to the Principal of the Trading

---

25. Thomas Bullock was another who recounted Brigham Young's speech in his account. Paralleling Jacob's report generally, he also stated that Young "counselled the brethren not to leave the Camp 20 rods, without orders from their Captains . . . . I see the hand of Providence in our journey to this place, that no man has been hurt . . . . [To avoid being "stript & robbed" by Indians,] Let every man have his guns & pistols in perfect order . . . . The historians & clerks have been so busy that I have not yet seen a copy of the rules of the Camp [given on 17 April]. Have them read at least on Sundays." Bullock, *Camp of the Saints*, 145. This was not the last of Young's pointed corrections to his brethren. By the end of the month, the pioneers' neglect of duty forced his scolding and reprimand again. Despite the complaints of some to his ponderous tactics, the Mormon leaders' influence, with or without accompanying verbal prodding, established the behavioral pace of the journey.
26. Charles Beaumont, the "Half-Breed Frenchman," was en route, with Pierre Papin and seven others, from Fort Laramie to Peter Sarpy's Missouri River trading post at Bellevue, Nebraska. Beaumont "stated that he wanted to see a white person once more" and that in their two years at Fort Laramie he and his men "had not seen neither bread or salt since they arived there and he wanted to get some bread of us and pay us in buffalo robes." The exchange was "3 robes for a very little bread." After the matter of carrying mail was raised, in reply to Beaumont's willingness to carry their mail to Winter Quarters, "Bread, Meat, Sugar, & coffee was given to him." Beaumont, thankful, "frequently begged not to be over loaded as he had got enough," though he was especially appreciative of obtaining bread, which "he had not eaten . . . for a long time. Beaumont's destination after Sarpy's post was St. Louis. Bullock, *Camp of the Saints*, 145–146; Atwood, Journal, 4 May 1847; Egan, *Pioneering*, 33; Goff, "Pierre Didier Papin," 9:316. Sarpy and his enterprise are described in Wickman, "Peter A. Sarpy."
27. The breadth of the Platte River a this place was estimated by Howard Egan to be double what Jacob stated, while William Clayton explained that the three brethren mentioned below who crossed the river, described the river to be "very good to cross, not being more than two feet deep in the deepest place, and the bottom good." Egan, *Pioneering*, 33; Clayton, *Journal*, 129.
28. Charles Beaumont gave the Saints five minutes to compose their letters, which numbered "about 50 [written] and packed up in 6 1/2 minits." When the "trader went back over

expedition & also to ascertain from him what could be learned with regard to the propriety of our crossing the river here as the feed is burnt up on this side by the Indians. wee proceeded on 3 miles & halted when our men came up & reported that the feed for Teams was better on that side than on this & there is the Orrigon road to travel in, while on this side ~~w~~ <we> hav had to break a new road ever since wee crossed the Loup Fork & shall continue to all the way up.[29] Yet after deliberating upon it wee concluded to continue on this side & some inconvenience for the sake of our Brethren who are to come after us. for although the <river> is fordable now it will not be in June when it is high. there are patches of grass here & there that wee can subsist our Teams upon until we get above where it is burnt.[30] wee proceeded 5 miles & camped.[31] Total 255 miles.

Wednesday 5th [May 1847] The Buffalo are in sight on all sides of us this morning. I was on guard with my Ten from 12 til 4 A.M. Started 1/2 past 7 & traveled 4 miles over burnt Prarie & halted where there was some small patches of grass. In about an hour wee proceeded on. After going 3 miles our hunters came in from the right with a report that they had killed a Buffalo cow & 5 calves & they brought one in alive, the boys foolishly thinking to take it along with the cows.[32] The President [Brigham Young] had directed

---

the river," William Clayton reported, "Thomas Woolsey, John Brown, and John Pack accompanied him on horses to speak with a person [part of Beaumont's group of nine] whom Brother Woolsey is acquainted with." Atwood, Journal, 4 May 1847; Clayton, *Journal*, 128–129.

29. While the absence of a visible route on the Platte's north bank may have led some of the Saints to believe themselves trailblazers, others, beginning at least as early as the eastbound Astorians in 1812–1813 paralleled the Platte overland on the north side. Army explorer Stephen H. Long used the north bank on his way west in 1820. Bagley in Bullock, *Camp of the Saints*, 22.
30. This is apparently the only time that the Saints contemplated traveling the Oregon Trail prior to Fort Laramie. Grass for their animals, burned on the north bank by Indians, and lack of Indian interference between their position and Fort Laramie reported by Charles Beaumont and his company caused them to consider crossing the Platte at this point. (While Beaumont's party reported that they had "not seen an Indian since they left Laramee," it must be understood that their travel was mostly by night in order to avoid the Native Americans.) Wilford Woodruff, like Jacob, noted that despite being at the forefront of the westward emigration that year, meaning their journey would likely be without competition, they "took into consideration the situation of the next company & thousands that would follow after" and determined to "brave the difficulties" of the trail on the Platte's north bank. The precedent would benefit those who followed. This example of sacrificing the convenience of an advance party for those who would follow generally characterized the Mormon immigration to Utah for the next two decades. Woodruff, *Journal*, 3:168; Goff, "Pierre Didier Papin," 9:316.
31. In the hastily written note Howard Egan sent to his wife Tamson via Charles Beaumont, he explained that they were then "traveling 5 wagons a breast of each other as there is Indians all around us." Howard Egan to Tamson Egan, 5 May 1847.
32. Heber C. Kimball, Orrin Porter Rockwell, and John S. Higbee were the three who brought in the calf. Clayton, *Journal*, 131.

them not <to> kill anny thing they could not bring in on their Horses, but the anxiety among some men to signaliz themselves by killing a Buffalo or an Antelope <is so great> that <they> cannot refrain from the shedding of blood without a commandment.[33] will they had better learn wisdom. The fires were burning so rapidly here that they concluded to stop til morning.[34] so the cutter (Leather Boat) went to bring in the cow while wee filed off to a small island & camped.[35] whole distance today 12 miles.

Thursday 6th [May 1847] Moved 3 miles before breakfast & having passed. the fire halted where there was green grass.[36] Here is immense herds of Buffalo in sight.[37] A drove of 13 Elk, the first we have <seen>, crossed the river Just above us. Started forward ~~after p~~. Saw a large drove of Elk off to the right. Traveled over a dry soil where the Buffalo have gnawed the grass into the ground. 7 miles. halted for dinner. Jack Reding [Redden] Shot an Antelope running past the waggons. one Horse in my Ten tired out, their corn having given out. Moved forward 8 miles & camped on the bank of the river in <a> verry eligible place.[38] Buffalo so plenty that it required a good deal of care to

---

33. Jacob did not exaggerate. During the season of plenty passing over Nebraska, Brigham Young regularly reproached the hunters for carelessness in how they dealt with wildlife.
34. Being "stopped about 4 P.M. by a wall of fire reaching from the river to the bluffs," the travelers "quarter[ed] back about a mile and camped by the Platte." The torched land, stirred by "the Wind blew the ashes of the burnt grass in all directions which soon caused us to look like [chimney] Sweeps." Smith (Carrington), History, 5 May 1847; Bullock, *Camp of the Saints*, 147.
35. Describing the manner of dividing the meat brought in by the "revenue cutter," William Clayton wrote, "The meat was divided amongst the companies of ten, each having either a calf or half a quarter of a cow." Clayton, *Journal*, 132.
36. Near the 100th meridian, the pioneer company faced a significant dilemma: scarcity of feed for their animals. The combination of grass burnt by the Indians and grazing buffalo eliminated much of the forage. The Saints, however, were given a partial reprieve at this spot; "During the night the Lord sent a light shower of rain which has put the fire out except in one or two places and made it perfectly safe traveling." While Jacob indicated they did encounter some grass for their stock, their animals still had difficulty; "where we have traveled today," Erastus Snow stated, "we are but little better off for feed, for it is nearly all eat up by the buffalos which have been driven here either by the fires or something else, in vast herds." Clayton, *Journal*, 132; Snow, "Journey," (April 1948): 117.
37. Jacob's understatement regarding the enormity of the region's buffalo population is supplemented by his fellow sojourners who quantified their amazement. During the day's travel, Erastus Snow estimated the buffalo numbers to be "five to ten thousand;" Thomas Bullock figured "about 10 or 15,000;" and a dazzled William Clayton wrote, "Some think we have passed fifty, and some even a hundred thousand during the day." "The prairie looks black with them, both on this and the other side of the river . . . . It is truly a sight wonderful to behold, and can scarcely be credited by those who have not actually seen them." Snow, "Journey," (April 1948): 117; Bullock, *Camp of the Saints*, 147; Clayton, *Journal*, 135.
38. Variations in the Platte's character regularly caught the sojourner's attention. In this spot it was noted that there was "No timber on either bank, nor on the small islands; it is getting scarce, but there are a few trees skirting along towards the foot of the bluffs." Smith (Carrington), History, 6 May 1847.

prevent our cows from running off with them. four came running up from the river & seemed determined to break through the line of waggons. the boys set the dogs <on> & they turned round the end of the line.[39] well, the commandment has at length come to cease slaying animals ~~well~~ until we need them for meat.[40] I am pleased with this regulation. <Lat 40° 48' 32">

a Buffalo calf followed one <of> our horsemen to the camp. the boys let it suck a cow & kept it. afterwards returned to look for a Spy glass lost by the President [Brigham Young] when a large white wolf was Just carrying off the remnant of the calf. <Lat 40° 51' 18">

Friday 7th [May 1847] A cold windy morning.[41] it <was> decided to give our Teams a longer time <to> graze in the morning because of the shortness of the feed & not start till 10 oclock.[42] the President [Brigham Young] chastned Br Erastus Snow for neglecting the driving of the cows wich caused him to loose his Spy Glass in riding after them to prevent thier running off with the Buffalo herd.[43] repaired a waggon & started 1/2 past 11 A.M. Traveled 7

William Clayton places in perspective the estimations at this point of mileage traveled by the company: "Some think we have traveled eighteen, some twenty and some even twenty-five miles today, but from the number of times we stopped and the slowness with which the teams moved, I feel satisfied that fifteen miles is plenty." Clayton, *Journal*, 134.

39. Seventeen dogs accompanied the pioneer expedition. Clayton, *Journal*, 76.
40. "It appears we have got as much meat in camp as can be taken care of," wrote William Clayton. *Journal*, 133.
41. The wind from the northwest was, according to William Clayton, "almost as cold as winter." Clayton, *Journal*, 135.
42. To illustrate the lengthy spread between the units of the pioneer camp, while Jacob stated they started at 10 A.M., others did not begin the day's travel until nearly an hour later. Smith (Carrington), History, 7 May 1847.
43. The circumstance of Brigham Young's chastening of Erastus Snow counts among the trek's most illustrative episodes regarding Young's leadership. The twenty-nine-year-old Snow had been assigned the previous day to watch the cattle, always an important duty, but particularly so at this juncture of the journey due to the livestock's propensity to merge with the ubiquitous buffalo, risking their separation from the pioneer company. Young, in riding hard to recover the animals which had wandered off, had lost his telescoping "Spy Glass," invaluable to the expedition's leader. The public exchange between Young and Snow proved a lesson to everyone who witnessed the showdown. Charles Harper's eyewitness account best summarizes the confrontation:

> Brother Erastus Snow received a severe reprimand from Brigham for not attending to his duty when it was his turn to drive the cows and for trying to excuse himself. Snow said he was able to roll off any plea [criticism] that could be brought against him and if he could not roll it off he would shoulder it. Brigham told him he would scold him or any other man when he pleased and he would put it on him so he could not roll it off. told him he was a lazy man and had neglected his duty and caled on the people for a vote w[h]ether Snow was to blame to which they said he was. and then Brigham told him to hold his tongue, say no more about it and tend to his business. Harper, *Diary*, 21.

Horace Whitney added that Young's excoriation, which began as a slight reproof before Snow began excusing himself, reminded Snow "that if he had been only a year

miles and camped where there was better grass than common in this immense Buffalo pasture.[44] thousands of them we passed today. they would come close up to us within gun shot & we had to drive them off to prevent their Breaking through our lines.[45] a calf turned aside and followed our cows & we were obliged to take him away to get rid of him & leave him out of sight ~~of them~~. <Total 283 miles>

Saterday 8th [May 1847] A white frost this morning but bids fair to be a warm day. Last night I was on guard with my Ten. in the fore part of the evining Br [Ezra] Benson called for the guard & said he thought he saw an Indian coming across the slough but it probably was some wild animal. Started 1/2 past 9 & traveled throug one continued herd of Buffalo for 8 miles[46] & halted to bate [bait][47] in a lowo bottom next [to] the river where our Teams could get a little grass for the whole face of the earth is eat up here by the thousands upon thousands of Buffalo.[48] Porter Rockwell shot one right by the side of our path. indeed wee had to stop to let them take their own time to get out of our way.[49]

---

or two in the church, he would be excusable; but, as he had been for a number of years therein, he ought to know better than to give way to a rebellious spirit; for he had seen a number of men go to the Devil from the same cause, like unto Warren Parrish & Sylvester Smith, who apostatized at Kirtland." Whitney, Diary, 7 May 1847.

Snow's own report for the day, after describing the circumstances provoking the "dressing," candidly concluded: "In attempting to exonerate myself from blame, I drew from him [Young] a severer chastisement; it is the first I have had since I have been in this Church, which is nearly fifteen years, and I hope it may last me fifteen years to come." Later "Brigham Young's spy glass was found by O. P. Rockwell." Snow, "Journey," (April 1948): 117; Smith (Carrington), History, 7 May 1847.

44. William Empey recorded the area to be "a valley of dry bones for . . . it appears as though there were milions of buffelows killed on this place." Empey, "Mormon Ferry," 124.

45. As part of Brigham Young's instruction for the day, he said, "I preached in Camp and advised the brethren not to kill any more buffalo or other game until the meat was needed." Young, *Manuscript History, 1846–1847*, 553.

46. The extent of the population of the American Bison on the Great Plains is illustrated here in miniature by the Mormon overlanders, unfathomable as it is: "Of all the sights of buffalo that our eyes beheld, this was enough to astonish man." Doubtless, their contemporaries in the East would have questioned the credulity of descriptions of the "countless numbers of buffaloes on both sides of the river, covering both bottoms a width of from four to five miles, and in length eight miles." Indeed, "It looked as though the face of the earth was alive & moving like the waves of the sea." Woodruff, *Journal*, 3:171; Smith (Carrington), History, 8 May 1847.

47. In the nineteenth century, "to bait" or "recruit" described the pause in travel for the feeding and rest of stock during a journey.

48. The buffalo "were so thick that the surface of the ground appeared black with them, and the grass is so eaten out that weeds are getting possession, as in an old pasture, and their dung is as plentiful as it commonly is, about a barnyard. In fact, the bottom today looks like an old yankee pasture that needs turning over without requiring any manure to be hauled on it." Smith (Carrington), History, 8 May 1847.

49. Thomas Bullock expressed gladness that the Saints had chosen to travel the north side of the Platte because "On the South side of the River the Buffalo was in one dense mass, several miles in length, covering the plain & marching towards the Mountains." But of a

if the Horsemen would chace them theyd turn round & look at them as soon as they stoped. travele[d] 3 miles & came to a place where the river runns close in to the Bluff. here wee camped in a barren sandy plain.[50] two Buffalo calves were killed Just at dusk. <Lat 40° 58' 14">

Sunday 9th [May 1847] After breakfast moved on over the Bluff a short distance & then on the Bottom again.[51] 3 miles & camped where the feed is somewhat better.[52] at 3 P.M. calld together for worship by the sound of the Bugle. Brethren [Wilford] Woodruff, 0[rson]. Pratt, A[masa]. Lyman, & [Ezra] Benson spoke & also Erastus Snow in which he said he could testify to <the> necesity of self government (Spoken of by Br Lyman). he was more particularly qualified to do so from the recnt dressing he had received from President Young. he felt that he deserved it, because he did <not> govern hymself but had been angry when he shoul have chawed Indea [India] rubber or something else rather than have spoken when angry. he had asked & obtained forgiveness from the President [Brigham Young] & now of the People but was afraid it [his misbehavior and verbal stance of 7 May] would be rembered.[53]

Br Pratt said that some had supposed we should be able to get over into Bear river valley in time to put in spring crops but he had not thought so.[54] but we must prepare for difficultys & we would be in a condition to cope with

---

sudden, upon rounding a hill, "there were the thousands & thousands of Buffalo ahead of us, marching directly in our Path & going the same way as the Camp. There were such a mass of living blackness that the Van Guard could not see the Prairie beyond them." Bullock, *Camp of the Saints*, 150.

50. This campsite was midway between present Gothenburg and Brady, Nebraska. Still wary of Indian threat, the travelers "camped in a semi-circle on the Platte just below where the bluffs make to the river for a short distance." Here the feed for the animals was "very scarce," with "very little wood" in the area, forcing the emigrants to "use buffalo chips to cook with." Unbeknown to them, they had recently crossed the 100th meridian "west of which rainfall would [later] prove so slight that irrigation would be required for most crops." Smith (Carrington), History, 8 May 1847; Egan, *Pioneering*, 35; Kimball, *Discovering Mormon Trails*, 27.
51. When circumstances required, the camp traveled on Sunday, though rest and worship were the usual objectives.
52. This Sabbath day also proved to be a day for cleanliness. "Soon as the camp was formed," William Clayton wrote, "I went about three quarters of a mile below to the river and washed my socks, towel and handkerchief as well as I could in cold water without soap. I then stripped my clothing off and washed from head to foot, which has made me feel much more comfortable for I was covered with dust." Horace Whitney explained the need to shake the dust from his clothes by adding they had not been able to do so "for 2 weeks or more." Clayton, *Journal*, 138; Whitney, Diary, 9 May 1847.
53. Ambitious, independent, and brash, Erastus Snow's contrite expression illustrated a personal dimension apparently appreciated by Brigham Young. Within two years, at age thirty, he was appointed by Young as one of the church's Twelve Apostles, which says something about Snow and also something about Young. Snow's diary contains nothing of his public contrition for this date.
54. The realities of trail difficulties, which restricted the speed of the company, were, by this time, understood by church leaders.

whatever circumstances we s[h]ould be thrown into & make the best of it. if we do not get there [in] time enough to return next fall we must winter there & make the best of it. Satterday Porter [Rockwell] went back & found the Spy Glass. <Lat 41° 2' 58">[55]

Monday 10 [May 1847] Started at 9 A.M. traveled 6 miles & halted in a wet Prarie.[56] Josep Hancock & Phineas Young killed the fattest young Buffalo we have had. they are generaly poor here. there is so many there is not feed sufficient for them.[57] this is a cold dry region of country: small stinted growth of cotonwood along the shores of the Islands.[58] moved on 4 miles & camped near a fine little Island where there is plenty of cottonwood for our Hórses as the grass is short. the Buffalo seem to have left so that the grass begins to spring up a little.[59] Just as we stoped P Young & Hancock shot a fine young Buck, the first venison we have had. we have passed the narrows & the Bottoms begin to widen out & [are crossing] better land than we have seen for above 90 miles.[60] <Total 316 miles.>[61]

---

55. William Clayton figured the camp had traveled 300 miles to this point, though Horace Whitney suggested Clayton exceeded the actual distance by three miles. Clayton, *Journal*, 139; Whitney, Diary, 9 May 1847.
56. 10 May became noteworthy as several of the company had been working on a mechanism to measure distance. Appleton Harmon and William Clayton are reputed by most as inventors of the device which became variously known as the roadometer, odometer, or wheelometer. In reality "the instrument's final design was a team effort"; "Capt. A. Harmon is busily engaged in constructing an apparatus, by which we can ascertain the number of miles we travel each day. It is to be found by means of <a wheel with 60> cogs, a screw &c., & is to be attached to the side of the wagon in which Wm. Clayton rides, communicating with the hind wheel of the same." Wright, "Mormon Pioneer Odometers," 89; Whitney, Diary, 10 May 1847.

    Orson Pratt claimed that Brigham Young, concerned about the measurement of travel, asked him to "give this subject some attention." Pratt claimed that while "Clayton, and several others" had been working on a device, he proposed a "double endless screw," the operation of which he detailed in his diary. However, Pratt's "original specifications . . . proved to be impractical and had to be modified significantly to simplify construction." Pratt, *Journals*, 391–392; Wright, "Mormon Pioneer Odometers," 89. See Wright's expanded description of odometers used by non-Mormons and Mormons alike, ibid., 82–115, and Wright, "Odometers," 14–24.
57. The previous day a "four year old Buffalo Bull" was captured and taken "to the River to water him." He was then turned loose "as he was not fat enough to kill." Bullock, *Camp of the Saints*, 151.
58. In the locale, the "hills are barren and cut up in many places on their sides and tops, by the effects of the winds and rain on the light soil." Smith (Carrington), History, 10 May 1847.
59. The company, according to Thomas Bullock, "set fire to the Prairies, that the next company may have some green grass for their cattle." Bullock, *Camp of the Saints*, 152.
60. "The face of the country here," wrote William Clayton, "is indeed bautiful, the soil rich on the bottoms, the ragged bluffs on each side of the river have a splendid appearance, and at about ten miles distance, west of where we now are, they seem to circle around until they form a junction." In this area, the tracks of any who had preceded them was absent with "no wagon track but our own." Clayton, *Journal*, 142; Smith (Carrington), History, 10 May 1847.
61. Before breaking camp, "the Twelve [Willard Richards] . . . planted a guide-post in the ground, at the camping place—on one side of the board was written the following

Tuesday 11th [May 1847] Traveled 8 miles[62] & Camped about 3 P.M. to give our animals a chance to graze on a small creek where we found much better grass than usual after passing all day over a dry naked sandy soil.[63] We are now opposite the Junction of the South Fork where the two Streams unite in the bottom among a number of Islands.[64] Lat 41° 7' 44", according to Professor [Orson] Pratt.[65]

Wednesday12th [May 1847] A cold East wind this morning. here the Saline ~~E~~ Efflorecence is more abundant than ~~we have~~ below. <Total 316 miles> it completely covers the ground in many places, produced by the salt water comeing upon the surface & being evaporated by the heat of the sun.[66] Started at 9 A.M. & traveled 8 miles.[67] halted on the bank of the North Fork

---

inscription—*'Look in this—316 miles from Winter Quarters—Camp of Pioneers, bound Westward—May 10. 1847.'* On the other side was written,—*'Look in this, & you will find a letter.'*" Whitney, Diary, 10 May 1847.

62. After rising at 4 A.M., work continued this day on the measuring device to accurately calculate distance. "Brother Appleton Harmon is working at the machinery for the wagon to tell the distance we travel and expects to have it in operation tomorrow," William Clayton wrote, "which will save me the trouble of counting, as I have done, during the last four days." Clayton, *Journal*, 143.
63. The campsite, according to Howard Egan, was a half mile from water so "the brethren dug two wells about four feet deep and found plenty of good water." The blacksmiths were busy making repairs at the camp. Egan, *Pioneering*, 37; Smith (Carrington), History, 11 May 1847.
64. The North and South Platte rivers diverge just east of the present-day community of North Platte, in west-central Nebraska. The Saints continued to parallel the North Platte into Wyoming. The South Platte courses through northeastern Colorado with its Rocky Mountain headwaters in the region of present-day Denver.
65. "Professor Pratt informed me," wrote Wilford Woodruff, "that He took an observation for the Longitude May 7th on the opposite bank of the Platt from whare Freemont gives the Longitude in his travels. Professor Pratt made the Longitude to be 100° 5' 45" making it two seconds of a degree less than Freemont, ownly about 10 rods which was vary Close calculating. He also found the Lat 1/2 a mile west of this nights encampment to be 41° 7' 44." Thomas Bullock added, "Barometer stood at 27.125. Attached Thermometer, 41°. Detached Thermometer 70°." Woodruff, *Journal*, 3:173; Bullock, *Camp of the Saints*, 153.
66. Jacob's description matches the dictionary definition of efflorescence: the "changing of certain crystalline compounds to a whitish powder or powdery crust through loss of their water of crystallization," or "the powder or crust thus formed." "[V]ast beds of salt, or rather dust with a salt taste," looking "something like dirty flour" is how William Clayton characterized the saleratus. *Webster's New World College Dictionary*; Clayton, *Journal*, 144.
67. From this time forward, the measurement of distance for the pioneers was scientific. Orson Pratt indicated that the Clayton/Harmon contraption attached to William Clayton's wagon for measuring mileage was now operational; "It is constructed upon the principle of the endless screw." Rockwood detailed the mechanics of the device consisting "of a wheel with 60 cogs which is attached to the side of the wagon back of the hind wheel." The "60 cog wheel" was driven by "what is called an Eternal Screw." The simplified tool provided that "Six revolution[s] of the wagon Wheel make one revolution of the Shaft sixty revolution[s] of the Shaft make one revolution of the 60 cog wheel which ~~which~~ denotes that the wagon has roled one mile." William Clayton, with relief,

[Platte] where grass is tolerably plenty. here is abundant signs of Indians.[68] our Hunters saw over a hundred Buffalo which have been slaughtered, the hides taken off, some of the flesh & marrow bones taken away & the remainder left upon the ground.[69] in one place some 30 or 40 calves were crushed to death on the bank of the river where a herd has ~~been~~ crossed fleeing before their [Indian] pursuers. passed on 4 miles & camped. nearby the Indians have been camped for sometime dressing their skins.[70] The hunters have killed a Small Buffalo. <Lat 41° 9’ 44”.>[71]

Thursday 13th [May 1847] Started at 9 A.M.[72] A high N. East wind this morning & which renders it verry uncomfortable.[73] traveled 11 miles to a point opposite the first high Land betwen the Forks of the river. The Bluff comes in ~~close~~ near the river on this side, & a fine Stream of clear water flows in from the North, from ten to twelve rods wide & from 6 inches to two feet deep, quick Sand bottom![74] we crossed over & camped on the right bank Just above its Junction with the Platte, the name of this river.

---

wrote, “I shall only have to count the number or miles, instead of the revolution of the wagon wheel.” Pratt, *Journals*, 393; Rockwood, *History*, 51; Clayton, *Journal*, 143; Wright, “Mormon Pioneer Odometers,” 113n39.

68. The emigrants “Camped in a circle near the mouth of a small run about one mile from the location of an Indian camp (probably Sioux), which had been vacated from seven to ten days. They had killed several buffaloes, and had left a good many old maccasins.” Smith (Carrington), History, 12 May 1847.
69. Numerous diarists in the pioneer camp, apparently surprised, noted this phenomenon. Wilford Woodruff estimated the size of the Sioux hunting party at between 500 and 1,000. He wrote that they “took the brains out of the large Buffalos, generally their Hides & some of the meet & broke up the bones for the marrow. 100 calves were found dead in one place with nothing taken but the tongues, legs to the knees & entrails.” Slaughter of this type has generally been laid only at the hands of whites. Woodruff, *Journal*, 3:174.
70. Scouting the area, Wilford Woodruff stumbled upon the site where the Sioux lodged during their hunt. Guessing that 400 lodges composed the mobile village, he said “There was Acres of ground covered with Buffalo wool whare they had dressed there skins. They left much stuff scattered over the ground such as peaces of dressed Buffalo & wolf skins magascins &c.” The following day when Thomas Bullock visited the site, finding “a pair of Macassins in pretty good condition,” he stated the remnants of meat, buffalo skins, moccasins, and halters found there suggested the Sioux “had been recruiting with new & casting away the old.” Woodruff, *Journal*, 3:174; Bullock, *Camp of the Saints*, 154.
71. Orson Pratt’s celestial calculations for the day included this geographical location and indicated the elevation at this point on the Nebraska plain was 2685 feet above sea level. Pratt, *Journals*, 393.
72. Though the starting time of 9 A.M. suggests a leisurely pace for the camp’s travel, Thomas Bullock states the “Horn was blown before 4 A.M.” indicating five hours of preparation before the days journey, which included paying “our Devotions to to [*sic*] our Father in heaven.” Bullock, *Camp of the Saints*, 154; Empey, “Mormon Ferry,” 125.
73. Thomas Bullock stated he “Got up, cold & raw.” William Clayton indicated “overcoats and buffalo robes” were required to blunt the cold. Bullock, *Camp of the Saints*, 154; Clayton, *Journal*, 145.
74. A number of teams crossing this stream running north to south lingered too long midstream and found their wagons and animals sinking in the quicksand requiring the

I was on guard with my Ten till 12 oclock. A mile above our camp the Platte runs in against the Bluff,[75] so we shall have to ~~climb over a gain~~ pass round through a <circuitous crooked> defile.

Friday 14th [May 1847] A cool cloudy morning, Sprinkled with rain a little. When the Bugle sounded to gather up our Teams, a Smart Shower of rain commenced from the S. East which detained us till ten oclock A.M., when we moved forward. The clouds began to break away in an hour or two with a prospect of having the grass grow some, for we have had one continued drouth during the whole Journey, while the Thermometer with few excptions has ranged verry low, so that it [is] impossible [that] there should be much vegetation.[76] Well we have at length wound round six miles to get half that distance through <between> these sand ridges on the rout.[77] Br [John] Higeby killed an Antelope.[78] the flesh of these animals is about like venison. after returning to the river bottoms we halted to bate. The broad valley of the Platte is contracted to A narrow compass, <being> here about a mile from Bluff to Bluff. hitherto our Journey, with few exceptions, has been over smoothe Bottom lands but to day it is sand hillocks & wet strips of Bottom.[79] we are now in the country of the Sioux. it was a hunting party of theirs whose signs we saw on the Bottoms below, which was determined by the peculiar shape of their mocasins, some of which was found by our men. they have pointed toes and [are] made to fit the foot, rights & lefts.[80] Moved on up the river 2 3/4 miles & camped a short distance below where the river runs in against the

assistance of other teams to extricate them. Of this stream, William Clayton wrote, "It appears that travelers have never discovered this stream for it is not noticed in any works that we have seen," prompting Brigham Young to name it, according to Erastus Snow and Albert Rockwood, "*Junction Bluff River*," though William Clayton and Horace Whitney stated Brigham Young called it "North Bluff Fork." Smith (Carrington)'s account also suggests an alternative: "passeda clear sand bottom creek, junction of Bluff Creek, about 10 rods wide, supposed to be the rawhide of the traders." Pratt, *Journals*, 395; Clayton, *Journal*, 146; Snow, "Journey," (April 1948): 119; Rockwood, *History*, 52; Whitney, Diary, 14 May 1847; Smith (Carrington), History, 13 May 1847.

75. This bluff is "the site of the Sand Hill Ruts, an imposing obstacle north of present Sutherland, Nebraska." The Sand Hill Ruts are extant, if difficult to visit. Bagley in Bullock, *Camp of the Saints*, 154n28; Kimball, *Historic Sites and Markers*, 64–65.
76. One report of the morning's travel stated, "Not a tree and hardly a bush in sight." Smith (Carrington), History, 14 May 1847.
77. The complicated terrain in the area not only proved problematic for travel, Wilford Woodruff reported, while out hunting he "got lost among the Bluffs but found my way out again." Woodruff, *Journal*, 3:176.
78. John Higbee also killed a badger, but it is not known if badger was considered repast for the camp. Smith (Carrington), History, 14 May 1847.
79. William Clayton described the "land between the two forks [of the Platte] for about 25 miles" as being "perfectly flat and very level without timber." Clayton, *Journal*, 147.
80. The absence of the recently present Sioux William Clayton credited to Providence who "hears the prayers of his servants and sends them [the Sioux] out of the way before we come up to them." Clayton, *Journal*, 148.

Bluff again which prevented our going further until a rout is explored.[81] our Hunters killed two Buffalo but at so late an hour that they did not get them in to <the> camp.[82] another Antelope also was killed. (This morning fed the last of my corn.) Total 347 3/4 miles.

Satterday 15th [May 1847] The prospect for warm grass-growing weather this morning is ~~slim~~ not verry flattering, a high north wind, wintry clouds, & cold, spatering rain at 8 oclock.[83] Our fuel will soon get so much soaked that we shall not be in a verry good condition to dry our selves when we get wet. The Buffalo dung is our principal resource with what little <drift> wood can be picked up along the banks of the river, principaly Pine & cedar. The Buffalo chips when dry burns verry well, especialy if one had a grate to burn it on, and the supply is most abundant.[84] At 9 A.M. moved on over around among Sand Knobs for 2 1/2 miles when we returned to the Bottoms at the confluence of a beautiful clear creek with the river where the grass is more abundant than at anny place we have seen.[85] So as there is a drisling rain we have turned out

---

81. Albert Rockwood described the bluffs as being "about 125 ft above the river. [They] have a commanding prospect of the river for maney miles." While Rockwood described the region as being "desolate as far as the Eye can reach Every direction," Orson Pratt reveled poetic in the variation of the plain:

> I ascended some of the highest of these hills, where a beautiful and extended prospect opened on every side. On the north, the surface of the country exhibited a broken succession of hills and ravines, very much resembling the tumultuous confusion of ocean waves, when rolling and tumbling in all directions by violent and contrary winds. On the east, the low level valley of the two forks of the Platte was visible to the junction, while the high peaks far below were distinctly seen resembling blueish clouds just rising in the distant horizon. On the south, the chain of bluffs beyond the south fork, stretched itself, apparently in one unbroken though gently undulating ridge, visible in extent from 30 to 40 miles, while the glistening waters of that river were here and there sweeping along its base. The bottom lands between the two forks continue in one unbroken level from the junction 18 or 20 miles west, where they gradually arise into broken hills, forming the high lands between these two affluents, which are here about six miles asunder. On the west, the roily yellow waters of the north fork were making their way over and between innumerable beds of quicksand, while the rich, level, green, grassy bottoms upon each side, formed a beautiful contrast, extending for miles in length." Rockwood, *History*, 52; Pratt, *Journals*, 395–396.

82. The "Revenue Cutter started at dusk after one of them [buffalo] 1 1/2 miles from here, but, it being so dark, the men ~~could~~ concluded to leave the wagon, & return to the camp on foot, on account of the difficulty of travelling through the sand heaps at night." Whitney, Diary, 14 May 1847.
83. It was cold enough, Levi Jackman said, that "overcoats, buffelo robes & mittens are all in fashion now." Jackman, Diary, 15 May 1847.
84. Because they had "no wood at this encampment," Albert Rockwood wrote they used buffalo dung. But because it was "rather damp" they gathered "Buffalow bones and build a great [*sic*] with them which answers a verry good purpose." Rockwood, *History*, 53.
85. Despite access to the water in this creek, the camp "dug two wells which afford a plenty of water for the whole camp." Four wells were dug the following day because the river water was "shallow and iron rusty." The soil, Albert Rockwood said, "is black mold for one foot, then light coulerd clay about 14 inches, then loos gravel. between the clay and gravel is

our Teams to bate. This morning before we started some of the men went out with the Cutter & brought in a four year old Bull that Luk Johnson & Br [Eric] Glines shot last evening which is fine fat meat. the other one that was killed was so far out into the sand knobs that it was thought they could not find it. The Bottoms are narrow on the river here ~~with~~ <and> a sucession of Sand Hills extending far back into the interior. Half past 12 oclock, the rain having ceased, we moved on 4 miles & camped.[86] in the evening the Hunters brought in another Bull. they report that there is no cows among the herds here.[87]

Sunday 16th [May 1847] Remained encamped. Br [Eric] Glines shot an Antelope near the camp. The President [Brigham Young] & some four or five others have gone up the river to explore the road as it runs in close to the Bluff about a mile above here.[88] at 3 P.M. Bugle Sounded for Publick worship. Just at the same time Br Glines, having went out to drive some Buffalo away from the cattle, commenced fireing at a large Bull. the first passed alongside his heart, when he run off some 60 or 80 rods. Glines followed up & fired three sohts [shots] through his lights & then he [the buffalo] turned upon his pursuer & ran some little distance when he turned & ran 40 or 50 rods farther & fell dead.[89] this was all within a mile & in full view of the whole

---

the water," which, he explained, was "cool, Soft, and good." Rockwood, *History*, 53; Smith (Carrington), History, 16 May 1847.

86. "The buffalo have eat down the feed between us and the hills which is the cause of our stopping in the middle of the bottom," was Erastus Snow's explanation for this campsite. "We camp where we can find feed irrespective of water or fuel," he concluded. Snow, "Journey," (April 1948): 120.

87. Although they were difficult to shoot, according to Wilford Woodruff, they found "the Bluffs dotted over with Buffalo." Woodruff, *Journal*, 3:176.

88. In an effort to de-myth the heralded Mormon venture, later observers have perhaps over-emphasized the Mormon reliance on existing trails forged by those who preceded them, precluding Mormon contributions to the westward venture. For example, Stanley Kimball declared that in *all* historic stretches of Mormon peregrinations, not to mention just the 1847 trek, the Saints "actually blazed less than one mile." In several trail sections, however, evidence from extant diaries indicates that Brigham Young and his advisors, from time to time, literally plotted new courses on the old roads. Despite others having traversed the Platte's north bank prior to 1847, the Oregon-California trail west of Fort Laramie, and a stretch of the Donner-Reed trail (Hasting's Cutoff), tracks or traces of the routes in some places proved negligible or were not conducive to travel by a large body. Numerous times during the 1847 journey, the Mormon vanguard had to innovate. Kimball in Brown, *The Mormon Trek West*, ix.

    One report for 16 May indicated that "about 3 miles ahead, the bluffs terminated abruptly at the bank of the river, & that we would ~~again~~ be obliged to go around them some 4 miles, before we could again come to the River bottoms." Whitney, Diary, 16 May 1847.

89. Thomas Bullock, impressed by the size of the animal, stated it weighed "about 800 pounds," though William Clayton estimated its size at 700 pounds, with "hair on his forehead [being] about a foot long and very shaggy." Bullock, *Camp of the Saints*, 156; Clayton, *Journal*, 151.

camp. While the meeting proceeded on the Hunters were dressing the beef which proved to be verry good & fat. after meeting the [Revenue] cutter, which had served for our Pulpit, was dispatched to bring in the meat. Br [Wilford] Woodruff opened the meeting by prayer when Doct [Willard] Richards proceeded to remark that he [thought] that ministers in the name of the Lord should do it with a pure heart & clean hands. for his part he had not <had> time to wash his hands today. as to the pure heart, others must Judge, for he had been busily employed all day in making some necessary repairs to his waggon and a Blacksmith with him, that he was used to such a course of life for when in Nauvoo, ever since he became the Hystorian of the Church, that business had confined him so much that he could never get a chance to attend meeting on the Sabbath unless important business was to <be> transacted or the Prophet was to preach. when he commenced the Labor of Hystorian it was 10 year[s] behind ~~& now~~ <but> he had brought the history of the church forward by constant labor & exertion until it now [was] about five years behind the present time.[90] But his whole object was to help to move the work of <the> Kingdom forward, which was the only reason he would ever consent to work upon the Sabbath, but he was su[r]e he would <not> kill Buffalo on the Sabbath when he had plenty of mea[t] on hand but he was not going to say anny thing about others doing [it].[91] <Total 354 1/4 miles.> Brother Brigham was not present. President H[eber]. C. Kimball called upon Bre[thren Stephen] Markum & [Albert] Rockwood to speak to the People. Their remarks were very appropriate upon the souject [subject] & necesssity of Subordination and obedience to council without waiting for the Lord to come out and comman[d] his people for then they might expect chastisement to follow immediately unless strict obedience was rendered. Br [Albert] Rockwood said that a Key of exaltation is found in being always ready to go when called, & then stop when the errand is performed and <not> do more than he [was] sent to do. Br Heber said that the Lord had prospered us continualy on this Journey, that his guardian Angels were with us on our right hand & on our left, our front & rear guard, only they were not visible to the natural eye but the Angels of <God> were nevertheless with the camp of the

---

90. The compilation, initiated by Joseph Smith as a dictated historical chronology and later known as *History of the Church*, was completed only to late 1838 by the Prophet at the time of his death in 1844. Thereafter, the work was brought to fruition in the mid-1850s by those who staffed the Church's Historian's Office, of which Willard Richards was a primary contributor until his death in 1853. See Jessee, "Writing of Joseph Smith's History," 439–473.

91. Willard Richards's comments about Sabbath behavior were prompted by Eric Glines's hunting performance that day before the camp. Richards's angle, like that of fellow apostle Wilford Woodruff, focused on the religious nature of the westward journey as reflected in Woodruff's journal entry for the day: "We are now in a place whare we are proving ourselves & if we are not faithful we shall Come under Condemnation." Woodruff, *Journal*, 3:177.

Pioneers. the Lord in answer to our prayers had turned aside the Indians so that wee were not molested by them. he had, indeed, a curiosity to see a Sioux but could not get an opportunity. It was necessary for us to reverence the word of the Lord & not take his name in vain, that the Lord would honor such persons & bless them. and if the Brethren of this camp would walk acording to the commandments & covenants of the Lord, not one of them would fall into the earth on this Journey, for the Lord was bound to honor the word of his servants by fulfiling whatever they promise in his name, whether it be blessing or cursing, but he felt to Bless the Brethren of this camp in the name of the Lord.[92] Lat 41° 12' 30".

Monday 17th [May 1847] A plasant morning & looks as though we might have Spring return again. Started at 9 A.M. & [traveled] two miles over the highest Sand hills we have passed yet, when we returned to the river again. we went 6 3/4 miles & halted for dinner. moved on some few miles fa[r]ther when the [Revenue] cutter brought up two Buffalo & returned for another. traveled 6 miles & camped 2 or 3 miles below cedar Bluffs on the other side of the river, & where there is ledges of rock, the first we have seen on the Platte. I was on guard with my Ten from 12 A.M. till day light.[93] much Springy Land in the region.[94]

---

92. Heber Kimball's sermon, also containing preachment against Sabbath hunting, offered universal encouragement to the pioneer camp at this time, testifying he had traveled with numerous camps previously, but that "he never was in a Camp or company that behaved themselves better than this Camp." Indicating the approval of God, Kimball continued, "These Pioneers were like clay in the hands of the Potter; they could be made into any thing that the Potter wanted to make of them." Egan, *Pioneering*, 40; Bullock, *Camp of the Saints*, 156.

93. Orson Pratt, two days previous, described the cautions taken by the pioneers, particularly those on guard in the night, regarding the Indians whom, he stated, "frequently . . . follow emigrants hundred of miles, keeping themselves secreted during the day, and watching the best opportunities for stealing during the night." He continued,

> Our wagons are generally organized in the circumference of a circle–a forward wheel of one locked into the hind wheel of another, forming a circular fortification, in the interior of which our horses are well secured during the night, while the whole camp is strongly guarded by a sufficient number of men. During the day, while our teams are grazing, about fourteen men usually encircle them on all sides, to prevent them from straying or being suddenly frightened away in case of any sudden incursion of Indians, accompanied by their horrid yells, which they frequently practice on purpose to scatter the horses and cattle of emigrants, and afterwards hunt them themselves at their leisure. Pratt, *Journals*, 397.

94. That afternoon, Erastus Snow stated, "we passed several spring fountains coming out of the foot of the Bluffs, and spread over the bottom, which was rather low and made it soft wheeling and many sloughs as the marshy places on the prairies are called." The nature of the area, according to Egan, was such that "One of Brother Phineas Young's horses got mired in a swamp where he went in to feed. The brethren hauled him out with ropes." Snow, "Journey," (April 1948): 120; Egan, *Pioneering*, 42.

Tuesday 18th [May 1847] President [Brigham] Young called the Captains together this morning & enquired if there were anny who had not a suply of meat. some had been grumbling. he wanted them to come and take away the meat that was on hand & not stick up their noses because it was a fore quarter, as though it was a stink offering from the Devil. the Lord had blessed us but there was a Spirit among some in this camp that was not right. some would fain kill all the game within a hundred miles if they could without one thought of who created it or formed those great pastures for the wild animals to feed in.[95] they <are> as thoughtless as the natural brute beasts made to be taken & destroyed & unless they would take heed to their ways they would be removed out of their place & it would not take much preaching to do it. he was not a going to preach to them but the captains of Tens must see that thier men remain with their Waggons & do their duty. <the President also reprimanded the Horsemen for neglect of duty.>[96] <[O]ne Antelope Killed yesterday. Total 382 3/4 miles.> Traveled this forenoon 6 1/2 miles. halted for dinner. moved on 9 1/4 miles and camped on a small creek. we have passed a great number of Spring creeks within three days. There is a ledge of sand rock of recent formation in <the> Bluff near where we camped.[97]

Wednesday 19th [May 1847] A rainy morning. went on 3 1/2 miles before breakfast to find feed & found but little.[98] a short distance below where the river runs in again to the Bluff passed on over the w<o>rst sand knobs of anny we have passed yet,[99] 2 1/2 miles, & turned out our teams to wait for the rain

---

95. Brigham Young's sensibility regarding the treatment of animals, while not unique for the time, was enlightened. Howard Egan reported him saying "that life was as dear to the animal, according to their understanding, as it was to us," and that "*it is a sin in the sight of the Lord to waste flesh*," as reported by Horace Whitney. Egan, *Pioneering*, 43; Whitney, Diary, 18 May 1847.

96. "As to the horsemen," wrote William Clayton of Brigham Young's preaching, "there are none with the exception of Brothers [Heber] Kimball, [Wilford] Woodruff and [Ezra] Benson, that ever take the trouble to look out a good road for the wagons but all they seem to care about is to wait till their breakfast is cooked for them, and when they have eaten it, they mount their horses and scatter away, and if an antelope comes across the track, the whole of us must be stopped perhaps half an hour while they try to creep up near enough to kill it, but when we come to a bad place on the route, all the interest they have is to get across the best they can and leave myself and one or two others to pick out a crossing place and guide the camp all the time. Such things are not right, and he wants them to cease and all take an interest in the welfare of the camp, be united, and receive the meat as a blessing from God and not as a stink offering from the devil." Clayton, *Journal*, 157.

97. "Today," Erastus Snow wrote, "we begin to find for the first time *ledges* of *rock* in the bluff on both sides of the river." Snow, "Journey," (April 1948): 120.

98. Describing the situation that morning and providing insight into how the camp sometimes moved, Howard Egan, also part of the advance group, stated, "Some of the teams are a quarter of a mile ahead of the main body of the camp." Egan, *Pioneering*, 44.

99. William Clayton called this stretch "the worst road we have had from Winter Quarters." Horace Whitney stated the sand was so deep, "It was with great ~~diffi~~ difficulty that our

to cease.[100] rain continued all day.[101] we moved on 2 miles and camped on the bank of the river.[102] I was on guard the first watch with my Ten. <Lat 41° 12' 50", 400 miles from Winter Quarters.>

Thursday 20th [May 1847] The rain has ceased & we hav a cool cloudy morning.[103] Started at the usual hour. my Team led this morning. we change puting a different Ten forward every day so as to divide the labor of breaking the road. traveled 7 3/4 miles & halted opposite cedar Bluffs and [a] small creek comeing in btween them.[104] our People have launchd the Boat & gone over to exmine some Timber in ~~the~~ a ravine.[105] about three miles below here there is a lone cedar tree, the first one I have seen on this side of the river,[106] and half a mile above is a beautiful little cedar Island in the middle of the river. We have found no Timber sinse we passed the Forks of the river excep the small scattering [of] cedar in some few places along the south Bluffs which here are more bold & prominent which relieves the monoting [monotony] of the scenery verry much. Our party returning from the other side report

---

horses came through," the sand being so deep that Erastus Snow stated their "Wheels rolled in the sand nearly to the hub." Clayton, *Journal*, 162; Whitney, Diary, 19 May 1847; Snow, "Journey," (April 1948): 121.

100. Heber Kimball, according to Howard Egan, at this point went ahead in search of a "road through the bluffs" and found himself, without a firearm, amid a pack of wolves who stood their ground despite his attempt to unnerve them. Egan, *Pioneering*, 44.

101. This was the most plentiful rain they witnessed to this point in the journey. Woodruff, *Journal*, 19 May 1847.

102. Describing the environment of this region, Levi Jackman wrote, "The sight of a tree is out of the question. It is seldom we see so mutch as a bush." The camp's configuration that night was, according to Appleton Harmon, "a semicircle at the river's edge," though Albert Rockwood denoted it "two wings of an Etchilong [echelon]." Jackman, Diary, 19 May 1847; Harmon, *Appleton Milo Harmon*, 19; Rockwood, *History*, 55.

103. The adverse effects of the cold, damp weather caused one of the roadometer's wooden teeth to break requiring Appleton Harmon to disassemble the device to remove the broken wheel resulting in William Clayton's return to counting each revolution of the wheel to determine distance. Clayton, *Journal*, 163.

104. Evidence that during their journey the vanguard used John Fremont's 1842–1843 report to Congress about his expedition west is found in William Clayton's account for the day which compares the vanguard's experience with Fremont's. Fremont's "map is not altogether correct in several respects," Clayton wrote, "and particularly in showing the windings of the river and the distance of the bluffs from it." Clayton, *Journal*, 164.

    Dale Morgan indicates Castle Creek, so-called by the Saints, is now Blue Creek. Morgan in Empey, "Mormon Ferry," 147n17.

105. The North Platte's rate of flow at this spot, though only two to three feet deep, was so strong that the party consisting of Orson Pratt, Amasa Lyman, Luke Johnson, and John Brown could not row the "revenue cutter" against the current. Brown jumped into the water and "dragged the boat over, the others assisting with the oars." Clayton, *Journal*, 164.

106. The "one cedar on the [North Platte's] north side" was a burial site, "with a young Indian laid on its top, covered in a buffalo hide, with his wooden bowl and spoon, and a small bag or pouch." Smith (Carrington), History, 20 May 1847.

that the Timber seen is Ash Hollow where the Orregon Road comes in from the South Fork.[107] Moved on 8 miles & camped near the Bluffs.[108] plenty of driftwood on a bar.

Friday 21st [May 1847] A fine, pleasant morning. Started at 8 oclock. the air is verry clear & serrene in this country.[109] objects are seen at do<u>ble the distance that they can be in the Mississippi valley. we are verry ~~much~~ liable to be deceived as to distances, frequently shoot at animals that <seem> to <be> quite near when the balls will fall to the ground before they reach the mark.[110] while <I> think of it, the Brethren have been quite orderly about shooting sinse they got such a dressing on Tuesday morning [18 May], not <a gun> having been fired at anny living object except a rattle snake lying the path [which] pitched battle when the President [Brigham Young] directed Br John Higby to kill it & he shot it with his rifle.[111] Buffalo appear to be scarce though they have been plenty here last winter. Started at 8 A.M. & traveled 7 3/4 miles and halted at a place where the grass has been burnt this Spring & now is up, finely. Perhaps some might ask how we measure the distance traveled with so much accuracy. About 10 days ago Br W[illia]m Clayton conceived the idea of measuring his waggon wheel and found that it took Just three hundred & sixty revolutions to make a mile. for several days he counted the revolutions made by his wheel, when, by Br Orson Pratt's instructions, Br Appleton Harmon constructed a Spiral shaft & toothed wheel which he attache[d] to the waggon wheel & thus we were enabled to ~~keep~~ measure our distance with ease & accuracy.[112] moved on 7 3/4 miles and camped in a circle. <Total 428 miles.>[113]

---

107. The Saints' interest in Ash Hollow, the significant milepost of the Oregon-California Trail near present-day Lewellen, Nebraska, was significant but to none more so than William Clayton who, as caretaker of the roadometer, was anxious to test "Fremont's distances to Laramie." David Miller later claimed that "Distances recorded in Clayton's 1848 *Emigrants' Guide*, which used Clayton's calculations of distance, check out perfectly with modern odometer readings." Smith (Carrington), History, 20 May 1847; Clayton, *Journal*, 164; Miller, "Parting of the Ways," 49.
108. During the day the camp came upon the grave of a man killed by an Indian the previous year whom John Brown helped bury when the Great Basin-bound Mississippi Saints traveled to Fort Laramie before returning to Pueblo, Colorado, to winter. In Dale Morgan's note about the incident he raises a question about the accuracy of Empey's entry: "Neither Brown nor the records of 1846 refer to such an incident, though at Ash Hollow Brown's party lost a few horses to Pawnees. Perhaps the man killed was Edward Trimble, but this happened farther east." Morgan in Empey, "Mormon Ferry," 127, 147n16.
109. "Today has seemed the most like spring of any day since we left Winterquarters, not only warm and pleasant but on every hand we have been greeted for the first time with the music of the quadrupeds [frogs] from the numerous little water ponds along the bottom," wrote Erastus Snow. Thomas Bullock called the performance "a full Frog Symphony, full of music & variety." Snow, "Journey," (April 1948): 121; Bullock, *Camp of the Saints*, 162.
110. This phenomenon was experienced by most upon their entry into the West.
111. Jacob's sensibility regarding man's proper stewardship over animals is illustrated again, evidenced by the fact that he mentioned these circumstances at all.
112. See editor's notes for 10 May 1847.

Just before we stoped, we met an Indian & his Squaw on horseback, belonging to a Band of the Sioux who are camped a short distance out among the hills to the North.[114] he could only converse with us by signs & soon went off to his camp. Near by we found the leg bone of some animal, four times as large as that of a Buffalo, completely petrified.[115] We are now [in] sight of a large grove of Pine Timber on the hills on the South side of the river. a large number of Indians are now in sight on a ridge to the North. <Lat 41° 24' 5">

Satturday 22d [May 1847] Clear & pleasant. Started at 8 oclock & traveled 7 1/4 miles & halted. grass is short. the country here is evidently geting dyer [drier].[116] we passd yesterday the bed of a creek that was dry & today another six rods wide. This afternoon we passed 8 1/4 miles over a Sterile tract of country & the dry beds of five large creeks. towards evening [we traveled] about 2 miles 'round over the Bluffs, all the way a good hard road.[117] at length, after decending into the bottom near the river, found a tolerable good supply of grass where we camped on a small eminence having a full view of the river & also the Bluffs in the rear which here are precipitous, partly rock & partly clay, worn into a variety of grand & picturesque forms by the force of the elements.[118] one, a mile & a <half> from the camp looks like an old ruined chimney.[119] it is about 60 or 80 feet high, 7 by 15 feet at the top, which <is>

---

113. Jacob's representation of distance traveled from Winter Quarters is at variance with others on the trek. For 21 May, Horace Whitney described William Clayton preparing a "guide post" for those who followed reading, "From Winter Quarters 409 miles—From the junction of North & South Forks 93 1/4 miles." He further stated, "According to *my* computation, we are 406 miles from Winter Quarters, being 3 miles less than Bro. Clayton's, as in the first part of our journey, we all depended upon *conjecture* as to the distance." Whitney, Diary, 21 May 1847.

114. Initially fearful of the white emigrants, "by signs" the Native Americans, who were apparently hunting, were disabused of their fear by the Mormons. They identified themselves as "cut throat sue [Sioux]," cut-throat being a definition of Sioux. Riding "work horses" thought by the overlanders to have been stolen from other emigrants, William Clayton described the male Indian as having "a good cloth coat on and appears well dressed." Clayton, *Journal*, 168; Atwood, Journal, 21 May 1847.

115. Wilford Woodruff indicated the bone "was 17 inches long, 11 inches wide & weighed 27 lbs," though Orson Pratt stated the weight was "after some had been broken from it." Woodruff, Pratt, and Horace Whitney surmised the bone belonged to "some animal of the mammoth species." Woodruff, *Journal*, 3:180; Pratt, *Journals*, 402; Whitney, Diary, 21 May 1847.

116. One effect of the climate change was noted by Albert Rockwood who wrote, "Frogs are peaping, musketoes busing [buzzing], though they are not thick by aney means; bugs, worms, reptiles, Flies, inseck of all kinds are scirs [scarce] when compa[r]ed with Missoura, Ilinois, or the Eastern States." Rockwood, *History*, 56.

117. During the day's travel, "Points of the Oregon Road [were] visible occasionally." Smith (Carrington), History, 22 May 1847.

118. Named Ancient Bluff Ruins by Brigham Young, the unusual formations, resembling "old fortifications, with their turrets, towers, walls, etc.," are located a few miles northwest of Lisco, Nebraska. "The Bluffs on our rout to day," wrote Wilford Woodruff, "have

composed of Sand rock of recent formation & texture as fine as the flour of Emery, which gradualy becomes softer towards the base, ~~until~~ which is broad, & ~~scatered~~ <covered> over with the broken fragments that have fallen from above. the lower part resembles gypsum. The softer part has crumbled out about 20 feet from the top so that it seems as though a gust of wind might throw it off. ~~Near by~~ Br George Grant found an Eagles nest on a cedar tree in the sides of the cliff & obtained from it a young Eaglet yet u[n]fledged as heavy as a goose.[120] another large petrified bone was found ~~meas~~ supposed to be a thigh bone measureing 16 inches in circumference in the smallest place.[121] rattle Snakes ar plenty.[122]

Sunday 23d [May 1847] Remained encamped. I was on guard with my Ten the morning watch. went up to visit the Bluffs before meeting. Br Orson Pratt aseertained by the Barometer that one of the highest points in these Bluffs is 235 feet above the level of the river.[123] at 10 oclock the Horses &c were brought up and fastened to stakes driven into the ground so that we might attend meeting without our minds being called off to watch our Teams, for we have [to] watch them night & day.[124] at 12 P.M. met for worship. President [Brigham] Young opened the meeting, after a hymn was sung, by an exclent Prayer. then called upon Br Erastus Snow to speak when he proceeded to remark upon the advantage we can derive from our experiance in passing

---

presented the most singular natural scenery that I ever beheld in my travels on the earth. It has the greatest appearance of the old walls & ruins of the castles of Europe from the size of chimneys to 100 feet square or more." To Horace Whitney, "The whole scene was one of romantic solitude, & inspired me with singular feelings, & reminding me forcibly of the descriptions I had read in my boyish days, of the fortified castles & watch-towers of the olden time." Smith (Carrington), History, 22 May 1847; Woodruff, *Journal*, 3:181: Whitney, Diary, 22 May 1847.

119. After five weeks on the trail, using John Fremont's guide, the travelers anxiously anticipated the significant overland milepost—Chimney Rock. However, some of the vanguard mistook this particular site for the famous chimney-shaped landmark which they would encounter four days later. Brigham's brother, Lorenzo Young, wrote "We are in sight of Chimney Rock, are in hopes to reach Fort Laramee this week." Young (Young), "Diary of Lorenzo Dow Young," 159.

120. Lorenzo Young stated the "young black eagle" had "just pinfeathered out, but [was] of An ormous [enormous] sise," "46 inches between the tips of his Wings," according to Thomas Bullock. Young (Young), "Diary of Lorenzo Dow Young," 159; Bullock, *Camp of the Saints*, 163.

121. The discovery of the fossils prompted Willard Richards to place a board at the site with this inscription: "Mammoth Bone Encampment 21 & 22 May 1847 Pioneers." The script read: "All well, Sioux Indians seen here." Bullock, *Camp of the Saints*, 162.

122. Thomas Bullock reported killing a rattler that day while "Luke Johnson killed 3 Rattler Snakes having 4, 8, & 12 rattles." Bullock, *Camp of the Saints*, 163.

123. Orson Pratt also calculated the site to be 3590 feet above sea level. Pratt, *Journals*, 405.

124. Regarding their animals, Brigham Young stated the following day that the "Horses failing, but the oxen are gaining." The cumulative travel taxed the animals significantly. Young, *Manuscript History, 1846–1847*, 555.

through adverse circumstance by calling into requisition the powers & energy of the soul. The President [Young] said he had frequently felt a desire to preach to us but an opportunity did not offer itself. he was well satisfied with our labors thus far. some expressed fears that we would not be able to get in crops. well, suppose we did not. we had done all we could & traveled as fast as our Teams were able to go, & when we had done all [we] could he felt Just as well satisfied as if we had a thousand acres planted with grain. the Lord would do the rest. He spoke also of [the] necessity of seizing upon every little item of instruction that might be given us from time to time, and also remembering & retaining that which was received. in this way the Elders might accumulate knowledge that [would] enable them to do great works, whereas <if> they sought the great things first, they would never be able to reach them. The Earth is composed of small particles and suppose, when organising it, they had rejected the small particles. it never could have been formed. He felt verry small when he reflected upon the small amount of Knowledge we have in possesion compared to that which is necessary to enable us to come into the presence of God to dwell in everlasting burnings. the common notions taught by the christian religionist comes far short of it. Something more than belief or faith is necessary. But we must go on to increase in Knowledge unto perfection. but the Knowlede pertaining to the Gospel & the things of God could ~~not~~ be commun<i>cated only in a proper place, hence the necesity of building another Temple in a place where we shall <not> be liable to be molested or disturbed & such a place we are seeking after. The Lord is with us & doth bless us continually.[125] Br [Nathaniel] Fairbanks got bit by a rattlesnake <on the Bluffs>.[126] <Total 451 3/4 miles.>

---

125. Brigham Young's remarks for the day were chronicled by several of the camp including Charles Harper who recorded that Young complimented the company, saying "that he never felt better in his life than he did on this journey and he felt to bless us in the name of the Lord." Harper, *Diary*, 22. John Brown's report of Young's several topics is particularly revealing:

> We are forming a character for eternity and have been, ever since we received the gospel and knew the right from the wrong way, hence how careful we should be in all our acts. A man of deep meditation and quick thought that will lay hold and go ahead would grow in the knowledge of the gospel faster than one of less perseverance. The mind of the faithful servant of God is ever active and full of meditation. If the Saints had obeyed counsel last year and let the authorities go ahead of the main camp, there could have been two hundred men here one year ago as easy as now, and the brethren would not have gone in the army for when the officers came to enlist them, the reply would have been, "the authorities have gone over the mountains and we cannot act without them," so it would have passed by, but the authorities were there and the call had to be responded to or we would never have gone to California. Brown, *Autobiography*, 74.

Young closed the meeting by stating: "on Sunday next he wants the brethren to understand that there will be meeting at eleven o'clock and the sacrament administered, and he wants the brethren to attend, all that can, and not ramble off and fatigue themselves but use the Sabbath as a day of rest." Clayton, *Journal*, 179.

Monday 24th [May 1847] <a cold winday morning & Snow Spitting>.[127] Started at 8 oclock, traveled 10 miles, & halted.[128] two Indians came across the river & went back to their camp.[129] we moved on 6 1/2 miles opposite to <a> large rock on the other side which looks like an old castle, battlments, Turret, Tower & all standing.[130] Some 20 or 30 Indians & Squaws came across to our camp, bearing the American Flag, to pay us a visit. we gave them some presents of Bread & Meal.[131] they presented Papers of recom[men]dation written in French, signed by the Traders at Fort Larimie.[132] Th[e]y are of the Sioux nation, noble looking fellows. Some of their Squaws are Pretty Brunetts. They were verry friendly & camped near by us for the night.[133] Br Higby Swaped Horses with one of them. they <are> neat & cleanly in their clothing & person.[134]

Tuesday 25th [May 1847] A White frost this morning. our friendly Indians

---

126. Nathaniel Fairbanks's encounter with the "large yellow" rattler caused him considerable suffering through the day, despite "remedies" of tobacco juice, leaves, turpentine, lobelia, and alcohol being applied. Fairbanks's leg swelled and his "tongue began to prick and feel numb," as well as his hands. He also complained of "sickness at his stomach and dimness in his eyes." Charles Harper stated that Fairbanks and "some of the other Brethren" had "been teasing a snake to make it mad." Not a half hour later, he said, Fairbanks was struck by the snake. Pratt, *Journals*, 405; Clayton, *Journal*, 177; Harper, *Diary*, 22.
127. One of the company stated that "I put off my flannel yesterday morning, it was so warm; this morning put on both cotton and flannel, it was so cold." Smith (Carrington), History, 24 May 1847.
128. "The bottom," along which they traveled for the morning, was "more rolling than usual," while the road was "hard and good." Smith (Carrington), History, 24 May 1847.
129. William Clayton said the object of the visit of the Indians was to retrieve their "dog which has followed us to this place. They tarried a little while and then went away taking the dog with them." Wilford Woodruff said the dog would not follow the Indians. Clayton, *Journal*, 180; Woodruff, *Journal*, 3:183.
130. Lorenzo Young described the formation as resembling "a stately courthouse;" indeed, his brother Brigham called it "an old court house." Young, "Diary of Lorenzo Dow Young," 159; Smith (Carrington), History, 24 May 1847.
131. An expression of friendship and trust toward the Native Americans occurred when the Saints "smoked the pipe with them." Rockwood, *History*, 57.
132. "Albert Carrington was sent out to meet them to read two letters they had, written in French, both found to be recommends. One O Washtecha-ow le belle journec, who understood four languages was a good pilot, and a good Indian, etc., signed P. D. Papin. The other was for Brave Bear, a good hunter and robe dresser, but was not signed." Smith (Carrington), History, 24 May 1847.
133. Despite the hospitality extended, the pioneers were suspicious of the Indians' intentions and "Plased a strong guard" to watch their animals for the night. Rockwood, *History*, 57.
134. William Clayton's characterization of the Sioux visitors, whom Orson Pratt identified as "Dacotah," is noteworthy. When the Indians were spotted, "Some of the brethren went to meet them carrying a white flag with them. When the Indians saw the flag, some of them began to sing, and their chief held up a U.S. flag." The Sioux party of thirty-five, according to Clayton, were made up of "about half squaws and children." The Mormons proved to be polite hosts showing them around the camp, including an exhibition of

came round & traded Some Buffalo Skins with our Boys for meal & another Horse with S[tephen]. Markum for a Mule.[135] we Started forward on our Journey & they returned back across the river. passed over a sand ridge, 2 1/2 miles, & halted where we found good grass.[136] moved on over a heavy, wet soil 4 3/4 miles & halted for dinner. A sultry, warm day. ~~we are a little below the celebrated chimney Rock on the other side.~~[137] passed on 4 3/4 miles and camped for the night on a wet piece of ground, & grass bad.[138] Killed two Antelopes.[139] <Lat 41> <Lat 41° 42' 46" & 1' 12" South of Chimney Rock>.

---

their firearms; "They were shown a six and fifteen shooter also the cannon and the gunners went through the evolutions a number of times which seemed to please them much." (Thomas Bullock's account varies slightly.) Clayton was obviously taken by their appearance:

> They are all well dressed and very noble looking, some having good clean blankets, others nice robes artfully ornamented with beads and paintings. All had many ornaments on their clothing and ears, some had nice painted shells suspended from the ear. All appeared to be well armed with muskets. Their moccasins were indeed clean and beautiful. One had a pair of moccasins of a clear white, ornamented with beads, etc. They fit very tight to the foot. For cleanness and neatness, they will vie with the most tasteful whites.

After the party returned to their camp on the other side of the river, a chief, named Owashtach, and his squaw visited where they were entertained for the evening, which included the chief amusing "himself very much by looking at the moon through a telescope for as much as twenty minutes." Clayton, *Journal*, 180–182; Pratt, *Journals*, 407; Harmon, *Appleton Milo Harmon*, 22.

135. "The Indians were in and round the Camp from Sunrise to the time of Starting," Thomas Bullock reported, "going about just as their curiosity led them, some to get bread & other things, some trading Moccassins, Blankets, Horses &c." Described as being "a good size and very good looking," they "behaved perfectly, satisfactorily." Bullock, *Camp of the Saints*, 166–167; Smith (Carrington), History, 25 May 1847.
136. The "widest place in the bottom" of the North Platte River valley in which they traveled on this day was "about 6 miles." Smith (Carrington), History, 25 May 1847.
137. It is not known why Jacob lined out this sentence about Chimney Rock, which lay just three miles west of the company's camp, according to Orson Pratt, who, at that distance, also projected the height of the formation to be 260 feet. Others diarists noted the imposing site, like Horace Whitney who wrote, "we can distinguish Chimney Rock, which appears from here similar to a church steeple." Pratt, *Journals*, 407; Whitney, Diary, 25 May 1847.
138. Camping "in a circle about 4 miles east north-east from Chimney Rock," William Clayton explained that one of the reasons they camped on the "very wet spot" was because "the feed [was] poor where it was drier." For water, camp members dug several wells. Smith (Carrington), History, 25 May 1847; Clayton, *Journal*, 183; Harmon, *Appleton Milo Harmon*, 23.
139. Having been out of buffalo country for several days, the antelope provided a welcome meal. Porter Rockwell, one of the hunters whom Albert Rockwood called "Our Nimrod," referring to the biblical hunter, killed the two antelope along with two wolves. Clayton, *Journal*, 184; Rockwood, *History*, 57.

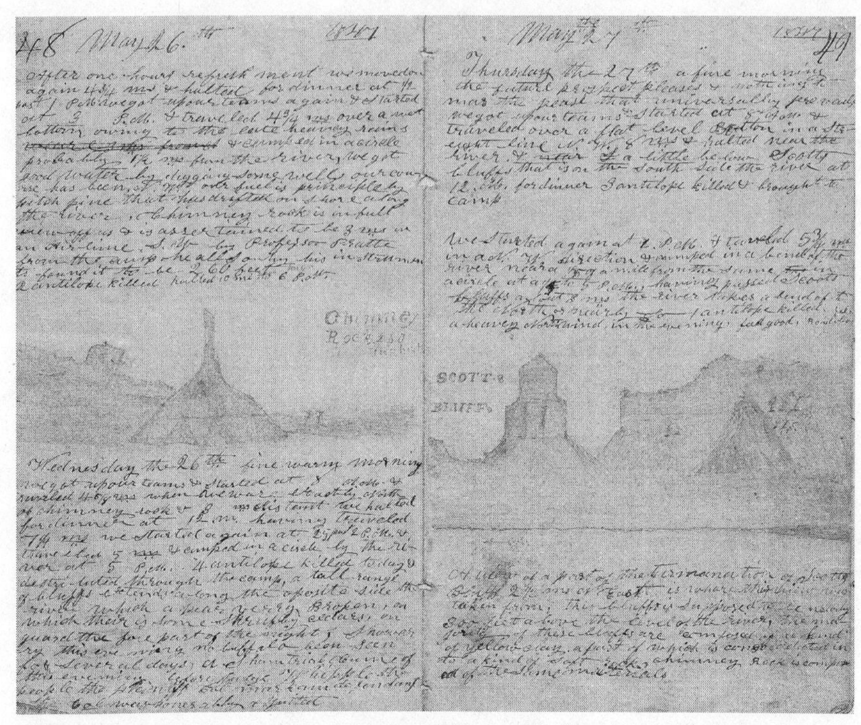

Appleton Harmon's diary entries and sketches of Chimney Rock and Scotts Bluff. Courtesy of the LDS Church Archives.

Wednesday 26 [May 1847] A Serrene, pleasant morning. Started at 8 oclock & after passing 4 5/8 miles came on a line directly North of the famous Chimney rock on the opposite side of the river.[140] it is two ~~one~~ hundred & fifty feet high & of the sam[e] formation as the one near where we camp[ed] on Sunday. traveled 7 1/4 miles and halted for dinner.[141] verry warm. Journeyed on 5

---

140. Chimney Rock is undoubtedly the most significant landmark on the "Great Platte River Road," the "ultimate in natural curiosities, the zenith of sight-seeing goals" for nineteenth-century overland sojourners. Located near what is now "the western edge of Morrill County, Nebraska, about three and a half miles southwest of Bayard and about twenty miles east of Scotts Bluff National Monument," a National Park interpretive center now informs the tourist. Exultant excerpts describing Chimney Rock from the writings of nineteenth-century emigrants who encountered the natural wonder are found in Mattes, *The Great Platte River Road*, 378–401.

    Howard Egan stated the landmark had been visible to the naked eye for "forty-one and a half miles." Horace Whitney, who drew an image of the formation in his diary, wrote that Chimney Rock was "situated on a small eminence, gradually sloping to the water's edge." "It is formed of clay," he continued, "& not of rock as I supposed, & the base or foundation, on which stands the object appearing like a Church steeple spoke of above, considerably resembles, ~~the~~ in shape, a volcano [with] The bluffs & crags in the background [being] much loftier than itself." Egan, *Pioneering*, 50; Whitney, Diary, 26 May 1847.

141. Wilford Woodruff described a potentially serious situation just before camping for noon, the injury-free aftermath of which he described as "truly A miricle."

miles & camped near the river in a most delightful spot of green grass.[142] our Hunters Killed four Antelopes. I was on guard with my Ten until 12 oclock last night.[143] The distance across this Stream is 792 yards here.[144] <Lat 41° 45' 58">[145]

Thursday 27th [May 1847] moved on in pleasant morning 8 miles & halted 2 or 3 miles below Scotts Bluff, which comes close to the river on the other side & is apparently 300 feet high or more.[146] passed on 5 3/4 miles and camped near the river.[147] we have had all day good grass next [to] the river.[148] Killed four Antelopes. <Total 505 3/4 miles>. <Lat 41° 50' 52">.

> An Indian Horse that was bought of the Sioux ran away with A singletree to his heels & gave A tremendious fright to the cows, oxen & horses that were Attached to the waggons. And in an instant A dozen or more waggons were darting by each other like lightning & the Horses & mules flying as it were over the ground. Some turned to the right & some to the left. Some run into other waggons. The Horse & mule that Br [John] Fowler was driving leaped with all spead. With Br [Jesse] Little hold of the lines & Br Fowler hold of the bits they darted by my carriage like electricity & came within one inch of A collission with my wheels. If they had locked we should have been a wreck.

After other associated close-calls, Woodruff stated, "A person can hardly concieve of the power that is manifest in Animals esspecially mules when in such A fright." Woodruff, *Journal*, 3:184–185.

142. Their camp for the evening was "nearly opposite Terrace Bluffs of morley clay constantly wasting away." Smith (Carrington), History, 26 May 1847.

That evening a "sham trial" was held involving Edson Whipple as judge, Stephen Markham as the defendant, with the people being plaintiffs. Fortunately, Markham was "honorably acquitted." Dale Morgan states their camp to be a mile southeast of modern Minitare, Nebraska. Harmon, *Appleton Milo Harmon*, 23; Empey, "Mormon Ferry," 148n24.

143. A reminder of the religious character of this expedition is found in Horace Whitney's diary entry for the evening of 26 May 1847. "By request of Bro. Heber [Kimball], I took a walk with him this evening out on the prairie near half mile. Here we knelt down, & each prayed alternately for our friends & relatives, whom we have left behind in Winter Quarters, & also for one another, & the Saints at large."

144. The breadth of the North Platte here was calculated by Orson Pratt. Whitney, Diary, 27 May 1847.

145. Orson Pratt estimated the North Platte Valley at this point to be 3790 feet above sea level. Pratt, *Journals*, 408.

146. William Clayton exuded his delight with the region at this spot. "We have seen a number of romantic spots on our journey, but I consider our view this morning more sublime than any other. Chimney Rock lies southeast, opposite detached bluffs of various shapes and sizes. To the southwest, Scott's Bluffs look majestic and sublime." Clayton, *Journal*, 186.

Scotts Bluff, which towers over the community of the same name today, received its name from American Fur Company clerk Hiram Scott, who died there in 1828. Bagley in Bullock, *Camp of the Saints*, 169n58.

147. Their camp "in a circle near the river" found them "just above where Scott's Bluffs come the nearest to the river." Smith (Carrington), History, 27 May 1847.

148. The "best grass since we left Bluff Ruins has been confined mostly to the river bank in a belt varying from one-fourth to one-half of a mile in width." Smith (Carrington), History, 27 May 1847.

Friday 28th [May 1847] A cloudy misty morning. tarryed in camp till half past ten A.M. when <we> moved on 11 1/2 miles & camped in a Sandy place where the feed is bad.[149] our Hunters P[orter]. Rockwell & T[homas]. Brown came in without anny game & report that they saw Indians in the Hills. A cloudy, Sour looking evening. Br B[r]igham [Young], whil Standing by the fire, was led to make some remarks upon the Spirit that prevails & has the ascendancy in the camp; levity, loud laughter, whooping, & hallooing ~~proceeds~~ among the Elders proceeds from an evil spirit.[150] "See," says the President, "all around us at this moment; what a Spirit of leveity. & it all arises from a neglect of ~~neglect~~ duty. for three or four men who do not belong to the church are enabled to insinuate [influence] the Spirit that rules them through the whole camp & overpower the other one hundred & forty men. dont you think I am ashamed of it? when, if ten men would be faithful before the Lord, they might controll all such Spirits. but those Negros want to dance.[151] others join in with them & they all become Negros together. there is no harm [that] will arise from meriment or dancing if Brethren, when they have indulged in it, Know when to stop. but the Devil takes advantage of it to lead the mind away from the Lord. they forget the object of this Journey & all feel well <to>gether. but if we travel in this way five hundred miles further, it will lead to the sheding of Blood & some will seek to destroy the Priesthood. it would be far better for three or four to go away together to pray than to engage in playing cards & thus forget the Lord. The men that compose this camp, if they would do right, might establish the Kingdom, <& it> would prosper from our hands. but if they do not do right, there will <be> such a scattering ~~as~~ among the Elders as you have never seen. we are the Pioneers for the whole church of God on the Earth seeking for a place to establish the ~~establish the~~ Kingdom. but we have not found it yet."[152] I remarked that I had thought of that. Br [Addison] Everet

149. Their late departure for the day's travel was due to the "fear of rain." One traveler noted, during the days journey, that the "river takes a sharp turn from Scott's Bluffs to the north-west, and almost north for a short distance." Smith (Carrington), History, 28 May 1847.

150. The men's behavior in the previous few days must have been particularly annoying to the expedition leaders as it was just six days earlier when Brigham Young heaped praise upon his followers. There likely had been some discussion of the camp's recent behavior between Brigham and Heber Kimball, as Kimball, earlier in the day within earshot of William Clayton, similarly to Young, reprimanded several whom he found playing cards. Appleton Harmon noted that both had "been privately exhorting some of the brethren to forsake an excess of mirthfulness and indulging in plays, dances, sham trials, etc., which have been carried to excess for the last few days." Clayton, *Journal*, 187; Harmon, *Appleton Milo Harmon*, 24.

151. Three African-Americans were among the 143 males who composed the camp. Hark Lay, Green Flake, and Oscar Crosby, while "owned by" Latter-day Saints, were Mormon converts prior to the 1847 trek. Lay was known for his musical talent and gifts.

152. While Brigham Young's verbal tactics may appear harsh and his tolerance level short, his religious motivation, exhibited throughout his life, fostered the success and efficiency of the vanguard and later the LDS Church in Utah. The circumstances that provoked this situation serve as an illustration, however, that the rank-and-file of the church did not

said he was willing to make every sacrific & do right. Br [Wilford] Woodruff said <he> felt that <the> coucil [counsel] of the President was right.[153]

Satturdy 29th [May 1847] Another misty morning. ~~Started after ten oclock~~. This morning the Camp has been verry quiet. The[y] have taken the hint from hearing what the President [Brigham Young] said last night. After the Teams were all harnessed onto our Waggons, about half past elevn oclock, the men were all called into the center of the circle when the President directed the captains of Ten to assemble their men seperately & Br [Thomas] Bullock to call the roll, when all were found to be present except Joseph Hancock & Andrew S. Gibbons.[154] The President, then standing in the Boat [Revenue Cutter] mounted on a Waggon, commenced addressing the congregation in the order in which they stood & "said he was now going to preach, had not preached much on the road, & his text would be that he did not feel like going anny farther with all this company of men & with the Spirit that prevails now in this camp.[155] from this text he would preach to them.[156] And first they <were> told before they left winter Quarters ~~that~~ and some here Know that because of our faith in the Gospel of Jesus Christ & on account of <the> doctrine taught by Joseph Smith, the church has suffered all manner of persecution, & we have been driven out from among the Gentiles for our religion, and you were all told before we started on this Journey that <it> was necessary for us to go & seek a place beyond the reach of the Gentiles, where the Kingdom of God may be established <&> a standard raised for all nations. & now we are

---

necessarily naturally subscribe always to the austere behavioral expectations counseled by Young and his lieutenants. As will be seen, on their return trip to Winter Quarters out of Young's imposing presence, the standards imposed by church leaders were regularly discarded.

153. After Brigham Young's scolding, Wilford Woodruff wrote that several of the Twelve Apostles met in Young's wagon where "Young wrote some of the word of the Lord Concerning the Camp & expressed his views & feelings concerning the camp that they must spedily repent or they would be cursed, that they were forgetting their mission." Woodruff, *Journal*, 3:186.

154. Joseph Hancock and Andrew Gibbons, hunters, plied their duty at the time of the meeting. Two others were "confined to their wagons but answered to their names." Clayton, *Journal*, 189.

155. William Clayton, one of the few to preserve contemporary reports of Joseph Smith's sermons in Nauvoo, Illinois, left a detailed account of Brigham Young's 29 May call to repentance which expands Jacob's report. (Howard Egan copied Clayton's copious notes into his own journal for an account of the meeting.) Clayton reported that Young titled his sermon, "That as to pursuing our journey with this company with the spirit they possess, I am about to revolt against it." Clayton, *Journal*, 189.

156. William Clayton captured an illustration of Brigham Young's instincts regarding the spiritual tone of the company when he quoted Young as declaring, "Nobody has told me what has been going on in the camp, but I have known it all the while. I have been watching its movements, its influence, its effect, and I know the result if it is not put a stop to." Clayton, *Journal*, 191.

~~beyond their~~ out of the reach of the Gentiles [so] that the Devil cannot stir them up against us. they know not where we are or what we are doing, but the Devil knows & he has no other way to opperate against us but to produce confusion, discord & contention in our mid[s]t. now," says he, "I am in no hrry to go on, nor do I intend to go anny farther, while ~~<things> remain their present condition with~~ <such a Spirit reigns in> this camp as has prevailed for several days, dancing, playing cards, chquers [checkers], domino[es], & giving way to a Spirit of gambling.[157] I want to know who is willing to pray, without my asking them to do it, & turn unto the Lord with full purpose to keep his commandments."[158] He then called for a division of the company & there was found to be 18 High Priests, 80 Sev[e]nties, 8 Elders, 13 members, 8 of the Twelve, & 6 that do not belong to the church.[159] The President now said that he was a going to ascertain how many were willing <to> return to the Lord and keep their covenants. he was averse to calling upon the Eldrs to enter into covenants unless it was necessary, but now was a time that all <should> remember the Lord. when putting it to vote all agreed unanimously to ~~abide their covenants~~ return unto the Lord, be sober & keep their former covenants—begining with the Twelve, through those of each quorum & also the members who do not hold the Priesthood. The President said one thing he wanted to be remembered, that in establising the Kingdom of God it is not necessary for a man to be a member of the Church in order to entitle him to the protection of the government. it matteres not whether he be a Mahometan, Pagan, or Jew. he is equaly entitled to protection under the Priesthood, but must honor that Priesthod.[160] he must ackowledge God & Jesus Christ to be

---

157. Had the company been composed of religious neophytes, Brigham Young said, he would preach to and nurture the men. But with priesthood holders and veterans of gospel protocols groveling in devilish behavior he could not restrain his inclinations to reprove and correct them. William Clayton noted Young's complete intolerance for card playing and the like but acknowledged an appropriate place for dancing as long as it was not to excess: "you want to keep it up till midnight and every night, and all the time. You don't know how to control your senses." Clayton, *Journal*, 193.
158. Following this phrase, William Clayton notes Brigham Young's resolution: "Give me the man of prayers, give me the man of faith, give me the man of meditation, a sober-minded man, and I would far rather go amongst the savages with six or eight such men than to trust myself with the whole of this camp with the spirit they now possess." Clayton, *Journal*, 191.
159. Jacob's tabulation leaves fifteen people for which there is no designation. Clayton's report of the sermon stated that in Young's attempt to obtain consensus from the company to change their ways, he called for the vote by priesthood assignment, i.e., four bishops, fifteen high priests, seventy-eight seventies, eight elders, and eight of the Twelve Apostles. Clayton, *Journal*, 197.
160. This posture on religious freedom echoes the sentiments of Joseph Smith in Nauvoo. William Clayton's phrasing of Brigham Young's words contains this statement: "I understand there are several in this camp who do not belong to the Church. I am the man who will stand up for them and protect them in all their rights. And they shall not trample on our rights nor on the priesthood." Clayton, *Journal*, 196.

the Savior of the world, but it matters not whether he be Baptised or obey the ordinances of the church. but they must [obey] the Laws that govern the Kingdom outwardly.[161] & if anny one shall attempt to introduce anny thing that is unlawful, secretly to carry their purpose into opperation without permission, I swear they shall not return home. notwithstanding, every one shall be protected in his rights but he shall not infringe upon mine. they may suffer evil Spirits to govern them if they please but they shall not govern me. the Priesthood shall be honored & respected, & rather than be broken up by the reb[e]lling of those that belong to the church, I will leave them upon the Prarie. yet no one has anny thing <thing to fear> from the opperation of the Gospel, for it is the Law of Liberty and will not harm a righteous person.[162] Br Heber [Kimball] now made some remarks approbating what had been said. Br [Wilford] Woodruff ~~ha~~ wanted the <Brethren> to be careful to keep their covenants lest the chastisements of the Lord come uppon us, & [there be] no power to avert it.[163] Br Orson Pratt said that prayer had been reccomded as a remedy against the evil of falling into temtation & being led by evil Spirits. he would also <mention> another remedy, which is to avoid idleness. let the mind <be> occupied by acquireing k[n]owledge.[164] The President said, when he took the vote concerning the covenant, that if there was anny who did not wish to enter into this covenant they were at liberty to take their waggons & return.[165] he also refered to <a> saying of Br Hiram Smith that he was afraid

161. Brigham Young's own report of his words reads: "I then told the few who did not belong to the Church that they were not at liberty to introduce cards, dancing, or iniquity of any description; but they should be protected in their rights and privileges while they conducted themselves well and did not seek to trample on the Priesthood nor blaspheme the name of God." Young, *Manuscript History, 1846–1847*, 555–556.

162. Of Brigham Young's speech, Appleton Harmon wrote, "there was not a man present that did not feel the weight of his remarks." Harmon, *Appleton Milo Harmon*, 24.

163. William Clayton's report of Wilford Woodruff's speech serves as a better report of Woodruff's language than Woodruff's own diary entry. Speaking of the ordeal of Zion's Camp in 1834, in which he said nine of the vanguard were apart, Woodruff stated, "Brother Joseph [Smith] stood up on a wagon wheel and told the brethren that the decree had passed and could not be revoked, and the destroying angel would visit the camp and we should die like sheep with the rot. He had repeatedly warned the brethren of their evil conduct and what it would lead to, but they still continued in their course." Soon, Woodruff said, "the destroying angel did visit the camp," and "We buried eighteen in a short time." Clayton, *Journal*, 200.

164. Orson Pratt's words, recorded by William Clayton, include this statement: "There are many books in camp and worlds of knowledge before us which we have not obtained, and if the brethren would devote all their leisure time to seeking after knowledge, they would never need to say they had nothing with which to pass away their time." Clayton, *Journal*, 199.

165. John Brown reported that after Brigham Young's reproof of the camp he "divided the camp, each quorum separate. He then asked the Twelve if they would repent and turn unto the Lord and remember their former covenants. The answer was in the affirmative, and the same passed all the quorums." Brown, *Autobiography*, 75.

of a man who did not love to pray.[166] The President proposed that tomorrow be set apart as a day of Fasting & prayer & that the Twelve would go away by themselves & select some to go with them, & we would now go on this afternoon and find a place to camp ~~whie~~ & tarry tomorrow.[167] moved at half past one P.M. made 8 1/2 <miles> & camped after five oclock this evening.[168] came in sight of cottonwood Timber on the islands, Small & scattering.[169] <Total 517 1/4 miles>[170]

Sunday 30th [May 1847] A quiet, peaceab[l]e Spirit prevails in camp.[171] had our prayer meeting at 10 A.M. & the sacrement at 12 oclock.[172] The Twelve, accompanyed by W[illia]m. Clayton, Shadrac Roundy, Albert Carrington, & Porter rockwell went up into the Hills to pray in their Robes before the Lord.[173] had some showers this afternoon. at 3 oclock broke our Fast. we had

---

166. William Clayton also wrote that Stephen Markham addressed the group. After Markham's display of emotion, admitting his indulgence in the idle pastimes Brigham Young condemned, Clayton stated that "Many of the brethren felt much affected and all seemed to realize for the first time, the excess to which they had yielded and the awful consequence of such things if they persisted [there]in. Many were in tears and felt humbled." Clayton, *Journal*, 200–201.
167. Horace Whitney, who also took notes of Brigham Young's sermon, wrote that the "meeting lasted near 2 hours." Whitney, Diary, 29 May 1847.
168. After the day's journey, Erastus Snow wrote, "The fruits of our morning's lecture was clearly seen, a very different spirit brooded over the camp." Snow, "Journey," (April 1948): 125.
169. Dale Morgan places this camp "nearly on, perhaps a little west of, the present Wyoming-Nebraska state line." Empey, "Mormon Ferry," 148n29.

    Another feature of the topography near their camp was a large rock that "resembled the Hull of A Steemboat loaded with freight," Wilford Woodruff wrote, "So I named it stone steem boat bluff." Also claiming he named the formation was Orson Pratt who wrote that because the rock resembled "the stern of a steam boat . . . I called it BOAT ROCK." Woodruff, *Journal*, 3:190; Pratt, *Journals*, 411.
170. William Clayton's figure for the trek's distance to this point is "514 1/2 miles from Winter Quarters." Clayton, *Journal*, 202.
171. Albert Rockwood wrote, "all is still and quiet about the camp save the tinklin of cow bells and now and then the Neigh of a horse. the meek & Quiet Spirit of the Lord broods over us." Rockwood, *History*, 58.
172. In this meeting, Howard Egan wrote that "Many of the brethren expressed their feelings warmly, and confessed their faults one to another," with Appleton Harmon adding that all determined "to profit by the reproof that was received yesterday." Egan, *Pioneering*, 61; Harmon, *Appleton Milo Harmon*, 26.
173. While removing themselves from the general company, the Twelve and those who accompanied them witnessed a spectacular panoramic view of the area when they "ascended the ridge and proceeded across the plain towards a high sandy point, about 2 1/2 miles from camp, which we also ascended and had a fine view of the main bluffs on either side of the river, from 20 to 30 miles apart, and of the intervening level, rolling and tumbled up surface along the course of the river for some distance and down." Albert Rockwood, who accompanied the group in their momentary isolation, wrote, "at this time the twelve and ten others of which I was one took our priestly apperral [Nauvoo Temple

a Pot of bo[i]led Beans ~~&~~ with hard Biscuit. our meat is getting scarse. my cow affords milks so that we have mush and milk every night for supper for nine of us.[174] The Black Hills are in sight.[175]

Monday 31st [May 1847] A White frost this morning but a fair & pleasant day. wind West. Traveled 9 1/2 miles before noon & halted. Br John Higby Killed <a> Deer & Charles Harper a Badger. There is manny Rabbits or Hares along this Valley of a large size. Afternoon made 7 miles over a sandy road & camped on a creek of muddy water 12 feet wide,[176] that well may be called Sand Creek, for it is the character of the whole country around, with scattering bunches of grass.[177] my Horses have got verry poor, while oxen that were poor when we started are thriving. they are decidedly the best Team for this Journey. Mules stand it well.[178] I was on guard till 12.[179] <Lat 42° 4' 30">

---

clothing] and retired to the bluffs and saught a retired place for prayer whare we cloathed and came before the Lord and patisione [petitioned] four the things we needed by Prayer and supplication." Smith (Carrington), History, 30 May 1847; Rockwood, *History*, 58–59.

174. The following day Appleton Harmon also mentioned that "Breadstuff is scarce with us, short allowance." Harmon, *Appleton Milo Harmon*, 26.

175. Orson Pratt's closure for the night indicates the romance the plains still held for camp. After the rain dissipated, he wrote, "The moon shone in brightness in the east, being about half an hour above the horizon, and by the refraction of its mild rays through the falling drops, it produced a beautiful lunar rainbow in the west, but little inferior in brightness to a solar rainbow." He closed: "Chimney Rock, though forty miles distant, can be seen from the bluffs, while the [t]owering peaks of the Black Hills, west of Laramie, present themselves like blue clouds stationary in the horizon." Pratt, *Journals*, 413.

176. The configuration of their camp was formed "in two parallel lines on the gravelly bank of a swift run 20 to 30 feet wide and about one mile about its outlet." Smith (Carrington), History, 31 May 1847.

177. Horace Whitney characterized the country where they camped as being "almost a barren, sandy desert, with here & there a few, scant tufts of grass, thus affording a very poor chance for horses & cattle." Whitney, Diary, 31 May 1847.

178. See the analysis of the nutritional and physiological advantages of the use of oxen over horses and mules in overland travel in Kauffman and Liebowitz, "Draft Animals on the United States Frontier," 13–26. The authors assert, along with other benefits, that though "an ox worked at two-thirds the speed of a horse," "oxen possess greater torque," "feeding oxen generally requires less care than feeding horses," and Indians were less inclined to steal the less versatile oxen. Mules, like oxen, "will stop working when exhausted where a horse can literally be worked to death."

179. The company camped this night at Rawhide Creek, having received its name during the fur trade, about eight miles northwest of present Torrington, Wyoming. Empey, "Mormon Ferry," 148n30.

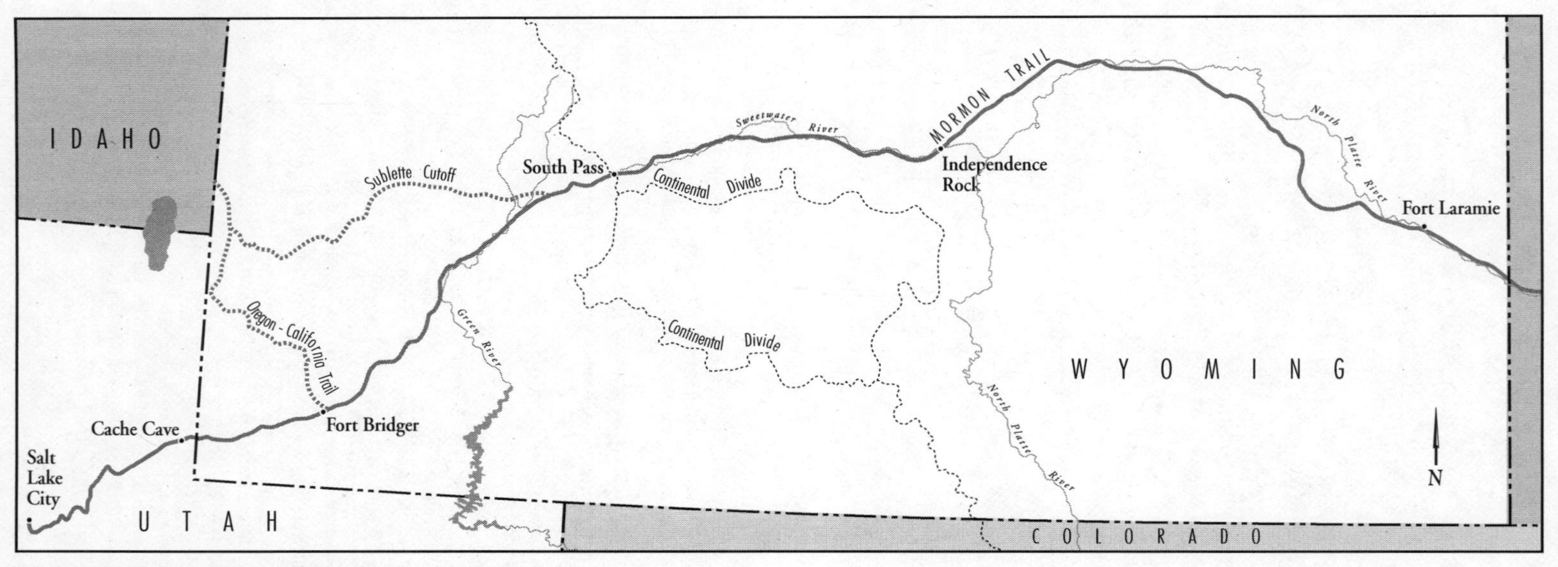

Mormon Trail across Wyoming. Map by Tom Child.

June 1847

THE SAINTS ARRIVED AT THE NEARLY twenty-thousand square foot Fort Laramie, located on the bank of Laramie's Fork in eastern Wyoming on 1 June. There the vanguard met and were joined by a group of Mississippi Mormons who had wintered at Pueblo, Colorado, with the Mormon Battalion's sick detachment, whose main body had traversed the American Southwest before finishing their Mexican War enlistment in California. From Fort Laramie on, the Saints shared the western trail with those bound for Oregon and California. Having passed buffalo country, feeding off the landscape became more difficult and nature's sustenance became scarce for a time. Following the North Platte River, by mid-month they, like all the other west-bound traffic on the Platte River highway, were required to cross the substantial river. To assist themselves and the non-Mormon emigrants as well, profiting from the latter by charging a toll, they established a ferry. The third week in June the vanguard passed Independence Rock and Devil's Gate, and thereafter followed the Sweetwater River across Wyoming's high plain. Arriving at the gateway to the Pacific slope, South Pass, on 27 June, they encountered the first of several mountaineers who informed the Saints of the Great Basin. At months end they rested at the Green River.

Tuesday first day of June 1847. A warm pleasant morning. all seem to be under the influance of the good Spirit. Br Heber [Kimball] was speaking of selvishness, that "every one should feel as though they could take hold & assist one another Just as quick as they would them selves: that when we could feel an interest in all our Brethren's welfare we would be filled with light & life: while selvishness tends to Death; it Kills the soul. one who acts for the good of the whole acts like a god, while he that coils hyself up in hymself & only strives to advance his own affairs will sink down to nothing." From the above I am led to deduce the following principles. The wise men of the world have this maxim, that self-love is the main spring of action in man. It tends only to promote act<ion> that is temporary, short lived, & ends in death. the Beasts act only from ~~the impulse of~~ self preservation which is the impulse of self love & such men are like them that are made to be taken & destroyd whos <only> motive of action is sevishness. Self-Love has no fell<ow>ship, fraternaty of feeling, or intercourse with Eternal things. it is not the Love of God, whereas Social Love is the grand moving principle of action in all imortal minds, whether [of] men, Ange[l]s, or gods, everlasting in duration, ceasless in opperation & is the Key of Eternal Lives. it is reciprocal in action. The Infant learns to love its mother because she gave it Birth & nourishes its frail infantile existence. It learns to love its Brothers & Sisters because she gave them Birth & nourishes their existance, and in more mature years it learns to love its Father because he gave it Life! hence the maxim that "we love him because he first loved us" is most assuredly true & based upon concert & unity of object, purpose, and design, increaseing in energy, strength & power until we arrive to the God Head. the Father, Son, & Holy Ghost are one!!![1]

This day we <traveld> 12 miles & camped <in a semicircle> on the North bank of the Platte one half mile above the Junction of Laramie's Fork[2] on the South & directly opposite <old> Fort Laramie <now Fort John>[3] distant 2 miles on the bank of Laramie's Fork, 40 yards wide.[4] the main Branch here is

1. Heber Kimball's sermon and Jacob's reflection again portray the religious character of the vanguard's participants often overlooked when tracking the pioneer transit to the West.
2. Fort Laramie represented a geographic and topographical demarcation for westbound emigrant companies. For overlanders traveling from the Missouri River to Salt Lake City, it was welcomed as something of a half-way station, even though distance-wise it was not. Horace Whitney described the physical setting as being "situated in an extensive valley, apparently 1 1/2 mile from the river, environed on all sides <except that next the river> by a lofty range of bluffs, which in the distance can be seen to the S. west, the dusky outlines of the 'Black Hills,' towering far above the surrounding scenery. . . . at this place the river is divided into 2 branches, one running [on] each side [of] the fort in an eastern direction, the one running on the south side is called the Laramie Fork of the Platte." The camps' accomplishment of arriving at Fort Laramie and the atmosphere surrounding their arrival stirred sentimental musings in some of the sojourners: "The camp fires have quite a cheerful appearance and old-fashioned look tonight." Whitney, Diary, 1 June 1847; Smith (Carrington), History, 1 June 1847.
3. The dimensions of the abandoned Fort John were, according to Wilford Woodruff, "144 by 132 outside" with the inside of the fort containing "16 rooms, 7 rooms on the North west & 7 on the South east one on the South, the largest on the north 98 feet long 47 wide." The walls were "11 feet high and 2 1/2 feet thick, with two entrances; one for stock and one for loads." Woodruff also stated that the "Oregon trail runs one rod from the S.W. corner of the fort." Smith (Carrington), History, 2 June 1847; Woodruff, *Journal*, 3:193.
4. The Saints arrived at Fort Laramie on the thirteenth anniversary of the fort's construction, initiated on 1 June 1834 by Robert Campbell and his partner William Sublette, for whom the structure received its first designation, Fort William. The lonely post symbolized to the Saints and all other westward travelers much more than Jacob entered into his account. Near the confluence of the Laramie and North Platte rivers, the fort served in the summer months as a refuge and recruiting station for the overlanders after weeks of dreary plains travel before entering the Rocky Mountains en route to the Pacific slope.

For most of its first decade the post was the center of Rocky Mountain fur trading activity. As demand for beaver pelts diminished in the 1840s, traders of buffalo hides and other commodities replaced the trappers as the businessmen of the high plains. Renamed Fort John in 1841 and reconstructed nearby of adobe for more substantial warehousing,

108 yards wide & runs rapidly.[5]

There was a Brother [Robert] crow at the Fort,[6] who met our advance guard at the river, having discovered us with a glass from the tower of the Fort when we were some distance below. he was much rejoiced to meet us.[7] he went up with the Missisippi company last summer to Fort Puerbelo [Pueblo, Colorado], 250 miles south of here & wintered there.[8] Br crow & his two

---

the nom de plume remained Fort Laramie. While westbound-travelers had utilized the fort since its mid-1830s construction, 1841 also witnessed the fort's first visit from a company specifically organized for transporting emigrants from the East to the West coast, the Bidwell-Bartleson company. Of course, tens of thousands followed. See Hafen and Young, *Fort Laramie*; and Lavender, *Fort Laramie*.

5. Orson Pratt, with instruments, measured the "North Fork" to be 108 yards wide and the "Laramie fork near the fort" to be 41 rods [yards] wide. The North Platte River transformed itself into a "river . . . much narrower," whose "Channel [was] much deeper and current strong," running "about three and one-half miles an hour." Pratt, *Journals*, 415–416; Smith (Carrington), History, 1 June 1847; Egan, *Pioneering*, 63.

6. Fort Laramie, Wilford Woodruff wrote, was "168 by 116 outside" with "6 rooms upon two sides, & 3 rooms upon the north & 3 upon the south occupied by stores Blacksmith & dwellings." To Woodruff, "It is quite A plesant situation for A fort." Orson Pratt determined the elevation of Fort Laramie to be 4090 feet above sea level, though Howard Egan noted that Fremont's calculation in 1842 for the elevation was 4470, a difference of 380 feet. The elevation is actually about that of Salt Lake City, 4260 feet above sea level. Woodruff, *Journal*, 3:193; Pratt, *Journals*, 416; Egan, *Pioneering*, 65; Rieck, "Geography of the California Trails," 15.

7. Regarding the company of southern Saints from Pueblo, Wilford Woodruff wrote that "They were truly glad to meet. No one can imagin the joy of friends on meeting each other under Such circumstances Away from the Abodes of white men whare they are ownly visited by Savages." Woodruff, *Journal*, 3:192–193.

8. LDS Church members who had converted in Monroe County, Mississippi, knowing of Mormon plans to settle in the West, moved westward themselves. They arrived at Grand Island, along the Platte River Road, to join the vanguard but were misinformed that Brigham Young's expedition had taken the South Platte into what is now Colorado. They were led by their misinformant to Fort Pueblo on the Arkansas River in what would become southeastern Colorado. Robert Crow's and William Kartchner's group of Mormon emigrants from Illinois had joined them. Together, forty-three people and nineteen wagons composed their party which arrived at Pueblo on 7 August 1846.

Only about a dozen then inhabited the small fort established a few years before. While there the Mormons heard the truth of Brigham Young's location and his designs for the following year. Some then returned to Mississippi to retrieve their families. These eastbound Mississippians encountered the Mormon Battalion on 12 September 1846. Learning of the Pueblo camp, the Battalion's commander sent the women and children of Battalion members, who accompanied the army from Fort Leavenworth, to join the other Mormons at Pueblo so the army could move faster and more efficiently. Eighty-six soldiers and twenty women and children traveled to Fort Pueblo. Twenty more able-bodied soldiers accompanied their wives from Santa Fe to Pueblo along with twenty-six men, too ill to walk. Their journey covered 18 October to 15 November 1846. A third detachment of the Battalion left Williamsburg, New Mexico, for Pueblo with fifty-five men. Approximately 275 Mormons spent the winter of 1846–1847 at Pueblo.

While it was an uncommonly mild winter, dissension wracked the military component of those in winter camp. Crow's company, with the Mississippi Saints,

Sons-in-Law, with their families, have been here two weeks anxiously waiting for some of the Saints to come up, ang [and] had heard nothing deffinite about our movements.[9] they were 15 days on their Journey & report that the detachme<nt> of our Soldiers [Mormon Battalion's sick detachment] at that place are prepareing to come on & Join us together with the other Brethren that are there.[10] 4 have died.[11] Three week[s] ago last Satturday the crow Indians came down from the Mountains & stole all the Horses belonging to the People of the Fort, 24 in number.[12] Some men have Just arrived here from Green river & report deep snows on the Mountains. where they traveled in snow can be seen from the Fort now on Laramie's Peak in the Black Hills.[13]

---

departed Pueblo before the Battalion to join the Mormon pioneers on the trail. They arrived at Fort Laramie just before the vanguard. Yurtinus, "Colorado, Mormons, and the Mexican War," 108–136.

9. Both Jacob's and William Clayton's entries for 4 June state that Robert Crow's party consisted of seventeen members.
10. The sojourn at Pueblo had been difficult physically and interpersonally for those forced to winter there. Ricketts, *Mormon Battalion*, 250–251.
11. Apparently four dead was the number reported to the emigrants, as Brigham Young's account uses the same figure. However, fifteen men associated with the three Mormon Battalion sick detachments died: seven expiring after separating from the battalion en route to Pueblo and eight during the winter at Pueblo. Ricketts, *Mormon Battalion*, 247.
12. Appleton Harmon stated that James Bordeaux, in charge of the fort, told the Saints that the Crow Indians "crept along under the bank of Laramie Fork until within eighty rods of the fort in the daytime, then rushed out between the fort and the horses and drove them off, in spite of the two guards herding them at the time." Learning of the Crow's raid on the fort's horses, and that it was "done in the day-time immediately before the eyes of the guard," Brigham Young instructed each captain of ten to select two "to act as a standing guard, to watch the cattle, &c. while we remain here." Harmon, *Appleton Milo Harmon*, 27; Whitney, Diary, 1 June 1847.

    The two western-most bands of the Teton or Lakota Sioux, the Oglala and Brules, centered their economic world on Fort Laramie at this time. The Crow Indians constituted the area's other dominant Native American tribe. Hostilities prevailed between the Sioux and the Crow, the former generally maintaining peaceful relations with Fort Laramie's white population at this time while the Crow saw the fort as an objective for plunder. Of course, by the mid-1850s, relations between the whites and the Sioux in the area had so degenerated that ponderous U.S. military and government initiatives were executed against the Sioux in 1855–1856. Lavender, *Fort Laramie*, 34; Clow, "William S. Harney," 133–151.
13. These, of course, are not the famed Black Hills of South Dakota but were similarly identified by the thick growth of cedar which covered them, though William Clayton indicated he was "satisfied that the Black Hills . . . are so named from the vast forests of pine trees covering their surface and being of a dark green color within a few miles of them." One reason the Native Americans gathered to the area was because the cedar made excellent lodge poles to use for constructing dwellings. Wade in Parkman, *Journals of Francis Parkman*, 2:629n125; Clayton, *Journal*, 221.

    Levi Jackman noted, as many other western sojourners did, that the "atmosphear [in the West] is very pure" and "the high hills that is said to be fiftey miles off . . . do not appear many [more] than 8 or 10" and that those ten or twelve miles away appear to be "not more than 2 or 3 at the most." Jackman, Diary, 2 June 1847.

There is some dwarf Pine on the Hills here & large Ash & Cottonwood along the stream.[14] <Total 554 1/4 miles.>[15]

Wednesday 2d [June 1847] Our Blacksmiths have set to work their three shops repairing & fitting up for a further prossecution of [our] Journey.[16] Mr [James] Bordeau[x],[17] the principal man at the Fort, kindly offered us an opportunity of useing their Smithy & was surprisid to learn that we had three already at work. The President [Brigham Young] & some others went over to the Fort today & chartered their Ferry Boat for $15.00 & brought it down the Laramie to the mouth & then up this stream.[18] we have dug down the banks & are prepared for ferrying our Waggons over.

---

14. John Smith, traveling in the second Mormon caravan of the season, as he approached the fort two months after the vanguard, noted that the physical character of the landscape had changed: "we saw Pine Tre for the first Time." Smith, Journal, 5 August 1847.
15. To illustrate the disparity of calculations made by various chroniclers on the journey, Jacob claimed the distance between Winter Quarters and Fort Laramie was 554 1/4 miles (though the source of this figure is not known), William Clayton declared the distance to be 543 1/4 miles, and Howard Egan's estimate was 541 1/4 miles. Clayton, *Journal*, 207; Egan, *Pioneering*, 62.
16. The few days at Fort Laramie provided opportunity for the Mormon emigrants to repair equipment as well to take care of other necessities precluded by their incessant westward march. On 3 June Wilford Woodruff wrote that besides setting up the blacksmiths for work, they also "made fires to do our washing, . . . the first time I have washed my clothing since I left winter quarters." Woodruff, *Journal*, 3:195.
17. James Bordeaux provided the Saints with "any information He could in relation to [their] rout," along with other news, including information about his Laramie enterprise which he said "sent six hundred bales of robes (10 in bl.) . . . over land 400 miles to Fort Pierre on the Missouri, where they are taken on steerage boats" earlier in 1847. The previous year California-bound Lilburn W. Boggs, former Missouri governor, visited Fort Laramie. Knowing the Mormons were en route to the West, Boggs warned Bordeaux to be wary of and distrust the Mormons, for whom he had held no affection for twenty years. After three days at the fort, however, Bordeaux told the Mormons they "were the best behaved Company that had passed there." In contrast, Bordeaux laughed, Bogg's company, composed of better "educated and cultivated" men than most other companies, "was quarrelling all the time & most of the company had deserted him." Bordeaux "finally told Boggs & co that, let the Mormons be as bad as they would, they could not be any wors than He & his men were." Smith (Carrington), History, 2 June 1847; Woodruff, *Journal*, 3:194; Bullock, *Camp of the Saints*, 180; Wade in Parkman, *Journals of Francis Parkman*, 2:630n136. Boggs's transit West in 1846 is treated in Marriott, "Lilburn W. Boggs," 52–62.

    Wallace Stegner, in appraising the encounter between Bordeaux and the Saints, explained that Bordeaux made the Saints "feel what in fact they were—disciplined and well-behaved—and demonstrated what has become a truism since: that no one is so popular among the Saints as a Gentile who expresses a good opinion of them." Stegner, *Gathering of Zion*, 144.
18. The Saints were pleased that James Bordeaux would rent his flat boat to them "on reasonable terms to assist us in ferrying the Platt." To test the craft, several of the Saints "got aboard and took a fine ride down the rapid current of Laramie to its mouth, about half a mile below our camp." Woodruff, *Journal*, 3:194; Smith (Carrington), History, 2 June 1847.

Fort Laramie (1853). Frederick Piercy, *Route from Liverpool to Great Salt Lake Valley* (1855).

Thursday 3 [June 1847] The right of the first Division began to cross a little after sunrise & at one oclock. P.M. had 38 Waggons over when a shower of rain came up, or rather down, from the South West.[19] There has been no rain here for 2 years till last week & now vegetation grows finely, thus the Lord Blesses the Saints.[20] Brethren Amasa Lyman, John Tibbits [Tippets], Thomas Woolsey, & Rawzel Stephens started at 12 oclock to go through to Fort Puerbalo to forward the Brethren that are there.[21] continued the ferrying

19. At 5 A.M., with the temperature at "51.5 deg.," the venture of transporting the wagons across the river began and continued at the rate of one crossing every fifteen minutes. The "hard storm" with attributes of "rain and hail accompanied by sharp lightening and heavy thunder . . . lasted one hour." Clayton, *Journal*, 212; Pratt, *Journals*, 417; Smith (Carrington), History, 3 June 1847.

20. Despite Fort Laramie's strategic location for the fur trade and later westward emigration, the environment, human and otherwise, generally proved difficult in sustaining life: "On account of Indian aggressions and the great droughts to which this country is subject," Orson Pratt explained, "agriculture is entirely neglected—they are dependent on the buffalo for meat, and on the States for articles of produce." Pratt, *Journals*, 416.

21. Brigham Young, Heber Kimball, Willard Richards, and Orson Pratt accompanied the four "to the Laramie fork and then held a council, kneeled down and dedicated them to God and blessed them." The emissaries were instructed by Young to assemble those at Fort Pueblo and lead them to join their brethren in the Great Basin. When the four met the main party from Pueblo on 11 June traveling toward Laramie they were hailed with much rejoicing, one of them running to Amasa Lyman "kissing him for joy." Lyman tempered lingering hostilities within the group from their winter together by giving them "a good [verbal] whipping . . . and a great deal of good council in relation to the course we should take." They arrived at Fort Laramie on 16 June 1847 and crossed the Continental Divide

at 4 oclock & put over 18 Waggons before dark, when it set in to rain.[22] I remained on the North side with my Ten. Lat 42° 12' 13".

Friday 4th [June 1847] Proceeded with our ferrying at sunrise & at 8 oclock all the Waggons [were] over, & while they were taking the Boat round up to the Fort, I walked across with some others to take a view of it.[23] there is 19 French & one Englishman here with numerous Squaws & half Breeds.[24] at 12 oclock we proceeded on up the South side of the Platte.[25] made 8 1/4 miles & camped in the Bottom which <is> narrow.[26] we came 3 miles over the Bluff to day. Br

---

the next month on 13 July. The main body of battalion veterans led by Captain James Brown entered the Salt Lake Valley, where they were grandly received, just days after the arrival of the vanguard. Clayton, *Journal*, 213; Ricketts, *Mormon Battalion*, 251–254; Yurtinus, "Colorado, Mormons, and the Mexican War," 137–138.

The history of the sick detachments of the Mormon Battalion and their connection with the Mormon vanguard can be found in Ricketts, *Mormon Battalion*, 229–259; Bigler and Bagley, *Army of Israel*, 277–303; and Yurtinus, "Colorado, Mormons, and the Mexican War," 126–135.

22. This storm was of such force, according to William Clayton, that they had to cease ferrying at 3:30 P.M. Once the storm passed the effort was renewed and by 5 P.M. the first division had crossed, the fastest having crossed in thirteen minutes. The second division then began transporting their wagons, although at a much faster pace than their predecessors, several crossing in only ten minutes. Only fifteen wagons were delayed crossing until the following day because of the revival of the storm. Clayton, *Journal*, 213.

23. When the Saints met James Bordeaux, according to Appleton Harmon, they were entertained in "a room upstairs which looked very much like a bar room of an Eastern hotel. It was ornamented with several drawings, portraits. A long desk, a settee, and some chairs constituted the principal furniture of the room. It was neat and comfortable." Harmon, *Appleton Milo Harmon*, 27.

24. "James Bordeaux and about 18 French, half breeds, and a few Sioux Indians" occupied the fort, according to Brigham Young's account, though Wilford Woodruff stated the fort was "occupied by 38 persons French mostly, who have Married the Sioux." Young, *Manuscript History, 1846–1847*, 556; Woodruff, *Journal*, 3:193.

While Jacob surveyed the fort, Young, Heber Kimball, Willard Richards, Albert Rockwood, and Thomas Bullock met with others at the fort who provided them with "very favorable reports about Bear River Valley [Salt Lake Valley], being well timbered, plenty of good grass, light winters, little snow and abundance of fish, especially spotted trout, in the streams." While the description of their destination was favorable, obstacles were noted for their immediate passage. Appleton Harmon said that traders who had just arrived at Fort Laramie from the west stated that "six days drive ahead the snow was middle deep ten days ago and that it would be difficult to find feed for our teams." It was also noted "that there were buffalo two days drive ahead and some grizzly bears." Clayton, *Journal*, 214; Harmon, *Appleton Milo Harmon*, 27.

25. Having been informed upon their arrival at Fort Laramie "that we could not travel more than four miles further on the north side of the Platte, the bluffs being impassable with wagons," the Saints used, thereafter, the south side of the North Platte, the Oregon-California Trail, to cross Wyoming. On 4 June emigrants bound for Oregon and California passed the Saints on the westward highway. Egan, *Pioneering*, 63; Brown, *Autobiography*, 76.

26. Entering the high Wyoming plain evoked a variety of exultations about the scenery, such as, "Stand and look all around our camp and you can hardly tell how we or the river got here, it being the most circumscribed view we ever had." Smith (Carrington), History, 4 June 1847.

[Robert] Crow & his company Joined us & consists of 9 men, 5 women, & 3 children, 5 Waggons & one cart, 24 oxen, 3 Bulls, 22 cows, 7 calves, and eleven Horses.[27] Mr [Lewis] Myars [Myers], Br Crows Hunter, Killed an Antelope.

Satturday 5th [June 1847] Started at 8 A.M., made 6 1/2 miles before dinner, one mile over the Bluffs and decended into the dry bed of a creek. in view of this place the river passes through a notch in the Black Hills which looks like a gate. the Precipi[ce] on either side [is] some 4 or 500 feet high so we passed up the creek, found in it two fine Springs of water & halted at one for dinner.[28] the Bluffs & Hills are scattered over with Pine & cedar. Eleven Waggons of Orregon Emigrants have Just come in above us on the road over the Hills from the Fort.[29] They have a Pilot by the name of Gabriel Predom [Prudhomme] who is attached to a Catholick Missionary Station on the river St. Marys [Bitterroot], a branch of the Columbia. <Total 568 miles, 14 3/4

---

27. The amalgamation of Robert Crow's seventeen members into the vanguard, minus the four who departed for Pueblo, brought the number of Salt Lake Valley-bound vanguard to 161, and their accompanying accouterments to "seventy-nine wagons, including a cannon, boat and cart, 96 horses, 51 mules, 90 oxen, 43 cows, 3 bulls, 9 calves, 16 dogs, and 16 chickens." However, the addition of Crow's company to the vanguard caused a stir at the outset. One of the Crow's camp found his team stuck in the sand. When approached by Brigham Young and others offering help, the newcomer "treated their assistance with contempt, all the time thumping away at [his] oxen." Young's outrage at the display provoked him to state "that there had been more abuse of cattle in those few minutes than by all the brethren since they left Winter Quarters." He then ordered Albert Rockwood to explain to Crow that "he did not nor would not suffer such abuse in the camp" and if the violator "did not reform from this moment he must leave the camp." Crow concurred, corrected the man, and the matter was resolved. It was apparent that despite the joining of the two bodies, Crow's group retained attachments according to their previous arrangement. Clayton, *Journal*, 215, 222–223; Bullock, *Camp of the Saints*, 180–181; Rockwood, *History*, 61.
28. Notable landmarks associated with the Oregon/Mormon Trail were passed by the vanguard on 4 and 5 June: Mexican Hill ("the most precipitous [descent] along the entire Oregon/Mormon Trail"), Register Cliff, and Deep Rut Hill. The springs mentioned here were known as "The Emigrant's Washtub," a "beautiful clear Spring, slightly warm & in sufficient quantity to turn a mill Wheel." Kimball, *Discovering Mormon Trails*, 27; Bagley in Bullock, *Camp of the Saints*, 181–182.
29. These emigrants were mostly from Michigan, according to Albert Rockwood, though Wilford Woodruff reported they were from Missouri. Two days previously, Erastus Snow and Woodruff reported that three westbound men arrived at the fort stating that behind them were "5000 emigrants" in "2,000 waggons on the road to Oregon from St Joes [St. Joseph, Missouri]," which, when compared to emigration data for the year, shows the numbers to be exaggerated. Divided "into companies of 20 to 50 waggons," the men expected the first of the emigrants to reach Fort Laramie on 4 June. Rockwood, *History*, 61; Snow "Journey," (April 1948):127; and Woodruff, *Journal*, 3:194–195, 197.

    Merrill Mattes's compilation of nineteenth-century Platte River Road travelers includes accounts of only a very few non-Mormons who wrote about encountering the Saints during their journey in 1847. Mattes, *Platte River Road Narratives*, 93, 96, 98.

from the Fort.> We followed on after them up the creek & out onto the table Land which is rooling [rolling] for several miles. we followed down another <dry> creek 1 mile, then up another that affords a beutiful stream of cold spring water. having made 10 1/2 miles this afternoon we camped 1/2 mile above the Emigrants.[30] we have fine showers & a growing time although the country exhibits marks of excessive drought.[31] There is four of the men belonging to the Fort camped with this company, on their way to Vancouvers Island to obtain Sea Shells to trade with the Indians.

Sunday 6th [June 1847] Held a fast & prayer meeting at 8 oclock.[32] met at 11 for Preaching. after singing & prayer by Br [Ezra] Benson, meeting was dismissed because of a shower of rain. Just at this time another company of Emigrants passed by us consisting of 22 Waggons, 2, 3, 4, & 5 yoke of oxen to a waggon & a large drove of cattle & horses.[33] The company that was camped near us passed on at 8 oclock & we proceded forward about one P.M. made 5 miles & camped between the two companies <of Emigrants> on this same creek, which is called 20 mile creek.[34] They came to us & hired Br [Burr] Frost to do some Black Smith work for them, having no Mechanicks with them. some of the them have been engaged with the Mobocrats heretofore.[35] ~~they started before us.~~ <My ten <were> on guard first w[a]t[ch]>.

30. The Mormon pioneers "Camped [on the] west side of Bitter Creek," according to Brigham Young. William Clayton, who had "put up two guide boards today" noting for subsequent emigrants distances from Fort Laramie, described the road that day as "very crooked, but not bad for traveling." Young, *Manuscript History, 1846–1847*, 557; Clayton, *Journal*, 218.
31. Despite evidence of drought, Orson Pratt saw beauty in the land: "The wild rose flourishes in great abundance" and the "principal herbs and plants of this elevated region are highly odoriferous, perfuming the atmosphere with their fragrance," while Wilford Woodruff noted evidence that they had moved into "elk, bear & mountain sheep country." Pratt, *Journals*, 419; Woodruff, *Journal*, 3:196.
32. William Clayton indicated that "many" neglected to join their brethren for meeting, but rather "kept about their wagons, some washing and some at other things." Clayton, *Journal*, 218.
33. The emigrants were identified by one Mormon as being "mostly from Illinois and Mississippi." Mormon diarists numbered the Oregon-bound emigrants as having between nineteen and twenty-two wagons. Smith (Carrington), History, 6 June 1847.
34. The guide of the larger Oregon-bound company, when the emigrants caught up to the Mormon vanguard, told church leaders that water could be found "six miles ahead" but that no more could be found for fifteen miles. So they would not "be obliged to travel over 20 miles to-morrow, before we can come to a convenient camping place, on account of the scarcity of water," the Saints determined, contrary to their normal practice, to move forward the six miles on the Sabbath. Egan, *Pioneering*, 66; Whitney, Diary, 6 June 1847.

    Appleton Harmon and Albert Rockwood indicated the encampment site was on Bitter Creek. Harmon, *Appleton Milo Harmon*, 29; Rockwood, *History*, 61.
35. Though Albert Rockwood said the emigrants were from "Mishigan," "four Missourians" visited the pioneer camp, according to William Clayton. They were "recognized by the

Monday 7th [June 1847] The road turns <to> the right here. up a dry valley, 7 3/4 miles, came to <a> Spring & halted for dinner. grass is scanty below. we have had excellent feed sinse we left the Fort. in this valley there is some verry good Pitch Pine Timber. while we were halted another Emigrant company of 13 Waggons, all ox Teams, passed us & the other ~~&~~ which started before us this morning ~~is~~ are in sight.[36] moved on 2 miles when we arrived at the sumit of a ridge of the Black Hills[37] & opposite Larimies' Peak crowned with his winter dress.[38] we have been in sight of it since a week ago last Satturday.[39] we now passed down another dry valley to Horse <shoe> creek, a fine Mill Stream about 2 rods wide.[40] it runs out from Laremie's Peak. Made 5 1/4 miles & camped in a wooded botom on the creek.[41] we are now in the midts of the Black Hills & have here the best grass we have had on the whole rout.[42] our

---

brethren," exhibiting some anxiety in meeting the Saints. They explained that Chariton, Missouri, a Missouri River town, had been abandoned by "the old settlers." Clayton, who emigrated to America after the Saints' Missouri troubles, had inherited animosity toward the Missourians as shown by his entry bidding the Missourians discomfort in their journey. Rockwood, *History*, 61; Clayton, *Journal*, 219.

36. William Clayton stated this company of thirteen wagons, with four yoke of oxen to each wagon, were driven by emigrants from Andrew County, Missouri, whose eastern border is less than thirty miles west of Far West, Missouri, from which the Saints were expelled in 1838–1839. Lorenzo Young stated they "seemed in a hurry to get away from us, and we was willing to have them." Clayton, *Journal*, 221; Young (Young), "Diary of Lorenzo Dow Young" 161.
37. The "many large cobble stones which lay in the road" in descending the summit, inhibiting travel, were removed by the "spare men" which made "it much better for other companies" traversing the road. Kimball, "Pioneer Journal," (April 1940): 83.
38. Orson Pratt thought the Laramie Peak's prominence controlled the area's weather by serving as "a condenser upon the vapour of the atmosphere which comes within its vicinity, generating clouds which are precipitated in showers upon the surrounding country." The area's thunder showers they experienced, he said, seemed "to originate in the vicinity of this peak." Pratt, *Journals*, 420.
39. Laramie Peak is the Laramie Range's highest, exceeding 10,200 feet above sea level.
40. John Fremont's 1842 account of his westward journey identified the place as Horseshoe Creek.
41. Heber Kimball, one of Brigham Young's chief lieutenants, routinely served as an advance scout for the party, and that day, having "discovered [a spring] before any of the rest of the brethren," he "named this spring as my spring." It was a "very large spring of pure water, about 8 feet in diameter and over 2 feet deep." The vanguard "encamped in a circle at 4 P.M.," located about four miles south of present-day Cassa, Wyoming, after traveling thirteen miles for the day. Kimball, "Pioneer Journal," (April 1940): 83; Whitney, Diary, 7 June 1847; Morgan in Empey, *Mormon Ferry*," 150n43.
42. The camp site located where they had access to "as good water as I ever drank," and "the highest & most luxuriant" grass since leaving Winter Quarters, caused Horace Whitney to describe the setting as "a perfect paradise." Howard Egan called their surroundings "truly romantic." Whitney, Diary, 7 June 1847; Egan, *Pioneering*, 67.

    It is important to note that nearly two months into the journey, one of the company stated "we are united in Love and in harmany. the spirit of the Lord is with us continuley." Many others of their countrymen who traversed the plains did not enjoy such cooperation

Hunters Killed two Black Tailed Deer & an Antelope. a heavy Shower of rain at 4 P.M.[43]

Tuesday 8th [June 1847] Started at 8 oclock, crossed the creek, & soon after, a Spring Branch. Saw a Buffalo.[44] about 2 miles ascended the highest & worst hill we have found.[45] passed over a rough, rooling [rolling] tract destitute of Timber.[46] plenty in sight to the left on the high Hills. Made 6 3/4 miles & halted on a small creek for dinner. [Lewis] M~~i~~<y>ars, Br [Robert] Crow's Hunter, brought in an Antelope.[47] ~~a~~ A dark wintry cloud arose from the West about 4 P.M. making it almost cold enough for Frost, but we decended at Evening into the Bottoms of Big Timber creek <8 3/4 miles> a rapid stream 2 rods wide where we campe in a place sheltered from the cold wind.[48] our Hunters brought in a Deer & an Antelope.[49] some of the Fur Co's Traders camped half a mile below us on their way in from Green River with four Teams laden with Peltry.[50] Emigrant camp 3 miles ahead. Total 612 <miles> & 58 3/4 from Fort John.[51]

---

within their companies. Empey, "Mormon Ferry," 131.

43. In planning to ferry the North Platte, a detail of men was sent to scout the route and make preparations. Young (Young), "Diary of Lorenzo Dow Young," 161.
44. This is the first buffalo seen in over two weeks.
45. William Clayton declared the ascent of the high bluffs to be "the worst we have ever had, being three quarters of a mile up, and having in that distance seven very steep rises," requiring double teaming. Clayton, *Journal*, 224.
46. Albert Rockwood, who had been appointed "Depity Superviser of the road" appointed ten others who, because of the rough road, "went forward of the teams & cleaned the road of stone," using "Axes, bars, spades &c." Rockwood, *History*, 62; Woodruff, *Journal*, 3:198.
47. The previous day Lewis Myers killed a deer for Robert Crow's company. When approached by Albert Rockwood to see if they were willing to divide it "according to the law of the Camp," Crow declined stating Myers, a non-Mormon, did not want to hunt for the other Mormons as he had an arrangement with Crow's family only. Kimball, "Pioneer Journal," (April 1940): 83.
48. John Fremont's map, according to William Clayton, identified this stream as "La Bonte river," which was "about 2 1/2 feet deep. Clear and rapid." Clayton, *Journal*, 225; Smith (Carrington), History, 8 June 1847.
49. Porter Rockwell and John Norton killed the deer and the antelope. Wilford Woodruff welcomed the harvest stating that upon arrival in camp, with the antelope waiting to be devoured, they "carved it up with our knives & stuck it on sticks & roasted it on the fire & satisfyed our Appetites finely without Salt." Whitney, Diary, 8 June 1847; Woodruff, *Journal*, 3:198.
50. The traders, en route to the Missouri River and captained by James Grieve, provided information to the Saints about crossing the North Platte, about Jim Bridger's fort farther west on the high Wyoming plain, and a favorable description of the Great Salt Lake Valley. One of them, William Tucker, being ill with "chills & Fever," was given a healing blessing from Luke Johnson. Woodruff, *Journal*, 3:199; Harmon, *Appleton Milo Harmon*, 30; Bullock, *Camp of the Saints*, 185.
51. It is not known for which day these figures were written given that they were entered at the page's bottom.

Wednesday 9th [June 1847] Started at Sunrise & moved down the creek a mile to get feed.[52] A [westbound] company of five Traders passed us with 12 Pack Horses <from Fort Bent on the Arkansaw> going to the mountains.[53] The [eastbound] party coming down made a Bull Boat of Buffalo Hides up at the crossing of the Platte and the President [Brigham Young] Started 19 Waggons this morning to go ahead & take possession of the Boat before the Emigrants get there.[54] we followed on 11 1/4 miles & halted for dinner.[55] passed a creek where there is abundance of red ocher in the Banks & Hills.[56] afternoon made 8 miles & camped on <a La Piere> creek [La Prele], about the same size as those described yesterday.[57] <this creek has cut its way through a high mountain & for ten rods [there is] a rock arch.>[58] we passed the Arkansaw Traders on the red Earth creek[59] & they passed us this

52. Feed for the animals as well as game for the emigrants proved less plentiful in this region.
53. The vanguard heard two different versions of this west-bound group's origin and destination: either Pueblo (or Fort Bent) to the Green River or Sante Fe to San Francisco. Thomas Bullock said the traders (identified as "Frenchmen" by Appleton Harmon), composed of "6 men & 15 horses," reported to them that the Mormon Battalion had embarked to California. Clayton, *Journal*, 226; Bullock, *Camp of the Saints*, 187; Harmon, *Appleton Milo Harmon*, 31.
54. These James Grieve-led eastbound "traders or mountaineers," upon meeting the Mormons, besides trading to the Saints such things as "robes mogazines & skins shirts & pants," told the Saints that they left a "ferry made of three buffalo skins hung in a tree on the Platte." The courtesy was due to their previous acquaintance with Lewis Myers; they wished to have Robert Crow's party use the ferry to cross the river. Determined to beat the Missouri emigrants to the North Platte crossing to control river passage, "about forty men," which included the entire Crow company, manned the nineteen-wagon express to cover the estimated seventy miles to the North Platte. Upon their arrival, according to John Brown, they "could find nothing of the boat." Woodruff, *Journal*, 3:199; Clayton, *Journal*, 226; Whitney, Diary, 9 June 1847; Brown, *Autobiography*, 76.
55. While the Oregon Trail was oft traveled by this time, it remained an uncomfortable ride. Orson Pratt described their work at this time: "We think that we fully work our road tax, for we have ten or twelve men detached daily, whose business it is to go in advance of the company with spades, iron bars, and other necessary implements to work the road." The previous day Albert Carrington "with several others worked on the road all day throwing away pebbles, etc." Pratt, *Journals*, 422; Smith (Carrington), History, 8 June 1847.
56. Ocher is an earthy clay colored by iron-oxide, usually yellow or reddish brown.
57. The pioneers noted "a grave just back of our camp, with a headstone marked 'J. Hembree, 1843.'" Smith (Carrington), History, 9 June 1847.
58. William Clayton described the creek being "about a rod wide, two feet deep and swift current." The arch was located about a mile from the road, the "tunnel" carved by the creek being "high enough for a man to stand upright in it." Clayton, *Journal*, 227; Egan, *Pioneering*, 69.
59. The hue from "Red Valley," as Thomas Bullock described it, extended "as far as the eye could reach," according to Howard Egan. William Clayton explained the "red earth or sand about the color of red precipitate . . . affected my eyes much from its brightness and strange appearance." Bullock, *Camp of the Saints*, 186; Egan, *Pioneering*, 69; Clayton, *Journal*, 226.

evening.[60] this country is covered with the wild Sage on the up Lands & Hills & destitute of Timber except on the Streams.[61] our boys Killed a Bird that the Traders call a Sage cock. it lives on the Sage & is a Species of Grouse. Three of ~~our boys~~ <them> brought in a Deer & an Antelope about 11 oclock at night. My Ten on guard the second watch.

Thursday 10th [June 1847][62] Moved on at 8 oclock. traveled 8 3/4 miles and halted in a fine Bottom of annother large creek.[63] Br [Edmund] Ellsworth Killed an Antelope. 4 1/2 miles from this place decended the Bluff to the [North Platte] River <91 1/4 miles from the Fort>.[64] I went out hunting this afternoon & Killed a Rabbit or Hare. we made 9 miles & camped in [a] grove on Deer creek.[65] three more Antelopes were Killed.[66] <Lat 42° 52' 50">[67]

---

60. The "19 1/4" miles traveled this day was said by Horace Whitney to be "the longest <ascertained> days journey ~~travel~~ we have accomplished since we left Winter Quarters." Whitney, Diary, 9 June 1847.
61. Despite the paucity of timber, the creek at which they stopped for the night was called Big Timber Creek, having passed Little Timber Creek earlier in the day. Jackman, Diary, 9 June 1847; Rockwood, *History*, 62.
62. It is important to note Horace Whitney's entry for this day stating that Heber Kimball identified their "destination" to be "the Salt Lakes." Clearly, church leaders knew their objective to be the Great Basin. Kimball, that day, included that he "learned today from one of the moutaineers that there is already one man living in the Bear River Valley and is to work making a farm," which, of course, referred to Miles Goodyear's enterprise on the Weber River near the future site of Ogden, Utah. Whitney, Diary, 10 June 1847; Kimball, "Pioneer Journal," (April 1940): 86.
63. Several diarists, including Orson Pratt, called the stream the "Fourche Boisee" though Horace Whitney identified the site as North Buffalo Creek. It is known today as Box Elder Creek. Pratt, *Journals*, 422; Whitney, Diary, 10 June 1847; Bagley in Bullock, *Camp of the Saints*, 188.
64. William Clayton continued to post "guide boards" every ten miles from Fort Laramie. Several of his comrades collected board scraps along the way, "enough to last 200 miles." Clayton, *Journal*, 231.
65. After stating he had been "agreeably disappointed in the country of the Black Hills" for the previous ninety miles, Erastus Snow described Deer Creek as "the most delightful place we have seen since we left the States." The stream was "about thirty feet wide and two feet deep, swift current and clear water." Interestingly, William Clayton, seven years after emigrating from England to the United States, wrote that the area reminded him of home. Perhaps Albert Carrington's discovery of a "coal bed," the "first ever reported to our knowledge on the Platte, or any of its tributaries," contributed to their feeling that the area was conducive to habitation. The Mormons established a way-station at Deer Creek in the mid-1850s to facilitate emigration, freighting, and carrying mail. Snow, "Journey," (July 1948): 264; Clayton, *Journal*, 229–230; Smith (Carrington), History, 10 June 1847.
66. While antelope and rabbit provided food for the pioneers this day, William Clayton caught two dozen fish in Deer Creek; others had comparable success. Clayton, *Journal*, 230.
67. Their camp's elevation, measured by Orson Pratt, was calculated to be 4,864 feet above sea level. Smith (Carrington), History, 10 June 1847.

Friday 11 [June 1847][68] Started half past seven.[69] traveled up the river 9 1/4 miles & halted for dinner. afternoon made 7 3/4 [miles] & camped on the river bank half a mile below where the [Missouri] Emigrants are crossing with a Scow Boat they brought on one of their Waggons.[70] 8 Antelopes b[r]ought into camp today. Snow on the high <Black> Hills to the left.[71] <Lat 42° 51' 50">

Satturday 12th [June 1847] Fine warm summer weather. I tried to ford the river this morning but found it too deep. Traveled 7 1/4 miles & halted for dinner on the bank where there is [an] excellent Ford. been much used by Emigrants. Brs [James] Case and [Stephen] Markum took their Horses & went across the river & found it to be mid sides to a Horse.[72] Br [Alexander] Chesley came down from where our company that was sent ahead under the direction of Bishops [Tarlton] Lewis and [John] Higby. are engaged in ferrying the company of 22 waggons of the Emigrants.[73] they get $33.00 for the Job

---

68. On this day Mormonism's second "cavalcade" of the year "began to roll out of Winter Quarters," numbering about 1,500 emigrants. The following day, when Eliza Snow left all that was familiar to her and joined the emigrants she lamented, "Bade farewell to many who seem dearer to me than life." Pioneers of 1847, Church Emigration, 1831–1847; Snow, *Personal Writings*, 177.
69. Describing the area that morning, Howard Egan wrote that "This is the first place I have seen since we left Winter Quarters, where I should like to live," the land being "good" with "plenty of timber and the warbling of the birds make it very pleasant." Egan, *Pioneering*, 71.
70. The Missouri emigrants told the Saints that the latter's advance detail was camped "at the ferry 10 miles or so Above us," though it was probably about half that distance. Beside the craft noted by Jacob, the Missourians had also constructed a raft to cross the river. Woodruff, *Journal*, 3:201; Clayton, *Journal*, 232.
71. Albert Carrington was taken with the scene of "snow banks" on the ridge "in spots, and at the head of ravines, contrasting vividly with the dark green of its pines, and the light green of its grass." Smith (Carrington), History, 11 June 1847.
72. Besides being "about four feet six inches deep," Stephen Markham and James Case also found the river, swelled by the spring runoff, to have a "very swift" current. When Brigham Young and others, on 13 June, measured the depth of the North Platte to find the right place to cross, they found it to be four to six feet deep. Clayton, *Journal*, 234; Bullock, *Camp of the Saints*, 191.
73. Ferrying the emigrants juxtaposed the Saints with Missourians, both groups harboring suspicion and resentment of each other. "When the brethren first commenced ferrying for them, they [the Missouri emigrants] were armed with Bowie Knives & Pistols, but before the brethren had finished their work the men had put them all away and having put away their fears also, were very civil and kind to the brethren." One of the Missourians tried "to swim across the river with his clothes on" and had to be rescued by the Saints in the Revenue Cutter or he would have drowned. The Missouri emigrants seemed "to feel well" toward the Mormons for the deed. Bullock, *Camp of the Saints*, 192; Clayton, *Journal*, 235.

    The good will displayed between the two camps included the Saints meeting "Judge Bowman," one of the Missouri emigrants. Bowman explained that it was his son, William Bowman, who was one of the guards enabling Joseph Smith and his associates to escape from Missouri authorities in April 1839. For the younger Bowman's compassion, he said,

& Flour at $2.50 per hundred.[74] besides, our Blacksmiths obtained Bacon & money for their work. After examining this Ford we concluded to go on up to where the Boys was. moved on 4 miles & camped on the bank 1 1/4 miles below their Ferry.[75] My Ten on Guard first watch. Artemus Johnson went out to the Mountains to Hunt this morning & has not come in at 8 oclock & Tunis Rappelle [Rappleye] started at 5 P.M. to go up to the top of the Mountain on a wager that he could go & get some Snow & come back in one hour if there was anny there, which manny have doubted, though some would tell them they had been there & seen it. Well, he having not returned, by the direction of the President [Brigham Young], Br Markum, with 6 or 7 Horsemen & the Bugler, Br [James] Craig, Started at 8 oclock to search in the Mountain for the fugitives, sounding the Bugle as they went. 18 minuits to elven Rappelle came in, directed by Fires we Kept burning, having tryed to get to the Bugle in the Hills but could not. We then fired guns & sounded the conk [conch] Shell for them to return.[76] at length the President, with three of us, took a lantern & went out to make Signals for them, when about a mile from camp we met them & soon after Johnson came to us, having followed the sound of the Bugle.[77] he brought part of a young Elk he had Killed. Rappelle's Snow melted in his hand by the time he got [to] the foot of the Mountain.[78] The Horsemen report it to be at least 8 miles, so deceiving are distances here. we

---

"Obediah Jennings" led a mob riding Bowman "on a bar of iron until they killed him." The elder Bowman also stated that "Morgan, the Sheriff, who had the custody of the Prophet Joseph, at the time of his escape from Mo., was in Oregon." Young, *Manuscript History, 1846–1847*, 558–559; Bullock, *Camp of the Saints*, 192; Egan, *Pioneering*, 72. The best description of Smith's escape and Bowman's role is Baugh, "We Took Our Change of Venue," 65–67, 80.

The portable leather skiff they carried, the "Revenue Cutter," capable of transporting "1500 or 1800 pounds," carried the emigrant's goods across the river. The "horses and cattle" swam. The wagons were then placed "in the cavity" of "2 logs that they had hewn out" and drawn across the swift-moving North Platte "by means of a rope fastened to the end of the tongue." Pratt, *Journals*, 424; Snow, "Journey," (July 1948): 265; Whitney, Diary, 12 June 1847; Harmon, *Appleton Milo Harmon*, 33.

74. The arrangement, Alexander Chesley reported, called for the emigrants to pay the Saints $1.50 per wagon load. One of the Mormons traded wagons with a Missouri emigrant, also obtaining in the deal a "horse, 100 lbs. flour, 25 lbs. of bacon and some crackers." Albert Carrington fixed the rate of transactions at "flour, $2.50 a hundred, and for trade and work bacon, cash $1." Clayton, *Journal*, 234–235; Smith (Carrington), History, 12 June 1847.
75. This ford became known as the "upper crossing of the Platte." The Mormons were now on the outskirts of modern Casper, Wyoming.
76. The conch, a large, spiral mollusk shell blown like a horn, likely referred to their bugle.
77. Artemas Johnson, according to Thomas Bullock, tired while hunting and simply "sat down on the hills," which delayed his return. Howard Egan said he got lost. Bullock, *Camp of the Saints*, 191; Egan, *Pioneering*, 73.
78. Tunis Rappleye, having believed he had but a three-mile journey, arrived in camp late due to misjudging the distance of mountain. His lengthy side trip provoked his declaration that "he would not go [on] another such a journey after a Snow Ball for 100 dollars." Bullock, *Camp of the Saints*, 191; Clayton, *Journal*, 235.

all returned to camp,[79] half past 12 oclock & I called up the Relief Guard. 5 Antelopes Killed, 4 Bears, 3 Buffalos, 10 [or] 12 Antelopes by the company that came ahead.[80] Total 678 1/2 miles and 125 from the Fort.[81] <Lat 42° 50' 18">

Sunday 13th [June 1847] Prayer meeting at 8 oclock.[82] after being opened Br H[eber]. C. Kimbal made some remarks concerning the necessity of our becoming one. he said it was natural for men to seek to go away by themselves & have a seperate interest & said that on this principle we cannot gather the House of Israel in six million probations. pursue this course & you will never advance one step & in the morning of the reserection you will find yourselves Just where you are now. the mission we are now engaged in is the greatest I have ever seen since I been in the Church & how do you regard it? why, it is of more importa[n]ce, Br [Robert] Crow, than to stay here & ferry over these gentiles if you could get 50 dollars a waggon. these are little things but it is necessary for us to be passive like clay in the hands of the Potter [Jesus] that we may become a vesel of honor.[83] then we shall come in honerable mansions, for the magnificence of the ma<nsion> will be in proportion [to the] honor of the vessel. When men walk in the Light & have the Spirit of God they view themselves to be the least, for they are enabled by the light to disern the small motes & their own imperfections are the more manifest. whereas, when a man is in the dark he can see nothing as it is, & hymself appears to be the largest object within the scope of his vision.[84]

Br Brigham [Young] then remarked when we are passive in the hands of the Lord we can receive Knwlidge but no truth can be written upon the tablet

---

79. With the camp's composition reconstituted after midnight, Tunis Rappleye and Artemas Johnson exhibited "extreme mortification at being the cause of so much anxiety and trouble in camp" which "served [to] greatly lighten the merited chastisement, which they received from the President." Snow, "Journey," (July 1948): 265.

80. The French traders told the Saints that the extraordinary abundance of wildlife had been driven into the area by Indians (Eastern Shoshone) hunting on the Sweetwater River, to the west of them. Clayton, *Journal*, 235.

81. The "Twelfth ten-mile stake [or board, was] put up" during the day, communicating information to the emigrants who followed. Smith (Carrington), History, 12 June 1847.

82. Others stated the meeting lasted from 9 A.M. to 12:30 P.M.

83. Heber Kimball's journal for this day notes his sermon's intent: "I endeavored to show them by the similitude of the Potter and the clay that the Lord designs to exalt us all to stations of honor and glory, if we will be passive in His hands, if not we shall mar in the process and be thrown back on the wheel again." John Brown wrote that Kimball, in emphasizing "the necessity of obeying counsel" in this sermon, related that "Brother Joseph [Smith] once told him to drive his team between two trees where one horse could not go through. He said he could not. Joseph stared at him. 'Drive through.' He jerked his reins and popped his whip. 'There,' said Joseph, 'that will do. I only wanted to see you try.'" Kimball, "Pioneer Journal," (July 1940): 152; Brown, *Autobiography*, 76.

84. Heber Kimball's "remarks were very touching and appropriate to our circumstances," according to William Clayton. Clayton, *Journal*, 236.

of the Heart unless that which has been written is first erased. when <we> are exalted to even to receive a fulness, does it follow that we canot <receive> anny more? if we understand what will save us today, that is a fulness of Knowledge but that will not be all that is <not> necessary for tommorrow. do men Know how to sereve the Lord & will you understand it if I tell you? It is to do that which will result in the greatest good. in order to do this it is necessary for you to Know & understand the result of all your actions. The gospel of Christ is the perfect Law of liberty.[85] what, say you, be subject <to> Law? is this liberty? yes, it is Liberty to increase without end but not to dethrone the Lord nor subvert his Laws while the liberty of the Devel is to injure your Brother & try to supplant him, run at large & Kill every thing you can whether you want it or not. well now, you are not at Liberty <to> do such things & thereby bring evil upon this camp, but anny one is at liberty to withdraw from us & go back or go with thos men who are going on ahead of us or go & live with the Indians, but if you stay here you must obey the Laws which are necssary for our preservation and for the building up the Kingdom of God. ~~at a certan~~ To the name of Je[s]us every <Knee> shall bow & reverenc must be paid to his Law whether men are willing [to] serve him in all things or not. they may serve the Devils and then bring them into bondage if they choose it, but to the name [of] God they must bow the Knee, & ackowledge his glory.[86]

After meeting the officers were called to the Presidents [Brigham Young] Waggon & agreed to go to the Mountain forthwith & get Poles to raft our Waggons across the Stream.[87] I went with a Team of four Horses from my Ten. we found beautiful Timber growing on the sides of this mountain, Norway Pine & Fir.[88] it is about six miles to the foot of the Mountain although it appears not half so far. ~~& it is~~ Br Heber's Boys made a raft.[89]

---

85. Brigham Young's sermon on agency and having unfettered liberty to exercise one's prerogatives represents another of Mormonism's timeless doctrines. Of course, Young's invitation to leave for those who chose not to harmonize with the whole is also a primary component of the principle of agency.

86. Mormon teaching that "every knee shall bow and every tongue shall confess that Jesus is the Christ" represents Latter-day Saint belief that a feature of the apocalyptic timetable includes Jesus' eventual triumph over the corrupted world.

87. The intent in this initial experiment of constructing a viable ferry was to lash the poles together to support four wagons tied abreast to be "drawn across the river without danger of being overturned." Whitney, Diary, 13 June 1847.

88. Those detailed to secure the poles reported "an abundance of splendid pine timber at the foot of the mountain and it is so thick with fir poles that a deer can scarcely get through. The poles and timber" harvested were "straight as an arrow." Kimball, "Pioneer Journal," (July 1940): 152.

89. Before the day was over flour, meal, and bacon were "distributed equally among the brethren in the camp, the provisions got of the Gentiles in payment for ferryage." Of this windfall, Wilford Woodruff wrote, "It looked as much of A miricle to me to see our flour & meal bags replenished in the midst of the black Hills as it did to have the Children of Israel fed with manna in the wilderness. But the Lord has truly been with us on this Journey." Whitney, Diary, 13 June 1847; Woodruff, *Journal,* 3:204.

Monday 14th [June 1847] Commenced crossing some waggons on a raft & Some floated with poles under & by the side of them. John Pack's turned over & over with box & cover all one. he lost a Plough, two bars of Iron & some Horse shoes.[90] the Poles brok under my waggon floating by the side of three others & it turned up sidewise but 'twas righted & all got ashore without much injury.[91] Some 12 or 15 waggons were got over during the day.[92] A copious shower with hail fell about 3 oclock,[93] after which I caryed over the loads belonging to my Ten in the Boat. the water is rising fast & we concluded not to float anny more wagons, as it is attended with much danger & risk.

Tuesday 15th [June 1847] I was engaged in towing up our raft with a yoke of oxen & hauling our waggons out from the beach till noon when I went with [Stephen] Markum, Lewis Barney, & George Mills up the river two miles & made another Raft out of dry cottonwood. they put oars to it & it worked better than running with Poles alone.[94] the wind severe downstream.

Wednesday 16th [June 1847] I was called to go with 16 or 18 others down the river in search of Timber for canoes, as the President [Brigham Young]

---

90. Howard Egan described the reason for John Pack's misfortune: "The second division then stretched a rope across the river at the narrowest place, and lashed two wagons together, and made the rope fast to them to float them across. When the wheels struck the sand on the other side, the current being so strong, it rolled them one over the other, and breaking the bows, and loosening the irons, etc., to the amount of $30." Egan, *Pioneering*, 73.

91. Jacob describes only part of the difficulties in crossing which, according to William Clayton, forced the decision that day to cross the river "one wagon at a time on a raft." Despite the procedure being "very slow," requiring "three or four days to get all the wagons across," caution tempered any urge to hurry. Clayton, *Journal*, 238.

92. "After toiling all day nearly up to our armpits in the water," Howard Egan reported, "we got over eleven wagons in the afternoon, making twenty-three during the day." Besides the wagons ferried during the day, "eleven waggon loads of goods" were transported via the "little leather boat." Others assisted in "driving cattle attached to the raft which [had to be towed] up stream some distance." Horace Whitney, one of the latter, said "I have done the hardest day's work to-day I ever recollect to have done in my life, & this evening I feel quite worn out with cold & fatigue." Egan, *Pioneering*, 74; Woodruff, *Journal*, 3:205; Whitney, Diary, 14 June 1847.

93. The storm, described by Albert Carrington as the "worst we have had," lasted about an hour. This cold blast followed a day described by several as being warm enough for summer. Smith (Carrington), History, 14 June 1847.

94. This raft was one of two of the pioneers' new ferry designs meant to fashion a safe and reliable means to transport their wagons. While twenty wagons were freighted across the North Platte, their first raft, like the others proved unstable and dangerous, though the two new rafts which employed oars proved "to be far superior to poles" in the strong current. With the exception of one horse which drowned that day, Robert Crow's "Indian pony" which became tangled in the "long rawhide rope, a piece of chain, and a billet of wood," the company's animals safely swam the river, though the rising river and high winds made for a dangerous crossing. Clayton, *Journal*, 238–240; Smith (Carrington), History, 15 June 1847.

said he was tired of experamenting with Rafts &c. after going about 3 miles we found two cottonwood trees near together of which we constructed two canoes 23 feet long, put them on the Waggons & hauled them up to camp at night.[95] I found that there was one hundred & eight Emigrant Waggons within four miles all wanting to cross the river.[96] Some hired us to cross them at $1.50 paid in flour at $2.50 per hundred, & others crossed themselves.[97]

Thursday 17th [June 1847] Crossed my Horses & cow over by s[wim]ming them this morning & then went with Barnabas Adams & two others to the Mountain to get Pine Poles to frame our canoes tgether to form a ferry Boat. While Capt [Thomas] Grover & others were engaged in cleaning out the canoes & the remainder of the Brethren completed the ferrying our camp over today.[98]

---

95. Lewis Barney, one of Jacob's ten detailed to obtain the trees necessary to build the raft, wrote that they "selected two large trees, 3 feet through. of these We made two large Canoes, 30 feet long. We then Cut two other trees and hewed them down to 2 inches thick and Straightened the edges making plank[s] of them, 14 inches wide and 30 feet long." They "then Lashed the two Canoes to geather and fastened the 2 plank[s] on the Canoes length-wais." (Barney exaggerated the length of the trees, though Clayton and Egan stated they were 25 feet in length.) Orson Pratt added this description of the craft, called by the Saints the "*Twins of the Black Hills*": "we made two large cotton wood canoes, and placing them parallel to each other, a few feet asunder, firmly pinned on cross pieces and flat slabs running lengthwise of the canoes, and having attached a rudder and oars, with a little iron work, we had a boat of sufficient strength to carry over the loaded wagons of the emigrants." The craft was manned by three men. Barney, Autobiography and diary, 38; Clayton, *Journal*, 239; Egan, *Pioneering*, 75; Pratt, *Journals*, 426; Whitney, Diary, 18 June 1847; Snow, Journey," (July 1848): 266.
96. Rumors circulated in camp that besides the "large collection of wagons" composing the "2d company of [Mormon] Pioneers" recently seen "above the head of Grand Island," another "1000 wagons of emigrants" filled "the road between here & Ft. John or Laramie," prompting the Saints to consider something more permanent for the ferry. William Clayton wrote that the purpose for the latest raft was twofold: "to ferry over the gentile companies" allowing for the acquisition of "a good stock of provisions for themselves," and also to "be prepared to set the brethren of the next company over without delay." Whitney, Diary, 15 June 1847; Clayton, *Journal*, 240.

    The "Twenty-one emigrant wagons [that] crossed below us four or five miles" were identified to be "from Pike and Adams Counties, Illinois," and who reported that they "buried two of their number within 150 miles of this place, the first deaths, to our knowledge, in any of the emigration companies." Smith (Carrington), History, 16 June 1847.
97. Horace Whitney reported a "company of about 21 wagons of emigrants, down the river about 3 miles near where our brethren were at work to-day, . . . managed to cross the river on a raft built by themselves." Thomas Bullock's account for the day indicates the flurry of activity, both the Mormon vanguard and Oregon emigrants, at the crossings. Whitney, Diary, 16 June 1847; Bullock, *Camp of the Saints*, 194.
98. The vanguard's crossing of the North Platte was completed about noon, including Brigham Young's wagon, when they "all moved up the river about 1 /2 mile & formed in a circle on its banks," though "It took till near dark before all the wagons got up." Because "it was too cold, and the wind blowed too strong" on the 17th, the remaining horses stayed on the river's south bank until the following day. Smith (Carrington), History, 17 June 1847; Whitney, Diary, 17 June 1847; Clayton, *Journal*, 241; Egan, *Pioneering*, 75.

we found the wind blowing on the Mountain cold as September. returned with Poles at evening.

Friday 18 [June 1847] A hard, white frost this morning. Started over at sunrise to finish our Boat.[99] got it completed & launched by two oclock P.M. & took on an Emigrant waggon with her load & carryed it safe over.[100] We have heard that our People from Winter Quarters are coming up with a large company, so we have built this Boat for their accomodation & in the meantime ferry all the Emigrants that wish to cross before they come.[101] so ten men were left to attend to this business with orders to charge $1.50, for crossing a Waggon & family, in Provisions, or young cattle at State prices, or $3.00 cash, to Keep a Just & acourate acount, & make the returns of the proceeds of their labor to the Authoritys of the Church & also to cross the Brethren & charge such as are able to pay a reasonable price to be determined by the council that shall come with the Camp. The Leather Boat [Revenue Cutter] was also left as church Property. the names of those 10 men are Tho[mas]. Grover, Capt., John S. Higby, his assistant, Luke Johnson, Edmund Elsworth, W[illia]m. Empy, Appleton Harmon, Francis M. Pomeroy, Franklin Stewart, James Davenport, the Blacksmith & Errick Glines who remained without counsel & on his own responsibility.[102] They were counciled to build themselves a

---

After the Saints were over, the Oregon-bound emigrants were ferried. After the initial company had arranged for passage at $1.50 per wagon, the second company "offered to pay the brethren 50¢ per man extra if they would set them over first, making $5.00 over the stated price for ferriage." Despite Albert Rockwood's arrangement with the first emigrant company, which he declined to break, because it was Stephen Markham's "day for the use of the boat," he took the offer and the second company prevailed. The ferriage of the Missourians, though one Saint claimed the second company to be from Iowa, "continued all night and till daylight," the night being so cold as to require coats for warmth. Clayton, *Journal*, 240–241; Empey, "Mormon Ferry," 133; Jackman, Diary, 17 June 1847.

99. After finishing the raft at 1 P.M., the vanguard could have continued their journey on 18 June, but determined it best to "wait and assist in finishing the boat and also to take the provisions on which will be realized from these two companies [of emigrants]." The "new canoe" proved to work "very well considering the wood [was] green," though Albert Carrington noted that, while they could not carry "a wagon with a full load," they did provide "quicker trips than our rafts." Whitney, Diary, 18 June 1847; Clayton, *Journal*, 241; Egan, *Pioneering*, 76; Smith (Carrington), History, 18 June 1847.

100. William Empey, one of those assigned to tend the ferry, stated they assisted eighty wagons across the river. Their payment for being ferried, taking most of the week, assisted the Saints significantly; the "263 pounds of flour, 100 pounds of meal and twenty-seven pounds of soap" figured to assist the Mormon vanguard for over three weeks. Empey, "Mormon Ferry," 133; Egan, *Pioneering*, 76–77.

101. Coincident to the vanguard's crossing, three westbound emigrant companies utilized the Mormon ferry. Whitney, Diary, 18 June 1847.

102. Eric Glines, for unknown reasons, determined to stay at the ferry, even though Brigham Young "wished [him] to go along with the [vanguard] company." He declined even though Young reproved him and, as Thomas Bullock stated, "those who were staying voted that they did not want Glines to stay." Charles Harper characterized the group as "9 of our

comfortable habitation & remain here till the camp comes up & then haul out their Boat & come on with the Brethren so as to have [a] chance to see the place of our Location.[103] <two Waggons [were] left here. Two Antelopes Killed by J[oseph] Hancock.>

Satturday 19th [June 1847] Frost again & a cool wind. at 8 oclock we got under way across the country towards the Sweet-water.[104] 11 1/2 miles came to a Spring & halted.[105] here is signs of coal & Iron in abundace. our course West. from here we traveled south Westerly 10 miles and camped after Sunset at a place called the Soap Springs, a perfect mire hole.[106] this is a sterile, barren region ex[c]ept low bottoms which afford good grass. but this is a place of most forbiding aspect, as one of my men expressed himself—"such a country! mire holes on the Mountains, Frost in July, Salt water & no wood to cook

---

good men" and "one indifferent one thrown in." Glines rejoined the main body about a week later. Woodruff, *Journal*, 3: 207; Bullock, *Camp of the Saints*, 195; Harper, *Diary*, 26.

James Davenport, also one of those assigned to the ferry, became, apparently on his own initiative, the first of the Mormon pioneers to return to Winter Quarters, encountering the second Mormon emigrating company on 31 July 1847 near Scott's Bluff while he traveled eastward. Historian's Office, Pioneers of 1847, Church Emigration, 1831–1847.

103. Those who remained were told, besides conducting their lives appropriately, to "attend strictly to their duty of ferrying over the emigrants," including the counsel to "Retain not that which belongeth to the Traveller." The "small house" they were instructed to build "on a gentle eminence on the other side of the river" was to be constructed, in part, "to secure them & their effects from the Indians, in case a war-party should come this way." (The written instructions, to which all of the nine subscribed, along with particulars of their ferry activities after the vanguard departed, was recorded by William Empey and Appleton Harmon.) By 18 July 1847, "they had ferried over four hundred Oregon waggons." Empey, "Mormon Ferry," 134; Harmon, *Appleton Milo Harmon*, 35; Whitney, Diary, 18 June 1847; Sessions, *Mormon Midwife*, 91. See also Bliss and Griffin, "Platte River Ferrymen."

This ferry and subsequent efforts by Mormons to establish ferries on the North Platte, including controversy over their precise locations, is described in Murray, "Trading Posts, Fort and Bridges of the Casper Area," 4–30.

104. Besides establishing a ferry to assist their fellow sojourners, Mormon and non-Mormon alike, the week's rest also restored the men and their animals: "good health and spirits" prevailed, and their "teams [were] in very good order." Clayton, *Journal*, 242.

105. Horace Whitney noted the spring was called "Cold Springs," while Wilford Woodruff identified them as "Willow Springs." They were, according to Albert Carrington, then "within sight of the high red banks of the Platte, or Red Butte." Whitney, Diary, 19 June 1847; Woodruff, *Journal*, 3:208; Smith (Carrington), History, 19 June 1847.

106. The twenty-one plus miles traveled that day was the "longest, ascertained distance we have made per day" since they left the Missouri River, according to Horace Whitney. Whitney, Diary, 19 June 1847.

The water at the site of their camp that night Wilford Woodruff called "poison water." He wrote that "the water tasted as though it run through A bed of salt, salts, saltpeter, sulpher," that it was "naucious Horrible." They had been informed by traders that the water would kill their animals, so they allowed their animals but little of it. Woodruff, *Journal*, 3:208.

with."[107] We had to resort to the Buffalo chips again & sage brush to cook our meat. John Norton & Andrew Gibbons went out to hunt where we halted. John came in about 11 P.M. but Gibbons remained out.[108] they had Killed a Buffalo. Gibbons went to a camp of Emigrants, got them to bring in his meat & tarried with them. Kiled three Antelopes, 1 deer <& 1 Buffalo>.[109]

Sunday 20th [June 1847] Started before breakfast.[110] 4 miles halted in green spot on the outlet of the willow Springs. Six miles from here South Westerly came to the Willow Spring.[111] 10 miles farther, same course. after decending into the valley of the SweetWater camped at dark near a creek.[112]

Monday 21st [June 1847] A Beautiful clear morning. moved on <S west> 7 1/2 miles & halted on the N bank of the Sweet-Water, one of the principal Sources of the Platte. This is a Beautiful Rivulet of clear water, 50 yards wide.[113] I visited the Soda Spring while we were halted here a mile & a half below. This Spring, or more properly a Pool, is a great natural curiosity. it [is] some 4 or 5 hundred yards in circumference, clear water without anny outlet & having the taste of Strong Lye, with a tincture of common

---

107. The area was "the most wretched of any ground we have found on the way," stated Wilford Woodruff. Brigham Young "thought it might properly be called Hell gate." An attack of mosquitos added "to the loathsome, solitary scenery around." Woodruff, *Journal*, 3:208; Clayton, *Journal*, 245.

108. Andrew Gibbons returned to camp the following evening.

109. Howard Egan noted that Lewis Meyers, the hunter for Crow's camp, killed two buffaloes that day but that he "took the tallow and tongues" only, and "left the meat to rot on the prairie." Egan, *Pioneering*, 77.

110. While Sabbath travel was unusual, several of the company, like Levi Jackman, stated that "For want of grass" they moved on. Undoubtedly, the need to make up for time lost at the ferry crossing also played into the decision. Jackman, Diary, 20 June 1847.

111. Willow Springs, a spring "about two feet wide and the water ten inches deep, perfectly clear, cold as ice water, and very good tasting," was a noted site on the Oregon Trail. The locale "looked like an oasis in this barren country," according to Albert Carrington. Clayton, *Journal*, 247; Snow, "Journey," (July 1948): 266; Smith (Carrington), History, 20 June 1847.

112. The company hoped to reach the Sweetwater River this day only to find they were "yet some miles from it." Their camp for the night was in a setting "entirely destitute of timber, not a tree to be seen, nor a shrub larger than the wild sage which abounds in all this region and will answer for cooking when nothing else can be found." Because Wilford Woodruff and John Brown, out exploring, had not returned to camp by midnight "the cannon was fired for them" to assist their return to camp in the dark. Clayton, *Journal*, 250; Smith (Carrington), History, 20 June 1847.

113. The course of the Sweetwater River, girdling the belly of Wyoming's high plains, served as the primary emigrant route across what became the Cowboy State. Generously serving emigrant needs after receiving the North Platte's handoff, the river led overlanders across Wyoming's mid-section to South Pass where their journey descended into the Pacific Ocean's drainage. Modern concerns about the river's fragile ecosystem symbolizes difficulties in the preservation of America's natural outdoor trail museums.

Independence Rock near the Sweetwater River (1853). Frederick Piercy, *Route from Liverpool to Great Salt Lake Valley* (1855).

Salt.[114] as the water is diminished by evaporation, the sand on the shore is covered with a substance white as the driven Snow & that answers every purpose of Saleratus.[115] I found it lying from 1/2 to 3 inches thick & soon gathered up a Bucket full. when I returned, our camp had started. 1 1/4 miles came to the Southern Point of Independence Rock on the bank of the Stream. this is a Pile of Granite standing in an Isolated position on a level grassy Plain & is 45 yards high & 600 by 300 yards in extent & with a round cap like summit on which there is Pools of water from five to ten feet in width, several feet deep.[116]

---

114. William Clayton reported three different bodies of saleratus-laced water. A remnant of this lake still exists on the high Wyoming plain. Clayton, *Journal*, 251.

115. Saleratus is the equivalent of sodium bicarbonate, baking soda. Overlanders harvested the valuable commodity by the bushel for use in raising their bread. Harriet Young, Lorenzo's wife, "made some bread by using this lake saleratus. When it was baked it was nice and light as bread could be, and has no unpleasant taste. She says that the saleratus is so much stronger than that bought at stores, that a person only needs to use about half as much of this as the other for the same quantity of flour." However, later in the month they found that "it being so much stronger than common saleratus, if the same quantity is used it makes the bread quite green." Kimball, "Pioneer Journal," (October 1940): 212–213; Clayton, *Journal*, 262.

116. Independence Rock, "shaped like an oblong loaf of bread" according to Albert Rockwood and referred to as "Rock Island" by Albert Carrington, is one of the most noted landmarks on the Oregon Trail. Fur-trader William Sublette dubbed the granite dome Independence Rock to note he and his companion's camp there on 4 July 1830. Government surveyor Ferdinand Hayden defined the size of the unusual geographic phenomenon as 1,552 yards in circumference in 1870. Reminded of the religious nature of the Mormon westward

High rocky ranges of Mountains on both sides of the Stream from 1/2 to a mile distant. in fact a Fortress on this Rock or on another Irregular cragged one five miles above would command the entrance into the Great South Pass of the Rocky Mountains. At the last mentioned place there is <a> chasm or rent in the Mountain some 80 feet wide & three hundred feet high through which the River rushes with great impetuosity for 20, 30 Rods into the plain below.[117] This Spur of the Mountains has evidently been subjected to Volcanic action.[118] Afternoon made 7 3/4 miles & camped on the bank of the River Just above the chasm on the South side having forded the Stream a mile above the Independence Rock.[119] two Antelopes were Killed today. the Mountain South has Snow near its summit.[120]

Tuesday 22 [June 1847] I was on guard from 12 oclock till daylight. at 8 oclock we were under way. made 10 miles over a rough, sandy road & halted on the

---

venture, Wilford Woodruff ascended the giant rock and "offered up . . . prayers according to the order of the priesthood" and rededicated himself to "the building up of Zions in the last days." Rockwood, *History*, 65; Smith (Carrington), History, 21 June 1847; Woodruff, *Journal*, 3:211.

Interestingly, while numbers of the vanguard probably scrawled their names on the rock, similar to hundreds of other nineteenth-century "trappers, traders, travellers, & emegrants," Jacob's, on the "top of the north end of the rock," is the only one of the pioneer company that is extant. Woodruff, *Journal*, 3:211; Bagley in Bullock, *Camp of the Saints*, 198n77–78; Hileman, *Tar and Paint and Stone*, 211–212.

117. The chasm, then and today known as Devil's Gate, was created by the Sweetwater which "had a channel of about three rods in width through the pass, which increases its swiftness, and it dashes furiously against the huge fragments of rocks, which has fell from the mountains, and the roaring can be heard a long distance." Orson Pratt measured the height of the cliffs looming over the stream to be four hundred feet in height, the same measurement pronounced by John Fremont. The unique formation is located near the site of the disaster nine years later where at least 145 Mormon emigrants attached to the Edward Martin handcart company died, having been caught in an early and lethal winter storm. A way station was established there by the Mormons to aid emigration in the mid-1850s. The LDS Church presently maintains a visitor's center there on the former Sun Ranch. Egan, *Pioneering*, 82; Rockwood, *History*, 65.

118. The Sweetwater's gorge at the base of Devil's Gate was, to William Clayton, "scenery . . . of romantic grandeur and it seems wonderful how the river could ever find a channel through such a mass of heavy, solid rock." Clayton described the rock formations of the area as appearing "as though giants had in by-gone days taken them in wheelbarrows of tremendous size and wheeled up in large heaps, masses of heavy clay which has consolidated and become solid, hard rock." Clayton, *Journal*, 252, 255.

119. The Sweetwater River's current, according to William Clayton, was "very swift, the water a little muddy, but pleasant tasting." Further, he said, "On the banks of the river there is plenty of good grass but destitute of wood there being only one solitary tree to be seen." Clayton, *Journal*, 252.

120. The nature of Sweetwater Valley, according to Orson Pratt, varied "in breadth from 5 to 8 or 10 miles, bounded upon the north and south by mountainous ridges, isolated hills, and ragged summits of massive granite, varying from 1200 to 2000 feet in height, those upon the southern boundary being the highest, and are partially covered with snow and well timbered with pine." Pratt, *Journals*, 429.

bank of the Stream directly opposite a Pass that goes out of the valley to the North. one Emigrant company passed us here & another came up.[121] Lorenzo Young broke his waggon axletry [axletree].[122] moved on in a deep dry sand 10 3/4 miles. passed the Emigrant camp a mile & camped in a beautiful spot on the bank of the River.[123] two Antelopes Killed. <Lat 42° 28' 28">

Wednesday 23d [June 1847] Charles Harper put in Lorenzo [Young]'s axletree last Night by Moon light & finished this morning.[124] Started 1/2 past 7 P.M. [*sic*][125] made 8 1/2 miles & halted on the bank of River where it enters a narrow defile in the Mountain.[126] moved on this afternoon over the most barren & deep sandy road that we found. hove in sight of a higher range of the Rocky Mountains to the West than anny we have seen & appears entirely covered with Snow.[127] made 8 1/2 miles & camped on the bank of the Stream with an Emigrant [company] above & another below us.[128] L[ewis]. Barney Killed two

---

121. Albert Carrington reported that while "nooning" he "learned that a young man eighteen or nineteen years old, belonging to the emigrant company just behind, named Columbus Austin, of Morgan County, Illinois, was drowned on the 18th [July] by swimming a horse across the north fork." Smith (Carrington), History, 22 June 1847.

    While the Mormons benefitted from westbound emigrants at the ferry, after the North Platte River crossing they proved competitors, although most interactions with emigrants were benign. Two days previously Howard Egan reported a half dozen of one particular party of Missourians disguised as Indians trying to detour the Mormons from a favorable campground. The Saints considered it "an old Missouri trick and an insult to our camp," and Brigham Young added that "should they attempt any more to play Indian tricks on us, it is very likely they will meet with Indian treatment." Egan, *Pioneering*, 79; Kimball, "Pioneer Journal," (July 1940): 157.

122. Lorenzo Young's axletree, a bar connecting two opposite wheels of a wagon, was "the first that has brook [broke] down on our journey." Illustrating that relations with Missouri emigrants were mixed, Howard Egan noted that after Young's axletree broke, "One of the Missouri company came up, and one of them took Brother Young's load into his wagon, and spliced his axletree, which enabled him to follow the camp." Rockwood, *History*, 65; Egan, *Pioneering*, 83.

123. The close proximity of the vanguard's travel at this time with Oregon-bound emigrants is shown in Snow's entry for this day: "We are camped tonight on the river at the base of an imposing butte about 250 feet High, with a company of Oregon Emigrants about three miles in advance of us, and another about the same distance in the rear; These two companies left the Platt, one about an hour before and the other about an hour after we did." Snow, "Journey," (July 1948): 267.

124. Charles Harper's skill was employed, he wrote, "at night by request of Brigham [Young, who asked that] I put another in so we were not detained from traveling as usual in the morning." Harper, *Diary*, 27.

125. It was the intention of church leaders to get an early start "to get ahead of the emigrants." Whitney, Diary, 22 June 1847.

126. The site was described by Albert Carrington as being at the "issu[e] of the river between two sloping granite walls fast abraiding." Smith (Carrington), History, 23 June 1847.

127. This is the famed Wind River range, noted by name by some of the vanguard, the most formidable mountain chain in Wyoming, stretching 100 miles from north to south and sporting Wyoming's highest peaks. Smith (Carrington), History, 23 June 1847.

128. The Mormons maintained contact with their fellow emigrants as they competed for forage and campsites. While caution tempered their association with each other, their interaction

Antelopes.[129] Lat 42° 31' 20".

Thursday 24th [June 1847] Started 1/2 past 6 without sound of Bugle so as not to give notice to the two camps ahead that we might gain on them but they got off first.[130] about 4 miles [on] a sandy road when we came to a Sulphur Spring, where we overtook the hindmost company.[131] here we found a great curiosity. 'twould seem that Vegetation & Frost had agreed to opperate in copartnership, for in digging through a grassy turf to open a Spring we found plenty of *Ice*![132] from this place the road is good, being hard gravel. about noon passed the hindmost company, but did not halt as there was no chance for feed.

The Wind river chain of the Rocky Mountains which was discovered yesterday, but the shaded side towards us shone dimly, now Stands for the

---

momentarily benefitted both groups: "It is stated that a man from one of these companies left his company a few days ago and went ahead to examine the route, etc . . . . He reports that he has been to the pass and that we shall find water about fourteen miles from here." On this day, Burr Frost also "set up his forge after we stopped and done some work for the Missourians." Clayton, *Journal*, 260; Egan, *Pioneering*, 84.

129. Lewis Barney's hunting prowess during this period provoked a humorous incident involving the notorious Porter Rockwell regarding their roles as hunters. One day in camp, about noon, after Barney's successful morning hunt for antelope, one of the company chided Rockwell for his dearth of success providing meat for the company: "here is Barney. he brings in Something every day." Rockwell defended his business explaining that Barney "kills does and all." While he could bring in "more than twenty does a day" if he wanted, Rockwell claimed, he preferred to kill only "nice fat Bucks." The following evening, after Rockwell brought in his "buck," Barney returned with "a buck and a doe." Rockwell said, defensively, "I Could have killed haff a dozen does if I wanted to." While Port explained his skill, Barney investigated the frontiersman's "buck." "I thought," he wrote, "that it was rather poor for a buck. So I took up the skin and examined it and found it was an old Suckling doe." Holding up the carcass to the others, he said, "See here boys, what nice tits Port's buck has. it must have gave a good mess of milk." While the others found great amusement in the incident, Rockwell "Sc[r]atched around for a while in a terible rage." Barney, Autobiography and diary, 37.

130. The following day, William Clayton summarized the vanguard's travel strategy vis-a-vis the much smaller numbered Missouri emigrants: "it is the intention to keep ahead of them and have the advantage of the good feed and camping grounds." Clayton, *Journal*, 266.

131. The Mormon vanguard traveled all day in proximity to the three westbound emigrants with whom they leap-frogged across the landscape.

132. Having temporarily left their parallel travel along the Sweetwater River, the ice spring, or Ice Spring Slough as it came to be known, was located by the road where there was about a half acre of "some water standing around a small, circular, swampy spot." Near "the northwest corner is a hole" where the "water in the hole smells strong of sulphur or alkali." But, according to William Clayton, "under the water which is over a foot deep there is as clear ice as I ever saw." Said to be "four inches thick" (though Wilford Woodruff figured the ice to be "about 18 inches thick"), Clayton wrote that, after breaking off some pieces of ice, he found it "tasted sweet and pleasant." The marked site is just off present U.S. 287, a few miles west of Jeffrey City, Wyoming, though the "actual springs are 1.5 miles north of the sign, on a rough road." Clayton, *Journal*, 262; Woodruff, *Journal*, 3:214; Kimball, *Historic Sites and Markers*, 87–88.

in all the noon-day Brilliancy of a Summer's Sun & robed in full Winter costume, presents a Scene Majestic, grand & imposing! The Eternal Snows, lifted up on those angular Peaks towards Heavn, an offering from Earth to Heavn's King, as though she would fain enjoy His Purity. (For *man* seeking the favor of his God, wishing the *best* to receive, of what he hath, in Sacrifice, the *best* presents.)[133] Old Nephi narrates that when upon the cross the Saviour died for man's sin & wickedness, darkness covered the Earth. She trembled & her Bosom heaved mightily; while some places Sinking became large Lakes & Pools of water.[134] here, upborn from their lowermos[t] foundations, these mighty Piles of Granite that ever since, despite the efforts of Summer's Suns, have held aloft the *Ensign of Peace*. And will not the Son of God respect the offering? Surely He will, for when to <bless the> Earth he comes again bringing Salvation. Her Sons will be Robed in purest *White*! and when celestialized, She herself transparant, will appear like unto a Sea of Glass mingled with fire.[135] Then let us pray "Thy Kingdom come, Thy *will* be done *upon the Earth*!!"[136] This afternoon a hard gravely road. we made in all today 17 3/4 miles & having left our little River to ramble among the Mountains all day till about 3 oclock, while we were decending a long sandy hill, suddenly through a small grassy bottom, winding, appeared its sparkling waters, a welcome sight to man & Beast & upon its bank we camped to rest & refresh ourselves & tired Teams,[137] several having failed on the way by reason of the heat of the Sun & fatigue of the Journey.[138] five Antelopes were brought in. a sad accident happened this evening. John Holman, driving in Br Brigham [Young]'s John Horse, poked his riffle out at him. the cock caught in his clothes, burst the cap & sent a ball into the belly of the Horse near the flank. he died in the course of the night, the best Horse in the

---

133. This unusual expression of emotive literary flurry by Jacob illustrates how the Mormons viewed heaven and earth conjoined to fulfill God's ultimate plan for the earth and its inhabitants.

134. This Mormon scriptural reference draws attention to Nephi's Book of Mormon narrative of the earth-wide, landscape-altering circumstances surrounding Jesus' crucifixion found in "The Book of Nephi," Chapter 4 (1830); 3 Nephi, chapter 8 (1981).

135. This mixed scriptural metaphor references the Apostle John's apocalyptic projections found in Revelations 6:11; 15:2; 21:21.

136. Jacob, like most of his fellow Mormon sojourners, was spiritually inclined, shown by his exultation of religious imagery at the sight of the majestic Wind River Mountains, denoting the release of his pent-up anticipation of being within reach of their goal of a new Zionic homeland. The scriptural citation here is, of course, from the Lord's Prayer, Matthew 6:10.

137. Characterizing the area, Albert Carrington stated the "valley has a slight smell like a salt marsh" surrounded by mountain ranges that "lose their rocky character and lower down into bluffs, table summits, and long swells, and look quite green and smooth." Smith (Carrington), History, 24 June 1847.

138. The nearly eighteen miles traveled this day, greatly taxing both man and beast, was due to finding "neither feed nor water to induce us to stop." Snow, "Journey," (July 1948): 268.

139. Returning to camp, the horse struggled prior to his expiration, his suffering and pain evident by "the sweat falling from his forehead in large drops," causing Brigham Young "deep sorrow," though he laid no blame to John Holman. Holman was beside himself over

camp, cost $150.00.[139] my Ten was on guard first watch. being unwell myself, I retired to rest & Br Erastus Snow attended to the duty of captain of the guard. F[rancis]. Pomeroy, having remained at the Ferry, I received Horrace Whitney in his place in the guard.

Friday 25th [June 1847] Started at 7 oclock, crossed over the River here, passed over a high Bluff, then down to the Stream again & pursued it up & having made 8 3/4 miles <halted> for dinner.[140] plenty of good grass for our Teams. moved on up the River about two miles when we left it & commenced [climbing] the Mountain against a verry Strong West wind blowing from the wind River chain some forty or fifty miles distant.[141] we continued ascending for about four miles over Lime stone, granete, and Slate. some excellent grind Stone grit was also found.[142] after arriving on the summit found a good road.[143] passed 3 ponds of water & a Spring & having made 11 1/2 miles halted on a smal Brook of pure soft water that runs to the left into the Sweet-water. the grass is short & mossy, Snow Banks in the ravenes all around us. two antelopes brought in.

Satturday 26th [June 1847] A hard frost.[144] Started at 7. passed two branches

---

the accident, and though Young and Rockwood tried to comfort him, he went "to bed sick of the horrows. [*sic*]" Clayton, *Journal*, 263; Rockwood, *History*, 65.

140. Heber Kimball's journal illustrates the routine reassessment of their route: "It is the opinion that by fording the [Sweetwater] river twice at the foot of the ridge we could save a mile." Albert Rockwood, as roadway engineer, concluded this day that with "1 hour's labor each for 100 men" they could "dig down the foot of the ridge so as to make it good passing and save rising the ridge and a miles travel without fording the river." Kimball, "Pioneer Journal," (October 1940): 217.

141. Orson Pratt, who chronicled characteristics of the journey's physical environment, noted here, "The country to-day begins to assume a more broken aspect, but not as mountainous and rugged as it is some 50 miles to the east." The climb in elevation affected their personal comfort, according to Erastus Snow: "It was quite warm in the morning but as we began to rise and meet the cold blasts from the mountains of snow and ice we began to gather our vests, then our coats, and finally before night our overcoats, and were cold at that." Pratt, *Journals*, 431; Snow, "Journey," (July 1948): 269.

142. After noting the "fine view" of the "Wind River Mountains gleaming with snow and ice," Albert Carrington described their day's travel crossing "an extensive bed of white and reddish fine grained sandstone of an excellent grit, then a very compact bluish brown limestone, then numerous and heavy bars of ferruginous and a light gray compact sandstone, cropping out and overlapping at an angle of about thirty degrees." Smith (Carrington), History, 25 June 1847.

143. This segment of the trail covers the famed and difficult "Rocky Ridge," made notable in Mormon circles from its challenging course in the 1856 Willie Handcart Company's tragedy.

144. Travel for the pioneers on the high Wyoming plain at summer's beginning was attended by very cold temperatures, "Thermometer at sunrise 28 degrees." Thomas Bullock reported this day that there was "Ice in the Buckets of Water," and that "A Pail of milk in Brother [Albert] Rockwood's Wagon frozen solid." Smith (Carrington), History, 26 June 1847; Bullock, *Camp of the Saints*, 202.

of the Sweet-water running out of those Snowy mountains on our right & having made 11 miles,[145] forded the river again where it is as wide & deep as where we first crossed it 90 miles below.[146] we halted here for dinner alongside a Snow Bank to cool our milk.[147] the best grass growing where the ground is moistened by the melting of the Snow. This afternoon passed over an undulating Sandy Plain & having made 7 3/4 miles,[148] turned aside half a mile to the right and camped on the bank of the River where we have plenty of grass & wood, such as it is, for the Sweet-Water [has] no Timber but dwarf willow throughout its whole length.[149] two antelopes brought in.

---

145. The vanguard passed Rock Creek in this stretch, another significant site associated with the tragedy of the Willie Handcart Company in 1856.

146. Wilford Woodruff explained that because of spring runoff from the Wind River Mountains, the Sweetwater was "Much larger than [the] original Stream." Consequently, the pioneers, in fording the river, found "The watter run into many of our waggons." Woodruff, *Journal*, 3:215.

147. Camping at what Erastus Snow said was known as the "Foot of the Pass," the trail was amidst snow banks allowing the almost-never-mentioned-children of the camp the enjoyment of "Snowballing each other." Snow, "Journey," (July 1948): 269; Bullock, *Camp of the Saints*, 202.

148. Albert Carrington, characterizing the area approaching the continental divide, "the great back bone of North America," stated that "with the exception of the snowy sumits of the Wind River chain, & the southern range of bluffs accompanied by the 2 table rocks, a few conical peaks & 1 large mount, you see nothing but shallow valleys, wide plains & low swelling hills, the road in fact for the last 34 miles, being much more level than in most prairies." Lyman (Carrington), Diary, 27 June 1847.

    Wilford Woodruff, anxiously anticipating South Pass, described their day's travel: "It was the best road we had had for many days & had it not have been for the wind river range of mountains full in view on our right & the rable coverd with eternal snow, & some snow banks 10 feet deep by the side of the road as we passed along & the table rock [Oregon Buttes] on the left I should have thought myself traveling over the beautiful prairies of Illinois & Missouri." He also found the area to be "perfectly strewn with vary handsom Cornelian stones," having seen "more in one hour this evening than I ever saw during my whole life either in the rude state or polished & set in breast pins in all the Jewellers shops I saw in my travels in the world from the sice of a goose egg to A pea." William Clayton described the stones as "hard flint rock . . . almost as clear as glass." Woodruff, *Journal*, 3:216; Clayton, *Journal*, 269.

149. Horace Whitney's summarization of their travel this day along the Sweetwater gives perspective: "we encamped in a circle <at 1/2 past 6 P.M.,> on the banks of the same stream we crossed at noon, in a small valley, environed by gentle, undulating hills, having come 18 3/4 miles during the day, & 129 3/4 miles during the week, & are this evening 276 1/4 miles from Ft. John, & 816 1/2 from Winter Quarters." Whitney, Diary, 26 June 1847.

    Also during the day, Eric Glines, the recalcitrant one who chose to stay with the ferrymen at the North Platte crossing, caught up with the vanguard and, though he did "not assign any reason why he followed us," repentantly reported the relocation of the ferry "8 miles lower." Bullock, *Camp of the Saints*, 202; Clayton, *Journal*, 268.

150. Though this was a Sabbath day and the third anniversary of Joseph and Hyrum Smith's martyrdom, the press of the "gentile companies" competing for scarce feed precluded worship or commemorative services. Clayton, *Journal*, 272.

Sunday 27th [June 1847] This morning,[150] after going about 2 miles, came to the summit of the Pass between the waters of the Atlantic & Pacific oceans & began to decend a little ravine that runs into Big Sandy creek.[151] after decending 3 miles came to water <The Pacific Springs>.[152] here we met a company of ten men from Orregon carrying the mail to the States.[153] one of the company, Major [Moses] Harris,[154] tarryed with us. we continued down the creek. having made in all today <6 1/4 miles>, halted for dinner. This Harris is an old Mountaineer, the one that explored a nearer rout from here to Orregon last year & he is now here for the purpose of Piloting through anny Emigrant company who may wish to avail themselves of his services. we obtained orregon Papers from him & one of Br [Samuel] Brannans papers from calafrnia.[155] This afternoon made 9 miles over a broad sandy Plain, paralel to our Snow clad Mountain on the North & 50 miles distant. came to creek called Dry Sandy & camped.[156] one Antelope Killed today.

Monday 28th [June 1847] We are now ~~at~~ <in> the ~~<Green> head of the~~ <the> Green River Valley, a most Barren, hard faced country, the soil being a pale

---

151. Despite Jacob's nondescript rendering of crossing South Pass, it was a significant day for the Saints in passing the barely discernible continental divide, "so gently rolling that independent of our geographical knowledge you would hardly suspect that you were crossing the backbone of North America." Having with them John Fremont's report, describing his journey five years previously, they noted that "he did not discover the highest point on account of the ascent being so gradual that they were beyond it before they were aware of it, although in company with a man who has traveled it back and forth for seventeen years." Orson Pratt, with his scientific bent, noted that "it was with great difficulty that we could determine the dividing point of land which separates the waters of the Atlantic from those of the Pacific," and that "the road gently rises about 40 or 50 feet, either of which elevations may be considered as the highest on our road in the Pass." Pratt determined the pass's elevation to be 7,085, slighting the actual figure by nearly five hundred feet. Smith (Carrington), History, 27 June 1847; Clayton, *Journal*, 267, 270; Pratt, *Journals*, 432–433.
152. Pacific Springs is a noted landmark in western overland travel.
153. Others in the Mormon camp indicate encountering only eight traders. While Moses "Black" Harris is the most noted of the party, Levi Scott captained the group which, after leaving Oregon City, Oregon, on 5 May, traveled eastward via Fort Hall, finally arriving in St. Joseph, Missouri, on 28 July. Bagley in Bullock, *Camp of the Saints*, 203n95.
154. Moses Harris's portrayal of the Salt Lake Valley (he called it the "Bear River Valley,"as the Bear empties into the north end of the Great Salt Lake) was described by the Saints as "very discouraging,"—the "country around Salt Lake was barren and sandy, destitute of timber and vegetation except wild sage"—but he "spoke in high terms" about Cache Valley to the north of the Great Salt Lake. He also advised the Saints to take the northern route westward rather than going via Fort Bridger. Young, *Manuscript History, 1846–1847*, 560; Egan, *Pioneering*, 87.
155. Providing the Saints with California newspapers, including Sam Brannan's sheet from Yerba Buena, the Saints read particulars about the Donner-Reed party's disaster in the Sierras the previous year. Whitney, Diary, 27 June 1847.
156. The Dry Sandy is the easternmost tributary of the Big Sandy River.

yellow sand & gravel, as hard as cast Iron in some places, others sandy, covered with the wild Sage & some little grass except on the Streams, where there is generaly pretty good grass & dwarf Willow. Major [Moses] Harris camped with us las<t> night and & bought two Rifles & some tobacco. paid in Deer and Elk SKins.[157] we Started at 8 oclock. traveled 13 1/2 miles & halted on the Little Sandy creek.[158] crossed over at a ford 2 rods wide & 2 feet deep. moved down the creek 1 3/4 miles & camped. here we met capt [Jim] Bridger[159] who commands Fort Bridgere, 100 miles ahead. he is on his way to Fort John, two men with him. he was verry obliging & gave all the information in <his> power concerning the Country & he has explored the Great Basin more than anny other white man living. the Twelve held a council with him.[160]

---

157. "[M]any of the brethren are trading with Mr. Harris for bucksins," wrote Howard Egan, though he declined the opportunity because "I considered [Harris's prices] too high." Harris, breaking from Levi Scott's eastbound company, stayed at the "Dry Sandy," telling the Saints he intended "waiting there for other emigrants" to guide, though he told his hosts that he would meet them at the Bear River. Egan, *Pioneering*, 87; Whitney, Diary, 28 June 1847; Woodruff, *Journal*, 3:219.

158. The Little Sandy, known today as a river, "being considerably swollen by the melting of the snow" was at the time "as large as [the] Sweet Water." Whitney, Diary, 28 June 1847. During this stretch of travel "without seeing wood or water or feed for our teams," the pioneers "came to a fork in the road." At the "Parting of the Ways," where the Oregon road split, the Saints "took the left for Bridger" while "the right leads to the Bear River bend." This significant western intersection divided the trail into the northern route, later known as the Sublette Cutoff, leading to Oregon via Fort Hall in Idaho, and the southern branch, known at the time as Hastings Cutoff, leading into the Salt Lake Valley. Egan, *Pioneering*, 87; Lyman, Diary, 28 June 1847. See Miller, "Parting of the Ways," 47–52, for a discussion of the subsequent error in identifying the place where the road split and the correct designation of the site.

159. It is not known if the coincidence of meeting within a day of each other two of the most notable frontiersmen in western history registered with the Saints. Jim Bridger knew of the Mormon expedition and anticipated their arrival in the region. George Smith, in advance of the company and, apparently, the first to meet Bridger, introduced the trader to church leaders. While Old Gabe provided the Saints with accurate and valuable information concerning conditions of the Great Basin's eastern rim ("He spoke more Highly of the great Salt Lake for a settlement than Major Harris did"), evidence by Mormon diarists suggest he distorted aspects of the region, including exaggerations that left his listeners suspicious. Clayton, *Journal*, 273; Woodruff, *Journal*, 3:219.

160. The council was held eight miles northeast of what is now Farson, Wyoming, where a monument commemorates the meeting. A summary of Jim Bridger's encounter with the Saints, including Mormon diary excerpts describing the meeting, and an appraisal of the controversial matter of Bridger's wager with the Saints for the production of corn, is found in Alter, *Jim Bridger*, 223–230. (For example, Brigham Young's account states that "he said he [Bridger] would give one thousand dollars for a bushel of corn raised in the Basin." Young, *Manuscript History, 1846–1847*, 561.) One of Bridger's tactics to impress the Saints, apparently, was to discredit Moses Harris's expertise and experience. Kimball, *Historic Sites and Markers*, 90; Egan, *Pioneering*, 89. The most extensive report of what Bridger told the Saints is Will Bagley's transcript of meeting minutes kept by Thomas Bullock, published in Bullock, *Camp of the Saints*, 209–213. See also William Clayton's extensive report of the meeting, Clayton, *Journal*, 273–278.

the information obtained concerning the Utaw country is verry encourageing which [is] from 3 to 4 hundred miles from here & twenty days travel.[161] from there, South throug a Sandy Desert, he found a country, the best he ever saw. it <is> bordering on the range of Mountains that constitutes the Southern boundary of the great Basin. he crossed that Desert in the month of January & found the sand so hot as to burn his Horses feet & was obliged to travel nights & lie by daytimes where he could find water.[162] A great portion of that country is yet unexplored & many Tribes of Indians. those he saw were engaged in cultivating the Earth.[163] there is a Tree peculiar to that country that produces a verry delicious fruit about the size of a Plumb. the Indians pound it & make bread of it which has a spicy taste like ginger cake.[164]

The Utaw [Uinta] Mountains are now in sight to the South, covered with Snow. also the three Tetons to the N. West.[165] I was on guard the morning watch. one Antelope Killed. no Buffalo in this region.

Tuesday 29th [June 1847] Capt. [Jim] Bridger left us this morning & pursued

161. The region known as Utah was probably first identified as "Yuta" in 1620 by Franciscan missionary Geronimo de Zarate Salmeron. The name, of course, denoted the area's dominant Indian population, the Utes. Tyler, "The Earliest Peoples," 30.

Horace Whitney's notation that Jim Bridger explained the Great Salt Lake to be but 200 miles farther, in contrast to Jacob's figures, suggests the disparity of Bridger's information distributed to the pioneer camp. Whitney, Diary, 28 June 1847.

162. This appears to be a description of southern Utah or Arizona.

163. Albert Carrington gleaned from Jim Bridger's portrayal that he spoke of "Piute country, where they raise wheat, corn, etc., of the best quality." Recent studies indicate that despite the "fragile environment" in which they lived, the "Paiutes were highly sophisticated botanists" who "used at least thirty-two families of flora encompassing some ninety-six species of edible plants." Smith (Carrington), History, 28 June 1847; Tom and Holt, "The Paiute Tribe of Utah," 124

164. In 1852 Hosea Stout, while visiting the Santa Clara region of southern Utah, noted that he "found a kind of mountain Plumb which is in great abundance & a most excellent fruit where we treated ourselves abundantly," likely the plant described by Jim Bridger. In the 1870s, scientific investigations of southern Utah flora were conducted by John Wesley Powell and Edward Palmer. More than 100 species of plants used by the Paiutes of southern Utah for food, medicine, and other domestic uses, including scrubs, trees, and berries, were described, classified, and cataloged. However, none of them match exactly the particulars of the fruit described by Jim Bridger. Stout, *On the Mormon Frontier*, 2:461. The plants of the nineteenth century identified by Powell and Palmer are described in Bye, "Ethnobotany of the Southern Paiute Indians," 90–98; with the more recent list in Martineau, *Southern Paiutes*, 135–148.

165. The mountains "to the south" are one of the most formidable mountain ranges in the American West, the Uintas. Called by Thomas Bullock the "Bear River Mountains" and located in present-day northeastern Utah, they run perpendicular to the north-south run of the other ranges in the Rocky Mountains. The Teton range to the north, of course, was noted from the period of the fur trade.

166. For Jim Bridger, Brigham Young sent a letter of introduction to Thomas Grover and company who were left to man the ferry at the North Platte. "We wish you to cross him and his two men on our account, because he was going to Laramie and expected to return

his Journey,[166] while we passed on down the creek 6 3/4 miles & crossed Big Sandy, where we halted for dinner.[167] the weather now is hot & sultry. in these Valeys it is generaly hot in the d<a>ytime but on account of the Snow on the Mountains it [is] verry cool at night. We proceeded down <the> river & continued on till 9 oclock at night before we found grass. made 17 mil[es] & camped on the bank of the river below the Forks.[168] it here [is] a large Stream but d<r>ys up entirely in the hot season. A few miles S. East there is <a> small mount called the Pilot But[t]e, <The name of "Bute" is applyed by the Mountaineers to eminences less than a Muntain> where there is Springs of living water. We are now in Calafornia, the Northern boundary being the paralel of 42° North Latitide.[169]

Wednesday 30th [June 1847] We moved on over to the Green river 8 miles & camped at 12 oclock on the bank.[170] afternoon I went up the River with twelve men to build a raft,[171] another raft having been built there by the Missourians. the Timber left was heavy & clumsy but we could get no better on the East side of the River, so we constructed our raft <12 by 24 feet> & brought it down to camp by sun Set. the Missourians Set their raft adrift lest it should

---

to his Fort in time to pilot the Pioneers through to Salt Lake." The later expectation, of course, did not materialize. Alter, *Jim Bridger*, 226.

167. The Big Sandy, "about 80 yards broad, with nearly 3 feet of water in the channel at the ford," is one of the primary tributaries of the Green River, the headwaters originating in the Wind River Range. Howard Egan noted that their rest stop midday found "Most of the second division stopped on the other side of the river, the first division stopping on the north side," giving insight into the company's travel arrangement. Pratt, *Journals*, 435; Egan, *Pioneering*, 89.

168. Wilford Woodruff and Porter Rockwell served as scouts for the day, six miles in advance of the company, to locate a suitable campsite for the night. Finally finding "the first place we Could get grass," it was, as Jacob noted, 9 P.M. before the company settled for the night, after "the longest days journey we had made on the whole route," nearly twenty-four miles. The "forks" spoken of are the Big and Little Sandy rivers. Woodruff, *Journal*, 3:220–221; Whitney, Diary, 29 June 1847.

169. Utah was known before settlement as Alta (upper) California and the property of the Mexican government. The forty-second parallel is the northern boundary of Utah today.

170. The ferry at the Green River, subsequently known at Lombard Ferry, is located near the bridge presently crossing Highway 28. The river at this place was described as being "quite deep & rapid," a "channel from 12 to 15 feet of water" according to Pratt. Estimations of the width of the stream varied from 100 to 180 yards. Bagley in Bullock, *Camp of the Saints*, 214n37; Whitney, Diary, 30 June 1847; Pratt, *Journals*, 436; Lyman, Diary, 30 June 1847.

171. After pausing for dinner at the Green River, "we were all busy washing, smithing, coal-burning and raft-making." By now the Mormon emigrants had become expert at crossing rivers and exhibited their prowess as "Immediately each Division was called together & men selected by Cols. [Stephen] Markham & [Albert] Rockwood to make 2 rafts, & stand guard." A raft was to be made for each division. Smith (Carrington), History, 30 June 1847; Whitney, Diary, 30 June 1847; Bullock, *Camp of the Saints*, 214.

172. Upon their arrival at the Green River, the Saints met "2 horsemen" who told them that the Oregon-bound emigrants, with whom the company had been jockeying for position

benefit us, so Col. [Albert] Rockwood <had> one built also.[172] John Brown killed an Antelope

~~Thurs~~ Br [Samuel] Brannan arrived from the Bay of San Francisco, having Started the same time we did from Winter Quarters.[173] has made a settlement on the Bay. reports that to be a beautiful rich country.[174] Old [Lilburn] Bog[g]s is on the opposite side of the Bay & dare not come over for fear of the Mormons. wants to get back to the States but is so poor that he cannot raise the wind.[175] Br Brannan fell in with a company of Emigrants, who by quarreling & fighting among themselves, delayed time until they got caught in the Snows on the Mountains last fall & could not extricat themselves.[176] the S[n]ows were much deeper in all this region than was ever Known before.

---

across Wyoming, had all crossed the Green and were "encamped some 5 miles above here." The two rafts were each "rigged with oars and rudder." Experience in making rafts allowed for them to cross safely "without taking out any of [the wagons'] contents." The animals, of course, swam the river. Whitney, Diary, 30 June 1847; Pratt, *Journals*, 436.

173. Samuel Brannan departed New York City 4 February 1846 for San Francisco leading an emigrant company of 238 Mormons aboard the ship *Brooklyn*, the same day the first refugees from Nauvoo crossed the Mississippi River. They arrived in Yerba Buena (San Francisco Bay) on 29 July 1846 after rounding Cape Horn and a ten-day stop in the Hawaiian Islands. Determined to coax the Saints to California, Brannan, with two companions, left San Francisco on 4 April 1847 to intercept Brigham Young on his westward journey. (Brannan's eastbound journey took him via Fort Hall.) Despite subsequent unfavorable characterizations of Brannan by the Mormons because of his defection from the faith, in part because the Saints dismissed his plea to continue to California, he was received by Young and the Saints at this time very favorably. Upon his departure westward on 4 July, Brigham Young "counselled brother Brannan how to proceed to California, for the best." Bagley, *Scoundrel's Tale*, 197, 209; Woodruff, *Journal*, 3:221; Bullock, *Camp of the Saints*, 219; Young, *Manuscript History, 1846–1847*, 561. Bagley details Brannan's life in *Scoundrel's Tale*.

174. Samuel Brannan's report included information about "our [Mormon] battalion in California, & the brethren who went round by sea." He said they were "settled in St Francisco, & neighboring villages, but will mostly move in to the valley of the San Joaquin, about 300 x 50 ms." and that "they have already begun to farm about 30 ms. above the settlements." Lyman (Carrington), Diary, 30 June 1847.

175. No other figure in Mormon history has generated the antipathy of Latter-day Saints quite like Lilburn Boggs, who, as Missouri governor, issued the infamous extermination order in October 1838 expelling the Saints from Missouri. Having traveled across the plains with the Donner-Reed company, Boggs escaped their fate by taking the northern route after separating from them at the "Parting of the Ways." He arrived at Sutter's Fort in October 1846. Unknown to most Mormons, Boggs's interactions with Mormons in California, including Samuel Brannan, apparently muted his hostility toward the Saints. Boggs's career in California, which included a significant political role for a time, is found in Marriott, "Lilburn W. Boggs," 63–92.

176. Of course, the company referred to is the tragedy-fated Donner-Reed company, caught by early snow in the Sierras the previous fall of 1846. Jacob apparently misunderstood Samuel Brannan's connection to the unfortunate emigrants, Brannan having encountered only the last of the relief parties. However, in crossing the Sierras, Brannan reported his group

their sufferings were incredible. manny of them perished with cold & hunger. all their cattle died & they [were] compeled to eat the flesh of those that died among them! In fact they Killd some & among the rest a Mormon woman by the name of [Levinah] Murphy, who formerly lived in Nauvoo.[177] Those people are in a wretched condition. their Teams all gone, they cannot get away until assistance shall be sent from Orregon.[178] Quarreling is a comon complaint among these Emigrants until they [are] all divided & subdivided into Small parties. cant agree to travel together in Peace, which fulfils Joseph Smith's Prophecy "that Peace is taken from the Earth." these are the men that have Mobed & Killed the Saints![179]

"passed directly over the camping ground where about 40 or 50 California emigrants [forty-two was the exact number] had perished, and been eaten up by their fellow sufferers . . . . Their skulls, bones, and carcasses lay strewed in every direction." Bagley, *Scoundrel's Tale*, 203; Pratt, *Journals*, 437.

177. Levinah (also spelled Lavinia and Lavina) Jackson Murphy became a Latter-day Saint in 1836, probably by Wilford Woodruff's hand in Weakly County, Tennessee. Her husband died about 1839, after which she moved her family to Nauvoo, Illinois. Not knowing precisely her reason for leaving Nauvoo for a temporary hiatus in Warsaw, Illinois, Wilford Woodruff likely misdiagnosed Levinah's status after she left Nauvoo, stating Murphy apostatized and "joined the mob." Daniel Tyler later explained her move to Warsaw, during the Saints' tenure in Nauvoo, to be more benign. She later removed to Tennessee. Widowed, and with a dozen other family members, including two sons-in-law, at the age of thirty-six she joined the Donner-Reed company intent on Sacramento, California. Levinah Murphy, having lost her sight during the ordeal in the Sierras, died at Donner Lake about 18 March 1847, one of the last to perish. The information Woodruff obtained about the tragedy, including rumor that Murphy "was killed & eat up," that her "bones [were] sawed to peaces for her branes & marrow," and that her remains were strewn upon the ground, may have been exaggerated, though her body was apparently mutilated when rescuers finally retrieved the dead. Dorius, "Crossroads in the West," 17–20; Woodruff, *Journal*, 3:227; Tyler, *Concise History*, 312–313; Johnson, *"Unfortunate Emigrants,"* 296, 306, 310; Johnson, "The Murphy Family," www.utahcrossroads.org/DonnerParty/Murphy.htm.

    The best summary of the Murphy's connections to Mormonism and to the Donner-Reed party is found in Dorius, "Crossroads in the West," 17–27. See also Campbell, "Mormons and the Donner Party," 307–311; Korns and Morgan, *West from Fort Bridger*, 199–200, 200n2; and Mullen, *Donner Party Chronicles*; Johnson, "The Murphy Family," www.utahcrossroads.org/DonnerParty/Murphy.htm.

178. George Stewart's *Ordeal by Hunger* is the standard account of the Donner-Reed party, but it is limited by his license for interpretation. For two recent scholarly overviews of the Donner-Reed tragedy see Johnson, ed., *"Unfortunate Emigrants,"* and Mullen, *Donner Party Chronicles*.

179. Jacob's generalization of non-Mormon emigrants is very telling regarding the view of Mormons toward those not of their stripe. The Saints' vivid memories of Midwestern injustices institutionalized, over time, a negative generalization of "Gentiles," particularly those from Missouri and Illinois. Many subsequent difficulties between Latter-day Saints and their countrymen were rooted in this attitude.

July 1847

THE LAST STRETCH OF THEIR JOURNEY faced the Mormon vanguard during the height of the western summer. It was to be the most physically formidable segment of the trek. Crossing the Green River, they pressed on past Black's and Ham's forks of the Green to Fort Bridger on 7 July, frontiersman Jim Bridger's trading post. They hardly stopped to recruit their animals. Many were afflicted in Wyoming by Colorado Tick Fever which slowed the journey, even disabling Brigham Young. Fording the Bear River, they soon entered Echo Canyon traveling downhill to the Great Salt Lake Valley, or so it seemed. The canyon of the Weber River, which they could have followed into the valley, proved not suitable for wagon travel. The alternative was the same route employed by the ill-fated Donner-Reed party the previous year. Breaking south at modern-day Henefer, Utah, they initiated their difficult climb over the Wasatch Mountains. The company, divided between the healthy and those afflicted with "mountain fever," sent the advance unit on to the valley, which they first entered on 22 July. Young followed two days later. Before the month was completed, streams were dammed, crops planted, and the region just south of the Great Salt Lake was explored.

Thursday 1st <day of July> [1847] On trial, found my raft to heavy to stem the violence of the current.[1] we were the first of our camp that crossed to [the] West side of Green River,[2] where by the request of Br Heber C. Kimbal I went to work with some men & built another raft out of dry cottonwood, ten

1. The craft of which Jacob spoke was simply "too unwieldy for use" because the "logs . . . [were] water soaked." The raft, according to Thomas Bullock, had to be "cut . . . to pieces" before they could "make a new one." A "very high wind" also complicated transporting wagons across the swollen river, prohibiting all but a few of the wagons from crossing, though the cattle with "great difficulty" swam the river. Whitney, Diary, 1 July 1847; Egan, *Pioneering*, 91; Bullock, *Camp of the Saints*, 216; Clayton, *Journal*, 281; Woodruff, *Journal*, 3:221–222.
2. Levi Jackman stated the river to be "about 40 rods wide" at the crossing. Jackman, Diary, 1 July 1847.

feet by twenty six, which we found to be better than 12 feet wide.[3] J[oseph]. Hancock Killed one Antelope.

Friday July 2d [1847] A Still hot day. went over with my company & finished our raft before breakfast & brought it over. it runs well. The first Division crossed 8 or 10 Waggons yesterday & our old raft, one. today both rafts are going it at the rate of 4 per hour. 45 Waggons ferryed over today. I was taken sick this afternoon with a fever, which has prevailed through the camp to a considerable extent since we left the Mountains,[4] supposed to be produced by a sudden change of climate.[5] we are now in the heat of Summer, while there we were in the midts of Frost & Snow. I bathed myself all over with warm water & went to bed in my Waggon & <was> took across the river.

Satturday 3d [July 1847] I sufferd excessively with pain in the Spine, Joints, & Head, with a high fever through the night. Charles [Harper] anointed my head & back & rubed it hard which caused the pain to cease in my back,

---

3. Albert Carrington stated the first division's raft measured "26 x 11 ft" while the second division's craft was "25 x 10." Lyman (Carrington), Diary, 2 July 1847.
4. Erastus Snow noted, on 3 July, that "about one-half the company had been attacked with the same complaint." Called "camp fever" or "mountain fever" by the travelers, Snow wrote that "Its first appearance is like that of a severe cold producing soreness in the flesh, and pains in the head and all parts of the body; and as the fever increases the pains in the head and back become almost insufferable." Their remedy: "an active portion of Physic [medicine] accompanied with warming and stimulating drinks, such as ginger and pepper tea, cayenne &c." Most recovered within a week, though as soon as some felt better, others were afflicted. Snow, "Journey," (July 1948): 270; Smith (Carrington), History, 2 July 1847; Lyman (Carrington), Diary, 2 July 1847.
5. The previous day Horace Whitney wrote that "more than 20 men [were] prostrated" by the "mountain fever." "Mountain fever" is the malady used to describe a number of illnesses emigrants encountered once they entered the American West, including the afflictions of the Saints. Wilford Woodruff stated, according to the prevailing belief, that the sickness was caused by "emegrants coming from the snowy mountains to the plains or valleys whare it is Hot wether," concurring with Jacob's analysis that the problem came from "a sudden change of climate." Without the ability through tests to properly diagnose the several illnesses which emigrants called "mountain fever," it is probably safe to state that the phrase was a catch-all for a number of debilitating infirmities which attacked westbound emigrants. The symptoms of gastrointestinal trauma and general body pain described by several of the Mormon diarists suggest the Saints were plagued by Colorado Tick Fever, a virus caused by the bite of the Rocky Mountain wood tick. The sickness, which delayed the company's progress considerably, generally afflicted its victims for nearly a week with relapses being frequent adding several more days of debility. One of the company, Solomon Chamberlain, said that "For six days and nights I took nothing into my stomach but cold water and that distressed me much." The symptoms of "Chills, muscle and joint pain, headache, deep pain behind the eyes, lumbar backache, and nausea and vomiting" characterized the complaint. Whitney, Diary, 1 July 1847; Young (Young), "Diary," 163; Woodruff, *Journal*, 3:222; Chamberlain in *Our Pioneer Heritage*, 2:599; Aldous, "Mountain Fever," 52–54; and Aldous and Nicholes, "What is Mountain Fever," 18–23.

but the fever still continued. I Kept in my Waggon through the day.[6] the remainder of Waggons were brought over & we moved down the river 3 miles & camped on its bank.[7] the <Musketos> here are verry troubelsom here during the sunshine of day but the nights are to cool for them & they leave us to rest quietly.[8] after arriving in camp Br Heber [Kimball] came to visit me & a[d]vised me to be baptized. So [we] went down to the water & Charles Harper baptised me for the restoration of my health,[9] which was confirmed upon me by Brethren Kimbal, Doct [Willard] Richards, [Stephen] Markum, [Lewis] Barney, & Charles [Harper]. the <administration> had the desired effect & broke my fever.[10] The Camp was called together at dusk, when arrangements were made to send five men back to meet the camp coming up from Winter Quarters & help them along. (I had forgot to notice the Br [Eric] Glines came from the ferry on the Platte & overtook us at the last crossing of the Sweet-water in the Pass.) Those ~~that were~~ selcted were Phineas Young, George Wood[w]ard, Aaron Farr, Rodney Badger, & Eric Glines.[11]

---

6. Perhaps because of his confinement, Jacob failed to note the terrible weather that hit the camp during the day: high wind, rain, thunder, and lightening.
7. The final wagon crossed the river at noon. Those conducting the crossing then "hauled one of the rafts up on the east side of the river for the next company." The "extensive bottom" of their encampment that day provided good grass and "plenty of underbrush for fuel." Egan, *Pioneering*, 91; Whitney, Diary, 3 July 1847.
8. Encountering "dense swarms" of the pesky irritants, Thomas Bullock wrote that they passed "a Mosquito manufactory" that day. William Clayton complained they were "more numerous here than I ever saw them anywhere, everything was covered with them, making the teams restive in the wagons." Pratt, *Journals*, 437; Bullock, *Camp of the Saints*, 218; Clayton, *Journal*, 282.
9. Mormons practice baptism for the remission of sins upon a candidate's entrance into the church to signify their acceptance of Jesus Christ's redemption. Rebaptism of persons for health purposes was a practice initiated in Nauvoo, Illinois, and was periodically employed by Latter-day Saints until the end of the nineteenth century. As will be seen upon the Saints' entrance into the Salt Lake Valley later in the month, rebaptism was also an ordinance of recommitment to the religion and its objectives, also abandoned at the turn of the century. Quinn, "Rebaptism at Nauvoo," 229–230, 232.
10. Latter-day Saints believe in the "gifts of the spirit," including the practice of healing the sick by the "administration" of olive oil, hearkening to the New Testament antecedent: "Is any sick among you? let him call for the elders of the church; and let them pray over him, anointing him with oil in the name of the Lord." James 5:14.
11. The evening's meeting had Brigham Young explain "that it was necessary that some individuals should go back to meet the next company of brethren, in order to pilot & assist them on the road." He said "it would be advisable to select *those* for that purpose that had families who would need their help." After the five to return were selected, Young "proffered them the use of the wagon which has formerly drawn the '*Revenue Cutter*'" to "carry their provisions." The group of five, soon to become six with the addition of Mormon Battalion veteran William Walker, took "with them instructions to the Saints whom they should meet, and also a short synopsis from some of our journals, containing the distances, good camping places, &c." Young and several of the Twelve accompanied them to the river the next morning to insure their safe crossing. Whitney, Diary, 3 July 1847; Egan, *Pioneering*, 91; Pratt, *Journals*, 437–438.

Sunday 4th [July 1847] This is uncle Sam's day of Independence.[12] well, we are independant of all the powers of the Gentiles. that's enough for us.[13] I rested verry well through last night. The President with Br Heber [Kimball], <Col> [Stephen] Markum, <&> Charles Harper went up to the Ferry to set Br Phineas [Young] & his company over[14] where they met Seagnt Thomas Williams with a detachment of twelve men from capt. [John] Brown's [Mormon Battalion] company from Puerblo going on to Fort Bridger in pursuit of some Horses stolen from them by the company of traders we crossed ove[r] dow[n] at the Platt.[15] they report capt. Brown to have left the Ferry on the Platte last

---

12. Their camp on this national day was "opposite to the junction of the Big Sandy and Green River," where on "the other side [of] the river there is a range of singular sandy buttes perfectly destitute of vegetation, and on the sides can be seen . . . two caves which are probably inhabited by wild bears." Clayton, *Journal*, 283.

    The previous day, Brigham Young, anticipating that he would accompany the returning brethren to the river the next day, instructed the company "that there should be no fishing, hunting, &c. on the *Sabbath Day*." But despite the Sabbath rest there was always something that had to be done. Though there was no hunting, "The horses & cattle were all drove down to a bottom about a mile . . . where the grass grows more luxuriant than at this place." Whitney, Diary, 3 July 1847.

13. John Smith, traveling in the second wave of Mormon migration following the vanguard that year, wrote on 4 July while camped on the Platte River: "we Do not feel to Celebrate it as the Birth day of the Independence of the united States As we have been Driven from her [borders] because we worship God according to his Laws." Smith, Journal, 4 July 1847.

    This posture reflected, more or less, Mormon attitudes toward the federal government during the rest of the nineteenth century. Latter-day Saints reverenced the heritage, philosophical moorings, and legal foundation of American government, believing its structure to be divinely inspired by God, who specially provided for the establishment of the United States of America and the ideology upon which it was founded. Mormonism's fracture in the nineteenth century with American culture was rooted in the hostility of state and federal governments to a theocratic organization inherently separate from American institutions and objectives.

14. George Woodward, one of the those selected to backtrack, noted Brigham Young's concern about those who followed, "Nothing having been heard from them." Upon receiving their assignments, the five men, after being given provisions, "were quickly off to fulfill the given mission." Young and those who accompanied him "went as far as the [North Platte] river," but when they reached the stream they "found that the water had fallen so low that fording was possible and there was no longer a necessity for them [Young and company] to stay." Woodward, *Auto-biography*, 10.

15. The thirteen Battalion returnees, "by riding hard," caught up to the vanguard company. Wilford Woodruff, who accompanied the "pilots" for the subsequent Mormon company to the Green River, described the surprise of the encounter: "when we arived at the river we saw 13 Horsman on the opposite bank with there baggage on one of our rafts. But to our great joy who should they be but our Brethren belonging to the Mormon Battalion. . . . We drew up the raft & crossed them all over but one who returned with our pilots to meet the company. When we met it was truly A Harty greeting & shaking of hands." Indeed, Brigham Young's account states that the "Pioneers were so pleased to behold the battalion brethren that they gave three cheers, and I led out in exclaiming, 'Hosannah! Hosannah! Give glory to God and the Lamb, Amen.'" Clayton, *Journal*, 282; Woodruff, *Journal*, 3:223; Young, *Manuscript History, 1846–1847*, 561–562. The thirteen horsemen are identified by Bagley in Bullock, *Camp of the Saints*, 219.

Wednesday [30 June] on his way up with forty three Waggons & ~~about~~ <about> two hundred men including this detacment.[16] they were received in our camp with demonstrations of Joy & thanksgiving to God that some of the Battalian had arrived safe. one of their number, W[illia]m. Walker, returned with our fivee men to assist his family. The Bishops held a meeting at 12 [P.] M.

Monday 5th [July 1847] Started at 9 [A.] M. Course 4 miles south down the River when we turned S. Westerly across the Hills,[17] making in all 20 miles without feed or drink for Teams except some who watered before we left the river.[18] we camped on ~~Ham's Branch of~~ Black's Fork of Green River.[19] one Antelope Killed. A Fish is caught here called mountain Trout.[20]

Determined to retrieve their horses taken by Tim Goodale's band of traders, most of which they retrieved at Fort Laramie, the thirteen were determined to replevin the remaining horse from Goodale whom they thought to be at Jim Bridger's fort. While the actual perpetrators had already moved on, Thomas Williams did apprehend Goodale there and "seized a horse belonging to Tim Goodale, for a mule stolen by one of his men at Pueblo," though Horace Whitney said Goodale willingly supplied the horse to Williams. Despite Williams's determination to exact justice from Goodale, Brigham Young gave him "no encouragement . . . to make the attempt." Williams gave Goodale a receipt for the horse anticipating that Goodale would recover its value from the man who took the Battalion's mule. However, on 9 July Brigham Young "gave the horse back to Goodale in the neatest, quietest, prettiest way possible; for which Goodale expressed his thankfulness to 'Captain Young.'" The pioneer camp revisited the "*Tim. Goodell affair*" at a Sabbath meeting on 8 August after their arrival in the Salt Lake Valley. Bagley in Bullock, *Camp of the Saints*, 219, 221–222; Clayton, *Journal*, 286; Whitney, Diary, 7 July 1847, 8 August 1847; Woodruff, *Journal*, 3:223.

16. John Brown's company brought details of the Mormon ferrymen at the North Platte. Despite the previous good will manifest by the Mormons and Missourians to each other, a later group of "Missourians" had proved troublesome at the ferry, threatening harm to the Mormons. But Luke Johnson, one of those left at the ferry, called them on, confident the nearby Saints from Pueblo would provide "plenty of assistance." This particular company was so ornery that upon crossing the North Platte, they "cut their rafts loose & let them drift away," being "so deficient in charity that they were not willing that numbers of their own companies should cross over without paying heavily for the use of them." Whitney, Diary, 4 July 1847.

    For an overview of the "Mississippi Saints" and their relationship to the Mormon Battalion and vanguard, see Carter, "Mississippi Saints," 2:421–476; and footnote #8 for 1 June 1847.
17. Their course this day was "over a stony, sandy, uneven road." Whitney, Diary, 5 July 1847.
18. Ever on the lookout for opportunities to shorten their route, both for themselves and for those who followed, after this day's journey William Clayton wrote, "There is one place in the road where we might have saved a crook of nearly a mile by digging down [a] bank which would probably have detained us about twenty minutes, but it was not discovered till most of the wagons had passed over." Brigham Young ordered the trail altered for those who followed "which was done." Clayton, *Journal*, 283; Bullock, *Camp of the Saints*, 219.
19. Black's Fork of the Green River "winds serpentinely in a s.e. direction, being about 8 rods in wideth, & quite deep & rapid." Whitney, Diary, 5 July 1847.
20. Wilford Woodruff, a skilled and passionate fly fisherman, rejoiced that the camp laid over. It was a time to fish: brook trout, "the first I had seen since I left England." The following day Woodruff "riged up my trout rod . . . fixed my reel, line, & Artificial fly & went to

Tuesday 6th [July 1847] I rest well & gain strength fast.[21] moved on up the Stream about 3 miles, crossed Ham's Fork.[22] about a mile farther crossed Black's Fork & continued up on the south side.[23] made 18 1/4 miles.[24] crossed back to the N. side & camped.[25]

Wednesday 7th [July 1847] There is flax along this Stream in full bloom, two feet high & in sufficient quantity that one could make a hand of gathering it. moved on up the Stream & about six miles crossed again. 3 or 4 miles further crossed the South Branch coming out of the Snow topd mountains which we saw a weak ago.[26] having made 9 miles, halted for

---

one of the brooks close by Camp to try my luck at catching trout." Arriving at the stream he stated that "a good many of the brethren were already at the creeks with their Rods & lines trying their skill baiting with fresh meat & grass hoppers., but no one seemed to ketch any." Undaunted, he "went & flung my fly . . . it being the first time that I ever tried the Artificial fly in America," and watched it floating down stream with "as much intens interest As Franklin did his kite when he tried to draw lightning from the skies." The success he obtained, a dozen fish after "two or three hours," gratified him as much, he said, as Franklin "when he saw electricity or lightning descend on his kite string." He caught more than the rest of the camp together "which was proof positive to me that the Artificial fly is far the best thing now known to fish trout with." Woodruff, *Journal*, 3:224–225.

While Woodruff identified the fish as a brook trout, Orson Pratt called it a "salmon-trout," weighing "from 1 to 10 pounds." Commonly called cutthroat trout today (*Salmo clarki*), the fish is native to the region and is known from the "red markings on the underside of the lower jaw." Pratt, *Journals*, 439; Slaughter in Richards, *Camping Out in Yellowstone*, 26n16.

21. Wilford Woodruff reported "The sick in Camp are most universally getting better." But within a few days, the illness, that had afflicted a large number of the company before diminishing some in its effect, returned to the camp. Albert Rockwood explained that one of the reasons they laid over at Fort Bridger on 8 July was to "recrute the sick." Woodruff, *Journal*, 3:224; Jackman, Diary, 7–8 July 1847; Rockwood, *History*, 67.
22. Ham's Fork, a major tributary of Black's Fork of the Green River, was named after the obscure mountaineer Zacharias Ham who discovered the stream in 1825. He was one of Ashley's men and later worked with Jedediah Smith, Etienne Provost, and William Wolfskill. Baur, "Zacharias Ham," 9:193–194.
23. Albert Carrington noted that "Black's Fork [is] 35 yards wide," and that the "names of the forks [Ham's and Black's] are according to Fremont's map." Smith (Carrington), History, 6 July 1847.
24. Wilford Woodruff described the day as being "warm windy [and] dusty." He said that from their day's travel, "man & beast Harnesses & waggons were all coverd with dust." Horace Whitney's eye were "quite sore this even, owing to the excess of dust encountered" during the day. Woodruff, *Journal*, 3:224; Whitney, Diary, 6 July 1847.
25. While it is not clear in Jacob's account, after crossing Ham's Fork, they "crossed Black['s] Fork twice" that day. Just before setting up camp, the company "met 2 men with 3 pack-horses," informing them that Fort Bridger was "about 15 miles" distance. Harper, *Diary*, 29; Whitney, Diary, 6 July 1847.
26. Albert Carrington noted that "Some distance on our left, a long range of snowy mountains extending north-west and south-east, and sloping down at their eastern extremity below the snow line." These were the Uinta Mountains in northeastern Utah. Smith (Carrington), History, 7 July 1847.

Millen Atwood

Lewis Barney

John Brown

Thomas Bullock

This page and following pages: Jacob's fellow chroniclers of the vanguard trek.

Albert Carrington

William Clayton

Howard Egan

William Empey

Appleton Milo Harmon

Charles Alfred Harper

Levi Jackman

Heber C. Kimball

Orson Pratt

Albert Perry Rockwood

George A. Smith

Erastus Snow

Horace K. Whitney

Wilford Woodruff

Brigham Young

Lorenzo Dow Young

dinner.[27] proceeded on up the main Stream. came to best valley we have seen for a long time producing good grass. Fort Bridger is seituated in this valley. below the Fort we saw Lodges of the Shoshonee, the first Indians we have seen since we lft Fort John.[28] made 8 3/4 miles & camped half a mile above the Fort, which is built of Logs. it [is] only a double Log House.[29]

Thursday 8th [July 1847] We remained encamped.[30] I traded my Bowie Knife with an Indian for a Buckskin Shirt & Pantaloons.[31] then I went to washing

---

27. Their travel this day, as recently experienced, was also complicated by high winds and trail dust making for "disagreeable traveling." Egan, *Pioneering*, 92.
28. As the pioneers entered this valley, the diarists saw a visionary landscape: "Turning round a bluff on our left hand saw 9 Wicka ups in a beautiful vale, also many horses grazing in a beautiful camp ground." As they pressed closer to Bridger's fort, they passed "6 more Wicka ups, crossing over three other small streams and halt in a beautiful vale where grass is 'knee deep, and deeper.'" This beauty was accented by "very clear" water and "excellent mill sites," with abundant timber. Together, "the Scene [was] lovely & delightsome to look at." Bullock, *Camp of the Saints*, 220.

    The Shoshone Indians, also known as the Snake Indians due to their proximity to the Snake River in Idaho and Wyoming, were described by Erastus Snow as having "a good reputation among the Mountaineers for honesty and integrity." Most of the Indian lodges near Fort Bridger were "occupied by half-breed traders," French mostly. Orson Pratt wrote that the nine lodges first encountered were located "half a mile" east of Jim Bridger's fort and that their inhabitants numbered "50 or 60." (The previous year when Edwin Bryant camped at the fort, as many as 500 "Snake Indians" were lodged nearby.) As the vanguard passed through the valley, they also witnessed "a full crop of young children, playing around the doors." The presence of the Shoshone and their families in the area, however, caused that there was "no fresh meat in Camp—game scarce." Egan, *Pioneering*, 92; Pratt, *Journals*, 439–440; Snow, "Journey" (July 1948): 272; Korns and Morgan, *West from Fort Bridger*, 55; Lyman (Carrington), Diary, 8 July 1847.
29. Jim Bridger constructed three forts, beginning in 1841, in proximity to the Green River. The fort in this story, the one whose remnants still remain as a historic site in southwestern Wyoming, was built in August 1843. Louis Vasquez was Bridger's partner in the enterprise and was the principal with whom the Mormons dealt when they purchased the fort in 1855. Gowans and Campbell, *Fort Bridger*, 10, 12.

    William Clayton described Bridger's fort as being "composed of two double log houses about forty feet long each and joined by a pen for horses about ten feet high constructed by placing poles upright in the ground close together." (Just a year earlier, Edwin Bryant described the fort as "two or three miserable log-cabins, rudely constructed, and bearing but a faint resemblance to habitable houses.") The double long houses, with dirt roofs, formed "an L." Clayton, *Journal*, 285; Pratt, *Journals*, 440; Korns and Morgan, *West from Fort Bridger*, 55; Lyman (Carrington), Diary, 7 July 1847.

    A description of emigrant portrayals of Bridger and his fort in the mid-1840s is found in Alter, *Jim Bridger*, 213–222.
30. They had located their camp "about half a mile past the fort," "in a circle" on an "Island formed by Black Fork." Egan, *Pioneering*, 92; Whitney, Diary, 7 July 1847; Harper, *Diary*, 29.
31. Brigham Young anticipated the interest of the pioneer camp in trading at Fort Bridger, and thus cautioned his charges on 3 July about trading strategy with those at the fort. Thomas Bullock noted that "few succeeded" with "trades with the French & Indians"

& washed 4 shirts, two garments & two pr socks.[32] White frost.[33] Lat 41° 19' 13[34]

Friday 9th [July 1847] Started at 9 [A.] M. moved on 6 3/4 miles to a watering place. passed on over the mountain.[35] Some Snow banks. came down onto the muddy fork [which] runs into Ham's fork.[36] made 6 1/4 miles & camped on the muddy fork.[37] good grass.

Saturday 10th [July 1847] A winding, mountainous rout. about the middle of the day came down upon another branch of the mudy fork where there is verry strong Sulphur Springs & evidence of copper, Iron, and Lead.[38] this afternoon passed the divide between the waters of the Gulf of Calafornia & the Great Salt Lake, which Divide is some 300 feet higher than the South Pass.[39] made 18 miles & camped on a Branch of Bear river.[40]

---

because "they could not obtain sufficient for their goods." However, others made bargains, though "The Articles generally at Bridger's fort were at least one third or one half higher than at any other traiding post in America," according to Wilford Woodruff. Whitney, Diary, 3 July 1847; Bullock, *Camp of the Saints*, 221; Woodruff, *Journal*, 3:225.

32. Jacob and others used the day's layover to clean personal articles while others "set some wagon tires." Egan, *Pioneering*, 93.
33. Orson Pratt wrote that "Ice was formed during the night, which, however, was soon melted by the rising sun." Pratt, *Journals*, 440.
34. Orson Pratt's scientific calculations for Fort Bridger placed the elevation at 6665 feet and the temperature for the day to be 66°. The distance of Bridger's fort from Fort Laramie was stated to be 397 miles. Pratt, *Journals*, 440; Bullock, *Camp of the Saints*, 221.
35. After traveling over a "table tolerably level for several miles," they began their descent which was "the steepest and most difficult we have ever met with, being long and almost perpendicular." Clayton, *Journal*, 287.
36. When they encountered the Muddy Fork, a "stream about twelve feet wide," it ran "North and winds round the hills to the North of Fort Bridger, forms a Junction with Ham's Fork, and so flows to Green River." Snow, "Journey" (July 1948): 272; Clayton, *Journal*, 287.
37. Their course that day over "Mr. [Lansford] Hasting's new route," was "dimly seen, as only a few wagons passed over it last season." Pratt, *Journals*, 440–441.
38. One of the evidences of mineral content in the area was the water which was "very clear but tastes very strong of copperas [ferrous sulphate, used in making dye and ink] and alum and has a somewhat singular effect on the mouth." Clayton, *Journal*, 287.
39. Orson Pratt figured the ridge to be 7,700 above sea level, though the "rim of the basin" at Aspen Divide rises to over 8,300 feet, making it "the high point on the pioneer trek." Korns and Morgan, *West from Fort Bridger*, 129n4; Bagley in Bullock, *Camp of the Saints*, 223n26.
40. Similar to the previous day, the company made another precipitous descent. The company wound down "two steep pitches, almost perpendicular, which on looking back from the bottom looks like jumping off the roof of a house to a middle story, then from the middle story to the ground." Three grizzly bears were seen during the course of the day. The night's camp "was on the south bank of Sulphur Creek, 1 3/4 miles east of the Bear River." Bullock, *Camp of the Saints*, 223; Woodruff, *Journal*, 3:227; Korns and Morgan, *West from Fort Bridger*, 130n4.

Sunday 11th [July 1847] Froze water in a Bucket but the day is warm. Some men returning from Calafornia to the States passed us this morning. also Mr Miles Goodye[a]r visited us, who lives about 60 miles from here near the Salt Lake.[41] he is on his way down the <Bear> River.[42] we remained encamped to day.[43] John Norton found a fountain of Petroleum or mineral Tar. it came verry opportunely for we were entirely out of Tar.[44] yesterday John Brown

---

41. The previous night Orson Pratt noticed smoke rising in the distance. Thinking it was an Indian camp, a detail of men however found Miles Goodyear with several others. Albert Carrington noted: "Miles Goodyear & 2 men & a Mr. [John] Craig of Ray Co Mo. & Mr. Truett of Shelby Co Ill & 2 other men, camped 1 1/2 ms. from us on Bear river; Goodyear & his men for Bridger, the other 4 for the States." John Craig, after descending from the Sierra Mountains the first week in June with seven pack mules, had visited Miles Goodyear's post near what became Ogden, Utah, on 4 July. He related to his listeners that while crossing the desert he lost five horses, and estimated their present location to be half way between San Francisco and St. Joseph, Missouri. Craig also noted in correspondence that the size and destination of the Mormon emigrant company to be "83 waggons being an advance party of the Mormons on thair way to the lake intending . . . to establish a colony." Mattes, *Platte River Road Narratives*, 93; Pratt, *Journals*, 442–443; Lyman (Carrington), Diary, 10 July 1847.

    Howard Egan noted the distance that Goodyear reported between their location and his fort to be seventy-five miles. Egan, *Pioneering*, 94.

42. Miles Goodyear had been in the West since 1836, initially trapping and trading out of Fort Hall and Fort Bridger. He established Fort Buenaventura in modern-day West Ogden, Utah, in September 1846 on the Weber River before it emptied into the Great Salt Lake. (The post was located about two miles above the Weber's junction with the Ogden River.) While not the first establishment built by white men in Utah, it was the only one functioning at this time. Goodyear's report to Mormon leaders about the favorable circumstances of his fort and garden reaffirmed their decision to settle along the eastern rim of the Great Basin. His close proximity to the Salt Lake Valley proved to be a boon for him when the Mormons, with $1950 in gold, purchased his claim on 25 November 1847.

    Jacob neglected to note the importance of Miles Goodyear's visit with the Saints. After their initial meeting, Goodyear accompanied several Mormons westward "to look out the road." The road temporarily forked here. One trail, the southerly and longer one, was that taken by the Donner-Reed party the previous year. The Saints took the northerly one, which proved to be the most suited for future travel. Egan, *Pioneering*, 94. The road's divide is discussed in Korns and Morgan, *West from Fort Bridger*, 132n7.

43. Not surprisingly, as the trek neared three months in duration, despite the knowledge that their objective was soon within reach, some complained about the journey. While resting in camp on the Sabbath Thomas Bullock "overheard several of the brethren murmuring about the face of the country," although Bullock felt that "it is very evident, to the most careless observer, that it is growing richer & richer every day." Bullock, *Camp of the Saints*, 224.

44. Of this petroleum spring, Albert Carrington wrote, "About a mile and a half nearly due south [from the Bear River], and about two hundred yards to the left, where the southern road begins its second rise, and near a black alder bush, is a fine spring of mineral tar exuding from the slope of the hill among the sandstone boulders and covering with its deposit of pitch and asphaltum a surface 30 feet by three yards." Lewis Barney, one of the hunters who likely teamed with John Norton, claimed that he "disCovered the tar or oil Springs." He said that he "tried Some of this oil and found that it would burn like a lamp. It also proved to be an excilent Remedy for Sore back horses and galded Shoulders." Upon

Killed an Antelope & L[ewis]. Barney one today. Last Friday morning Br [William] Casto, one of the Soldiers [Mormon Battalion], came to mess with us. I was on guard on the last watch.

Monday 12th [July 1847] Started at 8 [A.] M. a mile & an half crossed Bear river, a rapid Strem heads in the Snow toped to South & runs North almost to Fort Hall & then turns South & emties into the Salt Lake nearly West of here.[45] passed up a fine valley to the S West & down another where there is better Soil than we have found since we left the Big Platte.[46] made 9 3/4 miles & halted for dinner.[47] Br Brigham [Young] was taken Sick last

---

his return to Winter Quarters the following month William Clayton visited the tar spring on 21 August which he described: "The ground is black over with the oil for several rods but it is baked hard by exposure to the sun. It is difficult to get the clear oil, most of it being filled with dust and gravel. It smells much like British oil and is said to do well for greasing wagons." Smith (Carrington), History, 11 July 1847; Barney, Autobiography and diary, 38; Clayton, *Journal*, 351.

Thomas Bullock noted that along with oil springs the vicinity offered "Pure Water Springs, a creek, a Sulphur Spring, & a Pitchy or Greasy Spring within 1 1/4 miles of Camp." To him it seemed "as if Nature herself had separated her different productions for the especial use of the Persecuted Saints on their journey." The pool, or oil spring, is located twelve miles south of Evanston, Wyoming, and is still flowing. Bullock, *Camp of the Saints*, 224; Kimball, *Historic Sites and Markers*, 94–95.

45. At the Bear's crossing Howard Egan found the river to be "a very rapid stream about six rods wide ("about sixty feet," according to Orson Pratt) and two feet deep, the banks of which were lined with willows and a little timber." Pratt described the river bed as being "completely covered with rounded boulders, some of which were about as large as a human head." Egan, *Pioneering*, 94; Pratt, *Journals*, 443–444.

    The Bear River, originating in the northwestern portion of the Unita Mountains in northeastern Utah, flows northward into Wyoming and Idaho before bending southward into northern Utah. The river courses over 300 miles before emptying into the northeastern arm of the Great Salt Lake. Pratt placed the elevation of the river at 6836 feet "above the sea." Wahlquist, *Atlas of Utah*, 49; Pratt, *Journals*, 444.

46. This is the stretch of trail leading to Cache Cave, the vicinity of which can be seen today just south of I-80 about ten miles inside the Utah state line, near Castle Rock, Utah. The cave was called by the Saints "Reddin's Cave" due to Jackson Redden "being one of the first in our company who visited it." Cache Cave, while it was known by others as "Swallows" cave due to the bird nests within, became a noted landmark accumulating the numerous names of emigrants scrawled on its walls. Of the cave, William Clayton wrote that "It is supposed from appearances that there is some property cached in the cave," hence its name. The cave looked to be "about 8 feet high and 12 or 14 feet wide." (Others' approximations differed.) They entered "about 30 feet," Orson Pratt related, but "did not feel disposed to penetrate it any further." Wilford Woodruff, who carved his name in the soft rock, indicated "large wolf dens" may have been located at the rear of the cave, the fear of which may have precluded exploration. Kimball, *Historic Sites and Markers*, 96–97; Bullock, *Camp of the Saints*, 225; Clayton, *Journal*, 292; Pratt, *Journals*, 445; Woodruff, *Journal*, 3:228.

47. They encountered two forks in the road in the course of their day's travel, taking the "right hand fork" both times. The first fork "was the road [Heinrich] Lienhard took from Sulphur Creek to Yellow Creek on the advice of Lansford Hasting." The grass had

night.[48] he became so bad that he concluded to stop here [with] Br Heber [Kimball] with [obscure word crossed out] <3> of his Waggons, Br [Ezra] Benson with one Waggon & Lorenzo [Young] with two, while the remainder of the camp went on 6 3/4 [miles] through some fertile Valeys where that eye sore, the wild Sage, has disappeared. we camped on a Small Branch of the Weaver [Weber] river[49] which falls into the Salt Lake 10 miles below <or South> [of] the mouth of Bear river.[50] ten Antelopes Killed today.[51]

Tuesday 13th [July 1847] Brethren [Wilford] Woodruff, John Brown & Joseph Mathews went early this morning to Br Brigham [Young]'s camp to learn the state of his health &c. ~~about~~ while we remained encamped.[52] about noon they returned & Br Heber [Kimball] with them. report the President [Young] to [be] better[53] & he recommends that some twenty Waggons Start on to explore

---

grown sufficient that at times the road "was exceedingly difficult to find, excepting in places where the grass has not completely obscured it." Pratt, *Journals*, 443–444; Bagley in Bullock, *Camp of the Saints*, 225n33.

48. Near what is known as the Needles, located near the Wyoming-Utah border, Brigham Young took his turn in contracting the Colorado Tick Fever. Albert Rockwood, who was with Brigham Young and ill himself, said Young was "verry sick and much deranged." The illness completely sapped its victims. Erastus Snow described both Young and Rockwood "being nigh unto death." Kimball, *Historic Sites and Markers*, 95; Rockwood, *History*, 68; Snow, "Journey," (July 1948): 273.

    Orson Pratt described the Needles as "a pudding stone formation." He wrote that the "rocks are from 100 to 200 feet in height, and rise up in a perpendicular and shelving form, being broken or worked out into many curious forms by the rains." Wilford Woodruff reported the formations' "spires" reached "up like the pyramids of Egypt." Pratt, *Journals*, 444; Woodruff, *Journal*, 3:228.

49. The Weber River was sometimes known during the era of mountain men and trappers as Weaver's River. The Weber, akin to the Bear River, originates from the northwestern slope of the Uinta Mountains, although it runs northwesterly before it pours into the Great Salt Lake. Mormons, at this point, thought the Weber to be a fork of the Bear. The Weber River is one of the three primary drainage systems, the Bear and Jordan are the others, that feed into the inland sea. The origin of the names of Weaver and Weber as appellations to the river and valley in which Ogden, Utah, presently rests, have long been an object of conjecture. Whitney, Diary, 16 July 1847; Russell, *Journal of Trapper*, 114, 116; Wahlquist, *Atlas of Utah*, 49.

50. It is probable that this information was supplied to the pioneers by Miles Goodyear. The rivers empty into the Great Salt Lake about eighteen miles apart as the crow flies, the Bear on the north and Weber to the South.

51. As they began descent from the high Wyoming plain, they found the antelope "in great abundance, but rather wild." Pratt, *Journals*, 444.

52. The distance between Brigham Young's camp, who stayed behind due to the effects of the tick fever, and the main body had increased to nearly seven miles. Whitney, Diary, 13 July 1847.

53. While William Clayton wrote that Heber Kimball reported Brigham Young to be "a little better this morning," Kimball disclosed that the previous evening Young "was insensible and raving." Albert Rockwood was also described as being "very sick and quite deranged." Clayton, *Journal*, 292.

the road through the Bear river mountains which seperates the valley we are now in from the Great [Salt] Lake. a meeting was called by Br Heber to take this matter into consideration,[54] when it was resolved to send on the above named duty: captains Mathews, Brown, [Robert] Crow & [Seth] Tafts with their respective Tens, all to be under the direction of Br Orson Pratte, assisted by Col. Stephen Markum. 23 Waggons started about 2 oclock P.M.[55] Ten ~~five~~ Antelopes Killed today.[56] ~~I Killed one <a> fawn. the Brethren that went up to the President's camp returned at evening & report him to be convalescent. Br Rockwood has been verry sick but they intend to come down tomorrow.~~

Wednesday 14th [July 1847] Several taken sick yesterday & today.[57] Sultry, hot weather.[58] some went up to the other camp. I went hunting & Killed a fawn Antelope. four more were Killed today. the Brethren returned at

---

54. Apparently the decision to send an advance party to the Salt Lake Valley, a significant move, was discussed by Brigham Young and Heber Kimball prior to the council when the resolution was implemented. Pratt, *Journals*, 445; Lyman (Carrington), Diary, 13 July 1847.
55. The twenty-three wagons were manned by forty-two men, whom are identified in the accounts by Howard Egan, William Clayton, and Horace Whitney. (Erastus Snow wrote that the "best teams," mostly ox teams, were selected along with the "ablest men," which included the three African-Americans.) The objective of the advance party was ostensibly to define and clear the road for those who followed. They took "with them crowbars, & other implements, necessary to remove large obstacles from the path." Because church leaders had been "informed that it would be impracticable to pass through the [Weber] kanyon on account of the depth and rapidity of the water," Orson Pratt's charge was to "find Mr. [James] Reid's route across the mountains," referring, of course, to the Donner-Reed road created by that company the previous year. Egan, *Pioneering*, 95; Snow, "Journey," (July 1948): 274; Clayton, *Journal*, 292–293; Whitney, Diary, 13, 15 July 1847; Lyman (Carrington), Diary, 13 July 1847; Harper, *Diary*, 29; Pratt, *Journals*, 445.
56. Discussing the hunters' success the previous two days, Erastus Snow wrote that "there seems to be plenty of game west of Bear River, but between the [South] Pass and Bear River we saw but little." He also noted that they "saw the bones and ancient signs of buffalo, but we are told by Mountaineers that there have been none of these animals west of the Pass for some years." It may have been the case that the buffalo, some of which ranged into the Great Basin, were obliterated from the area during the extreme winter of 1830–1831. However, see Orson Pratt's notation for 19 July 1847 descending Big Mountain where he had viewed the Salt Lake Valley for the first time. He said he saw the "fresh track of buffalo." Snow, "Journey," (July 1948): 273; Pratt, *Journals*, 451.
57. "There are one or two new cases of sickness in our camp," William Clayton wrote. He reported the fever to be "very severe on the first attack, generally rendering its victims delirious for some hours, and then leaving them in a languid, weakly condition." Clayton, *Journal*, 292–293.

    Of interest, near the same location a year earlier, Oregon-bound emigrants were plagued with what may have been the same debility. Bryant in Korns and Morgan, *West from Fort Bridger*, 65.
58. Laying over for the day, despite the need for the repair of clothing and wagons, proved to be "Quite dull business" for those who sensed their closeness to their destination. Whitney, Diary, 14 July 1847.

evening. report the President [Brigham Young] to be convalescent. Br [Albert] Rockwood has been verry sick, but they intend to come down here tomorrow. my Ten on guard all night.

Thursday 15th [July 1847] I went down the creek with Major [John] Pack to look for a camping place.[59] Started back after going three miles when we met George A. Smith. the Major returned to camp, while we went down a mile & a half further & found a fine Spring, wood & grass. we returned & arrived at camp Just as the President [Brigham Young] & company did, Br [Wilford] Woodruff having gone up with his carriage for the President & Br [Albert] Rockwood to ride in.[60] they appeared verry cheerful & quite comfortable. we proceeded down to our Spring 4 1/2 miles & camped.[61] I went in company with Br George A. Smith & [Albert] carrington upon the mountains. North we found Shrub Oak on the side of the mountain & with a Spy glass saw large quantitys of Pine on the mountain to the South.[62] The sick are all getting better. one Antelope Killed.

Friday 16th [July 1847] A heavy Shower of rain this morning. in fact, we have had several small showers since we came into this valley which looks more cheering than the arrid desert we have been passing through. after the rain had ceased, we moved on down the creek between high mountains on either side, 6 3/4 miles.[63] we halted for dinner. Porter Rockwell met us here from

---

59. Jacob's note of traveling "down the creek" as they continued westward, is literally true. It is a significant descent in elevation from Cache Cave to Echo Canyon.

60. Wilford Woodruff provided beds in his carriage for Brigham Young and Albert Rockwood because it "was the easiest ve[h]icle in camp." Young's group of eight wagons rejoined their comrades about noon. Woodruff, *Journal*, 3:230; Bullock, *Camp of the Saints*, 227.

61. They formed camp in a "Circle" near what is now Castle Rock, Utah. Bagley in Bullock, *Camp of the Saints*, 227, 227n41.

62. It should be no surprise that the Saints, along the entire route, had noted circumstances favorable to the construction of way stations to assist those who followed and, as they neared their destination, settlements for those who would to gather to Zion. The following day Thomas Bullock noted, to his "great joy," that they had "found Hops flourishing, a pretty good proof of the absence of severe frosts & shews a mild climate." Bullock, *Camp of the Saints*, 228.

63. The route for the morning, "following the course of the creek," took them through "mountains [that] seem to increase in height, and come so near together in some places as to leave merely room enough for a crooked road." The company had entered Echo Canyon, which William Clayton described as having "a very singular echo," where "the rattling of wagons resembles carpenters hammering at boards inside the highest rocks." Further, he said, the "report of a rifle resembles a sharp crack of thunder and echoes from rock to rock for some time." And, besides the "lowing of cattle and braying of mules" seeming "to be answered beyond the mountains," musical instruments, "especially brass instruments, have a very pleasing effect and resemble a person standing inside the rock imitating every note." His description of the canyon concluded: "The echo, the high rocks on the north, high mountains on the south with the narrow ravine for a road, form a scenery at once romantic and more interesting than I have ever witnessed." Clayton, *Journal*, 294, 296.

the Pioneer camp 25 miles ahead.[64] moved on down the creek a S Westerly course 9 1/2 miles & camped within about a mile of Weaver [Weber] river.[65] S[olomon]. Chamberlin broke his Waggon axeltree two miles back & Captn [John] Wheeler unloaded his Waggon & went back & brought down the axltree to be mended.[66]

Satturday 17 [July 1847] Br [Thomas] Tanner set up his forge & welded the broken axeltree. nine Horses were lost this morning & the camp moved on

64. John Brown, who accompanied Orson Pratt's group, wrote that in determining whether the Weber River or the Donner-Reed route would best suit the Mormon pioneers, he and Pratt "went down [the river] and examined the [Weber] canyon but found it impassable." Pratt wrote that together they rode downriver "about 5 miles" from their encampment and being convinced they were in "the [impassable] 10 mile kanyon" of which they had heard reports, they returned to camp. Later they found the route the Donner-Reed party used the previous year, though it was "so dimly seen that it only now and then could be discerned." Brown, *Autobiography*, 77; Pratt, *Journals*, 447.

    Porter Rockwell had been sent back to report they "had found the new route [the Donner-Reed road], &c., which we had anticipated would be troublesome to find." They reported the road to be "about twenty-five or thirty miles to the canyon." Rockwell told them they had "found the road leading over the mountains to avoid the [Weber] canyon and expect to be on top today at noon." Pratt, *Journals*, 448; Clayton, *Journal*, 294–295.

65. The afternoon's stretch of road within Echo Canyon took them to where they "had to pass close to the foot of high, perpendicular red mountains or rock supposed to be from six hundred to a thousand feet high." Their campsite for the night, where they stopped at 7 P.M., was designated because it was "the first good camping place we have seen since noon, not for lack of grass or water, but on account of the narrow gap between the mountains." Erastus Snow noted their day's travel followed "a small creek fed by the spring of the Valley, which we had to cross about every have mile." Near evening, "for about a half or three-quarters of a mile the whole camp seemed perfectly emerged in a dense thicket of large shrubbery and weeds, with scattering trees which filled the Valley."

    Having established camp William Clayton then climbed up "the highest mountain on the south." He described the ascent as being "so steep that there is scarce a place to be found to place the foot flat and firm." Precariously finding his way to the top, which required him to rest "about half a dozen times," he said he "could see the fork of Weber River about a mile west of the camp" and while he could trace their route during the day, "in every other direction" he could see "nothing but ranges of mountains still as much bigger than the one I was on." The scenery, he exulted, was "truly wild and melancholy." Clayton, *Journal*, 295–297; Snow, "Journey," (July 1948): 274.

    Horace Whitney's account of the day's travel considered the topography in a prophetic manner. He wrote that "the pass between the mountains became quite narrow, & on looking up we could see huge fragments of rocks projecting immidiately over our heads." He continued that "this *pass* is so well fortified by nature, that I have no doubt but that 10 men could successfully dispute its passage for a long time, against 100 men." Of course, ten years later the Mormon militia employed the very tactic in preparing defense of the territory as the federal army marched against them in what was called the "Utah War." Whitney, Diary, 16 July 1847.

66. Earlier in the day "Harvey Pierce broke his wagon reach and bolster" indicating the difficulty of travel in Echo Canyon where, passing through "a deep ravine," most of "the teams had to double to get up." Clayton, *Journal*, 294.

while some went to carry [Solomon] Chamberlin's axeltree up to him while others went to hunt the lost Horses & found them 9 miles back on the road. we proceeded 2 1/2 miles when Br [Heber] Kimbal directed us to camp, as the President [Brigham Young] was so sick he could not travel.[67] we camped on Webber's River where The men caught <some of> the Speckled Trout.[68] [obscure word crossed out] In the afternoon 8 of the Brethren took their garments of [the] Priesthood & went up on the mountain & offered up prayers for the recovery of the President & those that are sick.[69]

Sunday 18th [July 1847] A severe white frost this morning but the vegetation here is of such a hardy nature that the frost do's [doesn't] seem to injure it.[70] President [Brigham] Young is verry sick this morning & President [Heber] Kimbal called the brethren together & proposed that we hold a prayer meeting at 10 oclock & humble our selves before the Lord that we may obtain power with him to turn away sickness & disease from our midst. all were requested [to] meet punctualy at the sound of the Bugle, but John Norton manifested a spirit of contention with the Brethren & instead of attending meeting went to bead [bed].[71] we had a good meeting. Br [Wilford] Woodruff said that the Devil was constantly striving to hinder our progress & thwart the purposes of God, & now, by causing the President to be sick, hinder our getting through in time to return to our families this fall.

The meeting was opened by Bishop [Tarlton] Lewis. President Kimbal proposed that the Camp go forward tomorrow morning & overtake the other company & go into the valley [on] the other side of the mountain & proceed

67. Albert Rockwood, who was so ill a few days before that he told his brethren that if he didn't get relief within "24 hour[s] they m[i]ght dig a hole to put me in," described Brigham Young's relapse as a "feaver" which "raged so high that he could not travel." With several other wagons, the ill stopped while the rest of the main camp continued. Rockwood, *History*, 68.

68. Echo Canyon, in which the pioneer camp had been traveling for two days, joins the Weber River at what is now the small town of Echo, Utah. The Weber River at this spot, with a "meandering" channel and "stony" bed, was noted to have a "very rapid" current, and to be "about 40 rods [yards] wide and on an average from one to one half foot deep." Smith (Carrington), History, 17 July 1847.

69. The clothing referred to was the ceremonial apparel associated with Nauvoo temple worship practiced by the Latter-day Saints. Five of the eight, Heber Kimball, Wilford Woodruff, Ezra Benson, George Smith, and Willard Richards, were members of the church's Twelve Apostles. En route to and on their return from their isolation, "All rolled stones" down the mountain. They were accompanied by Egan who explained, "We had a glorious time, and I thank the Lord for the privilege." Whitney, Diary, 17 July 1847; Egan, *Pioneering*, 97.

70. Several diarists noted the contrast of cold mornings and hot afternoons in the summer's mountain climate.

71. One of Jacob's ten, John Norton's exhibition of bad feelings and contentious disposition also showed up on the vanguard's return to Winter Quarters the following month. Barney, *One Side by Himself*, 107.

immediately to put all our seeds into the ground; while a few waggons should tarry here until the President should regain his health sufficient to be able to travel.[72] Doct [Willard] Richards & [Wilford] Woodruff aproved the plan posed by Br Heber. Willard Richards then moved that we start at an early hou[r] tomorrow morning, which was seconded & carryed unanimously. the meeting then adjourned to meet again at the sound of the Bugle to Break Bread. met according to adjournment & received some good instruction from Br Heber & partook [of] the sacrement.[73] Br Heber remarked that the Lord had heard & answered our prayers, for when they had washed & anointed him [Brigham Young], he fell into a sweet sleep & awoke much refreshed.

Monday 19th [July 1847][74] At 9 oclock a portion of the camp moved ahead,[75] but when we got to the forks of the road across the river, 3 miles, we were directed [to] halt as one of Doct [Willard] Richard's oxen was missing. after setting up a guide board directing to the left through [Orson] Pratt's Pass[76] to avoid the Kanyon through wihich Weber's river runs,[77] by the direction of

---

72. Another point of direction was given in the meeting with less-than-expected effect. Despite Heber Kimball's counsel in the meeting against hunting and fishing on the Sabbath, several successfully angled in the nearby stream, including Horace Whitney and Wilford Woodruff. Whitney, Diary, 18 July 1847; Woodruff, *Journal*, 3:231.
73. The periodic instruction of church leaders to company members was important to the men. Of Heber Kimball's teaching that day, Howard Egan reported that Kimball "gave us some good instructions, which done my soul good." Erastus Snow reported an "excellent meeting" where "The Holy Spirit was upon us, and faith seemed to spring up in every bosom." Egan, *Pioneering*, 97; Snow, "Journey," (July 1948): 275.
74. Orson Pratt and John Brown, examining "the road and country a-head" on 19 July, ascended a ravine before coming to a ridge where they tied their horses and climbed "a mountain . . . for several hundred feet." There, to the southwest from "the top of Big Mountain," they viewed for the first time "the extensive level prairie," the Great Salt Lake Valley. Returning to their camp, Pratt indicated they found the "fresh track of a buffalo," the hair of the animal "rubbed off" on the "brush in his path." He said it was "probably the only one within hundreds of miles." Brown's interesting entry for the day included the notation that Brigham Young had sent direction to them through a messenger from his camp that when Pratt's party got into the valley they were "to turn a little north" and begin planting. Pratt, *Journals*, 450–451; Brown, *Autobiography*, 78.
75. Forty-one wagons were designated to proceed while fifteen would remain behind with Brigham Young, though Thomas Bullock said only eight or ten wagons remained with Brigham Young. Woodruff, *Journal*, 3:231; Whitney, Diary, 19 July 1847; Egan, *Pioneering*, 97; Bullock, *Camp of the Saints*, 229.
76. William Clayton's guide board read "Pratt's Pass to avoid canyon. To Fort Bridger 74 1/4 miles." Clayton, *Journal*, 301.
77. The previous year, in the first week of August 1846, the Donner-Reed party found, near this point, the recently written note left for them by Lansford Hastings, who preceded them by two days, directing them to chase him down for direction in getting to the Salt Lake Valley. Sending three of their number ahead to find Hastings for clarification, the rest of their camp waited four days near Henefer, Utah, waiting for word from their advance men. Upon their return, after finding Hastings near the Great Salt Lake, the Donner-Reed company left the Weber and journeyed southwest over the mountains into the most

Major [John] Pack, who now has the comand of the camp, we proceeded on slowly up the Pass to the South S. West,[78] & when we had arrived to the top of the first ridge the Doct came up.[79] we now proceeded down a small creek to another larger one where it passes down through a Kanyon,[80] which is the name given to a narrow confined place of waters between perpendicular rocks.[81] here we camped & burned coal to set the t[i]re on George A Smith's waggon.[82] we made 13 miles. Henson Walker lay out on the mountains all night.[83]

Tuesday 20th [July 1847][84] S[t]arted after 10 [A.] M. up this creek to the South. left Br [Henry] Sherwood, he being verry sick (unable to travel) to

---

formidable stretch of road to the Salt Lake Valley. It was the beginning of numerous complications in crossing Utah which eventually led to their capture by the winter in the Sierra Nevadas. Korns and Morgan, *West from Fort Bridger*, 211–213, text and notes.

Orson Pratt and company, after determining the Weber Canyon route into the Salt Lake Valley to be inaccessible, broke southwest from the Weber River on 16 July at Henefer and followed the barely visible trail blazed by the Donner-Reed party. The road over the Hogsback Summit and down Dixie Hollow proved to be so difficult that an advance company of "about a dozen with spades, axes, &c." forged ahead "to make the road passable, which required considerable labor." After camping for the evening, near present-day East Canyon Reservoir at above 5600 feet, Pratt found evidence of the considerable road-clearing effort that taxed the Donner-Reed party the previous year before they had to abandon it for "a little more circuitous route over the hills." For most of the following day, 17 July, Pratt's group retraced the Donner-Reed route to better groom the road for those to follow. As they continued, they found the creek, which they had to cross thirteen times, to be "thickly covered with willows, from 5 to 15 rods wide, making an immense labour in cutting a road through" Dixie Hollow. Pratt, *Journals*, 448–449.

78. The efforts of Orson Pratt's advance party to clear the road for the remainder of the camp proved effective. Ascending the road to Hogsback Summit, Albert Carrington wrote that they "got to [the] top very easily & gradualy." Lyman (Carrington), 19 July 1847.
79. This ridge is what is known as Hogsback Summit.
80. The larger stream, named "Canyon Creek" by Orson Pratt, is today known as East Canyon Creek. (Several of the vanguard thought the creek to be "Ogdens fork" of the Weber River.) Wilford Woodruff called the trail that day "the worst road we have had on the Journey." Snow, "Journey," (July 1948): 276; Egan, *Pioneering*, 99; Woodruff, *Journal*, 3:231–232.
81. That Jacob felt it necessary to define "Kanyon," as others did, indicates the newness of the landscape to these eastern Americans. The "Kanyon" is known today as Dixie Hollow. William Clayton described the descent as being "not very steep but exceedingly dangerous to wagons being mostly on the side hill over large cobble stones, causing the wagons to slide very badly." Clayton, *Journal*, 301.
82. Descending from the summit, George Smith's "Wagon Wheels gave way going down the hill." The spokes were "loose in the hub, and worked about so that when the wagon slides they dish inward, etc." Several other "accidents occurred thro' the day, which caused [Burr] Frost to put up his Blacksmith's shop to repair the Wagons." Bullock, *Camp of the Saints*, 229–230; Clayton, *Journal*, 302.
83. Henson Walker rejoined his comrades the following morning. Smith (Carrington), History, 20 July 1847.
84. Brigham Young, and those who remained behind the main camp due to illness, reached William Clayton's guide board, directing them to the mountains to the southwest, early

camp here with three waggons.[85] found a good deal of labor to clear out the road notwithstanding it was cut through last summer by [James] Reed's company, they that were caught by the snows in the Calafornia mountains, & our Pioneers have done much & yet there is room for more labor.[86] One of the Pioneers met us this morning & reports Br [Orson] Pratt 7 miles ahead last night.[87] made 7 1/4 miles & camped, for we found a letter from Br Pratt informing us that it is 11 miles over the mountain to a camping place.

Wednesday 21st [July 1847][88] Started at 7 [A.] M. and soon turned to the N West <& West> up a narrow defile. This wild Pass has a familiar aspect by reason of the wild Wheat & oats growing along its sides, even to the tops of

---

in the morning of 20 July. Even after their brethren's work on the road the previous week, they still had to "repair the road" as they worked their way over the Hogsback Summit to Dixie Hollow. They continued on, finally camping with three wagons of comrades who stayed behind the main camp due to illness. At the end of the day, they projected themselves to be eight miles behind Orson Pratt's advance company. Egan, *Pioneering*, 98–99; Woodruff, *Journal*, 3:232.

85. Henry Sherwood, Benjamin Dewey, and Artemas Johnson were the three who stayed behind because of illness in wagons belonging to Stephen Goddard, James Case, and Benjamin Dewey. They were met by Brigham Young's camp later in the day. Whitney, Diary, 20 July 1847.

86. The company had to cross "Canyon Fork eleven times" during the day while contending with a road that was "stony and the hardest we have had on wagons, being so narrow in groves and willows, that one cannot walk and drive." The "awful" road ran "through willow bushes over twenty feet high," which had to be cut, and "Although there has been a road cut through, it is yet scarcely possible to travel without tearing the wagon covers." A swampy section had to be covered with willows to facilitate travel, and the water was bad and "dangerous for cattle." Smith (Carrington), History, 20 July 1847; Clayton, *Journal*, 303–304.

While Brigham Young and others of his camp rested on 21 July, Heber Kimball, Ezra Benson, and Lorenzo Young, who were part of Brigham Young's party, "rode out . . . to survey the country." Upon their return, they reported the terrain was so difficult to travel that "they were obliged to dismount from their horses & explore the passage on foot, the country being almost inaccessible." Whitney, Diary, 21 July 1847.

87. Thomas Bullock reported Robert Crow from Orson Pratt's advance group, visited their camp, and reported the distance between the camps to be nine miles. Bullock, *Camp of the Saints*, 230.

88. Orson Pratt and Erastus Snow, who had by this time caught up with Pratt, passed through what is now Emigration Canyon on 21 July and, after encountering "an exceedingly steep hill onto a Butte," which they thought to be "only an arm of Prairie," they ascended the butte and became ecstatic when they saw that they were in the valley. Snow said they "involuntarily, both at same instant, uttered a shout of joy at finding it to be the very place of our Destination." The valley that lay before them, according to Pratt, was "about 20 miles wide and 30 long." To the northwest they viewed the "broad waters of the Great Salt Lake." Though they had only one horse between them, they entered the valley and circled the area for "12 miles" before returning to camp. Snow, "Journey," (July 1948): 277–278; Pratt, *Journals*, 453.

On this same day of exultation for Pratt and Snow, several in Brigham Young's camp suffered so much, apparently from tick fever, that they laid over another day, hoping for recovery from the debilitating illnesses which had thwarted their progress for weeks.

the mountain, as though it had ben subjected to the cultivating hand of the hardy Mountaineer. at 12 oclock arrived at the summit of Pratts Pass of the Utah mountains,[89] 4 1/2 miles, <in sight of the Salt Lake Valley> then down a verry long steep mountain through <a> thickly wooded ravine with a rich soil, course West & S West about 10 miles, then N West over a high mountain & S West down another wooded ravine.[90] made 14 miles[91] & camped 1/2 half mile above Professor [Orson] Pratt's Pioneer company.[92]

Thursday 22d [July 1847] All hands engaged in working our way through to the Valley 4 miles,[93] making 110 miles from Fort Bridger, a fraction less

---

89. "Pratt's Pass" is the stretch of road named for Orson Pratt routed southwesterly from the Weber River, over the Hogsback, to Emigration Canyon, the same route taken by the Donner-Reed camp the previous year. Erastus Snow, who covered the pass earlier in the day, wrote that it "is the only notch or opening of the mountains known in this region of country that is at all practicable for a road except through the canyon, down the bed of Weber River." Pratt had determined the elevation at Big Mountain to be 7245 feet above sea level. Snow, "Journey to Zion," (July 1948): 276–277; Pratt, *Journals*, 451.
90. In contrast to the difficulty of traversing the area from the Weber River to the Salt Lake Valley as described in Mormon accounts, James Frazier Reed's account of the Donner-Reed party's journey the previous year reads like a summer excursion. Of course, it was hardly so. For example, Reed's record of crossing Big Mountain is placidly deceiving. "Tus 18 [August 1846] this Morning all started to Cross the Mountain which is a Natural easy pass with a little more work and encamped making this day." The ordeal down what is now Emigration Canyon was highlighted only by the nondescript phrase, "Clearing a road to the Vall[e]y of the Lake." The worked engineered by the Donner-Reed camp, without question, lessened their countrymen's difficulty the following year. Korns and Morgan, *West from Fort Bridger*, 216–218, text and notes.

    With the company's explorers in advance and Brigham Young's detail in the rear, for the main camp of Mormon pioneers, much of the day descending from the mountain heights on 21 July, through Mountain Dell Creek and Emigration Canyon, was filled with labor. "[C]utting down stumps, heaving out rocks and leveling the road," they "found the road down exceedingly steep and rendered dangerous by the many stumps of trees left standing in the road." Having to "cut up many of them . . . delayed us much." Descending into the ravine, Emigration Canyon east of Salt Lake City, Utah, the treacherous topography forced many to lock "both hind wheels" of their wagons to get into the valley without breaking apart. Clayton, *Journal*, 304–305.
91. The day's difficulty compelled the "Cannon wagon and Brother [Burr] Frost's team" to give out. Before the day was over, "All the teams [were] tired." Smith (Carrington), History, 21 July 1847.
92. Upon his return to camp after exploring the valley, Orson Pratt found his advance group situated "1 1/2 miles up the ravine [Emigration Canyon] from the valley." William Clayton explained that they determined that the ravine was actually a canyon "because of the very high mountains on each side leaving but a few rods of a bottom for the creek to pass through and hardly room for a road." Pratt, *Journals*, 453; Clayton, *Journal*, 306–307.
93. While the Donner-Reed effort the previous year had simplified the final stretch of road for the Saints in 1847, once the vanguard descended into the ravine near the mouth of the canyon they broke from their predecessor's road. Instead of evading the "trees and rock outcroppings" at the canyon's mouth by climbing the hill to the south like the Donner-Reed party the previous year, "the [Mormon] pioneers chose to take the time to

than 500 miles from Fort John & 1050 from Winter Quarters. after going 7 1/4 miles today, camped on Beaver creek, on a verry good soil.[94] Br George A Smith, with a number of horsemen,[95] took an excursion 10 miles down the Lake to the North about half the distance, a good soil & the N part Barren & with boiling hot Sulphur & Salt Springs.[96] they got within some 8 or 10 miles of the Great Salt Lake, but it is hemed in with small Lakes, Ponds, & Pools so that it appears difficult to get near it. in the midtst [of] the Lake there is two large, mountainous Islands.[97] we came into this valley opposite the South end of the Lake, which extends to the South some 20 or 30 miles & from 12 to 15 wide, encircled by mountains except to the North.[98] it <is> about 4000

---

clear a road through the dense growth along the creek rather than risk the steep incline of the hill." One of the reasons they decided to forge their way through the bottom of the canyon was because the route of the Donner-Reed party "over a very steep hill" appeared "almost impossible" to follow. Willard Richards directed the work in the canyon for the day. Bullock wrote that they "graded the hill [on] each side [of] the creek, when teams halted while extra hands go to repair the roads, then crossed over & entered the Kanyon; which required much hard work to make a road thro'." Horace Whitney, following two days later, wrote that as they made their way down the canyon, they "crossed the stream [Emigration Creek] 18 times." After the day's arduous labor on 22 July, Levi Jackman stated: "when we got through it seamed like bursting from the confines of a prison." Dixon, "From Emigration Creek to City Creek," 156; Bullock, *Camp of the Saints*, 231; Whitney, Diary, 24 July 1847; Jackman, Diary, 22 July 1847.

94. Once the initial division of the pioneer camp entered into the Salt Lake Valley on 22 July, they bore southwest following Emigration Creek (William Clayton called it Last Creek) out of the canyon before bearing northwest to rest that night near Parley's Creek (Jacob called it Beaver Creek, Clayton called it Brown's Creek) just south of what is now the intersection of Fifth East and Seventeenth South in Salt Lake City. (A park with informational signs commemorating the location of the first camp was established at the intersection in 1997.) Dixon, "From Emigration Creek to City Creek," 158–159, (see particularly the map on page 159).
95. William Clayton identifies George Smith's companions as John Brown, Joseph Matthews, John Pack, Porter Rockwell, and Jesse Little. Clayton, *Journal*, 308.
96. The several natural sulphur springs northwest of what became Salt Lake City, where the valley floor wraps around the base of the Wasatch Range, attracted the Saints' attention immediately. The temperature of the thermal waters varied by location, the springs mentioned in this entry being among the hottest. The report of those who explored the area stated that there may have been as many as fifty "hot sulphur springs issuing from the rocks," so hot that "a person cannot bear his hand in it but a very few seconds." Other warm springs, in closer proximity to the first camps, were soon claimed by some to have a medicinally therapeutic effect by bathing in the mineral-enriched waters (see Jacob's entry for 26 July 1847), just another indication to the Saints of their providentially appointed location. As the city grew, resorts were established north of town utilizing the springs. Clayton, *Journal*, 312.
97. While the lake actually has ten islands, or near islands, what are now called Antelope and Fremont islands are the land formations identified by Jacob and are the most apparent when viewed from Salt Lake City, Utah. Antelope, the largest island, is fifteen by four miles in size and is now a Utah state park. Fremont Island, north of Antelope Island and named after the government pathmarker, is seven by two miles in size.
98. Albert Carrington captured a first image of the Salt Lake Valley upon their arrival: "As we proceed down the run towards the lake, the small timber and brush give out and a few

feet above the level of the sea, the same as Fort John on the Platte.[99] we have here mild Summer weather, a serrene atmosphere, a most beautiful clear sky, with an excessive dry climate & arrid soil. if it could receive timely rains, it would be one of the most beautiful, fertile regions on the face of the earth, being watered by numerous Brooks & Rivulets perpetualy flowing out of the mountains on every side, filled with Trout, which, with the various kinds of rich grass & rushes, renders it one of the best grazing countrys that can be found.[100]

Friday 23d [July 1847] at 8 [A.] M. moved on to the North about 4 miles & encampe[d] for the present.[101] sent John Pack & Joseph Mathews back to meet the President's [Brigham Young] camp.[102] all were now assembled in the

---

clumps and fringes of willows and scattering cottonwoods and Box Elder trees on the runs is all the timber or shrubbery in the valley," though he also stated that there were a "few trees nearly one foot through near the mouth of the canyon." Smith (Carrington), History, 22 July 1847.

99. This generalization about the elevation of what became Salt Lake City and Fort Laramie is correct, both being about 4,300 feet above sea level, give or take fifty feet.

100. Most diarists in the Mormon vanguard company initially penned favorable reports of the climate and characteristics of the valley upon their initial entry, though concerns such as lack of water and timber were noted. Having finally arrived at what appeared to be their destination likely favorably colored some of their first conclusions about the valley, not shared by all, including at least one of the women. Harriet Young, Lorenzo Dow Young's wife, one of the three women on the expedition, upon her arrival on 24 July wrote in her husband's journal: "my feelings were such as I cannot describe. every thing looked gloomy and I felt heart sick." With an eye of domesticity, the bleak, unimproved landscape likely discouraged Harriet who undoubtedly envisioned the ordeal of rebuilding a life from scratch. Young, "Diary of Lorenzo Dow Young," 163.

Some of the pioneers' initial observations from a distance would prove inaccurate, such as William Clayton's who wrote that a mountain to "the northwest" of the Great Salt Lake, perhaps Promontory Point, was "rock salt from its white and shining appearance." Clayton, *Journal*, 308.

Most of the vanguard's descriptions of the valley belie the widely held views that the region was a desert, which it is not. Indeed, "While Utah is mostly an arid, desert-like region, a narrow strip of land bisecting the state and stretching from the northern boundary to almost the center of Utah has environmental characteristics unlike the rest of the state. It is this corridor that most of Utah's population [settled]. Designated a 'humid continental-hot summer' climatic zone and comprising only three percent of Utah's land mass, the primary geologic factor is the Wasatch Mountains, running north to south, which stalls and cools moist western clouds and winds forcing moisture to the ground, thereby creating mountain valleys conducive to farming and habitation. The cold winters and hot summers are separated by distinct springs and autumns making for a favorable place to reside." Barney, *One Side by Himself*, 140–141. See also Wahlquist, *Atlas of Utah*, 55.

101. The campsite for their second night in the valley, 23 July, was northwest of their camp the previous night, "on the eastern part of the [present] city block laying between Main and State and Third and Fourth South streets." Dixon, "On the Banks of a Beautiful Stream," 12–13.

102. John Pack later remembered, after stating that he "led the first company into the valley," that "on the 24th one of my company with me and went back on the road and

center of our camp, when Br [Orson] Pratt addressed us stating that we had been two years striving to get to this place which was had in contemplation before we left the Temple at Nauvoo as the place of our location somewhere in this great valley.[103] we have been greatly blessed in our Journey for which he now proposed to return thanksgiving to our heavnly Father, when the whole camp engaged in Prayer & thanksgiving,[104] after which several committees were selected to attend to the various branches of our labors in putting our seeds.[105]

Doct [Willard] Richards said some things had been manifested among this People in times past [that] has produced much evil, a Spirit of selvishness which we must now throw aside & go to work with all our might & energy to put in our seeds asking no questions who should eat the fruit of them lest the crickets should eat our turnips as they did last summer, for the Brethren eat their turnips before they were sown & so the crickets took them, & now if we go to disputing about who shall eat our crops we will not be blesed in our labors, but it will happen to us as it did to those people who undertook to cut throug the Kanyon we came down from the mountain ~~a~~ about a year ago, having got <to> quarreling, gave it up & climbed over the mountain & afte<r>wards starved & eat one another in the Calafornia

---

met Colonel Markham and company and escorted them in to the valley." Pack, [1847 Recollection].

Thomas Bullock stated that he prepared "a table of distances & route from Weber River" to the Salt Lake Valley which were given to the men to take to Brigham Young. Horace Whitney, who was with Young wrote that the letter and the messengers provided "an account of the roads ahead, the fertility of the soil, & general features of the country in their vicinity." Bullock, *Camp of the Saints*, 233; Whitney, Diary, 23 July 1847.

103. Some have argued, because of what appears to be confusing and contradictory evidence regarding the final objective of the Saints, that upon their departure from Nauvoo the matter was still undecided. "[C]ompelling evidence," Richard Bennett states, "indicates that late in Joseph Smith's life, he had begun to look to the Rocky Mountains as the probable place of temporary refuge." As Smith's successor, Brigham Young embraced Smith's instinct for the West. Indeed, Bennett declares, "their destination, at least in general terms, never was a question." Glen Leonard argues that talk of Vancouver Island or Oregon in the Pacific Northwest was nothing more than a diversionary tactic to veil their intent on the Great Basin. That generality likely narrowed to the Salt Lake Valley (also known as the Bear River Valley) before the vanguard pushed away from Winter Quarters. Bennett, *We'll Find the Place*, 8–10; Leonard, *Nauvoo*, 537, 566–567.

104. William Clayton's entry for the day indicates the focus of the camp's prayer at this meeting: "the brethren united in prayer and asked the Lord to send rain on the land, etc." Clayton, *Journal*, 313.

105. A "Committee of Five—Shadrach Roundy, Seth Taft, Stephen Markham, Robert Crow & Albert Carrington—were appointed to look out a place for planting Potatoes, Corn, Beans &c." Charles Harper, Charles Shumway and Elijah Newman were selected to "be a committee to Stock Plows & Drags & to call those men to their assistance that they want." Further, "Henson Walker, William Wadsworth [Wordsworth] & John Brown" were assigned to "be a committee to superintend the moving & rigging up of Scythes." Bullock, *Camp of the Saints*, 233.

mountains.[106] it will fare worse with us unless we go to work to preserve seed for the benefit of those that are to come after us. in fact, the temporal salvation of <our> families, our posterity, & the Nations of the earth depends upon the integrity of our conduct at the present time.[107] all seemed to partake of the unity of the Spirit & seperated each to his respective part of the labor.[108] I went to work with Lewis Barney & made two harrows by four oclock P.M.[109] Some Ploughs were put to runing & at night had brok 3 acres.[110] our mesengers returned from Br Brigham [Young]'s camp & reported him to be within ten miles & the sick all geting better.[111] met at evening[112] & organized our teams so as to have them work 4 hours & change four times each day.[113]

Satturday 24th [July 1847][114] I was engaged with the Plough makers making Ploughs.[115] a dam was constructed across the creek above the camp so as to irrigate our Ploughed Land.[116] all the Potatoes in <camp> were planted today

106. Willard Richards's conclusion about the Donner-Reed party undoubtedly came from Samuel Brannan when on 30 June the latter met the pioneer camp on the Green River.
107. Willard Richards's sermon on cooperation, selflessness, and working to make life easier for each other and those to follow, recognizing the Saints' shortcomings in this arena, nevertheless demonstrates an institutional theme that prevailed for a generation.
108. The "first furrow" was turned at noon. George Smith in Pratt, *Journals*, 457.
109. Orson Pratt recorded the afternoon temperature at 3 P.M. to be 96°. Besides feeling the effect of a very hot day, Jacob neglected to write that in the afternoon they had two hours of intermittent rain. Pratt, *Journals*, 457; Clayton, *Journal*, 313.
110. Soon after the gathering, "The brethren immediately rigged three plows and went to plowing a little northeast of the camp," along with one harrow. The shovels and ploughs first broke ground on land that is now "the northeast corner of State and Third South streets" in Salt Lake City. Clayton, *Journal*, 313; Smith (Carrington), History, 23 July 1847; Dixon, "On the Banks of a Beautiful Stream," 12.
111. Brigham Young's clerks later entered into his history Young's first impressions of seeing the Salt Lake Valley: "The spirit of light rested upon me and hovered over the valley, and I felt that there the Saints would find protection and safety." Young, *Manuscript History, 1846–1847*, 564.
112. William Clayton mentioned that at this gathering Willard Richards said some things "which seemed little welcome to many from the way it was handled." But despite the fact that "Some felt a little insulted," in the end "it all passed off well and jokingly." Clayton, *Journal*, 313.
113. "Stephen Markham was appointed to attend to the Teams & see that fresh sets were hitched up every four hours." The shifts were to "come in turns, 4 hrs each, from 4 A.M. to 8 P.M., 4 turns." Bullock, *Camp of the Saints*, 233; Lyman (Carrington), Diary, 23 July 1847.
114. William Clayton described the day to be "fine and hot with a nice breeze" and that in the late afternoon they "were favored with another nice shower accompanied by thunder and some wind." Clayton, *Journal*, 314.
115. The hardened, undisturbed soil proved to be so resistant that "A Lyman's & some other ploughs broke." Lyman (Carrington), Diary, 24 July 1847.
116. With the availability of water being one of the most important considerations in the final selection of a homeland, the pioneers' initial observations are very telling regarding their decision to settle in Salt Lake Valley. By William Clayton's account, on the east of "a beautiful table land, level and nicely sloping to the west," located about "three-quarters of

& some of <them> watered.[117] while we were eating Dinner, Br Brigham [Young]'s camp came in sight up towards the foot of the mountain & they soon arrived in camp greatly to the Joy of us all, <&> highly pleased with the valley.[118] three hunters [were] sent out today, one up the creek we are on & two went to the South up the Valley. Br [Joseph] Hancock returned at evening from up the creek and reports abundance of Bear signs & a large quantity of valuable Timber on the mountain & in the valley of the creek, Rock maple, White oak, Fir & Norway Pine suitable for sawing into Lumber.[119] Killed nothing but a Prarie chicken.

Sunday 25th [July 1847] I went & wartered [watered] our Potatoes by conducting it over the ground before breakfast. at 10 oclock [A.]M. attended

---

a mile north of the camp," is "a considerable creek of clear cold water descending from the mountains" which "branches into two forks, one running northwest the other southwest and the two nicely surrounding this place, and so well arranged that should a city be built here the water can be turned into every street at pleasure." The creek (named City Creek on 22 August, according to Wilford Woodruff), was dammed and a "narrow dike" was constructed "so as to throw the water at pleasure on the field . . . in case rain should not come sufficiently." Besides City Creek's water, Clayton noted that the "land is beautifully situated for irrigation, many nice streams descending from the mountains which can be turned in every direction so as to water any portion of the lands at pleasure." On 25 July, Sabbath morning, a number of the pioneers availed themselves of the opportunity of "bathing in the pure, cold water of the stream" that had been dammed. Clayton, *Journal*, 313, 318–319; Woodruff, *Journal*, 3:261; Whitney, Diary, 25 July 1847.

Randy Dixon, expert on the Saints' early settlement of Salt Lake City, details the first settlers' use and manipulation of the creek, as well as its history to the present time, in "Beautiful, Troublesome, City Creek," 24–29.

117. The "potato patch" of five acres was planted with seed potatoes and then watered by an irrigation ditch. "[E]arly corn" was also planted. Bullock, *Camp of the Saints*, 237; Snow, "Journey," (July 1948): 279.

118. Brigham Young and the others who were ill who traveled with him were reported by Orson Pratt to be "improving very fast" upon their arrival, being "able to walk around." (However, Albert Rockwood's entry for 23 and 24 July reads: "my health is so poor that I know but litt[l]e of what pas[s]es.") Pratt, *Journals*, 458; Rockwood, *History*, 68.

Wilford Woodruff, who escorted Young into the valley on 24 July began his diary entry for the day: "This is an important day in the History of my life and the History of the Church of JESUS CHRIST of Latter Day Saints. On this important day after trav[eling] from our encampment 6 miles through the deep ravene, valley, ending with the canion through the last creek we came in full view of the great valley or Bason [of] the Salt Lake and land of promise held in reserve by the hand of God for a resting place for the Saints upon which A portion of the Zion of GOD will be built." Woodruff, *Journal*, 3:234.

119. Two days later, Joseph Hancock with Lewis Barney entered what became City Creek Canyon and, climbing northwest to the top of the ridge, crossed over to the westward slope of the Wasatch Range north of what became Salt Lake City. Descending to the valley floor together on 28 July, they returned to the pioneer camp with the meat of a black-tailed deer and a report of seeing "plenty of Timber, fir, balsam & poplar," but stated that it was "difficult to get at it." Barney, Autobiography and diary, 43–44; Barney, *One Side by Himself*, 104; Bullock, *Camp of the Saints*, 241; Clayton, *Journal*, 325.

meeting.[120] we had a glorious time. all that spoke expressed themselves well pleased with this Land & the prospect before us.[121] afternoon partook of the sacrement. Br [Willard] Richards said that in order to go & proclaim the gospel to the Lamanites it was necessary for the Elders to enjoy the gifts of Speaking in Tounges, Interpretation of Tounges & the diserning of Spirits & how are they to obtain them?[122] by following council. Br Brigham [Young was] able to be out but quite feeble. at the close he said he had a few things to say. those that do not like our look & customs are at liberty to go where they please. but if they remain with us they must obey the Laws sanctioned by us. there must be no work done on the Sabbath[123] & as soon as we Select a place of permanent location we shall take the compass & chain & lay out a city & every man shall have his inheritance therein.[124] we shall also lay out ground for cultivation & every man shall have his inheritance & cultivate it as he pleases, only he must be industreous. we do not intind to buy anny Land or sell anny.[125] a hunter reports plenty of Timber up the Valley.

---

120. Another meeting was held in the afternoon and together they served as the forum for a great deal of public exhortation and preaching during the day by "Each one of the Twelve who were present" who "expressed their feelings and exhorted the brethren to righteousness." Others in the camp spoke as well. Pratt, *Journals*, 458.

121. Wilford Woodruff reported during the meeting that "there was one universal feeling of Satisfaction with the valley" continuing that "Evry man that spoke upon the subject said they were Joyfully disappointed that the whole appearance was Altogether better throughout the valley than they had Anticipated or even dreamed of." Erastus Snow stated that from the "excellent meeting" that "all felt satisfied that the Lord had led us to the very spot for a Stake of Zion [the gathering place for the Saints]." Woodruff, *Journal*, 3:235; Snow, "Journey," (July 1948): 279.

122. A Latter-day Saint "Article of Faith" prepared by Joseph Smith in 1842 affirms belief in "gifts of the spirit" described in the New Testament, such as the "gift of tongues [and] interpretation of tongues."

    Mormons incorporate within their theology provisions for the eventual flowering of Native Americans (Lamanites) and see themselves as instruments in the process. Book of Mormon, 2 Nephi 30:3–6; Doctrine and Covenants 49:24; *Times and Seasons* 3, no. 9 (1 March 1842): 709; "Indian Affairs," *Times and Seasons* 6, no. 4 (1 March 1845): 829–830. Mormon ideology and theology regarding Native Americans can be found in Walker, "Seeking the 'Remnant,'" 1–33.

123. Brigham Young, according to Wilford Woodruff, "Informed the brethren they must not work on Sunday that they would loose [*sic*] five times as much as they would gain by it, & they must not hunt or fish on that day." Woodruff, *Journal*, 3:236.

124. It should not be construed from this statement that Brigham Young considered anywhere but the Salt Lake Valley as the "permanent location" for the Saints. This reference merely refers to which parcel of ground within the valley the Saints would build into a city.

125. Wilford Woodruff's report of Brigham Young's sermon on how the land would be used stated: "He said that no man should buy any land that come Here. That He had no land to sell neither should He buy any but evry man should [have] his land measured of[f] to him for City & farming purposes what He could till. He might till it as he pleased but He should be industrious & take care of it." Woodruff, *Journal*, 3:236.

    Young further "wanted the brethren, in overhauling their wagons, to return everything that did not belong to them to the owner . . . even to the value of 6 1/4 cents,

Monday 26th [July 1847] I was called to go to the mountain for Timber for Ploughs. went with two Teams.[126] one of the men saw a gray Squirrel. the Teams continued Ploughing for corn & Beans.[127] Some of the Twelve, with the President visited the warm Mineral Springs 3 miles North.[128] Some of them bathed in them & think they possess verry valuable Medical qualitys.[129]

---

for if they retained it, it would leak out and be a spot in their character that neither time nor eternity would erase. They could not get rid of it until burned out in hell." Brown, *Autobiography*, 80.

126. Jacob's duty for the day was part of a cooperative plan to take care of their immediate needs and, just as importantly, to prepare for the future and for those to follow. Hundreds were planning on wintering in the valley and they had to be housed and fed. No haphazard operation, as expected, work and exploration efforts were centrally organized, including projects big and small. After rising on 26 July at 4 A.M. at the sound of the bugle, Stephen Markham "read over a list of names of those selected for farming operations," while fifteen others "were also chosen to go & make a road through the Kanyon . . . in order to obtain an easy access to places where there is supposed to be timber for building." Meanwhile "Ten men including the Twelve were appointed to go on an exploring expedition," taking them twenty miles around the northern portion of the valley. And, "Bros. [Robert] Byard [Baird?] & [Thomas] Cloward commenced their respective avocations of tailoring & shoemaking." The pattern of morning orders designating the day's work details continued for days. Whitney, Diary, 26 July 1847; Woodruff, *Journal*, 3:236.

127. Those who were selected for farming for the day were "to collect their horses and cattle to recommence ploughing & planting, & also at an interval of every 4 hours during the day, that the teams might be alternately relieved from labor, & others substituted in their place." Initially the cultivation was carried on somewhat "indiscriminately" but Brigham Young planned that "as soon as convenient, lines would be drawn, & each man allotted a portion of land, for his individual cultivation." Before the day was finished "three acres of potatoes, some peas, beans" and "four or five acres of corn" had been, or were in the processing of being, planted. William Clayton states that another plot of ground, a "garden," was being planted "about two miles to the southeast" and stated that "their operations and industry are truly pleasing and noble." Whitney, Diary, 26 July 1847; Clayton, *Journal*, 323.

128. Delayed a day by illness in embarking on a "northern expedition," and still feeling poorly, Brigham Young and his party on 26 July, besides visiting the mineral springs, also "went North of the Camp about 5 miles." En route they ascended a prominent peak, or knoll as some have suggested, just north of the newly founded settlement. After riding horseback two-thirds of the way to the top, they climbed the remainder of the way to "A high Peak in the edge of the Mountain which we considered A good place to raise An ensign upon which we named ensign Peak or Hill. " (Young claimed to coin the name.) Orson Pratt later calculated the elevation of the peak to be 1081 feet above the valley floor. Woodruff, *Journal*, 3:326; Clayton, *Journal*, 319; Young, *Manuscript History, 1846–1847*, 565; Smith (Carrington), History, 10 August 1847. Ronald W. Walker has characterized the importance of this exercise and the site in "A Banner is Unfurled," 71–91, and "A Gauge of the Times," 4–25.

129. The warm mineral springs, closer to the pioneer camp than the boiling springs farther north, were described by Albert Carrington as appearing "out from a small cave at the base of a spur of trapp rock, water very clear, forms a good sized pool & then runs off with a quick current, 3 ft wide & 1 deep, into a lake of considerable size, fed also by several other smaller hot springs." Others retaining the effects of the "mountain fever" also visited the hot mineral springs and found "the effects wonderfully beneficial." Commemorative markers now describe the site. Lyman (Carrington), Diary, 26 July 1847; Clayton, *Journal*,

John Brown & Joseph Mathews pursued the Emigrant road across the Valley West to the mountains 16 miles.[130] found a gray six year old Horse & brought him into camp & geave him to Br Brigham [Young].[131] they report a beautiful river runing through the Valley to the [Great Salt] Lake with a gentle current, 8 rods wide & 3 feet deep.[132] they crossed it 4 miles from here. after passing two miles the other side, found the country covered with Sage & Grease wood & soil perfectly barren.[133]

Tuesday 27 [July 1847][134] By the Presidents direction I went with two men to explore the mountains in search of Timber.[135] we found, on Red But[t]e creek,

---

318. See William Clayton's and Horace Whitney's more extensive descriptions of the springs and adjacent ponds, Clayton, *Journal*, 321–323; Whitney, Diary, 31 July 1847.

130. This, of course, was the trail taken by the Donner-Reed company the previous year.

131. They assumed the horse strayed from the California-bound emigrants the previous year. Clayton, *Journal*, 323.

132. This is the biblically-named Jordan River, running northward forty miles from fresh-water Utah Lake in Utah Valley to the Great Salt Lake, a parallel to the River Jordan running between the fresh-water Sea of Galilee and the salty Dead Sea in ancient Palestine.

John Brown and Joseph Matthews were not the only ones to explore the Jordan River that day. Farther to the north, William Clayton, George Smith, and Albert Carrington, after descending from Ensign Peak earlier in the day, and after visiting the area of the sulphur springs, bore westward hoping to find fresh water. After a time they "struck the old road made by emigrants" the previous year which they followed "about two miles" until they arrived at the Jordan. Approaching the "Emigrant Ford" of the river, which they noted had a "bed good for fording," the three observed "about two miles of fine rich land, well watered and covered with a luxuriant growth of fine grasses, meshes and prairie cane." Bounded by banks containing "muscle shells" about "five feet high" which were bereft of timber and with but few "willow bushes," they found the river to be "about 6 rods wide" with an "average depth [of] three feet." The slow-moving, but strong, current they said was "a dark lead color." Others apparently also visited the Jordan that day. Clayton, *Journal*, 321; Smith (Carrington), History, 26 July 1847.

133. Besides the information supplied by Jacob, Horace Whitney reported that Joseph Matthews and John Brown informed him upon their return that while the land beyond the river toward the mountain boundary to the west "is not quite so good," "the soil near the river, "if possible, is richer & more fertile than" where they were camped. Whitney, Diary, 26 July 1847.

134. In the morning Amasa Lyman, Samuel Brannan, Rodney Badger, and Roswell Stevens, according to William Clayton, arrived in camp stating that the Mormon Battalion members and Mississippi Saints who wintered in Pueblo, Colorado, were in Echo Canyon and would soon join the pioneer camp. (They arrived on Thursday, 29 July 1847.) They also reported that they had "heard of a large company" following them and expected their arrival in two or three weeks. This, of course, was the second company that year of Mormons to depart from Winter Quarters. (The first of this second wave of Mormon emigrants entered the Salt Lake Valley on 19 September 1847, though two of their expressmen arrived in the valley on 15 September carrying information to the valley's leaders.) Having been in the valley for most of the week, Clayton reported the "horses and cattle" to be "in good spirits and are getting fat," and that they were "full of life and ambition." Clayton, *Journal*, 324.

135. Jacob's charge, illustrating the pioneers' concern about the lack of timber, was, again, just one of many activities occupying the labor of the Saints. Cultivating and planting also

directly East of the camp 7 miles,[136] a fine g[r]ove of Spruce, Pine, also Rock maple & White oak, the fire having run throug[h] the whole of it last year. ther would be abundance of Timber in this country were it not for the fires. I also found some good grit for grind stones & a large quantity of sileceous Sand Stone ready quarryed for Building. we saw an Elk & abundance of Bear & Deer signs. The Twelve went with a company over to the West to explore the head of the [Great Salt] Lake.[137]

Wednesday 28 [July 1847] I went again searching for Timber up the creek where we are enca[m]ped. we found it runing in a Kanyon. some Timber on it, but impractible to get a road to it. we then turned & went over the mountain to the North.[138] visited the warm Springs which are numerous & are 3 miles from camp,[139] also a Boiling Spring 6 miles [away].[140] all this water is s[t]rongly empregnated with Salt, Sulphur & some other minerals. Some of the Utah Indians visited our camp yesterday & today & traded some Horses for guns, also skins for Powder, Lead &c.[141] they are small in stature

---

continued, probably accelerating in scope. Egan, *Pioneering*, 109–110.

136. Red Butte Creek and Canyon are now the eastern perimeter of the University of Utah campus in Salt Lake City.

137. Sixteen church leaders, all on horseback but Brigham Young and Wilford Woodruff who rode in Woodruff's carriage, composed this company of explorers. During the day, they traveled "over the plain about 16 miles from camp" before passing "on south-west for about six miles, between high cliffs and the lake." En route they found several springs, though they were somewhat brackish. As they bore westward they also came to "a point where [the] Emigrant road comes into [Lansford] Hastings' new route, both of which were traveled for the first time with wagons last year," a reference, of course, to the Donner-Reed party traversing northern Utah in 1846. Smith (Carrington), History, 27 July 1847.

The legendary Great Salt Lake, about which the Saints had heard and read so much, was the remnant of ancient Lake Bonneville, an inland sea of some 20,000 square miles existing about 10–30,000 years ago. The Great Salt Lake, still the largest body of water west of the Mississippi River, is about seventy-five miles long and thirty-five miles wide. An overview of the history of the lake and modern man's encounter with it is found in Morgan, *The Great Salt Lake*.

138. Apparently Jacob repeated the course north up City Creek Canyon, though it appears that he did not replicate the exploration over the mountain taken just days before by Joseph Hancock and Lewis Barney, who returned to camp that day, 28 July.

139. By 2 August, Thomas Bullock had applied his resources to harness what he called "Bullock's warm bathing Spring." He and two others excavated some of the ponds to facilitate better bathing. Bullock, *Camp of the Saints*, 247.

140. The spring of extremely hot mineral water, inhospitable at the time for human bathing, should not be confused with the warm springs more amenable to human use. The warm springs, more salubrious and inviting than the scalding springs, were captured the following year for a bathhouse. Whitney, *History of Utah*, 1:385.

141. Howard Egan reported about a half dozen Utes visited camp, though Wilford Woodruff recorded that on 28 July, he, returning from the west, three miles from camp, "discovered about 20 objects . . . [and] soon saw that they were Indians." While he tried to avoid them, "one mounted his horse & came after me with all speed." Woodruff found that he wanted

& appear to be a Shrewd, harmless People, verry familiar in their manners but not Beggars like the Iindians East of the mountains.[142] they slept in our camp & molested nothing.[143] The Twelve returned today from their excursion to the West.[144] went thirty miles along the South coast. saw much salt & other curiosities. bathed in the Lake & found the water so strong as to float a man on its surface.[145] it [is] warm, being no doubt kept in that state [by] the

---

to trade and "informed him by signs that our Camp was near so he went on with me to camp." Egan, *Pioneering*, 109; Woodruff, *Journal*, 3:238.

Ronald Walker, in a forthcoming book on Utah's Native American peoples, argues that the indigenous Indians of the region had heard of the Mormons' transit to the Great Basin and several score of them may have witnessed the Saints' arrival. Walker indicates that overall the white newcomers were well received and that several Indians soon submitted to Mormon baptism. I thank him for access to his manuscript.

142. This band of Utes were likely the Tumpanawach, though they were also known as Lagunas (fish-eaters), Timpanogos, or Northern Utes among whites who had visited the area. Centered by Utah Lake in Utah Valley, the next valley to the south of Salt Lake Valley, they dominated the region in size and strength. Conetah, *Northern Ute People*, 25.

143. Communicating with the whites "by signs," the Northern Utes, as they came to camp, conveyed "that there was a large party of them about forty miles" from the pioneer camp. Wilford Woodruff concurred with Jacob's assessment of the Natives. He said that while the "mountaineers" had given them a bad name, the pioneers found the Utes to be "friendly & not disposed to steal from [others]." Egan, *Pioneering*, 109; Woodruff, *Journal*, 3:238.

William Clayton mentioned a negative aspect of the Indians' visit to camp. While two of the men traded guns for horses, about which Clayton did not complain, he was troubled that, apparently to appease the Indians, several white men gave "twenty charges of powder and balls for a buck skin, while the usual price is three charges." If Clayton reflected the sentiments of others, like Heber Kimball (who made his views known on 1 August), it was thought to be foolish to supply the Native Americans with weapons and ammunition which could be used against the Saints and their animals. Clayton, *Journal*, 324, 335; Egan, *Pioneering*, 109.

144. While most of the Twelve explored the environs of the southern shore of the Great Salt Lake that day, their colleague Orson Pratt, with others, "journeyed [south] for about 10 miles along the eastern base of the range of mountains" but "found no water." Pratt then "went upon a rise of ground about 3 miles south of where our company stopped, " where, he said, "I could see Utah Lake, which appeared to be nearly 20 miles distant to the south." Pratt, *Journals*, 459.

145. Near the lake's southern beach they found a "perpendicular rock about 40 rods" from shore which they called Black Rock. (They also explored the nearby Black Rock Cave.) All of the company swam in the Great Salt Lake "which they found so very Salt[y], that no man could sink in it, & so warm that no one had a desire to retreat from it," and that "a man could sit in it as in a Rocking Chair." One of them noted the water to be "extremely limped and warm, perfectly saturated with salt and holding much in fine particles in suspension from the motion of the water." Yet another wrote that after floating "upon the surface" of the lake "like a cork," while dressing they found their "hair and skin perfectly coated with fine salt." One who "found the most beautiful white Salt that I ever saw lying in bunches," also thought the properties of the lake so amazing that he thought it "ought to be added as the eighth wonder of the world." After their frolic in the lake they "Passed on [the] same course about 3 miles to the mouth of a small valley [Tooele] apparently dry" and noted the western side of the Oquirrh range. Returning to the eastern side of the

multitude of warm & hot Springs that flow into it ~~which~~ making the wind that reaches us from the North West warm, which, together with the Saline particles that float in the atmosphere will make the climate mild & salubrious in the Winter & prevent much Snow falling in the Valley but rather rain. this [is] the testimony of the Traders.[146] Br [Heber] Kimbal & those that have been on the sea coast say that the smell & appearance of the air here is presisely the same as in the neighborhood of the ocean!! certainly I never was in anny place where the heat of midsummer was so tempered as it is here by the Salt. every one that came here sick are rapidly becomeing strong & healthy. manny have expereienced great benefit from bathing in the warm mineral Springs.[147] it appears the <Indians> have used them for the same purpose. two of our Hunters brought in a Deer.[148]

At 8 oclock P.M. the President [Brigham Young] sumoned all the camp to attend a council on the Spot intended for a Temple Lot in the Forks where this creek of pure cold Spring water spreads into several branches over this delightful plain & is capable of watering a city of one hundred thousand inhabitants.[149] It was a beautiful & instructing Scene. the soft mild air that always prevails here at night so that the men sit down comfortably in their

---

valley, they camped that night at one of the springs they found earlier in the day. Bullock, *Camp of the Saints*, 239; Snow, "Journey," (July 1948): 279; Woodruff, *Journal*, 3:237–238; Smith (Carrington), History, 27 July 1847.

146. This, of course, refers to the mountaineers whom they debriefed while crossing Wyoming.

147. It is fair to say that this idealistic characterization of and prognostication for the area's salubrious benefits proved to be wishful thinking, though the climate of the Wasatch Front has been noted by many since that time as being conducive to healthy living.

148. This likely referred to Joseph Hancock's and Lewis Barney's hunting and exploring venture, mentioned earlier. (William Clayton and Thomas Bullock both noted Hancock's and Barney's return to camp.) The scarcity of food in camp and how this particular venison was distributed is illustrated by Barney's description of their return to camp. They were met by Lorenzo Young upon their return, who said,

> "Well Boys, you have got back." I said, "yes, we have got Back and we have a little meat too." He Then [said], "Brother Barney, won't you let me have a piece of your venison?" I Said, "Brother Lorenzo, We have had a hard time to get this venison, Climbing mountains and Starving for over two days and nights. however, I will exchange a little of it for Bread." he then went to his wagon and brought a nice large loaf of Light Bread and handed it to me. I then Cut him of[f] a nice piece of venison an[d] gave [it to] him. We were both well pleased with our Bargain." Barney, Autobiography and diary, 44–45.

149. The previous day, Howard Egan received orders from Heber Kimball that Brigham Young wanted his wagons moved from the main camp (between what is now Third and Fourth South on State Street) northwest a few blocks to the northern fork of what became known as City Creek. Kimball wanted his wagons moved likewise. Egan found in making the move that others, Ezra Benson and Willard Richards included, had also moved there as well, which, he said, made "quite a number." Horace Whitney noted Young and the others who located "across the creek" did so to be "near the site of ground, where it is supposed the future city will be built." He also stated that the tent they had erected was also placed near the creek. Egan, *Pioneering*, 109; Whitney, Diary, 27 July 1847.

Shirt Sleeves. the full moon Shone over the Eastern mountain shedding her mild radiance on the quiet Valley of the Utah outlet, while we were seated on the <ground> engaged in council upon matters of vast importance. Cheerfulness & general hilarity prevailed in our little company, those that had been out exploring relating their adventures & the result of their observations. at length the President <said> that there wa[s] one question <he> wanted brought under the consideration of the council: Shall we look further or make a location upon this spot & lay out & build a city? we were the Pioneers of the Church & our business was to seek for a suitable location for the Church. the question is, shall this be the spot or shall we look further? I want all to freely express their minds & feelings. ~~I remarked~~ A motion was made to locate here. I seconded it & remarked that if we went up south to the utah Lake the country was ocupied by the Indians, while here it was unoccupied.[150] Br [Erastus] Snow said <he would> speak a few words & perhaps he might express the feelings of others. there was two reasons why he was in favor of this place. all that have been out exploring universaly returned satisfied with this place & the other is, the Lord has led us directly to it. he <was> well satisfied with it & he believe[d] all the Brethre[n] were generaly of the same feelings. the President said if this was their feelings he wanted them to manifest it by saing aye, when it was unanimously decided in the affirmative.[151] [He] then remarked the feelings of the Twelve was the same & he knew that as [a] general thing the minds of the Brethren were like this: if the[y] should say, by revelation, this is the spot they would be entirely satisfied if it wa[s] on a barren rock. well, I know it is the spot & we have com here according to the sugestion & direction of Joseph Smith who was martyred.[152] the word of the Lord was go to that Walley [valley] & the best place you can find in it is the Spot. well, I prayed that he would lead us directly to the best spot which he has done, for

150. As the newcomers found on 31 July, the Northwestern Shoshones claimed the region north of what became Salt Lake City and held that the Northern Utes' land was to the south. Ronald Walker notes in his forthcoming book on Utah's Indians that bands circulating in and near the Salt Lake Valley were allied with and intermixed with several of the tribes in the Ute and Shoshone homeland. Clayton, *Journal*, 329; Madsen, *Shoshoni Frontier*, 6.

151. While others, such as William Clayton, Thomas Bullock, Howard Egan, and Levi Jackman noted some of Brigham Young's comments on this occasion, Jacob's and Wilford Woodruff's accounts of Young's speech are the most extensive that are extant.

152. Of Joseph Smith, John Brown noted that part of Brigham Young's preachment that day included a statement about their past persecutions and that "Missouri might have been saved if [Lilburn] Boggs, [Thomas Hart] Benton and the rest of the leading men, after they had committed their crimes, had come to Joseph and said, 'We have shed innocent blood, wronged the Saints. Now here, take the sword and cut our heads off that our blood may run upon the earth that the smoke thereof may ascend to the throne of Jehovah for a witness and atonement of the crimes committed, that our spirits may be saved in the day of the Lord Jesus.'" But, Young said, "Now it is too late. Joseph is dead." Brown, *Autobiography*, 80.

after searching we can find no better.[153] Br W[illia]m Vance said his <feelings> had been different from his Brethren, but he supposed he was wrong. he felt as though we should go farther, perhaps on the other side of the Lake. the President replyed that Br Wm had a perfect right to his views, but if we were on the other side of the Lak we should not have the benefit of the warm North & West winds from the Lake. I knew this spot as soon as I saw it.[154] up there on that Table ground we shall erect the Standard of Freedom. [obscure word crossed out] ~~but I wanted you~~ The President then said, we [obscure word crossed out] shall have a committy to lay out the city & who shold it be, when it was unameously resolved that the "Twelve" be that commity & also to aportion the inheritances. says the President, we propose <to> have the Temple Lot contain 40 acres to include the ground we are now on.[155] what do you say to that? all right. that the Streets will be 88 feet wide, side walks 20 feet,[156] the Lots to contain 1 1/4 acre, 8 Lots in a Block, the houses invaribley set in the center of the Lot, 20 feet back from the Street,[157] with no shops or

---

153. Brigham Young's own account, later compiled by his clerks, states that "Some of the brethren talked about exploring the country further for a site for a settlement; I replied that I was willing that the country should be explored until all were satisfied, but every time a party went out and returned I believed firmly they would agree that this is the spot for us to locate." Young, *Manuscript History, 1846–1847*, 566–567. See Hartley, "Gathering the Dispersed Nauvoo Saints," 22, for an overview of Young's perceptions concerning the Salt Lake Valley site upon his arrival.

One of the effects of Young's reconnaissance south of the Great Salt Lake was after finding "no fresh water beyond the [Jordan] river . . . the brethren are more and more satisfied that we are already on the right spot." This lent to church leaders' earlier determination to locate in the general area of the Salt Lake Valley. Clayton, *Journal*, 325.

154. Levi Jackman confirmed Jacob's account of Brigham Young's declaration: "Pres Young said the [that] he knew that this is the place. he knew it as soon as he come in right [sight] of it and he hav [has] seen this verrey spot before." Jackman, Diary, 28 July 1847.

155. Brigham Young's clerks later quote him as stating that "I designated the site for the Temple block between the forks of City Creek, and on motion of Orson Pratt it was unanimously voted that the Temple be built on the site designated." Young, *Manuscript History, 1846–1847*, 567.

The forty acre temple site was later pared to the ten acres located between what is now North and South Temple streets and West Temple and State streets in Salt Lake City. Discussion between church leaders about reducing the size of the plot began as early as 2 August 1847 when it was proposed to half the forty acres. But objections were raised believing that "if we done it we should be sorry afterwards." Young closed that particular discussion stating "we Could eisier diminish than enlarge it afterward & finally decided to let it remain as it was." But on 4 August church leaders decided they "Could not do justice to 40 acres to begin with & finally concluded to confine the Temple & gard[en] to 10 acres." The discussion of the size of the temple site was likely forced because Orson Pratt and Henry Sherwood initiated a city survey on 2 August. Woodruff, *Journal*, 3:247–248; Bullock, *Camp of the Saints*, 247.

156. Later writers described the width of city streets to be 132 feet wide, failing to note that twenty foot sidewalks on each side of the street were added to the eighty-eight-foot wide streets Jacob describes.

157. Wilford Woodruff stated that one of the reasons for Brigham Young's proposed configuration was to insure that he "wished but one house built upon A lot & they being

other buildings on the corners of the Streets, neither will they be filled with cattle, Horses & hogs, nor children for they will hav yards & places appropriated for recreation & we will have a city clean and in order. no one will be allowed to divide his Lot or sell off a corner but when improved it may be right for him to sell the whole Lot or his inheritance in the country & gó to some other place, for many other places will be built up.[158] a man may live here with us & worship what God he pleases or none at all, but he must not blaspheme the God of Israel nor dam old Joe Smith <or his religion> for we will Salt him down in the Lake![159] We do not intend to have anny trade or commerce with the Gentile world, for so long as we buy of them we are in <a> degree dependant upon them. the Kingdom of God <cannot> rise independant of the Gentile nations until we produce, Manufacture & make every article of use, convenience, or necesity among our own People. we shall have Elders ab<r>oad among all nations & until we can obtain & collect the raw material for our Manufactures it will be their business to gather in such things as are <or> may be needed. So we shall need no commerc with the nations. I <am> determined to cut every thread of this Kind & live free & independant, untrameled by any of their detestable customs & practices. you dont know how I detest & despise them. we have suffered by persecution at their hands which makes me so sanguine with regard to Law & its execution upon this Land. you may think it oppression that your children are not permitted <to> run & ramble about the Streets. well, I have a Sermon to Preach to the Sisters concerning *their* duty & I believe I will give some of <it> to you now. let us have it, says Several voices. I will begin by saying that there's not a woman in this Church that Knows her duty. my <Wife> propably Knows as much as any woman in the church & she does not Know her duty!![160] Not many of the Elders Know their duty! every moment of my life I seek of my Heavnly Father to Know his will concerning me & what he requ[i]res me to do, & I am ready to [do] it & inasmuch <as> I e[n]quire, Lord what is thy will? my wife Should enquire, Husband what is thy will? Wife, it is my will that you take care of my clothes & keep them & your house clean. it is my will that you take care of that little Boy. see that he has a lesson given every day to learn & that he does not run about the Streets or associate with bad Boys. it <is> my will that you

---

in the centre if they took fire they would not burn up their neighbors." Woodruff, *Journal*, 3:239.

158. A description of early initiatives in the establishment of the Saints' headquarters in what became Salt Lake City are found in Arrington, *Great Basin Kingdom*, 45–63.

159. Brigham Young's response to the presence of non-Latter-day Saints in Utah Territory was mixed. He could be notably tolerant but within a context where the Saints lost their autonomy or were unduly influenced by non-Mormons, his rhetoric and behavior toward the latter were polemic and rigid.

160. It is not certain which of Brigham Young's wives this statement concerns. While Young's primary wife was his second wife, Mary Ann Angell, whom he married in 1834 after his first wife Miriam Works died, Clara Decker, whom he took as a plural wife in 1844, was the companion who accompanied him in the pioneer vanguard.

see to that little Girl & teach & instruct her in <her> duty! But instead <of> that she has so much to do to watch me that she can find no time <to> atend to these things as they should ~~be~~ be attended to. but if I am gone out & return is O Husband, I am so glad to see you. I was afraid something would happen to you. Wife, where is the Boys? O, I dont K[n]ow, I was so concerned about you. I guess they are over to neighbor such a one's. how have you been? I was <so> faaid [afraid] something would happen to you. Just as though Brigham did not Know enough to take care of hymself. so my Boys are allowed to run wild into all Kinds of difficulty before they are old enough for me to lay my hands upon them & assign them their business & caling or put them to learn a trade under a good master. All this arises from the Husbands not seeking to K[n]ow & do the will of ~~Lord~~ the Lord & from the <Wife> not seeking to Know & do the will of her Husband. How is it that men have such perverse disp<o>sitions? all Spirits are Pure whe[n] they enter the Tabernacle which is when, in a state of pregnancy, the woman first feels motion. then the Spirit is pure but it becomes united with flesh & is controled by it.[161] the woman then should never be crossed in anything, but treated as gentlle as an infant, her mind guided <& ruled> by the principles of righteousness & kept continualy upon Holy things. but, let her give way to temptation, Steal, get drunk, or any other evil, & her ofspring will partake of the same qualitys. whereas, if she will continualy resist all temptation she will be blessed herself & the <body of> her child will be larger, more strong & robust, <the Spirit mild & tractable> & [in] this way our race will become improved until the age of man Shall be as the age of a Tree.[162] at a late hour the meeting broke up.

Thursday 29th [July 1847] I was engaged in making [a] garden & in wartering our corn ground.[163] afternoon we had a fine shower. we have had several light showers since we came here, but the most of the rain falls on the mountains.[164]

---

161. John Brown's capture of Brigham Young's statement reads: "A woman, when pregnant, should receive proper care and consideration, as the embryo, previous to the spirit's entering, partakes of the mind and nature of the mother, and the spirit which is always pure and holy when entering the infant tabernacle, which takes place at the time life is first felt, partakes of the nature of the tabernacle." Brown, *Autobiography*, 80. Young's utterance, apparently noting the time when the fetus becomes a separate entity from its mother, was apparently not widely discussed in Mormon circles in the nineteenth century.
162. Brigham Young's sentiment regarding gender roles, as reported by Jacob, reflected a view that Young continued to hold later in his life. For example, an 8 April 1852 sermon by Young to the Saints in Great Salt Lake City reiterated the same particulars expressed in his 28 July 1847 speech. *Journal of Discourses*, 1:66–67. See also Young's sermon given 21 September 1856 wherein he discusses the relationship between men and women. *Journal of Discourses*, 4:55–57.
163. The "garden spot about three miles southeast of the camp," also received the attention of the pioneers. Egan, *Pioneering*, 111.
164. Wilford Woodruff wrote that while in Emigration Canyon, a "Heavy shower of rain . . . which sent down the water in the Creeks from the mountains with a rush & roar like

That portion of the Battalion under the command of Captain [James] Brown, comprising one third of the whole Battalion arrived this afternoon in good condition & were marched in Military Stile to their Quarters.[165] the Missisippi company are also with them. The "Twelve" & some others went up to the mountain & escorted them in.[166]

Friday 30th [July 1847] First Buckwheat sowed yesterday & today we were irrigating it.[167] In the evening a meeting was called at the Presidents Quarters 1/2 past 7 when he adressed the soldiers. after the whole congregation had engaged in Praiseing the Lord with three times three Hosannahs, meeting continued till nine oclock.[168] The President [Brigham Young] told the Soldie[r]s they would be quarterd here until their capt. [James Brown] could go over to the Bay & obtain their discharge.[169] in the mean time they could be engaged in getting their families from Winter Quarters, Building their houses, & making their farms while [the] Goverment will be obliged to you for your time until you are discharged, & if they will pay it, we will go and take it with good interest.[170]

---

thunder resembling the opening of a flood gate." The "first rush of the water came down with a front of 3 feet High." Woodruff, *Journal*, 3:242.

165. The Mormon Battalion veterans numbered about "140" with "about 100 of the Missippi saints," according to Wilford Woodruff. With them they brought "about 60 waggons [and] 100 Horses & Mules & 300 Head of cattle." (William Clayton said the group brought "twenty nine wagons . . . and one carriage," while Horace Whitney reported the vehicles numbered "14 Government wagons, & about 20 wagons belonging to the Mississippi company.") Their arrival came formalized with the "Council & Officers first, Infantry next with martial music [the "soul-stirring tones of the fife & drum"], then followed the Cavalry with the Baggage Wagons bringing up the rear." They "camped between the two creeks at 3 P.M.," a "little west" of the "lower camp." Woodruff, *Journal*, 3:242; Clayton, *Journal*, 326–327; Whitney, Diary, 29 July 1847; Bullock, *Camp of the Saints*, 245.

166. Upon their meeting, the "brethren were very much rejoiced at getting once more among their friends & a general congratulation took place." After the Battalion and the Mississippi Saints settled in, the Twelve "went over north to the mountains" to council about what lay ahead of them. Bullock, *Camp of the Saints*, 245; Clayton, *Journal*, 327.

    Albert Carrington, one of the welcomers, wrote that incident to their reunion, "Some of the boys hauled up a fine stick of balsam fir, 24 feet long and two feet at the butt for making a boat." Smith (Carrington), History, 29 July 1847.

167. Along with their return to horticulture, one group of men "erected a saw pit for the purpose of sawing lumber, with which to build a boat," the log for which was noted previously. Whitney, Diary, 30 July 1847.

168. Brigham Young pointedly told the Battalion veterans that their enlistment "proved our temporal salvation" by negating the schemes of government officials who "intended to distroy us from off the face of the earth." Woodruff, *Journal*, 3:244.

169. The main body of the Mormon Battalion which marched into California, was mustered out at Los Angeles on 16 July 1847. Samuel Brannan was designated to pilot Captain James Brown and those to accompany him to San Francisco where they were to make their report. Woodruff, *Journal*, 3:243.

170. Brigham Young closed the meeting, according to William Clayton, by "requesting the battalion to build a bower tomorrow on the temple lot where we can assemble for

Satturday 31st [July 1847] I was engaged in Harrowing.[171] another Shower.[172] Some of the [Northwestern] Shoshone Indians came here to trade. they got into a quarrel with a [Northern] Utah about a gun. one of them broke the gun over his head, when his Father i[n]terfered & gave them both a whipping & cut the young man's Bow String so he should do no mischief. Some time after, he found an opportunity to drive off one of their Horses. after he had got three or four miles the start, six of the Shoshones started across the Plain in pursuit mounted on their best Horses. in a couple of hours they returned & showed by signs that they had Killed him & his Horse. they brought back another Horse.[173] This evening arrangements were made to place the Soldiers under the direction of the President & that the might come into the general organization of the Pioneer Camp.

---

meetings, etc.," which they completed the following day. It measured 40 by 28 feet, the "good shade" being provided by "brush." Clayton, *Journal*, 327; Whitney, Diary, 31 July 1847; Bullock, *Camp of the Saints*, 245; Smith (Carrington), History, 31 July 1847.

171. Albert Carrington noted at the time that "Between sixty and seventy acres of ground are ploughed." Smith (Carrington), History, 31 July 1847.

172. Horace Whitney noted it rained "quite hard for 3/4 of an hour, accompanied by a strong breeze from the west, & a slight fall of hail, about the size of a kernal of corn, when it suddenly ceased." Whitney, Diary, 31 July 1847.

173. William Clayton's lengthy account of this encounter and his characterization of the Northern Utes and Northwestern Shoshones (distinct from their Eastern Shoshone cousins who the Saints encountered on their return to Winter Quarters) is an important perspective that merits rehearsal.

> There are from twenty to thirty of the Utah Indians here and some squaws trading with the brethren. They are generally of low stature, pleasing countenance but poorly clad. While we were there, a dispute arose between two of the young men and they went to fighting very fiercely. One broke his gun stock on the other's head and I expected to see a pretty serious affray, many of the others gathering around. Soon an old man came up, father to one of the young men engaged in the quarrel and he used his heavy whip very freely about both their heads and faces. The antagonist of the son struck the old man and he immediately gathered a long pole and broke it over the young man's head. He succeeded in quelling the broil and gave them a long lecture. They then mostly left and resumed their trading a little distance from the camp. . . . In the evening I walked down to the Pueblo camp and there learned the following particulars:
>
> These Indians who are now here are of the Shoshones, about fifteen or twenty in number, and several woman among them. There were four or five of the Utahs here this morning when the Shoshones came up. One of the Utahs had stolen a horse from one of the Shoshones and the latter party saw him with the horse here. He had traded the horse for a rifle but was unwilling either to give up the horse or rifle hence the quarrel spoken of above. When the old man separated them, the thief went down and hid himself in the camp below. Soon after, he saw another horse walking by, which he knew to belong to the Shoshones. He sprang on his own horse and drove the other one before him towards the mountains on the southeast as hard as he could ride. The Shoshones being informed of it, four of them started in pursuit and as he got in between the mountains they closed in on him, one of the pursuers shooting him dead while another one shot his horse. They returned and made this report to the others of the tribe at the camp at the same time exhibiting fresh blood

on one of the rifles. They appear to be much excited and continually on the watch. When the men returned, they sat down and made a meal of some of these large crickets. They appear to be crisped over the fire which is all the cooking required. Many of the brethren have traded muskets and rifles for horses and ordinary muskets will buy a pretty good horse. They appear to be displeased because we have traded with the Utahs and say they own this land, that that [*sic*] the Utahs have come over the line, etc. They signified by signs that they wanted to sell us the land for powder and lead. The Shoshones are poorer clad than the Utahs. They are about the same in stature and there are many pleasing countenances among them. Clayton, *Journal*, 327–329.

The dead bodies of two Indians, thought to be the victims in this fight, were found "about 10 miles" from the main pioneer camp by an exploring party to Utah Valley on 5 August. Clayton said the discovery proved "that there was one of each tribe killed" in the fray. They also came upon "the dead body of a horse, with its throat cut, some 6 miles from here" which they also thought to be involved in the inter-tribal confrontation. Whitney, 5 August 1847; Clayton, *Journal*, 341.

August 1847

WITH THE VANGUARD AND MISSISSIPPI SAINTS joined in the valley by the Mormon Battalion's sick detachment, the foundations of Great Salt Lake City, including a fort, were established in late July and early August 1847. (Before the month was over, they were joined by nine other companies of Mormon pioneers, numbering over 1,500 new settlers.) The 111 day journey to the Salt Lake Valley was only the first half of the season's travel for many of the vanguard. Joined by a number of their Battalion veteran comrades, four sections of the Saints organized for a return to Winter Quarters on the Missouri River. A four man express, dispatched to inform the Saints who followed the vanguard, left the valley on 2 August. They were followed on 11 August by an eleven-man detail of hunters, led by Norton Jacob, whose purpose it was to secure food for those who followed. On 16 August a company of seventy men driving ox teams followed. Brigham Young led the fourth sector returning eastward that year, numbering 107 men, leaving 25 August. The return to Winter Quarters that late summer and fall was expected to run as smoothly as the westward journey. It did not.

Sunday August first [1847] I did not got [go to] meeting this forenoon but was engaged <in> writing.[1] Afternoon we partook of the Sacrement when Br Amasa Lyman Preached upon the [subject] of humbling ourselves before the Lord upon this choice Land which he has held in reserve for the righteous. but before this Doct. [Willard] Richards read the revelation given at Winter Quarters Jan. 14, 1847.[2] Br Brigham [Young] being i[n]disposed again, Br

1. The meeting missed by Jacob, held in the new bowery on the temple lot, was filled with the leaders' sermons which included Orson Pratt's appraisal of the valley in light of biblical prophecy, stating that their arrival there was according to the designs of God as it fulfilled the Old Testament prophets' projections for the future of God's people. Heber Kimball spoke about the caution required by the Saints in their relations with the Native Americans. Clayton, *Journal*, 330–336; Woodruff, *Journal*, 3:245–246.
2. Clerk-of-the-camp Thomas Bullock penned numerous copies of Brigham Young's revelatory direction for the pioneer vanguard's leadership. A number of the copies, including what may have been the original document dictated by Young, are preserved in

Heber [Kimball] acted as President & enquired how the congregation liked the revelation, when it <was> received by acclamation by the Soldiers for they <were> hungry for the word of the Lord.[3] Arrangements were then made to burn lime & Brick, make adobies, & build a Stoc[k]ade of adobie Houses.[4]

Monday <2d> [August 1847] Br [Ezra] Benson Started back to meet the Big Camp, accompanyed by Porter Rockwell & three of the Soldiers.[5] we moved

---

the LDS Church Archives. The revelation was added in 1876 to the Mormon canon as Section 136 in the Doctrine and Covenants.

3. Mormon Battalion veterans had never heard of nor voted to sustain Brigham Young's revelation having been in southern California at the time of its reception.

4. A discussion ensued in the meeting concerning the materials with which they would build their dwellings in the valley. With timber being scarce, "The idea was suggested, & finally adopted, that we employ the spanish mode of building houses with '*adobies*'—clay or dirt moulded & dried in the sun." Erastus Snow explained the manufacture of adobe bricks: "To those unacquainted with this kind of buildings I will say that they are very common in New Mexico and other sparsely timbered countries. Dobies are brick made of gravelly soil and dried hard in the sun instead of being burned with fuel. Ours were moulded 18 by 9 inches in length and breadth, and four and one-half thick. The soil upon the ground of the Fort [the stockade] being well adapted for the dobies, it was plowed and water brought from the creek on to it, and mortar made with oxen." However, by 5 August conditions changed and consideration was made to "go into the mountain & draw out logs & build us some Cabins as the doby [adobe] houses might not be ready," though "1600 Adobies" had been formed that day. On 10 August, the day when about "4000 Dobies" were made, a council of leaders determined "to enclose one Block of 10 acres with dobys & log buildings as a fort or fortification." Whitney, Diary, 1 August 1847; Clayton, *Journal*, 337–338, 345; Lyman (Carrington), Diary, 1 August 1847; Snow, "Journey," (July 1948): 281; Woodruff, *Journal*, 3:248, 255; Bullock, *Camp of the Saints*, 249, 255. Snow added that "The planting of our seeds being pretty much over, with the exception of a few turnips, it was unanimously resolved in order to prepare winter quarters for those that are to tarry, and the balance of our brethren who are expected here, to go jointly to enclosing one of the public squares of the City, containing 10 acres or 40 rods square, by a wall of log and dobie houses, to be joined together with the exception of a gate on each of the four sides; buildings to be fourteen feet wide 9 feet high on the outside, roofs to slant a little inwards." Snow, "Journey," (July 1948): 280–281.

5. The express headed by Ezra Benson (which included Porter Rockwell and John Binley) was the first of four segments of returnees to Winter Quarters that year. (There were apparently some Battalion members, according to William Clayton, who were "getting dissatisfied at being kept here so long from their families and . . . several of them left the camp secretly to go to Winter Quarters." Clayton, *Journal*, 345.) The express was to be followed by a detail of hunters who were to supply a group of ox teams who were, in turn, to be followed by horse teams, the largest group led by Brigham Young, with designs for them all to get to Winter Quarters before bad weather hit the region. Ostensibly, the dual purpose of the express was to educate the "Big Camp," the second wave of westbound Mormon emigrants that year numbering over 1,500 persons, about particulars regarding the trail that lay ahead of them and to inform them that a location for settlement had been identified by the vanguard. (The express also carried mail from the valley for the pioneers' and soldiers' families at Winter Quarters.) The most complete overview of the four-part return of the Saints to Winter Quarters is found in Barney, *One Side by Himself*, 106–116. Benson's primary communication was directed to Charles C. Rich's company which followed the vanguard. Rich was told by Brigham Young that "about 450 souls" then

all together today & formed one encampment.[6] last Satturday we had broke 55 acres of Land & got 2/3 of it into crops.[7]

Tuesday 3d [August 1847][8] I made hoe handles [this] forenoon. afternoon sowowed [sowed] two acres of Buck Wheat for mine, the twelf[th] Ten.[9] engaged three yoke of cattle of Selden [Serbert] Shelton to go back to Winter Quarters which I am to deliver to Charles C Rich if I do not need them myself to move out here next Summer.[10] I engaged John Wristan to take my Horses, Harness, Plough, & Seeds & put ~~the~~ in a crop next Spring.

---

inhabited the valley, that they knew "of no one but who is pleased with our situation," and that they had commenced to build a city. Young inquired if any of his "camp is sick," if "your teams are worn out," or "if you are short of teamsters or any other circumstance impeding your progress." Young pledged that if they needed help, "we have help for you." Once Young's company was in the valley, their sights were focused on preparing for those to follow. Clayton, *Journal*, 338–339.

6. The "2 camps below commenced to move [to the encampment near the site designated for the temple] that we may all form our wagons into a circle." Also, "Those not engaged in moving [to the temple site] are occupied in ploughing, planting, sawing lumber for a boat, making coal pits, &c. &c." Another part of the preparations of the day included Orson Pratt's and Henry Sherwood's initiation of the city survey, a significant endeavor. Whitney, Diary, 2 August 1847; Bullock, *Camp of the Saints*, 247.

7. A report by Stephen Markham of the status of agricultural progress by the Saints on Saturday, 31 July, included the information "that there are three lots of land already broke. One lot of thirty-five acres of which two-thirds is already planted with buckwheat, corn, oats, etc. One lot of eight acres which is planted with corn, potatoes, beans, etc. And a garden of ten acres, four acres of which is sown with garden seed. He says there about three acres of corn already up and about two inches above the ground and some beans and potatoes up too. This is the result of eight days' labor, besides making a road to the timber, hauling and sawing timber for a boat, making and repairing plows, etc. There have been thirteen plows and three harrows worked during the week." William Clayton, on 10 August, wrote that Markham reported "that in addition to the plowing done week before last, they have plowed about thirty acres which is mostly planted, making a total of about eighty acres." The potential appeared immense to the new settlers. Upon the return of an exploring party to Utah Valley on 6 August, they reported "400 Square miles arable." Clayton, *Journal*, 329–330, 343; Bullock, *Camp of the Saints*, 250.

8. Howard Egan noted a change in the temperature: "It was warm and pleasant as usual but the last night was the coolest we have experienced for a long time." Egan, *Pioneering*, 114.

9. Each division of ten men was responsible to plant for their assigned brethren. Wilford Woodruff's entry for the day stated: "Our ten sowed our Buck wheat to day a little over one bushel on two acres," with Orson Pratt, George Smith, and himself doing the work. With "Considerable of the corn & beans planted [that] has already made its appearance above the ground" and being "in a flourishing condition," plowing more ground for cultivation neared completion. Once the bulk of the plowing and planting had been completed, the labor force directed their attention to cutting and hauling logs from the canyons and making adobes for housing and fortification. Woodruff, *Journal*, 3:247; Whitney, Diary, 3 August 1847; Clayton, *Journal*, 343.

10. Jacob delivered Sebert Shelton's oxen to Charles Rich, who captained the Big Company, on 31 August 1847 when the hunters intersected with Rich's company. The agenda for the pioneers' return to Winter Quarters was beginning to take shape. Brigham Young told Horace Whitney that he intended the ox teams, the third segment of the returnees,

Wednesday 4th [August 1847] I went wit[h] C[harles]. Harper up <to> the mountain after Timber.[11]

Thursday 5th [August 1847] Stocked my Plough. Professor [Orson] Pratt measured the Height of the Snowy Peaks which lie to the South East. one of them [is] 18 miles [away] & 6619 feet above the level of the Plain. another, 15 miles distant & 6319 feet above the valley.[12] Professor Pratt by observation finds the Latitude of this place 40° 46' 6".[13]

Friday 6th [August 1847] Lewis Barney, one of the Hunters that went back over the mountain last Tuesday, retururned today without any meat, while the others went on towards Bear River. my Ten is out of Bread Stuff except a little Seed corn which we can grind on a hand mill. Barney acted foolish in turning back without meat.[14]

Satturday 7th [August 1847] Got my rifle Sights fixed by Br [Thomas] Tanner preparatory for Starting back to Winter Quarters, also some chain

---

to leave the following week with the horse teams to follow two weeks thereafter. This schedule changed somewhat. Whitney, Diary, 3 August 1847.

11. The timber they retrieved from the nearby mountains was quite dissimilar to the eastern hardwoods to which they were accustomed, according to Erastus Snow, who noted the species was "a kind of timber called in the East 'Furr' [Fir] tree; Mountaineers, call it 'Pine.' Some call it 'spruce Pine.' It often grows on these mountains to a great size." Snow, "Journey," (July 1948): 282.

    Hauling timber into the valley from adjacent canyons was of highest priority and occupied several teams every day after the Saints' arrival. Lewis Myers, the Crow family's guide from Pueblo, who had accompanied the Mormons to the valley, and who would settle in the Ogden, Utah, area for a time, had visited Utah Lake and Utah Valley to the south the previous day and reported that "on the east side [there] is plenty of timber" which he said could "be easily floated down the [Jordan] river" to the Salt Lake Valley. The previous evening one team came into camp with "cedar with which to make bedsteads, pails, &c." Three other teams, besides Jacob and Charles Harper, returned the night of the 4th "with 3 loads of good logs got for the purpose of building a storehouse." Whitney, Diary, 3–4 August 1847.

12. Jacob's figures, attributed to Orson Pratt, of elevation and distance from the temple site in Salt Lake City regarding the two most prominent peaks along the eastern rim of the Great Basin, are the same as those used by Albert Carrington who kept George Smith's diary. Modern calculations show the peak closest to Salt Lake City, Twin Peaks, at 11,329 feet above sea level, and Lone Peak, the more southerly peak at 11,253 feet. Smith (Carrington), History, 6 August 1847.

13. Orson Pratt, on 11 August, measured, by "Barometric Observations," the "altitude of Temple Block to be 4309 feet above the Sea." Bullock, *Camp of the Saints*, 255.

14. Rectifying the absence of food became a priority for those in the new settlement. On a day calculated to be a very warm 98°, Lewis Barney, one of Jacob's ten who had managed to become appointed a hunter en route to the Salt Lake Valley, prided himself on his shooting prowess. While Barney accounted for his activity after his arrival in the valley, he did not mention in his memoir that he had disappointed Jacob in failing to secure meat on this outing. Barney, *One Side by Himself*, 103–105, 320n55; Lyman (Carrington), Diary, 6 August 1847.

hooks.[15] coul[d] not find my cow this morning so we had to do without our dinner. found my cow at evening.[16] I sold her to Thos. S Williams for 16 Indians Shirts, worth here $24.00. I reserved the use of her u[n]til I Start on my return. I also sold him a Yougher[17] for $12.00 in Skins, Powder, & Vermillion, & one Shirt.

Sunday 8th [August 1847] This morning I was Baptized <by Bishop [Tarleton] Lewis> for my Health & the remission of my Sins, confirmed by Willford Woodruff[18] unto all Blessings, privileges, authority & Keys which had before been Sealed upon my head by the Searvants of God by the Holy anointing. Night before last the "Twelve" were Baptized.[19] last evening 55 others & to day the greater part of the remainder of the Camp including several who had never Joined the Church before.[20] at ten oclock [A.]M. all except the

---

15. Thomas Tanner served as one of the expedition's blacksmiths. He and Burr Frost, the other blacksmith, established a "Blacksmith Shop" on 4 August, "the first house built of logs" covered with "bushes." Chain hooks were used for surveying land. Bullock, *Camp of the Saints*, 248; Whitney, Diary, 7 August 1847.
16. Others had similar experiences with their animals. Bullock, *Camp of the Saints*, 250; Woodruff, *Journal*, 3:248–249.
17. A youger, also called a jaeger, jager, or yager, refers to a European-style rifle used for hunting. My thanks to David Packard, an expert in Mormon firearms for this information.
18. The collective exhibition of devotion via rebaptisms was a significant symbolic gesture for unity among the several groups now joined in the Salt Lake Valley. None were excused, including the hierarchy. The previous evening "Tarlton Lewis, Charles Shumway, Erastus Snow, Stephen H. Goddard & Addison Everett" were appointed to perform the rebaptisms, while "Wilford Woodruff, Heber C. Kimball, Orson Pratt, Amasa Lyman & G.A. Smith" were assigned to conduct the confirmations, the ordinance where, according to Mormon theology, the gift of the Holy Ghost is bestowed to ratify the baptism and to endow the recipient with divine direction. The Mormons, being zealous record keepers at this time, insured that five others, including Thomas Bullock, kept records of the ordinances. Bullock, *Camp of the Saints*, 252.

    Baptisms, in this case rebaptisms, proved to be an oft-used gesture by nineteenth-century Saints to signify devotion to Mormon objectives including church membership, healings, repentance, or symbolizing commitments to the Mormon Reformation or United Orders.
19. Wilford Woodruff, who had worked himself to exhaustion harvesting timber for the settlement, wrote, "I had laboured so hard during the two days I Could hardly stand upon my feet. I went to my waggon & flung myself upon my bed to rest." However, he said,

    > I had not been on the bed but a short time before Br [Heber] Kimball called upon me & informed me that the Twelve were going soon to the water to be Baptized for the remission of their sins to set an example to the Church As they would be called upon on Sunday morning to be baptized by the Twelve those that wished. We considered this A duty & privlege as we come into a glorious valley to locate & build a temple & build up Zion we felt like renewing our Convenant before the Lord and each other."

    Brigham Young rebaptized his "Brethren [of] the Twelve." Woodruff, *Journal*, 3:249.
20. One of the reasons for the ordinance came from a decision made on 4 August to rebaptize all of the Battalion veterans in the valley due to "much wickedness in the Battalion" during their journey to Santa Fe, Pueblo, and on to Utah. Altogether, Thomas Bullock stated, "289 persons [Wilford Woodruff gave the number as 288] . . . went forward & renewed

necessary guard for the camp repaired to the Bowry & listened with attention & delight to Br Heber [Kimball] & Br [Wilford] Woodruff while they set forth the necessity of being rig[h]teous & concerning the invisable agency that has continualy buoyed up the minds of those who have been called to bear the Priesthood from the Prophet Joseph [Smith] down to the present time under the most forbiding & trying circumstances; stimulating them forward to accomplish the things required at their hands, even when all the power of the world was arrayed against them, at least of the United States.[21] what is it that can make men thus devoted & cheerful? braving every danger, regardless of Personal consequences. because they have Light & enjoy the Liberty of the Sons of Light, which is to be exempt from fear, from doubt, from anxiety about consequences, Knowing absolutely Knowing ~~Shall work together~~ that *all* things shall work together for *their* good & for establishing the Kingdom of God upon the Earth!![22]

Monday 9th [August 1847][23] Capt. [James] Brown, Br Samuel Brannan & eight of the Brethren Started for the Pacific coast by the way of the Bear river Valley & Fort Hall[24] <where> Captn Brown intends to obtain Provisions on

their Covenant to serve the Lord." Bullock, *Camp of the Saints*, 248, 253; Woodruff, *Journal*, 3:251.

Horace Frink and Stephen Kelsey, both teenagers, were baptized Mormons for the first time when their comrades were rebaptized. The record of these baptisms and all of the rebaptisms can be found in Salt Lake Stake, Record of Members.

21. Thomas Bullock's account of Wilford Woodruff's sermon, which Woodruff included in his record, illustrated this point stating "The Prophet Joseph, The Twelve Apostles, with many of the Elders of Israel & Saints Have been called to pass through seenes of suffering & privations that would have discouraged an Allexander [the Great]." Woodruff, *Journal*, 3:252.

22. Wilford Woodruff stated after making his remarks that he "was never blessed with greater liberty of speach in addressing a congregation." Woodruff's message largely discriminated between the Latter-day Saints who he declared represented righteousness and God's favor and the civilization from which they fled who were characterized as being "wicked men & devils." Jacob did not note the messages of the afternoon meeting where Brigham Young continued Woodruff's theme stating: "words & actions cannot exhibit what is in me—the hand of the Lord is stretched out—he will surely vex the nation that has driven us out—they have rejected the whole council of God. The nation will be sifted, & the most will come out chaff, & they will go to the fiery furnace—they will go to hell." Whitney, Diary, 8 August 1847; Woodruff, *Journal*, 3:251–3.

23. William Clayton noted on this day that the "Twelve had decided on a name for this place and a caption for all letters and documents issued from this place, which is as follows: Salt Lake City, Great Basin, North America." On 14 August the "quorum of the Twelve" confirmed "that the name of our City should be City of the Salt Lake, Great Bason, North America." Finally on 22 August, besides applying the name of City Creek to the stream running from the same canyon, a "conference with the Twelve & saints . . . resolved universally to Call this place City of the great salt lake of the great Bason North America." Clayton, *Journal*, 342; Woodruff, *Journal*, 3:256, 261.

24. James Brown, Samuel Brannan and their brethren were given "an 'Epistle of the Twelve' to the Battalion and the saints in California" to relay to their brethren and sisters on the coast. Several of those who accompanied Brown and Brannan intended "to accompany

Great Salt Lake (1853). Frederick Piercy, *Route from Liverpool to Great Salt Lake Valley* (1855).

the credit of Uncle Sam to supply the Soldiers under his comma[n]d as they cannot be discharged, although their time of service is expired, until he can go to the Pacific where there is a Superior officer & obtain authority to discharge his men.[25]

I Ploughed out my corn, which looks fine. one week from the time we stoped here we had corn up.

Tuesday 10th [August 1847] I went [to] work on the Skiff we are building to fish in the Utah Lake,[26] when Br Heber [Kimball] & Amasa Lyman came

them as far as Ft. Hall & a few only as far as Bear River." The small company who continued on to California, not unlike their brethren who departed the Salt Lake Valley for Winter Quarters a few days later, managed to accomplish their mission despite personality clashes. Abner Blackburn, one of their number, wrote that "Brannan and Cap Brown could not agree on anny subject. Brannan thought he knew it all and Brown thought he knew his share of it. They felt snuffy at each other and kept apart." Whitney, Diary, 9 August 1847; Egan, *Pioneering*, 117; Blackburn, *Narrative*, 65.

25. The pay for the sick detachment of the Mormon Battalion, which James Brown was commissioned on this venture to retrieve from military officials in California, proved to be the money by which the Mormon settlers purchased Miles Goodyear's property on the Weber River (near present-day Ogden, Utah) the following year. Another duty of the west-coast bound company was the delivery of "252 letters" which had been written by those in camp. Bullock, *Camp of the Saints*, 253.

26. On 11 August William Clayton wrote, "The brethren in camp have finished the skiff and launched her in the creek to soak." The following day "[Albert] Carrington & 4 others, started with the boat on wheels for Eute [Utah] Lake to fish & explore the country, got with the boat as far as top of the hill that forms outlet kanyon, & turned back with boat, as we had not enough men or team to haul up Lake hill if we went down." Clayton, *Journal*, 345; Lyman (Carrington), Diary, 12 August 1847; Carter, *Founding Fort Utah*, 42–43.

to me & Said that the President wanted me to take charge of a company of Hunters to Start back to Winter Quarters ahead of the Ox Teams, to obtain meat for them.[27] but Heber wanted I should go to the Salt Lake first. So I put off on Horseback in company with John Norton, Lewis Barney & John Wheeler. after a ride of 20 miles West across the Valley we came to the Lake Shore where there is a large Rock Standing out 40 or 50 rods into the water where we went in[28] & Bathed in [the most] Beautiful water I ever saw, so clear that you can see the bottom where it is 10 feet deep & can float or walk in it at pleasure as it is impossible to sink. Five of our men were here making Salt & with three Kettles can make 40 Bushels per day as white as the Liverpool Salt & as fine.[29] we tarryed here an hour & then returned to camp a little after dusk, having rode 40 miles without eating or drinking any thing but Brack[ish] water. on our way back fell in with some hundred & fifty Indians, Utahs, mostly naked, going to our camp. they arrived next morning.[30]

Wednesday 11th [August 1847] Our men commenced laying up the Adobie Houses & also Some Log Houses on the [fort's] East side.[31] A[t] 12 oclock

---

27. William Clayton had written upon their arrival in the valley that "If we stay here three weeks and our teams have any rest they will be in good order to return." The hunters' departure the following day, exactly three weeks after their arrival, fit Clayton's projection. Clayton, *Journal*, 313.

28. As noted previously, a number of the camp, particularly the leaders, had visited the lake, including Black Rock, at the lake's southern shore, now visited by Jacob and his associates.

29. In contrast to the scarcity of timber, salt, one of life's essentials, was so abundant it quickly became taken for granted. On 9 August "Stephen H. Goddard, [Alexander] Chesley, [Chauncey] Loveland & Zebedee Coltrin" were assigned the task of harvesting salt from the Great Salt Lake. In the evening on 10 August, William Clayton reported that the "brethren who went to the lake on Monday to boil down salt have returned this evening and report that they have found a bed of beautiful salt ready to load into wagons. It lies between two sand bars and is about six inches thick. They suppose they can easily load ten wagons without boiling." When the salt was delivered to camp Horace Whitney wrote that it "is the best kind I ever saw, being as white as snow, though somewhat course." Bullock, *Camp of the Saints*, 254; Clayton, *Journal*, 343; Whitney, Diary, 12 August 1847.

30. William Clayton's report of the Utes' visit the following day reads: "Early this morning, a large company of the Utah Indians came to visit the camp and it was with difficulty they could be kept outside the wagons. There are few of them who have any clothing on except the breech clout [cloth] and are mostly of low stature. They have scarcely anything to trade and not many women and children with them. They are camped about three miles north of west and supposed to be going north hunting. One of them was detected stealing some clothing which lay on the bushes to dry, but was made to leave it. When they found they were not permitted inside the circle, they soon moved off to their camp." Clayton, *Journal*, 344–345.

31. "The brethren," William Clayton wrote, "have commenced laying the adobe wall today which will be twenty-seven inches thick and nine feet high. The adobes are 18 inches long, 9 inches broad and 4 1/2 inches thick." The fort (also called the "stockade" and "fortress") built on what became known as Pioneer Square in Salt Lake City (the ten acres between today's Third and Fourth West and Third and Fourth South) and was a line of adobe huts placed together in a configuration formed like these brackets, [ ], with openings for entering and egress on the north and south. (The fort extended into the block to

[P.]M. I Started on my Homeward trip with three Waggons, one having gone ahead.[32] traveled 13 miles & camped all together. the Boys having Killed some Small Birds, we had a fine Supper, Br Heber having got us some flour.[33]

Thursday 12th [August 1847] After Breakfast I read to the company the following Instructions, which all agreed to observe & obey:

> Great Salt Lake City, Great Basin, North America, August 11th 1847
> Instruction to Norton Jacob, John Wheeler, John Norton, Joseph Hancock, Lewis Barney, Thomas Brown, Richard D. Smith, James Oakl[e]y, David M. Perkins, W[illia]m. E. Beckste[a]d, & Isaac Carpenter.[34]
>
> Brethren: As you are about to leave this place on your return homewards, we have thought best to select Norton Jacob to be your leader, which if you approve,

---

the north.) Twenty-seven log houses were built in the fort, with the intent to house 160 families for the winter of 1847–1848. Clayton, *Journal*, 345; Morgan, *The Old Fort*, 17.

32. While one can imagine the anxiousness of the men to return to the Missouri River settlements to reunite with their families, the reality of what faced them did not escape many. William Clayton, the day he got into the valley, recognized what lay in front of them: "I dread nothing so much as the journey back again and when I think of the many dangers from accident which families traveling this road are continually liable to and especially this last mountain road from Weber River, it makes me almost shudder to think of it." Clayton, *Journal*, 310.

    Thomas Bullock and Horace Whitney suggest one of the reasons for the hunters' early departure was the lack of provisions," confirmed by Jacob's description of their situation on 6 August. Bullock, *Camp of the Saints*, 255; Whitney, Diary, 11 August 1847.

33. Lewis Barney, one of Jacob's hunters, explained that Brigham Young appointed a committee to survey the camp for provisions to supply the hunters before their departure. He wrote that "The Commity, after going through the Camp to every wagon returned with 60 pounds of flour Stating that that was all they could posibly raise." Heber Kimball, according to Barney explained to him that "this is the best we can do for you. go and be blest." With that, they started on their journey. Barney, Autobiography and diary, 45.

34. The eleven hunters were composed of components of both the vanguard and the now healthy sick detachments of the Mormon Battalion who had spent the previous winter in Pueblo, Colorado. Norton Jacob, the captain, who turned 43 the day before their departure, was one of six from the vanguard. The vanguard's six were mature men in contrast to those of the six (all privates) from the Mormon Battalion, mostly in their early twenties. John Wheeler (45), John Norton (27), Joseph Hancock (47), Lewis Barney (38), and Thomas Brown (_), with the exception of John Norton, were father-age to Richard Smith (_), James Oakley (19), David Perkins (24), William Beckstead (20), and Isaac Carpenter (20). "1847 Pioneers," *1997–98 Church Almanac*, 124, 126, 136, 139, 144, 154–155; Larson, *Database of the Mormon Battalion*, 21, 54–55, 180, 187, 221.

    Much of the unruliness of the men and the personal confrontations afflicting the hunters on their return to Winter Quarters, later illustrated in Jacob's diary, can be attributed to the youthfulness of half of those who composed the group, but not all. Brown, who earlier in the year may have hidden under the Mormon blanket to escape detection from civil authorities who wanted him for complicity in a robbery-murder near Nauvoo, Illinois, was particularly obnoxious. A violent brawl the following year in the Kanesville, Iowa, area, proved to be Brown's last incident. Stegner, *Gathering of Zion*, 125–126.

we want you to agree that you will follow his council implicitly; and we desire that you will be agreed in all your opperations, acting in concert and Keeping together. We wish you to be cautious of the Teams intrusted to your care, and recruit them at every place where you find the feed and scituation will answer. Be prudent in all things and do not give way to a hurrying Spirit, not letting your Spirits run away to Winter Quarters before your bodies can arrive there. as soon as you arrive at a good hunting country, we wish you to stop & hunt, so as to supply the ox Teams that will start from here in a few days; and then you will not be detained any longer hunting, But will be able to pursue your Journey Steadily to the Buffalo country on the Platte. Be humble, be patient, be prayerful. listen to the council given you, and obey it, and you shall be blest, and in a short time we will be with you again, and go with you to your homes.

In behalf of the Council
Brigham Young, President
Willard Richards, Clerk[35]

We proceeded on over Pratt's pass to Beaver creek & having made 18 miles, camped near the Kanyon. after we were encamped Thomas Brown & Madison Welsh arrived on Horseback, having left the ~~camp~~ <city> this morning. they report the death of [George] Thurlkil's [Therlkill] child in the creek where a dam is thrown across to turn the water onto our Ploughed ground.[36] this creek has a de[s]cent of 251 feet in a mile above the city.[37]

Friday 13th [August 1847] Before Breakfast two Hunters went out & John Norton shot an Antelope but lost it in the Sage brush. we started late, having waited for our Hunters. in about three miles we fell in with two of our men by the names of [Lewis] Myars & [Alexander] Chesny, who went on Monday with Capt. [James] Brown's company up the Lake, to the North. they report

35. The retained copy of the letter of instructions can be found in the Brigham Young, Office Files, LDS Church Archives.

36. The tragedy, the first death of a Mormon in the valley, affected all in the camp. Between 4 and 5 P.M. on Wednesday, 11 August, Milton Howard Therlkill, "age 3 years 8 months 26 days," was "found [by his uncle] in the creek south of the camp . . . . Various efforts were made to restore it but unsuccessfully." The child's parents, George and Matilda Jane, mourned "the accident bitterly," but, according to Howard Egan, the "agonized mother baffles all description. She laughed, wept, walked to and fro, alternately, refusing all attempts at consolation from her friends, being, apparently unable to become resigned to her domestic and melancholy bereavement." The child's death pained the settlement which just two days before had welcomed the birth of the first child born in the valley, the daughter of Catherine and John Steele. The day of the first birth was also the day of the first divorce. Life's mixture of joys and vicissitudes appeared early in Great Salt Lake City. Bullock, *Camp of the Saints*, 253, 255; Whitney, Diary, 11 August 1847; Egan, *Pioneering*, 121; Clayton, *Journal*, 345.

37. On 10 August, Orson Pratt reported to Thomas Bullock that the previous day "he went 1 mile up the [City] creek & found the fall of Water to the meeting ground on Temple Block [to be a] 251 feet fall." Bullock, *Camp of the Saints*, 254.

having passed 17 creeks before they reached the mouth of the Weber [River], 35 miles & ricih [rich] fertile Vallys on all those Streams. near the Weber Mr Miles Goodye[a]r has a garden. his corn, Beans, onions, &c look finely, but they report the climate to be colder here than at our city as the North winds have a fair sweep from the Bear river Valley.[38] The Weber is well Timbered from the mouth up to the upper Kanyon in the mountains.[39] we proceeded on over to the Weber & up to where the road leaves it where we camped. Ezra [Isaac] Carpenter Killed a wild goose & a Duck & Joseph Hancock Shot a Deer which he did not get & Killed a Duck. we made 14 miles to the mouth of Echo creek, which is 45 miles from the city.

Saturday 14th [August 1847] Four Hunters went ahead & two took a circuit up the Weber & round on the mountains. we moved on up the creek 20 miles & camped in good feed near a small Spring. the Hunters that went ahead Killed nothing, but [Joseph] Hancock & [John] Norton, who went round on the mountain, Killed a black tailed Deer & an Antelope. I went out after we camped, shot at an Ante[lope] but did not Kill. there is abundance of game here, yet the Hunters who were sent out here to get meat for the camp did not Kill any. but Henson Walker & Joseph Rooker left their hunting & went on without orders or council to meet the Big Camp![40] Query? will they be blest in so doing. [41]

---

38. John Brown, accompanying James Brown and Samuel Brannan northward, wrote that as they moved north they "found the fort of Mr. [Miles] Goodyear, which consisted of some log buildings and corrals stockaded in with pickets. This man had a herd of cattle, horses and goats. He had a small garden of vegetables, also a few stalks of corn, and although it had been cultivated it would do well, which proved to us that with proper cultivation it would do well." The garden was reported to be "about 15 yards square, looking well." Wilford Woodruff reported on 14 August that "4 of the messengers returned from Bear River valley & cash [Cache] valley who started with Capt. [James] Brown that has gone with a Company to the Bay via Fort Hall. The messengers Bring a glorious report of cash valley & the Country between us & there, that is rich soil & well watered & well calculated for farming purposes Also bear river valley for stock grazing." Along with the glowing reports of the region, however, they also reported "game to be very scarce." Brown, *Autobiography*, 81; Smith (Carrington), History, 14 August 1847; Woodruff, *Journal*, 3:256; Whitney, Diary, 14 August 1847.

39. Despite the timbered character of Weber Canyon, when Lewis Myers returned to the settlement at Salt Lake City he reported "Weber River canyon roads [to be] very bad for traveling, and further than our route from [Orson] Pratt's Pass." Smith (Carrington), History, 14 August 1847.

40. Henson Walker (27) and Joseph Rooker (29) were not part of Jacob's hunters, but were assigned to provide meat for the Saints in the valley who lacked food. After abandoning their posts to join with the "Big Camp," the collection of companies composing the second wave of Mormon emigration that year, Walker joined with Jacob's hunters on 24 August. "1847 Pioneers," *1997–98 Church Almanac*, 147, 153–154.

41. Everyone not staying in the valley, vanguard and battalion veterans alike, had little else but their return to Winter Quarters on their minds, hard as the return venture promised to be. Perhaps the first of the Mormon sojourners to return to the Missouri River was

Sunday 15th [August 1847] I counciled the Boys not to hunt to day but rest, excep[t] some who were to go out & bring in the Antelope that was Killd last evening. in a Short time Br [Lewis] Barney returned having got a fine Buck Antelope.[42] about noon the other party <returned> with the one they went after. John Gould & Bail[e]y Jacobs passed us having been to Ft. Bridger & got two cows & an ox that Strayed from our camp in the Valley of the Salt Lake.[43] Some Emigrant gave them Provisions, as they <were out>.[44]

Monday 16th [August 1847][45] I sent out all the men to hunt on each side of the road except the Teamsters & we moved on ten miles & camped at a fine Spring on a Small Branch that runs into Bear river. the hunters came in & Killed nothing. Several of [them] went out & Isaac Carpenter Killed an Antelope. Joseph Hancock & John Norton grumbled & murmered because we did not stop as soon as they wanted, although we came to the verry place

---

James Davenport. One of those assigned to tend the North Platte ferry in June, the next month (23 July) Davenport left his brethren, harboring hard feelings. On 31 July 1847, near Scott's Bluff, the second emigrating company of the year met Davenport "who was returning to his family at Winter Quarters" with a group of Oregon pioneers returning to the States. Empey, "Mormon Ferry," 142; Historian's Office, Pioneers of 1847, Church Emigration, 1831–1847.

Others were anxious to return to their families. William Clayton explained on 12 August that "The soldiers are getting dissatisfied at being kept here so long from their families and yesterday several of them left the camp secretly to go to Winter Quarters and this morning others are gone. . . . about a dozen are already gone and others are preparing to follow them." The behavior of Henson Walker and Joseph Rooker, both young men numbered among the vanguard, reflected the restlessness of the men returning to their homes and families. Clayton, *Journal*, 345; Bullock, *Camp of the Saints*, 303.

A contingent of the Mormon Battalion, led by Nathaniel Jones, traveled eastward with General Stephen Kearney from Los Angeles to Fort Leavenworth. They met the second wave of Mormon migration that year on 3 August near Fort Laramie. Historian's Office, Pioneers of 1847, Church Emigration, 1831–1847.

42. Lewis Barney noted their camp that morning was at "the Cave rock [Cache Cave, also called Reddin's Cave] at the head of Echo Canion." Barney indicated that from this time on they generally "had all the meat we Could eat." Barney, Autobiography and diary, 46.

43. Jacob's account suggests that John Gould and Bailey Jacobs had been to Fort Bridger in advance of the hunters, presumably on assignment. Gould later joined with Brigham Young's party returning to Winter Quarters. Bullock, *Camp of the Saints*, 276.

44. While the Mormons were furbishing the Salt Lake Valley, the year's Oregon and California emigration continued northward through Fort Hall in what is now eastern Idaho.

45. "Most of the company of ox teams have started today [16 August 1847] for Winter Quarters." The ox teams preceded the main pioneer camp by ten days. This is the body for whom the hunters, who departed five days earlier, was to supply meat. The company was composed of 24 pioneers and 46 soldiers (Battalion veterans), with 34 wagons, 92 yoke of oxen, 18 horses, and 14 mules. An advance detail of the ox teamsters, which included William Clayton, preceded their brethren of the ox team's main body for much of the return trip to Winter Quarters. Clayton, *Journal*, 347; Bagley in Bullock, *Camp of the Saints*, 258–259.

we had agreed by a vote in the morning! They did the same thing under the same circumstances on Satturday. this evening John Norton thretened <to> cowhide John Wheeler in his absence, because he had cautioned him not to use the Flour too lavishly & said Flour was furnished by Wheeler.[46]

Tuesday 17th [August 1847] Lewis Barney, John Wheeler & myself went out to hunt before breakfast. I came in first, having shot twice at a Buck & missed. now [Joseph] Hancock & [John] Norton were murmering that we werere delaying too much & would get caught in the mountains by the Snow as the Gentiles did last winter!![47] I asked them where the "Twelve" would be then & [said] moreover, the remainder of our ox Team company were behind & that I sho[u]ld not start until those Hunters came in [even] if they all went & left me. John Norton had gone on & [Joseph] Hancock took his waggon & went on to the Tar Spring while David Perkins tarried with me. Thos. Brown, James Oakly, and Madison Welsh, without any council, Started off to Ft Bridger. about 11 oclock my hunters came in, having each Shot at Antelope but did not get any. we moved on 9 miles to the other waggon. Isaact Carpenter had Killed an Antelope. Josep[h] Hancock remained out till after dark but got nothing. we went to the Spring & got tar.[48]

Wednesday 18th [August 1847] We moved on over the mountain about 12 miles & halted for dinner. when we started, Ezra Becksted manifested a rebelious Spirit in leaving his place & Starting his Team in ahead of the company contrary to my council, producing disorder in the company. we made today 25 miles & camped after decending a mountain, which is the sevnth one we have crossed since we left the Valley.

Thursday 19th [August 1847] In going six <miles> came to Ft. Bridger Just as a company of Emigrants were starting out from there on their way to

---

46. The fractious rancor among Jacob's hunters within a week of their departure from the Salt Lake Valley portended two months of erratic behavior generally characterizing their return to Winter Quarters. Jacob was almost powerless to stifle the dissent exhibited by several of the hunters, primarily the young Battalion veterans. In the absence of the stern atmosphere of compliance expected by Brigham Young in the western trek, the yearning for their families on the Missouri, from whom the Battalion veterans had now been absent for over a year, countered the cooperative spirit marking much of Mormonism's endeavors in its early years.

    The contrariness within the group of hunters caught the attention of Wallace Stegner in *The Gathering of Zion*. Indeed, the company's return to Winter Quarters was generously peppered with disputes and willfulness that resembled a comedic ensemble. However, Stegner's apparently hasty read of Jacob's account led him to errantly generalize as negative Jacob's behavior and intent.

47. This, of course, is a reference to the Donner-Reed disaster discussed earlier.
48. The tar spring, of course, was discovered by Lewis Barney and John Norton on 11 July en route to Salt Lake Valley.

Orregon.[49] we halted a short time & moved on down Blacks Fork of Green river 14 miles & camped.[50] Bridger's People say they have had more rain in this parched Desert since the Mormons passed this way than they have had in three years before. well, the Lord has promised that the Desert places shall be made glad because of the Saints in the last days! there has been Showers almost every day since we started from the Valley & the grass is better than it was when we went up in July.[51] [Jim] Bridger sells Flour at $7.00 per hundred.

Friday 20th [August 1847] Moved on at an early hour. after going 7 or 8 miles, a fine Buck Antelope made his apearance in the road ahead. the Horsemen having passed on, Lewis Barney & Isaac Carpenter, after Shooting six times, Killed him. a few miles fa[r]ther we found another Buck by the side of the road that John Norton had Killed. made 18 miles & camped on Ham's Fork.

Satturday 21st [August 1847] Moved on down Black's Fork 3 miles & then across to green river & up it 3 miles where we campd making in all 22 miles.[52] after we camped John Norton said it was move[d] that the Captain cook Supper. I replyd I was going to cook. he then commenced abusing me in the most vulgar manner, threatning to whip me. I told him I was not concerned about his whiping, but I would bring him to an account for his conduct hereafter. once before, he rode into the road & without any ceremony asked what I was driving past all the game for. he was going to stop it. I told Br [John] Wheeler to drive on to the Spring half a mile ahead, but John never hunted any while we were here, neither could any of us Kill, though we had a fair opportuntys.

Sunday 22d [August 1847] We remained encamped. those Soldiers [the young Mormon Battalion veterans] were all full of curscing & Swearing, except David M. Perkins. Thomas Brown [was] as profane as any of them, Swearing they would leave the company & with their Horses go ahead to Winter Quarters when we get to Sweet Water![53]

---

49. One branch of the Oregon Trail continued on to Fort Bridger after the parting of the ways, the Sublette Cutoff, the road most Oregon-bound emigrants took en route to Fort Hall. While several companies of Oregon and California-bound emigrants in the early 1840s had traversed the Salt Lake Valley, none apparently used the Great Salt Lake route in 1847, breaking north for Fort Hall at Fort Bridger

50. The advance detail of the ox teams, now just four days behind the hunters, like the hunters stopped but briefly at Fort Bridger, resting only an hour and a half. Clayton, *Journal*, 351.

51. The Mormon sojourners saw providential markers in many particulars associated with their arrival and settlement in the West, including modification of the climate.

52. Still only four days behind the hunters, William Clayton, with the advance ox teams, noted after traveling roughly the same distance that they "found several places where the road is shortened some, but it is yet about sixteen miles from water to water." Clayton, *Journal*, 352.

53. Understanding why Thomas Brown was assigned to the company of hunters is confusing. Order, discipline, and willingness to fulfill an assignment for the good of the whole were

Monday 23d [August 1847] Started at an early hour. Forded green river above the mouth of Big Sandy. continued up that Stream & camped on its banks having made 28 miles over barren, Sandy plains.

Tuesday 24th [August 1847] I <was> taken unwell last night by eating late & too hearty of meat as we have but little Bread, having Started with only 60 pounds of Flour for five of us.[54] we made but 8 miles & camped on little Sandy, as there is a dry r[e]gion of over 20 miles that will take us a full day to cross & here we can get a little grass for our Teams. I was verry glad to stop as I needed rest. I found a little Tea <I> had brought along verry useful now. the Boys Killed some Sage chickens of which Br [John] Wheeler made me some verry nourishing broth. their flesh is white as any chicken. we had rain this evening accompanyed with a cold wind from the S West. ~~I felt~~ met [Henson] Walker & <he> turned back with us.

Wednesday 25th [August 1847] I rested well last night & feel much refreshed this morning, able to drive my Team. moved on at an early hour. after going about 10 miles me[t] Br E[zra]. T. Benson with the express from the Big Camp. he reports 556 Waggons & 3,000 People coming up.[55] John Norton & Thos. Brown returned with Br Benson to the first camping place to examine the List of those that are coming on. after 5 miles further we met over a hundred Snake Indians who gave us Buffalo meat & were verry friendly.[56] they

---

clearly expected of the hunters. Brown did not fit this profile. It was likely unknown by the Saints at the time that he joined the vanguard on 19 April, with three others, that he was wanted by an Iowa sheriff for an 1845 murder. But on 12 February 1847 Brigham Young received a credible report that Brown "was threatning the lives of the 12." That Brown was allowed to accompany the Saints westward two months later is difficult to explain. Stout, *On the Mormon Frontier*, 1:236, 236n32.

54. If there was a timely moment for the hunters and the ox teams to join as designed, it was at this spot. Three days after the hunters moved from this area, William Clayton noted that access to food was of concern to the ox teams, including a shortage of flour. They rejoiced when Bailey Jacobs "killed a large antelope" as they "were nearly out of bread stuff and had little meat for several days." Clayton, *Journal*, 353.

55. Westbound at this time, Ezra Benson encountered the advance of the ox teams the following day. To them he reported, according to William Clayton, that nine companies were en route to the valley, composed of "566 wagons and about 5,000 head of stock." (The LDS Church Historian's Office capitulation numbered 1,540 emigrants, with 580 wagons and 4,342 animals, including horses, mules, oxen, cows, sheep, swine, and chickens.) Clayton, *Journal*, 352; Historian's Office, Pioneers of 1847, Church Emigration, 1831–1847.

56. Escaping encounters with the Mormon overlanders on their venture to the Great Basin earlier in the year, the Snake Indians identified here were Eastern Shoshones, though the generic name of Snake Indians often denoted the several Shoshone groups, especially those more closely tied to the Snake River region. The Eastern Shoshone centered near Wyoming's Wind River Mountains and ranged through the Sweetwater River region of western Wyoming at this time. Regarding Shoshone relationships with emigrants during this period, as late as 1860, Washakie, the noted Shoshone leader of the second half of the nineteenth century, boasted "that the blood of the white man had never stained their soil."

were Just returning home from their Buffalo hunt on the Sweet Water.[57] as we approached the Pass we met a furious, cold East wind that continued on through the night. made 22 1/2 [miles] & camped [at] the outlet of the Pacific Springs. Some frost yesterday morning.

Thursday 26th [August 1847][58] moved on over the [South] Pass, the Storm of wind having abated. a cool, pleasant morning. Isaac Carpenter Killed two

---

Stamm, *People of the Wind River*, 19–40; Madsen, *Shoshoni Frontier*, 3–6; Simpson, *Report of Explorations*, 461. A contemporary appraisal of these "Sho-sho-nees," giving particulars of their seasonal movement, is found in former Utah Territory Indian agent Garland Hurt's report of 2 May 1860 to James H. Simpson in Simpson, *Report of Explorations*, 461. A view of Shoshone-white relations on the emigrant trails is found in Trenholm and Carley, *The Shoshonis*, 97–110.

57. Lewis Barney, one of Jacob's hunters, noted his personal encounter at this time with the Native Americans when the company traveled between the Green River and South Pass. Hunting alone during the day, he "fell behind the train eight or ten miles and being two or three miles from the road on a Smoth open plain, I discovered ahead of me about a mile a band of Indians about 15 in nunber Coming over a little hill right toward me." Frightened and realizing he had no opportunity to hide in the open, he walked toward them when the Indians noticed the lone white man. They "Shouted and [put the] whip to their horses and on they Come full speed." Quickly surrounded, he put on his brave face and, distracting them from his vulnerable plight, he said, "I made Signs that my feet was very Sore and that I was very hungary and wanted to buy a pair of mogisons And some buffalo Beef." Despite his precarious situation, the Indians "Seemed to Simpthise with me." Promptly, "One of the Squaws handed me a pair of mogisons." Asking "the price," the "Chief Said 20 loads of powder and balls" which Barney negotiated to ten. Hoping his openness and good-faith negotiation would influence the Native Americans, who clearly had the upper hand, he said "I then handed him my rifle to hold while I measured the 10 Charges of powder and balls." The result: "they then gave me a buffalo toung and my gun and went on their way."

    Barely recovered from this frightful situation, shortly Barney "met another band of Indiangs about the same number." Again he was quickly surrounded. And again he was frightened, although less so at first. But finding quite a different reception from this group of Eastern Shoshones, he said "Several of them made attemps to take my Riffle and powder." Not waiting around to passively await his fate, he "then made a rush and broke from them and went on my way" while "They Stood and watched me till I got 4 or 5 hundred yeards from them" and "went on there way." Barney, Autobiography and diary, 46–47.

    The following day, the ox teams met this band of Eastern Shoshone Indians, described as being "a large party of mounted Indians." Clayton, *Journal*, 352.

58. This is the day, 26 August, two weeks after the band of hunters left the valley, that the "Pioneer Camp with a large number of the [Mormon] Battalion Harnessed up our horses," wrote Wilford Woodruff, "& bid farewell to our friends who was to tarry" and, departing the Salt Lake Valley, took up the return trek to Winter Quarters. Woodruff, *Journal*, 3:262.

    The previous day, 25 August, Woodruff summarized their work in the Salt Lake Valley: "We as A pioneer company have accomplished more this season then can be found on record concerning any set of men since the days of Adam. . . . in one month after our arival [we have] laid out a city two miles square & built A fort & fortification of hewn timber drawn 7 miles from the mountains & of unburnt brick surrounding 10 acres of ground 40 rods of which was coverd with Block Houses, Besides planting about 100

Antelopes. we made 14 miles & camped on Sweet Water. I went out with [Henson] Walker. found plenty of Buffalo Signs, but the Indians have driven them all off.[59] Killed an Antelope. [John] Norton & [Alexander] Boss overtook us.

Friday 27th [August 1847] Before breakfast Some half dozen Snake Indians came to us. bought some Buffalo robes of them.[60] moved on down Sweet Water, over the mountain 22 miles, & camped. James Oakly found an Indians horse. A tremendous, hard frost this morning, but here under the mountain it is warm. Alekander Boss Killed an Antelope & Isaac Carpenter a mountain goat.

Satturday 28th [August 1847] Tarryed here to rest our Teams & hunt. Alexander Boss & James Oakly went on to meet the camp that is coming up. Br [Ira] Eldridge's camp arrived & stoped a little above us.[61] all well of

---

Acres of corn, potatoes, Buckwheat turnips gardens &c." Albert Carrington's 26 August summarization of their accomplishments over the previous month expanded Woodruff's appraisal, stating: "During the time we were in the valley, a little over one month, the pioneers, with the aid of the detachment and families from Pueblo broke, watered, planted and sowed upwards of one hundred acres with various kinds of seeds; nearly stockaded with adobies one public square (ten acres); explored the country north to Fort Hall, 216 miles, west, along the southern shore of the Salt Lake, from 30 to 40 miles; south, to Utah Lake, 40 miles, and ascended with barometer the highest mountain peak in the neighborhood of City Valley, and explored much of the neighboring hills, mountains and canyons, and building one line of log cabins in stockade." Woodruff, *Journal*, 3:262; Smith (Carrington), History, 26 August 1847.

A roster of Brigham Young's returning camp—107 persons—is provided in Bagley in Bullock, *Camp of the Saints*, 276–277.

59. Several of the advance detail of the ox teams, in the same vicinity two days later, "killed a buffalo a few miles back, but it is very poor." Clayton, *Journal*, 353.

60. While this meeting with the Eastern Shoshone at the Sweetwater River was now, by all appearances, routine to the hunters, two days later, on 29 August, the ox teams encountered a band of "about sixty in number, about twenty of them boys," likely attached to the half dozen met by the hunters, that for unfounded reasons gravely frightened them. The Shoshones, however, were entirely benign desiring only to trade, even offering to host the ox teamsters at their lodges. After trading, the Mormons moved on. Clayton, *Journal*, 354–355.

61. The hunters encountered Ira Eldredge's company of Mormon emigrants, one of nine "companies of fifty wagons" that departed from Winter Quarters two months after the vanguard left, almost two weeks after Eldredge's group met Ezra Benson's express. The second wave of Latter-day Saints bent on the Great Basin, of which Eldredge's was the most advanced, was composed of 1540 Saints, many with families, in 580 wagons. In an express sent to Brigham Young by John Taylor on 18 August, Taylor, explaining why their progress toward the Salt Lake Valley was retarded, wrote that "Our numbers far exceed that we anticipated, for instead of numbering one hundred wagons we have near six hundred." The first fifty arrived in the Salt Lake Valley on 19 September 1847, preceded by an express on 15 September. The last of the second wave of Mormons emigrants entered the valley on 8 October 1847. Historian's Office, Pioneers of 1847, Church Emigration, 1831–1847.

them.[62] I learned that my Father [Udney Hay Jacob] got disappointed in geting his wheat ground & is not coming up. I went out & got a shot at a Buffalo but did not get him. [Lewis] Barney Killed an Antelop.

Sunday 29 [August 1847] The Brethren went on up the mountain & we went down the river 10 miles & camped. towards night Parley [Pratt]'s company came up & camped with us.[63] John Norton began another quarrel with me this morning without any cause or provocation on my part. he also ~~told~~ gave an unfavorable account of the Great Salt Lake Valley to Br Parley's company, thereby creating uneasiness in the minds of some of the Brethren.[64]

Monday 30th [August 1847] moved on down the river 15 miles & camped

---

62. The advance detail of ox teamsters met Ira Eldredge's group two days later.

63. Parley Pratt was ostensibly *not* one of the division captains of the second companies. But he and John Taylor, because of their status within the Twelve Apostles, tended to serve as emigration leaders even though Ira Eldredge and Joseph Horne, respectively, were appointed to lead the apostles' companies of fifty on 17 June 1847 at the Elkhorn River. Eldredge and Horne, as "captains of fifty" were subordinate to Daniel Spencer and Edward Hunter who were two of four (Jedediah Grant and Abraham Smoot were the others) who headed companies of 100 in the second wave of emigrants. Added to the group was Charles Rich's "artillery company," who accompanied the emigrants. The nine "companies of fifty" stretched out, sometimes, across the Nebraska and Wyoming plains many dozens of miles between each other. Historian's Office, Pioneers of 1847, Church Emigration, 1831–1847.

When Brigham Young's eastbound camp met up with Pratt's company on 4 September, he learned from them the status of the church in the Missouri River settlements when they left in the middle of June. He was not pleased. At a council of the leading men, Young focused his disappointment on Pratt, reproving him "very strongly for disorganizing all the Winter's Work of the Quorum of the Twelve." Defensively, Pratt "manifested a contra[ry] Spirit" but "afterwards repented" and the council "proved a most glorious meeting to all." A final meeting between the eastbound and westbound brethren the next day so "mutually gratified" the men, "& such good feelings existed that we did not separate until 9." Bullock, *Camp of the Saints*, 279.

64. "We Crosed over the Rocky Ridge, went down on to the River, and made Camp for the night" where "we had the Satisfaction of meeting Parleys Pratt's Company of one hundred wagons," wrote Lewis Barney. Being "very anxious to hear from our friends," and the westbound emigrants being "equal[ly] as anxious to hear from us and know how we were and Where we had made a location for the Church," Barney said, "We gave them the desired information Relating many Circumstances that transpired on our journey and founding a City in the tops of the Mountains." He explained, with biblical flavor, that in their venture they emblemized "the geathering of Israel And that the ensign Spoken of by Isiah the prophet [that] was Raised for the geathering of the honest in heart from all nations to geather to." He also noted to his comrades that they "had hoisted the Stars and Stripes and it was fluttering in the breeze over Mexican Soil And that we had taken possesion of the Country in the Name of the god of Israel for the purpose of building up his kingdom in the valleys of the mountains." In exchange, Barney said, "They gave us encouraging news from our families." Barney, Autobiography and diary, 47–48.

The ox teamsters met Parley Pratt two days later on 1 September.

with Br [Abraham] Smoot's company & deliverd the Indian Horse to him that Br [Stephen] Markum obtained for Br Smoots Mule.[65]

Tuesday 31st [August 1847] moved on down 5 or six miles. met three fifties of our Brethren, one of them Br Charles Rich's. he was glad to see me & [I] delivered to him one yoke of Br [Sebert] Shelton's oxen & one Log chain.[66] continued down ~~to~~ 10 miles in all to day & camped with Br John Taylor's hundred. all the Brethren we have met appear to be in good health & Spirits. we enjoy fine weather. John Wheeler & [Henson] Walker, having met their families, turned back.[67] I was now out of bread. Br Charles Rich & old Father [Samuel] Merril[l] each gave me some crackers & I bought a dollars worth of W[illia]m. Lan[e]y. Br John Taylor directed his Hundred to raise a hundred lbs of Bread stuff for my company of 13 persons, but there was above 70 lb obtained. all the Brethren treated us [with] great friendship, cordialy inviting us to eat with them.[68]

---

65. For 30 August, John Smith, en route to the Great Basin in the second Mormon emigration of the year, reported that some of the "Pioneer Camp of Israel Camped near us on their Return for winter Quarters. they the Pioneers had ben to the valy of the Great Salt Lake & the 12 had Laid out a city there." Smith, Journal, 30 August 1847.
66. This fulfilled Jacob's commitment to Sebert Shelton made earlier in the month.
67. Besides the Wheeler and Walker families being reunited, others in the eastward Mormon companies found their families among the 1,500 who were Salt Lake Valley-bound and reversed their way intent on wintering in the Great Basin.
68. While foodstuffs were shared with Jacob's hunters by their westbound brethren, a consequence of the many coursing their way to the Great Basin was the depletion of resources upon which they had depended. "We Soon began to meet other Companies which gave us much Satisfaction," Lewis Barney wrote. "These Companies had drove the Buffalo and other Game from the Road making it Scarce and hard to get hold of. Consequenly We were under the necesity of going much further than we anticipated before we Could make a halt to kill and dry meat for the Company with the ox teams." Barney, Autobiography and diary, 48.

September–December 1847

Retracing their route from Winter Quarters, Norton Jacob's hunters and the ox teams who followed them eastward found themselves fraught with friction and frustration. Accusations and threats between the groups were followed by reconciliation, a return to strife, and another mending of feelings. The large Mormon body which moved westward earlier in the year tended to negate Native American mischief against emigrants. But with the Saints stretched out across the plains in smaller numbers on their return, the Plains Indians of Nebraska were emboldened. Threat of Indian depredations proved to be the stimulus for reconciliation between the fractious returnees who began arriving at the Missouri River the third week of October. Brigham Young's group entered Winter Quarters at month's end, October 1847. The remainder of the year found Jacob gathering resources to replenish his family, then living in western Iowa, from whom he had been absent for six months.

Wednesday first day of Sept. [1847] Left Br [John] Taylor's company to Journey on & proceeded down the river 19 miles & camped with Br Jedediah Grant's Hundred. they have been unfortunate in looseing cattle by poison, especialy Br Willard Snow's Fifty & there is some bickering among this company about assisting those that have lost their cattle.[1] Jack Reding [Redden] turned back to meet the ox <Teams>.

1. Accompanying the second companies were 124 horses, 9 mules, 2213 oxen, 887 cows, 358 sheep, 35 swine, and 716 chickens, a formidable number of animals which had to be cared for while crossing a third of the continent. As an illustration of the difficulty of transporting such an enormous portable barnyard, John Taylor, whose contingent trailed Parley Pratt's wrote an express to him from Independence Rock on 28 August to explain why they lagged behind: "Great numbers of the cattle have died, I believe for want of feed, and others have been poisoned. . . . I supposed that in three or four camps in four days past they are minus 40 head of cattle. The fifty that I am in have lost ten and one of [Jedediah] Grant's ten. I suppose the others [have lost animals] in the same ratio." Meeting Grant and Willard Snow two days later, William Clayton noted that their group had "lost many cattle and are so bad off for teams as not to be able to travel

Thursday 2d [September 1847] Moved down 5 miles & camped. to go through a gap in the mountains to hunt [was] contrary to my Judgment but I did it to please the whims of the men that were with me. we divided into two companies & went through different passes, 3 in one & 4 in the other.[2] Isaac Carpenter Killed a poor Bull Buffalo & with [Joseph] Hancock & [Lewis] Barney packed a part of the meat. the company I went <with> had <to go> much farther to get to where the Buffalo were. Killed two old Bulls. lef[t] Blankets over them to Keep off the wolves & started about sunset to go 12 miles to camp. In the midtst of a Shower of rain night overtook us. we could not find the pass & after cambering over the rocks several hours, having fatigued ourselves & horses, struck up a fire & camped where we found good feed for our Horses but no Supper for ourselves.

Friday 3d [September 1847] Started a little after sunrise for the camp where we arrived about 9 oclock. after geting some Breakfast moved on down 12 miles & camped below Independance Rock.[3]

Satturday 4th [September 1847] I concluded, as the Buffalo were poor here & those that were Killed would spoil before we could get to them with a Waggon, to go on to where we could find Buffalo that were fat.[4] traveled 14 miles & camped as Isaac Carpenter had Killd a fine yearling Bull that was fat. the feed is short here.[5]

Sunday 5th [September 1847] Tarryed here to dry our meat. Joseph Hancock said "he did not Know as he should ever go back to the Valley, for Joseph Smith had promised that he should have his inheritance in Jackson county [Missouri] & <if> he had to take a Squaw he would go & get a Potawatamie

---

more than ten miles a day." Along with Taylor's express, Pratt sent his own to Brigham Young seeking assistance for all of the trailing companies in their depleted circumstances. Historian's Office, Pioneers of 1847, Church Emigration, 1831–1847; Clayton, *Journal*, 357.

2. The two routes may refer to the primary road and a "new road on the north side of the Sweet Water," which was "sandy in places but much better than the old road." Clayton, *Journal*, 357.
3. Arriving at the granite dome two days later, William Clayton, roaming over the large rock "had some solemn meditations and felt to humble myself and call upon the Lord for myself and family, for this company, the twelve and all the companies on the road." Brigham Young's company camped near Independence Rock eleven days later on 14 September. Clayton, *Journal*, 358; Bullock, *Camp of the Saints*, 284.
4. The decision to move on from this place for more favorable prey instead of waiting to service the ox teamsters who followed likely factored into the hostility manifest later between the two groups.
5. Almost two weeks later on 15 September at the same place, Brigham Young's camp noted that the "grass is nearly all eat away by Buffalo and Emigrating Camps, which gives our teams but a poor chance." Bullock, *Camp of the Saints*, 285.

& then he would be right there on the Spot.[6] he did not believe in Building so many Temples & then sell them to the Gentiles. Heber Kimbal is as good a man as Brigham Young & he [Young] does not receive revelations & I do not believe that Brigham Young is a Prophet or that he ever received any revelations but what he got from Joseph Smith & they are all written down beforehand."[7] Who can wonder that men who do not understand or treat with contempt the authority of the "Twelve" should refuse to obey their council & despise those whoom they have set to rule? The Lord will recompense them. the men are all in a great hurry to get home. I do not Know as I shall be able to detain them until the ox Teams come up. there [are] good fat Buffalo here but the feed is scant for our Teams so I have decided to go on to the ferry, 34 <mils> where there is feed & wood to dry meat.[8] Killed an Antelope.

Monday 6th [September 1847] moved on at an early hour & traveled 22 mils when we met a terrible, cold N East Storm of wind & rain ~~&~~ <which> compeled <us> to camp sooner than we would,[9] though we got pretty good feed for our Teams.

Tuesday 7th [September 1847] The rain continued all night & in the morning the Black Hills to the South of the river was covered with Snow. during the night a pair of oxen came to us on the road from the West, supposed to belong to the camp behind us.[10] while we were getting breakfast they put ahead & our

---

6. When Joseph Smith envisioned the removal of the Latter-day Saints to Jackson County, Missouri, in the early 1830s they were promised by their Prophet that the general area would serve as the center of Mormonism prior to the Second Advent of Jesus Christ. Once the Mormons were expelled in the 1830s from Missouri, talk of returning to Jackson County to acquire their "inheritance" became a recurrent theme thereafter. As early as December 1833, William W. Phelps wrote the Missouri governor that the Saints planned "to return to Jackson County." Smith, *History of the Church*, 1:452.
7. The reasons for Joseph Hancock's sour attitude toward Brigham Young are not known. Hancock, a year older than Young at 47 years, was one of Mormonism's early converts, had served in Zion's Camp in 1834, and experienced the optimism and disappointments of Kirtland and Nauvoo. His nomadic behavior after returning to Utah two years later, described as a "wandering nature," included time in California, the East, and the Missouri River Valley, where he stayed until returning to Utah in 1882 where he died in 1893. "1847 Pioneers," *1997–98 Church Almanac*, 136–137.
8. Here, again, is another situation where Jacob, had he waited for the ox teams, may have mitigated the fracture that divided the groups later, though it is clear he had little influence over the hunters. One of the hunters, Lewis Barney, wrote that due to the lack of game "We were under the necesity of going much further than we anticipated before we Could make a halt to kill and dry meat for the Company with the ox teams." Barney, Autobiography and diary, 48.
9. On the same day, William Clayton, with the ox teams close on the heals of the hunters, noted the seasonal change, stating that "Some of the teamsters have only a light summercoat with them and they suffer considerably." Clayton, *Journal*, 359.
10. On the same day William Clayton noted the missing animals: "This morning our cattle were all missing." Two of the teamsters "started early on foot to hunt the cattle but after

horsemen did not overtake them u[n]till they were half way to the Ferry & then they could not stop them but they went on down the river. we moved on in the rain which became Snow as we were passing over a Spur of the Black Hills. about 11 oclock the clouds broke away & the Storm ceased a little. after noon we arrived <& camped> on the banks of the Platte above the upper Ferry & [the storm] became more moderate.[11]

Wednesday 8th [September 1847] Eight men went out [to] hunt Buffalo & about noon the Head of our ox Te[a]m company arrived, 4 Waggons led by Br W[illia]m Clayton who told <me> he should go right on & not stop to hunt but Kill meat by the way.[12] two hours after, the main body passed by but did not Stop to say how do you do, but moved on down the river! towards night our Hunters came in. Isaac Carpenter & L[ewis] Barney Killd each an Antelope.[13] Joseph Hancock wounded a Bear. four Horseme[n] went in pursuit but he escaped into the mountain. Jack Reding requested me to go on with him & [William] Clayton.[14]

Thursday 9th [September 1847] As Capt. [Tunis] Rappleye did not think proper to call on us to see whether we were Trappers, Indians, or White men, I do not think [it] proper to place myself & company under his Jurisdiction. so we started before sunrise & drove to the Lower Ferry 6 <1/4> miles where Br [William] Clayton, J[ohn]. Pack, & [Jack] Reding were camped before they got under way.[15] three miles after I forded the river, I passed the other company

---

following them over seven miles in the storm and seeing that they had kept on the road towards the Platte river, they returned to camp." Clayton, *Journal*, 359.

11. When Brigham Young's camp reached this area on 17 September, Thomas Bullock illustrated the speedier character of the westbound versus eastbound treks by observing that "We were 42 days going from this Spot to Great Salt Lake City, including stoppages. We are 23 days coming from Great Salt Lake City to this place, including stoppages or 19 *days* quicker on return journey." Bullock, *Camp of the Saints*, 286.
12. This four-wagon advance detail of the ox teams was apparently headed by William Clayton, whose chronicle augments Jacob's hereafter until their arrival at Winter Quarters.
13. Lewis Barney, one of Jacob's hunters and who turned 39 that day, wrote that at the "upper Crosing of the Plat River" they decided to "stop for the purpose of Laying in a Suply of Beef for the ox team Company." But upon the hunters' return in the evening they found "that the ox teams had past about the middle of the after noon and had gone on down the River never Stopping to Say, 'how do you doo,' 'good by' or any thing else. On hearing this our Company fell themselves Slighted and insulted. So they [the hunters] held a Council and it was Resolved to Start the next morning by Sunrise." Barney, Autobiography and diary, 48.
14. William Clayton's account for the day, which noted their finding "N. Jacobs and company there hunting," gives no hint at this point of bad feelings between the groups. Clayton, *Journal*, 360.
15. Upon reaching the camp which had passed them, Lewis Barney wrote, "We caled a halt and Asked them why they did not stop at our Camp, that we had killed a large qu[a]ntity of meat for them and as they did not stop we left it where it was killed for the wolves.

who stop[ped] here to hunt today. one of their Hunters came to my camp after dark last night expecting to find his company with us, having Killed two Buffalo 5 miles up the river & left a man to watch the meat through the night. after Joining Capt. Reding's company, we continued down the river 18 miles & halted for diner. while here J[oseph]. Hancock came in having shot an Elk up towards the foot of the mountain. six Horsemen went to get the meat & we moved on 12 miles & camped on deer creek. after dark our Hunters came in with the Elk. they found an Indian's arrow two thirds the length of it in his side. it had been recently shot. Our company now consists of sevn Waggons & 21 men.[16] We are now at the most Northern Point of the whole rout about 43°.

Friday 10th [September 1847] moved on down the river 5 miles then commenced winding our way over the Black Hills. made 17 1/2 miles & camped on Ra la Prele creek. [Ezra] Beksted [Beckstead] Killed a Buffalo & L[ewis]. Barney another. a few miles after we started this morning, [we] Saw a company of 6 or 7 men & 17 or 18 <horses> moveing down on the other side of the river, supposed to be Indians.

Satturday 11th [September 1847] Early this morning Brethren [Eric] Glines, N[orman]. Taylor, & [Lyman] Curtis arrived from the other camp & report 17 or 18 horses stolen from them night before last which are undoubtedly those we saw yesterday.[17] we moved on 19 1/2 miles & camped on Big Timber creek. Isaac Carpenter Killed a Buffalo.

Sunday 12th [September 1847] Traveled 15 1/2 miles & camped on Horse

---

They said they Could kill their own and wanted none of [our] help." The collective insult became personal when, according to Barney, "Lyman Curtis Came to me and demanded his horse he had agreed to let me have untill we got home." Barney, whose fine horse had been accidentally killed on 28 April near the Loup Fork River, was then required to team with John Norton and his mare for the remainder of the journey. Again, William Clayton's daily account for 9 September mentions nothing about hard feelings between the groups. Barney, Autobiography and diary, 49; Clayton, *Journal*, 360.

16. This is the count of the hunters and the advance of the ox teamsters.
17. Lewis Barney, having just had the use of Lyman Curtis's horse taken from him, took a little perverse pleasure in describing the circumstance. He noted that having noticed "a large band of Indians travling down the River on the opposite Side with a large band of horses" he said to his companions, "there is a horse in that band [that] looks like Lymans horse." The following morning, he wrote, "Erick glines and 2 other men Came to our Camp and enquired if we had Seen any thing of their horses, Stating that they had lost 18 head last night.' We then told them that we had seen a band of Indians traveling down the River on the other Side of with a large band of horses and that they had a large grey horse with them that looked very much like Lyman Curtises White horse that he took from me when we pased their Camp. They said that was one of the horses that was missing. We were then Satisfied that the Indians had the horses." They learned on 14 September that their animals had been taken by the Sioux Indians. Barney, Autobiography and diary, 49.

Shoe creek. for three days we have seen hundreds of Buffalo.[18] The Trees here exibit the yellow leaves of Autum.

Monday 13th [September 1847] moved on 14 miles & camped on Bitter creek.

Tuesday 14th [September 1847] Traveled 24 miles & camped on on the river 4 1/2 miles above the old Fort [John]. There [William] Empey, Luke Johnson, & Appleton Harmon[19] came to us from the Fort, an Indian having carried the news that we were over the Bluff. they gave us account of the Horses that [were] taken up at the crossing. a Band of Sio[u]x have them over on the Raw Hide, some 15 miles North. Phineas Young & W[illia]m Casto have gone on down the river.[20]

Wednesday 15th [September 1847] Thos Brown & the Soldiers, except David M. Perkins, have been, ever since we came into the Green river Valley, Bulling about going on ahead. this morning they, with W[illia]m. Clayton's & Jack Reding, made a break & away they went. W[illia]m Empy came in with his Waggon to travel with us. Luke Johnson went with an Interpreter in pursuit of the lost Horses & A[ppleton] Harmon hired to work at Black Smithing at the Fort, $25.00 per month.

We moved on 4 miles, crossed the river & down it 16 miles & camped, having overtaken our runaway company. their courage has failed them.[21]

---

18. While there was not much variation in their diets at this point, "bread stuff is now out," being in buffalo country was a blessing to the travelers. They recognized that they had "to live solely on meat the balance of the journey," but at least they could sustain themselves for a time. But all were not grateful. Shortages produced feelings. William Clayton noted that John Pack "has got flour enough to last him through," and that with the companies' staples gone he "proposes for each man to mess by himself." Clayton also described Pack concealing "his flour and beans together with tea, coffee, sugar, etc.," until "the rest have gone to bed" when he prepared his meals. Ten days later Clayton complained about Pack's repeated selfishness again declaring, "He has disgraced himself in the estimation of many within the past few days." Clayton, *Journal*, 361–362, 366.
19. These men were part of the detail left to man the ferry on the North Platte River earlier in the year.
20. Phinehas Young and several others were among those who independently returned to Winter Quarters outside of the organized parties. Hosea Stout noted their arrival and their report about the Salt Lake Valley on 3 October 1847, nearly three weeks before the company with which Jacob traveled arrived at Winter Quarters. Stout, *On the Mormon Frontier*, 1:277.
21. William Clayton, having previously neglected to identify rancor within the merged groups, reported on 15 September that, after having left his brethren behind, "The ox teams have kept nearly up with us and it is evident they intend to keep with us or kill their teams." He noted that "if the teams are injured we shall be blamed for it," so his small group, whom Jacob identified as "runaways," determined to "give up going ahead to save the teams," though Jacob claimed it was their "courage that failed them." Clayton, *Journal*, 363.

Thursday 16th [September 1847] We all moved on together again, made 20 miles & camped near the river where we camped going up when Br Brigham [Young] called the camp together & told them he was going no further until there was a different Spirit manifest.[22] well, would to God that a different Spirit preavailed in this camp, for I can discover that some are yet for going ahead & leave all the Waggons & take all the arms they can get. but Richard Smith & Isaac Carpenter say they will not go.

Friday 17th [September 1847] Moved on 18 miles. Thos. Brown, Ezra Becksted, W[illia]m Bird, David M. Perkins, Benjamin Roberts & Madison Welsh Started on ahead again for Winter Quarters.[23] after we camped there was a consultation among us whether we had not Stop here & rest our Teams, as the feed is good, until the Brethren who are behind come up with us.

Satturday 18th [September 1847] Five Lodges were seen three miles below on the other side of the river & two Frenchmen came up to our camp & said if we would come down they would like <to> trade some with us. accordingly, we moved our camp dow[n] & some of the Brethren went over.

Last night at 12 oclock John Pack's grey mare, a valuable animal, was stolen ~~from~~ being tied to the fore wheel of his [wagon] within ten feet of the dog & 20 or 30 from two men on guard. It made no small stir in [our] little camp. I immediately gave it as my opinion that it <was> done by some man acquainted with the manner pursued every night in fastening that mare & also with the dog who is verry cross. for giving this opinion I was, with some others, verry much sensured by W[illia]m Clayton, as though it was slandering the men who had Just left us. but, on examining, the mare was tracked to their camp five miles below.[24]

I went over & traded some shirts with the Frenchmen for five Buffalo Robes. they requested us to go down below with them to hunt.

Sunday 19th [September 1847] moved down sevn or eight miles. L[ewis]. Barney Killed an Antelope.[25] the French & Indians Killed two Buffalo.

---

22. This is a reference to Brigham Young's excoriation of the westbound vanguard on 29 May at Scotts Bluff, the site where the returnees were camped on 16 September.

23. This group, several of whom came from Jacob's band of hunters, left their brethren, according to William Clayton "in consequence of having no bread." Clayton, *Journal*, 363.

24. William Clayton's view of the matter on 18 September reads: "Last night John Pack's gray horse was stolen from his wagon. He lays it to the brethren ahead [the handful of men who left for Winter Quarters on 17 September] and with Norton Jacobs and Joseph Hancock has heaped a pretty long string of severe abusive language on them which I consider to be premature, unjustifiable and wicked." As events unfolded, Jacob's allegations were proven to be accurate. Clayton, *Journal*, 363; Barney, *One Side by Himself*, 110–111.

25. William Clayton noted the meat provided by Lewis Barney was much needed giving "us a little fresh meat," though he inferred it was a buffalo. Clayton, *Journal*, 364.

Monday 20th [September 1847] moved down about six miles to get better feed where we camped with intention of waiting until the Twelve overtak us.[26] Joseph Hancock Killed a Buffalo. there is thousands of them in sight & the cows are verry fat. the greatest number are Bulls & most of them poor. Isaac Carpenter Killed a fine cow.

Tuesday 21st [September 1847] Remained encamped. W[illia]m. Empey Shot a cow & drove her up to the camp where he Killed her.[27] [John Baptiste] Richards,[28] the Frenchman, & his Indians are daily Chasing them so that we have a poor chance.[29] A cold Storm of rain.

Wednesday <22d> [September 1847][30] We have had fine weather for 2 weeks past. the Buffalo are principaly out of sight now.

Thursday 23d [September 1847] A hard frost. Some of our men went down the river to look for Buffalo but found none fit to Kill. The Frenchmen went further down & Killed four cows. when thirsty in the chase, the Indians will cut a vein & drink the blood of the Buffalo & eat the liver raw. Capt. [Jackson] Redding & another man started back with the Spy glass to look for [the] other company. they found them & they camped about 5 miles above us, having obtained most of their lost Horses. last Satturday a Sio[u]x Indian brought down to Fort John nine Horses & mules which he stole from the "Twelve" at

---

26. Jacob may have inadvertently misrepresented what the camp had actually decided when he stated that they planned to stay in camp at Chimney Rock until Brigham Young's company arrived. William Clayton's parallel statement that they "concluded to wait here until the balance of the company arrives," suggests, because of what actually happened, that their intent was to wait for the trailing ox teamsters and not Young's company. The hunters and advance ox teamsters waited at Chimney Rock from Monday, 20 September, until Friday, 24 September, when they received word that the ox teams were just a few miles behind, while Brigham Young's company did not reach that place until the following Wednesday, 29 September. Clayton, *Journal*, 364; Bullock, *Camp of the Saints*, 299.
27. An arrangement between William Empey and Lewis Barney called for Barney to "kill game and he [Empey] would hawl it to Camp and we would devide the tallow between us." Barney, Autobiography and diary, 50.
28. This probably refers to John Baptiste Richard, "Reshaw" with French flavor, (1810–1875), who was born in Missouri. Involved in the fur trade from his youth, he partnered with four men in 1845 to build a rival post to Fort John (Laramie) called Fort Bernard, located eight miles east of the more famous fort. Richard ably led the party of Mississippi Mormons from Fort Laramie to winter at Pueblo, Colorado in 1846. While he was gone his fort was burned. He later located a trading post at Ash Point, about twenty miles below Fort Laramie. Richard's life is summarized in McDermott, "John Baptiste Richard," 289, 294–296.
29. The French hosted the Mormons for supper, who "went over the river and had a good feast on buffalo ribs" which were "cooked by a squaw but looked much cleaner than our men cook it." Clayton, *Journal*, 364.
30. Because the trailing teamsters had not arrived on this day, the advance men determined "there is something the matter with them." Clayton, *Journal*, 364.

the South Pass on the night of the Snow Storm,[31] which came on us the 7th inst. Luke Johnson, Col [Jesse] Little & some others, having obtained a part of the Horses, started back last Monday to meet the company.

Friday 24th [September 1847] Moved on, the company following us in sight.[32] Made 13 miles & camped on the river bank. they came up & camped near by. Joseph Hancock Killed a fine fat cow which we gave to the company as they were living on lean Bull meat.[33]

Satturday 25th [September 1847] This morning took our position with the first Ten of [the] second Division in the ox Team company.[34] moved on 20 miles & camped on the river bank.[35] saw thousands of Buffalo. 7 were Killed & brought into <camp>.

---

31. The confrontation between Brigham Young's company and the Sioux aroused great fear and anger among the Saints before ending peacefully. After a scene of great confusion, with "Indians after Indians . . . pouring into sight & sweeping thro' the valley like a torrent," the "Indians discovered that the horses belonged to a camp of White men [rather than being Shoshone horses]." Thomas Bullock reported that shortly afterwards they "saw 'Wash te cha' & several of the Indians who visited us on the 25th of May last & we found our old acquaintances of the Dacotah tribe. They appeared friendly, telling us thro' the Frenchmen that we should have all our horses again & several of the Indians were sent after them." Leaders of the Sioux and the Mormons "sat down to smoke the pipe of peace, while 200 [Indians] sat & or stood behind." Bullock, *Camp of the Saints*, 289; Clayton, *Journal*, 365.
32. Lewis Barney wrote that upon discovering the ox teamsters "in Sight about 7 miles up the River . . . orders was given to moove on which was quickly obeyed." Barney, Autobiography and diary, 50.
33. Lewis Barney's portrayal of the evening's events shows that brotherly affinity trumps hard feelings, especially when hunger dictates.

> about 10 o'clock in the evening the Camp of ox teams Came up and Called a halt. Brother John Gleason and Carpenter Came to my wagon and Said, "Barney, have you anything to eat?" I told them I had aplenty. They then replied, "Well, we have not had a morsel to eat for the last three days and the whole Camp is nearly Starved." I replied, "well John, what will you have? I have aplenty of dried and green meat fresh from the plains. but I have not a morsel of flour." I then handed them a quarter of Antelope and piece of buffalo beef. Joseph Hancock allso handed them the hind quarter of an elk. I then furnished them with Cooking vessels and Said, "now boys, help yourselves," Which they Readily did keeping up afire and roasting, boiling, and frying meat untill day light, The whole Camp following Suit. During the night all past feelings were droped and many hearty jokes past. To say the least it was a night long to be remembered for the good feeling and social that [we] enjoyed in a wildernes exposed to the ruthless savages and Starvation, driven by our enemies from the face of Civilation to Die in the wilderness. Yet the hand of providence alone delivered us from all these evils and Comforted our harts with his holy spirit. The next day we resumed our journey and travled to geather as a band of brethren should do. Barney, Autobiography and diary, 50–51.

34. Upon the hunters and ox teamsters joining together, according to William Clayton, "Most of the camp now begin to feel as it is necessary for us to make our way home as fast as possible to save our teams and escape the cold rain and snowstorms." Clayton, *Journal*, 366.
35. William Clayton identified the stream as Crab Creek. Clayton, *Journal*, 365.

Sunday 26 [September 1847] We have beautiful warm weather, so we tarryed here to dry our meat & all hands went out to Hunt who wanted to help themselves to meat.[36] 14 Buffalo were brought in by those of the second Division, while the first Killed none. we gave them one & a half.[37] I shot two down within six feet of each other & gave one to Tho. Clowerd [Cloward] for helping to dress & haul them in.[38] Isaac carpenter Killed one.

Monday 27th [September 1847] The first Division, together with [Lewis] Barney's, [William] Clayton's, [William] Empy's, & [Henry] Sanderson's Waggons & Jack Reding went on down the river 5 or 6 miles to Hunt while

---

36. The hunting free-for-all was due, according to William Clayton, to the abundance of game at this place, recognizing that the meat would have "to last us through as it is not likely we shall have another privilege as good as this" upon the Nebraska plain. Clayton, *Journal*, 366.
37. This disparity in success found William Clayton complaining that "During the day the second division killed more than enough meat to last them home, but were totally unwilling to let the first division have any although they killed none, not having but two or three guns in the division." One of the meatless, Clayton groused that the inequity "tended to increase the feeling of envy and bitterness which already exists too much." Clayton, *Journal*, 366–367.
38. Lewis Barney described a humorous incident amidst this flurry of hunting activity involving several of his brethren.

    With "Captain Wm. Clayton and william Empy and several others," he "Started out ahead of the train" and chanced upon "a small herd of buffalo feeding on our Course." Barney wrote that he "went on and Crept up to them and fired," downing one, while the others ran off "about a quarter of a mile" before they stopped. "as luck would have it," he continued, "Erick glines hapened to be in about 100 yards of them. he fired and brought one of them to the ground. by this time I Came in Shooting distance and shot another. this one ran a little off over a rise of ground and fell. Erick then Shot and killed another. I also kiled one more. he kiled his third bufalo, making six in all." As the smoke cleared, others in the company arrived on the scene where they found "five buffaloes laing dead on the ground as we suposed." Barney, sensing the moment, said "I thought I would have a little fun with Erick so I Said, 'Erick, which of these buffalo did you kill?'" Glines, "pointing to the ones [he] had kiled," said, "I killed this one and that one and that one," identifying the three he had shot. But Barney countered saying, "I know I killed this one," whereupon Glines, "Standing Close to it," emphatically stated, "I know I killed that one myself." Clayton and several others, watching the encounter, sensed Barney's mischief and played along. Barney, turning to Clayton, said "Captain, didn't you see m[e] kill three buffalo?" Clayton affirmed the suggestion: "'I know you killed thre for I seen them fall,' the rest of the Conpany Confirming his statement." Barney then set Glines up: "now Erick, I have proved that I killed three buffaloes and as there are but five here you Could not have killed but two." About this time, Barney said, "Erick was geting prety warm." The prankster "then said, 'now see here, Erick, . . . I believe I killed this one,'" and kicked it with his foot. As if on cue, Barney chortled, just "as soon as I gave it the kick," the buffalo "sprang to its feet and off it went at full spe[e]d as though nothing had been the mattere with it." With that Barney blandly acknowledged, "well Erick, I must have been mistaken. that must have been your Buffalo for I don't kill Buffalo like that So [that] they Come to liffe in half an hour after they have been killed." Everyone had a good laugh. Barney, Autobiography and diary, 51–53.

we tarryd to dry our meat.[39] five more Buffalo were brought in & two of them given to three Waggons of the first division that tarryed with us.[40] Joseph [Hancock] Killed one Buffalo.

Tuesday 28th [September 1847] Continued drying our meat till one oclock. moved on 20 miles & overtook the other company at 10 oclock at night.[41] some Dozen Indians came to us Just as we started.

Wednesday 29th [September 1847] traveled 19 1/2 miles & camped on the bank of the river Just below Sand Knobs.[42] an ox died last night.

Thursday 30th [September 1847] 4 miles, crossed Wolf creek. made 17 3/4 miles & camped at the mouth of rattle Snake creek.[43] By the request of Jackson Reding I took his place as captain of the first Ten in the second Division.

Friday first day of Oct [1847] moved on 20 miles.[44] John Norton Killed four Buffalo.

Satturday 2d [October 1847] traveled 19 1/2 miles.[45] Lewis Barney & Rawzell Stephens Killed each a Buffalo.

---

39. Having enough meat for themselves, this group, which William Clayton identified as Lisbon Lamb, Lewis Barney, and John Norton, "volunteered to go and kill what meat they can for those who have none." Clayton, *Journal*, 367.
40. William Clayton, with others "of the first division who [had] no meat," concluded "to move on a few miles to where there are more buffalo as they have mostly left here, but the second division will not move till they have dried their meat some." Clayton, *Journal*, 367.

    Jacob, at this point in his account, apparently concluded not to include the fractious conduct which still prevailed between the camp's divisions. Clayton, however, made sure to note his disgust with some of his brethren—some by name, including Jacob—of whom he said: "Such little, selfish, unmanly conduct as has been manifested by them, is rarely exhibited except by the meanest classes of society. A man who will openly and boldly steal is honorable when compared with some of their underhanded conduct." The pettiness and self-interest, quite uncharacteristic of many of the men involved, is mostly attributable to the anxiety tainting the camp's yearning to get home. Clayton, *Journal*, 367.
41. They camped that night, according to William Clayton, on "Sand Hill Creek about a mile from the river." During their day's travel, Clayton noted, he had "seen more buffalo today than I ever saw in one day, supposed to be not less than 200,000." Clayton, *Journal*, 367–368.
42. In contrast to buffalo filling every horizon on 28 September, the beasts were scarcely seen the following day. Clayton, *Journal*, 368.
43. At the end of the day's journey, William Clayton wrote that "It appears that some of the brethren left their fires burning this morning and the prairie has caught fire and is still burning furiously." Clayton, *Journal*, 368.
44. The travelers camped on Bluff Creek. Clayton, *Journal*, 368.
45. It was a difficult day's trek. Intending to travel but eleven miles, they found there to be "no grass and were compelled to continue on." During the day, "Two of the oxen gave out and had to be left on the road." Clayton, *Journal*, 368–369.

Sunday 3d [October 1847] Moved on 3 miles to get feed & camped.[46]

Monday 4th [October 1847] Traveled 19 3/4 miles & camped near the Bluf.[47]

Tuesday 5th [October 1847] moved on 19 miles. camped on the river. Eight or ten Buffalo were Killed today. so as they were for stopping to dry their <meat>, Capt [Jackson] Reding, with the first Ten & 4 other waggons, moved forward, with <the> view of spurring forward the camp inasmuch as they have all the meat their Teams can haul. ~~we made 17 mile & camped on the rivir~~.

Wednesday 6th [October 1847] made 17 miles & camped on the river.[48]

Thursday 7th [October 1847] moved on 19 miles & camped on the river. we now decided to move slower until the company overtake us.

Friday 8th [October 1847] Just as we were moveing from our camp,[49] two Pawnee Indians were seen coming toward us on foot with a flag. in a few minuites a Dozen were gathered around & stopped our Teams, Seized a Horse & made signs for us to leave our waggons. we gave them some Salt & turned our course back towards the other company when they left us, driving off some loose oxen.[50] we proceeded back 5 miles when we met our company

46. On the first Sabbath of October they "camped opposite some islands [in the Platte River] where there is pretty good feed and willows." Clayton, *Journal*, 369.
47. William Clayton's account of the day reads: "We traveled twenty and three quarters miles and found that the last company have made a new road near the bluffs to avoid a very bad slough. We went a little on the old road and then struck across to the new road but had considerable difficulty in crossing the slough. We camped beside a small lake of not very good water and several miles from timber." Clayton, *Journal*, 369.
48. Jacob neglected at this point to note a significant division within the camp, which included him. Lewis Barney wrote that "A debate arose in Camp about remaining in Camp the next day to dry our beef. The Camp was devided on the Subject; about two thirds voted to Stop, the other third, not being Satisfied, Said they would not Stop. I told the Company that we were hurrying on too fast that we should wait here untill the twelve Came up. But few seemed willing [to] wait for them. Here then was another Split in Camp." Eleven wagons and twelve anxious men decided to move on toward home on the Missouri, including Norton Jacob, William Clayton, Jackson Redden, William Empey, Roswell Stevens, George Cummings, Joseph Hancock, Henry Sanderson, John Pack, Thomas Cloward, Zebedee Coltrin, and Barney, even though he initially weighed against the move. Barney, Autobiography and diary, 53–54; Clayton, *Journal*, 369–370.
49. The anxiousness, and poor judgment, of the men when they broke camp is shown in Lewis Barney's account: "as Soon as it was light, our little Camp was astir. every man Seemed to be his own Captain and apearantly tried to see who should be off first. Accordingly the first that Could get breakfast and harness up was the first to Start. So by the time the Sun was fairly u[p] the Camp was on the move, the first teams being a mile ahead by the time the last left the Camp ground." Barney, Autobiography and diary, 54.
50. While William Clayton, in his diary, added detail to this story, Lewis Barney prepared a lengthy and much more complicated account, illustrating that the encounter was not

& all moved down the river together & having made 5 miles,[51] camped at dark on the river bank.[52] recoverd the oxen from the <Indians>.

Satturday 9th [October] moved on at daylight to a small creek & halted for breakfast. in a couple of hours proceeded forward & having made 17 miles, camped opposite the head of Grand Island. here we fell in with some United States Soldiers exploreing the country for a Seite [site] for a Fort. the company consists of 60 men.[53]

---

just a robbery run amuck, but that the white men's lives were in peril. After parrying and fending with the Indians as they brashly tried to steal goods from the overlanders' wagons, as well as trying to relieve them of their animals, a show down materialized.

> At the same time, the Indian Chief Shouted to his men and in an instant they formed a line, every man with his gun Cocked and ready for the word for action. Their line was about 15 feet from us. It so hapened the Chies [Chief] Stood in front of me not more than 15 feet off, his gun in his hands nearly in a shooting position. I also had my rifle Cocked and elevated a little above his head with my eye fixt on his. he also had his eye on me. In this position we Stood about two minutes. not a word was spoken on either side. I was determind; if the chief made the least move to Shoot I would put a ball through his breast. He Seeing the position and danger he was in made a quick turn on his heel and gave a Shout to his men. they all whirled round and Started off full Speed. they went as fast as they Come and was soon out of Sight.

Barney was so unnerved by the confrontation that he babbled to his comrades "that we go back to the other Company, repeating it perhps fifty times." Clayton, *Journal*, 370–371; Barney, Autobiography and diary, 56; Barney, *One Side by Himself*, 113–114.

51. The anxious twelve, upon their return to their brethren with their tails between their legs, suffered the humiliation of having to acknowledge their poor judgment, as described by William Clayton: "After traveling back about six miles, we met the company, told the story and bore their slang and insults without saying much, but not without thinking a great deal." Clayton, *Journal*, 371.

52. William Clayton, very sensitive to the humiliating situation, stated that upon camping that night he endured "Many hard speeches [passing] among the brethren, such as 'damned hypocrites,' 'damned liars,' 'mutineers,' etc., and most of those who started ahead are ordered to travel in the rear all the time." After several more ugly gestures between the groups, Clayton resolved: "For my part, I shall be glad when I get in more peaceable society, and I think I shall not easily be caught in such a scrape again." Lewis Barney, who did not take it nearly as hard as Clayton, once the awkwardness was over, stated, "We again Resolved to travel togeather as brethren and no more Seperate untill we reached winter quarters. all former feelings and difficulties was again laid aside." Clayton, *Journal*, 371; Barney, Autobiography and diary, 56.

53. In September 1847, Lt. Daniel Woodbury, a U.S. Army topographical engineer, with seventy men, departed his post at Fort Kearny (at present Nebraska City, Nebraska) under orders to select a site for a military post on the Platte River. The installation was planned to protect emigrant travel along the Platte River road from Indian depredations. The new post, also named Fort Kearny, after the Nebraska City location was abandoned, was established 117 miles west of its predecessor which was located on the Missouri River. The original intent was to use Mormons at Winter Quarters to help supply the site. The fort was completed in 1848. Frazer, *Forts of the West*, 88–89; http://kearnykomets.sdcs.

    William Clayton's particulars about their meeting on 9 October with the U.S. military varies some from Jacob: "A United States soldier came up to the wagons and went

Sunday 10<th> [October 1847] Held council to consider the propriety of stoping here for the "Twelve" when it [was] dicided to move on slowly.[54] The Soldiers Started down on the opposite side of the river & <we> moved on 16 miles & camped in the bottom on the river.[55]

Monday 11th [October 1847] A cold rainy morning but broke away towards noon. traveled 17 1/4 miles and camped on a Slough.[56]

Tuesday 12th [October 1847][57] Started out this morning, when we were delayed by some oxen being missing, till eleven oclock when we proceeded on, crossed Wood river & bore off towards the Loup Fork. made 15 3/4 miles & camped on Prarie creek.

Wednesday 13th [October 1847] moved on over the Sand Hills 21 1/4 miles & camped on the bank of the Loupe Fork.

Thursday 14th [October 1847] Just as we were fileing out of camp to go

---

with us a few miles. He says there are ninety of them on the island surveying and looking out a place to build a fort." The Mormons learned, after a "number of the soldiers came over to camp," that "the Pawnees are perfectly enraged and savage and that the worst band of between four and five hundred are on the north side of the Platte about forty miles below." This, of course, elevated the anxiety of the men who recognized they had to pass through this vicinity to get back to Winter Quarters. Clayton, *Journal*, 372.

54. The vote, according to William Clayton, was "Thirty men voted to go on, seventeen voted to wait and the remainder did not vote." Clayton, *Journal*, 372.
55. Hosea Stout, with a relief party of fifteen having left Winter Quarters to intercept those returning to the Missouri River from the Salt Lake Valley, upon hearing about the federal troops from the advance team of pioneers was suspicious "that some trickery was afoot" on the part of the government toward the Latter-day Saints. Stout, *On the Mormon Frontier*, 1:281.
56. The travelers were "much dissatisfied with the camping place" at the slough, though it was "amongst high grass close to timber." Clayton, *Journal*, 372–73.
57. While there had been no communication between Brigham Young's company and the hunters and ox teamsters, the former had drawn a conclusion about the latter expressed on this day, 12 October: "In talking about the Ox Teams the Doctor [Willard Richards] said they were rebellious & if they did not think they were, they had only to look at their instructions, which they had in their pockets." And on 16 October, after noting "many signs of the ox teams having gone this route," Thomas Bullock stated "they were perfectly satisfied that the Ox teams were running ahead at 25 miles a day, perfectly reckless of their promises & determined to leave us at the mercy of the weather." Bullock, *Camp of the Saints*, 309, 312.

The very real hardship in which Young's group found themselves is expressed in John Brown's summarization of their plight after they left Fort Laramie. With their "teams being so reduced, we feared that we should not be able to get our wagons in, and lest the ox teams should not wait for us, at the head of Grand Island, they having surplus teams, it was thought best to send an express after them." Brown, one of twelve who raced ahead of Young's group on foot to catch the ox teams, gave up the chase after ten days of fruitless pursuit, having "suffered much from fatigue and cold." Little wonder some in Young's group felt disgust toward the ox teamsters. Brown, *Autobiography*, 86.

up the river a mile to cross at a ford I had Searched out, we discovered a number of men on the opposite Bluff whoom we took to be Indians but they displayed a white flag & fired one round & gave three cheers. we ~~then~~ were then Satisfied they were some of our People. proceeded to cross over our Teams & found it to be Col. Hosea Stout with 15 men & two waggons, having come out to meet us.[58] we were rejoiced to meet <each other>. got our Teams all over by two oclock when we all camped together. Harmon D. Pearson's [Pierson] Team tired out yesterday & this evening he burnt his Waggon & put his Team on with another, saving the Irons. A hard frost this morning.

Friday 15th [October 1847] Col [Hosea] Stout's party crossed over the river & went on to meet the Twelve.[59] we were hindered till 9 1/2 oclock by an ox being lost. when we moved on 10 1/2 miles & camped on the river.

---

58. The sixteen men composing Hosea Stout's "Relief Party," called by William Clayton "the old police," departed Winter Quarters on 8 October 1847 to assist their brethren returning from the West. The men are identified by Stout, along "with [the] numbers of rounds of shot each one had in case we were attacted," in all 111 "rounds which would [have] enabled us to make a good defence if occasion had required." Nearing the "Upper Ford of the Loup Fork" on 14 October, Stout and his companions "discovered a white man on the other side of the river which was soon followed by a long train of waggons which we soon knew to be brethren so we drew up in order & fired a Salute to them which gave them to know who we were."

    Stout, after obviously having interviewed several of the men, wrote that those in this group were "but a portion of the pioneers who had been sent ahead with the ox teams to lay up Buffalo meat for the company who were to follow in a short time." He stated that "insted of [catering to the needs of Brigham Young and the Twelve, who were following several days behind,] they proceeded on & were now out of the Buffalo count[r]y leaving those who were to follow to shift for themselves." Stout blamed John Pack and William Clayton, "with some more to back them up," for instigating the abandonment of Young's company. However, to the others in this advance company, Stout called them "true and faithful Saints and viewed this treacherous act in its true light." In summary he wrote, "This is their own story and you may immagine our feeling of joy, anger & supprise on meeting them and recieving this intelligence." Stout, *On the Mormon Frontier*, 1:278–279, 281.

    Two weeks later, some in Young's company, as they neared Winter Quarters, were still complaining about the negligence of the ox teams and hunters. Thomas Bullock's closure to his comprehensive account of the vanguard's venture to and return from the West concludes with this statement: "At this place there was beautiful feed when our brethren passed, but the ox team company appears to be determined we should not have any of it for what they did not eat, they set fire to, leaving us a prairie of burnt ashes. The Doctor [Willard Richards] says 'the ox team company have gone on like a parcel of Geese: they eat all before them and shit on all behind them.'" Bullock, *Camp of the Saints*, 318.

59. Assisting Brigham Young's company was the primary objective of Hosea Stout's relief party, causing a disappointed Lewis Barney to write: "Not finding President young with us he went on not leaving a morsel of provisions with us." Stout's detail, on 18 October, eventually met up with Young's company "strung along the road some on foot & some a Horse back for three or four miles." Barney, Autobiography and diary, 58; Stout, *On the Mormon Frontier*, 1:283.

Satturday 16th [October 1847] Moved on at an early hour. crossed cedar creek, a large Stream 7 or 8 rods wide & 2 feet deep. 10 1/2 miles to the old Missionary Station. here was some three or four hundred Indians, Squaws & children engaged in gathering their corn & carrying it across the river as the Sioux have driven them away from here once this fall & they are fearful they will be upon them again.[60] moved on to Beaver creek 9 1/2 miles & camped. two Indians came to us with ears of corn to trade. Knowing the treachery of these Indians, we raised our camp & moved on by Moon light 5 miles & camped half past eight oclock without fire.

Sunday 17th [October 1847] Moved on to Looking Glass creek 1 mile & got our Breakfast, when we proceeded on down the river 15 miles & camped on its bank.

Monday 18th [October 1847] Traveled 16 miles & camped on Shell creek.

Tuesday 19th [October 1847] Moved on [blank] miles & camped at the Liberty Pole on the Platte.[61] here the Prarie is burnt.[62]

Wednesday 20th [October 1847] Move[d] on to the Elk Horn river 11 3/4

---

60. A small group of hunters, including William Clayton, Jackson Redden, William Empey, Joseph Hancock, and Lewis Barney, went in advance of their brethren "looking for game, being two or three miles ahead of the Camp." As related by Barney, the group,

> on reaching the Summit of a hill looking ahead 2 or 3 miles We saw the Missionary farm Covered with Pawnee Indians geathering Corn. No Sooner than we reached the Summit of the hill with our Covered wagons, the Indians discovered us And 5 of them Mounted their horses and Came dashing toward us at full speed. They dashed up to our wagons with long Spears in their hands in a State of great excitement. after pow wowing and maneuvering for a few minutes they exquired if we had seen anything of the Sioux Indians. As a Stratagem we told them we had and that they were Coming this way and would be here in two Sleeps. As they were at war with them this Stratagem had the desired affect. On learning this 2 of their number Started back back for the Station. as soon as they reached the field we Could see a general move among the Indians. the whole Camp was in motion geathering up their horses and in fifteen or 20 minutes there was a line of them Stringing out a mile or more long leaving the way Clear. Barney, Autobiography and diary, 57.

See also William Clayton's account of meeting the Pawnee, whom he said "show great fear of the Sioux." Clayton, *Journal*, 374.

The fear by the Pawnees of the Sioux at the time was exacerbated by a huge Sioux war party of 700 to 800, in May 1847, that fired the Loup Fork Pawnee village and later attacked a camp of 200 Pawnees killing eighty-three. Hyde, *Pawnee Indians*, 227.

61. The distance for the day, according to William Clayton, was "twenty-three and a quarter miles. Clayton, *Journal*, 375.
62. William Clayton, commenting on the burned prairie which he speculated stretched "probably to the Elk Horn [River]," also stated that they were "cheered by a view of the timber on that stream," knowing they were close to home. Clayton, *Journal*, 375.

m[iles] & crossed at the upper Ford.[63] then to the Papeau<n> [Papillon River] 8 1/4 miles where we camped after dark.

Thursday 21st [October 1847] This <day> went through to Winter Quarters 18 miles.[64] found the Brethren here enjoying peace & plenty, the earth having produced & brought forth in her Strength.[65]

Friday 22 [October 1847] I crossed the river & started late in the afternoon to go to my family. proceeded down the Missourie river 8 miles where I met Br Joel Ricks, from Nishnebotana [River in southwestern Iowa], who stopped & camped with me. we were rejoiced to see each other. he gave me inteligence of my family being will [well] & my having an heir, a female born on the 12th day of August last. my wife named her Emily Amelia.

Satturday 23d [October 1847] Just at day light Br [Joel] Ricks Started for Town. after he was gone I observed a singular Sign in the Heavns. the <full> Moon was near the Western Horizen & the first streaks of day light in the East. a broad crimson belt extended from East to West, forming a splendid Arch about as much inclined to the North as the Sun's path to the South. the belt was intersected in its whole length by divergeing rays of light whos center appeared to be in the Sun's place when on the merridian. This is one of the Signs of the Last days.[66] I moved on before Sun rise & arrived at Baker's camp,[67] the residence of my family, a little before Midnight, having traveled

---

63. Fording the Elkhorn River, they found the "water was nearly three feet deep and the bottom somewhat soft." Clayton, *Journal*, 375.
64. The 21 October arrival of the returnees to Winter Quarters included seventy-one men in thirty-three wagons with ninety-two yoke of oxen, their journey taking nine weeks and three days. Historian's Office, Manuscript History, Winter Quarters, 21 October 1847.
65. William Clayton's first view of the circumstances at Winter Quarters was not nearly as cheery as was Jacob's. He wrote upon meeting his family, "Their circumstances are not good, but in other respects they have been prosperous for which I thank my God. There has been much sickness here and many deaths during the fall and many are now suffering for lack of some of the comforts of life." Clayton, *Journal*, 376.
66. At this time, the anxiousness for the millennial reign of Jesus influenced the Latter-day Saints so completely that any extraordinary (to them) celestial phenomenon portended the imminence of its inauguration. Jacob, reflecting the views of his fellow Saints, exhibits this characteristic throughout the period covered by his record.
67. Jacob writes in his genealogy, accompanying this record as Appendix 1, that his daughter Emily Amelia was born on Silver Creek just two months before his return from the Great Basin, which suggests that Baker's Camp may have been located on Silver Creek in western Iowa. However, as Jacob also references his family's stay during his absence in proximity to Joel Ricks on the West Branch of the Nishnabotna River, the exact location of Baker's Camp is not known, though the latter location for Baker's Camp seems the most reasonable.

    The West Branch of the Nishnabotna River, somewhat paralleling nearby Silver Creek, served as the water supply for several temporary Mormon settlements in what is now western Mills County, in southwestern Iowa, located twenty miles or so southeast of Kanesville (Council Bluffs, Iowa). Baker's Camp, like Edwards's Camp and

30 miles.[68] I found my family al[l] well, though some of them have had the chill feever.

Sunday 24th [October 1847] attended meeting at Br Joel Ricks when the Brethren requested me to deliver a Lecture. I spoke to them concerning our Mission to the West & the Spot for the Location of the church according to the word of the Lord given to Br Joseph Smith, the Martyr.[69]

Sunday 31st [October 1847] The past week I have been engaged prepareing my family for winter. Br [Joel] Ricks & Br [Benjamin] Cross say that [I] had better not go down to Missourie to get work, for my labor will be required here to fit out waggons, yokes, &c, & they will be able to furnish me with what I want to fit out for the West next Spring. Held meeting to day at Br Ricks. Br [Thomas] Whittle Presided. Sister Shepherdson introduced a difference existing between her & Sister [Roxana] Cross, &, being counciled, they agreed to settle the affair.

Sunday 7th November [1847][70] Held our meeting as usual. Br [Benjamin] Cross Presided. the past week we have been engaged gath[er]ing corn. today got news of the safe return of the "Twelve" [to Winter Quarters] a week ago.

Monday 8th [November 1847] The first Snow fell <here>.

Sunday 14th [November 1847] having finished gathering corn, I went to mill & returned yesterday. Br [Lyman] Stoddard, who Presides over this District

---

Alpheus Cutler's "Big Grove on Silver Creek," was inhabited by those who planned to emigrate to Utah the following spring. Thomas Kane, who befriended the Saints in their lowly condition during this time referred to these temporary Mormon settlements as "Tabernacle Camps," some having Mormon "tabernacles" gracing the settlements. Historian's Office, Manuscript History, Cutler's Park.

68. Prior to the Mormons' temporary settlements in the region, the area had been uninhabited by Anglos. *History of Mills County, Iowa*, 515.

69. This references what had become, by this time, the widespread understanding among the Saints that Joseph Smith had prophesied the relocation of the Mormons to the Rocky Mountains. Christian, "Mormon Foreknowledge of the West," 12–14.

70. During the previous week on 4 November 1847, church leaders in Winter Quarters discussed the "advisability of selecting a gathering place for the Saints on the *East* side of the Missouri River." Four days later "At a meeting of the Twelve at Winter Quarters it was voted that the Saints vacate Winter Quarters in the spring of 1848 and go westward." The Saints, by previous agreement, were required to abandon Winter Quarters the following year. Of course, some had Utah on their minds. Those who were not prepared were required to relocate across the river in what became Pottawattamie County, Iowa. On 19 November 1847, Brigham Young solicited direction from the local government Indian agent regarding their future relocation. Historian's Office, Manuscript History, Winter Quarters, 4, 8, 14, 19 November 1847.

of country, visited our Branch yesterday. Preached to us last evening & also today, at Br [Joel] Ricks' house. Continued our meetings every Sunday at 10 oclock A.M. I went down to Missouri & worked a few days & earned 5 1/4 dollars which I laid out for necessarys for my family.[71]

[18 December 1847] Br [Lyman] Stoddard visited us again on Satturday, the 18th of Dec. Preached in the evening & also on Sunday following. Br [Joel] Ricks & my self now began to make arrangements to attend a conference of the Saints to commence on Friday the 24 instant[72] near the old Block <House>,[73] West of Muqueto [Mosquito] Creek, a conference having convened there some three weeks ago & adjourned, to build an House.[74]

Wednesday, 22d [December 1847] wee, <Br [Joel] Ricks & myself>, left home on Thursday, went over to Winter Quarters, had an interview with Br Heber C. Kimbal & received council from him about our preparations to fit ourselves to go West to the Valley of the Mountains next Spring.

Friday, 24th of Dec. [1847] Conference commenced in the commodious Logg House built by the Saints, being 40 by 60 feet, the Biggest Logg Cabin in the World![75] Much valuable instruction was given to the Saints during this

71. Hundreds of Latter-day Saint refugees temporarily settled in camps in the Missouri River Valley and, with local resources limited, traveled south into Missouri for supplies and to augment their desperate circumstances. The residents of Savannah, Weston, Westport (near Independence), and St. Joseph, Missouri, among other locations, provided opportunities for Mormons to sustain themselves during their temporary stay in their Missouri River camps. See Bennett, "Mormons and Missourians."

72. At this time, the factor of time characterized in conversation, correspondence, and elsewhere was generally designated by "instant" (indicating the present month), "ultimo" (the previous month), and "proximo" (the following month).

73. The "Old Block House," constructed of "logs and rough puncheons," was built in 1837 by United States military troops for defensive purposes and to keep peace among the Native Americans in the area. The following year the site became a Jesuit Mission, lasting until 1841. The site, called a fort by many, existed until 1857. The complex was built on the bluff in the east part of what is now Council Bluffs, Iowa. Babbitt, *Early Days at Council Bluffs*, 43–44.

74. Brigham Young proposed on 4 December 1847 the building of "a big log house in Miller's Hollow for the temporary use of the Saints, telling the congregation not to be surprised if a city should be built there." He later explained on 23 January 1848, "In December last we appointed a day to hold a conference on the other side of the [Missouri] river [from Winter Quarters], in a large double block house, occupied by one of the brethren, where the Saints congregated in such large numbers that we found it impracticable to continue our conference, the house being so crowded and many shouting at the windows to get in, so that we adjourned for three weeks to build a house capable of holding the Saints." Historian's Office, Manuscript History, Winter Quarters, 4 December 1847; Young to Orson Spencer, 23 January 1848, in Clark, *Messages*, 1:337.

75. The "Log Tabernacle" built by about 200 Mormon workmen, "erected in a short time, during the severest weather we have had this winter," was a "well-constructed, capacious

meeting, there being present of the "Twelve" Pres. Brigham Young, W[illard]. Richards, H[eber]. C. Kimbal, Orson Pratt, W[ilford]. Woodruff, G[eorge]. A. Smith, Amasa Lyman, and ~~Seth~~ <E[zra]. T.> Benson. at the close of the meeting on Sunday there was found to be present 700 persons & Notice was given that on the morrow every officer & member in this part of the <Land> Should be present & Br Kimbal prophesied that we be enabled to Kindle up such a fire among us that it would not soon go out.

Monday, 27th [December 1847] Conference remained in session all day, being addressed by Br Brigham [Young], H[eber]. C. Kimbal & others under the influence of the power of the Holy Ghost interspersed with most Heavnly music from the Brass Band. In the afternoon Br Orson Pratt introduced ~~of~~ the ~~reorganisei~~ subject of the reorganiseing [of] the Church by Electing a first Presidency, when after som<e> remarks by G[eorge]. A. Smith & A[masa]. Lyman, a motion was carried that this conference proceed to reorganise the church with a First Presidency, & also that Brigham Young be the First President. Heber C. Kimbal & Willard Richards wer chosen by President Young for his councilers which was sanctioned by the conference all without a dissenting voice.[76] when the conference wa[s] adjourned to meet at the same place on the 6th day of April next. the conference was closed by all the congregation uniting to praise the Lord with loud Hosanahs according to the order of the Priesthood in [the] manner following, Striking the right hand into the Palm of the left at the end of each word, Hosanah! Hosanah! Hosanah! To God and the Lamb! Amen! Amen! Amen! and Amen! Repeated three times.[77]

---

log house, 60 by 40 feet inside," seating "1000 persons, with a recess or stand 20 by 10 feet for the priesthood and clerk's bench." With "logs cut three miles away and carted to the site," the walls grew to "eight logs high," the "log roof was covered with willow, straw, and dirt," and a "large fireplace angled outward at the west end, and two stoves were placed in the building." Brigham Young characterized the building as "an ornament to this new country, and shows a little of Mormonism." Young to Orson Spencer, 23 January 1848, in Clark, *Messages*, 1:337; Bennett, *Mormons at the Missouri*, 212 (which also shows the building's configuration on page 213). Private parties recently reconstructed the structure, termed the Kanesville Log Tabernacle, in Council Bluffs, Iowa, at a location near the original site. LDS Church president Gordon Hinckley dedicated the reconstructed structure in 1997.

76. See Bergera, *Conflict in the Quorum*, 53–83, which contains a transcription of minutes of leadership meetings in November and December 1847 detailing the process to reconstitute the church's First Presidency. See also Bennett's discussion of Brigham Young's acquisition of complete control over church leadership and the Latter-day Saints at this time. Earlier in December 1847, private meetings were held by the Twelve Apostles where they acquiesced to Young's determination to reorganize the First Presidency, even though several had previously expressed opposition to the action believing the Twelve could lead the church as a quorum. Bennett, *Mormons at the Missouri*, 199–212.
77. This ritual known in the LDS Church as the "Hosanna Shout" is used when each new church president is accepted by church members in the transition from one church

A general meeting of the Saints was appointed to [be] held at this place on the 16th of January next [1848] as a Kind of Jubilee or time of rejoiceing & thanksgiving before the Lord.

One thing I would commemrate from the time of Joseph Smith's death to the time of Brigham Young's appointment to the first Presidency was Just three years & six months & took place about the same hour of the day!

---

president's administration to another, with one modification in procedure. Rather than the fist-to-palm described here, today a white handkerchief is held above and circled around the head while repeating the words "Hosanna, Hosanna, Hosanna, to God and the Lamb." The ritual is also employed in the dedication of the church's temples. See Woodbury, "Origin and Uses of the Sacred Hosanna Shout," 17–22.

1848

NORTON JACOB'S PLAN IN 1848 WAS to adequately outfit his wife and family for their journey to the Great Basin that summer. Preparing for months with hundreds of fellow Saints for their final push to the West, Jacob equipped his family and assisted his neighbors for their western adventure. Departing the first part of June, his family's overland travel, retracing the vanguards' route the previous year, found them in the Salt Lake Valley the third week of September. Before their arrival, Jacob's oldest son Oliver, ill since their departure, finally succumbed upon reaching Independence Rock. Once in Utah, Jacob quickly found employment constructing a mill for Heber Kimball north of Great Salt Lake City in what is now Bountiful. There he temporarily established his family.

Jan. first 1848. my wife made a New Year's Supper & invited the neighbors to partake of the feast. about a dozen attended & old Farther [Timothy Baldwin] Clark[1] from Winter Quarters, on a mission to Saints scatered through the country, happened to arrive Just at this time & partook of the feast with us. In the evening he preached to us at the house of Br [Joel] Ricks on the necissity of a reformation among the Saints.[2] next day, being Sunday, he preached to us again & in the evening. also Monday evening.

Having received a letter from my Daughter Elsie who, with her Husband Jesse Snyder, lives near St Jo[seph] in Mo.[3] I sent an answer to it by Father

1. This is probably Timothy Baldwin Clark.
2. Others have written about the notion of "reformation" among the Mormons during the 1840s and 1850s. The premise was not to reform the church's organization or doctrines but rather to refine the Saints' behavior. Regular preachments against iniquity and transgression filled the ears of Mormon congregations. The attempt by church leaders to arouse a righteous people prepared to receive Jesus upon his Second Advent is so central to Mormonism that its importance should not be minimized. See Peterson, "The Mormon Reformation of 1856–1857," 59–87; Peterson, "Brigham Young and the Mormon Reformation," 244–261; and Bennett, *We'll Find the Place*, 77–80.
3. Hundreds of Mormon refugees found economic subsistence in Missouri's northwestern towns and villages during the Saints' temporary hiatus along the Missouri River. St. Joseph, Buchanan County, is located in northwestern Missouri.

Clark who left us on his way <East>.[4]

14th [January 1848] I with my son Oliver [Jacob] took a Team & carryed a load of corn, 22 bush[el] sent by our Branch to Elder [Orson] Hide who is absent on <a> mission East.[5] we staid at his house over night & 15th [January 1848] went [to] Br Killy's[6] on Musqueto Creek[7] with whoom I had some business. tarryed over night. in the morning sent Oliver home with the Team while I tarryed with Br Killy & attended the Jubilee, or Jubilo as Br Brigham [Young] called it.[8]

Sunday 16th [January 1848] was spent in Preaching & teaching by Br Brigham [Young] & others & Monday [17 January], Tuesday [18 January], Wednesday [19 January] & Thursday [20 January] each day till one P.M. occupyed in Preaching & teaching & the remainder in praiseing the Lord with Singing, Instrumental music & the dance wherein old & young enjoyed themselves with much satisfaction.[9] From this meeting I went up to the big Camp <Winter Quarters> & returned home in company with Father [Alpheus] Cu[t]ler & his wife in their Buggy on Monday, the 24th [January 1848].[10] the same evening we were visited by Br [Lyman] Stod[d]ard & Bishop [Daniel] Corking [Carn?][11] soliciting aid for the Police. I gave a Buffalo Robe [worth] $3.00. The Branch was organised for going West in [the] manner following:

---

4. Timothy Baldwin Clark died later that year in Illinois.
5. George Smith and Orson Hyde were initially assigned to preside over the numerous Mormon settlements on the Missouri River, though, later Hyde became the principal ecclesiastical and temporal leader of the Saints in the region.
6. This may be Elick Kelly, though other Church members named Killy and Kelly lived in the area at the time. Also men with surnames of Keley and Kellie appear on the 1850 Pottawattamie County, Iowa, census list.
7. Evidence from the 1850 census of Pottawattamie County, Iowa, indicates numerous Mormons lived along Mosquito Creek, a substantial stream draining a portion of the county in a southwestern direction into the Missouri River.
8. As Jacob notes in his record, the Jubilee celebration, organized by the seventies quorums and held in the Log Tabernacle, lasted for most of the week. As many as 600 "saints and strangers" attended the meeting on 17 January. Brigham Young explained in a letter he wrote to Orson Spencer that while the seventies called the observance a jubilee, "I told them it could not be considered a Jubilee spoken of in the Revelations, for all bands were not broken, and I called it Jubilo." Young to Spencer, 23 January 1848, Clark, *Messages*, 1:339; Journal History, 16–17 January 1848.
9. Another action taken during the jubilee celebration was application to the Iowa legislature for county status for the region comprising the small but numerous Mormon settlements along the eastern bank of the Missouri River. Journal History, 16 January 1848.
10. Alpheus Cutler and his family also lived near the Nishnabotna's west branch, at a place called Silver Creek.
11. This may be Bishop Daniel Carn, though there is no explanation as to how Jacob could be so far off in the spelling of Carn's name. Carn was a bishop in both Nauvoo and Winter Quarters.

A Return of the Ten Norton Jacob Captn Company Being the Hundred in the 2nd Grand Division under H. C. Kimball

Names		Age	Teamsters	Wagons	Horses	Mules	Yoke of Oxen	Cows	Sheep	Bush Buck Wheat	Bush Corn	lbs Meat	cash Tools & Seeds
Norton	Jacob	43	1	1	-	-	2	1	-				Carpenter Tools
Emily	Jacob	37											Expect to go to the
Oliver B.	Jacob	14	1										
Lucian H	Jacob	12	1										Mountains
Ira N	Jacob	7											
Joseph	Jacob	3											
Emily Amelia	Jacob	6 months											
Joel	Ricks	44	1	6	5	-	13	13	18	20	200	200	Farmers Tools
Eleanor	Ricks	40											
Thomas C.	Ricks	19	1										
Lewis	Ricks	17	1										
Sally Ann	Ricks	15											Expects to go to the
Clarinda	Ricks	13											
Temperance	Ricks	11											Mountains
Wm	Ricks	9											
Jonathan	Ricks	7											
Mary E	Ricks	5											
Josiah	Ricks	3											
Bejamin	Cross	58	1	2	-	-	2	3	-	-	-	100	Expects to go to the
Roxana	Cross	55											Mountains
Thomas	Whittle	35	1	2	1	-	4	3	-	-	60	200	Farmers Tools
Mary	Whittle	30											Expects to go to the
Olive	Whittle	14											
John C	Whittle	12	1										Mountains
Mary E	Whittle	10											
George	Whittle	7											
Zerah	Whittle	5											
Emeline	Whittle	3											

This page and facing page: Norton Jacob's company of 1848 emigrants to Utah. Courtesy of the LDS Church Archives.

Name	Age												Remarks
[illegible]	8												
Dexter Stillman	48	1	1	-	-	2	1	3					Cant go
Barbara Stillman	39												
Clark Stillman	20	1											
Franklin Stillman	13	1											
Mary Stillman	11												
Elizabeth Stillman	8												
Asa Davis	65	1	1	-	1	1	2						Expects to go to the
Sally Davis	56												
Corydon Davis	16	1											Mountains
Rhoda Ann Davis	14												
Roxana Davis	39		1	-	-	1	2	-	4	100			A Widow
Charlotte Ann Davis	16												mountains
Philetus G. Davis	11	1											Expects to go to the
Squire Egleston	46	1	2	-	-	3	4	7		200	400		Carpenter & Farm Tools
Caroline Egleston	45												
[illegible] Egleston													Cant go
Wm Mathews	20	1											
Amanda M. Mathews	17							Young Stock	[illegible] Stock	Chickens	Dogs	Cats	
Jesse Folks	40	1	2	1	-	6	4	-	4	5	1	2	
Mary "	33												
Juliette Kay	21	1											
Amirica Folks													
Stephen D. "													
Teresey "													
Mary E "													

While at the Jubilee[12] I sent a letter to my friends in Hancock County Ill, the <following> being a coppy of it:

Winter Quarters, Camp of Isreal
Jan. 20th 1848
Dear Friends:

Mother, Brothers, & Sisters (though last, not least in my affections), having an opportunity of sending to you by Brother [Almon] Babbitt who has Just arrived from the lower world, I most cheerfuly embrace it to communicate a few thoughts. I have recently heard of the death of David Thompson[13] but not a word concerning anny others of my friends since I left the Land stained with the blood of the Martyrs![14] I feel to sympathise with <those> who have lost a Father. Of the acts & doings in your midst of the "Mob of Upper Standing," I am fully advertised, but what part, if anny, my Kinsmen have borne in that Tragedy I <am> not apprised but shall Know here after, & in the name of the Lord, whose servant I am, beseech my Friends to be careful that their hands be not found stained with the blood of the Saints, for a terrible retribution awaits all such, & is close at the door, except an atonement be made. now, I say this not to give uneasiness, but I feel a deep interest in your Salvation. and if anny have need of the benefit of an atonement, flee to the Saints who are prepared to give all necessary council & will afford the utmost relief, aid & assistance in the day of your calamity. Last Spring I went with the Pioneers led by the "Twelve" to seek the hiding place (an assylum of rest for all who are weary, borne down & oppressed with the corruption, abomination & wickedness of this generation) "until the indignation of the Lord shall pass over the nations."[15] After Journeying two & a half months in the wilderness & among the Mountains, the Lord led us to a Beautiful Spot in a Secluded Valley, recognised by us to be the identicle Spot as described by Joseph [Smith] the Martyr, Shown by the Lord to him and to others during the endowments in the Temple at Nauvoo,[16] Where they will establish a Stake of Zion & cause the Ensign of Freedom to be reared, Where the honest in heart & the oppressed of all nations, Kingdoms & countries may flee for

---

12. During the celebration, Jacob and hundreds of others also signed a petition, dated 20 January 1848, appealing to the federal government to establish a post office in Pottawattamie County, which request was granted for a Kanesville post office. The complete list of petitioners is published in Ward and Woods, "The 'Tabernacle Post Office.'"
13. David Thompson, the father-in-law of Jason Jacob, Norton Jacob's brother, is shown to own property in Hancock County, Illinois, in 1842 in Range 6N 6W. Hancock (Ill.: County) Assessor's Office, Books of Assessment, 1840, 1842, and 1850, p. 183.
14. The latter phrase is a reference to the assassination of Joseph and Hyrum Smith on 27 June 1844.
15. This passage states a sentiment expressed in numerous passages from the Mormons' Doctrine and Covenants, e.g., 45:47; 56:1; 84:96; 97:24; 101:11, 98.
16. Lewis Christian argues that Joseph Smith had visionary conception of the location of the Saints' future home in the Rocky Mountains much earlier than Jacob's statement indicates. Christian, "Mormon Foreknowledge of the West," 12–14.

reffuge when the overflowing Scourge shall pass through, and it matters not what may be their religion or Politicks, whether they worship one God, three, or none at all. But they must honor the God of Israel, <& must> not blaspheme his name, or the Saints' religion. Where equal & Just Laws will opperate for the protection, safety, & benefit of all of every nation, color & clime on the face of the whole Earth.[17] I returned to my family here on the 22 day of Oct. last, having traveled & drove my Team since the 7th day of April [1847] about twenty one hundred miles! I found my family all well with the addition of a Daughter born on the 12th of August [1847], named Emily. during my absence Father left this region of country for parts unknown to us, since which we have not heard from him.[18] I found, on my return, the Lord had prospered the Saints exceedingly having according to his promise, caused the Earth to bring forth in her s[t]rength so that we have an abundance of the good things of this Life, with Peace in our borders and are now engaged in celebrating a Period of praise & thanksgiving to the Lord, wherein wee partake largely of the good things of the Life to come, being the happyest People on the face of this Earth! In the comeing Spring we shall, with thousands of our Brethren & Sisters, flee to the Valley of the Mountains. Elsie P. [Norton Jacob's daughter] & her Husband [Jesse Snyder] intend to go with us. She has a Son about three weeks old.[19] Manny of the Saints will remain in this region preparing an outfit to go another year, so that whoever wish[es] can come on here & winter, as there will be companys fitting out from this point for several years to come.[20] This

17. The Latter-day Saints had, for the time, an unusually liberal posture regarding religious freedom and tolerance, undoubtedly formed by the absence of the same for them in the previous decade. Joseph Smith presented a bill to the Nauvoo City Council on 1 March 1841 as "An ordinance in relation to Religious Societies" that called for "Catholics, Presbyterians, Methodists, Baptists, Latter-day Saints, Quakers, Episcopals, Universalists, Unitarians, Mohammedans, and all other religious sects and denominations whatever" to have "free toleration, and equal privileges" in the city. In Brigham Young's and the Twelve Apostle's "General Epistle" to the church, written 23 December 1847, they reiterated the Saints' pledge to religious toleration and freedom in the spirit of Smith's call. Identifying the same religious groups as Smith, as well as "pagans," the epistle reads, "it mattereth not what a man's religious faith is . . . if he will bow the knee and with his tongue confess that Jesus is the Christ, and will support good and wholesome laws for the regulation of society, we hail him as a brother, and will stand by him while he stands by us in these things; for every man's religious faith is a matter between his own soul and his God alone." Nauvoo City, Council Proceedings, 1 March 1841; Smith, *History of the Church*, 4:306; General Epistle from the Council of the Twelve Apostles," 23 December 1847, in Clark, *Messages*, 1:334–335.
18. Udney Hay Jacob had apparently returned to be near his children in northeastern Hancock County, Illinois, near La Harpe, the very ones Norton addressed.
19. Elise Jacob Snyder and Jesse Snyder, with their child, did not accompany Norton Jacob's family to Utah in 1848. In a letter to his father, Norton Jacob, on 20 March 1849, wrote that Jesse Snyder had emigrated to Utah prior to that time. See the letter in the following chapter.
20. The Saints mostly evacuated the nearly one hundred Mormon settlements near the Missouri River in 1852, the heaviest year of Mormon emigration to the West when one-seventh of the entire pre-railroad emigration to Utah took place. It is important to note

Potawatomy district will probably soon be organised into a county of the State of Iowa, which comprises a large tract of rich soil with many good mill privileges.[21] I want you to write as soon as you receive this. if you send by private conveyance, direct your letters to Winter Quarters, Council Bluffs. if by mail, direct to Austin, Atchison Co., Mo.[22] Show this letter to all enquiring friends, especialy Thomas Gilmore[23] & John Houston [Huston][24], to whoom I promised to give information concerning the administration of Law &c among the Saints when untrameled by the world. Please to receive this as a testimony of the Love and fidelity of your Brother & friend, Norton Jacob. To Elizabeth, Jason K. [Jacob], & Stephen Jacob, Eliza Ann Andrus, & Mary Jaane Hamilton.[25]

Feb 16th [1848] Br Joel Ricks started to St Louis & to Illinois to get his money, returned the last of March, having had good success & laid in Supply to go over the mountains.

March 13th [1848] Br [William] Steel[26] & myself went down about forty miles into Mo. & took a Job building a mill dam.[27] we finished it about the first of April [1848]. for my share I received $11.85. I bought me ten Sheep at .75 per head, the wool off. after we returned home, Br [Abraham] Hodge, our Black Smith, having arrived, we set in to complete ~~our~~ fitting out our waggons &c for our Journey.

April 16th [1848] Father [Alpheus] Cutler arrived with his family from Winter Quarters,[28] having bought out Br [Joel] Ricks & let him have a yoke of oxen

---

that 1852 was also the largest year of travel to Oregon and California as well, meaning the overland roads were traveled as never before or after. Unruh, *The Plains Across*, 120.

21. Pottawattamie County, Iowa, (in the southern third of the western-most part of the state, with the Missouri River forming its western border) was organized by the Iowa legislature on 21 September 1848, though the county's southern section was subdivided to create Mills County in 1851, as was the northern part in 1853 to form Harrison County.
22. Atchison County, Missouri, is the northwestern-most county in that state.
23. Thomas Gilmore is shown as owning property in Hancock County, Illinois, in 1842 in Range 7N 6W. According to the 1842 tax assessment, he lived in proximity to the Jacob families in the county. Hancock (Ill.: County) Assessor's Office, Books of Assessment, 1840, 1842, and 1850, p. 183.
24. Three families of Hustons lived in proximity to the Jacobs in Range 6N 6W in Hancock County, Illinois, in 1842. Hancock (Ill.: County) Assessor's Office, Books of Assessment, 1840, 1842, and 1850, p. 183.
25. The addressees include Norton Jacob's mother and his siblings, Jason and Stephen Jacob, and Eliza Ann Jacob Andrus and Mary Jane Jacob Hamilton, all of whom lived in Hancock County, Illinois.
26. This is probably William Steele.
27. This is another evidence of the importance of the northwestern Missouri citizens and settlements to the Saints during their sojourn along the Missouri River.
28. Jacob's language suggests Alpheus Cutler and his family were about to join with the others intent on the Salt Lake Valley in the spring of 1848. This is not the case. Cutler, already

& Waggon. I received two letters from my Father in Hancock Co., Ill. under date of Feb 13th & 27th [1848], wherein he complains most bitterly of his seituation while here in the wilderness,[29] & it seems he is not much better pleased where he is as he says he is in the midtst of inveterate enemies. The following is an extract <of> a letter I returned in answer to his:

Baker's Camp,[30] April 23, 1848
Dear Father

When I came home last fall I had promised myself a great deal of pleasure in describing to you the countries & curiosities I had seen, especialy the rich & extensive Valley chosen for our present location, possesing a Beautifuly dry & salubrious climate & exilerating atmospere so admirably calculated to renovate your constitution by reason of the regular Bracing Salt Breeze coming from the N. West off the Great Salt Lake, being a verry large body of water 20 miles distant from & in sight of our camp, where we have laid out the Great Salt Lake City, Great Bason, North America, Latitude 40° 46". But I was deprived of this pleasure & the additional one of assisting you to remove in your old age to [this] most favored spot for health, even surpassing anny place that can be found on the sea coast.[31] Because for the want of faith you must needs go back after the Leeks & onions, thus distrusting the honor, the probity & the promise of God that when he went to cause Israe[l] to rest, the Earth, no longer bearing briars & thorns, should bring forth in her strength! There's no briars or thorns in the valley of the Utah, but an exceedingly fertile soil. and, if in your "Assylum" you & your children should meet with famine, pestilence & Sword, you will then remember the Prophesy which says, The time shall come that he that will not take up his sword against his neighbor must needs flee to Zion for safety, as they are the only people that are not at war among themselves.[32] Zion are the pure in heart[33] & they

---

at odds with Brigham Young and the Twelve Apostles, had designs to create a ministry to Native Americans in Kansas on the Delaware River. He moved between his Silver Creek settlement in southwestern Iowa and the mission on the Delaware River until being severed from the LDS Church in 1851, about the time he gave up his mission to the Indians. Jorgensen, "Cutler's Camp," 42; and Jorgensen, "The Cutlerites of Southwestern Iowa," 136–137, 141, 143.

29. Udney Jacob apparently never did have the comfortable fit for Mormonism acquired by his son Norton. The elder Jacob's tenuous posture regarding the LDS faith during this period is suggested by his action of leaving the body of Saints at the Missouri to return to Illinois and his other loved ones where he remained until 1850. It appears that he may have retained a feature of heterodoxy, even after his emigration to Utah and embrace of Mormon plural marriage.

30. It is not known exactly where this temporary camp was located along the Nishnabotna's west branch.

31. This, and Jacob's subsequent optimistic characterization in this letter of the region of the Great Basin, is yet another reflection that the Saints viewed their future in the Rocky Mountains to be providential.

32. Doctrine and Covenants 45:68, dated 7 March 1831.

33. Doctrine and Covenants 97:21, dated 2 August 1833.

shall dwell in peace & abundance. while speaking of war, I will remind you of the Prophesy of Joseph [Smith] concerning the appearance of a Sword for a long time han[g]ing so portentously in the S. West in Winter '43. He said it was the Sign of a long & bloody war that should commence in the S. West & finaly proceed to the East! (the direction the sword pointed)[34] Now, tell me why this government have not been able to make peace with Mexico, having constantly carryed the S[w]ord in one hand & the olive Branch in the other?[35]

April 25th [1848] Left Baker's Camp for the mountains at the head of my company consisting <of> Joel Ricks & family, 11 persons; Tho. Whittle & family, 8 persons; & Benj[amin] Cross & wife; with my own family [of seven] in all 28 persons, 11 Waggons, 5 Horses, 77 cattle, 54 sheep & 5 hogs.[36]

Friday 28th [1848] arrived at the Missouri River.

Monday May first [1848][37] the last of our company got over the river & we camped North of the [Turkey] creek in Winter Quarters waiting for the Presidency to get ready.[38] Br [Thomas] Whittle returned to our former camp to get oxen for Br [Heber] Kimbal. Br [Joel] Ricks gave Br H. C. Kimbal a Horse.

Friday 5th [May 1848] I went <to> work repairing Waggons for Br [Heber] Kimbal. they are waiting for a Boat to come up.

---

34. Joseph Smith's diary entry for 10 March 1843 (kept by Willard Richards) reads: "I, Willard W. Richards, discovered a stream of light in the South West quarter of the heavens. The pencil rays of light /were/ in the form of a broad sword with the hilt downward. The blade [was] raised, pointing from the west southwest raised at an angle of 45 degrees from the horizon, and extending nearly /or within 2 or 3 degrees/ to the Zenith of the degree where the sign appeared. This sign gradually disappeared from 7 1/2 o'clock and at 9 had entirely disappeared." Smith, *An American Prophet's Record*, 331; Smith, *History of the Church*, 5:300–301.
35. James Polk, eleventh United States president, and an enthusiastic expansionist, included the Mexican territory known as New Mexico and California on his agenda for acquisition after taking office in 1845. He attempted to diplomatically negotiate his design without success. In April 1846 hostilities erupted opening the war between the North American neighbors. After American troops gained the upper hand through strategic victories, a treaty was finally signed in February 1848 in Guadalupe-Hidalgo, Mexico, giving the United States the vast region Polk coveted in exchange for $15 million.
36. The company roster leaving Baker's Camp, listed on pages 262 and 263 , indicates that as many as twenty-five others, composing several families, planned to go but did not make the venture at the time. Once Jacob's company crossed the Missouri River, they were amalgamated into other, larger companies for crossing the plains.
37. On this date, Brigham Young "proposed that the companies emigrating west [that year] be organized at the Elkhorn [River]," about eighteen miles west of Winter Quarters. Historian's Office, 1 May 1848, First Division, 1848, Church Emigration, 1848–1849.
38. Getting ready would take one month before the huge companies departed the Elkhorn River for the Great Basin. The preparation for the 1848 emigration is discussed in Hartley, "Howard Egan," 38–40.

Sunday 7th [May 1848] attended meeting. Br Orson <Pratt> delivered an excelent discourse taking leave of his Brethren, prepareing to go to England.[39] My Son Oliver [Jacob] taken Sick with inflamatory Rheumatism.[40]

Tuesday 9th [May 1848] moved out 6 miles & being Joined [by] 8 of Br [Heber] Kimbals Waggons, formed a camp of 21 Waggons. Br Brigham [Young] accompanyed us. I returned to work at the Big Camp [Winter Quarters].

Friday 12th [May 1848] By Br Heber [Kimball]'s council I went out to our camp, Oliver [Jacob]'s Sickness requiring my presence.

Sunday 14th [May 1848] By external aplications, Sweating & administering in the name of the Lord, we obtained some power over the disease.[41] Received accessions to our camp so that it now numbers 50 Waggn.

Friday 19 [May 1848] Having continued to work until Wednesday, Br Heber [Kimball] requested me to go & examine a rout for a new Bridge on the Papilan [Papillion] Creek.[42] went in company with Joel Ricks, Daniel davis & Br [Timothy] Fooke [Foote],[43] reconoitered the route & returned to camp in the evening & reported. after deliberation it was decided to build the Bridge in <a> fine Grove a mile above the old one by which a good camping ground will be obtained & a mile or two saved in going to the Elk Horn [River].[44]

Satturday 20 [May 1848] Traveled over to the Papalan [Papillion Creek] with our company of 16 Waggons.[45] Br Lorenzo Snow's Pisgah co[mpany].,[46] &

---

39. Orson Pratt appointed to another tour of service to Great Britain, was commissioned to be president of the church's European Mission. Accompanied by his wife Sarah, the couple arrived in Liverpool on 20 July 1848. England, *Orson Pratt*, 142–143.
40. This is the beginning of the demise of Jacob's oldest son, fourteen-year-old Oliver, who had shouldered many adult responsibilities for his father.
41. Mormons, then and now, generally employ both faith ("administering in the name of the Lord") and science ("external applications") in matters of healing.
42. Nebraska's Papillion Creek flows southeasterly into the Missouri River and is located about eighteen miles west of Winter Quarters.
43. This is probably Timothy Foote.
44. Daniel Davis's diary entry for Wednesday, 17 May 1848, reads: "In the Morning Father [Heber Kimball] spoke to the company A short time & then Wanted Joel Rix, [Norton] Jacobs & I to go And look out A new road to the [Elk]horn River. We did so & Returned at four oclock. We could not find any better chance for A new road than the <Pioneer road>." Davis, Diaries, 17 May 1848.
45. Daniel Davis wrote on 20 May 1848, "This day [Joel] Rix & Family, Bro [Norton] Jacob, [Thomas] Whittle With their Familes moved on to the Papao [Papillon] to Build a Brige by Fathers [Heber Kimball] Request." Davis, Diaries, 20 May 1848.

    The Elkhorn River encampment where those bound in 1848 for the Great Basin gathered prior to departure is described in Hartley, "Howard Egan," 40–41.
46. Lorenzo Snow became presiding church authority at Mt. Pisgah in Iowa, in the spring of 1847, replacing Charles Rich. After a difficult year at the temporary settlement, in the

Some others making in all 61 Waggons, 12 miles.

Sunday 21st [May 1848] Went to work and built our Bridge [on Papillon Creek], having it completed by two oclock after which the camp came together at the sound of the horn & held publick meeting. Br [Lorenzo] Snow preached to us concerning the advantages of trials to the Saints & the necesity of their exercising themselves in Patience & forbearance tow[a]rds one another. A heavy shower of rain fell in the evening.

Monday 22d [May 1848] On account of the ground being wet we remaind encamped, & in the afternoon had heavy Showers again. a large number of waggons arrived & some went over on our new Bridge, the mud being verry bad.

Tuesday 23d [May 1848] rained hard through the night & continued until 12 oclock when it cleared off with N winds. one hundred Waggons arrived here today wallowing through the mud.

Wednesday 24th [May 1848] Washed our Sheep & I went back to Town. about a hundred Waggons Started for the [Elk]Horn [River].

Thursday 25 [May 1848] This morning I had the good fortune to trade the demand I held against Capt. [James or John] Brown[47] for repairing Waggons to Cyrenus Taylor for which I received $9.25 in cash which enabled me to obtain some necessary articles of clothing &c. I returned to our camp.

Friday 26th [May 1848] Our Camp Journeyed over to the [Elk]Horn [River] 8 miles.[48] arrived about noon & found our Brethre[n] had constructed a raft & comenced crossing yesterday, having over a hundred Waggons across.

Satturday 27th [May 1848] Continued ferrying over Waggons. Br [Albert] Gregory's[49] Waggon accidentally ran off the raft into the river which damaged very much his provisions, clothing etc. Br Brigham [Young] arrived in the evening with his company. Sister [Susannah] Neff's[50] Son was drowned.[51]

---

spring of 1848 Snow led about twenty-five families to join the huge Mormon emigrating companies at the Elkhorn River. Smith, *Lorenzo Snow*, 89–95.

47. This is likely James Brown, who became noted as a captain in the Mormon Battalion, although John Brown had also filled the role of captain during the western emigration.
48. The difficulty in crossing the Elkhorn River was significant for all westbound Mormon emigrants. But that was only one of a number of formidable barriers. The preparatory time before embarking on the overland venture was conducted with caution in assembling the hundreds who would be attached to Heber Kimball's division. A myriad of concerns compounded the assemblage, which took several weeks to accomplish.
49. This is probably Albert Gregory.
50. Susannah Gazy Neff (1806–), from England, was married to John Neff.
51. Of this incident, John Pulsipher recorded: "While we were here our joyful camps were suddenly changed to *mourning* by the Death of Charley Beer, Step-son of Bro John Neff,

Sunday 28th [May 1848] A tremendous, heavy rain this morning.[52] we rem[a]ined encamped. no crossing today.

Monday 29th [May 1848] The President's [Brigham Young] company & family crossed over today.[53]

Tuesday 30th [May 1848] I repaired Doct [Samuel] Sprague's Waggon & received in pay some medicine for Oliver [Jacob]. he is rendered helpless by rheumatic pains.

Wednesday 31st [May 1848] We made an early move & crossed my Ten over, encamped & made report of ~~my Ten~~ to Br [Thomas] Bullock the Recorder.

Thursday first day of June [1848] The Camp of Israel began its march to the mountains by sending forward Capt Lorenzo Snow's company of Waggons.[54] H[eber]. C. Kimbal arrived with about fifty.[55]

Friday 2d [June 1848] Another company under Capt. [Zera] Pulcipher [Pulsipher].[56] a great deal of electioneering [was conducted] by some persons

---

a lively little Boy who accidently *fell* into the River & was drowned. We all turned out & searched 'til the body was found. A coffin was made by Geo. Alger & others out of a solid log of wood like a trough & lid, Hewn & smoothed up nice. The child was buried near the liberty Pole." Stout, *On the Mormon Frontier*, 1:313n77.

52. The terrific storm, described by one as a "hurricane," tore "to shreds" the wagon covers of the now mobilized refugees and "whistled fearfully through the empty dwellings" they left behind. Historian's Office, 9 May 1848, Second Division, 1848, Church Emigration, 1848–1849.

53. Three days earlier, Brigham Young's record reads: "On the 26th, I started from Winter Quarters on my journey to the mountains, leaving my houses, mills and the temporary furniture I had acquired during our sojourn there. This was the fifth time I had left my home and property since I embraced the gospel of Jesus Christ." Young, *Manuscript History, 1847–1850*, 105.

54. The day before, on 31 May, Lorenzo Snow had been appointed one of two captains of one hundred for the pending emigration. Young, *Manuscript History, 1847–1850*, 105.

55. The 1848 emigration of Latter-day Saints to the Rocky Mountains, according to Andrew Jenson, one of the emigration's more comprehensive chroniclers, was composed of three major divisions: Brigham Young's, with 1,229 people in 397 wagons; Heber Kimball's, with 552 people (though Brigham Young's *Mansucript History, 1847–1850* places this number at 662) in 226 wagons; and, leaving about a month later than the Young/Kimball companies, Willard Richards's (and Amasa Lyman's), with 526 people in 169 wagons. The total numbered 2,417 souls with 792 wagons. (Norton Jacob and his family were a part of Kimball's company.) Jenson, *Church Chronology*, 35.

    In contrast to Mormon numbers crossing the plains in 1848, the West Coast migration of Americans was light with 1,300 venturing to Oregon and 400 to California, totaling 1,700 persons. The Oregon/California emigrants of 1848 numbered less than half of those emigrating the previous year, and a thousand less than each of 1845 and 1846. Unruh, *Plains Across*, 119.

56. Zera Pulsipher, like Lorenzo Snow, was appointed captain of one hundred emigrants. Young, *Manuscript History, 1847–1850*, 105.

to those who have formerly belonged to Elder [Heber] Kimbal's company to Join others & in many cases they succeeded to draw them off.

Satturday 3d [June 1848] W[illia]m Perkins' hundred Started & moved on in the rain. our Ten was now increased by the arrival of Jerry Root & Alfred Randal[l] to 18 Waggons, & Joel Ricks appointed captain. Two more children & a woman buried here.

Sunday 4th [June 1848] A small <number> gathered & held meeting at Br [Heber] Kimbals camp where we received some excelent instruction from Presd [Isaac] Morley, Bishop [Newel] Whitney, & H. C. Kimbal.[57]

Monday 5th [June 1848] President [Brigham] Young moved on with his company & some more arrived from Winter Quarters.

Tuesday 6th [June 1848] About 10 oclock A.M. an alarm was raised that the Indians were driving off our cattle.[58] in a few minutes several men were in pursuit, following them to the river. they took one ox from them, but they had killed one. Br [Hiram] Clawson got sight of one in the act of tying up his meat & fired upon him. the Indians fled across the river, W[illia]m Kimbal, Howard Egan, Thomas Ricks, Willis Barthalomew [Bartholomew] followed the Indians across the river[59] & coming up with them they presented their guns when our Boys commenced fireing with their revolvers. the Indians returned the fire. Shot Ricks in the back with three Buck Shot[60] & Egan through the wrist with a ball Just as he was fireing his revolver which threw the Pistol from his hand & he lost it. his Horse was also shot in the top of the neck & Kimbal's in the top of the hip. the Indians, altho the most numerous, finaly fled & our Boys brot off their wounded man, the news comeing to Br [Joel] Ricks. he &

57. The subjects addressed included the "necessity of walking humbly and righteously before God, so that all might realize the blessings needed during the journey, etc." Historian's Office, 4 June 1848, Second Division, 1848, Church Emigration, 1848–1849.

58. This aggressive action on the part of the area's Native inhabitants was, undoubtedly, provoked by a sense of frustration that the Anglos had proffered them little for utilizing their resources. Two years later a more civilized policy was exacted upon white emigrants by the Oto Indians. When Jacob Hamblin's company embarked for the West from their staging ground on 10 June 1850 they "ware visited by the Chiefs of the Oto tribe of Indians" who, through their interpreter, "demanded ten cents a wagon f<o>r the privilige of pasing through thare teritory." Hamblin, Journal, 10 June 1850, p. 47.

59. See the lengthier report of the encounter, which required a six-mile chase of the ten Indians, and an overview of the skirmish are found in Historian's Office, 6 June 1848, Second Division, 1848, Church Emigration, 1848–1849; and Hartley, "Howard Egan," 41–45, which includes a map showing the range of the encounter.

60. Thomas Ricks, during the westward journey, was incapacitated for three months due to his injuries. Jenson, *Latter-day Saints Biographical Encylopedia*, 1:455–456.

Tho. Whittle & a Boy started with a Buggy to meet them, but they missed the company & fell in with the Indians who threatened their lives & robbed them of a yearling Colt, about thirty dollars worth of clothing & some other articles, when they told them to go home, saying that <they> had four men Killd & some wounded.[61]

This was a foolish affair on the part of our men. Elders of Israel are not called to make war upon the Lamanites.

Some forty Waggons crossed over today & President [Heber] Kimbal broke up his camp here & moved out two miles & formed a corel [corral] with some hundred & fifty Waggons & set a strong guard.

Wednesday 7th [June 1848] Moved over to the Platte [River], made 15 miles & camped.

Thursday 8th [June 1848] This morning my wife [Emily Jacob] Sprained & bruised her ancle severely. our wounded man [Thomas Ricks] is doing well & Oliver [Jacob] is much better, but we have our share of invalids.

moved on eight miles & camped on the bank of the river in three companys <225 Wag[ons]>. Br [Heber] Kimbal's company contained 104 Waggons. he called us together and organised his company,[62] with Henry Hariman, capt of hundred, Titus Billings, & John Pack, capts of fifty; with six capts of Ten in our fifty. W[illia]m Clayton was elected clerk of this company & Norton Jacob capt of the guard.[63]

---

61. The party of Indians numbered twenty to thirty. Historian's Office, 6 June 1848, Second Division, 1848, Church Emigration, 1848–1849.

62. Heber Kimball, reminding the camp of the religious nature of their journey, at this time also exhorted those in his charge proclaiming the need "for a reformation in the camp in regard to conduct and then exhorted the brethren to commence it, by reforming themselves in the first place, and then reforming their families. He knew there were but few who attended to family prayers and exhorted them to have prayers with their families twice a day, to pray for the cattle, for the wagons, for the stock, for the camp and the presidency and promised if they would do this the Lord would remember them and they would go safely and have the blessings of the Lord with them day by day." He concluded by asking the questions: "Shall we begin from this night to have a reformation, to cease from swearing, profane language, murmuring, angry feelings to our cattle and each other, and begin to attend to family prayers, etc." The answer: "It was decided by unanimous vote that the camp would do so." Historian's Office, 8 June 1848, Second Division, 1848, Church Emigration, 1848–1849.

63. The Fifty of which Jacob was a part was led by:
Titus Billings, Captain of the 1st Fifty.
William Burgess, Captain of the 1st Ten.
Joseph G. Hovey, Captain of the 2nd Ten.
Newel K. Whitney, Captain of the 3rd Ten.
John Cox, Captain of the 4th Ten.
Albert P. Griffin, Captain of the 5th Ten.
Joel Ricks, Captain of the 6th Ten.
Norton Jacob, Captain of the Guard.
William Clayton, Clerk.

The essential animal entourage accompanying this company of fifty of "64 wagons, [and] 179 souls," was constituted of "21 horses, 16 mules, 19 oxen, 93 cows, 27 loose

112

Saturday 10th Camped 12 miles above Shell creek on the bank of the river

Sunday 11 remained encamped & having a little leisure to take tending upon my sick folks I make the following list of the Guard of the first fifty—

1 Charles Hubbard Seargent of the first company of 8 men as follows
2 Alfred Billings
3 Melancton Burgess
4 James Bess
5 Orlando D Hovey
6 George Pitkin
7 ~~Wm S Covert~~
7 Charles Carnover
8 Abram Carnover

1 Peter Carnover Seargent of second company
2 ~~Charles Carnover~~
3 Amos Harmon
4 Henry Owatt
5 Edward Martin
6 Franklin Edwards
7 Wms Mathews
George Billings
8 James Steel

Joseph G. Hovey Searg't 3d com.
1 ~~George Billings~~
2 George Clauson
4 Dan Davis
5 Hosea Cushin
6 Asahel Harmon
7 George Roads
Spencer Millbank
8 Abram Losee

1 George Myers Searg't 4th company
2 ~~Spencer Millbank~~
3 H. K. Whitney
4 O. K. Whitney
5 Solon McFarlin
6 Jason Haws
7 Everet Van Orden
Jackson Redin
8 Charles Williams

1 John Cox Searg't 5th company
~~Henry E. Gibson~~
2 ~~Jackson Redin~~
3 Obed Thompson
4 Arvit Hale
5 Joseph Henry
6 Ozro Eastman
7 James Duncan
8 George Duncan
~~Hubert H Foster~~
8 ~~Charles Foster~~

1 Albert Griffin Searg't 6th com.
2 Charles Foster
3 ~~Hubert H Foster~~ H. Foster
4 Ezra Thompson
5 Alonzo H Rolly
6 Thomas Colburn
7 Epraim Badger
8 Robert Blackman
~~Thomas Corbit~~
~~Wm Cayton~~

Fred Ricks Searg't 7 company

This page and facing page: guard for the First Fifty, 1848 emigrants. Courtesy of the LDS Church Archives.

~~Thomas Corbit~~
~~Wm Cayton~~

Joel Ricks Searg't 7 company
2 W. Cayton
3 ~~Thomas Corbit~~ remain
~~Jesse Folks~~
4 Elick Kelly
5 Wm Kelly
6 Jonathan Pugmire
7 Lewis Ricks
8 Benjamin Croft
~~Daniel McKay~~
8 ~~Norton Jacob~~

1 Thomas Whittle Searg't 8th company
2 ~~Norton Jacob~~
3 ~~Jesse Folks~~ 2
4 ~~Daniel McKay~~ 3
5 Alfred Randall 4
3 Jerry Root 5
7 Almerin Root 6
5 John Calvert 7
5 ~~John C Whittle~~
10 Wm Barnet 8
7 ~~Horace Hill~~

1 Elbridge Tufts Searg't 9th com
2 ~~John Calvert~~
3 ~~Thomas King~~ Phiny Wells
4 Schyler Jennings
5 Thomas Chappell
6 Edward ~~Thomas~~ Chappell
Alfred D Young
Oliver Bess
8 Isaac Ferguson

1 Benjamin F. Mitchell Searg't 10th company
~~Victor L Cool~~
2 Elias Gardner
3 Walter E. Gardner
4 John W Tuttle
5 George Teeples
6 Alvah Tippets
7 John H. Tippets
8 Hiram Tippets

Satturday 10th [June 1848] Camped 12 miles above Shell Creek on the bank of the river.[64]

Sunday 11 [June 1848] remained encamped & having a little leisure while tending upon my sick folks, I make the following list of the guard of the first fifty.

Thursday 15th [June 1848] Passed the old & new Pawnee Missionary Stations yesterday & camped on Cedar Creek. The Sio[u]x have burned their new Missionary house that was built last Summer![65]

The Lord intends the Saints shall have a free passway through this region so he has removed our enemies, this being the third time they have been burned out by the Sioux![66]

Today John [Jehu] Cox's Daughter [Lucretia], 6 years old, was Killed by a Waggon running over it.[67] Camped near an old Indian Town in ruins. A tremendous Storm of rain thunder & lightning accompanyed with wind & hail, but our encampment being formed, our cattle remained quietly within our carell by close watching, A[lbert]. Griffin's Company being on guard.

A Messengers arrived from Br Brigham [Young]'s camp & informed that his company crossed over the Loup Fork about noon.[68]

---

cattle, 74 sheep, 28 hogs, 71 hens, 22 dogs, and 5 cats." Historian's Office, 8 June 1848, Second Division, 1848, Church Emigration, 1848–1849.

64. The company camped on the Platte River "to give the women a chance to do their washing, etc., which was attended to with alacrity." Historian's Office, 10 June 1848, Second Division, 1848, Church Emigration, 1848–1849.

65. This is the Pawnee Missionary Station complex encountered the previous year on 22 April 1847.

66. The Mormons' thinking in terms of providential intervention on their behalf, even in settings of extreme hardship and disappointment, was incessant and ubiquitous.

67. In a 23 July 1848 letter from William Thompson, the clerk of Heber Kimball's company, to Willard Richards's trailing company, he wrote "We moved along in peace and order, every thing harmonizing like clock work until we came opposite the old Pawnee village. Going down a little pitch, Bro. Cox's daughter Lucretia fell of[f] the wagon tongue and was run over, the body by the fore wheel and and [sic] over the neck by the hind wheel of the wagon; she died almost instantaneously. We interred the body on the north side of the road, probably you have seen the grave." The only other human death on the journey took place on 14 July 1848 when Sarah Twitchell, 28, died of consumption. William Thompson to Willard Richards and Amasa Lyman, 23 July 1848, in Historian's Office, 23 July 1848, Second Division, 1848, Church Emigration, 1848–1849; William Thompson, Journal, 14 July 1848, in Historian's Office, Journal History, 24 September 1848, p. 31.

68. The following day, 16 June 1848, because of their perceived vulnerability to Indian depredations, "Young instructed Pres. [Heber] Kimball to bring his division to the camp of the First Division and about 2 o'clock . . . Elder Kimball's company appeared on the north bank of the Loup Fork where they formed their corral." Historian's Office, 16 June 1848, Second Division, 1848, Church Emigration, 1848–1849.

Brigham Young's camp at this point was composed of "1229 souls, 397 wagons,

Friday 16th [June 1848] It rained the forepart of the day but we Journeyed on to the ford of the Loup [River] & in the evening we had another tremendous Storm of wind & rain, which was severe on our sick.

Satturday 17th [June 1848] All the Brethren that came on are encamped on the right bank of the [Loup] river & they sent over about a hundred yoke of oxen to assist us to move over & by the middle of the afternoon we had moved over 225 Waggons & several hundred head of loose cattle & Sheep & hogs without anny accident.[69]

Sunday 18th [June 1848] The Saints gathered midway between camps on the bank of the river for worship. Br Brigham [Young] opened the meeting by Prayer & then addressed the Saints on the object that should be constantly Kept in view on this Journey, the building up [of] the Kingdom of God on the Earth, that an individual might believe mormonism to be true & be all his life in the midtst of the Saints, & be damned & go to hell at last because they did not keep & retain the influence of the holy Ghost within their own breasts to govern & rule the whole man. Br [Heber] Kimbal & some others spoke when the President proposed the following order of march from here: Br [Lorenzo] Snows company first, four Waggons abreast; [William] Perkins & [Zera] Pulsipher forming one company next, his own next & Br Kimbals in the rear, which motion was carried when meeting was dismissed by E[rastus] Snow.

---

74 horses, 19 mules, 1275 oxen, 699 cows, 184 loose cattle, 411 sheep, 141 pigs, 605 chickens, 37 cats, 82 dogs, 3 goats, 10 geese, 2 hives of bees, 8 doves and 1 crow." With Heber Kimball's company of "662 souls, 226 wagons, 57 horses, 25 mules, 737 oxen, 284 cows, 150 loose cattle, 243 sheep, 96 pigs, 299 chickens, 17 cats, 52 dogs, 3 hives of bees, 3 doves, 5 ducks, and 1 squirrel," images of Moses' exodus from ancient Egypt were vivid in the minds of the Saints and are to modern observers as well. On 20 June 1848, Kimball's train of wagons was described as appearing "like an army." Young, *Manuscript History, 1847–1850*, 107; Historian's Office, 20 June 1848, Second Division, 1848, Church Emigration, 1848–1849.

69. William Thompson, Heber Kimball's company clerk, noted to Willard Richards's company who trailed behind, that the herculean effort of getting the company and their animals across the river "was a sight that would have truly pleased you, to see and hear the brethren greet each other. Every heart was glad, and every countenance smiling." Of this incident-free effort, Brigham Young "returned thanks to the brethren who had assisted to bring Bro. Kimball's company over the river; they had done well and he was satisfied." Historian's Office, 17 June 1848, 23 July 1848, Second Division, 1848, Church Emigration, 1848–1849.

Transporting the hundreds of animals essential to the emigrants was an enormous task. The following day, 18 June 1848, "Cornelius P. Lott was chosen Captain of the Herd." The following morning the routine for the rest of the trek was established: "The herd was sent out a[t] 3:30 A.M." followed over four hours later by the emigrants whose starting time was 8 A.M. 18–19 June 1848, in Journal History, 24 September 1848, p. 4.

Satturday 24th [June 1848] Encamped near the head of Grand Island.[70]

Sunday 25th [June 1848] remained encamped & was visited by 8 or 10 Soldiers from where they are building a fort 10 or 12 miles below here on the South side of Grand Island.[71]

Friday 30th [June 1848] Killed the first Buffalo at the head of the Pawnee Swamps a few miles below the forks of the river.[72]

This was a pell mell hunt, a small Band being started down the Swamps towards the river came running up & dashed through our lines receiving showers of bullits & being pursued by men, women, & children until most of the Buffalo were destroyed.

Satturday first of July [1848] moved on 12 or 15 miles & camped on the river above the forks, 303 1/2 miles from Winter Quarters.[73]

Sunday 2d [July 1848] remained encamped[74] & attended meeting & received excellent instruction from President [Brigham] Young. In the evening our com[pany] was called together & selected six hunters, all others to abstain from Killing game.[75] There was also a reorganizing of the Guard by appointing

70. The vanguard reached this point the previous year at the end of April.
71. This detail of soldiers were attached to the same military project that Jacob noted on 9 October the previous year. Whereas the Mormons' first encounter with these men was while the latter were searching for a site on which to build a post on the Platte River to protect overland emigration, by this time, Lieutenant Daniel Woodbury's men had "arrived at the head of Grand Island" to erect the "first military station on the route to Oregon." As many as 175 labored to construct the fort. Called Fort Childs initially, after Woodbury's father-in-law, on 30 December 1848 the War Department determined the "new post established at Grand Island, Platte River, will be known as Fort Kearny." http//www2.sandi.net/kearny/history/swk/fk.html.

    William Burton, for this day, wrote: "A visit was made by Lieutenant Craig and ten privates belonging to the Oregon Battalion Station near the head of Grand Island. The visitors were given refreshments, remained about three or four hours and returned to their encampment apparently pleased with their reception." 25 June 1848, in Journal History, 24 September 1848, p. 5.
72. One part of this fork with the Platte River may be a stream known at the time as Carrion Creek. Historian's Office, 1 July 1848, Second Division, 1848, Church Emigration, 1848–1849.
73. Heber Kimball's encampment trailed Brigham Young's company by a mile at this point. Historian's Office, 1 July 1848, Second Division, 1848, Church Emigration, 1848–1849.
74. An unusual event of the day transpired when "Bro. John Pack baptized a man and his wife that started from McDonough county, Illinois, for the Bay of San Francisco." Historian's Office, 23 July 1848, in 23 July 1848, Second Division, 1848, Church Emigration, 1848–1849.
75. Associated with the evening meeting, "two persons were baptized . . . . There are a number of families going with us who do not belong to the church." 2 July 1848, in Journal History, 24 September 1848, p. 6.

a sufficient number of Seargents of the Guard with Elias Gardner captain, which relieved me from the duties of that office on account of the sickness of my Son [Oliver Jacob], as I have to attend upon him every night.

Friday 7th [July 1848] Halted at camp creek & remained here two days & hunted Buffalo on Satturday [8 July 1848] & killed four or five. Br Brigham [Young] & Br [Isaac] Morley came back 17 miles on Sunday [9 July 1848] to visit our camp[76] & gave information that some men had met their camp from the "Valley" who gave encouraging information concerning the prospects for a crop there.[77]

Satturday 15th [July 1848] Arrived in the vicinity of Chimney Rock late in the evening[78] & encamped with Br Brigham [Young]s camp about a mile from us. last Friday [14 July 1848] we met Br [Shadrach] Roundy with 12 Teams from the Valley, he having left a number more at Ft John unable to come farther on account of lamness.

Sunday 16th [July 1848] Arrangments were made for dividing these two Camps into 8 companys[79] & also to send three men as an Express to the Vally for more Teams to meet us at Green river.

Tuesday 18th [July 1848] Br Heber [Kimball]'s camps crossed over the Platte [River] by fording about half way between Chimney Rock & Scots Bluffs[80]

---

76. The seventeen miles difference, at this point, between the Brigham Young and Heber Kimball companies, was due to Kimball's group halting because of the strain on some of the oxen in Kimball's company, several "suffering with sore necks." During Young and [Isaac] Morley's visit, Kimball told Young he would endeavor to have his company "within four miles of the advance division by the next Sunday." Historian's Office, 9 July 1848, Second Division, 1848, Church Emigration, 1848–1849.
77. John Greene and Joseph Young led the group who brought to Brigham Young "several letters and 18 wagons sent from the Valley to help the companies in." Ten wagons were retained to assist Young's and Heber Kimball's companies into the valley, while "[e]ight of these wagons were sent to Winter Quarters." Historian's Office, 11 July 1848, Second Division, 1848, Church Emigration, 1848–1849.
78. The vanguard reached this point the previous year on 26 May 1847.
79. At the Sabbath day meeting, "After some preaching and teaching, Isaac Morley moved that we break up both companies into four companies each, <it being more convenient to travel in smaller companies.> The motion was seconded and carried." Historian's Office, 16 July 1848, Second Division, 1848, Church Emigration, 1848–1849.
80. The Platte River's width at this fording point was about a mile. In crossing the river, the emigrants "generally had to put on the strength of three wagons, as the falloes of each wagon generally buried themselves in gravel and sand." Crossing the river at this point "saved about ten miles travel, and the road is much the best." Hosea Stout noted that the Platte River, near this spot, "looses its wide shallow watters and is a narrow deep swift running stream of good water." Historian's Office, 23 July 1848, Second Division, 1848, Church Emigration, 1848–1849; Stout, *On the Mormon Frontier*, 1:319.

while Br Brigham [Young]s camps continued their rout up the North side. our camp now consists of four Tens under Capt [Henry] Heriman.

Friday 21st [July 1848] encamped about 10 oclock near Racheau's [John Baptiste Richard] camp 20 miles below Fort John.[81] Br [Heber] Kimbals companys having encamped here last night.

Satturday 22d [July 1848] Br [Heber] Kimbals company went on ahead but we hired Racheau's Blacksmith tools, built a coal pit & made arrangements for Br [Jonathan] Pugmire to do our Smith work here. we understand that Br Brigham [Young]s company cross[ed] yesterday about 8 miles above here.

Tuesday 25th [July 1848] We moved on after having set about 40 Waggon tires. Passed Fort John Wednesday 26th [July 1848] & overtook some of Heber [Kimball]s company on Bitter Creek.

Friday 28th [July 1848] we remained here two days to recruit our Teams and make tar. The feed in the Black Hills much scarser than it was last year.[82] made our way through them safely & camped on Deer creek 3 miles above the road on [*sic*].

Satturday the 5th day of August [1848] remained here Sunday [6 August 1848] & were obliged to stop Monday [7 August 1848] on account of the sickness of Br [William] Claytons wife, who was delivered of a Daughter. Br Jesse Folks also had a Daughter born Tuesday the fir<st> of August on the La Bonte river in the Black Hills.

On Wednesday the 9th [August 1848] we overtook all of Brother [Heber] Kimbals companys about noon encamped on the Platte [River], a few miles below the ford.

On Friday the 11th [August 1848] <This morning Br [Thomas] Whittle Baptized Oliver [Jacob] in the Platte> [River].[83] crossed the river, moved on to 12 Mile Creek & encamped in one corell [corral] with Br [Heber] Kimbal. here our cattle began to get Poison, either from some vegetable or mineral. I had one ox verry sick, but he recovered.[84]

81. This refers to John Baptiste Richard, "Reshaw" as spoken by the French, whom the 1847 Saints encountered near Fort Laramie.

82. One of the reasons the feed near the Black Hills was scarcer during the 1848 trek than the previous year was that the vanguard reached this place in the first week of June and was one of the first emigrating companies of the season.

83. This was a baptism for health purposes.

84. Two days later, after the company voted to stop and rest, "There was some dissatisfaction in the company because of the cattle, fearing that they would be poisoned with the alkali. A

Sunday 13th [August 1848] moved on from the Willow Spring over into the Sweetwater Valley & camped on Grease-Wood creek eight miles N. East from the Independence Rock. here my Son Oliver Bar Jacob died on Monday the 14th of August [1848] at < 8 oclock A.M> after having suffered incredably for above 3 months with Black Scurvy, Black Canker & the Liver complaint, all of which he bore with great patience & resignation. he was a good Boy and a verry promising youth, Aged 14 years 7 months & 9 days. We buryed him on a small eminence near our camp 1/2 mile S. East of the road & marked the Spot with a heap of rough Stones and a lettered Board. here with sorrow & mourning we left him to rest in the Wilderness! Haven been worn out, a Martyr to the cause of righteousness.[85]

Satturday, 19th [August 1848] Being unwilling longer to travel in so large a company, we remained encamped on the Sweet water while Brother [Heber] Kimbal's companies went on ~~& Kept~~ remained Sunday.[86]

Monday 21st [August 1848] moved on 8 miles leaving 7 Waggons, so many cattle having died & for several days we were obliged to halt occasionaly & send back Teams to bring up those whose Teams were deficient, the <cattle> dying every day until Sunday the 3d day of Sept. [1848],[87] Teams having

---

number of these persons did not belong to the church; some said they would go at all hazards. They brought up their cattle and some of them took sick, therefore they were willing to stop." 13 August 1848, in Journal History, 24 September 1848, p. 12.

85. Jacob's writings suggest that once-able Oliver's slow demise exacted a considerable tax upon his father's spirit.

86. The Mormon camps by this time were stretched out on the trail farther than any time previously. On 24 August 1848 Brigham Young's account of the trek notes that Heber Kimball's companies were over twenty miles behind his group: "the cattle [of] many of them worn out, and four or five [are] dying every day," while "three or four dying daily" was the count affecting Young's own companies. Historian's Office, 24 August 1848, Second Division, 1848, Church Emigration, 1848–1849.

87. Once the advance companies arrived at the last crossing of the Sweetwater River, Brigham Young and Heber Kimball wrote a letter characterizing the trek to those who remained behind in the Missouri River settlements.

> We have been sixty three days in travelling from the Elk Horn to the last crossing of the Sweetwater at an average of 12 miles per day, resting 22, including Sundays, to recruit and strengthen our cattle. The very dry season, the scarcity of grass, the heavy dragging, dusty roads and inhaling so much of the alkali by breathing, eating and drinking has been the cause of our losing many of our cattle; some have died with appearances of the bloody murrain, others by the hollow horn and a few by an unusual swelling of the melt, which on examination was generally putrid; several worn out animals have been devoured by the wolves which abound in great numbers on the route; the cattle that have died without any appearances of sickness were the best and fattest.
>
> The health of the camp has been generally good, although there have been some 20 cases of the mountain fever, all of which are recovered or recovering.
>
> Young and Kimball to Hyde, Smith, and Benson, [n.d.], in Young, *Manuscript History, 1847–1850*, 120.

arrived to our assistance from the Valley. we moved on over the South Pass & camped at the Pacific Springs.[88]

Satturday 9th [September 1848] encamped on Black's fork having made 91 miles in 7 days.

Sunday [10 September 1848] remained encamped.

Satturday 16th [September 1848][89] Encamped 2 miles below Reden's [Cache] cave on Echo creek & remained over Sunday [17 September 1848].[90]

Satturday 23d [September 1848] Encamped at the mouth of the Kanyon in the Valley, every thing appears much more fresh & green than last year, there having been plenty of rain this season.[91]

Sunday 24th [September 1848] Br [Heber] Kimbal having arrived, his whole camp moved on in order down to the City of the Saints, passed through the Fort & encamped on the wester side.[92]

Tuesday 26th [September 1848] By the council of Br [Heber] Kimbal, Br [Joel] Ricks, Br [Benjamin] Cross & myself moved 12 miles North to finish building his mill.[93]

---

88. Jacob's enthusiasm for chronicling the journey had obviously ebbed by this time. Unquestionably, Oliver Jacob's death enervated his father's outlook and dimmed his imagination. Besides the relatively uneventful remainder of the trek, Jacob's brief entries with significant gaps in his record, suggest a man worn out and distracted.
89. It was in this general area traveled by Jacob's fellow sojourners during the previous week that the vanguard in 1847 was afflicted with mountain fever. The malady had little effect upon the 1848 sojourners, save it be for the few mentioned by Brigham Young in his letter to Orson Hyde, et al, mentioned above.
90. The gap between Heber Kimball's and Brigham Young's companies at Cache Cave had narrowed to the latter being one day in front of the former. Historian's Office, 17 September 1848, Second Division, 1848, Church Emigration, 1848–1849.
91. One report to Brigham Young of the valley while he was gone stated, "there has much more rain fallen since the 22nd of last July [1848] than during the same dates last year, which has greatly favored irrigation." Pratt, Taylor, and Smith to Young, 23 August 1848, Great Salt Lake City, in Young, *Manuscript History, 1847–1850*, 117.
92. A report to Brigham Young written in late August 1848 reported the progress of the settlement since the previous year: "There are 450 buildings in the forts [*sic*], besides quite a number of temporary farm buildings; 3 saw mills in operation, and 1 partly finished; 1 temporary grist mill, and an excellent one nearly finished." (For a description of the fort referred to by Jacob, see the entry and notes for 11 August 1847.) Pratt, Taylor, and Smith to Young, 23 August 1848, Great Salt Lake City, in Young, *Manuscript History, 1847–1850*, 116.

    At the end of the summer's emigration, the Salt Lake Valley's population numbered about 5,000. Alexander and Allen, *Mormons & Gentiles*, 28.
93. This mill, one of the first operations of its kind in Utah, is generally not acknowledged in the literature about Utah's milling industry, grist, saw, or otherwise, likely because Jacob's

Sunday first day of October [1848] went down to the city [Great Salt Lake City] to meeting. a resolution was pass[ed] to build a Council House by Tything & to commence now to Tythe ourselves of our time.[94]

Monday 2d [October 1848] Brethren H[eber]. C. Kimbal, E[dson]. Whipple, W[illia]m. Wallace & [John] Nebecer [Nebeker] came up to the place where they had commenced to build a mill & all together agreed that Br [Joel] Ricks & myself should go on & finish the mill & they would back up Br Ricks & would pay me for my work & when done I should have a chance to run the mill.[95]

Tuesday 3d [October 1848] raised Br [Joel] Ricks' and [Benjamin] Cross's houses.

Wednesday 4th [October 1848] I moved my family into a cabin near the Mill belonging to the Brethren Just named & proceeded to repair it.

Satturday 7th [October 1848] I commenced work on the mill by repairing a wheel barow. Found the plan of the Mill defective & by the advice of the Brethren engaged Br Ezra Thompson to assist in making a new plan & also to put up the mill. (4 days work on <W[h]eelbarrows.)>

Monday 16th [October 1848] Procured Timber for cogs & Pins.

---

diary account of the endeavor has not received wide attention. Jacob had, of course, plied his labor at Brigham Young's mill on Turkey Creek in Winter Quarters previously. This new undertaking was the first of several mill-building enterprises in Utah involving Norton Jacob's considerable skill, something for which he became noted in early Utah.

This particular venture on North Mill Creek, named such because it was north of the Great Salt Lake City settlement, became a sawmill operation initiated in what is now Bountiful, Utah, located nine miles north of the temple site in Great Salt Lake City and just south of what is now Bountiful High School. While the mill was built for Heber Kimball, the enterprise later became known as Edson Whipple's sawmill. Kimball later received an exclusive grant from the territorial legislature in 1851 to use the canyon and water of North Mill Creek to power what later became a successful flour mill that was built on the stream beginning in 1852. A plaque and a model of the latter mill commemorates the site. Leonard, *History of Davis County*, 114; Roberts, "Pioneer Mills and Milling," 7:120–122.

94. At a meeting of the city's High Council on 30 September 1848, Brigham Young proposed to build "a council house by tithing labor." The following day at a meeting in the makeshift meeting structure, a bowery, "The congregation voted to build a council house by tithing labor and that Daniel H. Wells superintend the building of the same." Young, *Manuscript History, 1847–1850*, 124.

95. This employment opportunity for Jacob is of some consequence. The paltry harvest of 1848 in the midst of the burgeoning demand for domestic resources, including food, due to the influx of new emigrants, placed most of Utah's settlers in precarious circumstances.

The story of Utah's early mills is best told in Roberts, "Pioneer Mills and Milling," 7:85–136, though Roberts only mentions this endeavor of Jacob's in passing.

Wednesday 18th [October 1848] Br Ezra Thomson arrived & I went to Town to Procure materials. returned on Thursday [19 October 1848].

Friday 20th [October 1848] Proceeded to Level & make a plan for the Mill with Br [Ezra] Thompson. wrought 3 days this week, & Thompson 1 day on the Mill.

Tuesday 24th [October 1848] A Snow Storm here in the Kanion though quite warm & Snow soon melted off. discovered today that the n[a]ture of the Soil is such here that our mill-dam, which Br [Joel] Ricks has partly erected, will not hold the water, as it leaks out in the botom of the creek. [obscure word crossed out] Br E[lijah]. Newman & P[hineas]. Wright have come to assist us in Building the Mill.

Wednesday 25th [October 1848] All hands went up the creek half a mile selecti[n]g a new Mill scitie [site] & commenced to build another dam in which Br [Joel] Ricks & his hands did not Join us, but wished he never had seen it.

Satturday 28th [October 1848] I made 4 1/2 days this week [working on the mill], [Ezra] Thompson 4, [Elijah] Newman 3 1/2, & [Phineas] Wright 3 1/2 days, while [Joel] Ricks continued to fool away his time on the old dam.

Tuesday 31st [October 1848] Br [Joel] Ricks now coming in with us, we held council in which we concluded, on account of difficulties attending it, to abandon the building [of] a dam at our new scite & bring the water in a Trunk made of plank some 20 rods onto an over shot Wheel & Gear it with cogg Wheells.

Satturday 4 Nov. 4th [1848] I made 5 days this week, [Ezra] Thompson 5 1/2, [Elijah] Newman 4 1/2, & [Phineas] Wright 6 days.

Satturday 11th [November 1848] I made 6 days, [Ezra] Tho[mpson] 6, [Elijah] Newman, & [Phineas] Wright 6 days.

Satturday 18th [November 1848] went to Town with Br [Ezra] Thompson. I made 4 days, Thompson 4, [Elijah] Newman 4, & [Phineas] Wright 4 days.

Satturday 25th [November 1848] I made 5, [Ezra] Thompson 5, [Elijah] Newman 4, & [Phineas] Wright 5 days.

Satturday Dec. 2d [1848] all four of us Mill wrights turned out.

Sunday 3d [December 1848] I brot up Br [John] Nebaker's 5 cows to keep upon Shares & cut Saw Loggs to day, inasmuch as the rest of the men <[Joel] Ricks & [Benjamin] Cross> employed on the mill were verry egarly engaged cutting down the timber so as to monopolise it to themselves with the intention of paying us off in Lumber of their own procuring & deprive us of the privilege of sawing our own Loggs & thereby obtain our pay from the mill according to previous arrangements. This course of ours mad[e] a mighty stir among them & [Joel] Ricks refused to furnish us the Beef he had before promised. I worked 5 days this week, [Ezra] Thompson <5>, [Elijah] Newman 3 1/2, & [Phineas] Wright 5 days.

Satturday 9th [December 1848] In consequence of a Snow Storm & excessive cold weather we were hindred from our work, so we proceeded to erect a Logg shop, Br [Joel] Ricks continuing obstinate in his course. by our council & advice Br [Ezra] Thompson prop[o]sed to him three alternatives, either to furnish us with Beef, or sell to us his interest in the Mill, or wee will stop work & quit the Job, & as he does not comply with our propositions we have sent Br [Phineas] Wright to inform Br [Heber] Kimbal of the state of our affairs.

I made 2 1/2 days, [Ezra] Thompson 3, [Elijah] Newman 3, & [Phineas] Wright 3.

Monday 10th [December 1848] Br [Phineas] Wright returned with an order from Br [Heber] Kimbal to Br [Joel] Ricks directing him to get Br [Benjamin] Cross' oxen & turn them out to us for Beef. wee accordingly took them at $50.00 on foot. Killed one & he weighed 513 lb.

Satturday 16th [December 1848] I made 1 day, [Ezra] Thompson 3, [Elijah] Newman 2, and [Phineas] Wright 2 1/2 days.

Monday 18th [December 1848] Br [Heber] Kimbal & his wife Lucy came to visit us & called all the people in this Kanion together at Br [Alfred] Randal's. we had a social meeting in which all parties seemed well pleased & we received much valuable instruction from Br Heber.

Satturday 23rd [December 1848] I made 3 1/2 days, [Ezra] Thompson 4 1/2, [Elijah] Newman 5, & [Phineas] Wright 5 days.

Satturday 30th [December 1848] For the want of timber we are not able to prossecute our work verry fast, but worked for ourselves on the mill. I made 2 days, [Ezra] Thompson 3, [Elijah] Newman 3, & [Phineas] Wright 3 days.

1849–1852

NORTON JACOB CONTINUED HIS WORK IN 1849 working to build one of the first mills constructed in Utah, a vocation as a millwright that he continued during much of the remainder of his life. Immersed in religious faith, Jacob entered the unique practice of Mormon plural marriage in 1851. (He later multiplied his vows with two other women.) At the time this record terminates he has selected as his residence Great Salt Lake City, though this would later change.

Satturday Jan. 6th 1849 The Council & Brethren in the City have ordained & established a Bank of deposit so as to Keep the gold which is brought in abundance from the mines from going out from among us. The Presidency isue notes payable on demand bearing the Great Seal of the Priesthood.[1] This week I made [worked] 6 days, [Ezra] Thompson 6, [Elijah] Newman 3 1/2, & [Phineas] Wright 5 1/2 days.

<Wednesday 10 [January 1849] Br Ep[h]raim B. Green commenced boarding with me>.

Satturday 13th [January 1849] I made 5 1/2 days, [Ezra] Thompson none, [Elijah] Newman 4, & [Phineas] Wright 1 day.

Satturday 20th [January 1849] I worked on the mill 1/2 day & [Elijah] Newman 3 days. We have a thaw comenced & pleasant weather after about six weeks

1. The Latter-day Saints coined gold from the dust brought to Salt Lake City by Mormon Battalion veterans who worked the gold fields of California after their discharge in 1847. The first gold dust was deposited in LDS Church coffers on 10 December 1848. Coins from the dust, first in $10 denominations, were soon minted. The crucibles broke, however, and further coinage was delayed until dies were received from the East in September 1849. In the meantime, the Saints issued a paper currency beginning on 2 January 1849. Denominations of "50 cents, $1.00, $2.00, $3.00, and $5.00 were distributed, most of them being of the $1.00 denomination. The bills were written out by hand on plain white paper with pen and ink." Subsequently, paper scrip was produced, the first printed items in Utah territory. Arrington, *Great Basin Kingdom*, 55–56, 71.

of Storm & Snow which has fallen here two & three feet deep, though in the Valley but about 12 inches.

Satturday 27th [January 1849] I made 3 1/2 days, [Ezra] Thompson 5 1/2, [Elijah] Newman 4, & [Phineas] Wright 2. I went to Tow<n> [Great Salt Lake City] thursday. found Br Heber [Kimball] quite sick.

Satturday Feb. 3d [1849] I made 6 days, [Ezra] Thompson 5 1/2, [Elijah] Newman 2, & [Phineas] Wright 5.

Monday 12th [February 1849] Received 46 lbs of meal & 30 3/4 of Beef of Br [Heber] Kimball. Last week I made 6 days, [Ezra] Thompson 6, & [Elijah] Newman 3 days.

Friday 16th [February 1849] Received 190 lbs of beef of H[eber]. C. Kimball by Dan Davis.

Satturday 17th [February 1849] I made 6 days, [Ezra] Thompson 6, [Elijah] Newman 5, & [Phineas] Wright 3 days work. An estimate has been made of the People & provisions now in the Vally & there is found to be nearly 4000 Inhabitants over one year old & over 3/4 of a pound of bread stuff to each person <pe[r] day> till harvest.[2]

Satturday 24th [February 1849] I made 6 days, [Ezra] Thompson 3, [Elijah] Newman 2 1/2, & [Phineas] Wright 2 day. Br [Alfred] Randal commenced work on the [mill's] cogs, monday 19 [February 1849]. made 5 days. Hosea Cushing commenced thursday march first [1849].

Satturday March 3d [1849][3] I made 5 days, [Ezra] Thompson 1, [Elijah] Newman 4 1/2, [Phineas] Wright 3 1/2, [Alfred] Randal 4 1/2, & [Hosea] Cushing 2 1/2.

Wednesday 28th Feb [1849] I received 136 lbs of meal of Br [Heber] Kimbal & [Ezra] Thompson 184 lbs.

---

2. At a meeting held by city leaders on 3 February 1849, "the cries & Sufferings of the Poor were called up in question. The council wer of the opinion that a sufficiently of Bread Stuf was in the valley to sustain all the inhabitants, till more could be raised, could it be eaqually distributed." Recognizing that some were in difficult straits, "It was then decided that Bishop Whiting [Newel Whitney] call a meeting of the Bishops in the several wards & instruct them to go to every man's House & assertain the true amount of Bread stuf, Seed, grain, cows & calves & report at the next session of the council." Lee, *A Mormon Chronicle*, 1:87–88.

3. There is no explanation for this chronological irregularity in Jacob's record.

February 16th [1849][4] [Ezra] Thompson Rec[eived] 202 lbs Beef & 64 of meal.

Satturday March 10th [1849] I received of Joel Ricks 182 lbs of Beef <Fore Quarter>, & [Ezra] Thompson 167 lbs Hind Quarter. I made this week 5 days, Thompson 6, [Elijah] Newman 4 1/2, [Phineas] Wright 6, [Alfred] Randall 1 1/4, & [Hosea] Cushing 5 days.

Monday 12th [March 1849] there was an election held at the City when Brigham Young was elected Governor of the Teritory & Magistrates & other officers were also chosen[5] & also commenced a reorganization of the Nauvoo Legion.[6]

Satturday 17th [March 1849] I made 5 days, [Ezra] Thompson 5, [Elijah] Newman 5, [Phineas] Wright 4, [Alfred] Randal 4 1/2, & [Hosea] Cushing 3 1/2 days work.

Satturday 24th [March 1849] I made 5, [Ezra] Thompson 6, [Elijah] Newman 5, [Phineas] Wright 6, [Alfred] Randal 4 1/2, & [Hosea] Cushing 5 days work. John G[h]een began work Wednesday 21 [March 1849] & made this week 3 1/2 days. I received 19 1/2 lbs of meal.

In answer to <a> letter I received from my father, Hancock County, Illinoi, July 10th 1849 [1848], I wrote the following:

Great Salt Lake City March 20th 1849
Dearly Beloved Father:

---

4. There is no explanation for this chronological irregularity in Jacob's record.
5. Early in February 1849, notice was given that a "convention" would be held on 5 March 1849 "for the purpose of taking into consideration the propriety of organizing a Territorial or State government." On Sunday, 4 March 1849, at a meeting of the Council of Fifty, a non-ecclesiastical body of Mormon leaders that met privately, this council determined the election for a civil government would be held 12 March, instead, "for the purpose of Electing the following men to fill the different Stations in office. Namely: Pres. Brigham Young, govenor; Heber C. Kimble, Supreme Judge; Willard Richards, Secretary of State; Newel K. Whitney & John Taylor, associate Judges; Horace K. Eldridge, Marshal," etc. A committee to draft a constitution was appointed, and on 8 March they submitted their preamble and constitution for approval, which passed. On 12 March 1849, the "election" was held in Great Salt Lake City's Bowery, where 674 votes endorsed the proposed ticket. Morgan, *State of Deseret*, 30–33; Lee, *On the Mormon Frontier*, 99.

   A description of the prelude to the events noted above and the organization of a territorial government in Utah is found in Morgan, *State of Deseret*, 7–57.
6. The first action in reorganizing the Nauvoo Legion, the military entity dubbed Utah's "minute men," took place later in the month on 28 March 1849, when Daniel Wells was appointed major-general, and the first company was organized with George Grant as captain. Jenson, *Church Chronology*, 37.

here the first of Dec. last [1848], I received your <letter> by our mail which arrived at the close of it. I discover a Key which unlocks the msytery of your present forlorn condition, <&> also reveals the cause of the numerous miscalculations & mistakes you have fallen into. dear Father, you are under the influence of a false & lying Spirit, & when I make it manifest to you, I hope I shall enable you to see the Truth & embrace it. And first, you say that we must soon be destitute of money, whereas we are in the midtst of the mountains that are filled with the precious metals! Last Spring Some of our Soldier-Boys in digging a mill race for Capt. [John] Sut[t]er on the American Fork of the Sacramento [River] about two hundred miles from the coast, discovered a gold mine,[7] the richest & most extensive in California, So that before Winter there were hundreds of People at work gathering gold over a space of country extending along the Western side of the Siera Nevada [Mountains] 50 miles wide & three hundred long.[8] After a considerable quantity had been obtained by our People (often gathering fifty, Sevnty-five & hundreds of dollars worth in a day) a portion of them started for this Valley.[9] on this side of the mountains they found gold & in many places saw signs of it on their way home. Thus we are enabled to make a pure gold coin of our own free [will] from the alloy that other nations put into theirs.[10] While the country that you was so anxious for the Church to go to is totaly ruined! cultivating the soil, Building mills, & all Kinds of of business stopped to runn into the mountains to gather gold! Suter's Large Flouring mill, with much of the machiniry Just ready to put into opperation, Stands right where it did when the gold was first discovered in the race! Clerks leave their counters, Husbandmen their harvest fields with the grain standing, & Soldiers desert their posts to seek for the yellow dust! Even Vessels dare not land in the harbors, for fear their crews will desert & leave them lying at the wharves, But are forced to ly off many miles, Keep a strong guard, & send ther cargoes on shore in lighters. And at this remote distance, this "yellow fiver" rages to such a degree that nothing but the power of the Priesthood strengthened by the faith of the New & everlasting covenant & the sanctions of Eternity can control the People & prevent their rushing off into the mountains where Bread does not grow & a Beef will cost them a hundred dollars & Flour forty & fifty dollars per Barrel, when here an abundance of the best of wheat can be raised & money is more plenty than any place I have ever lived. Potatoes, Beans, corn & all Kinds of garden vegetables thrive well.

---

7. Mormon Battalion veterans were working for Johann (John) Sutter near Sacramento, California, when James Marshall discovered gold at his mill at present-day Coloma, California, in January 1848. For descriptions of circumstances surrounding the event by Battalion veterans who first recorded the discovery, see Bishop, *Henry William Bigler*, 49–64; and Smith, *Gold Discovery Journal of Azariah Smith*, 108–119.
8. For an overview of the Mormon involvement in the beginnings of the California Gold Rush see Davies, *Mormon Gold*; Rohrbough, *Days of Gold;* and Owens, *Gold Rush Saints.*
9. Walter Barney, a Mormon Battalion veteran who worked the California mines in 1848, told his nephew that when he and his companions "couldn't wash out $50.00 per day they quit that place and hunted new diggings." Barney, *One Side by Himself*, 120.
10. See the note for 6 January 1849.

Your next grand mistake is in supposing that Iron must needs be verry dear in this place. I can buy tons of it for a bit a pound, furnished from the thousands of old waggons necessarily brought here. besides there is plenty of ore & coal in the mountains & it will not take many years to convert it into Iron & Steel. You boast of the advantages of commerce. how ~~has~~ strangely has your intellect become darkened! how has the precious metal become tarnished, the fine gold grown dim! What can be the advantages of commerce in the regeneration of the world, the restoration of the House of Israel to all the blessings promised by the Father? and has he not also promised, by his servants, the destruction of the traffic of Babylon in the last days, the entire overt<h>row of her merchants & utter worthlessness of their merchandise? Israel can never be gathered & become an independant Nation so long as we hold commerce with the Nations of the Earth, for with whatever People we hold commerce, upon that People we are dependant. What else has empoverished Orregon? & w[h]at else has humbled & enslaved the celestial Empire of China that maintained her independance for so many ages, the old[e]st nation on Earth? Formerly she sent abroad her products but would receive none in return! nothing but Specie would buy her Teas, & Silks, ginghams, 'till Britain forced upon her the opium trade at the point of the Bayonet! The principle upon which all commerce is carr[i]ed on is to buy cheap & sell dear, & is founded in corruption & supported by the Sword, Till such time as we can produce & manufacture all things that we need, the constant gathering of the Saints from all parts of the world will enable them to furnish us with raw materials & various articles which we want & they will receive in exchange provisions & the products of our mechanicks labor or money, if the[y] need it. But our money will not be sent abroad for foreign articles for our principle circulating medium is a paper currency Just equal in amount to the Gold & Silver in the Vault So that merchants coming here to trade must become one of us or they can do nothing, because we shall not give them our Gold & Silver for Gewgaws and trifles. nevertheless persons in whoom the Presidency have confidence may from time to time receive, in exchange for the paper foreign coin, for we are not verry desirous of Keeping it with the pure metal. Now the Key of which I speak I find in these words. you say speaking of faith "Would to God such gifts & such power could be found on Earth, But hitherto I have not found it." Well, a certain degree of Kowledge is necessary to enable one to exercise the power of faith, & how will you obtain it except you condecend to learn of those who have it in possession?[11]

As a proof of the truth of this work, I will relate an account given by Elder [Addison] Pratt who has been for five years on a mission to the Society Islands & arrived here last fall. He found them a verry honest, Inteligen & hospitable People.[12] They entertain a great affection for him & told him what they Know

11. Jacob's preachment typifies Mormon attitudes regarding their particular approval by God in contrast to the "the world," who were generally characterized by the Saints in negative terms.
12. Addison Pratt and three companions, Knowlton Hanks, Noah Rogers, and Benjamin

of their history. according to their tradition, theirs Fathers, a great while ago in a large Ship, were driven by Eastern winds from the main Shore & wrecked on one of those low coral Islands which cannot be seen far in the night time. Out of the wreck they constructed several small craft in wich they tryed to get back to the main Land, But were <driven> on several other Islands of the same group, & being acquainted with the art of constructing water craft, they & their decendants scattered themselves over many other Islands of the Pacific. now read in the Book of Mormon, page 395, 3d Ed., & you have the whole story told![13] You wanted me to help make a farm on the Missouri [River]. We stayed to long in that sickly Land. While I was out with the Pioneers, the children were all sick, & last Spring Just as we left Winter Quarters, Oliver was taken sick with that dreadful disease so prevelant there, the Black Canker and Black Scurvy, & after suffering 'till reduced to a mere skeleton for three months, died on the 14th of August [1848] & we buried him in the wilderness Just before we reached the Sweet-Water [River]. Since, we have had no sickness in our family. Capt [Caleb] Baldwin & Wife recovered their health & came out here,[14] also Jesse Crosby,[15] John Scott[16] & Esq [Daniel] Wells. Old Brother [Hezekiah] Peck[17] & family & all the Snyders except Jane Richards, are b[e]hind, also John Crosby. When we want roses, Haws, "Briars & thorns," we go to the mountains where we also find abundance of Service Berries, But no Whortle Berries nor Winter Green. Green river, the main Branch of the colerado [River], heads near the South Pass, about 250 miles N East of here. There is no outlet to the Salt Lake, nor this part of the Great Bason. But three hundred miles South, the

Grouard, departed Nauvoo in June 1843 to begin what became the first Mormon endeavor with a non-English speaking people. Embarking from New Bedford, Massachusetts, in October 1843, the missionaries began their journey to the Pacific Islands. The following month, the leader of the four, Hanks died at sea from consumption. They were side-tracked from their initial objective, the Sandwich Islands by docking at Tubuai in April 1844. The group also proselyted in Tahiti. By the time the mission was halted by the French government in the early 1850s, over a thousand Polynesians had joined the Mormon ranks. Rogers, discouraged early, returned to the United States in 1845. Pratt left Tahiti in March 1847, and after a stay in California, arrived in Great Salt Lake City on 28 September 1848. Pratt's mission among the Polynesians in the Society Islands during the 1840s and 1850s is found in Pratt, *Journals of Addison Pratt*. For an overview of this mission through the early 1850s see Ellsworth and Perrin, *Seasons of Faith and Courage*, 1–30, and Britsch, *Unto the Islands of the Sea*, 3–20.

13. Page 395 of the Book of Mormon, 3rd edition, published in Nauvoo, Illinois, in 1840, (Book of Mormon, Alma 63:5–6, 1981) repeats the brief story of a Nephite man named Hagoth. From a point on the west coast of the western hemisphere, Hagoth and a number of his people built a ship and with "many women and children "launched it forth into the west sea" (construed by the Saints to be the Pacific Ocean), and by his efforts populated some of the Pacific Islands. For a view of how this story is interpreted by some Mormons see Parsons, "Hagoth and the Polynesians."
14. Caleb Baldwin was also part of Heber Kimball's 1848 emigrating company to Utah.
15. Jesse Crosby emigrated to Utah in 1847.
16. John Scott emigrated to Utah in 1848.
17. This is likely Hezekiah Peck.

water frows [flows] into the colerado. There is a mountaineer residing here who says he has visited a Tribe of White People who live on the colerado Eight hundred miles S East of this place. they have fortified themselves on a mountain & raise cotton, grain & vegetables in the Valley of the river.[18] A Brother [Ephraim] Green has boarded with me who says that when going out with the Mormon Battalion, on the river Hela [Gila], a Branch of the colerado, they passed through the Pema [Pima] Indians, the most friendly People he ever saw any where. they do not live by the chase, But raise Cotton (of which they make Blankets) also Wheat, Corn, Beans, Pumpkins & melons, the finest he ever saw, having to irregate their fields by ditches from the riveer 4 & 5 miles long, dug with wooden shovels. they have no trade with the Whites as they have no furs nor peltry to excite their avarice, are not Warlike. the Spaniards tried to tempt them to fall upon our People by offering them the Booty, But could not.[19] much more I could [tell you], but have not room. We hope you will not long defer the visit you speak of. We shall ever cherish the remembrance of our Brothers & Sisters & wish we could say they were in the bonds of the New & everlasting covenant.

Norton Jacob
Mr. Udney H. Jacob

P.S With respect to the Gentiles enjoying our Temple & dancing in it, you may tell them that <we> shall not only make them pay the Fidler one of these days, but dance to another tune & remember, the Lion will rise up out of his thicket for the destroyer of the Gentiles is on his way.[20]

April 6th
N. Jacob

April 7th [1849] I made 5, [Ezra] Thompson 6, [Elijah] Newman 5, [Phineas] Wright 5, [Alfred] Randal 2, [Hosea] Cushing 4, & [John] Geen 5 days work. I received 29 1/2 lbs meal & Thompson same.

[April] 9th [1849] I received 26 1/4 lbs of coarse flour of H[eber]. C. Kimball

18. See the brief discussion of white Indians lore in Sorenson, *An Ancient American Setting*, 351–352.
19. The Pima Indians, a name given them by early Spanish explorers/settlers, were indigenous to the desert American Southwest for at least two millennia. Centered in the Gila and Salt River valleys in Arizona, their origins are from Mexico rather than the north like their Athapascan Navajo neighbors. They were agricultural and characterized as peaceful by the white Anglos who encountered them in this period. When Dr. George Sanderson, the army surgeon assigned to the Mormon Battalion, visited the Pima Indians in Arizona in December 1846 he wrote: "They are savages but they are honest and industrious . . . [the] happiest [people] to all appearances I have ever seen." Sanderson, Diary, 22 December 1846.
20. Jacob's sentiment represents the universally held view by Mormon believers at the time that, through the intervention of God, they would soon subdue every impediment to the progress of the Mormon kingdom, i.e., the wicked. The climax of this epic would be the return of Jesus Christ to initiate his millennial reign.

& [Ezra] Thompson 25 1/2.

[April] 18th [1849] I received of H[eber]. C. Kimball 78 lbs of meal & [Ezra] Thompson 90 lbs. I Bought a Beef ox on foot of Brother [Alexander] Shoemaker[21] at $5.00 per hundred for the Quarters which weighed 544 pounds <$27.20>. I <let> Br Thompson have one Hind Quarter weighing 127 lbs & [Elijah] Newman a Fore Quarter 149 lbs.

Satturday [April] 28th [1849] I went to Town to attend the organization of the Legion.[22] Six companys were formed in the first cohort & five in the second cohort. Daniel H. Wells was Elected Major General, Jedediah M. Grant Brigadier of the first cohort, & Horace H. Eldridge Brigadier of the second Cohort, ~~Almon~~ <John S> Fulmer Colonel of the first Regiment, first cohort, & John Scott Colonel of the first Regmt, second Cohort. I Joined the Artillery company. Willard Snow & Ira Eldridge Majors in Fulmer's Regmt. John Pack rejected by a vote of the People. Andrew Litle [Lytle] & Henry Heriman, Majors in Scotts Regmt. John D. Lee rejected by a vote of the people.[23]

President Young remarked that the People had not been called upon to spend much time in preparing to defend themselves against their enemies since Joseph [Smith]'s death. during his lifetime much time was spent in dfending him & ourselves against mobs. When the Elders are prepared to go into the field of Battle in defense of the Truth, they are in the line of their duty, even to lay down their lives for the cause of God & the support of his Kingdom on the Earth. But not in a spirit of revenge against our enimies will we ever be sent, But in the strength of Israels God & by the Power of the Holy Ghost, doing the work because it ought to be done.[24]

---

21. This may be Alexander Shoemaker.
22. The first action in reconstituting the Nauvoo Legion, as mentioned above, occurred just the month before.
23. Hosea Stout revealed in his diary, the attitude of the men who voted against John Pack and John Lee as Legion officers.

> One circumstance took place today which I never saw before. John Pack & John D. Lee were each put in nomination for Majors by regular authority & both most contemptestously hissed down. When any person is thus duly nominated, I never before knew the people to reject it. But on this occasion it appears that they are both a perfect stink in every body's nose. The reasons of which is not needful to relate.

The censure was provoked, apparently, by the questionable behavior of Pack and Lee in the community effort to exterminate predatory animals and birds pestering the early settlers. Stout estimated that between fourteen and fifteen thousand "skelps" of wolves, foxes, and wild cats, and wings of eagles, hawks, owls, ravens, and magpies were taken during the purge. Lee, *A Mormon Chronicle*, 1:82–85, 100; Stout, *On the Mormon Frontier*, 2:351.

24. There is very little information available about the initial reorganization of the Nauvoo Legion in Utah, according to Hamilton Gardner who has described the formation of the Mormon military division in Utah. Jacob's account of Brigham Young's speech gives

Monday May first [1849] I received of H[eber]. C. K[imball] 56 1/2 lbs of meal & [Ezra] Thompson received 68 1/2 lbs of meal

May 28 [1849] I received of H[eber]. C. Kimball 15 1/2 lbs of meal, 14 1/2 of Flour & one lb of coffe. [Ezra] Thompson had 15 1/2 lbs of meal.

June 4 [1849] Started the mill. Br [Heber] Kimball present & dedicated the mill & all things pertaining to it to the Lord before it Started. it bids fair to do good business.

June 10 [1849] Brs [Heber] Kimball, [William] Wallace, [Joel] Ricks, & [John] Nebekar made a feast for the men who had built the <mill> & were present with their families which was verry acceptable as we were living on verry short rations, it [being] almost impossible to procure provisions.

After I left the mill I took up a farm on the North side of North Mill creek & built a Shanty of Boards and moved on to it on Monday the 9th of July [1849]. not being able to buy Bread-stuff for money, I was forced to go with my wife & children & glean wheat in Br [Alexander] Shoemaker's field!

Sept first [1849] I went to work for John Neff in company with Br [Ezra] Thompson repairing his Grist mill[25] by which I was enabled to pro cure Bread & other necessaries for my family. I continued at this business till February [1850] at $2.00 per day, amounting [to] $127.00.

After leaving Neff's I worked 26 days repairing Samuel Thompson's Saw mill on South Mill Creek at $3.00 per day, amounting to $78.00. I trade[d] a part of the improvement on my farm, including 20 acres of ground, to Alondus Backland [Buckland] for $80.00.

Worked at opening my farm putting in crops till the elevnth of June [1850] when by the solicitation by President [Brigham] Young I commenced work on the council House & other Publick works.[26] Boarded with Jane

---

insight into Young's primary defensive concerns at the time, though the interaction with Utah's Native Americans proved to be the Legion's early foil in territorial history.

As an illustration of the kinds of matters that occupied the attention of leaders and settlers alike during Salt Lake City's early years, one of the other actions transacted during this meeting was that "it was decided by vote that every man who allowed his cattle to trespass upon ploughed ground should be fined $1.00, and that any Bishop who neglected making a bridge across the ditches running through his ward should also be fined." Journal History, 28 April 1849, p. 3.

25. Utah Territory's second gristmill, producing the first white flour in the territory, was built in late 1848 by John Neff in Mill Creek Canyon in Salt Lake Valley. Roberts, "Pioneer Mills and Milling." 7:92, 103.

26. On 26 January 1850, Jacob had been appointed by church leaders to be the church's foreman of "joiners and carpenters" at the time Great Salt Lake City's Public Works program was initiated. This significant enterprise, which employed between 200 to 500

[Snyder] Richards one week & 5 days at .50 cts per day. ~~Commenced~~ Boarded one week & two days with br [Stephen] Winchester[27] when I came home to harvest my Wheat. Paid him $3.33.

July 4th [1850] my work had amounted to 19 days at $ [blank]. Received of the Tything office for my labor, $56.71.

July 8 [1850] returned to work at noon. [July] 17th [1850] had made 8 1/2 days & received $30.12. Boarded with [Stephen] Winchester 9 days at .50. Paid him 134 lbs of flour at $.10 = 13.40 & 13 1/2 lbs of mutton at .10. [$13.40 +] 1.35 [=] 14.75.

Sept. 10th [1850] Father Udney H. Jacob arrived quite unexpected to us from the States in good health & Spirits & took up his abode with my family. In accordance with Br Brigham [Young]'s council I purchased Leonard E. Harrinton's Hous & improvements on Block No. 104, Lot No 1[28] for five hundred dollars, one half to be paid this fall & one half in one year from the 15th of Sept having also rented my farm to Charles Hancock for one year for one third of the prodducts. I moved my family on to my new place in the city about the first of October [1850]. On the 7th [October 1850] I hired Henry. L Cook for one year at three hundred dollars.

Nov. 10th [1850] I have paid him one par of boots $5.00, & one coat & vest 12.00.

A Short time after I moved to the City we were afflicted by a sad accident. Br [Henry] Cook & Lucian [Jacob] going to red Bute Canion after wood, Lucian was riding on the forward axeltree, his feet hanging down, when one foot caught against a stump and broke his leg. But Doct [Hiram] Cannon set the bone so well that in 5 weeks he was enabled to walk with the aid of crutches which he used but one week when he laid them bye.

About the middle of Nov. [1850], Br [Henry] Cook quit work with me as he thought coul[d] do better in cutting wood in the canion & making coal.

Charles Hancock also left my farm to go to little Salt Lake [Valley] with Georg A Smith's company w<h>o started about the first of Dec. [1850] to go & make

---

men per year during the 1850s, served as the territory's largest employer which built the infrastructure of the Mormons' capital city. At the outset, joiners and carpenters earned $2 per day. Journal History, 26 January 1850; Arrington, *Great Basin Kingdom*, 108–112.

27. This may be Stephen Winchester.
28. The present location of this property, Block 104, Lot 1, in Salt Lake City, Utah, is the southeast corner of 200 North and West Temple Street, catty-corner from the northwest

a Settlement there with the view of making Iron, as that part of the country abounds in Iron ore & other min[in]g.[29]

I continued at work on the Publick works throug[h] the winter. my family suffered much by living in a cold Log cabin, which cost me much of my labor to Keep it warm enough to prevent our freezing.

Julia Ann Cook came to my house in September [1850] & remained until she was taken sick by reason of exposure & cold. at the same time my Father, from the same causes, was taken dangerously ill, but through the laying on of hands by Bishop [Joseph] Heywood & myself he was healed & gradualy recovered his health. Julia went to Br [Daniel] Bull's[30] where she could be better taken care of where she recovered her health.

On the 27th of Nov. [1850] Myself and wife received a Card from Presidents Brigham Young, H[eber]. C. Kimball, & Willard Richards to attend a Supper Party & Ball for the dedication of the Bath House. a large Party was convened & we had a verry pleasant time.[31]

In February [1851] the upper room of the Council House was finished, dedicated & the People commenced receiving their endowments[32] ~~on the 27th~~ On Thursday evening the 27th of Feb. 1851 I was called to Preside over a quorum of 12 persons to meet weekly in Prayer circle in the upper rooms of the Council House, according to the Holy order of the Priesthood.[33]

---

corner of the LDS Church's Conference Center. Norton Jacob sold this property to Orson Hyde in November 1852.

29. George Smith and his role in founding the Iron Mission in southern Utah, an initiative of LDS Church leaders to manufacture iron in their effort to become self-sufficient, is described in Shirts and Shirts, *A Trial Furnace*. After identifying iron ore, in what later became known as Iron County, Utah, a significant endeavor was mounted in the calling of "Farmers, Blacksmiths, Carpenters, Joiners, Mill Wrights, Bloomers, Moulders, Smelters, &c., Stone Cutters, Brick Layers, Stone Masons, one Shoemaker, one Tailor, &c. &c" to man the mission. The objective for the missionaries was to "saw, build and fence; erect a saw and grist mill; establish an iron foundry . . . for the furnishing of provisions and lumber for the coming year for a large number of emigrants, with their families, and castings of all kinds for the mountain settlements." *Deseret News*, 27 July 1850, quoted in Shirts and Shirts, *A Trial Furnace*, 17.

30. This may be Daniel Bull.

31. "The Warm Springs Bath House, near G. S. L. City was opened with a festival attended by the First Presidency, a number of the Apostles and other leading men. Heber C. Kimball offered the dedicatory prayer." Journal History, 27 November 1850.

32. The same religious rituals performed in the Nauvoo Temple by the Mormons before their exile from Illinois were temporarily performed in the Council House in Salt Lake City, anticipating the construction of a more appropriate building. Located on the southwest corner of what is now South Temple and Main Street, the Council House, one of the first public buildings built in Salt Lake City, served as the site for Mormon temple rites until an Endowment House (1855–1889) was built on Temple Square. The Salt Lake Temple then served as the setting for the sacred Mormon services after 1893.

33. Prayer circles are generally associated with LDS temple ceremonies. However, from 1851

My wife has hitherto been rather opposed to the Holy order of the Seal of the Covenant and of my getting other wives but about this time her mind was wrought upon by the Spirit of God to cease her resistance & <in> consequenc the Lord gave her a greater testimony of the work of the last days than she had ever received before & being through weakness & debility unable to perform alone her duties of House-wife, she put herself about seeking for another Help-mate for me, & hearing <heard> of [a] girl that wanted employment & a home, she sent to her & on Sunday the 30th day of March [1851] Maria Van Valkenburg came to reside at my House & Sunday the 20th day April [1851] ~~She~~ She was Sealed to me as my Second wife at 5 oclock P.M. by Pres. Brigham Young in his office in the upper <N West> room of the Council House, her Farther being present & also W[illard] Richards, H[eber]. C. Kimball, Joseph Young, Jed[ediah]. Grant, T[ruman]. O Angel[l], D[aniel]. H Wells, T[homas] Bullock & others.[34]

Mariah Van Valkenburg was born June 23, 1835 in the Town of Hecter, Steuben Co., New York, the daughter of Peter & Margaret Van Valkenburg. She is a Kind, obedient, & effectionate wife living in love, harmony, & Friendship in my family as though she had always been a member of it. On the 4th of July [1851] a pick nick Party was attended over at the Black Rock on the Salt Lake by the Presidency & all the Principal men of the Kingdom together with their families. I attended with my two wives & Miss Julia Ann Cook. we had a beautiful ride and a pleasant time encamped over night & returned the next day.

~~April~~ on the 24th of July [1851] the aniversary of the Entrance of the Pioneers into the Valley was celebrated <with> great rejoicing. I attended & marched in the Procession with the Pioneers, who were provided with the various Tools & implements used by them in their Pioneer campaign. I carried the Square & compass.[35]

About this time [I] Lost a valuable Horse, being drowned by O[rlando] F Mead & my Son Lucian [Jacob] in the Jordan Slough. I made application to Bishop [Edward] Hunter & <he> Sold me two Horses for $150. the last of

---

to 1878, prayer circles were held by local priesthood quorums outside of temples. See Tate, "Prayer Circle," 3:1120–1121.

34. The unique Mormon practice of polygamy was contemplated by Joseph Smith in 1831 and initiated by him in the mid-1830s in Kirtland, Ohio. While never publicly admitted by the LDS Church during Joseph Smith's lifetime, because of its assault upon monogamous sensibilities of Americans, in August 1852 apostle Orson Pratt was asked by Brigham Young to publicly announce the marital practice by the Saints. At the time of Jacob's plural marriage to Mariah Van Valkenburg, polygyny, the practice's technical nomenclature, was more openly practiced in Utah territory though not yet publicly announced. Mormon polygamy has been described in Daynes, *More Wives Than One*, Van Wagoner, *Mormon Polygamy*, and Hardy, *Solemn Covenant*.

35. The square and compass, of course, are tools of precision used by craftsman in construction. But to Latter-day Saints, as well as other cultural entities, they hold a special

August one of them Strayed or was stolen from me. I continued to Work on the Publick works at $3.00 per day & having obtained some Lumber from Br H[eber]. C Kimball's mill in pay for my work in Building it & some Adobies from Br Henry J. Cook. I set about Building me a House so that my family may be better sheltered from the inclemency of the coming Winter. I had the good fortune to fall in with Br Abraham Day & John [blank] who Laid the first foundation Stone on the first day of October [1851] and had reared the walls by the 20th [October 1851]. on the first day of January 1852 my family had moved into it & having Bishop [Joseph] Heywood, the Bishop of our Ward (17th) together with his Ladies & above fifty othe[r] persons.[36] we gave them a Feast & Dedicated the Hous in the <name of the> Lord as a Habitation of Peace & righteousness with Hymns, Prayer, thanksgiving, & rejoiceing together with musick & the Dance.

Towards the Last of Feb. [1852] Lucian [Jacob] & Mariah [Van Valkenburg Jacob] removed up to our Farm to make preperations for putting <in> our crops, Br John Crosby having farmed for us the past year upon the Shares. We concluded this year we would manage it our Selves. Mariah appeared well pleased to have an opportunity of Keeping house by herself, as some little misunderstanding had arrisen between her & my Wife Emily ~~wich~~ which grieved me verry much. But <I> hoped that our present arrangement of our domestic affairs would tend <to> produce peace and union. in this I was disappointed. Mariah in her new home associated herself with persons in possession of untrained Spirits who were in the habit of Speaking against the principals of our Holy religion & making derision of our domestic relations which served to alienate her affections from the Truth & in the same ratio to dissolve her attachments to me though I strove with all my power to do her good, give her good council & make her happy. Forseeing the tendency of these things, I resolved to again rent out my farm & remove her to a place nearer to the City where I had an opportunity of taking a da<i>ry upon Shares. one evening while conversing with her upon this subject, she verry abuptly to<ld> me she [end of document]

---

symbolic meaning regarding man's relationship to God. See Brown and Smith, *Symbols in Stone*, 105–106, 141–142, for a description of their use in Mormon temple construction.

36. At the end of the year, 1852, a census of wards in Utah Territory found fifty-two heads of households in the Salt Lake 17th Ward, located just northwest of Salt Lake City's temple block. In contrast, the adjacent ward to the west, the Salt Lake 16th Ward, where Jacob later moved in the 1850s, had 107 heads of households. Registry of Names of Persons Residing in the Various Wards . . . , 1852.

For comparison, a county census taken the previous year, indicated that Salt Lake County had 6,155 persons, about evenly distributed between men and women. Davis

Appendix 1

Norton Jacob's Family Record

NORTON JACOB, REMINISCENCE AND JOURNAL, 1844 May–1852 January, LDS Church Archives, Family and Church History Department, The Church of Jesus Christ of Latter-day Saints, Salt Lake City, Utah. The family information below is the preface to Jacob's reminiscence and diary. Jacob's diary entry for 25 January 1846 suggests the date of this genealogy's creation: "I remained at home in the forenoon & employed myself in writing the Genealegy of our family as I received from my Father [Udney Hay Jacob]." Genealogical entries identifying Norton Jacob's last seven children, all post-dating 25 January 1846, were obviously added after that date.

I was born the 11th day of August 1804 in the Town of Sheffield Berkshire County Mass. the son of Udney <H> & Elizabeth Jacob, ~~who~~ the Grand son of Richard & Elizabeth Jacob, the Gr Grand son of Richard & Thankful Jacob! the Gr. Gr. Grand Son of Joseph Jacob! He was Born about the year 1693 and died 1790, Aged 97 <years>. We supose he was born in England or Wales. Richard, his only Son, was Born about the year 1720 near Boston Mass. Died in the year 1809, aged, 88 <years>. his wife was Tha[n]kful Kellogg. Richard, <Second> Son of his Father, Richard Jacob, was born July 24th 1760, was drowned in March 1796, Agd 36 <years 8 mo>. his wife was El<i>zabeth Kellogg, the Daugter of Elisha Kellogg. She was born in Berkshire Co., Mass in the year 1758. Died 1826 Agd 68.

Step[h]en Jacob, the Elder Brother of <Grnd Father> Richard, removd to Winsor in Vermont where he Died. he had a Son Richard who died when young.

Israel Jacob, also a Brother to <Grnd Father> Richard, had a large family by two Wives. by the first he had three Sons, Sherman, Richard, & Francis.

(1)

The Record of Norton Jacob

I was born the 11th day of August 1804 in the Town of Sheffield Berkshire county Mass. the Son of Udney & Elizabeth Jacob. the Grand Son, of Richard & Elizabeth Jacob the Gr Grand son of Richard & Thankful Jacob! the Gr" Gr" Grand Son, of Joseph. Jacob.! He was Born about the year 1693 and died 1790. Aged 97 years we supose he was born in England or Wales. Richard his only Son was born about the year 1720 near Boston Mass. Died in the year 1809 aged 88 years his wife was Thankful Kellogg. Richard Second Son of his Father Richard Jacob was born July 24th 1760 was drowned in March 1796 Ag. 36 years his wife was Elizabeth Kellogg the Daugter of Elisha Kellogg She was born in Berkshire co. Mass in the year 1758. Died 1826 Agd 68

Stepen Jacob the Elder Brother of Grand Father Richard removed to Winsor in Vermont where he Died. he had a Son Richard who died when a young

Israel Jacob also a Brother to Gr. Grd Father Richard had a large family by two Wives, by the first he had three Sons Sherman, Richard & Francis

Mary Jacob the Eldest Sister of Richard was born Sheffield maried to Jonathan Curtis in Sheffield, where She Died. She had three Sons Abijah, Joseph, & Josiah who are all dead. they had Six Sisters Amanda, Thankful, Orra, Sabra, Pamela & Adelia- Amanda Married Isaac Rice in Sheffield

Keziah Jacob also a Sister of Richard was born in Sheffield & Married there to Capt Aaron Trowbridge had one Son Richard [illegible] Trowbridge one Daughter Polly

Thankful Jacob also a Sister of Richard [illegible] was born in Sheffield & Married there to Benjamin Franklin Holms, She had two Sons, Richard & William one Daughter Elizabeth who was my Nurse— her Husband's name is Wires (Lives near Hudson N.Y. 1829)

Udney Hay Jacob eldest Son of Richard Jacob Jun, was Born April 24th 1781 in Sheffield was Married there to Elizabeth Hubbard Daughter of Prosper Hubbard. She was born in Middletown in connecticut August 24, 1784 She had three Brothers Comfort dead, Prosper dead & Josiah dead.

two Sisters Martha dead & Huldah dead. Martha Married [illegible] Winslow Bierce, had one Son Sydney

Udney Hay Jacob recived his middle name in Honor of Col. Udney Hay a revolutionary officer and companion of his Father—

The beginning of Norton Jacob's record. Courtesy of the LDS Church Archives.

Mary Jacob, the Eldest Sister of Richard, was born <in Sheffield>, maried to Jonathan Curtis in Sheffield where She Died. She had three sons, Abijah, Joseph, & Josiah who are all dead. they had Six Sisters, Amanda, Thankful, Orra, Sabra, Pamela, & Adelia. Amanda Married Isaac Rice in Sheffield. Keziah Jacob, also a Sister of Richard, was born in Sheffield & Married there to Capt Aaron Trowbridge, had one Son Richard Jun Trowbridge, one Daughter, Polly.

Thankful Jacob, also a Sister of Richard Jacob, was Born in Sheffield & Married there to Benjamin Franklin Holms, She had ~~three~~ <two> Sons, Richard & Willian, one Daughter Elizabeth who was my Nurse. her Husband's name is Winis. (he lives near Hudson NY 1829)

Udney H<ay> Jacob, eldest Son of Richard ~~was born~~ Jacob Jun., was Born April 24th 1781 in Sheffield, was Married there to Elzabeth Hubbard, Daughter of Prosper Hubbard. She was born in Middletown in Connecticut <August 24, 1781> She had three Brothers, Comfort, <dead> Prosper, <Dead> & Josiah <dead>, two Sisters Martha <dead> & Huldah <Dead>. Martha Married Winslow Bierce, had one Son Sydney.

Udney Hay Jacob re[c]eived his middle name in Honor <of> Col. <Udney> Hay, a revolutionary officer and companion of his Father.

Orson Jacob, Brother of Udney, was Born in Sheffield 1785, was burned to death when two years of age.

Stephen Jacob, also Brother to Udney, was Born in Hampton Washing<ton> Co., N.Y. 1789, Died in Newburgh Agd about 33 years, had one Son Richard. Elisha Pelham Jacob, youngest Brother of Udney was born 1797 in Saratoga Co., N.Y., Town of Half moon. U[r]sula Jacob, Eldest Sister of Udney, was born in Sheffield Dec. 2d 1782, Married in Saratoga Co., N.Y. to Daniel McLeland, had 3 or 4 Sons, Richard, William. (Ursula is dead)

Thankful Jacob, <dead> Sister of Udney, was born in Hampton, Washington Co., N.Y. 1787, was Married to David Conklin in Saratoga Co., N.Y., had several Sons, John, <dead>

Eliza Jacob, Sister of Udney, was Born 1791 in Half Moon, Saratoga Co., N.Y., was Married there to Samuel Luckey, died in the city of N. York. Jason Kellogg Jacob, 2d Son of Udney, was Born in Sheffield <August 24> 1806. Married in Hancock Co., Ill. 1840 to Sarah Thompson (Daughter of David Thompson), had 3 Sons, Orson, Milton, Richford.

Prosper Hubbard Jacob, Son of Udney, was Born in Sheffield Oct. 31, 1808. Married in Busti, Chautauque Co., N.Y. to Hannah Curtis <dead>.

Stephen Jacob, Son of Udney was Born in Renselar [Renssalaer] Co., N.Y., July 30, 1811. Married in Busti to Minerva Ostrander, had two Sons & three Daughters Abram, Marvin, Elisha, & Margaret, Mary, <Amy>.

Elisha P Jacob, Son of Udney, was born in Scipio, Cayuga Co., N.Y. May 8th 1813.

Eliza <Ann> Jacob, Daughter of Udney, was Born in Chenango Co., N.Y. May 20th 1816. Married in Busti 1838 to Merrils Andrus (Son of Asahel Andrus), had three Sons, Charles, Udney, & Asahel.

Mary Jane Jacob, Daughter of Udney, was Born in Hartford, Dearborn Co., I[ndian]a, Dec. 2, 1822. Married to Milton Hamilton in Pilot-Grove, Hancock Co., Ill. August, 1839, had 1 Daughter, Lois Ann, 1 Son, Jason Adam.

I am the Eldest Son of Udney <Hay> Jacob. Married in Busti, Nov. 20th 1830 to Emily Heaton. had 5 Sons & 3 Daghters. the Eldest son, Benjamin, was born Jan. 1833. Died of Small Pox <when 2 days old>. Oliver Barr Jacob, born Jan. 5th 1834, in Jamestown Chautauque Co., N.Y. <Died August 14, 1848, near Independence Rock, Sweetwater>. Lucian Heaton Jacob, born Feb. 22d 1836, near Warsaw, Hancock Co., Ill. <died June 1876 drowned>. <carried over to 9th page> Family record <(9)> brot over from page 2.

Ira Norton Jacob was born Pilot Grove, Hancock Co., Ill. Oct. 16th 1840.

Jos[e]ph Jacob was born in Nauvoo, Hancock Co., Ill. May 20th 1845 <named after the Prophet Joseph Smith.>

Elsie P<amela> Jacob was born in Busti, Chauque [Chautauqua] Co., N York, May 13, 1831. Married in Nauvoo to Jesse Snyder, May 17, 1846.

Elizabeth Jane Jacob wa[s] born in ~~Nauvoo~~ <Pilot Grove, Hanc> ok, Co., April 8, 1838. Died same place August 24, 1839. burryed on the ridge East of my house.

Emma Jacob was born in Nauvoo, Nov. 16, 1842. Died Oct. 27, 1844. Burryed on the ridge North of my House. Emily Amelia Jacob was Born in the Land of the Potowatomy Nation near Council Bluffs, <on Silver Creek on> August 12, 1847 while I was out with the Pioneers & the day after I started from the camp of Israel in Salt Lake Valley to return home.

Mary Eliza Jacob was Born in North Kayon Ward, Salt Lake Valley, December 25th, 1849.

Isaac Jacob was born in the 17th Ward, Salt Lake City, June 24th 1852.

Norton Kellogg Jacob was Born <April 2d 1860> in Spa[n]ish Fork City, U.T. Co., Utah Teritory. Fra[n]k Graham Jacob was born <May 7th 1862> in Mound City, Provo Valley, Wasatch Co., U.T.

[In a hand other than Norton Jacob's.] Sidney Osborn Jacob, Born March 22 1865 in Mound City, ~~Provo V~~ Wasatch Co., U.T.

Benjamin Alonzo Jacob, Born June 18th 1868 in American Fork, Utah Co., U.T.

Appendix 2

Roster of the Pioneer Camp

Bagley in Bullock, *Camp of the Saints*, 130; Roberts, *Comprehensive History of the Church*, 3:186–187.

1st Ten [nine]. Wilford Woodruff, John S. Fowler, Jacob D. Burnham, Orson Pratt, Joseph Egbert, John M. Freeman, Marcus B. Thorpe, George A. Smith, George Wardle.

2nd Ten [eleven]. Thomas Grover, Ezra T. Benson, Barnabas L. Adams, Roswell Stevens, Amasa M. Lyman, Starling G. Driggs, Albert Carrington, Thomas Bullock, George Brown, Willard Richards, Jesse C. Little.

3rd Ten. Phinehas H. Young, John Y. Green, Thomas Tanner, Brigham Young, Addison Everett, Truman O. Angell, Lorenzo D. Young, Bryant Stringham, Albert P. Rockwood, Joseph S. Scofield.

4th Ten [eleven]. Luke S. Johnson, John Holman, Edmund Ellsworth, Alvarus Hanks, George R. Grant, Millen Atwood, Samuel B. Fox, Tunis Rappleye, Eli Harvey Peirce, William Dykes, Jacob Weiler.

5th Ten. Stephen H. Goddard, Tarlton Lewis, Henry G. Sherwood, Zebedee Coltrin, Sylvester H. Earl, John Dixon, Samuel H. Marble, George Scholes, William Henrie, William A. Empey.

6th Ten. Charles Shumway, Andrew Shumway, Thomas Woolsey, Chauncey Loveland, Erastus Snow, James Craig, William Wordsworth, William Vance, Simeon Howd, Seeley Owen.

7th Ten [twelve]. James Case, Artemas Johnson, William C. A. Smoot, Franklin B. Dewey, William Carter, John or Franklin G. Losee, Burr Frost, Datus Ensign, Franklin B. Stewart, Monroe Frink, Eric Glines, Ozro Eastman.

8th Ten [thirteen]. Seth Taft, Horace Thornton, Stephen Kelsey, John S. Eldredge, Charles D. Barnum, Almon W. Williams, Rufus Allen, Robert T. Thomas, James W. Stewart, Elijah Newman, Levi N. Kendall, Francis Boggs, David Grant.

9th Ten. Heber C. Kimball, Howard Egan, William A. King, Thomas Cloward, Hosea Cushing, Robert Byard, George Billings, Edison Whipple, Philo Johnson, Carlos Murray.

10th Ten [eleven]. Appleton M. Harmon, William Clayton, Horace K. Whitney, Orson K. Whitney, Orrin P. Rockwell, Nathaniel T. Brown, R. Jackson Redden, John Pack, Francis M. Pomeroy, Aaron Farr, Nathaniel Fairbanks.

11th Ten. John S. Higbee, John Wheeler, Solomon Chamberlain, Conrad Kleinman, Joseph Rooker, Perry Fitzgerald, John H. Tippetts, James Davenport, Henson Walker, Benjamin Rolfe.

12th Ten [nine]. Norton Jacob, Charles A. Harper, George Woodward, Stephen Markham, Lewis Barney, George Mills, Andrew Gibbons, Joseph Hancock, John W. Norton.

13th Ten [nine]. Shadrach Roundy, Hans C. Hansen, Levi Jackman, Lyman Curtis, John Brown, Matthew Ivory, David Powell, Hark Lay (Black), Oscar Crosby (Black).

14th Ten [eight]. Joseph Mathews, Gilbard Summe, John Gleason, Charles Burke, Alexander P. Chesley, Rodney Badger, Norman Taylor, Green Flake (Black), [Ellis Eames, who returned to Winter Quarters from the Pioneer camp on the 18th of April on account of sickness.]

Clarissa Decker Young, Ellen Sanders Kimball, Harriet Young, Perry Young (child), Sabriski Young (child).

~

Biographical Notes

~

Sources

Information for the brief biographical notes used to identify those mentioned in the text were assembled from a wide variety of sources, but are particularly reliant upon information compiled by, in alphabetical order, the Ancestral File of the Family and Church History Department of the LDS Church; Will Bagley, "Galaxy of Mormon Pioneers" in Bullock, *The Pioneer Camp of the Saints*; Susan Easton Black, comp., *Membership of the Church of Jesus Christ of Latter-day Saints*; Susan Easton Black, comp., *Early Members of the Reorganized Church of Jesus Christ of Latter Day Saints*; Kate B. Carter, comp., "First Company to Enter Salt Lake Valley"; Lyndon W. Cook, *Revelations of the Prophet Joseph Smith*; "1847 Pioneers," *Deseret News 1997–98 Church Almanac*; Frank Esshom, *Pioneers and Prominent Men of Utah*; Historian's Office, Iowa Branch Index, 1839–1859; Andrew Jenson, *Latter-day Saints' Biographical Encyclopedia*; Dean C. Jessee, "Biographical Register," *The Papers of Joseph Smith*; Carl V. Larson, *A Database of the Mormon Battalion*; Nauvoo Legion (Ill.), Files 1841–1845; Nauvoo Restoration, Nauvoo Seventies List; Nauvoo Stake, Nauvoo Ward Census, 1842; *Nauvoo Temple Endowment Register*; Marvin E. Wiggins, comp., *Mormons and Their Neighbors*; Historical Department, "Winter Quarters Ward Membership Lists, 1846–1848"; Florence C. Youngberg, ed., *Conquerors of the West*; and Zarahemla Stake, Record of Members.

Definitions

Mormon, LDS, and Saints refer to members of The Church of Jesus Christ of Latter-day Saints.

RLDS refers to members of the Reorganized Church of Jesus Christ of Latter Day Saints, now the Community of Christ.

Kirtland is located in Lake County in northeastern Ohio, near Cleveland and Lake Erie.

Nauvoo, in Hancock County, Illinois, was founded by the Mormons on a peninsula of the Mississippi River.

Winter Quarters later became part of Florence, Nebraska, a northern suburb of Omaha, on the Missouri River.

The LDS Church branches in western Iowa, such as Pottawattamie, Blockhouse, Council Point, were located in Iowa's Pottawattamie County, bounded on the west by the Missouri River.

Salt Lake City is located in northern Utah and was the territorial and later state capital.

Priesthood offices in the LDS Church mentioned below include apostles (or members of the Quorum of Twelve Apostles), bishops, elders, seventies, high priests, and patriarchs, all lay offices.

Zion's Camp, a Mormon military brigade, in 1834 marched to Missouri in two segments, one from Kirtland, Ohio, and the other from Pontiac, Michigan, to recover property and resources owned by Latter-day Saints who had been expelled from Jackson County in the previous year.

The military and security component for the Saints in Nauvoo, Illinois, was known as the Nauvoo Legion, organized in 1841.

The Council of Fifty, generally composed of as many members, was formed by Joseph Smith in 1844 as a secretive advisory group regarding political, economic, and social matters of the Saints. A few non-Latter-day Saints were part of the body.

In ecclesiastical jurisdictions, generally a branch is a small unit of the LDS Church led by a lay presidency, while a ward is a larger unit, governed by a lay bishopric, and is usually organized in a more populous Mormon center. Both branches and wards were attached to stakes, larger geographical designations, though at the outset a branch and a stake could be the same entity.

NAMES THAT APPEAR IN NORTON JACOB'S RECORD

Arza Adams (1804–1889), from Ontario, Canada, was baptized a Mormon in 1836. Ordained an elder the following year, he served as a missionary before moving his family to Missouri in 1838. After leaving that state, he moved to Nauvoo where he became a policeman, and was one who carried documents to Nauvoo from John Taylor and Willard Richards who described the Smiths' murders in Carthage, Illinois. A seventy and a carpenter on the temple, he was endowed in the Nauvoo Temple. He later lived in the Pottawattamie Branch before joining the Mormon vanguard brigade in 1847. He emigrated to Utah with his family in 1849.

Barnabas (Barnaby) L. Adams (1812–1869) was a Canadian who converted to Mormonism at age 23. He was one of the original company of pioneers to Utah in 1847 and after returning to Winter Quarters, took his family to Utah in 1848. He was a lumberman who furnished lumber for several important Salt Lake City buildings, including the tabernacle and theater. He died in Salt Lake City after an accident.

James Allred (1784–1876), from North Carolina, was baptized in 1834, the same year he joined Zion's Camp. He became a high priest, one of the Nauvoo Legion, a bodyguard for Joseph Smith, and was endowed in the Nauvoo Temple. An influential community leader while the Saints temporarily gathered in settlements on the Missouri River, he served on the local high council and lived in the Council Point Branch. He emigrated to Utah in 1851 and became one of the early settlers of Sanpete County. He died in Spring City, the community he helped found.

Augustus Leander Anderson (1832–1846) was the oldest of four children of William Anderson and Emeline Tilton Stewart. He was killed with his father by a county militia during the battle at Nauvoo in September 1846.

William Anderson (1809–1846), born in Maine, joined the LDS Church in 1841. A seventy, his missionary work in the area of Chicago, Illinois, produced several dozen converts to Mormonism. He moved to Nauvoo in September 1844 and was later endowed in the Nauvoo Temple in December 1845. He was killed by a county militia in the attack upon Nauvoo in September 1846.

Truman O. Angell (1810–1887), born in Rhode Island, was a brother of Brigham Young's wife Mary Ann. He joined with the Mormons in 1833. When he moved to Kirtland in 1835 he became a seventy and worked on the temple's construction, something he later did as well in Nauvoo. There he lived in the 4th Ward, served in the Nauvoo Legion, and was endowed in the temple. A member of the pioneer vanguard to Utah in 1847, he was later appointed Church architect, and built Young's Beehive and Lion houses, though his principle work was the St. George and Salt Lake temples. He died in Salt Lake City.

Almon W. Babbitt (1813–1856), from Massachusetts and a lawyer, he joined the LDS Church in the early 1830s. One of Zion's Camp, he later became Kirtland (Ohio) Stake president in 1841, and led the church for a time in Ramus, Illinois. In 1844 Babbitt was elected to the Illinois legislature from Hancock County, and was endowed in the Nauvoo Temple. When the Saints evacuated Nauvoo, he became one of the trustees of church property. He emigrated to Utah in 1848 where he later became territorial secretary. While traveling between Washington, D.C., and Salt Lake City, he was killed in Nebraska by Cheyenne Indians.

Adolphus Babcock (1800–1872) was born in Massachusetts. After joining the LDS Church, he moved to Jackson County, Missouri, and later to Nauvoo, where he lived in the 2nd Ward. He participated in Nauvoo Temple rites in

February 1846. Babcock and his family wintered at the Pawnee mission for the winter of 1846–1847. A farmer, he emigrated in 1847 to Utah, and died there in Spanish Fork.

Jacob Benjamin Backenstos (1811–1857), born in Pennsylvania, moved to Illinois in 1838. He was appointed clerk of the Hancock County court in 1841. He led local Democrats in 1843. In August 1844 he was elected to represent Hancock County in the state legislature, and the next year in August 1845 became county sheriff. He fought to save the Nauvoo Charter which was defeated by state leaders. He was arrested, tried, and acquitted for Franklin Worrell's 1845 death. He had close ties to the Mormons, though he never became one of them. After he resigned as sheriff in 1846, he was commissioned a captain in the Mexican War, though he finally resigned his commission in 1851. After lingering difficulties with the military, he took his own life in Oregon in 1857.

Rodney Badger (1823–1853) was from Vermont and became a Latter-day Saint in 1838. He helped his family move to Nauvoo, where he was endowed in the temple. One of the first pioneers to Utah in 1847, he went part-way and returned to help those following, which included his wife. They continued on to Utah where, after arriving, he served in a bishopric and as a member of Utah's Nauvoo Legion. He died by drowning in a swollen river while trying to save a family in distress.

Eli Bagley (1804–1889) was born in Ohio. During the Nauvoo, Illinois, period of Mormonism, he lived nearby in Appanoose. He died in Ferndale, California.

Caleb Baldwin (1791–1849), born in New York, was a War of 1812 veteran. After becoming a Mormon in 1830, he endured the Mormon persecution in Missouri, including incarceration with Joseph Smith in the Liberty Jail through the winter of 1838–1839. He lived in the Nauvoo 3rd and 4th wards, and was endowed in the Nauvoo Temple. In Winter Quarters, he lived in the 21st Ward. He emigrated to Utah in 1848 where he died the following year.

James Baldwin (1791–1875), from England, after emigrating to Nauvoo was endowed in the temple. He later joined the Saints in exile on the Missouri River, where he was a member of the Winter Quarters 21st Ward. He was ordained a high priest in the Mormon priesthood in 1851. He died in Salt Lake City.

Lewis Barney (1808–1894), born in New York, became a Latter-day Saint in 1840. Ordained a seventy in Nauvoo, he worked on the Nauvoo Temple and was endowed there in February 1846. He joined the pioneer vanguard to Utah in 1847, one of Norton Jacob's ten, before returning to retrieve his family in western Iowa. Finally relocating to Utah in 1852, he helped settle ten valleys in Utah, Arizona, New Mexico, and in Colorado, where he died.

Noah Willis Bartholomew (1808–1876), from New York, became a Mormon in 1844. He was part of the Winter Quarters 15th Ward before emigrating to Utah in 1848. After first settling in the Salt Lake Valley, he was one of the southern Utah expedition in 1849–1850. He was later called to settle in Fillmore, Utah, where he became the first bishop and where he died.

William Ezra Beckstead (1827–1909), from Canada, converted to Mormonism in 1839. Ordained a seventy, he later enlisted in the Mormon Battalion in 1846 and was one of those who wintered at Pueblo, Colorado, before joining with the pioneer vanguard in the Salt Lake Valley in 1847. He later removed to California where he died.

John Cook Bennett (1804–1867), a physician from Massachusetts, after his Mormon baptism in 1840 he acquired one of the highest profiles among the Saints. Mayor of Nauvoo, general in the Nauvoo Legion, counselor to Joseph Smith, Bennett's influence was great, including his instrumentality in securing a city charter for Nauvoo from the Illinois legislature. However, Bennett fell out of favor the following year when his errant moral behavior became known. He later became an opponent of Joseph Smith and the Mormons and briefly connected with James Strang's movement. Bennett later died in Polk City, Iowa.

Ezra T. Benson (1811–1869), from Massachusetts, became a Mormon in 1840 and moved to Nauvoo the following year. He served a mission in 1842–1843 in eastern America. Upon his return he became a Nauvoo high council member, and was endowed in the Nauvoo Temple. During the Saints' exile from Nauvoo in 1846, he was ordained one of the Mormon Twelve Apostles. He lived for a time in the Pottawattamie Branch before joining with the pioneer vanguard to Utah in 1847. After relocating his family to Utah, he served several other missions for the LDS Church before his death in Ogden, Utah.

Samuel Bent (1778–1846), a Massachusetts native, grew up a practicing Congregationalist and served as a colonel in the Massachusetts militia. Baptized in Pontiac, Michigan, in 1833, he joined Zion's Camp in 1834. He was later imprisoned in Richmond, Missouri, during Mormon troubles in 1838. In Nauvoo he became a colonel in the Second Cohort of the Nauvoo Legion, a member of the Nauvoo High Council and the Council of Fifty, and was endowed in the Nauvoo Temple. In 1844 he served a mission to Illinois, Indiana, and Michigan. Designated to lead 100 Saints in the evacuation of Nauvoo, he later served as presiding officer for the LDS Church at Garden Grove, Iowa, where he died in August 1846.

John M. Bernhisel (1799–1881), born in Pennsylvania, was a medical doctor when he embraced Mormonism. Ordained a high priest, he became a church leader in New York. In 1843 he moved to Nauvoo where he became an intimate of Joseph Smith. Immigrating to Utah in 1851, he was elected Utah's first delegate to Congress, where he served for eight years, thereby becoming one of Utah Territory's most influential figures before his death in Salt Lake City, Utah.

Titus Billings (1793–1866), from Massachusetts, was the second person baptized a Mormon in Kirtland in 1830. Ordained an elder in 1832, he later became a counselor to the church's first bishop, Edward Partridge. He was involved in the Mormon difficulties in Missouri and emigrated to Lima, Illinois, in 1839. He became an officer in the Nauvoo Legion in 1841 and was endowed in the Nauvoo Temple. Billings was involved with George Miller's group at the Ponca River and lived in the Winter Quarters 11th Ward. He emigrated to Utah in 1848, was an early settler of Manti, and later died in Provo, Utah.

John Bills (1819–1850) from Pennsylvania and a tailor, was baptized a Mormon in 1836. He became a seventy, lived in the Nauvoo 4th Ward, and was a Nauvoo Legion officer. He tailored Joseph Smith's Legion uniform. He was endowed in the Nauvoo Temple. Emigrating to Utah in 1848, he later relocated to California where he died.

Charles Bird (1803–1884), from New Jersey, after becoming a Mormon, emigrated to Nauvoo. There he lived in the 1st Ward, served in the Nauvoo Legion, and was endowed in the Nauvoo Temple. He later played an important role in establishing the LDS Church on the Missouri River, where he was a member of the Winter Quarters 17th Ward and Council Point Branch. He was one of three, while the Saints were on the Missouri River, who negotiated with the local Indian tribes on behalf of the church. After emigrating to Utah, he lived in Mendon, Utah, where he was major and justice of the peace, and where he died.

William Bird (1823–ca. 1892) was born in New York. He joined the Mormon Battalion in 1846 and was discharged in 1847. Returning to Iowa, he affiliated with the Pottawattamie Branch. He later relocated to Utah and later still to Idaho, where he is buried in Paris, Idaho.

Lilburn W. Boggs (1792–1860) was a Kentuckian who married the granddaughter of frontiersman Daniel Boone. After moving to St. Louis, Missouri, where he was a merchandiser, he settled in Independence, Missouri. Following his service as lieutenant governor, he became governor of Missouri from 1836–1840. He is most noted for the extermination order he enacted in

October 1838, expelling the Saints from Missouri. He emigrated to California in 1846 where he later died in Napa Valley.

James Bordeaux (1814–1878), the son of a French-Canadian, was born and lived near St. Louis, Missouri, for two decades. He may have entered the fur trade and ventured to the West at the early age of twelve. Having worked for the American Fur Company at Fort Laramie for over a decade, he was the acting bourgeois when the Saints arrived. His positive relationships with the Sioux, in part due to his marriage to a Brule woman, contributed to his success. After the U.S. government purchased the fort in 1849 Bordeaux stayed in the region for another twenty years before relocating to South Dakota where he died.

Alexander Boss (1822–1904) was in the emigrating companies that followed the pioneer vanguard to Utah in 1847. He later removed to California, where he died.

William Boyce (1823–1887) was born in New York. He later emigrated in 1847 to Utah, where he lived out his life in South Cottonwood.

James (Jim or Old Gabe) Bridger (1804–1881) was a Virginian. His family moved near St. Louis, Missouri, when he was a boy. While still a teenager in 1822 he answered William H. Ashley's call for 100 young men to ascend the Missouri River. He was, perhaps, in 1824 the first Anglo to see the Great Salt Lake. He became one of the most noted of western frontiersmen. After his venture in the fur trade, he established, with Louis Vasquez, a strategically placed fort on Black's Fork of the Green River in southwestern Wyoming. After a fracture with Bridger, the Mormons bought the fort from Vasquez. After leaving the West, he moved to the Independence, Missouri, area where he died in 1881.

James S. Brown (1801–1863), born in North Carolina, joined the LDS Church in 1838. He later served as a missionary to the Southern States and was endowed in the Nauvoo Temple. He joined the Mormon Battalion where he became captain of Company C, and accompanied the sick detachment of the Battalion who wintered in Pueblo, Colorado, before joining the vanguard in Utah in 1847. Brown went on to California where he obtained the pay for the Battalion's service during the Mexican War. Returning to Utah, he used some of the money to purchase for the Mormons Miles Goodyear's property at Ogden, Utah. He later served a brief mission to British Guiana and became an Ogden city councilor. He died in Ogden, the result of an accident.

John Brown (1820–1897) was from Tennessee and became a Mormon in 1841. He served a mission to the American South and was later endowed in the Nauvoo Temple. He helped organize the Mississippi Saints who wintered at Pueblo, Colorado, and who later joined the vanguard pioneers in 1847 in Utah. Brown, himself, previously returned to Winter Quarters in early 1847 and joined the pioneer vanguard. He was a mayor and bishop in Pleasant Grove, Utah, where he died.

Nathaniel Thomas Brown (–1848) was one of the original pioneers to Utah in 1847. He was killed in 1848 in Council Bluffs, Iowa, while planning to return to Utah.

Alondus De Lafayette Buckland (1823–1852/53) was from Vermont. Not long after his baptism into Mormonism, he was one of the *Brooklyn* Saints who journeyed to California from New York in 1846. He lived for a time in California before emigrating in 1849 to Utah, where he lived briefly in Bountiful. He died from cholera on the plains out of Ft. Leavenworth while returning to Utah from a mission to eastern Canada.

Daniel B. Bull (1814–1885), born in England, was baptized a Mormon in 1844. Ordained a high priest, he emigrated to Utah in 1849 where he was a gunsmith, including service for Brigham Young. He died in Morgan, Utah.

Thomas Bullock (1816–1885), from England, became a Mormon in England in 1841. After emigrating to Nauvoo, he became a clerk to Joseph Smith, and was endowed in the Nauvoo Temple. In Iowa, Bullock was a member of the Winter Quarters 17th Ward. One of the original company to Utah in 1847, he was official clerk of the trek and rendered one of the most important accounts of the journey. He took his family in 1848 to Utah, where he served as clerk of Salt Lake and Summit counties, the territorial House of Representatives, and the LDS Church Historian's Office. He died in Coalville, Utah.

Harrison Burgess (1814–1883), from New York, was baptized a Mormon in 1832. He moved to Jackson County, Missouri. He later joined Zion's Camp in 1834 and became a seventy the following year, eventually serving as a quorum leader. He was endowed in the Nauvoo Temple. Serving as a missionary in the United States and England, after emigrating to Utah, he was sent to the Southern Utah Mission. He was appointed bishop in Pine Valley, where he later died.

William Burton (1809–1851), an Englishman, immigrated to Upper Canada where he was baptized a Mormon in 1837. Ordained an elder, he moved to Illinois where he lived in Walnut Grove. He was endowed in the Nauvoo Temple. While among the Saints on the Missouri River, he lived in the Blockhouse Branch. He emigrated to Utah and later served a mission in England.

Reynolds Cahoon (1790–1861), a New Yorker, served during the War of 1812. He was baptized in October 1830. A high priest and counselor to Bishop Newel Whitney in 1832, later at Adam-Ondi-Ahnman, in Missouri, he became counselor in the stake presidency. In Nauvoo he served in the Nauvoo Legion and in the Council of Fifty and was endowed in the temple. He emigrated in 1848 to Utah in 1848 and later died in South Cottonwood.

Hiram (also Hyrum) Cannon (1786–), born in Massachusetts, after joining with the Saints on the Missouri River was a member of the 15th and 21st wards in Winter Quarters. A medical doctor in early Utah, he had a reputation for being resistant to Mormonism, though his son Marsena became a notable photographer among the Saints. The elder Cannon died in Salt Lake City.

Daniel Carn (1802–1872), born in Pennsylvania, was baptized a Mormon in 1830. After removing to Nauvoo, he lived in the 4th Ward before being appointed bishop of the Nauvoo 6th Ward. He was endowed in the Nauvoo Temple in December 1845. He was a policeman, flour inspector for Nauvoo city, Nauvoo Legionaire, and a trustee of the Nauvoo Mercantile and Mechanical Association. He was appointed bishop of the Winter Quarters 10th Ward before emigrating to Utah. He served a mission to Germany in 1851 as mission president and later died in Salt Lake City.

Isaac Carpenter (1827–1910), lived in Hancock County, Illinois, after his baptism. He later enlisted in the Mormon Battalion in 1846 and was one of those who wintered at Pueblo, Colorado, before joining with the pioneer vanguard in the Salt Lake Valley in 1847. He helped to colonize the Fort Supply area in Wyoming, and later lived in Nevada, California, and Colorado, where he died.

James Case (1794–1858) was born in Connecticut. He was employed at a missionary outpost for Native Americans in Nebraska where he became a Mormon. He became one of the pioneer vanguard in 1847, and after locating his family to Utah, he went to Sanpete County where he was appointed to the Utah legislature. Besides a mission to Illinois, determined to assist the Indians, he later served an Oklahoma mission to the Native Americans. He died in Sanpete County, Utah, soon after his return.

William W. Casto (1816–1894), from Indiana, was endowed in the Nauvoo Temple. With his brother James, he joined the Mormon Battalion in 1846 and was one of the company who had wintered at Pueblo, Colorado. Upon connecting with the pioneer vanguard he was numbered with Norton Jacob's ten. Casto later settled in the Salt Lake Valley where he died.

Solomon Chamberlain (1788–1862), from Connecticut, was one of the earliest converts to Mormonism in 1830 and one of the earliest promoters of Joseph Smith. He lived among the Saints in Kirtland, Jackson County, Missouri, and Nauvoo, where he lived in the 2nd Ward and was endowed in the temple. After living among the Saints on the Missouri River in the Winter Quarters 22nd Ward, he was one of the older men to accompany the pioneer vanguard to Utah in 1847. He later went to California as part of the gold rush before returning to Utah where he died in Washington, Utah.

Alexander P. Chesley (1814–1884), from Virginia, was a lawyer. After his conversion to Mormonism, he was endowed in the Nauvoo Temple, and later settled with the North Pigeon and Macedonia branches in Iowa before becoming one of the pioneer vanguard to Utah in 1847. He was a teacher and lawyer in Provo, Utah, until going on a mission to Australia in 1856. He never returned to the United States, dying in Australia.

Benjamin L. Clapp (1814–1860) was born in Alabama. After his conversion to Mormonism he served as a missionary in Kentucky and Alabama. He joined the Saints during their persecution in Missouri. After removing to Nauvoo, where he lived in the 1st Ward, Clapp was chosen as one of three replacements in the presidency of the First Quorum of Seventy, the body just junior to the Twelve Apostles. He was endowed in the Nauvoo Temple. Among the Saints on the Missouri River, he lived in the Winter Quarters 14th and 15th wards and the Pottawattamie Branch. After emigrating to Utah, he was excommunicated from the LDS Church in 1859 and departed for California where he died the following year.

Timothy Baldwin Clark (1778–1848), born in Connecticut, became a Latter-day Saint in 1832. He was later ordained a high priest and endowed in the Nauvoo Temple in January 1846. He died in Illinois.

Hiram B. Clawson (1826–1912) was a New Yorker. His family became Mormons in 1838 and they moved to Nauvoo in 1841, where he was endowed in the temple. At Winter Quarters he was a member of the 17th Ward. After emigrating to Utah in 1848, he became business manager for Brigham Young. He also supervised construction of Salt Lake City's Council House and was later instrumental in the operation of Zion's Cooperative Mercantile Institution. He died in Salt Lake City.

William Clayton (1814–1879), an Englishman, after converting to Mormonism, emigrated to Nauvoo, where he lived in the 4th Ward. He became a secretary to Joseph Smith and city treasurer of Nauvoo, where he was also endowed in the temple. He wrote the famous Mormon anthem "All is Well"

(Come, Come Ye Saints) in 1846 while crossing Iowa during the exodus. In Winter Quarters he lived in the 17th Ward. One of the pioneer vanguard to Utah in 1847, he helped develop the "roadometer," measuring the trek, and kept the most comprehensive account of the journey. He later died in Salt Lake City.

Thomas P. Cloward (1823–1909), from Pennsylvania, was a shoemaker. After becoming a Latter-day Saint, he located at Nauvoo before emigrating west where he became a member of the Winter Quarters 13th Ward and later the Rocky Ford Branch in Iowa. One of the original pioneers to Utah in 1847, he took his family to Utah in 1852 where he was a shoemaker in Utah County. He died in Payson, Utah.

Andrew Colton (1817–1894) was a New Yorker. After becoming a Mormon, he was a member of the Nauvoo 2nd Ward and of the Winter Quarters 3rd Ward before emigrating to Utah in 1850, where he lived in Weber County. He later moved to Kansas where he died.

Zebedee Coltrin (1804–1887), born in New York, was baptized a Mormon and ordained an elder in 1831. He followed the church in Ohio, Missouri, and then Nauvoo, before returning to Kirtland. He became president of the Seventies quorum in Kirtland in 1835, where he was also appointed a counselor in the Kirtland Stake presidency. Later ordained a high priest, he was part of the Kalamazoo Conference meeting at the beginning of June 1844. He was endowed in the Nauvoo Temple. At Winter Quarters he lived in the 22nd Ward and, in Iowa, the Pottawattamie Branch. Coltrin later emigrated to Utah, where he died in Spanish Fork.

Henry Lyman Cook (1803–1869), born in New York, was baptized a Mormon in 1837. He was ordained a seventy in 1844, served in the Nauvoo Legion, and was endowed in the Nauvoo Temple in January 1846. Norton Jacob performed his marriage in 1843 in Nauvoo. After emigrating to Utah, he died in Goshen, Utah.

Julia Ann Cook (1836–1911), born in Canada, was the daughter of Henry Cook. She married Asa E. Bigelow in 1853 and later died in Wallsburg, Utah.

Jehu Cox (1803–1893), from Kentucky, became a Mormon in 1838. He moved to Nauvoo in 1841 and was endowed in the temple in February 1846. He emigrated with his family to Utah in 1848. He became a bishop's counselor in Salt Lake County before moving to Sanpete Valley, where he later died in Fairview, Utah.

James Craig (1821–1868), from Ireland, after joining the Saints on the Missouri River, was a member of the Winter Quarters 11th Ward. One of the original pioneer company to Utah in 1847, he lived for a time in Mill Creek and later served a mission to England and Ireland. He was called to help colonize southern Utah and died in Santa Clara, Utah.

Jesse Wentworth Crosby (1820–1893), from Nova Scotia and a brother of John Crosby, was baptized a Mormon in 1838. He traveled to Nauvoo the following year. He began a series of missions in 1840 that led him to Canada, Illinois, Michigan, New York, and Massachusetts. He worked on the Nauvoo Temple and was endowed in January 1846. He emigrated to Utah in 1847 and later served a mission to Britain in 1850–1852. He died in Panguitch, Utah.

John Knowles Crosby (1812–1898), from Nova Scotia and a brother of Jesse Crosby, he was endowed in the Nauvoo Temple and was later appointed leader of the Macedonia Branch in 1849. After emigrating in 1850 to Utah, he lived in Davis County where he died in Bountiful.

Benjamin Cross (ca. 1789/91–), with his wife Roxana, emigrated to Utah in 1848. A farmer, he was the first LDS bishop in Payson, Utah, in 1851.

Robert Crow (1794–1876), from Tennessee, converted to Mormonism in 1838. He led a group of seventeen from Mississippi to Utah in 1846–1847. After he determined the pioneer vanguard was going to wait until 1847 to go to Utah, his company wintered in 1846–1847 with the Mormon Battalion's sick detachment at Pueblo, Colorado, and joined the original pioneers in the Salt Lake Valley the next summer. He later lived in southern Utah before relocating to California where he died.

Lyman Curtis (1812–1898), from Massachusetts, was baptized a Latter-day Saint in 1833. He assisted in the Kirtland Temple's construction and joined Zion's Camp in 1834. He endured the Mormon difficulties in Missouri and Nauvoo, where he lived in the 2nd Ward and was endowed in the temple. After temporarily settling on the Missouri River he became a member of the Winter Quarters 3rd Ward. One of the pioneer vanguard to Utah in 1847, he later took his family to Utah in 1850, and eventually ended up living in southern Utah. After serving a mission to the Indians in that region, he moved to Utah County and died in Salem, Utah.

Hosea Cushing (1826–1854), born in Massachusetts, was baptized a Mormon in 1844 and ordained an elder, and immediately began serving a mission. Arriving in Nauvoo in 1845, he worked on and was endowed in the Nauvoo Temple, and later endured the Saints' exile from Illinois. He was part of the pioneer vanguard in 1847, and after returning to the Missouri River settlements to retrieve his family, he took them in 1848 to Utah. One of Utah's Nauvoo

Legion, he died in Salt Lake City, suffering from the effects of starvation during the Walker Indian War.

Alpheus Cutler (1784–1864), born in New Hampshire, was a War of 1812 veteran. He joined Mormonism in 1833. He followed the Mormon course through Ohio and Missouri before locating in Nauvoo. Later he joined the Nauvoo Legion, became a member of the Nauvoo High Council, and the secretive quasi-political body known as the Council of Fifty. He was captain of Joseph Smith's bodyguards, and was endowed in the Nauvoo Temple. Upon the expulsion of the Saints from Nauvoo, he crossed Iowa in 1846 and formed one of the first settlements for the Mormons in Nebraska, Cutler's Park. He acquired a significant position of influence for the Saints on the Missouri River. Though he initially planned to go West with the Saints, after friction with the LDS Church's apostolic leadership over Cutler's designs and activity among Iowa Indians, he was excommunicated in April 1851. Cutler became one of the fragmentary alternatives for those previously attached to Mormonism. He died in southwestern Iowa.

Charles Dalton (1810–1891), from Pennsylvania, after his baptism was appointed to preside over church matters in the Michigan counties of Calhoun and Jackson. He was endowed in the Nauvoo Temple. After emigrating to Utah, he served in the Salmon River Mission for the LDS Church. He died in Ogden, Utah.

James Davenport (1802–1885), born in Vermont, was a blacksmith and an early convert to Mormonism in 1830. Emigrating to Nauvoo in 1845, he was endowed in the Nauvoo Temple. He later plied his trade for the original pioneer company to Utah in 1847, though he was assigned to assist in running the ferry on the North Platte River. After removing his family to Utah, he lived in several communities, including two in Cache Valley. He died in Richmond, Utah.

Daniel Davis (1808–1892), born in Massachusetts, became a Latter-day Saint in 1845, the same year he was ordained a seventy. He was one of Sheriff Jacob Backenstos's posse in Hancock County, Illinois, in the prelude to the Mormon expulsion from the state. Endowed in the Nauvoo Temple in January 1846, he was adopted into Heber Kimball's family. He lived in the Winter Quarters 17th Ward before going west. He died in Bountiful, Utah.

Abraham Day III (1817–1900) was a Vermonter. A machinist, he joined the Latter-day Saints in 1838 and later became a member of the Mormon Battalion. After emigrating to Utah in 1851, he built the first grist mills in Springville, Mt. Pleasant, and Nephi, Utah. He died in Lawrence, Utah.

Moses Deming (1804–1871), from Massachusetts, became a Mormon in 1841. He was ordained a seventy, was part of the Nauvoo Legion, and was endowed in the Nauvoo Temple. A farmer, he emigrated to Utah in 1847 and died in Salt Lake City.

Osmyn Merrit Deuel (1802–1889), from New York, resided in northern Illinois before removing to Nauvoo where he joined the Nauvoo Legion and lived in the 3rd Ward. He was also endowed in the Nauvoo Temple. He arrived in Utah in 1847 with Charles Rich's company. His log cabin built that fall is purported to be among the oldest structures surviving from the pioneer period in Utah, and is on display adjacent to the Museum of Church History and Art in Salt Lake City.

Jonathan Dunham (1800–1845), from New York, participated in LDS Church activities in Ohio and Missouri. He served in Nauvoo public functions, becoming, among other things, a captain of the Nauvoo police and a colonel in the Second Cohort of the Nauvoo Legion. He later was appointed acting major general in the legion. He died while on a mission to the Indians.

Crandell Dunn (1817–1898), born near Palmyra, New York, his family moved to Michigan where he became a Mormon in July 1840. After affiliating with the LDS Church, he moved to La Harpe in northeastern Hancock County, Illinois, and served a mission to Michigan. While among the Saints on the Missouri River he lived in the Pottawattamie Branch. After emigrating to Utah, he died in Beaver Dam, in southern Utah.

Edmund (also Edmond) Durfee (1788–1845), from Rhode Island, was baptized a Mormon in 1831. A carpenter and millwright, he was ordained a high priest, served missions, and helped construct the Kirtland Temple. After relocating to Missouri and then to Hancock County, Illinois, near Morley's settlement, his home was burned in September 1845 by an anti-Mormon mob. He fled to Nauvoo but returned to his farm in mid-November to harvest his crop. While dousing a haystack fired by the mob, he was shot and killed on 15 November 1845. The alleged perpetrators were apprehended, but later released.

William Dykes (1815–1879), from Pennsylvania, moved to Nauvoo after becoming an LDS Church member. There he was ordained a seventy, and later became a member of the first company to Utah in 1847. After settling for a time in Utah, he returned eastward and later died in Nebraska.

Ellis Eames (1809–1882), from Ohio, ordained an elder, lived in the Nashville Branch across the river from Nauvoo, Illinois. After joining the Saints in the

Missouri River settlements, he lived in the Pottwattamie Branch. He was one of the original company of Mormons signed on to travel to Utah but dropped out from the expedition. After living for a time in Utah, he emigrated to California where he died in San Bernardino.

Justus Eames (1791–), from Maine, and his wife Betsey (ca. 1795–), who married in 1813, were baptized in September 1837 by Wilford Woodruff on the Fox Islands in Maine. Their Illinois home served as a resting stop for many Saints en route to and from Nauvoo.

James Eastman (1786–1847), from New Hampshire, became a Mormon in 1842. He moved to Nauvoo in 1843 and became a high priest near the time he received the Nauvoo temple endowment in January 1846. While with the Saints on the Missouri River, he lived in the Winter Quarters 3rd Ward and later the Pottawattamie Branch. He died near Keg Creek, Iowa, just five days before the pioneer vanguard departed Winter Quarters in 1847. His son, Ozro, who never became a Mormon, was, due to his father's legacy, invited to accompany the pioneer vanguard to Utah in 1847.

Howard Egan (1815–1878) was an Irishman, who became a Mormon in 1842. He emigrated to Nauvoo where he became a major in the Nauvoo Legion and a city policeman. There he also was endowed in the temple. While living with the Saints on the Missouri River, he lived in the Winter Quarters 17th Ward before joining the pioneer vanguard to Utah in 1847. His diary is a notable chronicle of the vanguard's journey. A pony express rider in Utah, he also was a Salt Lake City policeman. He died in Salt Lake City.

Horace S. Eldredge (1817–1888), from New York, joined with the Saints in 1836. Moving from Indiana to Missouri before returning to Indiana, he moved to Nauvoo in 1840, where he lived in the 1st Ward. After being endowed in the Nauvoo Temple, he temporarily settled near the Missouri River, and lived in the Winter Quarters 5th Ward. Emigrating to Utah in 1848, he resumed his role of marshal and became a brigadier general in the Utah militia, and became the church emigration agent in St. Louis in the 1850s. He served in the First Council of the Seventy until his death. A successful merchant, he was instrumental in the establishment of ZCMI. He died in Salt Lake City.

Ira Eldredge (1810–1866) was a Vermonter. Temporarily settling near the Missouri River en route to the West, he lived in the Winter Quarters 5th Ward. He emigrated in 1847 to Utah where he became a member of the Salt Lake Stake high council and territorial legislature. He was later ordained a church bishop and captained three emigrating companies to Utah, where he died in Hoytsville.

Edmund Ellsworth (1819–1893), born in New York, became a Mormon in 1840. Later ordained a seventy, he married one of Brigham Young's daughters. He was endowed in the Nauvoo Temple. One of the original company to Utah in 1847, he helped man the ferry on the North Platte River. His family, following, joined him and they all journeyed to Utah. He later served a mission to England, and upon his return was an alderman in Salt Lake City. He eventually moved to Arizona where he died at Show Low.

James Emmett (1803–1852), from Kentucky, joined with the Saints in 1831. An eyewitness to Mormon difficulties in Missouri, he became a Nauvoo policeman, one of a dozen official bodyguards of Joseph Smith, one of the Nauvoo Legion, and a member of Mormonism's secret multifunctional Council of Fifty. He lived in the Nauvoo 1st Ward. He later made several expeditions to Iowa and South Dakota, anticipating the Mormon move to the West. He later separated from the LDS Church and died in California.

William A. Empey (1808–1890) was a Canadian. After becoming a Mormon he moved to Nauvoo, where he was ordained a seventy and was endowed in the temple. One of the pioneer vanguard in 1847, he worked at the North Platte Ferry and never made it to Salt Lake Valley that year, accompanying Brigham Young on his return to Winter Quarters. After taking his family to Utah in 1848, he served a mission to England, which was followed by his call to settle in southern Utah. He died in St. George, Utah.

Addison Everett (1805–1885), from New York, joined the LDS Church in 1837. He located at Nauvoo in 1844, where he was also endowed in the temple. Among the Saints on the Missouri River, he became bishop of the Winter Quarters 21st Ward. He was one of the pioneer vanguard in 1847, and later took his family to Utah. He was appointed a bishop in Salt Lake City and was later called to colonize southern Utah. He helped to build the temple in St. George, where he died.

Nathaniel Fairbanks (1823–1853) was a New Yorker who was baptized a Mormon in 1843 and moved to Nauvoo the following year. He was one of the original pioneers to Utah in 1847. Crossing a river while driving cattle to California in 1853, he was thrown from a mule and accidentally drown.

John W. Farnham (1793/94–1846), from Massachusetts, had been endowed in the Nauvoo Temple in December 1845. A seventy, he died in a Mormon camp near Winter Quarters, Nebraska.

Aaron F. Farr (1818–1903), from Vermont, was baptized a Mormon in 1832. He moved to Kirtland and then to Nauvoo to be with the Saints. There he was endowed in the Nauvoo Temple. Among the Saints on the Missouri River, he lived in the Winter Quarters 1st Ward. One of the early Utah pioneers in 1847, after settling his family in Utah, he and his brother Lorin were important to Ogden's early development. A lawyer, he was city alderman, a deputy marshal, probate judge, and he also served in the territorial legislature. He died in Logan, Utah.

William Felshaw (1800–1867), from New York, became a Mormon convert in Boston in 1832. He was endowed in the Nauvoo Temple. En route to the West, he lived in the Winter Quarters 21st Ward. A carpenter, he worked on temples in Kirtland, Nauvoo, and Salt Lake City, where he relocated in 1851. He became a Utah territorial legislator and died in Fillmore, Utah.

Amos Fielding (1792–1875) converted to Mormonism in his native England, where he served as church agent until 1845. After emigrating to Nauvoo, he became a member of the Council of Fifty. He emigrated to Utah where he died in Salt Lake City.

James Flack (–), after becoming a Latter-day Saint, worked to protect Joseph Smith when Smith was threatened with arrest by Missouri and Carthage lawmen in June 1843. During this period he also was involved in timber harvesting in Wisconsin. He became an officer in the reorganization of the Nauvoo Legion at Winter Quarters, and lived there in the 21st Ward.

Jesse Folks (1808–1890), from Maryland, emigrated to Utah in 1848 and then to San Bernardino, California, in 1851. A farmer, he returned to Utah in 1856, but later relocated to San Bernardino where he lived in 1880.

Timothy B. Foote (1799–1886), from New York, removed to Nauvoo, where he joined the Nauvoo Legion, lived in the 3rd Ward, and was endowed in the temple. He emigrated to Utah in 1848 and died in Nephi, Utah.

Thomas Ford (1800–1850), from Pennsylvania, became a superior court judge in Illinois in 1837, and justice of the Illinois state supreme court, 1841–1842. He was elected Illinois governor and served from 1842 to 1846. Though the Saints heavily supported him for governor in 1842, he later lost their confidence. He died in Peoria, Illinois.

Horace M. Frink (1832–1874), born in New York, moved to Nauvoo, Illinois, with his family. He later lived in the Zarahemla (Iowa) Stake. He joined the first pioneers to Utah in 1847 as a boy of fifteen. He was baptized a Mormon for the first time when the rest of the pioneer camp were rebaptized upon their arrival in the Great Salt Lake Valley. Emigrating to San Bernardino, California, he stayed, after the Saints were called to return to Utah, where he later died.

Burr Frost (1816–1878), from Connecticut, became a Mormon and was ordained a priest in 1842 and two years later a seventy. He was endowed in the Nauvoo Temple. He lived in the Winter Quarters 14th Ward. He later served as a blacksmith for the pioneer vanguard to Utah in 1847. He served as an LDS missionary to Australia in the 1850s and later became president of his seventies quorum. His family later settled in Salt Lake City, where he died.

David Fullmer (1803–1879), born in Pennsylvania and the brother of John Fullmer, was baptized a Mormon in 1836. He was a veteran of Mormon difficulties in Missouri before settling in Nauvoo, where he lived in the 3rd Ward, was a member of Nauvoo High Council and the city council, and otherwise served an important role in the city. He was endowed in the Nauvoo Temple. En route to the West, he presided over the Mormon settlement of Garden Grove in Iowa. After emigrating to Utah he became a member of the territorial legislature and treasurer of Salt Lake City. He also served as a church patriarch. He died in Salt Lake City.

John S. Fullmer (1807–1883), a Pennsylvanian and brother to David Fullmer, later moved to Tennessee and studied to be a Baptist minister. Traveling to Nauvoo to investigate Mormonism, he was baptized in 1839 and moved his family there the following year. A colonel and paymaster in the Nauvoo Legion, he became closely associated with Joseph Smith and was with him the evening before Smith and his brother were killed. He was endowed in the Nauvoo Temple. One of three trustees appointed to liquidate church property in Nauvoo, Fullmer finally left the city for the West in 1848. He later served in the territorial House of Representatives in Utah, where he later died in Springville, Utah.

Elias Gardner (1807–1890), born in New York, lived in New York City. The leader of a brass band, he was baptized a Mormon in 1841 and later ordained a seventy. He was endowed in the Nauvoo Temple. After leaving Nauvoo, he lived in the Winter Quarters 5th Ward before serving as a hunter during the 1848 emigration to Utah. He died in Annabella, Utah.

Chauncey Gaylord (1821–1885), from New York, was ordained a seventy after his baptism. He joined the Nauvoo Legion, and was endowed in the Nauvoo Temple on 31 December 1845. He was excommunicated from the LDS Church on 22 February 1846.

John Gheen (1806–1856), from Pennsylvania, after emigrating to Nauvoo, he was endowed in the Nauvoo Temple. He later lived in the Pottawattamie Branch in western Iowa, and while protecting his interests there in April 1848, he killed a man. Ten years after emigrating to Utah in 1848, he was acquitted of the killing. The year following his acquittal, however, he was found dead of a gunshot in Salt Lake City, Utah. Two of his sisters became plural wives of Heber Kimball.

Andrew S. Gibbons (1825–1886), from Ohio, after becoming a Mormon, moved to Nauvoo where he was endowed in the Nauvoo Temple. He joined the first group of pioneers to Utah in 1847 before returning to the Missouri River. Relocating to Utah in 1852, he settled in Davis County for a time before going to southern Utah and then to Arizona, where he later died at St. Johns.

Flora Clarinda Gleason (1819–1900), born in Massachusetts, who lived with the Jacob family for a time as an unmarried young woman, became the wife of Abraham Washburn in 1849. She had been endowed in the Nauvoo Temple. She died in Monroe, Utah.

John S. Gleason (1819–1904), from New York, after joining the LDS Church, served missions in Canada and the eastern United States. His family settled in Nauvoo, where he lived in the 3rd Ward and was endowed in the temple. He became one of the pioneer vanguard in 1847 and, after permanently settling in Utah, he became a Nauvoo Legionaire there. He later served as a county commissioner and justice of the peace. He died in Pleasant Grove, Utah.

Eric Glines (1822–1881), from New Hampshire, was reared in Canada. He was endowed in the Nauvoo Temple. After joining with the original pioneers to Utah in 1847, he lived in western Iowa in the Pottawattamie Branch upon his return. He later moved to California where he died in Santa Rosa.

Stephen H. Goddard (1810–1898), a New Yorker, became a seventy in 1845 in Nauvoo. There he lived in the 3rd Ward, joined the Nauvoo Legion, was a policeman, and was endowed in the temple. He later joined the vanguard to Utah in 1847. With musical talent, once in Utah he became the first conductor of the choir that performed in the old tabernacle in Salt Lake City. He spent the rest of his life in Utah, until the year before his death when he moved to California.

Miles Goodyear (1817–1849), Connecticut-born, had been in the West since 1836, initially trapping and trading out of Fort Hall. He began his connection with Fort Bridger in 1843. He married the daughter of Ute chief Peteetneet. He established Fort Buenaventura in modern-day Ogden, Utah, in September 1846 on the Weber River, about two miles above its junction with the Ogden River, before it emptied into the Great Salt Lake. While not the first establishment built by white men in Utah, it was the only one functioning when the Mormons arrived in Utah. Goodyear's report to Mormon leaders about the favorable circumstances of his fort and garden reaffirmed their decision to settle along the eastern rim of the Great Basin. His close proximity to the Salt Lake Valley proved to be a boon for him when the Mormons, with $1950 in gold, purchased his claim on 25 November 1847. Goodyear died in November 1849 in the Sierra Nevada Mountains.

John Calvin Gould (1821–1850), from Virginia, was a member of the Mormon Battalion's sick detachment that wintered in Pueblo, Colorado, in 1846, before joining with the pioneer vanguard in Salt Lake Valley in 1847. He died in California.

George R. Grant (1820–1889) was a New Yorker, and after removing to Nauvoo, he was endowed in the Nauvoo Temple. Among the original pioneers to Utah in 1847, he later lived in the Block House Branch in western Iowa. After returning to Utah in 1848 he lived in Davis County for a time. One of the Salmon River Mission party to what is now Idaho, he taught the Indians agriculture and home building. After moving to Carson City, Nevada, he eventually relocated to California where he died.

Jedediah M. Grant (1816–1856), born in New York, was baptized a Mormon in 1833. He joined with Zion's Camp the following year when he was eighteen. Involved in missionary work, he was ordained an elder and then a seventy in 1835. In Nauvoo, he was endowed in the temple. He became one of the First Council of Seventy in 1846, and later lived in the Winter Quarters 17th Ward. After emigrating to Utah he became mayor of Salt Lake City and speaker of the Utah House of Representatives. He was ordained an apostle and made a counselor to Brigham Young in 1854. He died in Salt Lake City.

Edward M. Green (1817–1879), born in New York, became a Mormon in Michigan in 1844. He was endowed in the Nauvoo Temple in February 1846. He took his family to the Mormon settlements on the Missouri River where he lived in the Winter Quarters 21st Ward and the Big Pigeon Branch, but then returned to Michigan. He later joined the RLDS Church in 1874 and died in Missouri.

Ephraim Green (1807–1874), from New York, was baptized a Mormon in 1841. Ordained a high priest, he was endowed in the Nauvoo Temple in January 1846. He joined the Mormon Battalion, and later mined gold in California after his discharge. He served as a missionary in Hawaii and later died in Utah.

Harvey (also Hervey) Green (1806–1875), born in New York, was baptized a Mormon in 1831. He served a mission in Illinois in 1834. A farmer, he served as elders' quorum president in the Nauvoo 2nd Ward and later as a high priest. Green, with Charles Rich, had been appointed at the Kalamazoo conference on 1 June 1844 to responsibility for the LDS Church in Michigan. He was endowed in the Nauvoo Temple. Before emigrating to Utah in 1848, he lived in the Winter Quarters 15th Ward. He later moved to California where he died at Sacramento.

Albert Gregory (1802–1855), from Connecticut, was ordained an elder and then a seventy in the LDS Church. He was endowed in the Nauvoo Temple in January 1846. He died in Kansas returning from a church mission.

Albert B. Griffin (1804/09–1894), born in Vermont, was baptized a Mormon in 1842. He became a seventy in Nauvoo and was endowed in the temple in February 1846. In the emigration to Utah in 1848, he was a captain of ten emigrants. He died in Kannaraville, Utah.

John Groesbeck (1801–), was born in New York. After his baptism he became a bishop's counselor in Augusta, Iowa. He was a seventy, and was endowed in the Nauvoo Temple in January 1846. In Winter Quarters he lived in the 21st Ward.

Thomas Grover (1807–1886), born in New York, was baptized a Mormon in 1834. He supported construction of the Kirtland Temple and served several missions for the LDS Church. In Nauvoo he was a high councilor, joined the Nauvoo Legion, and was endowed in the temple. One of the pioneer vanguard to Utah in 1847, en route, he led the company who stayed at the North Platte Ferry. Returning to the Missouri River settlements, he lived in the Pottawattamie Branch. After settling in Utah, he made several expeditions for the church, served in the territorial legislature, and as probate judge in Davis County. He died in Farmington, Utah.

Zenos Hovey Gurley (1801–1871), from Connecticut or New York, became a Latter-day Saint in 1838 in Ontario, Canada. He was a seventy and later served a mission in Illinois, where in March 1841 he baptized Norton Jacob. He was an officer in the Nauvoo Legion, and was later endowed in the Nauvoo Temple. After Joseph Smith's death, Gurley affiliated with James Strang before becoming one of the early principals in the RLDS Church in 1852.

Joseph Hancock (1800–1893), born in Massachusetts, was an 1830 convert to Mormonism. He moved to Kirtland and became a member of Zion's Camp in 1834. In Nauvoo he joined the Nauvoo Legion and was endowed in the temple. He lived for a time in the Mt. Pisgah Branch in Iowa and later became a member of the pioneer vanguard to Utah in 1847. After returning to the Missouri River settlements, he lived in the Mill Branch.

Before permanently settling in Utah (where he died in Payson), he lived for a time in California.

Hans Christian Hansen (1806–1890), a Dane, converted to Mormonism in 1842 while aboard a ship that docked briefly in Boston. In Nauvoo, he was endowed in the temple. The only person from Scandinavia that accompanied the vanguard to Utah in 1847, he was noted for his musical ability en route. He later returned to Denmark as a missionary. Never marrying, in Utah he settled in Salina where he died.

John J. Hardin (1810–1847) was a Kentuckian. A lawyer, he served in the Black Hawk War in Illinois, and in 1844 became a brigadier general (and later a major general) in the Illinois Militia. He served in the Illinois legislature and was later elected as a Whig to the U.S. Congress, 1843–1845. He was commissioned a colonel in the U.S. war with Mexico, where he was killed at the Battle of Buena Vista in February 1847.

Appleton Milo Harmon (1820–1877) was from Pennsylvania. After joining the LDS Church, he served a mission in 1843. He was appointed a Nauvoo policemen, was a Nauvoo Legionaire, and was endowed in the Nauvoo Temple. During the pioneer vanguard trek of 1847, he helped construct the "roadometer," measuring distances. He was one appointed to operate the ferry on the North Platte River. He relocated his family to Utah in 1848, and later served a mission to England in 1850–1853. He helped construct saw mills, a furniture factory, and a woolen mill in Utah, where he died in Holden.

Charles Alfred Harper (1816–1900), born in Pennsylvania, became a Mormon in Nauvoo. A wagonmaker, he was well educated, graduating from college. Endowed in the Nauvoo Temple, he joined the pioneer vanguard to Utah in 1847. After returning to Winter Quarters to retrieve his family, they emigrated to Utah in 1848. He died in Holladay, Utah.

Henry Harriman (1804–1891) from Massachusetts, joined the Mormons in 1832. A veteran of Zion's Camp in 1834, he also participated in the evacuation of Kirtland in the Kirtland Camp in 1838. That same year he became one of the First Council of Seventy, a position he held until his death. In Nauvoo he joined the Nauvoo Legion. He emigrated in 1848 to Utah in 1848, where he later died at Huntington, Utah.

Leonard Ellsworth Harrington (1816–1883) was from New York. Baptized in 1840, he moved to Nauvoo in 1842 where he became justice of the peace the following year. A farmer, he emigrated to Utah in 1847 where he lived for a time in Salt Lake City. Later he became a bishop, a member of the territorial legislature, mayor of American Fork, and chairman of the territorial judiciary committee for twenty-eight years. He died in American Fork, Utah.

George W. Harris (1780–1857), a Massachusetts native, became a Mormon in 1834. Emigrating from Missouri to Nauvoo, he lived in the 4th Ward and became a stake high councilor and city alderman. He was president of the Coach and Carriage Manufacturing Association in Nauvoo, where he was also endowed in the Nauvoo Temple. After leaving Nauvoo he lived in the Pottawattamie Branch, and became a bishop and high councilor in Council Bluffs, Iowa, where he died.

Martin Harris (1783–1875), from New York, was one of Mormonism's earliest and most important benefactors. He helped subsidize Joseph Smith and funded the Book of Mormon's publication. After significant influence in Mormonism's first years, he became disenchanted and left the LDS Church in 1837. He aligned with James Strang for a time, even touting in England Strang's successorship to Joseph Smith. Harris finally reconciled with Mormonism, emigrating in 1870 to Utah where he died in Clarkston.

Moses "Black" Harris (–1849) was, by the time he met the 1847 Mormon vanguard, already a reputed fur-trader and mountaineer. Born in South Carolina, he likely traveled West as early as 1822. He was also likely one of the four men who first circumnavigated the Great Salt Lake in 1826. With the decline of the fur trade in the early 1840s, he served as a western guide. Having traversed the region for over twenty years, his disclosure of information about the Great Basin to the Saints suggested his hope that the Mormons would hire his services and knowledge. Failing to attach himself to the Saints as a guide, he later hooked up with Commodore Robert Stockton, of California fame, and led him east that season. Harris died in Independence, Missouri, in 1849.

Elias Heaton (ca.1779–1842), Norton Jacob's father-in-law, was married to Mary Heaton, and, while never becoming a Latter-day Saint, died at age sixty-three from typhus fever in Nauvoo, where he apparently lived with Jacob.

Joseph Leland Heywood (1815–1910), from Massachusetts, moved to Quincy, Illinois, in 1839 where he became a merchant. Joining with the Mormons in 1842, he moved to Nauvoo in 1845. Endowed in the Nauvoo Temple, he was appointed one of the trustees to liquidate Mormon holdings after the Saints departed Nauvoo. After emigrating to Utah in 1848 he became the first bishop of the Salt Lake City 17th Ward, city postmaster, and United States marshal for Utah Territory. He died in Panguitch, Utah.

John S. Higbee (1804–1877) and his family, from Ohio, became Mormons in 1832. Higbee endured the Saints' difficulties in Missouri and Illinois. In

Nauvoo, he lived in the 1st Ward, was a member of the Nauvoo Legion, and was endowed in the temple. Before joining with the pioneer vanguard to Utah in 1847, he lived in the Mt. Pisgah (Iowa) Branch. After settling in Provo, Utah, he served a mission to England. He also lived for a time in Weber County, Utah. Sent to settle in southern Utah, he later died in Toquerville.

John Hill (1814–1863), born in Scotland, emigrated with his family to Upper Canada in 1821. Baptized a Mormon in 1840, he relocated to Nauvoo by 1842, and was ordained a seventy in 1844. He was endowed in the Nauvoo Temple. He lived in the Lake Branch in Iowa, and later emigrated to Utah where he died in Salt Lake City.

Abraham (also Abram) C. Hodge (1806–1882), from New York, was baptized a Latter-day Saint in 1840. Later he was ordained a seventy and a high priest and was endowed in the Nauvoo Temple in January 1846. He also served as a policeman in Nauvoo. He lived in the Mill Branch in Iowa and later emigrated to Utah, where he died in Lehi, Utah.

John G. Holman (1828–1888), from New York, was baptized at age eight into Mormonism. Having lived in Ohio and Missouri, after moving to Nauvoo he was endowed in the temple. In the Missouri River settlements he lived in the Winter Quarters 20th Ward and then the Coonville Branch in Iowa. He was one of the youngest men to join the pioneer vanguard to Utah. He later served a mission to England, and settled in Utah, in Pleasant Grove and Santaquin, and later Idaho, where he died in Rexburg.

Jacob Houtz (1814–1896), born in Pennsylvania, became a Mormon in 1844. In Winter Quarters he lived in the 11th Ward. After emigrating to Utah in 1847, he served a mission to Prussia for the church in the early 1850s. He settled in Springville, Utah, where he died.

Edward Hunter (1793–1883), from Pennsylvania, became a Mormon in 1840. After moving to Nauvoo, he became a member of the city council and a financial benefactor for the Saints. He was endowed in the Nauvoo Temple. In Winter Quarters he lived in the 1st and 15th wards before emigrating to Utah in 1847. A bishop in Nauvoo, Winter Quarters, and the first bishop of the Salt Lake City 13th Ward, he became in 1851 the LDS Church's third Presiding Bishop. He died in Salt Lake City.

Orson Hyde (1805–1878), from Connecticut, converted to Mormonism in 1831. A very influential missionary, he later served with Zion's Camp in 1834. He became one of the LDS Church's Twelve Apostles in 1835. In the heat of the Mormons' 1838 struggle in Missouri, he temporarily lost fellowship with the church but was readmitted the following year. He served important church missions to England and Palestine. He gave chaplain service in the Nauvoo Legion and was endowed in the Nauvoo Temple. He lived in the Pottawattamie Branch, supervised church settlements on the Missouri River, and published the *Frontier Guardian* in Kanesville, Iowa. Arriving in Utah in 1852, he became a territorial government leader and presided over settlements in Sanpete and Sevier counties. He died in Spring City, Utah.

Mathew Ivory (1800–1885), a mechanic and carpenter from Pennsylvania, became a Mormon in 1840. He was one of the pioneer vanguard to Utah in 1847, and later served a church mission to New Jersey. He moved to Beaver, Utah, where he was killed in an accident.

Emily Heaton Jacob (1810–1859), Norton Jacob's first wife, was born in Chittenden County, Vermont, and married Jacob in 1830. Together they had eleven children. She was endowed in the Nauvoo Temple. After emigrating to Utah in 1848, she later died in Spanish Fork, Utah.

Jason Kellogg Jacob (1806–1882), Norton Jacob's younger brother, was born in Massachusetts. He married Sarah Thompson in 1840. He lived his adult life in Hancock County, Illinois.

Lovisa Comstock Snyder Jacob (1789–1856), Udney Jacob's second wife, was from Massachusetts. She had married Isaac Snyder (who died in February 1844 in Nauvoo, Illinois) in 1807. She married Udney Hay Jacob on 17 May 1846. She later emigrated to Utah where she died in Salt Lake City.

Mariah Van Valkenburg Jacob (1835–) was born June 23, 1835 in Hecter, Steuben County, New York, the daughter of Peter & Margaret Van Valkenburg. She became the second wife of Norton Jacob on 20 April 1851 in Salt Lake City.

Oliver Barr Jacob (1834–1848), Norton Jacob's oldest son who survived infancy, was born in Jamestown, New York, and died near Independence Rock in Wyoming en route to the West with his family.

Stephen Jacob (1811–1899), Norton Jacob's younger brother, was born in New York and emigrated with his family to Hancock County, Illinois, in 1837. He was married to Minerva Ostrander of New York and became a farmer who was noted later in the century as "one of the old pioneers of this county [Hancock]," where he died.

Udney Hay Jacob (1781–1860), the father of Norton Jacob, was born in Massachusetts. Unusually interested in the Christian religion and originally opposed to Mormonism, he was later baptized a Latter-day Saints, and was endowed in the Nauvoo Temple. He later joined the Saints in exile near the Missouri River where he lived in the Winter Quarters 21st Ward. Later still, he emigrated to Salt Lake City where he died.

Bailey Jacobs (–1847) was a member of the Mormon Battalion in 1846, wintering with the sick detachment in Pueblo, Colorado, before joining with the pioneer vanguard in Salt Lake Valley in 1847. He died in California.

Oren Jeffords (or Jefferds) (1801–1869), born in Vermont, became a Mormon in 1840. He emigrated to Nauvoo where he owned land and where he was ordained a seventy in 1844. He was endowed in the Nauvoo Temple. He was later involved in church work in Oakland, Michigan in 1845. He emigrated in 1852 to Utah and died there in Union, Salt Lake County.

Aaron Johnson (1806–1877), from Connecticut, after becoming a Latter-day Saint, relocated to Nauvoo, where he lived in the 4th Ward, was a high priest, and a Nauvoo Legionaire. He was one of the building committee for the Nauvoo Masonic Temple. He was endowed in the Nauvoo Temple. In the Missouri River settlements, he lived in the Pottawattamie and Big Pigeon branches. He emigrated to Utah in 1850 where he was a founder of Springville and the community's first bishop until 1870. There he died.

Artemas Johnson (1809–) was a New Yorker, who was ordained an elder in Nauvoo in 1839. Before joining with the original pioneers to Utah in 1847, he lived in the Winter Quarters 21st Ward. He returned to Winter Quarters later in the year. It is believed he later returned to Utah.

Luke S. Johnson (1807–1861), a Vermonter, was baptized a Mormon in 1831. His family had hosted Joseph Smith in Hiram, Ohio. He was very successful as an early Latter-day Saint missionary. He was one of the original Twelve Apostles of the LDS Church. After breaking with Smith and the church in Kirtland, Ohio, he moved to Virginia and became a physician. He later returned to the LDS Church and joined the vanguard pioneers in 1847 where he helped man the North Platte River ferry. In the Missouri River settlements, he lived in the Pottawattamie Branch. He later became a bishop in Utah where he died in Salt Lake City.

Thomas L. Kane (1822–1883), born in Pennsylvania to an influential family, he had a military career, including service in the Civil War where he was wounded. He became acquainted with the Latter-day Saints in May 1846 and thereafter became an important advocate for them in the middle of the nineteenth century, beginning with his assistance in arranging for the Mormon Battalion, and especially in mitigating the Utah war crisis in 1857–1858. He died in Philadelphia, Pennsylvania.

James Keeler (1817–1907), from Vermont, after emigrating to Utah, served as a missionary in Hawaii. He lived in Stockton, California, and Richfield, Utah. He died in Monroe, Utah.

Levi N. Kendall (1822–1903), from New York, became a Mormon in Michigan, and was later ordained a seventy in 1844. He returned to Michigan to serve a mission. He was endowed in the Nauvoo Temple. One of the original pioneers to Utah in 1847, he moved his family to Utah the following year. He later helped with subsequent Mormon emigration. He lived in Utah County, dying in Springville.

Heber C. Kimball (1801–1868), born in Vermont, became a significant leader in Mormonism after his conversion in 1832. After his duty in Zion's Camp, he became one of the LDS Church's original Twelve Apostles in 1835. His missionary success in the 1830s and 1840s in England was legendary. In Nauvoo he served as a chaplain in the Nauvoo Legion and was endowed in the temple. He lived in the Pottawattamie Branch while one of the church's primary leaders with Brigham Young on the Missouri River. He was one of the 1847 vanguard and became a counselor in the First Presidency that December, where he served until his death in 1868 in Salt Lake City.

William H. Kimball (1826–1907), a son of Heber Kimball, was born in New York. He was endowed in the Nauvoo Temple. He emigrated to Utah in 1848. After a mission to England in the mid-1850s, he became a U.S. Marshall in Utah and a brigadier general in the Nauvoo Legion. He died in Coalville, Utah.

Thomas Rice King (1813–1879), a New Yorker and younger brother of Timothy King, their father became a Mormon in 1838. Thomas joined two years later. Emigrating from New York to join the Saints, he settled in Iowa, across the Mississippi River from Nauvoo. After serving as a missionary to Michigan in 1842, he was ordained a seventy in 1844. He lived in the Winter Quarters 22nd Ward. After emigrating in 1851 to Utah, he was a probate judge in Fillmore where he also served in the local stake presidency. He died in Kingston, Utah.

Timothy H. King (1803–1867), older brother of Thomas King, was born in New York. He was baptized a Mormon in 1840 and later ordained a seventy. He lived in the Winter Quarters 22nd Ward. After emigrating to Utah, he settled in Millard County, and died in Fillmore.

Vinson Knight (1804–1842), from New York, became a Mormon in 1834. A druggist, he joined the Nauvoo Legion, and was appointed a counselor to

Bishop Newel Whitney in 1836 who later was appointed presiding bishop of the LDS Church. Knight died the following summer in Nauvoo.

William Laney (1815–1891), from Kentucky, joined the LDS Church in 1843. He emigrated to Utah in 1847 after living among the Saints in the Missouri River settlements. Once in Salt Lake City, he moved to Parowan and then Harrisburg, both southern Utah villages. He later had a falling out with the LDS Church. He died in Harrisburg, Utah.

Asahel A. Lathrop (1810–), from Connecticut, was ordained a seventy in 1839. Endowed in the Nauvoo Temple, he later joined with George Miller and his company and was one of twelve men chosen to lead the camp as the Saints prepared to embark for the West. Lathrop emigrated to Utah in 1847.

Ezekiel Lee (1795–1877), born in Massachusetts, was a medical doctor. He and his family became Mormons in February 1843. An important Latter-day Saint personality in the area, he was appointed president of the church's Comstock, Michigan, branch. Lee immigrated to Nauvoo in 1845. He died in Salt Lake City.

John D. Lee (1812–1877), born in Illinois, became one of the most controversial characters in Mormon history. He became a Latter-day Saint in 1838 and emigrated to Nauvoo in 1840, where he was a city policeman, one of the Nauvoo Legion, and lived in the 3rd Ward. He was endowed in the Nauvoo Temple. Serving as a church missionary, he later campaigned for Joseph Smith's run for the United States presidency. He lived in the Winter Quarters 17th Ward. An adopted son of Brigham Young, he became a leader in southern Utah after emigrating to the territory in 1848. He was one of the principals who planned and carried out the Mountain Meadows Massacre, was excommunicated from Mormonism, and later executed at Mountain Meadows for his role in the murders. He is buried in Panguitch, Utah.

Tarlton Lewis (1805–1890), from South Carolina, was baptized a Mormon in 1836. After relocating to Nauvoo, as a cabinet maker and carpenter, he helped build the Nauvoo Temple and joined the Nauvoo Legion. He was bishop of the Nauvoo 4th Ward and was endowed in the Nauvoo Temple. He joined the pioneer vanguard to Utah in 1847. After settling his family in Utah, he was called as a bishop, leading congregations in Salt Lake City, Parowan, and Richfield. He died at Teasdale, Utah.

Jesse C. Little (1815–1893), from Maine, after joining the LDS Church in New Hampshire, was ordained a high priest, and later was appointed the church's Eastern States mission president. He helped negotiate with federal government leaders to enlist the Mormon Battalion. In the Missouri River settlements, he lived in the Pottawattamie Branch. One of the first company to Utah in 1847, he finally relocated his family there in 1852. He was a bishop and later served as a counselor to the church's presiding bishop. He died in Littleton, Utah.

Amasa Mason Lyman (1813–1877), from New Hampshire, embraced Mormonism in 1832. His early missionary work was influential for the growing church. In Nauvoo, where he was one of the Nauvoo Legion, he rose to leadership in the church's First Presidency and Twelve Apostles. He was endowed in the Nauvoo Temple. His role in the emigration of 1847 included retrieval of the Mormon Battalion sick detachment from wintering in Pueblo, Colorado. Co-leader of the church enterprise in San Bernardino, California, in the 1850s, he later fell out of favor with Brigham Young over doctrinal matters. He was excommunicated from the LDS Church in 1870 and later died in Fillmore, Utah.

Andrew Lytle (1812–1870), born in Pennsylvania, lived through Mormon troubles in northern Missouri. After relocating to Nauvoo, he became a seventy and one of the police. He was endowed in the Nauvoo Temple. He joined the Mormon Battalion as an officer. His family emigrated to Utah in 1848. He later moved to San Bernardino, California, before returning to Utah. But in 1860 he returned to San Bernardino where he later died.

John Lytle (1803–1892), born in Pennsylvania, became a Mormon in 1836. He was ordained a seventy in 1838 and after relocating to Nauvoo, he lived in the 4th Ward, joined the Nauvoo Legion, and became a city policeman. There he was also one of those arrested for the destruction of the *Expositor* that eventually led to the death of the Smith brothers in June 1844. He was endowed in the Nauvoo Temple. He lived in the Winter Quarters 21st Ward. Lytle emigrated to Utah in 1848 where he became a bishop in Salt Lake City. He died in St. George, Utah.

Wandle Mace (1809–1890), from New York, was baptized a Mormon in the winter of 1837–1838. He moved to Missouri in 1838 and then to Illinois upon the Saints' removal there. Involved in inventive enterprises before he became a Mormon, he started an iron foundry in Nauvoo and became one of the Nauvoo Legion. He was endowed in the Nauvoo Temple. He emigrated in 1859 to Utah and later died in Kanab, Utah.

Asa Manchester (1809–1901), from Rhode Island, who lived near Newark, Illinois, served as the clerk for the LDS conference at Newark in May 1844.

He was endowed in the Nauvoo Temple in January 1846. He died in Kendall County, Illinois.

Stephen Markham (1800–1878), from New York, became a Latter-day Saint in 1837. Closely attached to LDS Church leaders in Nauvoo, where he lived in the 1st and 3rd wards, he became a colonel in the Nauvoo Legion. He was endowed in the Nauvoo Temple. Helping to manage the Mormon transit of Iowa in 1846, he lived in the Winter Quarters 17th Ward, and later served as an officer in the 1847 vanguard to Utah. He became a bishop in Utah after emigrating. He died in Spanish Fork, Utah.

Joseph L. Matthews (1809–1886), from North Carolina, joined the LDS Church in 1845. Before joining the advance group of Saints to Utah, he lived in the Winter Quarters 7th Ward. He helped settle the Mormon colony in San Bernardino, California. Resettling in Utah, he later moved to Arizona where he died at Pima.

James McGaw (1823–1872), born in Upper Canada, moved to La Harpe, Illinois, where he became a Mormon in 1841. Ordained an elder and then a seventy, he served a mission to Indiana the year after his baptism. It was the first of seven he would serve for the church, including one to England. He was endowed in the Nauvoo Temple. He led an emigrating company in 1852 to Utah, where he later became a city councilor and bishop's councilor in Ogden where he died.

Orlando Fish Mead (1823–1897), born in Connecticut, was baptized a Mormon in 1839. After moving to Nauvoo in 1841, he was ordained a seventy. He became a member of the Mormon Battalion and later a shoemaker for John Sutter in California. He died in Price, Utah.

Samuel Merrill (1780–1878), born in New York, was a veteran of the War of 1812. He was endowed in the Nauvoo Temple. Several of his children, including a son and two daughters joined the Mormon Battalion. Merrill emigrated to Utah in 1847 or 1848. He died in Salt Lake City.

George Miller (1794–1856), a Virginian who grew up in Kentucky, later moved to Illinois where he became a Mormon in 1839. He was ordained a Nauvoo bishop in 1841. He became a central figure in the construction of the Nauvoo House and the new temple, where he was later endowed. Militarily he quickly rose from captain in 1841 to brigadier general of the Nauvoo Legion in 1842. He led the timber harvest in Wisconsin for lumber to build the Nauvoo Temple. Serving on both the Nauvoo City Council and the Council of Fifty, he became an important figure in the Saints' plan to evacuate Illinois.

Providing leadership in the exodus across Iowa, he later had a falling out with Brigham Young leading to his severance from the LDS Church in 1848. He later aligned himself with Lyman Wight and James Strang before Miller's death in Illinois.

Henry W. Miller (1807–1885) was a New Yorker. He became a Mormon in 1839 in Illinois and soon moved to Nauvoo where he joined the Nauvoo Legion. He helped provide timber for both the Nauvoo House and Nauvoo Temple where he was endowed. Departing Nauvoo, he settled in western Iowa in what became Miller's Hollow, named after him, which became the site of Kanesville (Council Bluffs), Iowa. There he lived in the Pottawattamie Branch. A high councilor in the Pottawattamie Stake, he was a principal in constructing Kanesville's huge log tabernacle for Mormon worship in Kanesville. He led immigrant companies bound for Utah in 1852 and 1862. He died in Farmington, Utah.

William Miller (1814–1875), a New Yorker, became a Latter-day Saint in 1834. He relocated to Missouri and later to Illinois. He was endowed in the Nauvoo Temple. After he emigrated to Utah in 1849, he became a territorial legislator and an officer in Utah's Nauvoo Legion. He served as a bishop and stake president in Utah. He died in Provo, Utah.

George Mills (–1854) was from England. In Winter Quarters, he lived in the 13th Ward. One of the first group of pioneers to Utah in 1847, he later died during surgery for cancer in Salt Lake City.

Isaac Morley (1786–1865), from Massachusetts, was a War of 1812 veteran and captain in the Ohio militia when he converted to Mormonism in 1830. Living near Kirtland, he became important to Mormonism as it sought a foothold in the area. He was in 1831 appointed a counselor to Bishop Edward Partridge, a role he played until 1840. He became a church patriarch in Far West, Missouri, in 1837. After fleeing Missouri, he founded a settlement south of Nauvoo in Hancock County which eventually bore his name, spelled backwards: Yelrome. He was endowed in the Nauvoo Temple. On the Missouri River, he lived in the Winter Quarters 5th Ward and the Pottawattamie Branch. He emigrated to Utah in 1848 and became a church and civic leader in Sanpete County, Utah. He died in Fairview, Utah.

Levinah Jackson Murphy (ca.1810–1847), born in South Carolina, became a Latter-day Saint in Tennessee in 1836. Widowed in 1839, she then moved to Nauvoo for a period before eventually returning to Tennessee. She joined the ill-fated and California-bound Donner-Reed party in 1846 and proved to be among the first Mormons to enter Utah. Her emigrant party, stranded in the Sierra Nevadas during an early snowstorm, suffered horribly in the extreme conditions. Almost half of the party of over eighty died in the mountains. Murphy was one of the last of the unfortunate emigrants to die.

Lewis Myers (–), a veteran mountain man in the West for nearly a decade, served as the guide and hunter for Robert Crow's company of Mississippi Saints. His unusual taste for eating roasted deer antlers caught the attention of the Mormon emigrants. Encountering the Mormon vanguard, Myers debated between returning to his family or continuing with Crow and his family, who had joined the vanguard, finally deciding on the latter. Once in the Salt Lake Valley, Myers served as a guide for the Saints on initial exploring ventures in surrounding areas, being the first to investigate Utah Valley. In 1848 he settled with the Crows near Ogden before departing for California the following year.

John Nebeker (1813–1886), from Delaware, converted to Mormonism during the winter of 1845–1846. He emigrated in 1847 to Utah, and was an early horticulturalist there. There he also served as a deputy marshal, justice of the peace, probate judge, and in the territorial legislature. He lived for a time in Toquerville, Utah, but died in Laketown, Utah.

John Neff (1794–1869), from Pennsylvania, was baptized a Mormon in 1842. He emigrated to Utah in 1847. He had helped sponsor the journey of the ship *Brooklyn*, which transported Mormons from New York to San Francisco in 1846. Among the Saints on the Missouri River, he lived in the Pottawattamie Branch. A miller, Neff built in 1848 a flour mill near the mouth of Mill Creek Canyon in the foothills of the Wasatch Range in Salt Lake County. He died in East Mill Creek, Utah.

Elijah Newman (1793–1872), a Virginian, was baptized in 1832. He was endowed in the Nauvoo Temple. Ordained a seventy, he was one of the pioneer vanguard in 1847, and after settling in Utah worked on the Salt Lake City public works as a carpenter in 1852. Called to settle in southern Utah, he was an early resident of Parowan, where he was ordained a high priest, served as a justice of the peace, and on the town council. He died in Parowan, Utah.

Freeman Nickerson (1779–1847), from Massachusetts, was baptized a Mormon in 1833. He served missionary duty to several locales in the 1830s, including having a significant impact on the reestablishment of Mormonism in Boston in the early 1840s. He was endowed in the Nauvoo Temple. He died in Iowa before going West.

Joseph B. Noble (1810–1900), born in Massachusetts, was baptized a Mormon in 1832. He joined Zion's Camp in 1834 and was ordained a seventy. He endured the Missouri and Illinois difficulties. In Nauvoo, he lived in the 4th Ward, was one of the Nauvoo Legion, and was a bodyguard to Joseph Smith. There he was also endowed in the temple. He also lived in the Zarahemla (Iowa) Stake. He was a bishop in the Winter Quarters 20th Ward. Emigrating in 1847 to Utah, there he also served as a bishop. He died in Dingle, Idaho.

David Norris (1800–1846) was born in New York. He was baptized a Mormon in 1840, and was ordained a seventy. He was endowed in the Nauvoo Temple in January 1846 before he was killed during the attack upon Nauvoo in September 1846.

John W. Norton (1820–1901) was from Indiana. He became a Mormon in 1838 and lived for several years in Kirtland, before moving to Nauvoo where he was ordained a seventy and endowed in the temple in 1846. He was in the first group of pioneers to Utah in 1847. In 1848, Norton moved his family to Utah, where he was employed in Salt Lake City's public works. He then served a mission to Australia. He lived for a time in southern Nevada and died in Panguitch, Utah.

James D. Oakley (1826/1828–1915), from New York, was baptized a Mormon in 1844. He joined the Mormon Battalion, and was one of the detachment that wintered at Pueblo, Colorado, before joining with the pioneer vanguard in Salt Lake Valley. He settled in Utah and died at Springville.

John Pack (1809–1885) was born in New Brunswick, Canada. Becoming a Mormon in 1836, he moved to Kirtland, and then to Missouri. After moving to Nauvoo, where he lived in the 3rd Ward, he became a major in the Nauvoo Legion and a city policeman. There he was endowed in the temple. He lived in the Winter Quarters 17th Ward. One of the Mormon vanguard of 1847, after his family's emigration to Utah, he assisted in the settlement of Carson Valley, Nevada. Pack's widowed mother married Udney Hay Jacob, Norton Jacob's father.

Noah Packard (1796–1860), from Massachusetts, became a Mormon in 1832. A member of the Kirtland High Council, he became a high priest quorum leader in Nauvoo, where he lived in the 1st Ward. He was endowed in the Nauvoo Temple. Among the Saints in the Missouri River settlements, he lived in the Pottawattamie Branch. He emigrated to Utah in 1850 and settled in Springville, where he was a community leader and where he died.

John E. Page (1799–1867), born in New York, joined the LDS Church in 1833. After moving to Kirtland, in 1835, he had phenomenal success as a missionary in Canada. Called to be one of the Twelve Apostles in 1838, he later led the church in Pittsburgh, Pennsylvania. In Nauvoo, he joined the

Nauvoo Legion and was endowed in the temple. His problems with his fellow church leaders began when he reneged on the call of the Twelve to Great Britain and his call to accompany Orson Hyde to Palestine. After his excommunication from the LDS Church he lived in Wisconsin and Illinois. He died in Sycamore, Illinois.

Hezekiah Peck (1782–1850), from Vermont, was one of Mormonism's earliest converts, joining in the summer of 1830. A brother-in-law to Joseph Knight, one of Joseph Smith's early benefactors, Peck was a millwright and became a Mormon bishop in Nauvoo, where he lived in the 3rd Ward. He was endowed in the Nauvoo Temple. He also lived in the Zarahemla (Iowa) Stake and later in the Winter Quarters 7th Ward. He died in Missouri before he could emigrate to the West.

David M. Perkins (1823–1874), from Tennessee, joined the LDS Church in 1840. He lived in the Ramus/Macedonia Branch in Hancock County, Illinois. He later joined the Mormon Battalion in 1846 and was one of the company who wintered in Pueblo, Colorado. He is buried in Salt Lake City, Utah.

William G. Perkins (1801–1886), born in South Carolina, after settling in Sangamon County and then Hancock County, Illinois, became a Mormon in 1838. He was endowed in the Nauvoo Temple. He was the bishop of the Mormon settlement at Macedonia, Illinois, where he frequently entertained church leaders. He led the congregation westward as they emigrated together. After relocating to Utah in 1848, he became the first bishop of the Salt Lake 7th Ward and a city councilor. He later moved to southern Utah. He was later ordained a church patriarch before he died in St. George, Utah.

William W. Phelps (1792–1872) hailed from New Jersey. Before his conversion to Mormonism in 1831, he worked for an anti-Masonic newspaper. He later served as editor of the church's first organ, *The Evening and the Morning Star* in Independence, Missouri, and helped with other church publications. His literary skills were utilized by Joseph Smith on numerous occasions. Phelps separated from the LDS Church in 1838 but reaffiliated in 1840. He was endowed in the Nauvoo Temple. Among the Saints on the Missouri River, he lived in the Winter Quarters 11th Ward. He emigrated in 1849 to Utah, where he died in Salt Lake City.

Harmon D. Pierson (1818–1891), from Connecticut, converted to Mormonism in 1842. He enlisted in the Mormon Battalion in 1847 and spent the winter at Pueblo, Colorado, with the sick detachment of the soldiers. He later joined with the pioneer vanguard in the Salt Lake Valley in 1847. He died in Willard, Utah.

William Warner Player (1793–1873), an Englishman, was baptized a Mormon in 1841. In Nauvoo he joined the Nauvoo Legion and plied his skill as a stone mason and cutter on the Nauvoo Temple, where he was later endowed. He was privileged to place the last trumpetstone and the first starstone in place on the temple in April and May 1845. He also supervised construction of the temple's baptismal font, including the carving of the oxen holding the large bowl. He lived in the Pottawattamie Branch in Iowa before emigrating to Utah. He died in Salt Lake City.

Francis M. Pomeroy (1822–1883), from Connecticut, after a short career on a whaling vessel, became a Mormon in 1844. Before leaving for the West, he was endowed in the Nauvoo Temple. He lived in the Winter Quarters 17th Ward. He was one of the first company bound for Utah in 1847, although he was assigned to assist at the North Platte River ferry in Wyoming. There his wife joined him and they finished the journey to Utah before serving a mission to southern California. He later lived in Idaho and Arizona, being one of the founders of Mesa, Arizona. He headed the mission to the Indians before he died in Mesa.

Addison Pratt (1802–1872), born in New Hampshire, lived in the 1st Ward and was one of the Nauvoo Legion after emigrating to Nauvoo. There he was also ordained a seventy before being, in June 1843, one of four who left Nauvoo to serve in the Pacific Islands, the church's first foreign-language mission. He landed on Tubuai the following year and had notable success among the Polynesians there and in Tahiti. He returned to the United States in 1848 and, after a stay in California, later arrived in Salt Lake City. He returned to Tahiti later in the 1850s, and died in California.

Orson Pratt (1811–1881), born in New York, was a younger brother of Parley Pratt. One of the early converts to Mormonism, he spent the early years of the 1830s as a missionary in the eastern United States. He participated in Zion's Camp in 1834. In February 1835 he became one of the LDS Church's Twelve Apostles. Noted for his academic and scientific prowess, he was attached to Mormon educational endeavors in Illinois and Utah. He was a chaplain in the Nauvoo Legion and was endowed in the Nauvoo Temple. Leaving Nauvoo, he lived in the Winter Quarters 15th Ward before joining the Mormon vanguard in 1847. He also had an important career as a missionary to Great Britain. A member of the Utah territorial legislature, he was later also assigned as LDS Church historian. He died in Salt Lake City.

Parley P. Pratt (1807–1857), born in New York, became one of the earliest baptized Mormons in 1830. Once a Campbellite preacher, he later became an influential Mormon missionary. A member of Zion's Camp in 1834, he was ordained one of the initial Quorum of Twelve Apostles in 1835 with his brother Orson. His literary skills fostered Mormonism through books and pamphlets that had a significant impact on investigators and members during the religion's first generation. He gave chaplain duty in the Nauvoo Legion and was endowed in the Nauvoo Temple. Among the Saints on the Missouri River he lived in the Pottawattamie Branch. After a mission to England, he joined one of the emigrating companies to Utah following the vanguard in 1847. He was later murdered in Van Buren, Arkansas, in 1857.

Gabriel Prudhomme (1817?–), once one of Peter Skene Ogden's trappers, later lived among the Flathead Indians prior to the Catholic missionaries' arrival and served the latter's interests in establishing their presence among the Indians at a mission station on St. Mary's (Bitterroot) River in Montana. He had also served as Father Pierre DeSmet's interpreter and guide in 1841.

Edward Pugh (1824–1900) was born in England. He was endowed in the Nauvoo Temple and was ordained a seventy in 1846. He later emigrated to Utah where he died in Kanab.

Jonathan Pugmire (1823–1880), an Englishman and blacksmith who converted to Mormonism in 1841, emigrated to Nauvoo in 1844 and there was ordained a seventy. He was endowed in the Nauvoo Temple. He joined the Mormon Battalion and, after returning to the Missouri River Valley, took his family to Utah in 1848, where he became a major in Utah's Nauvoo Legion. He later emigrated to Idaho, where he died at St. Charles.

Zera Pulsipher (1789–1872), born in Vermont, became a Mormon in 1832. The following year he baptized Wilford Woodruff, part of the former's several years of missionary activity in the 1830s. A seventy, he was a member of Kirtland Camp in 1838 and, after relocating to Missouri, was then driven from there as well. He settled in Nauvoo in 1840, where he lived in the 3rd Ward and was endowed in the temple. He lived in the Winter Quarters 14th Ward before emigrating in 1848 to Utah, where he lived to the end of his life in southern Utah.

Alfred Randall (1811–1891), from New York, became a Latter-day Saint in 1840 and moved to Nauvoo, where he was endowed in the temple. Among the Saints on the Missouri River, he lived in the Winter Quarters 13th and 15th wards. A farmer and carpenter, he emigrated to Utah in 1848 and later served several LDS missions, including twice to Hawaii. He died in North Ogden, Utah.

Ammon Tunis Rappleye (1807–1883), from New York, became a Mormon in 1832. He helped build the Kirtland Temple, and later lived near Crooked

Creek, Missouri. In Hancock County, Illinois, he lived in the Ramus/ Macedonia Branch. He was one of the original pioneer company to Utah in 1847 and later filled a mission to the Eastern States before returning to Utah. He helped settle Millard County and died in Kanosh, Utah.

Return Jackson Redden (1817–1891), was from Ohio, and became a Latter-day Saint in 1841. One of Joseph Smith's bodyguards, he later lived in the Sand Prairie Branch. He was endowed in the Nauvoo Temple and was a seventy. One of the first company to Utah in 1847, en route he discovered Cache Cave, then called Redden's Cave. He took his family to Utah in 1848. After a venture in California and Carson Valley, Nevada, he returned to Utah, where he lived in several locations and served as a justice of the peace. He died in Hoytsville, Utah.

James Frazier Reed (1800–1874), from Ireland, emigrated to Virginia and then to Springfield, Illinois, where he manufactured cabinet furniture. He served in the Black Hawk War in Illinois in 1831–1832. Emigrating to California in 1846, he was one of the principles in what came to be known as the Donner-Reed party. Disaster visited him on the trek when he killed another emigrant and was banished from the train and later his family was caught in the early winter snow in the Sierra Nevadas, where about half of the party of over eighty died. Reed later died in San Jose, California.

Daniel M. Repsher (1804–) was born in Pennsylvania. He was president of a seventy's quorum in Kirtland, and later became a policeman in Nauvoo at the end of 1843 as well as a member of the Nauvoo Legion. He managed the *Maid of Iowa*, Joseph Smith's steamboat on the Mississippi River. He, as part of a committee to provide for the poor, was sent by the Nauvoo City Council to regions north of Nauvoo to solicit assistance for the destitute in the city. In November 1845, he was, with John Scott, appointed as captain of ten in preparation for emigration the following spring. In February 1846 he became sergeant of the guard for Nauvoo's police force. He was endowed in the Nauvoo Temple.

Charles C. Rich (1809–1883), a Kentuckian, became a Mormon in 1832 in Illinois. After service as a missionary, in Nauvoo, where he lived in the 3rd Ward, he became a religious, civic, and military leader, as well as a city policeman. He became commander of the Nauvoo Legion in April 1844. He was endowed in the Nauvoo Temple. He later became one of Mormonism's Twelve Apostles, appointed by Brigham Young, in February 1849 with Erastus Snow and Franklin Richards. After emigrating to Utah, he helped found settlements in the Bear Lake Valley of Utah and Idaho and remained a significant influence in Utah affairs. He died in Paris, Idaho.

John Baptiste Richard (1810–1875), pronounced "Reshaw," was born in Missouri. Involved in the fur trade from his youth, he partnered with four men in 1845 to build a rival post to Fort John (Laramie) called Fort Bernard, located eight miles east of the more famous fort. Richard ably led the party of Mississippi Saints from Fort Laramie to winter at Pueblo, Colorado in 1846. While he was gone his fort was burned. He later located a trading post at Ash Point, about twenty miles below Fort Laramie.

Jane Snyder Richards (1823–1912), a sister to Norton Jacob's son-in-law Jesse Snyder, was born in New York. She was endowed in the Nauvoo Temple. She lived in the Winter Quarters 8th Ward. She emigrated to Utah in 1848, where her husband Franklin Richards became a Mormon apostle the following year. Jane became president of the Weber County Relief Society in 1877 and counselor to the general Relief Society president in 1888, where she served until 1901. She died in Ogden, Utah.

Willard Richards (1804–1854) was from Massachusetts and a cousin of Brigham Young. A physician, he became a Latter-day Saint in 1836. He served a mission to England and became a member of the LDS Church's Twelve Apostles and later the First Presidency. He was a clerk to Joseph Smith in Nauvoo, where he also served in the Nauvoo Legion and was endowed in the temple. He lived in the Winter Quarters 17th Ward and the Pottawattamie Branch in Iowa. He was the first editor of the church's *Deseret News* in Salt Lake City, where he died.

Joel Ricks (1804–1888), a Kentuckian, was a Campbellite in Illinois before being baptized a Mormon in 1841. He was endowed in the Nauvoo Temple in January 1846. Ricks helped care for Norton Jacob's family while the later accompanied the vanguard to Utah. Emigrating to Utah in 1848, Ricks worked with Jacob in building a mill in what is now Bountiful. Ricks lived for a time in Centerville, Utah, before settling in Cache Valley, where he also built a mill and became county treasurer for thirty years. He was ordained a patriarch in the LDS Church. He died in Logan, Utah.

Thomas E. Ricks (1828–1901), a son of Joel Ricks, was born in Kentucky. He was baptized a Mormon in 1845 and worked on the Nauvoo Temple. He emigrated to Utah in 1848. One of the Southern Utah Exploring Expedition of 1849–1850, he later moved to southeastern Idaho where he became an LDS stake president. Ricks College (now Brigham Young University-Idaho) in Rexburg, Idaho, where he died, was named for him.

Sidney Rigdon (1793–1876) was a Pennsylvanian who gained regional fame while contributing to the formation with Alexander Campbell of the Disciples of Christ. But converting to Mormonism in November 1830, he later became Smith's scribe before becoming his counselor in 1832, a position he held until 1844. He was a leading orator in the LDS Church. After Smith's martyrdom in June 1844, already somewhat estranged from the church, Rigdon managed to alienate himself entirely from Brigham Young and the Twelve Apostles. He was unchurched in September 1844. He went on to form his own church in Pennsylvania. He died in Friendship, New York.

Benjamin Roberts (1827–1891), from Pennsylvania, was baptized a Mormon in 1840. He enlisted in the Mormon Battalion in 1846 and was one of the company who wintered at Pueblo, Colorado, eventually joining the pioneer vanguard in Utah in 1847. After settling in Utah, he died in Provo.

William Robison (1829–1897) was a Pennsylvanian. After his baptism he was ordained an elder. He emigrated to Utah in 1860. He lived in Morgan, Utah, in 1880.

Orrin Porter Rockwell (1815–1878), from New York, was a friend of Joseph Smith's family and an early convert to Mormonism in 1830. He was endowed in the Nauvoo Temple. He gained a reputation as being a devoted, if ruthless, defender of the LDS Church in Nauvoo and in Utah. One of the pioneer vanguard to Utah in 1847, he rode for the Pony Express, and later was a marshal in Salt Lake City, where he died.

Albert Perry Rockwood (1805–1879), was born in Massachusetts. He became a Mormon in 1837. After relocating from Missouri to Nauvoo, where he lived in the 1st Ward, he became a general in the Nauvoo Legion. He commanded Joseph Smith's Life Guard as well. In 1845 he was appointed as a president of all the seventies where he served until his death. He was endowed in the Nauvoo Temple. An adopted son of Brigham Young, he was one of the most responsible leaders in the vanguard to Utah in 1847. After settling in Salt Lake City, he became warden of the territorial penitentiary. He died in Salt Lake City.

Noah Rogers (1797–1846), from Connecticut, after becoming a Mormon, in 1840 was, with three others, kidnapped, whipped, and beaten by Missourians, who imprisoned them. In June 1843, living in the Nauvoo 1st Ward, he was one of four who left Nauvoo, to serve in the Pacific Islands, the church's first foreign-language mission. Upon his return to Nauvoo he had become the first Mormon to circumnavigate the globe as a missionary. He was endowed in the Nauvoo Temple. Rogers died in May 1846 while living at Mount Pisgah, Iowa, before he could depart for the West.

Samuel J. Rolfe (1794–1869) hailed from New Hampshire, but was converted to Mormonism in Maine. Emigrating to Kirtland and later Nauvoo, he worked on both city temples. In Nauvoo he lived in the 1st Ward and was one of the building committee for the Nauvoo Masonic hall. He was endowed in the Nauvoo Temple. He became bishop of the Winter Quarters 13th Ward. After emigrating to Utah, he later settled in San Bernardino, California, and became a civic and church leader there. Later he died in Lehi, Utah.

Joseph Alva Rooker (1818–1901), born in Indiana, was ordained a seventy and moved with the Saints to Council Bluffs, Iowa, before joining with the original band of pioneers to Utah in 1847. In Utah he lived at Black Rock in Salt Lake County and was a seventy there as well. In 1857 he left Utah for southern California, where he died in Oceanside.

Jeremiah (or Jerry) Root (1801/02–1898) was a Vermonter who was baptized a Mormon in 1835. Ordained a seventy, he was endowed in the Nauvoo Temple in January 1846. Though he emigrated to Utah, he later joined the RLDS Church.

Shadrach Roundy (1789–1872) was a Vermonter who was an early convert to Mormonism. He endured the difficulties of the Mormons in Ohio and Missouri, and upon removing to Nauvoo, he lived in the 4th Ward. He also became one of the Nauvoo Legion, a captain of the city's police, and was endowed in the Nauvoo Temple. He lived in the Winter Quarters 5th Ward before joining with the vanguard pioneers to Utah in 1847. He became one of the first members of the Salt Lake Stake high council, a bishop, and a member of the territorial legislature. He was one of the founders of Zion's Cooperative Mercantile Institution. He died in Salt Lake City.

Henry W. Sanderson (1829–1896) was born in Massachusetts. Enlisting in the Mormon Battalion in 1846 while a teenager, he was one of those who wintered with the sick detachment in Pueblo, Colorado, before joining with the pioneer vanguard in Utah in 1847. He eventually settled in Sanpete County, Utah, and died in Fairview.

David Sanger (1782–1851) was born in Massachusetts. He was ordained a high priest and participated in the Nauvoo Temple ordinances in January 1846. He died in Ottawa, Illinois.

Peter A. Sarpy (1805–1865), described as being "a legend in his own time," operated at Bellevue, "one of the most strategically located posts on the Missouri River." During and after the fur trade, Sarpy "cultivated a mounting trade by supplying travelers, army units, and the Indians tribes of the area, and by developing ferrying services across the Missouri River."

John Scott (1811–1876) immigrated to Canada in 1819 with his family from his Irish homeland. His father's family converted to Mormonism in their new home. John Scott moved to Far West, Missouri, in 1838, and near Nauvoo about 1841. He became a president in a seventy's quorum in Nauvoo where he also became a city policeman and a colonel in the Second Cohort of the Nauvoo Legion. He was one who retrieved the bodies of the martyrs from the Carthage Jail in 1844. He was endowed in the Nauvoo Temple and lived in the Winter Quarters 15th and 21st wards on the Missouri River before emigrating to Utah in 1848. He died in Millville, Utah.

Lucius N. Scovil (1806–1889), born in Connecticut, became a Mormon in 1836 and was ordained a seventy in 1839. In Nauvoo, where he lived in the 2nd Ward, he owned a bakery, served in the Nauvoo Legion, and was involved in the city's mercantile and manufacturing association. There he was also one of the Masonic Temple building committee and became the warden of the lodge of Freemasons. He was endowed in the Nauvoo Temple. Called to serve a mission in England in 1846, he returned to Winter Quarters in August 1847. He lived in the Pottawattamie Branch in Iowa. He later became church emigration agent in New Orleans before settling in Utah, where he died in Springville.

Thomas C. Sharp (1818–1894), from New Jersey, was a lawyer and editor of the *Warsaw Signal*, published in Warsaw, Illinois, a rival to Nauvoo thirteen miles downriver. He proved to be the most vocal and visible opponent of Mormonism in Illinois. He was one of those indicted for the murder of Joseph Smith, though later absolved. He died at Carthage, Illinois.

Sebert Crutcher Shelton (1793–1857), from Virginia, was quartermaster sergeant of the Mormon Battalion's Company D. He was one whose wife and children accompanied the Battalion. He died in Petaluma, California.

Henry G. Sherwood (1785–1857), after becoming a Mormon, emigrated to Nauvoo where he joined the Nauvoo Legion and became a city marshal. There he also was endowed in the temple. He lived in the Winter Quarters 11th Ward, before joining with the original pioneers to Utah in 1847. In Utah he later served in important capacities in Salt Lake City, including being a member of the high council. He helped colonize San Bernardino, California, for the LDS Church, eventually dying there.

Alexander M. Shoemaker (1813–1872), from Kentucky, emigrated to Nauvoo after his baptism, where he was also endowed in the temple. He lived for a time in the Mt. Pisgah settlement in Iowa. A farmer, after the journey to Utah in 1847, he lived in Plain City, Utah, where he died.

Charles Shumway (1808–1898), from Massachusetts, became a Mormon in 1841 and moved to Nauvoo, where he became a police officer. Before he was the first to cross the Mississippi River in the evacuation of Nauvoo, he was endowed in the Nauvoo Temple. He became one of the pioneer vanguard the following year in 1847. He built gristmills in Utah and Arizona after removing his family to the West. He died at Shumway, Arizona.

Mephibosheth Sirrine (1811–1848), born in New York, raised up an LDS Church branch in Lenawee County, Michigan in August 1838. He later served the church in Connecticut and England. After returning from England he was appointed president pro tem of eastern states church branches. Starting for the West in 1848, he died of consumption near the mouth of the Ohio River. His body was transported to Winter Quarters, Nebraska, for burial.

Aaron Smith (1797–1856), from Vermont and a brother of Moses Smith, became a Mormon in 1831. After removal to Nauvoo, he apparently joined the Nauvoo Legion. For a time, after the death of Joseph Smith, he became an influential follower of James Jesse Strang. He later broke with Strang over the acceptance of John Bennett into Strang's church. He later affiliated with the RLDS Church, but eventually left that church as well, forming his own Church of Christ. Later, still, he joined with Henry Deam's organization, as his counselor, after Deam separated from the RLDS Church. Smith died in Mentor, Ohio.

Don Carlos Smith (1816–1841), younger brother of Joseph Smith, played an important role in Nauvoo, religiously and civically. Besides serving in a high administrative position in the LDS Church's Melchizedek Priesthod, he also served as a Nauvoo city council member, and a lieutenant colonel in the Hancock County militia along with being a high-ranking officer in the Nauvoo Legion. Co-editor of the LDS Church's organ, *Times and Seasons*, at the time, he died on 7 August 1841 in Nauvoo, Illinois.

George A. Smith (1817–1875), born in New York and a cousin to Joseph Smith, at twenty-two became an apostle and was called to missionary service in England. He later became a Nauvoo city councilman and alderman, one of the Nauvoo Legion, and was endowed in the Nauvoo Temple. In the Missouri River settlements he lived in the Winter Quarters 15th Ward and Pottawattamie Branch. After relocating to Utah he became LDS Church historian and later a counselor to Brigham Young in the Church's First Presidency. He died in Salt Lake City.

John Smith (1781–1854), an uncle of Joseph Smith, Jr., was from New Hampshire. He joined his nephew's church in 1832. He proved an able leader in several localities, including leadership of the Saints in eastern Iowa, where he lived in the Zarahemla Stake. He later served as Nauvoo Stake president and as church patriarch (until his death) and was endowed in the Nauvoo Temple. When the pioneer vanguard departed Winter Quarters, he was left in charge. He emigrated to Utah in one of the companies that followed the vanguard. As in Winter Quarters, when the Twelve Apostles departed the Salt Lake Valley for the Missouri River settlements, Smith was left in charge. Uncle John Smith, as he was known, died in Salt Lake City.

Joseph Smith (1805–1844), born in Vermont, founded and became the first president of the Church of Christ (later the Church of Latter Day Saints, 1834, and the Church of Jesus Christ of Latter-day Saints, 1838) in western New York in 1830. He lived and struggled with the Saints in Ohio, Missouri, and Illinois, where he, in each place, became a city builder and civic, political, and military leader. He was assassinated in June 1844 at Carthage, Illinois, and buried in Nauvoo.

Lucy Mack Smith (1775–1856), from New Hampshire, "the aged and honored parent of Joseph Smith," mothered both the Smith family and church since its inception. After the deaths of her sons, Joseph and Hyrum, she prepared to accompany the Saints to the West, was endowed in the Nauvoo Temple, but later changed her mind and stayed in Nauvoo, where she was buried near her children.

Moses Smith (1800–1849), from Vermont, converted to Mormonism in 1832 in Ohio. Moving to Wisconsin in 1835, followed by his brother Aaron the following year, he is reputed to be the first "significant" Mormon to settle in the state and the first to organize an LDS branch there, in Burlington. He moved to Nauvoo in 1842–1843 where he opened a mercantile store. He was the brother-in-law of James Strang. After Joseph Smith's death he aligned with the Twelve Apostles, initially rejecting Strang's claims while his brother was one of Strang's chief lieutenants. But after returning to Burlington in 1845, he became sympathetic to Strang's position. Appealing Strang's case to the Twelve, he was excommunicated in early 1846, becoming a Strangite apostle in April 1846. Moses later rejected Strang and moved to northwestern Wisconsin where he died in May 1849.

Richard D. Smith (–), a private in company C of the Mormon Battalion, was one of the sick detachment of the group who wintered in Pueblo, Colorado, 1846–1847, before joining with the pioneer vanguard later in the Salt Lake Valley.

William B. Smith (1811–1893), younger brother of Joseph Smith and a member of Zion's Camp, was later appointed one of the Twelve Apostles in 1835. He became a member of the Illinois House of Representatives. He was an influential preacher and became editor of the Nauvoo newspaper, *The Wasp*. After Joseph Smith's death, William could not accommodate the authority of Brigham Young and the Twelve, believing his brother intended for a lineal priesthood order similar to Old Testament models where leadership was retained within a leader's family. William also served as Church patriarch after his brother Hyrum was killed, a lineal priesthood legacy. William was excommunicated from the LDS Church by the Twelve Apostles in 1845. He later affiliated with James Strang before attaching himself to the RLDS Church. He died in Iowa.

Abraham O. Smoot (1815–1895), born in Kentucky, converted to Mormonism in 1835. He later located in Kirtland and Missouri, where he endured Mormon difficulties there. He was a city policeman in Nauvoo, where he was also endowed in the temple. He also lived in the Zarahemla (Iowa) Stake. He became the bishop of the Winter Quarters 14th Ward and lived in the Pottawattamie Branch. After his arrival in Utah, he became the first bishop of the Salt Lake City 15th Ward, second mayor of Salt Lake City, and later the mayor of Provo. A member of the territorial legislature, he was also a justice of the peace, and a church stake president. He died in Provo, Utah.

William Cockran Adkinson Smoot (1828–1920) was a Tennessean who became a Mormon in 1836. He lived with the Saints in Far West, Missouri, and Nauvoo, and helped on the city's temple. He was a seventy and was endowed in the temple. One of the pioneer vanguard to Utah in 1847, he was noted for being the last of the company to enter the valley, but also as being the last of the group to die. He assisted in the emigration of other Mormons to Utah for several years. He died in Salt Lake City.

Erastus Fairbanks Snow (1818–1888), born in Vermont and brother of Willard and William Snow, converted to Mormonism in 1833. He resided in Ohio, Missouri, and Illinois during Mormon periods in those states. A significant church leader and missionary in New England during the early 1840s, after returning to Nauvoo he became a Council of Fifty member and was endowed in the temple. One of the vanguard to Utah in 1847, he opened Scandinavia to Mormon missionary work in 1850, where he was also instrumental in translating the Book of Mormon into Danish, the first foreign language translation of the book. Ordained a Mormon apostle in 1849, he became presiding church authority in southern Utah in 1861. He died in Salt Lake City.

Lorenzo Snow (1814–1901), born in Ohio, became a Latter-day Saint in 1836. Ordained an elder, he soon began missionary service for the church. Later accepting a mission to England in the early 1840s, he led the church in London. He joined the Nauvoo Legion and was endowed in the Nauvoo Temple. In Iowa he led the Mt. Pisgah Branch and later lived in the Pottawattamie Branch. Snow became one of the Twelve Apostles in 1849. He became a counselor to Brigham Young in 1873 and the fifth president of the LDS Church in 1898. He died in Salt Lake City.

Willard Trowbridge Snow (1811–1853), born in Vermont, and brother of Erastus and William Snow, was baptized in 1833. The following year he joined Zion's Camp. He became a seventy in 1835 and did missionary service. He was endowed in the Nauvoo Temple and lived in the Zarahemla (Iowa) Stake. He was bishop of the Winter Quarters 22nd Ward. Emigrating to Utah in 1847, he later presided over the church's Scandinavian Mission in the early 1850s. He died en route from Denmark to England in 1853.

William Snow (1806–1879), a Vermonter and brother of Erastus and Willard Snow, was baptized a Mormon in 1832. He did missionary work soon after his baptism. Having been endowed in the Nauvoo Temple and as a high priest, he lived in the Council Point Branch in Iowa. After emigrating in 1850 to Utah, he became a territorial legislator, probate judge, church bishop, and patriarch. He helped settle Fort Supply in Wyoming. He died in Pine Valley, Utah.

Elsie Pamelia Jacob Snyder (1831–1891), a daughter of Norton Jacob, was born in New York. She married Jesse Snyder in 1846, just as the Jacob family was preparing to depart Nauvoo. After Jesse died in 1853, Elsie married his brother George Gideon Snyder. She died in Park City, Utah.

George Gideon Snyder (1819–1887) came from New York. He was the son of Udney H. Jacob's second wife, Lovisa, and older brother of Jesse Snyder, Norton Jacob's son-in-law. After leaving Nauvoo, he moved to Missouri, and then to California before settling in Utah. After his brother Jesse died in 1853, he married Jesse's widow, Norton Jacob's daughter, Elsie Pamelia. He died in Park City, Utah.

Jesse Snyder (1825–1853) was born in New York. In Nauvoo he served in the Nauvoo Legion and was endowed in the temple. He emigrated to Utah with his wife, Norton Jacob's daughter Elsie, and died in Salt Lake City. His older sister Jane Snyder married Franklin Richards, who became a Mormon apostle in 1849.

Samuel L. Sprague (1807–1886), born in Massachusetts, was one of the early Mormon physicians. He was endowed in the Nauvoo Temple. His role in the Nauvoo exodus and Missouri River hiatus, considering the difficulties visited upon the Saints, was significant. Emigrating to Utah in 1848, he personally attended to Brigham Young in a number of circumstances. He died in Salt Lake City.

Roswell Stevens (1808–1880), from Canada, was baptized a Mormon in 1834. After removing to Nauvoo, where he lived in the 1st Ward, he became one of the Nauvoo Legion and the police force and was endowed in the temple. In Iowa he lived in the Pottawattamie and Council Point branches.

He joined the Mormon Battalion but returned to Winter Quarters once the men reached Santa Fe, New Mexico, to carry back wages and other materials. He was one of the pioneer vanguard to Utah in 1847, and was assigned to retrieve the Mississippi Saints and sick detachment of the Battalion at Pueblo, Colorado. After living in Alpine and Weber Valley, Utah, he was one of the exploring party that settled southeastern Utah, where he died in Bluff.

Benjamin Franklin Stewart (1817–1886), from Ohio, became a Mormon in 1844. He was one of the pioneer company to Utah in 1847, though he was one of those appointed to build a ferry on the North Platte River and later accompanied his family to the Salt Lake Valley. He operated a sawmill in Utah and later served a mission to Iowa and Illinois. He died in Benjamin, Utah, named for him, after being struck by lightning.

George P. Stiles (1816–1885), from New York, after becoming a Mormon became a lawyer in Nauvoo, where he also served in civic positions and was endowed in the temple. In Iowa he lived in the Pottawattamie Branch. He became an associate justice for Utah Territory where his dissonance with Mormonism led to his excommunication in 1856. His library was destroyed by Mormon vigilantes in Salt Lake City. He died in Texas.

Lyman Stoddard (1795–1854), from Connecticut, served several missions for the LDS Church in the United States. He presided in a number of church settings where he served. He was endowed in the Nauvoo Temple. In Iowa he lived in the Blockhouse, North Pigeon, and Pottawattamie branches. After emigrating to Utah, he died in Davis County.

Hosea Stout (1810–1889), born in Kentucky, was baptized a Mormon in Missouri in 1838. Fleeing to Nauvoo, where he lived in the 4th Ward, he soon became an officer in the Nauvoo Legion, eventually serving as an acting brigadier general. He became captain of the Nauvoo police force and there was endowed in the temple. His role in law enforcement continued in the Mormon settlements on the Missouri River. He was a member of the Winter Quarters 11th and 15th wards. He emigrated to Utah in 1848 where he became an attorney and a member of the territorial legislature. He died in Holladay, Utah.

Matilda A. Stowell (1827–1851), born in New York, was endowed in the Nauvoo Temple and later married Orrin Packard in 1849. After emigrating to Utah in 1850, she died in Springville, Utah.

James Jesse Strang (1813 –1856), a New Yorker, practiced law before accepting Mormonism. Influenced toward Mormonism by his brothers-in-law, Moses and Aaron Smith, he was baptized and ordained an elder in early 1844. After Joseph Smith's death, Strang produced an 18 June 1844 letter, alleged to have been written by Joseph Smith, appointing him Smith's successor and directing the Saints to gather to a small town in southeastern Wisconsin called Voree. After being unchurched by Brigham Young and the Twelve Apostles, he proved to be, for a time, the most formidable opponent of Young's leadership and organization. The church he created picked up many of those who rejected Young, including several former church leaders such as William Smith, John Page, William Marks, George Adams, and John Bennett. He gathered as many as 3,000 from the former ranks of the LDS Church. Strang was later killed in 1856 in Wisconsin by a disenchanted disciple.

Johann (John) Augustus Sutter (1803–1880), born in Germany, emigrated to America at the age of 31. In 1838 he joined a company of trappers who traveled to the West Coast. With supplies he obtained on credit, he traveled up the Sacramento River in August 1839 to establish a post. After becoming a Mexican citizen, he received a grant of nearly 49,000 acres, which he called New Helvetia after his homeland. He started building his fort in 1840. He became an important entrepreneur in that region of California. It was at his mill on 24 January 1848 that James Marshall found the gold that inaugurated the California Gold Rush.

Seth Taft (1796–1863), from Massachusetts, became a Mormon in 1841 in Michigan. He relocated to Nauvoo and among the Saints on the Missouri River was a member of the Winter Quarters 5th Ward and Pottawattamie Branch. He later became one of the pioneer vanguard to Utah in 1847. He became the first bishop of the Salt Lake City 9th Ward and later a church patriarch in Salt Lake City, where he died.

Tanner, Thomas, not John as written by Jacob, (1804–1855), from England, emigrated to America in 1831 and was baptized a Mormon ten years later. He was endowed in the Nauvoo Temple. One of the first company to arrive in Utah in 1847 and a blacksmith, he was responsible for the cannon accompanying the group. He plied his trade for the public works in Salt Lake City, where he died from an accident.

Cyrenus Taylor (1826–1854), born in New York, was a carpenter. He would be ordained a seventy later in the year after arriving in 1848 in Utah, where he would become the first county clerk for Sanpete County in Manti. He died in Manti, Utah.

John Taylor (1808–1887), born in England, became a Mormon convert in Canada in 1836. He became a Mormon apostle in 1838 and served in the apostolic mission to England in 1839–1841. In Nauvoo he became editor of the *Times and Seasons* and *Nauvoo Neighbor*, and in New York edited *The Mormon*. He was badly wounded in the killings of Joseph and Hyrum Smith in June 1844. He was endowed in the Nauvoo Temple. He lived in the Winter Quarters 3rd and 11th wards. He emigrated to Utah in 1847, and became the third president of the LDS Church after Brigham Young's death. He died in Kaysville, Utah.

Norman Taylor (1828–1899), born in Ohio, became a Mormon in 1844. He joined the Mormon Battalion, though he did not go with the expedition. In Iowa he lived in the Macedonia Branch. He became one of the original pioneers to Utah in 1847. He took his family to Utah in 1850, and later removed to San Bernardino, California, though he returned to Utah, eventually locating and ranching in Moab, Utah, where he died.

Otis Terry (1796–1887), from Massachusetts, was baptized in 1843/1844 and was later ordained a high priest. He was endowed in the Nauvoo Temple. He served as an acting bishop in Iowa at Honey Creek while waiting to depart for the West. He emigrated in 1850 to Utah, and later lived in Millcreek and Fairview, Utah, where he died.

George Therlkill (ca. 1832–), a relative of Robert Crow, with his family were among the Mississippi Saints who wintered at Pueblo, Colorado, in 1846 with the sick detachment of the Mormon Battalion.

Ezra Thompson (1797–1873), from Connecticut, after becoming a Latter-day Saint, moved to Nauvoo, where he lived in the 3rd Ward and was endowed in the Nauvoo Temple in 1846 before emigrating to Utah. A millwright, he died in Salt Lake City.

Samuel Thompson (1813–1892), from New York, was endowed in the Nauvoo Temple before enlisting in the Mormon Battalion in 1846. After settling in Utah, he died in Vernal.

John Harvey Tippets (1810–1890), from New Hampshire, was baptized a Mormon in 1832. He endured Mormon difficulties in Ohio, Missouri, and Illinois. He was endowed in the Nauvoo Temple. He joined the Nauvoo Legion, and later joined the Mormon Battalion; he became part of the sick detachment that wintered in Pueblo, Colorado, and joined the pioneer vanguard to Utah in 1847. He took his family to Utah in 1848 and later served a mission to England. He was ordained a church patriarch and died in Farmington, Utah.

William P. Vance (1822–1914), from Tennessee, became a Mormon in 1839. Joining the Saints in Nauvoo, where he lived in the 3rd Ward, he was ordained a seventy and learned stenography. He later returned to Tennessee as a missionary. He was endowed in the Nauvoo Temple. One of the original pioneers to Utah in 1847, he became an early settler in southern Utah, where he lived in Parowan, St. George, and Pine Valley. He was a probate judge. He later moved to Lund, Nevada, in 1902, where he died.

Moses Vince (1801–) was born in New York. A seventy, he was a member of the church's Council Point, Buoyo, and Union branches in Iowa, local congregations at the time the Saints lived in proximity to the Missouri River.

Henson Walker (1820–1894) was a New Yorker who became a Mormon in 1840. After emigrating to Nauvoo, he worked on the temple. He was one of the first pioneers to Utah in 1847. He became a bishop in Pleasant Grove, Utah, where he was also first mayor. He later served missions to England and Scotland and to the Northern States. He died in Pleasant Grove.

William H. Walker (1820–1908), from Vermont, became a Mormon in 1835. He arrived in Missouri just in time to be evicted. His father was wounded at Haun's Mill in 1838. After locating in Nauvoo, he became an employee of Joseph Smith. He was endowed in the Nauvoo Temple. He later enlisted in the Mormon Battalion in 1846 and with the sick detachment, wintered in Pueblo, Colorado, before joining with the pioneer vanguard in Utah in 1847. After living for a time in Salt Lake City, he later died in Idaho.

William Wallace (–) worked on Salt Lake City's public works crews in 1852.

Charles W. Wandell (1819–1875), a New Yorker, joined with the Mormons in 1837. He became a clerk in the Church Historian's Office, working for Willard Richards, in Nauvoo. He was endowed in the Nauvoo Temple. His career in the church was tumultuous. It included missionary work in Australia in the early 1850s, but later resulted in his leaving Mormonism and becoming a critic of Brigham Young. Later, in 1873, he joined the RLDS Church and died in Australia in their service.

William Weeks (1813–1900), from Massachusetts, was trained as an architect by his father. Born a Quaker, he converted to Mormonism while visiting the southern states. Trained in the Greek Revivalist school, he was appointed by Joseph Smith to be architect of the temple in Nauvoo, where he was endowed. He lived in the 3rd Ward and otherwise served an important role in Nauvoo. He lived for a time in the Winter Quarters 21st Ward. He became an 1847 emigrant to Utah, where he had a falling out with church leaders. He left Utah for San Bernardino, California.

Daniel H. Wells (1814–1891), born in New York, was a constable and justice of the peace in Commerce, Illinois, and an officer in the county militia before the arrival of the Mormons. While still a non-Mormon, he became a Nauvoo alderman, city councilman, Nauvoo University regent, and brigadier general in the Nauvoo Legion. He was baptized a Mormon in August 1846 and was a principal defender of the Saints in the Battle of Nauvoo. He emigrated in 1848 to Utah, where he became principal officer of the reconstituted Nauvoo Legion and second counselor to Brigham Young (till 1877). He died in Salt Lake City.

Madison Welsch (1828–), from Ohio, enlisted as a private in the Mormon Battalion's Company C in 1846 and was one of those who wintered at Pueblo, Colorado, before uniting with the pioneer vanguard in the Salt Lake Valley in 1847.

John Wheeler (1802–), born in South Carolina, after becoming a Mormon, was ordained an elder in 1842 and lived in the Nashville (Iowa) Branch. He was endowed in the Nauvoo Temple. He was one of the first pioneers to Utah in 1847. He returned to Utah in 1851 and later removed to California.

Edson Whipple (1805–1894), born in Vermont, became a Mormon in 1840. He emigrated to Nauvoo in 1842. In 1844 he served a mission to Pennsylvania to promote Joseph Smith's campaign for the U.S. presidency and afterward was endowed in the Nauvoo Temple. He lived in the Pottawattamie Branch in Iowa. One of the Mormon vanguard in 1847, he returned to Utah again in 1850, where he became an officer in Utah's Nauvoo Legion. He settled in southern Utah and later lived in Provo. He died in Mexico.

Horace K. Whitney (1823–1884), born in Kirtland, Ohio, was the son of Newel Whitney, one of Mormonism's early leaders. In Nauvoo, he lived in the 4th Ward and was endowed in the temple. He was a major in the Nauvoo Legion's Topographical Engineers. He joined the pioneer vanguard to Utah in 1847 and became one of its most able chroniclers. He later joined Utah's Nauvoo Legion. He was involved in drama and music in early Utah, where he was also involved for over twenty years in the production of the *Deseret News*. He died in Salt Lake City.

Newel K. Whitney (1795–1850), a Vermonter, was a Kirtland, Ohio, merchant in 1831 when Joseph Smith called upon him. After his baptism he was appointed a bishop in 1831, a position he later held in Nauvoo and Salt Lake City. His leadership role as bishop played a significant role in the first generation of Mormonism. He was endowed in the Nauvoo Temple. He lived in the Winter Quarters 15th Ward before immigrating to Utah in 1848. He died in Salt Lake City.

Thomas L. Whittle (1812–1868), born in Upper Canada, was baptized a Mormon in 1837. In Nauvoo, where he lived in the 2nd Ward, he was ordained a seventy in 1844 and endowed in the temple in January 1846. After emigrating to Utah in 1848, he later served the church as a missionary to Hawaii. He died in Richmond, Utah.

Lyman Wight (1796–1858), from New York, became a Mormon in Ohio in 1830. A zealous convert, he proved influential in the church in Missouri, where he was imprisoned with Joseph Smith in Liberty in 1838–1839. Appointed to the Twelve Apostles in 1841, his allegiance to Brigham Young never equaled his devotion to Joseph Smith. After his unilateral move to Texas in 1845, his connection to Mormonism waned. Church leaders excommunicated him in 1848. He died in Texas.

Thomas S. Williams (1827–1860), born in Tennessee, was endowed in the Nauvoo Temple. The 21-year-old sergeant in the Mormon Battalion's Company D wintered with the sick detachment at Pueblo, Colorado. Williams had an independent spirit, which he appears to have come by genetically, though he later conformed some and became a successful lawyer and businessman in Salt Lake City. He died in California in 1860 at the hands of Indians, though some question the circumstances.

Stephen Winchester (1795–1873), born in Vermont, was baptized a Mormon in 1833. In 1834, he became a member of Zion's Camp and suffered the persecutions of Mormons in Missouri. Apostle David Patten, after the battle of Crooked River in Missouri, died in Winchester's home. In Nauvoo, he lived in the 3rd Ward, was one of the Nauvoo Legion, and was endowed in the temple. He was the father of the noted Mormon author and pamphleteer Benjamin Winchester. A farmer, he emigrated to Utah in 1849. He died in Salt Lake City.

Jesse Atwater Wixom (1807–1884), from New York, and his wife Artimesia Rich Wixom (1811–1880), from Indiana, Charles Rich's sister, were married in 1831 in Tazewell County, Illinois.

Wilford Woodruff (1807–1898), from Connecticut, baptized a Mormon in 1833, became one of the Mormon apostles in 1839 prior to his missionary service in England. Later in 1844 he became the Church's European Mission president. He was endowed in the Nauvoo Temple. He lived in the Winter Quarters 14th Ward before joining the Mormon vanguard to Utah in 1847. He is noted for keeping a diary during his entire tenure as a Mormon, 1833–1898. He became LDS Church president in 1889 and terminated the Mormon practice of plural marriage in 1890. He died in San Francisco, California, and was buried in Salt Lake City.

George Woodward (1817–1903), from New Jersey, was baptized a Mormon in 1840. He moved to Nauvoo the following year and was ordained a seventy and worked on both the Nauvoo House and Nauvoo Temple, where he was later endowed. He was a member of the Winter Quarters 17th Ward before joining the pioneer vanguard in 1847 to Utah, where he later became a bishop's counselor. He settled in southern Utah where he died in St. George.

Thomas Woolsey (1806–1897) was a Kentuckian and became a Mormon there in 1838. After removing to Nauvoo and being endowed in the Nauvoo Temple, he lived for a time in the Mt. Pisgah Branch in Iowa and later joined the Mormon Battalion, becoming one of the sick detachment that wintered in Pueblo, Colorado, 1846–1847. The group entered the Salt Lake Valley in 1847 shortly after the pioneer vanguard. After taking his family to Utah in 1852, he lived in several Utah communities, dying in Wales, Sanpete County.

William S. Wordsworth (also Wardsworth) (1810–1888), from New Jersey, was baptized a Mormon in 1841 or 1843. Ordained a seventy and endowed in the Nauvoo Temple in 1846, he later lived in the Winter Quarters 3rd Ward. He then became one of the pioneer vanguard to Utah in 1847. After removing his family to Utah, he was a farmer and lived in Springville, where he died.

Franklin A. Worrell (–1845), from Pennsylvania, immigrated to Illinois with his mother and brothers. He was one of the early settlers of Carthage, Illinois. A public-minded merchant in Carthage, he was also a lieutenant in the local militia organization, the Carthage Greys. He was, when Joseph and Hyrum Smith were killed in June 1844, reputed to be captain of the guard at the Carthage jail, whose ostensible duty was protection but who, in fact, conspired to murder the Smiths. Worrell, on 16 September 1845, was killed in Hancock County by Orrin Porter Rockwell, in defense of Hancock County, Illinois, sheriff Jacob Backenstos.

Phineas Reddington Wright (1816–), from New York, was ordained a seventy and was endowed in the Nauvoo Temple in January 1846. A member of the Mormon Battalion, he later emigrated to Utah where he was a farmer and an officer in Utah's Nauvoo Legion.

John Price Wriston (1823–1899) was endowed in the Nauvoo Temple and was later a private in Company C of the Mormon Battalion. He maintained, at this time, the surname his grandfather had adopted from the latter's stepfather. Later the junior Wriston changed his surname to Clifford, his family's true name, by which he was thereafter known on church and civil records.

Brigham Young (1801–1877), born in Vermont, was baptized in 1832. A member of Zion's Camp in 1834, he became one of the original Twelve

Apostles in 1835. He helped with the evacuation of Mormons from Missouri and led the apostolic mission to Great Britain in 1839, where he became quorum president. Instrumental in Nauvoo events, including Nauvoo Temple ceremonies, he held religious, civic, and military positions. In the turmoil after Joseph Smith's assassination, Young prevailed over his rivals to lead most of the Saints to the Missouri River, where he led the temporary settlements there. There he officially became second president of the LDS Church. He led the pioneer vanguard in 1847 to Utah, where he became territorial governor and led the settlement of the Intermountain West until his death in Salt Lake City.

John Young (1791–1870), born in Massachusetts and an older brother of Brigham Young, served as a missionary in Ohio, Pennsylvania, and New York in 1834–1836. He later became Kirtland Stake president. He was endowed in the Nauvoo Temple. He emigrated in 1847 to Utah where he later died.

Joseph Young (1797–1881), born in Massachusetts, was an older brother of Brigham Young. After converting to Mormonism in 1832, he became a member of Zion's Camp in 1834 and became the senior president in the First Council of Seventy in 1835, in which position he served until his death. He endured the Mormon difficulties in Missouri and later moved to Nauvoo, where he lived in the 4th Ward. He also joined the Nauvoo Legion and was endowed in the Nauvoo Temple. He emigrated in 1850 to Utah, where he died in Salt Lake City.

Lorenzo Dow Young (1807–1895), born in New York and a younger brother of Brigham Young, became a Mormon in 1832. He endured Mormon difficulties in Missouri and Illinois, where he lived for a time in the Ramus/Macedonia Branch in Hancock County. He was endowed in the Nauvoo Temple. He also lived in the Winter Quarters 5th Ward before accompanying the original pioneer company to Utah in 1847. After settling in Utah, he became bishop of the Salt Lake 18th Ward for twenty-seven years. He was later ordained a church patriarch. He died in Salt Lake City.

Phinehas Howe Young (1799–1879), from Massachusetts, was an older brother of Brigham Young. An early convert to Mormonism in 1830, he served a mission to Ohio in 1841. He was endowed in the Nauvoo Temple before he became one of the pioneer vanguard to Utah in 1847. At Green River, Wyoming, he was sent back to guide the following companies. He later served a mission to Great Britain and was ordained a bishop. A Salt Lake City lawyer, he lived for a time in Summit County, Utah, but returned to Salt Lake City where he died.

Bibliography

THE SHORT FORM OF EACH CITATION is used throughout the text.

Books

Alexander, Thomas G. and James B. Allen. *Mormons & Gentiles: A History of Salt Lake City.* Boulder, Colorado: Pruett Publishing Company, 1984.

Allen, James B. *No Toil Nor Labor Fear: The Story of William Clayton.* Provo, Utah: Brigham Young University Press, 2002.

Allen, James B., Jesse L. Embry, and Kahlile B. Mehr. *Hearts Turned to the Fathers: A History of the Genealogical Society of Utah, 1894–1994.* Provo, Utah: BYU Studies, 1995.

Alter, J. Cecil. *Jim Bridger.* Norman, Oklahoma: University of Oklahoma Press, 1962.

Arrington, Leonard J. *Great Basin Kingdom: An Economic History of the Latter-day Saints, 1830–1900.* Cambridge, Massachusetts: Harvard University Press, 1958.

———. *Charles C. Rich: Mormon General and Western Frontiersman.* Provo, Utah: Brigham Young University Press, 1974.

———. *Brigham Young: American Moses.* New York: Alfred A. Knopf, 1985.

Babbitt, Charles H. *Early Days at Council Bluffs.* Washington, D.C.: Byron S. Adams, 1916.

Bagley, Will, ed. *Scoundrel's Tale: The Samuel Brannan Papers.* Spokane, Washington: The Arthur H. Clark Company, 1999.

Ballowe, Patricia Jewell, Violet Michaelis Jewell, and Carol Watkins Lundgren, comps. *The 1850 Census of Illinois, Hancock County.* Richland, Washington: Locust Grove Press, 1977.

Bancroft, Hubert Howe. *History of Utah.* San Francisco: History Company, 1889.

Barney, Gwen Marler. *Anson Call and the Rocky Mountain Prophecy.* Salt Lake City: Call Publishing, 2002.

Barney, Ronald O. *One Side by Himself: The Life and Times of Lewis Barney, 1808–1894.* Logan, Utah: Utah State University Press, 2001.

Bashore, Melvin L. and Linda L. Haslam. *Mormon Pioneer Companies Crossing the Plains (1847–1868) Narratives: Guide to Sources in Utah Libraries and Archives.* [Salt Lake City]: Historical Department, The Church of Jesus Christ of Latter-day Saints, 1990.

Bates, Irene M. and E. Gary Smith. *Lost Legacy: The Mormon Office of Presiding Patriarch.* Urbana, Illinois: University of Illinois Press, 1996.

Baur, John E. "Zacharias Ham." In LeRoy R. Hafen. ed., *The Mountain Men and the Fur Trade of the Far West.* 10 vols. Glendale, California: The Arthur H. Clark Company, 1965–1972. Vol. 9, 1972.

Bennett, Richard E. *Mormons at the Missouri, 1846–1852: "And Should We Die."* Norman, Oklahoma: University of Oklahoma Press, 1987.

———. *We'll Find the Place: The Mormon Exodus, 1846–1848.* Salt Lake City: Deseret Book Company, 1997.

Bergera, Gary James. *Conflict in the Quorum: Orson Pratt, Brigham Young, Joseph Smith.* Salt Lake City: Signature Books, 2002.

Bigler, David L. and Will Bagley, eds. *Army of Israel: Mormon Battalion Narratives.* Logan, Utah: Utah State University Press, 2000.

Bishop, M. Guy. *Henry William Bigler: Soldier, Gold Miner, Missionary, Chronicler.* Logan, Utah: Utah State University Press, 1998.

Bitton, Ronald Davis. *The Redoubtable John Pack: Pioneer, Proselyter, Patriarch.* Salt Lake City: Eden Hill, 1982.

Black, Susan Easton, comp. *Membership of the Church of Jesus Christ of Latter-day Saints: 1830–1848.* 50 vols. Provo, Utah: Brigham Young University, Religious Studies Center, 1984–1988.

———. *Early Members of the Reorganized Church of Jesus Christ of Latter Day Saints.* 6 vols. Provo, Utah: Brigham Young University, Religious Studies Center, 1993.

Black, Susan Easton and William G. Hartley, eds. *The Iowa Mormon Trail: Legacy of Faith and Courage.* Orem, Utah: Helix Publishing, 1997.

Blackburn, Abner. *Frontiersman: Abner Blackburn's Narrative.* Will Bagley, ed. Salt Lake City: University of Utah Press, 1992.

Blender, Edie. *This Township Called Durham.* Bushnell, Illinois: McDonough Democrat, 1993–1994.

Bradley, James L. *Zion's Camp, 1834: Prelude to the Civil War.* Salt Lake City: Publisher's Press, 1990.

Britsch, R. Lanier. *Unto the Islands of the Sea: A History of the Latter-day Saints in the Pacific.* Salt Lake City: Deseret Book, 1986.

Brown, John. *Autobiography of Pioneer John Brown, 1820–1896.* Arranged and published by John Zimmerman Brown. Salt Lake City: Stevens & Wallis, Inc., 1941.

Brown, Joseph E. *The Mormon Trek West.* Garden City, New York: Doubleday & Company, Inc., 1980.

Brown, Matthew B. and Paul Thomas Smith. *Symbols in Stone: Symbolism in the Early Temples of the Restoration.* American Fork, Utah: Covenant Communications, Inc., 1997.

Bullock, Thomas. *The Pioneer Camp of the Saints: The 1846 and 1847 Mormon Trail Journals of Thomas Bullock.* Will Bagley, ed. Spokane, Washington: The Arthur H. Clark Company, 1997.

Bye, Robert A., Jr. "Ethnobotany of the Southern Paiute Indians in the 1870s: With a Note on the Early Ethnobotanical Contributions of Dr. Edward Palmer, in Don D. Fowler, ed. *Great Basin Cultural Ecology, a Symposium.* Reno, Nevada: Desert Research Institute Publications in the Social Sciences, No. 8, 1972.

Campbell, Eugene E. "Miles Morris Goodyear." In LeRoy R. Hafen, ed., *The Mountain Men and the Fur Trade of the Far West.* 10 vols. Glendale, California: The Arthur H. Clark Company, 1965–1972. Vol. 2, 1965.

Cannon, D. James. ed. *Centennial Caravan: Story of the 1947 Centennial Reenactment of the Original Mormon Trek.* N.p.: Sons of Utah Pioneers, 1948.

Carter, D. Robert. *Founding Fort Utah: Provo's Native Inhabitants, Early Explorers, and First Year of Settlement.* N.p.: Provo City Corporation, 2003.

Carter, Kate B. "Pioneer Mills and Milling." In Kate B. Carter, comp., *Heart Throbs of the West.* 12 vols. Salt Lake City: Daughters of Utah Pioneers, 1939–1951. Vol. 3, 1941.

———. "They Came in '47." In Kate B. Carter, comp., *Heart Throbs of the West.* 12 vols. Salt Lake City, Daughters of the Utah Pioneers, 1939–1951. Vol. 8, 1947.

———. comp. "Mississippi Saints." In Kate B. Carter, comp., *Our Pioneer Heritage.* 20 vols. Salt Lake City: Daughters of Utah Pioneers, 1958–1977. Vol. 2, 1959.

———. comp. "The First Company to Enter Salt Lake Valley." In Kate B. Carter, comp., *Our Pioneer Heritage.* 20 vols. Salt Lake City: Daughters of Utah Pioneers, 1958–1977. Vol. 2, 1959.

Carvalho, Solomon Nunes. *Incidents of Travel and Adventure in the Far West: with Col. Fremont's Last Expedition across the Rocky Mountains: including Three Months' Residence in Utah and a Perilous Trip across the Great American Desert to the Pacific*. New York: Derby & Jackson, 1857.

Chamberlain, Solomon. [Autobiography]. In Kate B. Carter, comp. *Our Pioneer Heritage*. 20 vols. Salt Lake City: Daughters of Utah Pioneers, 1958–1977. Vol. 2, 1959.

Christian, Lewis Clark. "Mormon Foreknowledge of the West." In James B. Allen and John W. Welch, eds. *Coming to Zion*. Provo, Utah: BYU Studies, Brigham Young University, 1997.

Clayton, William. *The Latter-Day Saints' Emigrant' Guide: Being a Table of Distances, showing all the springs, creeks, rivers, hills, mountains, camping places, and all the other notable places, from Council Bluffs to the Valley of the Great Salt Lake. Also, the latitudes, longitudes, and altitudes of the prominent points of the route. Together with remarks on the nature of the land, timber, grass, &c. The whole route having been measured by a Roadometer, and the distance from point to point, in English miles, accurately shown*. St. Louis: Republican Steam Press, Chambers and Knapp, 1848. Reprinted in Stanley B. Kimball, ed. St. Louis: Patrice Press, 1983.

———. "The Journal of William Clayton." In Kate B. Carter, comp. *Heart Throbs of the West*. 12 vols. Salt Lake City: Daughters of Utah Pioneers, 1939–1951. Vol. 6, 1945.

———. *William Clayton's Journal.* Salt Lake City: Deseret News, 1921, reprinted L.K. Taylor Publishing Company, 1973.

———. *An Intimate Chronicle: The Journals of William Clayton*. George D. Smith ed. Salt Lake City: Signature Books, 1995.

Coates, Lawrence G. "Refugees, Friends, and Foes: Mormons and Indians in Iowa and Nebraska." In James B. Allen and John W. Welch, eds. *Coming to Zion*. Provo, Utah: BYU Studies, Brigham Young University, 1997.

Coleman, Ronald G. "Blacks in Utah History: An Unknown Legacy." In Helen Z. Papanikolas, ed., *The Peoples of Utah*. Salt Lake City: Utah State Historical Society, 1976.

Colvin, Don F. *Nauvoo Temple: A Story of Faith*. American Fork, Utah: Covenant Communications, 2002.

Conetah, Fred A. *A History of the Northern Ute People*. Kathryn L. MacKay and Floyd A. O'Neil, eds. Salt Lake City: Uintah-Ouray Ute Tribe, 1982.

Cook, Lyndon W. *The Revelations of the Prophet Joseph Smith*. Provo, Utah: Seventy's Mission Bookstore, 1981.

———. comp. *Nauvoo Deaths and Marriages, 1839–1845*. Orem, Utah: Grandin Book Company, 1994.

Crawley, Peter. *A Descriptive Bibliography of the Mormon Church, Volume One, 1830–1847*. Provo, Utah: Religious Studies Center, Brigham Young University, 1997.

Curtis, Luceal Rockwood. *Compiled and Assembled History of Albert Perry Rockwood*. Salt Lake City: N.p., 1968.

Davies, Joseph Kenneth. *Mormon Gold: The Story of California's Mormon Argonauts*. Salt Lake City: Olympus Publishing, 1984.

Daynes, Kathryn M. *More Wives Than One: Transformation of the Mormon Marriage System, 1840–1910*. Urbana, Illinois: University of Illinois Press, 2001.

Dellenbaugh, Frederick Samuel. *A Canyon Voyage: The Narrative of the Second Powell Expedition Down the Green-Colorado River from Wyoming, and the Exploration on Land, in the Years 1871 and 1872*. New York: G. P. Putnam's Sons, 1908.

Dorius, Guy L. "Elder" in Arnold K. Garr, Donald Q. Cannon, and Richard O. Cowan. *Encyclopedia of Latter-day Saint History*. Salt Lake City: Deseret Book Company, 2000.

Douglas, Stephen A. *The Letters of Stephen A. Douglas.* Robert W. Johannsen, ed. Urbana, Illinois: University of Illinois Press, 1961.

Edwards, Paul M. "William B. Smith: 'A Wart on the Ecclesiastical Tree.'" In Roger D. Launius and Linda Thatcher, eds., *Differing Visions: Dissenters in Mormon History*. Urbana, Illinois: University of Illinois Press, 1994.

Egan, Howard. *Pioneering the West, 1846 to 1878: Major Howard Egan's Diary*. Richmond, Utah: Howard R. Egan Estate, 1917.

"1847 Pioneers." *Deseret News 1997–98 Church Almanac*. Salt Lake City: Deseret News, 1996.

Ellsworth, S. George and Kathleen C. Perrin. *Seasons of Faith and Courage: The Church of Jesus Christ of Latter-day Saints in French Polynesia, A Sesquicentennial History, 1843–1993*. N.p.: Yves R. Perrin, 1994.

England, Breck. *The Life and Thought of Orson Pratt*. Salt Lake City: University of Utah Press, 1985.

Esshom, Frank. *Pioneers and Prominent Men of Utah*. Salt Lake City: Utah Pioneers Book Publishing Company, 1913.

Federal Writers' Project. *Old Bellevue*. Papillion, Nebraska: Papillion Times, 1937.

Fitzpatrick, Doyle C. *The King Strang Story: A Vindication of James J. Strang, the Beaver Island Mormon King*. Lansing, Michigan: National Heritage, 1970.

Flanders, Robert Bruce. *Nauvoo: Kingdom on the Mississippi*. Urbana, Illinois: University of Illinois Press, 1975.

Foster, Lawrence. *Religion and Sexuality: The Shakers, the Mormons, and the Oneida Community*. Urbana, Illinois: University of Illinois Press, 1984.

Franzwa, Gregory M. *Maps of the California Trail*. Tucson, Arizona: Patrice Press, 1999.

———. *Maps of the Oregon Trail*. Gerald, Missouri: Patrice Press, 1982.

Frazer, Robert W. *Forts of the West: Military Forts and Presidios and Posts Commonly Called Forts West of the Mississippi River to 1898*. Norman, Oklahoma: University of Oklahoma Press, 1972.

Garr, Arnold K. "Joseph Smith: Candidate for President of the United States." In H. Dean Garrett, ed., *Regional Studies in Latter-day Saint Church History: Illinois*. Provo, Utah: Department of Church History and Doctrine, Brigham Young University, 1995.

Gentry, Leland H. "The Mormon Way Stations: Garden Grove and Mt. Pisgah." In James B. Allen and John W. Welch, eds., *Coming to Zion*. Provo, Utah: BYU Studies, Brigham Young University, 1997.

Givens, Terryl L. *By the Hand of Mormon: The American Scripture that Launched a New World Religion*. New York: Oxford University Press, 2002.

Goff, William A. "Pierre Didier Papin." In LeRoy R. Hafen. ed., *The Mountain Men and the Fur Trade of the Far West*. 10 vols. Glendale, California: The Arthur H. Clark Company, 1965–1972. Vol. 9, 1972.

Goss, C. Chaucer. *Bellevue, Larmier & Saint Mary: Their History, Location, Description*. Bellevue, Nebraska: John Q. Goss, 1859.

Gowans, Fred R. and Eugene E. Campbell. *Fort Bridger: Island in the Wilderness*. Provo, Utah: Brigham Young University Press, 1975.

Gregg, Th[omas]. *History of Hancock County, Illinois, together with an Outline History of the State and a Digest of State Laws*. Chicago: Chas. C. Chapman & Co., 1880.

Hafen, LeRoy R. and Francis Marion Young. *Fort Laramie and the Pageant of the West, 1834–1890*. Glendale, California: The Arthur H. Clark Company, 1938.

Hallwas, John E. "Mormon Nauvoo from a Non-Mormon Perspective." In Roger D. Launius and John E. Hallwas, eds. *Kingdom on the Mississippi Revisited: Nauvoo in Mormon History*. Urbana, Illinois: University of Illinois Press, 1996.

Hallwas, John E. and Roger D. Launius, eds. *Cultures in Conflict: A Documentary History of the Mormon War in Illinois*. Logan, Utah: Utah State University Press, 1995.

Hamilton, Marshall. "From Assassination to Expulsion: Two Years of Distrust, Hostility, and Violence." In Roger D. Launius and John E. Hallwas, eds. *Kingdom on the Mississippi Revisited: Nauvoo in Mormon History*. Urbana, Illinois: University of Illinois Press, 1996.

Hardy, B. Carmon. *Solemn Covenant: The Mormon Polygamous Passage*. Urbana, Illinois: University of Illinois Press, 1992.

Harmon, Appleton Milo. *Appleton Milo Harmon Goes West*. Maybelle Harmon Anderson, ed. Berkeley, California: Gillick Press, 1946.

Harper, Charles Alfred. *The Diary of Charles Alfred Harper* N.p.: n.p., ca. 1971.

Hartley, William G. *The 1845 Burning of Morley's Settlement and Murder of Edmund Durfee*. Salt Lake City: Primer Publications, 1997.

———. *My Best for the Kingdom: History and Autobiography of John Lowe Butler, a Mormon Frontiersman.* Salt Lake City: Aspen Books, 1993.

Hileman, Levida. *In Tar and Paint and Stone: The Inscriptions at Independence Rock and Devil's Gate.* Glendo, Wyoming: High Plains Press, 2001.

Hine, Robert V. and John Mack Faragher. *The American West: A New Interpretive History*. New Haven, Connecticut: Yale University Press, 2000.

History of Mills County, Iowa. Des Moines: State Historical Company, 1881.

Holzapfel, Richard Neitzel. *Their Faces toward Zion: Voices and Images of the Trek West.* Salt Lake City: Bookcraft, 1996.

Hoogs, Cynthia Tryon. *Sheffield, Massachusetts: Cemetery Inscriptions.* Great Barrington, Massachusetts: N.p., 1987.

Hyde, George E. *The Pawnee Indians.* Norman, Oklahoma: University of Oklahoma Press, 1988.

Jackman, Levi. [Diary] *An Enduring Legacy.* 12 vols. Salt Lake City: Daughters of the Utah Pioneers, 1978–1989. Vol. 9, 1986.

Jacob, Norton. *The Record of Norton Jacob.* C. Edward Jacob and Ruth S. Jacob, eds. Salt Lake City: The Norton Jacob Family Association, 1949.

Jacob, Udney Hay. *An Extract from a Manuscript Entitled the Peace Maker or the Doctrines of the Millennium being a Treatise on Religion and Jurisprudence or a New System of Religion and Politicks for God, My Country and My Rights.* Nauvoo, Illinois: J. Smith, Printer, 1842.

Jenson, Andrew. *Church Chronology: A Record of Important Events Pertaining to the History of the Church of Jesus Christ of Latter-day Saints.* 2nd ed. Salt Lake City: Deseret News, 1899.

———. *Latter-day Saint Biographical Encyclopedia.* 4 vols. Salt Lake City: Andrew Jenson History Company/Andrew Jenson Memorial Association, 1901–1936.

———. *Encyclopedic History of the Church of Jesus Christ of Latter-day Saints.* Salt Lake City: Deseret News Publishing Co., 1941.

Jessee, Dean C. *The Papers of Joseph Smith.* 2 vols. Salt Lake City: Deseret Book Company, 1989, 1992.

———. "Joseph Smith and the Beginning of Mormon Record Keeping." In Larry C. Porter and Susan Easton Black, eds. *The Prophet Joseph: Essays on the Life and Mission of Joseph Smith.* Salt Lake City: Deseret Book Company, 1988.

Johnson, Kristin, ed., *"Unfortunate Emigrants": Narratives of the Donner Party.* Logan, Utah: Utah State University Press, 1996.

Jorgensen, Danny L. "The Old Fox: Alpheus Cutler." In Roger D. Launius and Linda Thatcher, eds. *Differing Visions: Dissenters in Mormon History.* Urbana, Illinois: University of Illinois Press, 1994.

Journal of Discourses, by Brigham Young, President of the Church of Jesus Christ of Latter-day Saints, His Two Counsellors, the Twelve Apostles and Others. 26 vols. Liverpool: F. D. Richards, et al., 1855–1886.

Kimball, Stanley B. *Discovering Mormon Trails: New York to California, 1831–1868.* Salt Lake City: Deseret Book Company, 1979.

———. *Heber C. Kimball: Mormon Patriarch and Pioneer.* Urbana, Illinois: University of Illinois Press, 1981.

———. *Historic Resource Study: Mormon Pioneer National Historic Trail.* N.p.: United States Department of the Interior, National Park Service, 1991.

———. *Historic Sites and Markers along the Mormon and Other Great Western Trails.* Urbana, Illinois: University of Illinois Press, 1988.

King, Larry R. *The Kings of the Kingdom: The Life of Thomas Rice King and His Family.* N.p.: Larry R. King, 1996.

Korns, J. Roderic and Dale L. Morgan. *West from Fort Bridger: The Pioneering of Immigrant Trails across Utah, 1846–1850.* Revised and Updated by Will Bagley and Harold Schindler. Logan, Utah: Utah State University Press, 1994.

Krakauer, Jon. *Under the Banner of Heaven: A Story of Violent Faith*. New York: Doubleday, 2003.

Larson, Carl V, comp. and ed. *A Database of the Mormon Battalion: An Identification of the Original Members of the Mormon Battalion*. 2nd ed. Salt Lake City: U.S. Mormon Battalion Inc., 1997.

Lavender, David. *Fort Laramie and the Changing Frontier*. Washington, D.C.: U.S. Department of Interior, 1983.

Lee, John D. *A Mormon Chronicle: The Diaries of John D. Lee, 1848–1876*. Robert Glass Cleland and Juanita Brooks, eds. 2 vols. Salt Lake City: University of Utah Press, 1983.

Leonard, Glen M. *Nauvoo: A Place of Peace, a People of Promise*. Salt Lake City: Deseret Book Company and Brigham Young University Press, 2002.

LeSueur, Stephen C. *The 1838 Mormon War in Missouri*. Columbia, Missouri: University of Missouri Press, 1987.

Linforth, James, ed. *Route from Liverpool to Great Salt Lake*. Illustrated with steel engravings and wood cuts made from sketches made by Frederick Piercy. Liverpool: Franklin D. Richards, Latter-day Saints' Book Depot, 1855.

Littlefield, Lyman O. *The Martyrs: A Sketch of the Lives and a Full Account of the Martyrdom of Joseph and Hyrum Smith*. Salt Lake City: Juvenile Instructor Office, 1882.

Madsen, Brigham D. *The Shoshoni Frontier and the Bear River Massacre*. Salt Lake City: University of Utah Press, 1985.

Madsen, Carol Cornwall. *Journey to Zion: Voices from the Mormon Trail*. Salt Lake City: Deseret Book Company, 1997.

Map of Hancock County, Illinois. N.p.: Harold & Arnold, 1859.

Martineau, LaVan. *The Southern Paiutes: Legends, Lore, Language, and Lineage*. Las Vegas, Nevada: KC Publications, 1992.

Mattes, Merrill J. *The Great Platte River Road: The Covered Wagon Mainline Via Fort Kearny to Fort Laramie*. N.p.: Nebraska State Historical Society, 1969.

———. *Platte River Road Narratives: A Descriptive Bibliography of Travel Over the Great Overland Route to Oregon, California, Utah, Colorado, Montana, and Other Western States and Territories, 1812–1866*. Urbana, Illinois: University of Illinois Press, 1988.

McDermott, John Dishon. "John Baptiste Richard." In LeRoy R. Hafen, ed., *The Mountain Men and the Fur Trade of the Far West*. 10 vols. Glendale, California: The Arthur H. Clark Company, 1965–1972. Vol. 2, 1965.

Miller, David E. and Della S. Miller. *Nauvoo: The City of Joseph*. Santa Barbara, California: Peregrine Smith, Inc., 1974.

Morgan, Dale L. *The State of Deseret*. Logan, Utah: Utah State University Press and Utah Historical Society, 1987.

Morgan, Nicholas Groesbeck, Sr., comp. *The Old Fort: Historic Mormon Bastion, the Plymouth Rock of the West*. Salt Lake City: Nicholas Groesbeck Morgan, Sr., 1964.

Mortimer, William James. *How Beautiful upon the Mountains: A Centennial History of Wasatch County*. Salt Lake City: Wasatch County Chapter, Daughters of Utah Pioneers, 1963.

———. "Patriarchal Blessings." In Daniel H. Ludlow, ed., *Encyclopedia of Mormonism*. 4 vols. New York: Macmillan Publishing Company, 1992.

Mouritsen, Robert G. *Mantle: Windy Day in August, at Nauvoo*. [Salt Lake City]: Westheather Development Company, 2004.

Mullen, Frank, Jr. *The Donner Party Chronicles: A Day-by-Day Account of a Doomed Wagon Train, 1846–1847*. N.p.: Halcyon Imprint of the Nevada Humanities Committee, 1997.

Nauvoo Temple Endowment Register, 10 December 1845 to 8 February 1846. Salt Lake City: Temple Records Index Bureau, The Church of Jesus Christ of Latter-day Saints, 1974.

Newbold, Bruce. *In Our Fathers' Footsteps: Inspiring Stories from the Mormon Trek Re-enactment*. Salt Lake City: Bookcraft, 1998.

Nibley, Preston. *Exodus to Greatness: The Story of the Mormon Migration*. Salt Lake City: Deseret News Press, 1947.

Noord, Roger Van. *King of Beaver Island: The Life and Assassination of James Jesse Strang*. Urbana, Illinois: University of Illinois Press, 1988.

Nugent, Walter. *Into the West: The Story of Its People*. New York: Alfred A. Knopf, 1999.

Owens, Kenneth N. *Gold Rush Saints: California Mormons and the Great Rush for Riches*. Spokane, Washington: The Arthur C. Clark Company, 2004.

Parkman, Francis. *The Journals of Francis Parkman*. Mason Wade, ed. 2 vols. New York: Harper & Brothers Publishers, 1947.

Parsons, Robert E. "Hagoth and the Polynesians." In *The Book of Mormon: Alma, the Testimony of the Word*. Provo, Utah: Religious Studies Center, Brigham Young University, 1992.

Peterson, Paul H. "Brigham Young and the Mormon Reformation." In Susan Easton Black and Larry C. Porter. *Lion of the Lord: Essays on the Life & Service of Brigham Young*. Salt Lake City: Deseret Book Company, 1995.

Pratt, Addison. *The Journals of Addison Pratt: Being a Narrative of Yankee Whaling in the Eighteen Twenties, a Mormon Mission to the Society Islands, and of Early California and Utah in the Eighteen Forties and Fifties*. S. George Ellsworth, ed. Salt Lake City: University of Utah Press, 1990.

Pratt, Orson. *The Orson Pratt Journals*. Elden J. Watson, ed. Salt Lake City, Utah: Elden J. Watson, 1975.

Pratt, Parley P. *Mormonism Unveiled: Zion's Watchman Unmasked and Its Editor, Mr. L. R. Sunderland, Exposed: Truth Vindicated: the Devil Mad, and Priestcraft in Danger!* New York: Printed for the Publisher, 1838.

Pratt, Parley P., John Taylor, and John Smith. Letter to Brigham Young, 23 August 1848, Great Salt Lake City. In Brigham Young, *Manuscript History of Brigham Young, 1847–1850*. William S. Harwell, ed. Salt Lake City: Collier's Publishing Co., 1997.

Preiss, Lillian E. *Sheffield: Frontier Town*. North Adams, Massachusetts: Sheffield Bicentennial Committee, 1976.

Prince, Gregory A. *Power from on High: The Development of Mormon Priesthood*. Salt Lake City: Signature Books, 1995.

Quaife, Milo M. *The Kingdom of Saint James: A Narrative of the Mormons*. New Haven, Connecticut: Yale University Press, 1930.

Richards, Mary Bradshaw. *Camping Out in the Yellowstone, 1882*. William W. Slaughter, ed. Salt Lake City: University of Utah Press, 1994.

Ricketts, Norma Baldwin. *The Mormon Battalion: U.S. Army of the West, 1846–1848*. Logan, Utah: Utah State University Press, 1996.

Roberts, Allen D. "Pioneer Mills and Milling." *An Enduring Legacy*. 12 vols. Salt Lake City: Daughters of Utah Pioneers, 1978–1989. Vol. 7, 1984.

Roberts, B. H. *A Comprehensive History of the Church of Jesus Christ of Latter-day Saints, Century I*. 6 vols. Provo, Utah: Brigham Young University Press, 1965.

Rohrbough, Malcolm J. *Days of Gold: The California Gold Rush and the American Nation*. Berkeley, California: University of California Press, 1997.

Russell, Osborne. *Journal of a Trapper: 1834–1841*. Lincoln, Nebraska: University of Nebraska Press, 1965.

Schelsinger, Arthur, Jr., ed. *The Almanac of American History*. New York: G. P. Putnam's Sons, 1983.

Sessions, Patty Bartlett. *Mormon Midwife: The 1846–1888 Diaries of Patty Bartlett Sessions*. Donna Toland Smart, ed. Logan, Utah: Utah State University Press, 1997.

Shipps, Jan. *Sojourner in the Promised Land: Forty Years Among the Mormons*. Urbana, Illinois: University of Illinois Press, 2000.

Shirts, Morris A. And Kathryn H. Shirts. *A Trail Furnace: Southern Utah's Iron Mission*. Provo, Utah: Brigham Young University Press, ca. 1998.

Simpson, James H. *Report of Explorations Across the Great Basin of the Territory of Utah for a Direct Wagon-Route from Camp Floyd to Genoa, in Carson Valley, in 1859*. Washington: Government Printing Office, 1876, reprinted as James H. Simpson, *Report of Explorations Across the Great Basin in 1859*. Reno, Nevada: University of Nevada Press, 1983.

Slaughter, William W. and Michael Landon, *Trail of Hope: The Story of the Mormon Trail*. Salt Lake City: Shadow Mountain, 1997.

Smith, Azariah. *The Gold Discovery Journal of Azariah Smith*. David L. Bigler, ed. Logan, Utah: Utah State University Press, 1996.

Smith, Brian L. "Ephraim." In Daniel H. Ludlow, ed., *Encyclopedia of Mormonism*. 4 vols. New York: Macmillan Publishing Company, 1992.

Smith, Eliza R. Snow. *Biography and Family Record of Lorenzo Snow*. Salt Lake City: Deseret News Company, 1884.

Smith, Joseph Jr. *History of the Church of Jesus Christ of Latter-day Saints: Period I: History of Joseph Smith, the Prophet*. Edited by B. H. Roberts, 2d ed., rev. 7 vols., Salt Lake City: Deseret Book Company, 1971. (Also includes Period 2, from the Manuscript History of Brigham Young.)

———. *An American Prophet's Record: The Diaries and Journals of Joseph Smith*. Scott H. Faulring, ed. Salt Lake City: Signature Books, 1989.

Snow, Eliza Roxcy. *The Personal Writings of Eliza Roxcy Snow*. Maureen Ursenbach Beecher, ed. Logan, Utah: Utah State University Press, 2000.

Sorensen, A. D. "Zion." In Daniel H. Ludlow, ed. *Encyclopedia of Mormonism*. 4 vols. New York: Macmillan Publishing Company, 1992.

Sorenson, John L. *An Ancient American Setting for the Book of Mormon*. Salt Lake City and Provo, Utah: Deseret Book Company and Foundation for Ancient Research and Mormon Studies, 1985.

Stamm, Henry E., IV. *People of the Wind River: The Eastern Shoshones, 1825–1900*. Norman, Oklahoma: University of Oklahoma Press, 1999.

Stegner, Wallace. *The Gathering of Zion: The Story of the Mormon Trail*. New York: McGraw-Hill Book Company, 1964.

Stevens, Michael E. and Steven B. Burg. *Editing Historical Documents: A Handbook of Practice*. Walnut Creek, California: AltaMira Press, 1997.

Stewart, George R. *Ordeal by Hunger: The Story of the Donner Party*. Boston: Houghton Mifflin Company, 1960.

Stout, Hosea. *On the Mormon Frontier: The Diary of Hosea Stout*. Juanita Brooks, ed. 2 vols. Salt Lake City: University of Utah Press, Utah State Historical Society, 1982.

Sunderland, LaRoy. *Mormonism Exposed and Refuted*. New York: Piercy & Reed, 1838.

Swinton, Heidi S. *Sacred Stone: The Temple at Nauvoo*. American Fork, Utah: Covenant Communications, 2002.

Szasz, Ferenc Morton. "How Religion Created an Infrastructure for the Mountain West." In Jan Shipps and Mark Silk, eds. *Religion and Public Life in the Mountain West: Sacred Landscapes in Transition*. Walnut Creek, California: AltaMira Press, 2004.

Tate, George S. "Prayer Circles." In Daniel H. Ludlow, ed., *Encyclopedia of Mormonism*. 4 vols. New York: Macmillan Publishing Company, 1992.

Tom, Gary and Ronald Holt. "The Paiute Tribe of Utah" in Forrest S. Cuch, ed., *A History of Utah's American Indians*. Salt Lake City: Utah State Division of Indian Affairs–Utah State Division of History, 2000.

Trenholm, Virginia Cole and Maurine Carley. *The Shoshonis: Sentinels of the Rockies*. Norman, Oklahoma: University of Oklahoma Press, 1972.

Tyler, Daniel. *A Concise History of the Mormon Battalion in the Mexican War, 1846–1848*. Glorieta, New Mexico: The Rio Grande Press, Inc., 1980 (1881).

Tyler, S. Lyman. "The Earliest Peoples." In Richard D. Poll, Thomas G. Alexander, Eugene E. Campbell, and David E. Miller, eds. *Utah's History*. Logan, Utah: Utah State University Press, 1993.

Udall, Stewart L. *The Forgotten Founders: Rethinking the History of the Old West*. Washington, D.C.: Island Press, 2002.

Under Wasatch Skies: A History of Wasatch County, 1858–1900. Salt Lake City: Deseret News Press, 1954.

Unruh, John D. *The Plains Across: The Overland Emigrants and the Trans-Mississippi West, 1840–1860*. Urbana, Illinois: University of Illinois Press, 1979.

Van Orden, Bruce A. "W. W. Phelps: His Ohio Contributions, 1835–36." In Milton V. Backman, Jr., ed. *Regional Studies in Latter-day Saint Church History: Ohio*. Provo, Utah: Department of Church History and Doctrine, Brigham Young University, 1990.

Van Wagoner, Richard S. *Mormon Polygamy: A History*. 2nd ed. Salt Lake City: Signature Books, 1989.

Wahlquist, Wayne L., ed. *Atlas of Utah*. Provo, Utah: Weber State College and Brigham Young University Press, 1981.

Waldman, Carl. *Encyclopedia of Native American Tribes*. New York: Facts on File Publications, 1988.

Warnock, Irvin L. and Lexia D. Warnock, eds. *Our Own Sevier*. Richfield, Utah: Richfield Reaper, 1965.

Warrum, Noble, ed. *Utah Since Statehood: Historical and Biographical*. 4 vols. Chicago: The S. J. Clarke Publishing Company, 1919.

Webster's New World College Dictionary, 3rd edition, New York: Macmillan, 1997.

White, Richard. *"It's Your Misfortune and None of My Own": A History of the American West*. Norman, Oklahoma: University of Oklahoma Press, 1995.

Whitney, Orson F. *History of Utah*. 4 vols. Salt Lake City: George Q. Cannon & Sons Co., 1892 1904.

Wickman, John E. "Peter A. Sarpy." In LeRoy R. Hafen, ed., *The Mountain Men and the Fur Trade of the Far West*, 10 vols. Glendale, California: The Arthur H. Clark Company, 1965–1972. Vol. 4, 1966.

Wiggins, Marvin E., comp. *Mormons and Their Neighbors: An Index to Over 75,000 Biographical Sketches from 1820 to the Present*. 2 vols. Provo, Utah: Brigham Young University, Harold B. Lee Library, 1984.

Wight, Jermy Benton. *The Wild Ram of the Mountain: The Story of Lyman Wight*. Afton, Wyoming: Star Valley Llama, 1996.

Woodruff, Wilford. *Wilford Woodruff's Journal, 1833–1898, Typescript*. 9 vols. Edited by Scott G. Kenny. Midvale, Utah: Signature Books, 1983–1985.

Woodbury, Lael J. "The Origin and Uses of the Sacred Hosanna Shout." In *Sperry Lecture Series*. Provo, Utah: Brigham Young University Press, 1975.

Woodward, George. *Auto-biography of George Woodward*. N.p.: Dixie Advocate Print, 1903.

Young, Brigham. *Manuscript History of Brigham Young, 1846–1847*. Elden J. Watson, ed. Salt Lake City: by the editor, 1971.

———. *Manuscript History of Brigham Young, 1847–1850*. William S. Harwell, ed. Salt Lake City: Collier's Publishing Co., 1997.

———. Letter to Orson Spencer, 23 January 1848, Winter Quarters [Nebraska]. In James R. Clark, ed. *Messages of the First Presidency of the Church of Jesus Christ of Latter-day Saints, 1833–1964*. 6 vols. Salt Lake City: Bookcraft Inc., 1965.

——— and Heber C. Kimball. Letter to Orson Hyde, George A. Smith and Ezra T. Benson, n.d., Last Crossing of the Sweetwater River. In Brigham Young, *Manuscript History of Brigham Young, 1847–1850*. William S. Harwell, ed. Salt Lake City: Collier's Publishing Co., 1997.

Youngberg, Florence C., ed. *Conquerors of the West: Stalwart Mormon Pioneers*. 4 vols. Salt Lake City: Agreka Books, 1999.

Zinn, Howard. Preface to Ray Raphael, *A People's History of the American Revolution: How Common People Shaped the Fight for Independence*. New York: The New Press, 2001.

PERIODICALS

Adams, Kellene Ricks. "'She's Going': Three Women, Two Children Made 1847 Pioneer Trek." *Pioneer* (spring 1997).

Aldous, Jay A. "Mountain Fever in the 1847 Mormon Pioneer Companies." *Nauvoo Journal* 9, no. 2 (fall 1997).

——— and Paul S. Nicholes. "What is Mountain Fever?" *Overland Journal* 15, no. 1 (spring 1997).

Allen, James B. "Was Joseph Smith a Serious Candidate for the Presidency of the United States, or Was He Only Attempting to Publicize Gospel Views on Public Issues?" *Ensign* 3, no. 9 (September 1973).

Allis, Samuel. "Forty Years among the Indians and on the Eastern Borders of Nebraska." *Transactions and Reports of the Nebraska State Historical Society* 2 (1887).

Baugh, Alexander L. "'We Took Our Change of Venue to the State of Illinois': The Gallatin Hearing and the Escape of Joseph Smith and the Mormon Prisoners from Missouri, April 1839." *Mormon Historical Studies* 2, no. 1 (spring 2002).

Beecher, Maureen Ursenbach, ed. "'All Things Move in Order in the City': The Nauvoo Diary of Zina Diantha Huntington Jacobs." *BYU Studies* 19, no. 3 (spring 1979).

Bennett, Richard E. "Mormons and Missourians: The Uneasy Truce." *Midwest Review* 9 (spring 1987).

———. "'A Samaritan had passed by': George Miller—Mormon Bishop, Trailblazer, and Brigham Young Antagonist." *Illinois Historical Journal* 82, no. 1 (spring 1989).

Black, Susan Easton. "How Large was the Population of Nauvoo?" *BYU Studies* 35, no. 2 (1995).

Bliss, Sharon Mangum and Kaylene Allen Griffin. "The Platte River Ferrymen: Making the Trek Safer and Easier for Hundreds of Pioneers." *Pioneer* (spring 1997).

Brown, Lisle G. "The Sacred Departments for Temple Work in Nauvoo: The Assembly Room and the Council Chamber." *BYU Studies* 19, no. 3 (spring 1979).

———. "Temple Ordinances as Administered in Nauvoo, Illinois, 1840–1846." *Research Report: A Bi-Monthly Publication of the Southwest Center for Religious Research* 1, no. 5 (March–April 1990).

Buckley, Jay H. "Crossing the Great Plains: A Sesquicentennial Look at the 1847 Mormon Pioneer Trek West." *Overland Journal* 15, no. 3 (autumn 1997).

Campbell, Eugene E. "The Mormons and the Donner Party." *BYU Studies* 11, no. 3 (spring 1971).

Clark, David L. "Moses Smith: Wisconsin's First Mormon." *Journal of Mormon History* 21, no. 2 (fall 1995).

Clayton, William. "An Interesting Journal." *Juvenile Instructor* 21, nos. 2–20 (15 January–15 October 1886).

Clow, Richmond L. "Mad Bear: William S. Harney and the Sioux Expedition of 1855–1856." *Nebraska History* 61, no. 2 (summer 1980).

Davis, Richard M. "Where Have All the Wagons Gone? Gone, Gone Long Ago, or Very Near So." *Overland Journal* 15, no. 3 (autumn 1997).

Dixon, W. Randall. "Beautiful, Troublesome, City Creek." *Pioneer* (winter 1996).

———. "From Emigration Canyon to City Creek: Pioneer Trail and Campsites in the Salt Lake Valley in 1847." *Utah Historical Quarterly* 65, no. 2 (spring 1997).

———. "On the Banks of a Beautiful Stream." *Pioneer* (summer 1997).

Dockstader, Julie A. "'With the Just We Shall Dwell': 1847's Non-Mormon Pioneers." *Pioneer* (spring 1996).

Dorius, Guy L. "Crossroads in the West: The Intersection of the Donner Party and the Mormons." *Nauvoo Journal* 9, no. 1 (spring 1997).

Dunn, Crandall. Letter to William Appleby, 4 August 1846, New York, New York. *Latter-day Saints' Millennial Star* 8, no. 6 (15 October 1846).

Empey, William A. "The Mormon Ferry on the North Platte: The Journal of William A. Empey, May 7–August 4, 1847." Dale L. Morgan, ed. *Annals of Wyoming* 21, nos. 2–3 (July–October 1949).

England, Eugene. "George Laub's Nauvoo Journal." *BYU Studies* 18, no. 2 (winter 1978).

Foster, Lawrence. "A Little Known Defense of Polygamy from the Mormon Press in 1842." *Dialogue* 9, no. 4 (winter 1974).

Gardner, Hamilton. "The Nauvoo Legion, 1840–1845: A Unique Military Organization." *Journal of the Illinois State Historical Society* (summer 1961).

Godfrey, Audrey M. "No Small Miracle: The Movement of Domestic Animals Across the Plains." *Nauvoo Journal*. 9, no. 1 (spring 1997).

Godfrey, Kenneth W. "A New Look at the Alleged Little Known Discourse." *BYU Studies* 9, no. 1 (autumn 1968).

Hartley, William G. "From Men to Boys: LDS Aaronic Priesthood Offices, 1829–1996." *Journal of Mormon History* 2, no. 1 (spring 1996).

———. "Gathering the Dispersed Nauvoo Saints, 1847–1852." *Ensign* 27, no. 7 (July 1997).

———. "Howard Egan, the Elkhorn Skirmish, and Mormon Trail Emigration in 1848." *Mormon Historical Studies* 1, no. 1 (spring 2000).

———. "Nauvoo Stake, Priesthood Quorums, and the Church's First Wards." *BYU Studies* 32, nos. 1–2 (winter-spring 1992).

———. "The Pioneer Trek: Nauvoo to Winter Quarters." *Ensign* 27, no. 6 (June 1997).

Hickman, Martin B. "The Political Legacy of Joseph Smith." *Dialogue* 3, no. 3 (autumn 1968).

Irving, Gordon I. "The Law of Adoption: One Phase of the Development of the Mormon Concept of Salvation, 1830–1900." *BYU Studies* 14, no. 3 (spring 1974).

Jensen, Richard E. "The Pawnee Mission, 1834–1846." *Nebraska History* 75, no. 4 (winter 1994).

Jenson, Andrew. "The Pioneers of 1847." *The Historical Record* 9, nos. 1–12 (January–December 1890).

Jessee, Dean C. "The Writing of Joseph Smith's History." *BYU Studies* 11, no. 4 (summer 1971).

———, ed. "The John Taylor Nauvoo Journal." *BYU Studies* 23, no. 3 (summer 1983).

Jorgensen, Danny L. "Cutler's Camp at the Big Grove on Silver Creek: A Mormon Settlement in Iowa, 1847–1853." *Nauvoo Journal* 9, no. 2 (fall 1997).

———. "The Cutlerites of Southwestern Iowa: A Latter-day Saint Schism and Its Role in the Early Setttlement of Iowa." *Annals of Iowa* 58, no. 2 (spring 1999).

Jorgensen, Lynn Watkins, et al. "The Mantle of the Prophet Joseph Passes to Brother Brigham: A Collective Spiritual Witness." *BYU Studies* 36, no. 4 (1996–1997).

"Kalamazoo Conference." *Times and Seasons* 5, no. 13 (15 July 1844).

Kauffman, Kyle D. and Jonathan J. Liebowitz. "Draft Animals on the United States Frontier." *Overland Journal* 15, no. 2 (summer 1997).

Kimball, Heber C. "The Pioneer Journal of Heber C. Kimball." *Utah Genealogical and Historical Magazine* (January 1939–October 1940).

Kimball, Stanley B. "The Iowa Trek of 1846." *Ensign* 2, no. 6 (June 1972).

———. "The Mormon Trail Network in Iowa, 1838–1863: A New Look." *BYU Studies* 21, no. 4 (fall 1981).

Knight, Gregory R., ed. "Journal of Thomas Bullock (1816–1885): 31 August 1845 to 5 July 1846." *BYU Studies* 31, no. 1 (winter 1991).

"Letters Concerning the Presbyterian Mission in the Pawnee Country, Near Bellevue, Neb., 1831–1849." *Collections of the Kansas State Historical Society* 14 (1915–1918).

Leonard, Glen M. "Cannon was First 'Pulpit' in Salt Lake Valley." *LDS Church News*, 17 March 1990.

Limerick, Patricia Nelson. "Peace Initiative: Using the Mormons to Rethink Ethnicity in American Life." *Journal of Mormon History* 21, no. 2 (fall 1995).

Lloyd, R. Scott. "Pioneer Trek 1997: Sesquicentennial Celebration Extends Across Miles, Faiths and Families." *Pioneer* (summer 1997).

Marty, Martin. "It Finally All Depends on God: A Conversation with Martin Marty." *Sunstone* 11, no. 2 (March 1987).

Miller, David E. "The Parting of the Ways on the Oregon Trail—the East Terminal of the Sublette Cutoff." *Annals of Wyoming* 45, no. 1 (spring 1973).

———. "Miles Goodyear and the Founding of Ogden." *Utah Historical Quarterly* 21, no. 3 (July 1953).

Murray, Robert A. "Trading Posts, Fort and Bridges of the Casper Area—Unraveling the Tangle on the Upper Platte." *Annals of Wyoming* 47, no. 1 (spring 1975).

Nealon, John S. "'Morning Fair, Roads Bad': Geology, Topography, Hydrology, and Weather on the Iowa and Nebraska Mormon Trails, 1846–1847." *Nauvoo Journal* 10, no. 1 (spring 1998).

Peterson, Paul H. "The Mormon Reformation of 1856–1857: The Rhetoric and the Reality." *Journal of Mormon History* 15 (1989).

Peterson, Paul H. and Ronald W. Walker. "Brigham Young's Word of Wisdom Legacy." *BYU Studies* 42, nos. 3–4 (2003).

Poll, Richard D. "Joseph Smith and the Presidency, 1844." *Dialogue* 3, no. 3 (autumn 1968).

Potter, Gail DeBuse. "A Note on the Samuel Allis Family: Missionaries to the Pawnee, 1834–1846." *Nebraska History* 67, no. 1 (spring 1986).

Pratt, Orson. "Interesting Items Concerning the Journeying of the Latter-day Saints from the City of Nauvoo, Until Their Location in the Valley of the Great Salt Lake." *Latter-day Saints' Millennial Star* 11–12 (1849–1850).

———. "Extracts from the Journal of Orson Pratt." *Utah Genealogical and Historical Magazine* 15–17 (1924–1926).

Quinn, D. Michael. "The Practice of Rebaptism at Nauvoo." *BYU Studies* 18, no. 2 (winter 1978).

Rieck, Richard L. "Geography of the California Trails—Part I." *Overland Journal* 11, no. 4 (1993).

Saunders, Richard L. "Officers and Arms: The 1843 General Return of the Nauvoo Legion's Second Cohort." *BYU Studies* 35, no. 2 (1995).

Schindler, Harold. [Serial entries for the Mormon Sesquicentennial Celebration, 1997]. *Salt Lake Tribune*, April–July 1997.

Smith, George A. "My Journal." *Instructor* 83, no. 6 (June 1948); 83, no. 7 (July 1948).

Snow, Erastus. "From Nauvoo to Salt Lake in the Van of the Pioneers: The Original Diary of Erastus Snow." Moroni Snow, ed. *Improvement Era* 14–15 (May 1911–October 1912).

———. "Journey to Zion." *Utah Humanities Review* 2, nos. 2–3 (April, July 1948).

Van Orden, Bruce A. "William W. Phelps's Service in Nauvoo as Joseph Smith's Political Clerk." *BYU Studies* 32, nos. 1–2 (winter–spring 1992).

Walker, Margaret F. "'. . .Written Under Very Adverse Circumstances': The 'Awful Hard Work' of Chronicling the Westward Journey." *Overland Journal* 15, no. 2 (summer 1997).

Walker, Ronald W. "'A Banner is Unfurled': Mormonism's Ensign Peak." *Dialogue* 26, no. 4 (winter 1993).

———. "A Gauge of the Times: Ensign Peak in the Twentieth Century." *Utah Historical Quarterly* 62, no. 1 (winter 1994).

———. "Lucy Mack Smith Speaks to the Nauvoo Saints." *BYU Studies* 32, nos. 1–2 (winter and spring 1992).

———. "Martin Harris: Mormonism's Early Convert." *Dialogue* 19, no. 4 (winter 1986).

———. "Seeking the 'Remnant': The Native American during the Joseph Smith Period." *Journal of Mormon History* 19, no. 1 (spring 1993).

Ward, Maureen Carr and Fred E. Woods. "The 'Tabernacle Post Office' Petition for the Saints of Kanesville, Iowa." *Mormon Historical Studies* 5, no. 1 (spring 2004).

Watson, Elden J. "The Nauvoo Tabernacle." *BYU Studies* 19, no. 3 (spring 1979).

Watt, Ronald G. "A Tale of Two Bells: Nauvoo Bell and Hummer's Bell." *Nauvoo Journal* 11, no. 2 (fall 1999).

Whitney, Horace K. "Westward with the Saints: Excerpts from the Hitherto Unpublished Journal of Horace K. Whitney, 1847." *Improvement Era* 50, nos. 4–7 (April–July 1947).

Wright, Norman E. "Odometers: Distance Measurement on Western Emigrant Trails." *Overland Journal* 13, no. 3 (fall 1995).

———. "Mormon Pioneer Odometers." *BYU Studies* 37, no. 1 (1997–1998).

Young, Lorenzo Dow. "Diary of Lorenzo Dow Young." *Utah Historical Quarterly* 14, nos. 1–4 (January, April, July, October 1946). (This account kept by Young's wife, Harriet.)

Yurtinus, John F. "Colorado, Mormons, and the Mexican War: A History of the Mississippi Saints and the Sick Detachments of the Mormon Battalion." *Essays in Colorado History* 1 (1983).

MANUSCRIPTS

LDS Church Archives, LDS Church Historical Library, and Family History Library are part of the Family and Church History Department,The Church of Jesus Christ of Latter-day Saints, Salt Lake City, Utah.

Atwood, Millen. Journal, 1847, April–July. LDS Church Archives.
Barney, Lewis. Autobiography and diary, ca. 1878–1882. LDS Church Archives.
———. Reminiscences, ca. 1886. LDS Church Archives.
[Black], Susan Easton. "Impact of the Original Pioneer Company of 1847." Paper delivered at Mormon History Association, 1984. LDS Church History Library.
Burton, William. Diaries, 1839–1851, LDS Church Archives.
Davis, Daniel. Diaries, 1846–1892. LDS Church Archives.
Dunn, Crandell. Journals, 1842–1880. LDS Church Archives.
Egan, Howard. To Tamson Egan, 4 May 1847. Daughters of Utah Pioneers, Salt Lake City, Utah.
Everett, Addison. Diary, 1847, April. LDS Church Archives.
Glenwood Ward. Record of Members, 1871–1877. LDS Church Archives.
Hamblin, Jacob. Journal, Papers, 1850–1877. LDS Church Archives.
Hancock (Ill.: County) Assessor's Office. Books of Assessment, 1840, 1842, and 1850. LDS Church Archives.
Hancock (Ill.: County) School Commissioner. Nauvoo School Schedules, 1842–1845. LDS Church Archives.
Higbee, John S. Reminiscences and diaries, 1845–1866. LDS Church Archives.
Historian's Office. Bishop's List of Widows, Women whose Husbands are in the Army and others. LDS Church Archives.
———. Church Emigration, 1831–1849. LDS Church Archives.
———. History of the Church, 1839–[ca. 1882]. LDS Church Archives.
———. Iowa Branch Index, 1839–1859, (1991). LDS Church Archives.
———. Journal History of The Church of Jesus Christ of Latter-day Saints, 1830–present. LDS Church History Library.
———. Letterpress Copybook, 1854–1879; 1885–1886. LDS Church Archives.
———. Manuscript History, Cutler's Park. LDS Church Archives.
———. Manuscript History, Winter Quarters. LDS Church Archives.
Historical Department. Winter Quarters Wards Membership Lists, 1846–1848. LDS Church Archives.
Jackman, Levi. Journal, 1847–1849. LDS Church Archives.
Jackson, Michigan, Convention Minutes, 6 June 1844, Charles C. Rich, Collection, 1832–1908. LDS Church Archives.
Jacob, Phylotte. To Brigham Young (Salt Lake City), 2 March 1852, Salt Lake City, Utah. Brigham Young Papers, Incoming Correspondence. LDS Church Archives.
Jacob, Udney Hay. To Joseph Smith, 6 January 1844, Nauvoo, Illinois. Joseph Smith Papers, Incoming Correspondence. LDS Church Archives.
———. To Martin Van Buren (Washington, D.C.), 19 March 1840, La Harpe, Illinois. Illinois State Historical Library, Springfield, Illinois.
———. To Oliver Granger (Commerce, Illinois), 3 March 1840. LDS Church Archives.
Illinois. Hancock County. Nauvoo Precinct. Election Returns, 1842 Aug. 1. LDS Church Archives.
Lyman, Amasa M. Diary, 1847. LDS Church Archives. (This account was kept by Albert Carrington.)
Mace, Wandle. Autobiography, ca. 1890. LDS Church Archives.
Nauvoo (Ill.) City Council. Proceedings, 1841 February–1845 February. LDS Church Archives.
Nauvoo Legion (Ill.). Files, 1841–1845. LDS Church Archives.
Nauvoo (Ill.) Registry of Deeds. Record of Deeds, Book B, 1843 September–1846 February. LDS Church Archives.

Nauvoo Restoration. Nauvoo Seventies List, 3 vols. LDS Church Archives.
Nauvoo Stake. Nauvoo Ward Census, 1842. LDS Church Archives.
Pack, John. Papers 1833–1882. LDS Church Archives.
Petition for post office near log tabernacle. Brigham Young, Papers, Administrative Papers. LDS Church Archives.
Registry of Names of Persons Residing in the Various Wards, &c., as p. Bishop's Reports, December 28th, A.D. 1852. Brigham Young, Office Files, LDS Church Archives.
Rich, Charles C. Diaries. Charles Coulson Rich Collection. LDS Church Archives.
Salt Lake Stake. Record of Members. LDS Church Archives.
Sanderson, George B. Diary. Special Collections, Marriott Library, University of Utah.
Scott, John. Journals 1847–[1848] and 1855–1856. LDS Church Archives.
Sevier County, Utah. Tax Assessment and Military Enlistment Records, 1873–1918. Microfilm in LDS Church Archives.
Smith, George A. History of George A. Smith (typescript), George A. Smith, Papers. LDS Church Archives. (This account was kept by Albert Carrington.)
Smith, John. Papers, 1833–1854, Journals. LDS Church Archives.
Tippets, John Harvey. Autobiography [ca. 1882]. LDS Church Archives.
Whitney, Horace K. Diary, 1847 (typescript). LDS Church Archives.
Woodruff, Wilford. Letter to Thomas L. Kane, 8 March 1859, Great Salt Lake City, Historian's Office, Letterpress Copybooks, 1854–1879; 1885–1886, LDS Church Archives.
Zarahemla Stake. Record of Members. LDS Family History Library.

Newspapers and Periodicals

Latter-day Saints' Millennial Star
Times and Seasons
Warsaw Signal

Dissertations

Barrett, Gwynn William. "John M. Bernhisel: Mormon Elder in Congress." Ph.D. Diss., Brigham Young University, 1968.
Marriott, L. Dean. "Lilburn W. Boggs: Interaction with Mormons following Their Expulsion from Missouri." Ed.D. Diss., Brigham Young University, August 1979.

Internet Sites

"The History of Fort Kearny." www2.sandi.net/kearny/history/swk/fk.html.
Johnson, Kristin. "The Murphy Family." www.utahcrossroads.org/DonnerParty/Murphy.htm
Kearny High School. "The History of Fort Kearny." www.kearnykomets.sdcs.k12.ca.us/history/html/fort_kearny.html
Lapriano, Don. "Pompey Lamb Revisited: Black Soldiers in the American Revolution." www2.lhric.org/spbattle/Pomp.html
Oregon-California Trails Association. www.octa-trails.org/JumpingOffToday/VirtualTour/PlatteNE.asp.

Films

Groberg, Lee, written by Heidi Swinton. *Trail of Hope: The Story of the Mormon Trail.* Public Broadcasting System Television, in partnership with KUED Television, 1997.

Index